WILLIAM WORDSWORTH

Selected Poems and Prefaces

RIVERSIDE EDITIONS

RIVERSIDE EDITIONS

UNDER THE GENERAL EDITORSHIP OF

Gordon N. Ray

WILLIAM WORDSWORTH

Selected Poems
and Prefaces

EDITED WITH AN INTRODUCTION AND NOTES BY

Jack Stillinger

UNIVERSITY OF ILLINOIS

HOUGHTON MIFFLIN COMPANY · BOSTON

CONTENTS

Prefaces

INTRODUCTION

"In truth," Wordsworth told a correspondent on 9 April 1801, "my life has been unusually barren of events, and my opinions have grown slowly, and I may say insensibly." The year-by-year outward events of his life are recorded in the Chronology. A central biographical fact, his close attachment to the English Lake District, will be obvious to the most casual reader of the pieces included in this volume. The poems are commented upon, in some instances explicated, in the Notes. Matters of style, technique, source, influence, reputation — even "philosophy" — are amply taken care of in works listed in the Select Bibliography and referred to in the Notes. In this brief essay I would concentrate narrowly on the question of what Wordsworth's poems are principally about.

Nothing is more easily documented, when we take an over-all view, than the apparently contradictory character of the English Romantic poets. In a letter to Benjamin Bailey (22 November 1817) Keats affirms his faith in "the authenticity of the Imagination," which he illustrates by a comparison with Adam's dream in *Paradise Lost* ("he awoke and found it truth"); a day or two later he writes down Endymion's fervent denial of this same authenticity: "I have clung / To nothing, lov'd a nothing, nothing seen / Or felt but a great dream!" Byron tells Tom Moore (28 January 1817) about the writing of the third canto of *Childe Harold,* "I was half mad during the time of its composition, between metaphysics, mountains, lakes, love un-extinguishable, thoughts unutterable, and the nightmare of my own delinquencies," and goes on to say, "I should, many a good day, have blown my brains out, but for the recollection that it would have given pleasure to my mother-in-law." Wordsworth is especially full of such oppositions of statement and tone. He laments in the Intimations ode the loss of "celestial light," "the visionary gleam . . . the glory and the dream," seeming not to resolve the loss in the "sober colouring" that the clouds take on at sunset — and then, possibly only a week or so after finishing that poem, asserts in *The Prelude* (VI.50–52) that for him "Life's morning radiance hath not left the hills, / Her dew is on the flowers." He lays down in "Expostulation and Reply" the supreme importance of "wise passiveness," and in *The Prelude* and other poems speaks of such passiveness as a second-rate condition, a degradation of man's mental powers. Lines in the Prologue to *Peter*

Bell — "The common growth of mother-earth / Suffices me . . . . what more need I desire / To stir, to soothe, or elevate?" — are countered by lines in *The Prelude* (V.573–77) saying that the "most noble attribute of man" is "That wish for something loftier, more adorned, / Than is the common aspect, daily garb, / Of human life." Natural and supernatural concerns appear to be elbowing one another throughout *The Prelude*.

Probably we should remain content with what Keats called "uncertainties, Mysteries, doubts . . . half knowledge," and not go irritably "reaching after fact & reason" in our poets. We do well to remind ourselves of R. D. Havens' observation, based on forty years' familiarity with the poet's writings, that "Any study of Wordsworth's religion must inevitably come to the conclusion that no formulation of his beliefs is possible. He was himself not clear about them; he did not follow up their implications or concern himself about possible inconsistencies. He felt differently at different times and expressed in his poetry the sincere feeling of the moment . . ." (*The Mind of a Poet,* 1941, p. 197). Havens' words apply to other things besides religion; a more recent critic says he "can think of no interpretative task so difficult as trying to define Wordsworth's concept of the imagination on the basis of utterances found in his poetry" (Herbert Lindenberger, *On Wordsworth's "Prelude,"* 1963, p. 91). But an over-all view is still desirable; the mind has to synthesize and unify. With a Romantic poet one best uses a method analogous to holding up a deck of IBM cards to see which of the many holes the light shines through. The beam shining through Wordsworth's deck spotlights his central concern with the workings of the human mind. Quite simply — though the result was the greatest achievement in poetry since Milton's — he looked into the mind of man, found it good, and was consoled.

The very simplicity is misleading. We may not be much impressed by the "infant Babe" of Book II of *The Prelude* who can "create" unity — his mother, "one dear Presence" — out of the separate parts of an arm, a breast, an eye, and so on. And yet it is this same faculty that creates an entire world, that enables Wordsworth to proclaim the mind "lord and master" over outward sense, and to say at the end of *The Prelude* that "the mind of man becomes / A thousand times more beautiful than the earth / On which he dwells." The Prospectus to "The Recluse" is throughout based upon a paradoxical notion of the marvelousness of the ordinary, of "high argument" out of the "simple produce of the common day." In speaking "of nothing more than what we are" he felt that he had a theme greater than Milton's (just as Milton had considered his greater than Homer's or Virgil's):

                                    Not Chaos, not
The darkest pit of lowest Erebus,
Nor aught of blinder vacancy, scooped out
By help of dreams — can breed such fear and awe
As fall upon us often when we look
Into our Minds, into the Mind of Man —
My haunt, and the main region of my song.

Milton of course had a somewhat different problem to deal with. In the Renaissance and earlier it had been taken for granted that man and nature fitted together in a perfect unity held together by God. With a half-century of thought culminating in Newton, however, nature lost its purpose, and, after Locke and his disciple David Hartley had finished theorizing about it, the mind was viewed as having only the most mechanical relationship to a lifeless external world. As the Romantics came into it, it was (to quote Keats) an age "too late for the fond believing lyre, / When holy were the haunted forest boughs, / Holy the air, the water, and the fire." Now rather than find meaning in nature it became necessary for man to create it. But Locke and Hartley denied the mind's creativity: sense impressions could be linked and combined, simple sensations built into complex, but nothing new could result. Each of the Romantics tried in his own way to circumvent this negative decree — the young Keats, for example, positing a realm beyond "our mortal bars" to which the visionary imagination could penetrate. Wordsworth early reverted to a pre-Newtonian, in some ways pantheistic conception of a universe alive with deity and purpose, and there are a number of passages — chiefly in manuscripts written before 1796 or 1797 — to prove it. But though vestiges remain (e.g., "Soul of Nature . . . [overflowing] With an impassioned life" in *Prel.*, XII.102–104), there is very little of this notion in the poems we care about today. Rather, Wordsworth came to pin his hopes on man's inner faculties, and to justify creativity through the imagination.

The mind's active ability to create as it perceives, to manipulate and modify sensations, may be seen quite plainly in the boatstealing episode of *The Prelude* (I.357–400). Already feeling guilty, the boy takes a boat that does not belong to him and rows out into the lake, his eye fixed, as he sits facing the stern of the boat, "Upon the summit of a craggy ridge, / The horizon's utmost boundary." As he rows further from the shore, his angle of vision changes, and he discovers a mountain peak *rising* behind the ridge —

                    a huge peak, black and huge,
          As if with voluntary power instinct

> Upreared its head. I struck and struck again,
> And growing still in stature the grim shape
> Towered up between me and the stars, and still,
> For so it seemed, with purpose of its own
> And measured motion like a living thing,
> Strode after me.

We know, of course, and so did Wordsworth when he wrote down the incident (note the qualifiers "As if," "so it seemed," "*like* a living thing"), that the peak was always there, mindless and unmoving. But the boy's imagination endows it with life, motion, a "purpose of its own." For him it is a moral agent; "With trembling oars" he returns the boat to its mooring-place, and for days and nights afterward the fearful experience affects him. Clearly he has mentally added a great deal to the scene that surrounds him; and there is no idea of an inherently active universe, no hint of a religious or philosophical basis for what happens — it is, rather, a perfectly natural experience in the process of growing up.

In *The Prelude* Wordsworth's first theoretical statement about the faculty that he praises so highly comes in the passage beginning "Blest the infant Babe" in Book II (232 ff.). Almost from the first, in the simplest acts of perception — recognizing the "one dear Presence," his mother, or constructing the idea that a flower, because it is associated with his mother's affection, is beautiful — the infant mind unifies as it perceives, organizing and adding to the sensations taken in:

> For feeling has to him imparted power
> That through the growing faculties of sense
> Doth like an agent of the one great Mind
> Create, creator and receiver both,
> Working but in alliance with the works
> Which it beholds. — Such, verily, is the first
> Poetic spirit of our human life,
> By uniform control of after years,
> In most, abated or suppressed; in some,
> Through every change of growth and of decay,
> Pre-eminent till death.

Practically all the Wordsworthian ideas are here: that this unifying, modifying, new-creating "power" is based on (but not restricted to) the "growing faculties of sense"; that it is a god-like power (cf. "Creation and divinity itself" in the summary passage at III.174); that it works in alliance with nature in a giving-receiving process (the "ennobling interchange" talked about at the end of *Prel.*, XIII); that it operates at its best in youth, and fades (except in those few who remain strong, who therefore become "poets," regardless of whether or not they write poetry) in the course of growing up. The power is called here "the first / Poetic spirit," a few lines later "this infant sensibility," and still later "My first creative sensibility." The last term is the most appropriate, since it embraces both sensation and creation, denoting a process whereby outer and inner are combined.

As he most frequently writes about it in his poems, Wordsworth's concept of imagination is identical with the "shaping spirit" of Coleridge's "Dejection: An Ode" (1802) —

> O Lady! we receive but what we give,
> And in our life alone does Nature live:
> Ours is her wedding garment, ours her shroud!
>   And would we aught behold, of higher worth,
> Than that inanimate cold world allowed
> To the poor loveless ever-anxious crowd,
>   Ah! from the soul itself must issue forth
> A light, a glory, a fair luminous cloud
>   Enveloping the Earth —

and it is very much like the combined faculties of primary and secondary imagination as they are defined in Coleridge's brief remarks at the end of chapter XIII of *Biographia Literaria:*

> The IMAGINATION . . . I consider either as primary, or secondary. The primary IMAGINATION I hold to be the living Power and prime Agent of all human Perception, and as a repetition in the finite mind of the eternal act of creation in the infinite I AM. The secondary Imagination I consider as an echo of the former, co-existing with the conscious will, yet still as identical with the primary in the *kind* of its agency, and differing only in *degree,* and in the *mode* of its operation. It dissolves, diffuses, dissipates, in order to re-create; or where this process is rendered impossible, yet still at all events it struggles to idealize and to unify. It is essentially *vital,* even as all objects (*as* objects) are essentially fixed and dead.

Both Wordsworth and Coleridge employ images of projection (especially of light) and spreading abroad to describe this power: e.g., "An auxiliar light / Came from my mind, which on the setting sun / Bestowed new splendour" (*Prel.,* II.368–70); "moments awful . . . When power streamed from thee, and thy soul received / The light reflected, as a light bestowed" (Coleridge's "To William Wordsworth," written after Wordsworth read *The Prelude* to him). The mind projects life, meaning, and value onto the external world in this giving-receiving process; without man, Wordsworth wrote in an early manuscript of *The Prelude*, "the Earth / Is valueless." Hopkins has the same idea in "Hurrahing in Harvest":

> These things, these things were here and but the beholder
>   Wanting; which two when they once meet,
> The heart rears wings bold and bolder
>   And hurls for him, O half hurls earth for him off under his feet.

And like Hopkins here, Wordsworth constantly uses the language of explosion and fireworks ("flash," "gleam," "burst") in recounting the most ordinary interactions of mind and nature.

Later in Book II of *The Prelude* Wordsworth entertains the idea that this unifying, new-creating faculty is responsible for a feeling of "one life" in the universe, a "sentiment of Being spread / O'er all," and that he coerces "all things into sympathy," transferring "To unorganic natures . . . My own enjoyments." Here he offers an alternative possibility — that he "did converse / With things that really are" — but in Book III he is more decisive: he "spread [his] thoughts / And spread them with a wider creeping," and in return "felt / Incumbencies more awful, visitings / Of the Upholder of the tranquil soul"; "To every natural form, rock, fruit or flower, / Even the loose stones that cover the high-way, / I gave a moral life . . . . I had a world about me — 'twas my own; / I made it." It ought to be clear, even in these early books, that creative sensibility is not primarily a producer of mystic experiences. Wordsworth's immediate concern is always psychological; in the most impressive passages of the later books of *The Prelude*, the "spots of time" in Book XII and the ascent of Mt. Snowdon in Book XIV, no direct religious experience is involved.

The passage on "spots of time" (XII.208 ff.) is of crucial importance in showing Wordsworth's ultimate view of the greatness of man's mental powers. Again, its simplicity may mislead us. Having told in the first eight books how his upbringing in nature led to a love of man, and in the next three (IX–XI) how this love fostered an interest in man's betterment through revolutionary activities in France, how his enthusiasm turned out to be invested in a defective cause, and how, as a result, his imagination was "impaired" until a return to nature (his sister leading him by the hand) effected a restoration, he now says that he "again / In Nature's presence stood . . . A sensitive being, a *creative* soul." He then goes on, beginning a new paragraph:

> There are in our existence spots of time,
> That with distinct pre-eminence retain

A renovating virtue, whence . . .
                              our minds
Are nourished and invisibly repaired;
A virtue, by which pleasure is enhanced,
That penetrates, enables us to mount,
When high, more high, and lifts us up when fallen.
This efficacious spirit chiefly lurks
Among those passages of life that give
Profoundest knowledge to what point, and how,
The mind is lord and master — outward sense
The obedient servant of her will.

Two exemplifying incidents follow. In the first, Wordsworth tells that once as a boy he became separated from his father's servant, came to a place where a murderer had been hanged, and fled from that to the bare common, where he saw "A naked pool that lay beneath the hills, / The beacon on the summit, and, more near, / A girl, who bore a pitcher on her head, / And seemed with difficult steps to force her way / Against the blowing wind" — an ordinary sight, Wordsworth says, and yet one of "visionary dreariness." Years later, when he returned to the same spot with his loved one, the scene was transformed:

Upon the naked pool and dreary crags,
And on the melancholy beacon, fell
A spirit of pleasure and youth's golden gleam;
And think ye not with radiance more sublime
For these remembrances, and for the power
They had left behind?

The point is not just that his early fear made the landscape seem dreary and his later happiness in love made it seem pleasant, but that the later pleasure was heightened, "with radiance more sublime," *because* of its association with the earlier terror. The second example again involves a mental combining — of the anticipation of joy in going home for the Christmas holidays with the grief and "chastisement" of his father's death ten days later — and the emotions are again associated with elements of the landscape, a single sheep and a blasted hawthorn. In representing the combination of sensations ("So feeling comes in aid / Of feeling") into something not inherent in the scene itself, both passages illustrate how "The mind is lord and master" over outward sense. And in them, and similar recollected experiences, Wordsworth thought he found an answer to a major problem of the poem, "A more judicious knowledge of the worth / And dignity of individual man" (XIII.80–81).

The most difficult task in understanding Wordsworth is that of reconciling creative sensibility, as just described, with the infinity-questing imagination that takes on considerable prominence in several passages of *The Prelude*. Wordsworth thought of them as operations of the same faculty, and we do wrong to separate them (especially by calling one fancy, the other imagination, on the basis of distinctions that he made some years after writing his major poems). But we are faced, no matter which way we turn, with apparent contradictions: the state of being "laid asleep / In body," for example, is at odds with "the language of the sense" in "Tintern Abbey."

A possible solution to the difficulty turns on Wordsworth's special meaning of "infinity," which in Book VI of *The Prelude* he describes as "hope . . . expectation, and desire, / And something evermore about to be," and in Book XIV symbolizes by "waters, torrents, streams / Innumerable, roaring with one voice . . . voices issuing forth to silent light / In one continuous stream." In these passages infinity is the opposite of limitation or confinement; as an expression of freedom it is specifically set against the tyranny of the senses, that "Single vision & Newton's sleep" (Blake's terms) whereby the mind is arrested and held captive by whatever the senses are immediately taking in. In Wordsworth's thinking, creative sensibility is a power of infinite possibilities (among which the feeling of God or divine life in nature may be included). In Book II, for example, the "growing faculties" of sense lead to "possible sublimity" —

> With growing faculties she [the "soul" or mind] doth aspire,
> With faculties still growing, feeling still
> That whatsoever point they gain, they yet
> Have something to pursue.

In Books VI and VII we are shown ways in which the natural world leads the mind to an idea of something beyond nature: "The immeasurable height / Of woods decaying, never to be decayed, / The stationary blasts of waterfalls," and other images of permanence are seen as "types and symbols of Eternity"; and "the everlasting streams and woods, / Stretched and still stretching," and other impressions shape "The views and aspirations of the soul / To majesty." In Book XIV the "mind / That feeds upon infinity" is "sustained / By recognitions of transcendent power, / In sense conducting to ideal form."

"Infinity," however, is not so important as the interplay of mind and nature producing less supernatural effects. In the over-all view, both nature and mind, both sensations and imagination working upon those sensations, are necessary to the ideal human condition. On the one hand, separated from "forms and images" of nature, the mind loses itself in a "blank abyss" (VI.470), "in endless dreams / Of sick-

liness, disjoining, joining, things / Without the light of knowledge"
(VIII.435–37); on the other, overwhelmed by sensible impressions,
by "the bodily eye . . . held . . . In absolute dominion," the inner
faculties are laid asleep (XII.128–47) — either condition is bad. The
ideal is

> A balance, an ennobling interchange
> Of action from without and from within;
> The excellence, pure function, and best power
> Both of the object seen, and eye that sees. (XIII.375–78)

It is not necessary for nature to be alive or active in any romantic
sense; it is enough that nature exists as a basis (in both perception and
memory) on which the "excited spirit" can work its infinite creations.
The mind is lord and master, outward sense the obedient servant; but
both mind *and* outward sense ("action from without") are essential
in Wordsworth's "high argument" in "The Recluse":

> How exquisitely the individual Mind
> (And the progressive powers perhaps no less
> Of the whole species) to the external World
> Is fitted: — and how exquisitely, too —
> Theme this but little heard of among men —
> The external World is fitted to the Mind;
> And the creation (by no lower name
> Can it be called) which they with blended might
> Accomplish . . . .

All this at first glance may seem very remote from twentieth-century
concerns. In Wordsworth's chief meaning of the word, we are all of
us these days "poets" — creating as we perceive, combining past impressions with new ones, experiencing an "interchange / Of action
from without and from within." Wordsworth's ideas, for him a tremendous discovery, are now commonplace (though the extent to which
the mind modifies perception is a subject of increasing interest in
modern psychology). What we forget, and what Wordsworth may
remind us of, is the "ennobling" that attends contemplation of the
human mind. "Genius, power, / Creation and divinity itself" — we
can if we wish omit divinity and still admire what Wordsworth came
to know,

> how the mind of man becomes
> A thousand times more beautiful than the earth
> On which he dwells, above this frame of things
> (Which, 'mid all revolution in the hopes

>   And fears of men, do h still remain unchanged)
>   In beauty exalted, as it is itself
>   Of quality and fabric more divine.

For a while longer, Wordsworth's ideas will continue valid. And when the machines finally usurp pre-eminence we can still read him, reminiscently, as we now sometimes read Chaucer and Spenser and Milton, for an illumination of the past, the good old days, when the mind *was* lord and master.

A NOTE ON THE EDITING

FROM 1815 on, Wordsworth arranged his poems and printed them in categories that he defended and theorized about at some length — "Poems Written in Youth," "Poems Referring to the Period of Childhood," "Poems Founded on the Affections," "Poems on the Naming of Places," and so on. Apart from the fact that critics have never made much sense of his classifications ("ingenious but far-fetched," Arnold called them), the usual debate over the adoption of Wordsworth's arrangement vs. a chronological ordering is not a consideration in a selection like the present volume, which includes, for example, only two of Wordsworth's thirty-three "Poems of the Fancy" but twenty-three of the fifty-two "Poems of the Imagination." The poems are here given in chronological order, as nearly as I have been able to determine it, according to the dates of substantial completion. The texts of the shorter poems and the prefaces (except for the 1798 Advertisement to *Lyrical Ballads*) are taken from the six-volume *Poetical Works* of 1849–50, generally considered the last edition that Wordsworth had a hand in. (Although he altered his texts constantly, sometimes making extensive revisions, the latest texts do not in any significant way misrepresent the originals at the time of first completion.) Except for correcting printer's errors and making about thirty-five minor changes in punctuation, spelling, and capitalization, I have followed these texts, along with their inconsistencies and occasional archaisms, verbatim. For *The Prelude* my text is that of the edition of 1850, corrected and emended in some eighty places mainly on the basis of manuscript readings given in de Selincourt's apparatus and notes. Oddly enough, because de Selincourt — while pointing many of them out — never incorporated these corrections into his own text, the present text is a more accurate rendering of Wordsworth's final version than any that has hitherto been printed.

"A correct text is the first object of an editor," Wordsworth told Walter Scott in 1805; "then such notes as explain difficult or unintelligible passages, or throw light upon them; and lastly, which is of much less importance, notes pointing out passages or authors to which the Poet has been indebted." While aiming to preserve Wordsworth's emphases, I have, like other editors, given a good deal of space to his own notes on the poems that he dictated to Isabella Fenwick in 1843 (except in one instance, they are here printed from the *Poetical Works* of 1857, in which they were first published). It still seems reasonable that, of all persons commenting on the poems, Wordsworth — even as much as forty or fifty years afterward — was in a better position than anyone else to suggest what *may* have been in his mind at the time he wrote them. My considerable indebtedness in the notes to earlier editors and critics of Wordsworth will be obvious; here I would acknowledge a special obligation to the Oxford editions of Ernest de Selincourt and Helen Darbishire and to R. D. Havens' *The Mind of a Poet*.

CHRONOLOGY

1770   William Wordsworth is born on April 7, the second son of John and Ann Wordsworth, at Cockermouth, Cumberland, where his father is an attorney and chief law-agent to Sir James Lowther (later the first Earl of Lonsdale). Other children are Richard (1768–1816), Dorothy (1771–1855), John (1772–1805), and Christopher (1774–1846).

1776–77   Attends the grammar school at Cockermouth and Mrs. Ann Birkett's school at Penrith.

1778   Mother dies in March.

1779–87   Attends the Hawkshead grammar school, lodging with Mrs. Ann Tyson.

1783   Father dies at the end of December, and the Wordsworth children are left in the guardianship of two uncles.

1787   Reunion (after a nine-year separation) with his sister Dorothy at Penrith in July–August. Enters St. John's College, Cambridge, in October.

1788   Long vacation (July–October) at Hawkshead.

1789   Long vacation with Dorothy at Forncett Rectory near Norwich, and with Thomas and Mary Hutchinson at Sockburn-on-Tees in Durham. Perhaps first visits London during the Christmas vacation.

1790   Long vacation spent in a walking tour with Robert Jones through France and Switzerland across the Alps into Italy.

1791   B.A. degree (without honors) in January. Afterwards goes to London and, at the end of May, to Wales to visit Robert Jones (on a walking tour they climb Mt. Snowdon). Departs for France in November (in Paris at the beginning of December, and then on to Orleans).

1792   At Orleans (winter and the next fall) and Blois (spring and summer); friendship with Michel Beaupuy; affair with Annette Vallon, to whom is born his daughter, Caroline, in December. Returns to Paris at the end of October, and to England in December.

1793   *An Evening Walk* and *Descriptive Sketches* published at the beginning of the year. Britain declares war on France in February. Goes to the Isle of Wight with William Calvert at the end of June, then on a walking tour over Salisbury Plain and across the Severn into Wales (visiting Tintern Abbey in the Wye Valley). Possibly returns to France, getting as far as Paris, in October.

1794   Joins Dorothy at Halifax in February, and they sojourn for six weeks at the Calverts' Windy Brow farmhouse near Keswick in April–May. Except for a month's visit to Rampside on the Furness coast (near Peele Castle) in August, spends June–January 1795 at Keswick and Penrith with the ailing Raisley Calvert.

1795   Calvert dies in January, leaving him £900. Goes to London in February, to Bristol in August. First meets Coleridge probably in September. From the end of September through June 1797, resides with Dorothy and Basil Montagu's young son (b. 1793) at Racedown farmhouse in Dorsetshire (near Crewkerne, Somersetshire).

1797   Visited by Mary Hutchinson in the spring, and by Coleridge in June. Settles with Dorothy at Alfoxden (three miles away from Coleridge at Nether Stowey, Somersetshire) in July.

1798   Leaves Alfoxden in June to visit Bristol, Wales (and Tintern Abbey), London. With Dorothy and Coleridge, sails for Germany in September and settles at Goslar. *Lyrical Ballads, with a Few Other Poems* published in October.

1799   Travels in Germany, February–April, after which he returns to England and spends several months with the Hutchinsons at Sockburn. Walking tour through the Lake District with Coleridge in October–November. With Dorothy moves into Dove Cottage, Town End, Grasmere, in December (his principal residence until 1808).

1800   Visited by John Wordsworth (January–September), Coleridge, and Mary Hutchinson. Coleridge settles at Keswick in July.

1801   Second edition of *Lyrical Ballads* (dated 1800) published in January. Short visit to Scotland at the end of the summer.

1802   On the death of the Earl of Lonsdale (in May) the Wordsworths begin to recover £8500 owed by him to their father's estate (William's and Dorothy's share, paid in installments through 1804, is £3825). Meets Annette Vallon and daughter Caroline at Calais in August. Returns to London in September, and marries Mary Hutchinson on October 4. Five children are born to them: John (1803–75), Dora (1804–47), Thomas (1806–12), Catharine (1808–12), and William (1810–83).

1803   With Dorothy and Coleridge, tours Scotland in August–September.

1804   Coleridge sails for Malta in April (returning to England in August 1806).

1805   John Wordsworth is drowned in a shipwreck off Weymouth in February.

1806   Visits London in April–May. Moves into Sir George Beaumont's farmhouse at Coleorton, in Leicestershire, at the end of October. Visited by Coleridge during the winter.

1807   *Poems, in Two Volumes* published in May. Travels in Yorkshire during the summer, returning to Grasmere in August.

1808   Moves from Dove Cottage into Allan Bank, Grasmere, in June (his residence until 1811). De Quincey and Coleridge come to stay with him in September (remaining until November 1809 and May 1810, respectively).

1809   His tract *Concerning . . . the Convention of Cintra* published in May.

1810   "A Description of the Scenery of the Lakes" published as the introduction to Joseph Wilkinson's *Select Views in Cumberland, Westmoreland, and Lancashire.* Gradual estrangement from Coleridge (lasting until May 1812).

1811   Moves from Allan Bank into the Rectory, Grasmere, in May (his residence until 1813).

1812   Visits London and is reconciled with Coleridge in May. Deaths of a daughter and a son in June and December.

1813   Appointed Distributor of Stamps for Westmorland in March (an office he holds until 1842, when he is granted a pension of £300). Moves from the Rectory into Rydal Mount, Grasmere, in May (his residence for the rest of his life).

1814   *The Excursion* published in July. Tours Scotland with Mary and his sister-in-law in July–September.

1815   *Poems* (the first collected edition) and *The White Doe of Ryl-stone* published in March and May.

1819   Appointed J.P. for Westmorland in January. *Peter Bell* and *The Waggoner* published in April and May.

1820   *The River Duddon* and the four-volume *Miscellaneous Poems* published in May and July. Tour with Mary and Dorothy through Switzerland to the Italian lakes in July–November.

1822   *Ecclesiastical Sketches* and *Memorials of a Tour on the Continent* published in the spring.

1823 ff.   Various travels include trips to the Netherlands (1823), to North Wales (1824), up the Rhine (1828), through Ireland (1829), to the Highlands (1831), to the Isle of Man and Scotland (1833), through France and Italy (1837). Important collected editions of poems are published in 1827, 1832, 1836–37, 1845, and 1849–50.

1835   *Yarrow Revisited, and Other Poems* published at the beginning of the year.

1843   Appointed Poet Laureate in April.

1850   Dies on April 23, and is buried in Grasmere churchyard. *The Prelude* published in July.

POEMS

AN EVENING WALK

ADDRESSED TO A YOUNG LADY

General Sketch of the Lakes—Author's regret of his Youth which was passed amongst them—Short description of Noon—Cascade—Noon-tide Retreat —Precipice and sloping Lights—Face of Nature as the Sun declines— Mountain-farm, and the Cock—Slate-quarry—Sunset—Superstition of the Country connected with that moment—Swans—Female Beggar—Twilight-sounds—Western Lights—Spirits—Night—Moonlight—Hope—Night-sounds —Conclusion.

FAR from my dearest Friend, 'tis mine to rove
Through bare grey dell, high wood, and pastoral cove;
Where Derwent rests, and listens to the roar
That stuns the tremulous cliffs of high Lodore;
Where peace to Grasmere's lonely island leads,   5
To willowy hedge-rows, and to emerald meads;
Leads to her bridge, rude church, and cottaged grounds,
Her rocky sheepwalks, and her woodland bounds;
Where, undisturbed by winds, Winander sleeps
'Mid clustering isles, and holly-sprinkled steeps;   10
Where twilight glens endear my Esthwaite's shore,
And memory of departed pleasures, more.

    Fair scenes, erewhile, I taught, a happy child,
The echoes of your rocks my carols wild:
The spirit sought not then, in cherished sadness,   15
A cloudy substitute for failing gladness.
In youth's keen eye the livelong day was bright,
The sun at morning, and the stars at night,
Alike, when first the bittern's hollow bill
Was heard, or woodcocks roamed the moonlight hill.   20

    In thoughtless gaiety I coursed the plain,
And hope itself was all I knew of pain;
For then, the inexperienced heart would beat
At times, while young Content forsook her seat,
And wild Impatience, pointing upward, showed,   25
Through passes yet unreached, a brighter road.
Alas! the idle tale of man is found
Depicted in the dial's moral round;
Hope with reflection blends her social rays
To gild the total tablet of his days;   30
Yet still, the sport of some malignant power,
He knows but from its shade the present hour.

3

But why, ungrateful, dwell on idle pain?
To show what pleasures yet to me remain,
Say, will my Friend, with unreluctant ear,   35
The history of a poet's evening hear?

When, in the south, the wan noon, brooding still,
Breathed a pale steam around the glaring hill,
And shades of deep-embattled clouds were seen,
Spotting the northern cliffs with lights between;   40
When crowding cattle, checked by rails that make
A fence far stretched into the shallow lake,
Lashed the cool water with their restless tails,
Or from high points of rock looked out for fanning gales;
When school-boys stretched their length upon the green;   45
And round the broad-spread oak, a glimmering scene,
In the rough fern-clad park, the herded deer
Shook the still-twinkling tail and glancing ear;
When horses in the sunburnt intake stood,
And vainly eyed below the tempting flood,   50
Or tracked the passenger, in mute distress,
With forward neck the closing gate to press —
Then, while I wandered where the huddling rill
Brightens with water-breaks the hollow ghyll
As by enchantment, an obscure retreat   55
Opened at once, and stayed my devious feet.
While thick above the rill the branches close,
In rocky basin its wild waves repose,
Inverted shrubs, and moss of gloomy green,
Cling from the rocks, with pale wood-weeds between;
And its own twilight softens the whole scene,
Save where aloft the subtle sunbeams shine
On withered briars that o'er the crags recline;
Save where, with sparkling foam, a small cascade
Illumines, from within, the leafy shade;   65
Beyond, along the vista of the brook,
Where antique roots its bustling course o'erlook,
The eye reposes on a secret bridge
Half grey, half shagged with ivy to its ridge;
There, bending o'er the stream, the listless swain   70
Lingers behind his disappearing wain.
— Did Sabine grace adorn my living line,
Blandusia's praise, wild stream, should yield to thine!
Never shall ruthless minister of death
'Mid thy soft glooms the glittering steel unsheath;   75
No goblets shall, for thee, be crowned with flowers,
No kid with piteous outcry thrill thy bowers;
The mystic shapes that by thy margin rove

A more benignant sacrifice approve —
A mind, that, in a calm angelic mood   80
Of happy wisdom, meditating good,
Beholds, of all from her high powers required,
Much done, and much designed, and more desired, —
Harmonious thoughts, a soul by truth refined,
Entire affection for all human kind.   85

  Dear Brook, farewell! To-morrow's noon again
Shall hide me, wooing long thy wildwood strain;
But now the sun has gained his western road,
And eve's mild hour invites my steps abroad.

  While, near the midway cliff, the silvered kite   90
In many a whistling circle wheels her flight;
Slant watery lights, from parting clouds, apace
Travel along the precipice's base;
Cheering its naked waste of scattered stone,
By lichens grey, and scanty moss, o'ergrown;   95
Where scarce the foxglove peeps, or thistle's beard;
And restless stone-chat, all day long, is heard.

  How pleasant, as the sun declines, to view
The spacious landscape change in form and hue!
Here, vanish, as in mist, before a flood   100
Of bright obscurity, hill, lawn, and wood;
There, objects, by the searching beams betrayed,
Come forth, and here retire in purple shade;
Even the white stems of birch, the cottage white,
Soften their glare before the mellow light;   105
The skiffs, at anchor where with umbrage wide
Yon chestnuts half the latticed boat-house hide,
Shed from their sides, that face the sun's slant beam,
Strong flakes of radiance on the tremulous stream:
Raised by yon travelling flock, a dusty cloud   110
Mounts from the road, and spreads its moving shroud;
The shepherd, all involved in wreaths of fire,
Now shows a shadowy speck, and now is lost entire.

  Into a gradual calm the breezes sink,
A blue rim borders all the lake's still brink;   115
There doth the twinkling aspen's foliage sleep,
And insects clothe, like dust, the glassy deep:
And now, on every side, the surface breaks
Into blue spots, and slowly lengthening streaks;
Here, plots of sparkling water tremble bright   120
With thousand thousand twinkling points of light;

There, waves that, hardly weltering, die away,
Tip their smooth ridges with a softer ray;
And now the whole wide lake in deep repose
Is hushed, and like a burnished mirror glows, 125
Save where, along the shady western marge,
Coasts, with industrious oar, the charcoal barge.

Their panniered train a group of potters goad,
Winding from side to side up the steep road;
The peasant, from yon cliff of fearful edge 130
Shot, down the headlong path darts with his sledge;
Bright beams the lonely mountain-horse illume
Feeding 'mid purple heath, "green rings," and broom;
While the sharp slope the slackened team confounds,
Downward the ponderous timber-wain resounds; 135
In foamy breaks the rill, with merry song,
Dashed o'er the rough rock, lightly leaps along;
From lonesome chapel at the mountain's feet,
Three humble bells their rustic chime repeat;
Sounds from the water-side the hammered boat; 140
And *blasted* quarry thunders, heard remote!

Even here, amid the sweep of endless woods,
Blue pomp of lakes, high cliffs and falling floods,
Not undelightful are the simplest charms,
Found by the grassy door of mountain-farms. 145

Sweetly ferocious, round his native walks,
Pride of his sister-wives, the monarch stalks;
Spur-clad his nervous feet, and firm his tread;
A crest of purple tops the warrior's head.
Bright sparks his black and rolling eye-ball hurls 150
Afar, his tail he closes and unfurls;
On tiptoe reared, he strains his clarion throat,
Threatened by faintly-answering farms remote:
Again with his shrill voice the mountain rings,
While, flapped with conscious pride, resound his wings! 155

Where, mixed with graceful birch, the sombrous pine
And yew-tree o'er the silver rocks recline;
I love to mark the quarry's moving trains,
Dwarf panniered steeds, and men, and numerous wains:
How busy all the enormous hive within, 160
While Echo dallies with its various din!
Some (hear you not their chisels' clinking sound?)
Toil, small as pigmies in the gulf profound;
Some, dim between the lofty cliffs descried,

O'erwalk the slender plank from side to side;   165
These, by the pale-blue rocks that ceaseless ring,
In airy baskets hanging, work and sing.

Just where a cloud above the mountain rears
An edge all flame, the broadening sun appears;
A long blue bar its ægis orb divides,   170
And breaks the spreading of its golden tides;
And now that orb has touched the purple steep
Whose softened image penetrates the deep.
'Cross the calm lake's blue shades the cliffs aspire,
With towers and woods, a "prospect all on fire;"   175
While coves and secret hollows, through a ray
Of fainter gold, a purple gleam betray.
Each slip of lawn the broken rocks between
Shines in the light with more than earthly green:
Deep yellow beams the scattered stems illume,   180
Far in the level forest's central gloom:
Waving his hat, the shepherd, from the vale,
Directs his winding dog the cliffs to scale, —
The dog, loud barking, 'mid the glittering rocks,
Hunts, where his master points, the intercepted flocks.   185
Where oaks o'erhang the road the radiance shoots
On tawny earth, wild weeds, and twisted roots;
The druid-stones a brightened ring unfold;
And all the babbling brooks are liquid gold;
Sunk to a curve, the day-star lessens still,   190
Gives one bright glance, and drops behind the hill.

In these secluded vales, if village fame,
Confirmed by hoary hairs, belief may claim;
When up the hills, as now, retired the light,
Strange apparitions mocked the shepherd's sight.   195

The form appears of one that spurs his steed
Midway along the hill with desperate speed;
Unhurt pursues his lengthened flight, while all
Attend, at every stretch, his headlong fall.
Anon, appears a brave, a gorgeous show   200
Of horsemen-shadows moving to and fro;
At intervals imperial banners stream,
And now the van reflects the solar beam;
The rear through iron brown betrays a sullen gleam.
While silent stands the admiring crowd below,   205
Silent the visionary warriors go,
Winding in ordered pomp their upward way
Till the last banner of their long array

Has disappeared, and every trace is fled
Of splendour — save the beacon's spiry head   210
Tipt with eve's latest gleam of burning red.

   Now, while the solemn evening shadows sail,
On slowly-waving pinions, down the vale;
And, fronting the bright west, yon oak entwines
Its darkening boughs and leaves, in stronger lines;   215
'Tis pleasant near the tranquil lake to stray
Where, winding on along some secret bay,
The swan uplifts his chest, and backward flings
His neck, a varying arch, between his towering wings:
The eye that marks the gliding creature sees   220
How graceful pride can be, and how majestic, ease.
While tender cares and mild domestic loves
With furtive watch pursue her as she moves,
The female with a meeker charm succeeds,
And her brown little-ones around her leads,   225
Nibbling the water lilies as they pass,
Or playing wanton with the floating grass.
She, in a mother's care, her beauty's pride
Forgetting, calls the wearied to her side;
Alternately they mount her back, and rest   230
Close by her mantling wings' embraces prest.

   Long may they float upon this flood serene;
Theirs be these holms untrodden, still, and green,
Where leafy shades fence off the blustering gale,
And breathes in peace the lily of the vale!   235
Yon isle, which feels not even the milk-maid's feet,
Yet hears her song, "by distance made more sweet,"
Yon isle conceals their home, their hut-like bower;
Green water-rushes overspread the floor;
Long grass and willows form the woven wall,   240
And swings above the roof the poplar tall.
Thence issuing often with unwieldy stalk,
They crush with broad black feet their flowery walk;
Or, from the neighbouring water, hear at morn
The hound, the horse's tread, and mellow horn;   245
Involve their serpent-necks in changeful rings,
Rolled wantonly between their slippery wings,
Or, starting up with noise and rude delight,
Force half upon the wave their cumbrous flight.

   Fair Swan! by all a mother's joys caressed,   250
Haply some wretch has eyed, and called thee blessed;
When with her infants, from some shady seat
By the lake's edge, she rose — to face the noontide heat;

Or taught their limbs along the dusty road
A few short steps to totter with their load.   255

   I see her now, denied to lay her head,
On cold blue nights, in hut or straw-built shed,
Turn to a silent smile their sleepy cry,
By pointing to the gliding moon on high.
— When low-hung clouds each star of summer hide,   260
And fireless are the valleys far and wide,
Where the brook brawls along the public road
Dark with bat-haunted ashes stretching broad,
Oft has she taught them on her lap to lay
The shining glow-worm; or, in heedless play,   265
Toss it from hand to hand, disquieted;
While others, not unseen, are free to shed
Green unmolested light upon their mossy bed.

   Oh! when the sleety showers her path assail,
And like a torrent roars the headstrong gale;   270
No more her breath can thaw their fingers cold,
Their frozen arms her neck no more can fold;
Weak roof a cowering form two babes to shield,
And faint the fire a dying heart can yield!
Press the sad kiss, fond mother! vainly fears   275
Thy flooded cheek to wet them with its tears;
No tears can chill them, and no bosom warms,
Thy breast their death-bed, coffined in thine arms!

   Sweet are the sounds that mingle from afar,
Heard by calm lakes, as peeps the folding star,   280
Where the duck dabbles 'mid the rustling sedge,
And feeding pike starts from the water's edge,
Or the swan stirs the reeds, his neck and bill
Wetting, that drip upon the water still;
And heron, as resounds the trodden shore,   285
Shoots upward, darting his long neck before.

   Now, with religious awe, the farewell light
Blends with the solemn colouring of night;
'Mid groves of clouds that crest the mountain's brow,
And round the west's proud lodge their shadows throw,   290
Like Una shining on her gloomy way,
The half-seen form of Twilight roams astray;
Shedding, through paly loop-holes mild and small,
Gleams that upon the lake's still bosom fall;
Soft o'er the surface creep those lustres pale   295
Tracking the motions of the fitful gale.
With restless interchange at once the bright

Wins on the shade, the shade upon the light.
No favoured eye was e'er allowed to gaze
On lovelier spectacle in faery days;   300
When gentle Spirits urged a sportive chase,
Brushing with lucid wands the water's face;
While music, stealing round the glimmering deeps,
Charmed the tall circle of the enchanted steeps.
— The lights are vanished from the watery plains: 305
No wreck of all the pageantry remains.
Unheeded night has overcome the vales:
On the dark earth the wearied vision fails;
The latest lingerer of the forest train,
The lone black fir, forsakes the faded plain;   310
Last evening sight, the cottage smoke, no more,
Lost in the thickened darkness, glimmers hoar;
And, towering from the sullen dark-brown mere,
Like a black wall, the mountain-steeps appear.
— Now o'er the soothed accordant heart we feel   315
A sympathetic twilight slowly steal,
And ever, as we fondly muse, we find
The soft gloom deepening on the tranquil mind.
Stay! pensive, sadly-pleasing visions, stay!
Ah no! as fades the vale, they fade away: 320
Yet still the tender, vacant gloom remains;
Still the cold cheek its shuddering tear retains.

   The bird, who ceased, with fading light, to thread
Silent the hedge or steamy rivulet's bed,
From his grey re-appearing tower shall soon   325
Salute with gladsome note the rising moon,
While with a hoary light she frosts the ground,
And pours a deeper blue to Æther's bound;
Pleased, as she moves, her pomp of clouds to fold
In robes of azure, fleecy-white, and gold.   330

   Above yon eastern hill, where darkness broods
O'er all its vanished dells, and lawns, and woods;
Where but a mass of shade the sight can trace,
Even now she shows, half-veiled, her lovely face:
Across the gloomy valley flings her light,   335
Far to the western slopes with hamlets white;
And gives, where woods the chequered upland strew,
To the green corn of summer, autumn's hue.

   Thus Hope, first pouring from her blessed horn
Her dawn, far lovelier than the moon's own morn,   340
Till higher mounted, strives in vain to cheer

The weary hills, impervious, blackening near;
Yet does she still, undaunted, throw the while
On darling spots remote her tempting smile.

Even now she decks for me a distant scene,   345
(For dark and broad the gulf of time between)
Gilding that cottage with her fondest ray,
(Sole bourn, sole wish, sole object of my way;
How fair its lawns and sheltering woods appear!
How sweet its streamlet murmurs in mine ear!)   350
Where we, my Friend, to happy days shall rise,
Till our small share of hardly-paining sighs
(For sighs will ever trouble human breath)
Creep hushed into the tranquil breast of death.

But now the clear bright Moon her zenith gains,   355
And, rimy without speck, extend the plains:
The deepest cleft the mountain's front displays
Scarce hides a shadow from her searching rays;
From the dark-blue faint silvery threads divide
The hills, while gleams below the azure tide;   360
Time softly treads; throughout the landscape breathes
A peace enlivened, not disturbed, by wreaths
Of charcoal-smoke, that o'er the fallen wood,
Steal down the hill, and spread along the flood.

The song of mountain-streams, unheard by day,   365
Now hardly heard, beguiles my homeward way.
Air listens, like the sleeping water, still,
To catch the spiritual music of the hill,
Broke only by the slow clock tolling deep,
Or shout that wakes the ferry-man from sleep,   370
The echoed hoof nearing the distant shore,
The boat's first motion — made with dashing oar;
Sound of closed gate, across the water borne,
Hurrying the timid hare through rustling corn;
The sportive outcry of the mocking owl;   375
And at long intervals the mill-dog's howl;
The distant forge's swinging thump profound;
Or yell, in the deep woods, of lonely hound.

LINES

LEFT UPON A SEAT IN A YEW-TREE, WHICH STANDS NEAR
THE LAKE OF ESTHWAITE, ON A DESOLATE PART OF THE
SHORE, COMMANDING A BEAUTIFUL PROSPECT

NAY, Traveller! rest. This lonely Yew-tree stands
Far from all human dwelling: what if here
No sparkling rivulet spread the verdant herb?
What if the bee love not these barren boughs?
Yet, if the wind breathe soft, the curling waves,   5
That break against the shore, shall lull thy mind
By one soft impulse saved from vacancy.
——————————— Who he was
That piled these stones and with the mossy sod
First covered, and here taught this aged Tree   10
With its dark arms to form a circling bower,
I well remember. — He was one who owned
No common soul. In youth by science nursed,
And led by nature into a wild scene
Of lofty hopes, he to the world went forth   15
A favoured Being, knowing no desire
Which genius did not hallow; 'gainst the taint
Of dissolute tongues, and jealousy, and hate,
And scorn, — against all enemies prepared,
All but neglect. The world, for so it thought,   20
Owed him no service; wherefore he at once
With indignation turned himself away,
And with the food of pride sustained his soul
In solitude. — Stranger! these gloomy boughs
Had charms for him; and here he loved to sit,   25
His only visitants a straggling sheep,
The stone-chat, or the glancing sand-piper:
And on these barren rocks, with fern and heath,
And juniper and thistle, sprinkled o'er,
Fixing his downcast eye, he many an hour   30
A morbid pleasure nourished, tracing here
An emblem of his own unfruitful life:
And, lifting up his head, he then would gaze
On the more distant scene, — how lovely 'tis
Thou seest, — and he would gaze till it became   35
Far lovelier, and his heart could not sustain
The beauty, still more beauteous! Nor, that time,
When nature had subdued him to herself,
Would he forget those Beings to whose minds
Warm from the labours of benevolence   4C

The world, and human life, appeared a scene
Of kindred loveliness: then he would sigh,
Inly disturbed, to think that others felt
What he must never feel: and so, lost Man!
On visionary views would fancy feed,   45
Till his eye streamed with tears. In this deep vale
He died, — this seat his only monument.

    If Thou be one whose heart the holy forms
Of young imagination have kept pure,
Stranger! henceforth be warned; and know that pride,   50
Howe'er disguised in its own majesty,
Is littleness; that he who feels contempt
For any living thing, hath faculties
Which he has never used; that thought with him
Is in its infancy. The man whose eye   55
Is ever on himself doth look on one,
The least of Nature's works, one who might move
The wise man to that scorn which wisdom holds
Unlawful, ever. O be wiser, Thou!
Instructed that true knowledge leads to love;   60
True dignity abides with him alone
Who, in the silent hour of inward thought,
Can still suspect, and still revere himself,
In lowliness of heart.

THE REVERIE OF POOR SUSAN

At the corner of Wood Street, when daylight appears,
Hangs a Thrush that sings loud, it has sung for three years:
Poor Susan has passed by the spot, and has heard
In the silence of morning the song of the Bird.

'Tis a note of enchantment; what ails her? She sees   5
A mountain ascending, a vision of trees;
Bright volumes of vapour through Lothbury glide,
And a river flows on through the vale of Cheapside.

Green pastures she views in the midst of the dale,
Down which she so often has tripped with her pail;   10
And a single small cottage, a nest like a dove's,
The one only dwelling on earth that she loves.

She looks, and her heart is in heaven: but they fade,
The mist and the river, the hill and the shade:
The stream will not flow, and the hill will not rise,   15
And the colours have all passed away from her eyes!

THE OLD CUMBERLAND BEGGAR

The class of Beggars, to which the Old Man here described belongs, will probably soon be extinct. It consisted of poor, and, mostly, old and infirm persons, who confined themselves to a stated round in their neighbourhood, and had certain fixed days, on which, at different houses, they regularly received alms, sometimes in money, but mostly in provisions.

I saw an aged Beggar in my walk;
And he was seated, by the highway side,
On a low structure of rude masonry
Built at the foot of a huge hill, that they
Who lead their horses down the steep rough road   5
May thence remount at ease. The aged Man
Had placed his staff across the broad smooth stone
That overlays the pile; and, from a bag
All white with flour, the dole of village dames,
He drew his scraps and fragments, one by one;   10
And scanned them with a fixed and serious look
Of idle computation. In the sun,
Upon the second step of that small pile,
Surrounded by those wild unpeopled hills,
He sat, and ate his food in solitude: 15
And ever, scattered from his palsied hand,
That, still attempting to prevent the waste,
Was baffled still, the crumbs in little showers
Fell on the ground; and the small mountain birds,
Not venturing yet to peck their destined meal,   20
Approached within the length of half his staff.

   Him from my childhood have I known; and then
He was so old, he seems not older now;
He travels on, a solitary Man,
So helpless in appearance, that for him   25
The sauntering Horseman throws not with a slack
And careless hand his alms upon the ground,
But stops, — that he may safely lodge the coin
Within the old Man's hat; nor quits him so,
But still, when he has given his horse the rein,   30
Watches the aged Beggar with a look
Sidelong, and half-reverted. She who tends
The toll-gate, when in summer at her door
She turns her wheel, if on the road she sees
The aged Beggar coming, quits her work,   35
And lifts the latch for him that he may pass.

The post-boy, when his rattling wheels o'ertake
The aged Beggar in the woody lane,
Shouts to him from behind; and, if thus warned
The old man does not change his course, the boy   40
Turns with less noisy wheels to the roadside,
And passes gently by, without a curse
Upon his lips, or anger at his heart.

    He travels on, a solitary Man;
His age has no companion. On the ground   45
His eyes are turned, and, as he moves along,
They move along the ground; and, evermore,
Instead of common and habitual sight
Of fields with rural works, of hill and dale,
And the blue sky, one little span of earth   50
Is all his prospect. Thus, from day to day,
Bow-bent, his eyes for ever on the ground,
He plies his weary journey; seeing still,
And seldom knowing that he sees, some straw,
Some scattered leaf, or marks which, in one track,   55
The nails of cart or chariot-wheel have left
Impressed on the white road, — in the same line,
At distance still the same. Poor Traveller!
His staff trails with him; scarcely do his feet
Disturb the summer dust; he is so still   60
In look and motion, that the cottage curs,
Ere he has passed the door, will turn away,
Weary of barking at him. Boys and girls,
The vacant and the busy, maids and youths,
And urchins newly breeched — all pass him by: 65
Him even the slow-paced waggon leaves behind.

    But deem not this Man useless. — Statesmen! ye
Who are so restless in your wisdom, ye
Who have a broom still ready in your hands
To rid the world of nuisances; ye proud,   70
Heart-swoln, while in your pride ye contemplate
Your talents, power, or wisdom, deem him not
A burthen of the earth! 'Tis Nature's law
That none, the meanest of created things,
Of forms created the most vile and brute,   75
The dullest or most noxious, should exist
Divorced from good — a spirit and pulse of good,
A life and soul, to every mode of being
Inseparably linked. Then be assured
That least of all can aught — that ever owned   80
The heaven-regarding eye and front sublime

Which man is born to — sink, howe'er depressed,
So low as to be scorned without a sin;
Without offence to God cast out of view;
Like the dry remnant of a garden-flower   85
Whose seeds are shed, or as an implement
Worn out and worthless. While from door to door,
This old Man creeps, the villagers in him
Behold a record which together binds
Past deeds and offices of charity,   90
Else unremembered, and so keeps alive
The kindly mood in hearts which lapse of years,
And that half-wisdom half-experience gives,
Make slow to feel, and by sure steps resign
To selfishness and cold oblivious cares.   95
Among the farms and solitary huts,
Hamlets and thinly-scattered villages,
Where'er the aged Beggar takes his rounds,
The mild necessity of use compels
To acts of love; and habit does the work   100
Of reason; yet prepares that after-joy
Which reason cherishes. And thus the soul,
By that sweet taste of pleasure unpursued,
Doth find herself insensibly disposed
To virtue and true goodness.
                                    Some there are,   105
By their good works exalted, lofty minds
And meditative, authors of delight
And happiness, which to the end of time
Will live, and spread, and kindle: even such minds
In childhood, from this solitary Being,   110
Or from like wanderer, haply have received
(A thing more precious far than all that books
Or the solicitudes of love can do!)
That first mild touch of sympathy and thought,
In which they found their kindred with a world   115
Where want and sorrow were. The easy man
Who sits at his own door, — and, like the pear
That overhangs his head from the green wall,
Feeds in the sunshine; the robust and young,
The prosperous and unthinking, they who live   120
Sheltered, and flourish in a little grove
Of their own kindred; — all behold in him
A silent monitor, which on their minds
Must needs impress a transitory thought
Of self-congratulation, to the heart   125
Of each recalling his peculiar boons,
His charters and exemptions; and, perchance,

Though he to no one give the fortitude
And circumspection needful to preserve
His present blessings, and to husband up   130
The respite of the season, he, at least,
And 'tis no vulgar service, makes them felt.

    Yet further. —— Many, I believe, there are
Who live a life of virtuous decency,
Men who can hear the Decalogue and feel   135
No self-reproach; who of the moral law
Established in the land where they abide
Are strict observers; and not negligent
In acts of love to those with whom they dwell,
Their kindred, and the children of their blood.   140
Praise be to such, and to their slumbers peace!
— But of the poor man ask, the abject poor;
Go, and demand of him, if there be here
In this cold abstinence from evil deeds,
And these inevitable charities,   145
Wherewith to satisfy the human soul?
No — man is dear to man; the poorest poor
Long for some moments in a weary life
When they can know and feel that they have been,
Themselves, the fathers and the dealers-out   150
Of some small blessings; have been kind to such
As needed kindness, for this single cause,
That we have all of us one human heart.
— Such pleasure is to one kind Being known,
My neighbour, when with punctual care, each week   155
Duly as Friday comes, though pressed herself
By her own wants, she from her store of meal
Takes one unsparing handful for the scrip
Of this old Mendicant, and, from her door
Returning with exhilarated heart,   160
Sits by her fire, and builds her hope in heaven.

    Then let him pass, a blessing on his head!
And while in that vast solitude to which
The tide of things has borne him, he appears
To breathe and live but for himself alone,   165
Unblamed, uninjured, let him bear about
The good which the benignant law of Heaven
Has hung around him: and, while life is his,
Still let him prompt the unlettered villagers
To tender offices and pensive thoughts.   170
— Then let him pass, a blessing on his head!
And, long as he **can** **w**ander, let him breathe

The freshness of the valleys; let his blood
Struggle with frosty air and winter snows;
And let the chartered wind that sweeps the heath   175
Beat his grey locks against his withered face.
Reverence the hope whose vital anxiousness
Gives the last human interest to his heart.
May never HOUSE, misnamed of INDUSTRY,
Make him a captive! — for that pent-up din,   180
Those life-consuming sounds that clog the air,
Be his the natural silence of old age!
Let him be free of mountain solitudes;
And have around him, whether heard or not,
The pleasant melody of woodland birds.   185
Few are his pleasures: if his eyes have now
Been doomed so long to settle upon earth
That not without some effort they behold
The countenance of the horizontal sun,
Rising or setting, let the light at least   190
Find a free entrance to their languid orbs.
And let him, *where* and *when* he will, sit down
Beneath the trees, or on a grassy bank
Of highway side, and with the little birds
Share his chance-gathered meal; and, finally,   195
As in the eye of Nature he has lived,
So in the eye of Nature let him die!

ANIMAL TRANQUILLITY AND DECAY

THE little hedgerow birds,
That peck along the road, regard him not.
He travels on, and in his face, his step,
His gait, is one expression: every limb,
His look and bending figure, all bespeak   5
A man who does not move with pain, but moves
With thought. — He is insensibly subdued
To settled quiet: he is one by whom
All effort seems forgotten; one to whom
Long patience hath such mild composure given,   10
That patience now doth seem a thing of which
He hath no need. He is by nature led
To peace so perfect that the young behold
With envy, what the Old Man hardly feels.

A NIGHT-PIECE

—— THE sky is overcast
With a continuous cloud of texture close,
Heavy and wan, all whitened by the Moon,
Which through that veil is indistinctly seen,
A dull, contracted circle, yielding light   5
So feebly spread, that not a shadow falls,
Chequering the ground — from rock, plant, tree, or tower.
At length a pleasant instantaneous gleam
Startles the pensive traveller while he treads
His lonesome path, with unobserving eye   10
Bent earthwards; he looks up — the clouds are split
Asunder, — and above his head he sees
The clear Moon, and the glory of the heavens.
There, in a black-blue vault she sails along,
Followed by multitudes of stars, that, small   15
And sharp, and bright, along the dark abyss
Drive as she drives: how fast they wheel away,
Yet vanish not! — the wind is in the tree,
But they are silent; — still they roll along
Immeasurably distant; and the vault,   20
Built round by those white clouds, enormous clouds,
Still deepens its unfathomable depth.
At length the Vision closes; and the mind,
Not undisturbed by the delight it feels,
Which slowly settles into peaceful calm,   25
Is left to muse upon the solemn scene.

GOODY BLAKE AND HARRY GILL

A TRUE STORY

OH! what's the matter? what's the matter?
What is 't that ails young Harry Gill?
That evermore his teeth they chatter,
Chatter, chatter, chatter still!
Of waistcoats Harry has no lack,   5
Good duffle grey, and flannel fine;
He has a blanket on his back,
And coats enough to smother nine.

In March, December, and in July,
'Tis all the same with Harry Gill;   10

The neighbours tell, and tell you truly,
His teeth they chatter, chatter still.
At night, at morning, and at noon,
'Tis all the same with Harry Gill;
Beneath the sun, beneath the moon,   15
His teeth they chatter, chatter still!

Young Harry was a lusty drover,
And who so stout of limb as he?
His cheeks were red as ruddy clover;
His voice was like the voice of three.   20
Old Goody Blake was old and poor;
Ill fed she was, and thinly clad;
And any man who passed her door
Might see how poor a hut she had.

All day she spun in her poor dwelling: 25
And then her three hours' work at night,
Alas! 'twas hardly worth the telling,
It would not pay for candle-light.
Remote from sheltered village-green,
On a hill's northern side she dwelt,   30
Where from sea-blasts the hawthorns lean,
And hoary dews are slow to melt.

By the same fire to boil their pottage,
Two poor old Dames, as I have known,
Will often live in one small cottage;   35
But she, poor Woman! housed alone.
'Twas well enough when summer came,
The long, warm, lightsome summer-day,
Then at her door the *canty* Dame
Would sit, as any linnet, gay.   40

But when the ice our streams did fetter,
Oh then how her old bones would shake!
You would have said, if you had met her,
'Twas a hard time for Goody Blake.
Her evenings then were dull and dead: 45
Sad case it was, as you may think,
For very cold to go to bed;
And then for cold not sleep a wink.

O joy for her! whene'er in winter
The winds at night had made a rout;   50
And scattered many a lusty splinter
And many a rotten bough about.

Yet never had she, well or sick,
As every man who knew her says,
A pile beforehand, turf or stick,   55
Enough to warm her for three days.

Now, when the frost was past enduring,
And made her poor old bones to ache,
Could any thing be more alluring
Than an old hedge to Goody Blake?   60
And, now and then, it must be said,
When her old bones were cold and chill,
She left her fire, or left her bed,
To seek the hedge of Harry Gill.

Now-Harry he had long suspected   65
This trespass of old Goody Blake;
And vowed that she should be detected —
That he on her would vengeance take.
And oft from his warm fire he'd go,
And to the fields his road would take;   70
And there, at night, in frost and snow,
He watched to seize old Goody Blake.

And once, behind a rick of barley,
Thus looking out did Harry stand:
The moon was full and shining clearly,   75
And crisp with frost the stubble land.
— He hears a noise — he's all awake —
Again? — on tip-toe down the hill
He softly creeps — 'tis Goody Blake;
She's at the hedge of Harry Gill!   80

Right glad was he when he beheld her:
Stick after stick did Goody pull:
He stood behind a bush of elder,
Till she had filled her apron full.
When with her load she turned about,   85
The by-way back again to take;
He started forward, with a shout,
And sprang upon poor Goody Blake.

And fiercely by the arm he took her,
And by the arm he held her fast,   90
And fiercely by the arm he shook her,
And cried, "I've caught you then at last!"
Then Goody, who had nothing said,
Her bundle from her lap let fall;

And, kneeling on the sticks, she prayed   95
To God that is the judge of all.

She prayed, her withered hand uprearing,
While Harry held her by the arm —
"God! who art never out of hearing,
O may he never more be warm!"   100
The cold, cold moon above her head,
Thus on her knees did Goody pray;
Young Harry heard what she had said:
And icy cold he turned away.

He went complaining all the morrow   105
That he was cold and very chill:
His face was gloom, his heart was sorrow,
Alas! that day for Harry Gill!
That day he wore a riding-coat,
But not a whit the warmer he: 110
Another was on Thursday brought,
And ere the Sabbath he had three.

'Twas all in vain, a useless matter,
And blankets were about him pinned;
Yet still his jaws and teeth they clatter,   115
Like a loose casement in the wind.
And Harry's flesh it fell away;
And all who see him say, 'tis plain,
That, live as long as live he may,
He never will be warm again.   120

No word to any man he utters,
A-bed or up, to young or old;
But ever to himself he mutters,
"Poor Harry Gill is very cold."
A-bed or up, by night or day;   5
His teeth they chatter, chatter still.
Now think, ye farmers all, I pray,
Of Goody Blake and Harry Gill!

THE EXCURSION

BOOK FIRST

THE WANDERER

ARGUMENT

A summer forenoon. — The Author reaches a ruined Cottage upon a Common, and there meets with a revered Friend, the Wanderer, of whose education and course of life he gives an account. — The Wanderer, while resting under the shade of the Trees that surround the Cottage, relates the History of its last Inhabitant.

'Twas summer, and the sun had mounted high:
Southward the landscape indistinctly glared
Through a pale steam; but all the northern downs,
In clearest air ascending, showed far off
A surface dappled o'er with shadows flung   5
From brooding clouds; shadows that lay in spots
Determined and unmoved, with steady beams
Of bright and pleasant sunshine interposed;
To him most pleasant who on soft cool moss
Extends his careless limbs along the front   10
Of some huge cave, whose rocky ceiling casts
A twilight of its own, an ample shade,
Where the wren warbles, while the dreaming man,
Half conscious of the soothing melody,
With side-long eye looks out upon the scene,   15
By power of that impending covert thrown
To finer distance. Mine was at that hour
Far other lot, yet with good hope that soon
Under a shade as grateful I should find
Rest, and be welcomed there to livelier joy.   20
Across a bare wide Common I was toiling
With languid steps that by the slippery turf
Were baffled; nor could my weak arm disperse
The host of insects gathering round my face,
And ever with me as I paced along.   25

    Upon that open moorland stood a grove,
The wished-for port to which my course was bound.
Thither I came, and there, amid the gloom
Spread by a brotherhood of lofty elms,
Appeared a roofless Hut; four naked walls   30
That stared upon each other! — I looked round,

And to my wish and to my hope espied
The Friend I sought; a Man of reverend age,
But stout and hale, for travel unimpaired.
There was he seen upon the cottage-bench,   35
Recumbent in the shade, as if asleep;
An iron-pointed staff lay at his side.

  Him had I marked the day before — alone
And stationed in the public way, with face
Turned toward the sun then setting, while that staff   40
Afforded, to the figure of the man
Detained for contemplation or repose,
Graceful support; his countenance as he stood
Was hidden from my view, and he remained
Unrecognised; but, stricken by the sight,   45
With slackened footsteps I advanced, and soon
A glad congratulation we exchanged
At such unthought-of meeting. — For the night
We parted, nothing willingly; and now
He by appointment waited for me here,   50
Under the covert of these clustering elms.

  We were tried Friends: amid a pleasant vale,
In the antique market-village where was passed
My school-time, an apartment he had owned,
To which at intervals the Wanderer drew,   55
And found a kind of home or harbour there.
He loved me; from a swarm of rosy boys
Singled out me, as he in sport would say,
For my grave looks, too thoughtful for my years.
As I grew up, it was my best delight   60
To be his chosen comrade. Many a time,
On holidays, we rambled through the woods:
We sate — we walked; he pleased me with report
Of things which he had seen; and often touched
Abstrusest matter, reasonings of the mind   65
Turned inward; or at my request would sing
Old songs, the product of his native hills;
A skilful distribution of sweet sounds,
Feeding the soul, and eagerly imbibed
As cool refreshing water, by the care   70
Of the industrious husbandman, diffused
Through a parched meadow-ground, in time of drought.
Still deeper welcome found his pure discourse:
How precious when in riper days I learned
To weigh with care his words, and to rejoice   75
In the plain presence of his dignity!

Oh! many are the Poets that are sown
By Nature; men endowed with highest gifts,
The vision and the faculty divine;
Yet wanting the accomplishment of verse,   80
(Which, in the docile season of their youth,
It was denied them to acquire, through lack
Of culture and the inspiring aid of books,
Or haply by a temper too severe,
Or a nice backwardness afraid of shame)   85
Nor having e'er, as life advanced, been led
By circumstance to take unto the height
The measure of themselves, these favoured Beings,
All but a scattered few, live out their time,
Husbanding that which they possess within,   90
And go to the grave, unthought of. Strongest minds
Are often those of whom the noisy world
Hears least; else surely this Man had not left
His graces unrevealed and unproclaimed.
But, as the mind was filled with inward light,   95
So not without distinction had he lived,
Beloved and honoured — far as he was known.
And some small portion of his eloquent speech,
And something that may serve to set in view
The feeling pleasures of his loneliness,   100
His observations, and the thoughts his mind
Had dealt with — I will here record in verse;
Which, if with truth it correspond, and sink
Or rise as venerable Nature leads,
The high and tender Muses shall accept   105
With gracious smile, deliberately pleased,
And listening Time reward with sacred praise.

    Among the hills of Athol he was born;
Where, on a small hereditary farm,
An unproductive slip of rugged ground,   110
His Parents, with their numerous offspring, dwelt;
A virtuous household, though exceeding poor!
Pure livers were they all, austere and grave,
And fearing God; the very children taught
Stern self-respect, a reverence for God's word,   115
And an habitual piety, maintained
With strictness scarcely known on English ground.

    From his sixth year, the Boy of whom I speak,
In summer, tended cattle on the hills;
But, through the inclement and the perilous days   120
Of long-continuing winter, he repaired,

Equipped with satchel, to a school, that stood
Sole building on a mountain's dreary edge,
Remote from view of city spire, or sound
Of minster clock! From that bleak tenement   125
He, many an evening, to his distant home
In solitude returning, saw the hills
Grow larger in the darkness; all alone
Beheld the stars come out above his head,
And travelled through the wood, with no one near   130
To whom he might confess the things he saw.

So the foundations of his mind were laid.
In such communion, not from terror free,
While yet a child, and long before his time,
Had he perceived the presence and the power   135
Of greatness; and deep feelings had impressed
So vividly great objects that they lay
Upon his mind like substances, whose presence
Perplexed the bodily sense. He had received
A precious gift; for, as he grew in years,   140
With these impressions would he still compare
All his remembrances, thoughts, shapes, and forms;
And, being still unsatisfied with aught
Of dimmer character, he thence attained
An active power to fasten images   145
Upon his brain; and on their pictured lines
Intensely brooded, even till they acquired
The liveliness of dreams. Nor did he fail,
While yet a child, with a child's eagerness
Incessantly to turn his ear and eye   150
On all things which the moving seasons brought
To feed such appetite — nor this alone
Appeased his yearning: — in the after-day
Of boyhood, many an hour in caves forlorn,
And 'mid the hollow depths of naked crags   155
He sate, and even in their fixed lineaments,
Or from the power of a peculiar eye,
Or by creative feeling overborne,
Or by predominance of thought oppressed,
Even in their fixed and steady lineaments   160
He traced an ebbing and a flowing mind,
Expression ever varying!
                                        Thus informed,
He had small need of books; for many a tale
Traditionary, round the mountains hung,
And many a legend, peopling the dark woods,   165
Nourished Imagination in her growth,

And gave the Mind that apprehensive power
By which she is made quick to recognise
The moral properties and scope of things.
But eagerly he read, and read again,   170
Whate'er the minister's old shelf supplied;
The life and death of martyrs, who sustained,
With will inflexible, those fearful pangs
Triumphantly displayed in records left
Of persecution, and the Covenant — times   175
Whose echo rings through Scotland to this hour!
And there, by lucky hap, had been preserved
A straggling volume, torn and incomplete,
That left half-told the preternatural tale,
Romance of giants, chronicle of fiends,   180
Profuse in garniture of wooden cuts
Strange and uncouth; dire faces, figures dire,
Sharp-kneed, sharp-elbowed, and lean-ankled too,
With long and ghostly shanks — forms which once seen
Could never be forgotten!
             In his heart,   185
Where Fear sate thus, a cherished visitant,
Was wanting yet the pure delight of love
By sound diffused, or by the breathing air,
Or by the silent looks of happy things,
Or flowing from the universal face   190
Of earth and sky. But he had felt the power
Of Nature, and already was prepared,
By his intense conceptions, to receive
Deeply the lesson deep of love which he,
Whom Nature, by whatever means, has taught   195
To feel intensely, cannot but receive.

   Such was the Boy — but for the growing Youth
What soul was his, when, from the naked top
Of some bold headland, he beheld the sun
Rise up, and bathe the world in light! He looked —   200
Ocean and earth, the solid frame of earth
And ocean's liquid mass, in gladness lay
Beneath him: — Far and wide the clouds were touched,
And in their silent faces could he read
Unutterable love. Sound needed none,   205
Nor any voice of joy; his spirit drank
The spectacle: sensation, soul, and form,
All melted into him; they swallowed up
His animal being; in them did he live,
And by them did he live; they were his life.   210
In such access of mind, in such high hour

Of visitation from the living God,
Thought was not; in enjoyment it expired.
No thanks he breathed, he proffered no request;
Rapt into still communion that transcends   215
The imperfect offices of prayer and praise,
His mind was a thanksgiving to the power
That made him; it was blessedness and love!

A Herdsman on the lonely mountain tops,
Such intercourse was his, and in this sort   220
Was his existence oftentimes *possessed*.
O then how beautiful, how bright, appeared
The written promise! Early had he learned
To reverence the volume that displays
The mystery, the life which cannot die;   225
But in the mountains did he *feel* his faith.
All things, responsive to the writing, there
Breathed immortality, revolving life,
And greatness still revolving; infinite:
There littleness was not; the least of things   230
Seemed infinite; and there his spirit shaped
Her prospects, nor did he believe, — he *saw*.
What wonder if his being thus became
Sublime and comprehensive! Low desires,
Low thoughts had there no place; yet was his heart   235
Lowly; for he was meek in gratitude,
Oft as he called those ecstasies to mind,
And whence they flowed; and from them he acquired
Wisdom, which works thro' patience; thence he learned
In oft-recurring hours of sober thought   240
To look on Nature with a humble heart,
Self-questioned where it did not understand,
And with a superstitious eye of love.

So passed the time; yet to the nearest town
He duly went with what small overplus   245
His earnings might supply, and brought away
The book that most had tempted his desires
While at the stall he read. Among the hills
He gazed upon that mighty orb of song,
The divine Milton. Lore of different kind,   250
The annual savings of a toilsome life,
His School-master supplied; books that explain
The purer elements of truth involved
In lines and numbers, and, by charm severe,
(Especially perceived where nature droops   255
And feeling is suppressed) preserve the mind
Busy in solitude and poverty.

These occupations oftentimes deceived
The listless hours, while in the hollow vale,
Hollow and green, he lay on the green turf   260
In pensive idleness. What could he do,
Thus daily thirsting, in that lonesome life,
With blind endeavours? Yet, still uppermost,
Nature was at his heart as if he felt,
Though yet he knew not how, a wasting power   265
In all things that from her sweet influence
Might tend to wean him. Therefore with her hues,
Her forms, and with the spirit of her forms,
He clothed the nakedness of austere truth.
While yet he lingered in the rudiments   270
Of science, and among her simplest laws,
His triangles — they were the stars of heaven,
The silent stars! Oft did he take delight
To measure the altitude of some tall crag
That is the eagle's birth-place, or some peak   275
Familiar with forgotten years, that shows
Inscribed upon its visionary sides,
The history of many a winter storm,
Or obscure records of the path of fire.

    And thus before his eighteenth year was told,   280
Accumulated feelings pressed his heart
With still increasing weight; he was o'erpowered
By Nature; by the turbulence subdued
Of his own mind; by mystery and hope,
And the first virgin passion of a soul   285
Communing with the glorious universe.
Full often wished he that the winds might rage
When they were silent: far more fondly now
Than in his earlier season did he love
Tempestuous nights — the conflict and the sounds   290
That live in darkness. From his intellect
And from the stillness of abstracted thought
He asked repose; and, failing oft to win
The peace required, he scanned the laws of light
Amid the roar of torrents, where they send   295
From hollow clefts up to the clearer air
A cloud of mist, that smitten by the sun
Varies its rainbow hues. But vainly thus,
And vainly by all other means, he strove
To mitigate the fever of his heart.   300

    In dreams, in study, and in ardent thought,
Thus was he reared; much wanting to assist
The growth of intellect, yet gaining more,

And every moral feeling of his soul
Strengthened and braced, by breathing in content   305
The keen, the wholesome, air of poverty,
And drinking from the well of homely life.
— But, from past liberty, and tried restraints,
He now was summoned to select the course
Of humble industry that promised best   310
To yield him no unworthy maintenance.
Urged by his Mother, he essayed to teach
A village-school — but wandering thoughts were then
A misery to him; and the Youth resigned
A task he was unable to perform.   315

   That stern yet kindly Spirit, who constrains
The Savoyard to quit his naked rocks,
The free-born Swiss to leave his narrow vales,
(Spirit attached to regions mountainous
Like their own stedfast clouds) did now impel   320
His restless mind to look abroad with hope.
— An irksome drudgery seems it to plod on,
Through hot and dusty ways, or pelting storm,
A vagrant Merchant under a heavy load
Bent as he moves, and needing frequent rest;   325
Yet do such travellers find their own delight;
And their hard service, deemed debasing now,
Gained merited respect in simpler times;
When squire, and priest, and they who round them dwelt
In rustic sequestration — all dependent   330
Upon the PEDLAR's toil — supplied their wants,
Or pleased their fancies, with the wares he brought.
Not ignorant was the Youth that still no few
Of his adventurous countrymen were led
By perseverance in this track of life   335
To competence and ease: — to him it offered
Attractions manifold; — and this he chose.
— His Parents on the enterprise bestowed
Their farewell benediction, but with hearts
Foreboding evil. From his native hills   340
He wandered far; much did he see of men,
Their manners, their enjoyments, and pursuits,
Their passions and their feelings; chiefly those
Essential and eternal in the heart,
That, 'mid the simpler forms of rural life,   345
Exist more simple in their elements,
And speak a plainer language. In the woods,
A lone Enthusiast, and among the fields,
Itinerant in this labour, he had passed
The better portion of his time; and there   350

Spontaneously had his affections thriven
Amid the bounties of the year, the peace
And liberty of nature; there he kept
In solitude and solitary thought
His mind in a just equipoise of love.   355
Serene it was, unclouded by the cares
Of ordinary life; unvexed, unwarped
By partial bondage. In his steady course,
No piteous revolutions had he felt,
No wild varieties of joy and grief.   360
Unoccupied by sorrow of its own,
His heart lay open; and, by nature tuned
And constant disposition of his thoughts
To sympathy with man, he was alive
To all that was enjoyed where'er he went,   365
And all that was endured; for, in himself
Happy, and quiet in his cheerfulness,
He had no painful pressure from without
That made him turn aside from wretchedness
With coward fears. He could *afford* to suffer   370
With those whom he saw suffer. Hence it came
That in our best experience he was rich,
And in the wisdom of our daily life.
For hence, minutely, in his various rounds,
He had observed the progress and decay   375
Of many minds, of minds and bodies too;
The history of many families;
How they had prospered; how they were o'erthrown
By passion or mischance, or such misrule
Among the unthinking masters of the earth   380
As makes the nations groan.
                           This active course
He followed till provision for his wants
Had been obtained; — the Wanderer then resolved
To pass the remnant of his days, untasked
With needless services, from hardship free.   385
His calling laid aside, he lived at ease:
But still he loved to pace the public roads
And the wild paths; and, by the summer's warmth
Invited, often would he leave his home
And journey far, revisiting the scenes   390
That to his memory were most endeared.
— Vigorous in health, of hopeful spirits, undamped
By worldly-mindedness or anxious care;
Observant, studious, thoughtful, and refreshed
By knowledge gathered up from day to day;   395
Thus had he lived a long and innocent life.

The Scottish Church, both on himself and those
With whom from childhood he grew up, had held
The strong hand of her purity; and still
Had watched him with an unrelenting eye.   400
This he remembered in his riper age
With gratitude, and reverential thoughts.
But by the native vigour of his mind,
By his habitual wanderings out of doors,
By loneliness, and goodness, and kind works,   405
Whate'er, in docile childhood or in youth,
He had imbibed of fear or darker thought
Was melted all away; so true was this,
That sometimes his religion seemed to me
Self-taught, as of a dreamer in the woods;   410
Who to the model of his own pure heart
Shaped his belief, as grace divine inspired,
And human reason dictated with awe.
— And surely never did there live on earth
A man of kindlier nature. The rough sports   415
And teasing ways of children vexed not him;
Indulgent listener was he to the tongue
Of garrulous age; nor did the sick man's tale,
To his fraternal sympathy addressed,
Obtain reluctant hearing.

                              Plain his garb;   420
Such as might suit a rustic Sire, prepared
For sabbath duties; yet he was a man
Whom no one could have passed without remark.
Active and nervous was his gait; his limbs
And his whole figure breathed intelligence.   425
Time had compressed the freshness of his cheek
Into a narrower circle of deep red,
But had not tamed his eye; that, under brows
Shaggy and grey, had meanings which it brought
From years of youth; which, like a Being made   430
Of many Beings, he had wondrous skill
To blend with knowledge of the years to come,
Human, or such as lie beyond the grave.

                    ————————

So was He framed; and such his course of life
Who now, with no appendage but a staff,   435
The prized memorial of relinquished toils,
Upon that cottage-bench reposed his limbs,
Screened from the sun. Supine the Wanderer lay,
His eyes as if in drowsiness half shut,

The shadows of the breezy elms above   440
Dappling his face. He had not heard the sound
Of my approaching steps, and in the shade
Unnoticed did I stand some minutes' space.
At length I hailed him, seeing that his hat
Was moist with water-drops, as if the brim   445
Had newly scooped a running stream. He rose,
And ere our lively greeting into peace
Had settled, " 'Tis," said I, "a burning day:
My lips are parched with thirst, but you, it seems,
Have somewhere found relief." He, at the word,   450
Pointing towards a sweet-briar, bade me climb
The fence where that aspiring shrub looked out
Upon the public way. It was a plot
Of garden ground run wild, its matted weeds
Marked with the steps of those, whom, as they passed,   455
The gooseberry trees that shot in long lank slips,
Or currants, hanging from their leafless stems,
In scanty strings, had tempted to o'erleap
The broken wall. I looked around, and there,
Where two tall hedge-rows of thick alder boughs   460
Joined in a cold damp nook, espied a well
Shrouded with willow-flowers and plumy fern.
My thirst I slaked, and, from the cheerless spot
Withdrawing, straightway to the shade returned
Where sate the old Man on the cottage-bench;   465
And, while, beside him, with uncovered head,
I yet was standing, freely to respire,
And cool my temples in the fanning air,
Thus did he speak. "I see around me here
Things which you cannot see: we die, my Friend,   470
Nor we alone, but that which each man loved
And prized in his peculiar nook of earth
Dies with him, or is changed; and very soon
Even of the good is no memorial left.
— The Poets, in their elegies and songs   475
Lamenting the departed, call the groves,
They call upon the hills and streams to mourn,
And senseless rocks; nor idly; for they speak,
In these their invocations, with a voice
Obedient to the strong creative power   480
Of human passion. Sympathies there are
More tranquil, yet perhaps of kindred birth,
That steal upon the meditative mind,
And grow with thought. Beside yon spring I stood,
And eyed its waters till we seemed to feel   485
One sadness, they and I. For them a bond

Of brotherhood is broken: time has been
When, every day, the touch of human hand
Dislodged the natural sleep that binds them up
In mortal stillness; and they ministered   490
To human comfort. Stooping down to drink,
Upon the slimy foot-stone I espied
The useless fragment of a wooden bowl,
Green with the moss of years, and subject only
To the soft handling of the elements: 495
There let it lie — how foolish are such thoughts!
Forgive them; — never — never did my steps
Approach this door but she who dwelt within
A daughter's welcome gave me, and I loved her
As my own child. Oh, Sir! the good die first,   500
And they whose hearts are dry as summer dust
Burn to the socket. Many a passenger
Hath blessed poor Margaret for her gentle looks,
When she upheld the cool refreshment drawn
From that forsaken spring; and no one came   505
But he was welcome; no one went away
But that it seemed she loved him. She is dead,
The light extinguished of her lonely hut,
The hut itself abandoned to decay,
And she forgotten in the quiet grave.   510

   "I speak," continued he, "of One whose stock
Of virtues bloomed beneath this lowly roof.
She was a Woman of a steady mind,
Tender and deep in her excess of love;
Not speaking much, pleased rather with the joy   515
Of her own thoughts: by some especial care
Her temper had been framed, as if to make
A Being, who by adding love to peace
Might live on earth a life of happiness.
Her wedded Partner lacked not on his side   520
The humble worth that satisfied her heart:
Frugal, affectionate, sober, and withal
Keenly industrious. She with pride would tell
That he was often seated at his loom,
In summer, ere the mower was abroad   525
Among the dewy grass, — in early spring,
Ere the last star had vanished. — They who passed
At evening, from behind the garden fence
Might hear his busy spade, which he would ply,
After his daily work, until the light   530
Had failed, and every leaf and flower were lost
In the dark hedges. So their days were spent

In peace and comfort; and a pretty boy
Was their best hope, next to the God in heaven.

"Not twenty years ago, but you I think   535
Can scarcely bear it now in mind, there came
Two blighting seasons, when the fields were left
With half a harvest. It pleased Heaven to add
A worse affliction in the plague of war:
This happy Land was stricken to the heart!   540
A Wanderer then among the cottages,
I, with my freight of winter raiment, saw
The hardships of that season: many rich
Sank down, as in a dream, among the poor;
And of the poor did many cease to be,   545
And their place knew them not. Meanwhile, abridged
Of daily comforts, gladly reconciled
To numerous self-denials, Margaret
Went struggling on through those calamitous years
With cheerful hope, until the second autumn,   550
When her life's Helpmate on a sick-bed lay,
Smitten with perilous fever. In disease
He lingered long; and, when his strength returned,
He found the little he had stored, to meet
The hour of accident or crippling age,   555
Was all consumed. A second infant now
Was added to the troubles of a time
Laden, for them and all of their degree,
With care and sorrow: shoals of artisans
From ill-requited labour turned adrift   560
Sought daily bread from public charity,
They, and their wives and children — happier far
Could they have lived as do the little birds
That peck along the hedge-rows, or the kite
That makes her dwelling on the mountain rocks!   565

"A sad reverse it was for him who long
Had filled with plenty, and possessed in peace,
This lonely Cottage. At the door he stood,
And whistled many a snatch of merry tunes
That had no mirth in them; or with his knife   570
Carved uncouth figures on the heads of sticks —
Then, not less idly, sought, through every nook
In house or garden, any casual work
Of use or ornament; and with a strange,
Amusing, yet uneasy, novelty,   575
He mingled, where he might, the various tasks
Of summer, autumn, winter, and of spring.

But this endured not; his good humour soon
Became a weight in which no pleasure was:
And poverty brought on a petted mood   580
And a sore temper: day by day he drooped,
And he would leave his work — and to the town
Would turn without an errand his slack steps;
Or wander here and there among the fields.
One while he would speak lightly of his babes,   585
And with a cruel tongue: at other times
He tossed them with a false unnatural joy:
And 'twas a rueful thing to see the looks
Of the poor innocent children. 'Every smile,'
Said Margaret to me, here beneath these trees,   590
'Made my heart bleed.' "
            At this the Wanderer paused;
And, looking up to those enormous elms,
He said, " 'Tis now the hour of deepest noon.
At this still season of repose and peace,
This hour when all things which are not at rest   595
Are cheerful; while this multitude of flies
With tuneful hum is filling all the air;
Why should a tear be on an old Man's cheek?
Why should we thus, with an untoward mind,
And in the weakness of humanity,   600
From natural wisdom turn our hearts away;
To natural comfort shut our eyes and ears;
And, feeding on disquiet, thus disturb
The calm of nature with our restless thoughts?"

HE spake with somewhat of a solemn tone: 605
But, when he ended, there was in his face
Such easy cheerfulness, a look so mild,
That for a little time it stole away
All recollection; and that simple tale
Passed from my mind like a forgotten sound.   610
A while on trivial things we held discourse,
To me soon tasteless. In my own despite,
I thought of that poor Woman as of one
Whom I had known and loved. He had rehearsed
Her homely tale with such familiar power,   615
With such an active countenance, an eye
So busy, that the things of which he spake
Seemed present; and, attention now relaxed,
A heart-felt chillness crept along my veins.
I rose; and, having left the breezy shade,   620

Stood drinking comfort from the warmer sun,
That had not cheered me long — ere, looking round
Upon that tranquil Ruin, I returned,
And begged of the old Man that, for my sake,
He would resume his story.

                           He replied,   625
"It were a wantonness, and would demand
Severe reproof, if we were men whose hearts
Could hold vain dalliance with the misery
Even of the dead; contented thence to draw
A momentary pleasure, never marked   630
By reason, barren of all future good.
But we have known that there is often found
In mournful thoughts, and always might be found,
A power to virtue friendly; wer't not so,
I am a dreamer among men, indeed   635
An idle dreamer! 'Tis a common tale,
An ordinary sorrow of man's life,
A tale of silent suffering, hardly clothed
In bodily form. — But without further bidding
I will proceed.

                 While thus it fared with them,   640
To whom this cottage, till those hapless years,
Had been a blessed home, it was my chance
To travel in a country far remote;
And when these lofty elms once more appeared
What pleasant expectations lured me on   645
O'er the flat Common! — With quick step I reached
The threshold, lifted with light hand the latch;
But, when I entered, Margaret looked at me
A little while; then turned her head away
Speechless, — and, sitting down upon a chair,   650
Wept bitterly. I wist not what to do,
Nor how to speak to her. Poor Wretch! at last
She rose from off her seat, and then, — O Sir!
I cannot *tell* how she pronounced my name: —
With fervent love, and with a face of grief   655
Unutterably helpless, and a look
That seemed to cling upon me, she enquired
If I had seen her husband. As she spake
A strange surprise and fear came to my heart,
Nor had I power to answer ere she told   660
That he had disappeared — not two months gone.
He left his house: two wretched days had past,
And on the third, as wistfully she raised
Her head from off her pillow, to look forth,

Like one in trouble, for returning light, 665
Within her chamber-casement she espied
A folded paper, lying as if placed
To meet her waking eyes. This tremblingly
She opened — found no writing, but beheld
Pieces of money carefully enclosed, 670
Silver and gold. 'I shuddered at the sight,'
Said Margaret, 'for I knew it was his hand
That must have placed it there; and ere that day
Was ended, that long anxious day, I learned,
From one who by my husband had been sent 675
With the sad news, that he had joined a troop
Of soldiers, going to a distant land.
— He left me thus — he could not gather heart
To take a farewell of me; for he feared
That I should follow with my babes, and sink 680
Beneath the misery of that wandering life.'

"This tale did Margaret tell with many tears:
And, when she ended, I had little power
To give her comfort, and was glad to take
Such words of hope from her own mouth as served 685
To cheer us both. But long we had not talked
Ere we built up a pile of better thoughts,
And with a brighter eye she looked around
As if she had been shedding tears of joy.
We parted. — 'Twas the time of early spring; 690
I left her busy with her garden tools;
And well remember, o'er that fence she looked,
And, while I paced along the foot-way path,
Called out, and sent a blessing after me,
With tender cheerfulness, and with a voice 695
That seemed the very sound of happy thoughts.

"I roved o'er many a hill and many a dale,
With my accustomed load; in heat and cold,
Through many a wood and many an open ground,
In sunshine and in shade, in wet and fair, 700
Drooping or blithe of heart, as might befal;
My best companions now the driving winds,
And now the 'trotting brooks' and whispering trees,
And now the music of my own sad steps,
With many a short-lived thought that passed between, 705
And disappeared.
                          I journeyed back this way,
When, in the warmth of midsummer, the wheat
Was yellow; and the soft and bladed grass,

Springing afresh, had o'er the hay-field spread
Its tender verdure. At the door arrived,   710
I found that she was absent. In the shade,
Where now we sit, I waited her return.
Her cottage, then a cheerful object, wore
Its customary look, — only, it seemed,
The honeysuckle, crowding round the porch,   715
Hung down in heavier tufts; and that bright weed,
The yellow stone-crop, suffered to take root
Along the window's edge, profusely grew
Blinding the lower panes. I turned aside,
And strolled into her garden. It appeared   720
To lag behind the season, and had lost
Its pride of neatness. Daisy-flowers and thrift
Had broken their trim border-lines, and straggled
O'er paths they used to deck: carnations, once
Prized for surpassing beauty, and no less   725
For the peculiar pains they had required,
Declined their languid heads, wanting support.
The cumbrous bind-weed, with its wreaths and bells,
Had twined about her two small rows of peas,
And dragged them to the earth.

                            Ere this an hour   730
Was wasted. — Back I turned my restless steps;
A stranger passed; and, guessing whom I sought,
He said that she was used to ramble far. —
The sun was sinking in the west; and now
I sate with sad impatience. From within   735
Her solitary infant cried aloud;
Then, like a blast that dies away self-stilled,
The voice was silent. From the bench I rose;
But neither could divert nor soothe my thoughts.
The spot, though fair, was very desolate —   740
The longer I remained, more desolate:
And, looking round me, now I first observed
The corner stones, on either side the porch,
With dull red stains discoloured, and stuck o'er
With tufts and hairs of wool, as if the sheep,   745
That fed upon the Common, thither came
Familiarly, and found a couching-place
Even at her threshold. Deeper shadows fell
From these tall elms; the cottage-clock struck eight; —
I turned, and saw her distant a few steps.   750
Her face was pale and thin — her figure, too,
Was changed. As she unlocked the door, she said,
'It grieves me you have waited here so long,
But, in good truth, I've wandered much of late:

And, sometimes — to my shame I speak — have need   755
Of my best prayers to bring me back again.'
While on the board she spread our evening meal,
She told me — interrupting not the work
Which gave employment to her listless hands —
That she had parted with her elder child;   760
To a kind master on a distant farm
Now happily apprenticed. — 'I perceive
You look at me, and you have cause; to-day
I have been travelling far; and many days
About the fields I wander, knowing this   765
Only, that what I seek I cannot find;
And so I waste my time: for I am changed;
And to myself,' said she, 'have done much wrong
And to this helpless infant. I have slept
Weeping, and weeping have I waked; my tears   770
Have flowed as if my body were not such
As others are; and I could never die.
But I am now in mind and in my heart
More easy; and I hope,' said she, 'that God
Will give me patience to endure the things   775
Which I behold at home.'
                         It would have grieved
Your very soul to see her. Sir, I feel
The story linger in my heart; I fear
'Tis long and tedious; but my spirit clings
To that poor Woman: — so familiarly   780
Do I perceive her manner, and her look,
And presence; and so deeply do I feel
Her goodness, that, not seldom, in my walks
A momentary trance comes over me;
And to myself I seem to muse on One   785
By sorrow laid asleep; or borne away,
A human being destined to awake
To human life, or something very near
To human life, when he shall come again
For whom she suffered. Yes, it would have grieved   790
Your very soul to see her: evermore
Her eyelids drooped, her eyes downward were cast;
And, when she at her table gave me food,
She did not look at me. Her voice was low,
Her body was subdued. In every act   795
Pertaining to her house-affairs, appeared
The careless stillness of a thinking mind
Self-occupied; to which all outward things
Are like an idle matter. Still she sighed,
But yet no motion of the breast was seen,   800

No heaving of the heart. While by the fire
We sate together, sighs came on my ear,
I knew not how, and hardly whence they came.

"Ere my departure, to her care I gave,
For her son's use, some tokens of regard,   805
Which with a look of welcome she received;
And I exhorted her to place her trust
In God's good love, and seek his help by prayer.
I took my staff, and, when I kissed her babe,
The tears stood in her eyes. I left her then   810
With the best hope and comfort I could give:
She thanked me for my wish; — but for my hope
It seemed she did not thank me.
                                        I returned,
And took my rounds along this road again
When on its sunny bank the primrose flower   815
Peeped forth, to give an earnest of the Spring.
I found her sad and drooping: she had learned
No tidings of her husband; if he lived,
She knew not that he lived; if he were dead,
She knew not he was dead. She seemed the same   820
In person and appearance; but her house
Bespake a sleepy hand of negligence;
The floor was neither dry nor neat, the hearth
Was comfortless, and her small lot of books,
Which, in the cottage-window, heretofore   825
Had been piled up against the corner panes
In seemly order, now, with straggling leaves
Lay scattered here and there, open or shut,
As they had chanced to fall. Her infant Babe
Had from its Mother caught the trick of grief,   830
And sighed among its playthings. I withdrew,
And once again entering the garden saw,
More plainly still, that poverty and grief
Were now come nearer to her: weeds defaced
The hardened soil, and knots of withered grass: 835
No ridges there appeared of clear black mold,
No winter greenness; of her herbs and flowers,
It seemed the better part were gnawed away
Or trampled into earth; a chain of straw,
Which had been twined about the slender stem   840
Of a young apple-tree, lay at its root;
The bark was nibbled round by truant sheep.
— Margaret stood near, her infant in her arms,
And, noting that my eye was on the tree,
She said, 'I fear it will be dead and gone   845

Ere Robert come again.' When to the House
We had returned together, she enquired
If I had any hope: — but for her babe
And for her little orphan boy, she said,
She had no wish to live, that she must die   850
Of sorrow. Yet I saw the idle loom
Still in its place; his Sunday garments hung
Upon the self-same nail; his very staff
Stood undisturbed behind the door.
                                    And when,
In bleak December, I retraced this way,   855
She told me that her little babe was dead,
And she was left alone. She now, released
From her maternal cares, had taken up
The employment common through these wilds, and gained,
By spinning hemp, a pittance for herself;   860
And for this end had hired a neighbour's boy
To give her needful help. That very time
Most willingly she put her work aside,
And walked with me along the miry road,
Heedless how far; and, in such piteous sort   865
That any heart had ached to hear her, begged
That, wheresoe'er I went, I still would ask
For him whom she had lost. We parted then —
Our final parting; for from that time forth
Did many seasons pass ere I returned   870
Into this tract again.
                          Nine tedious years;
From their first separation, nine long years,
She lingered in unquiet widowhood;
A Wife and Widow. Needs must it have been
A sore heart-wasting! I have heard, my Friend,   875
That in yon arbour oftentimes she sate
Alone, through half the vacant sabbath day;
And, if a dog passed by, she still would quit
The shade, and look abroad. On this old bench
For hours she sate; and evermore her eye   880
Was busy in the distance, shaping things
That made her heart beat quick. You see that path,
Now faint, — the grass has crept o'er its grey line;
There, to and fro, she paced through many a day
Of the warm summer, from a belt of hemp   885
That girt her waist, spinning the long-drawn thread
With backward steps. Yet ever as there passed
A man whose garments showed the soldier's red,
Or crippled mendicant in sailor's garb,
The little child who sate to turn the wheel   890

Ceased from his task; and she with faltering voice
Made many a fond enquiry; and when they,
Whose presence gave no comfort, were gone by,
Her heart was still more sad. And by yon gate,
That bars the traveller's road, she often stood,   895
And when a stranger horseman came, the latch
Would lift, and in his face look wistfully:
Most happy, if, from aught discovered there
Of tender feeling, she might dare repeat
The same sad question. Meanwhile her poor Hut   900
Sank to decay; for he was gone, whose hand,
At the first nipping of October frost,
Closed up each chink, and with fresh bands of straw
Chequered the green-grown thatch. And so she lived
Through the long winter, reckless and alone;   905
Until her house by frost, and thaw, and rain,
Was sapped; and while she slept, the nightly damps
Did chill her breast; and in the stormy day
Her tattered clothes were ruffled by the wind,
Even at the side of her own fire. Yet still   910
She loved this wretched spot, nor would for worlds
Have parted hence; and still that length of road,
And this rude bench, one torturing hope endeared,
Fast rooted at her heart: and here, my Friend, —
In sickness she remained; and here she died;   915
Last human tenant of these ruined walls!"

  The old Man ceased: he saw that I was moved;
From that low bench, rising instinctively
I turned aside in weakness, nor had power
To thank him for the tale which he had told.   920
I stood, and leaning o'er the garden wall
Reviewed that Woman's sufferings; and it seemed
To comfort me while with a brother's love
I blessed her in the impotence of grief.
Then towards the cottage I returned; and traced   925
Fondly, though with an interest more mild,
That secret spirit of humanity
Which, 'mid the calm oblivious tendencies
Of nature, 'mid her plants, and weeds, and flowers,
And silent overgrowings, still survived.   930
The old Man, noting this, resumed, and said,
"My Friend! enough to sorrow you have given,
The purposes of wisdom ask no more:
Nor more would she have craved as due to One
Who, in her worst distress, had ofttimes felt   935
The unbounded might of prayer; and learned, with soul

Fixed on the Cross, that consolation springs,
From sources deeper far than deepest pain,
For the meek Sufferer. Why then should we read
The forms of things with an unworthy eye? 940
She sleeps in the calm earth, and peace is here.
I well remember that those very plumes,
Those weeds, and the high spear-grass on that wall,
By mist and silent rain-drops silvered o'er,
As once I passed, into my heart conveyed 945
So still an image of tranquillity,
So calm and still, and looked so beautiful
Amid the uneasy thoughts which filled my mind,
That what we feel of sorrow and despair
From ruin and from change, and all the grief 950
That passing shows of Being leave behind,
Appeared an idle dream, that could maintain,
Nowhere, dominion o'er the enlightened spirit
Whose meditative sympathies repose
Upon the breast of Faith. I turned away, 955
And walked along my road in happiness."

    He ceased. Ere long the sun declining shot
A slant and mellow radiance, which began
To fall upon us, while, beneath the trees,
We sate on that low bench: and now we felt, 960
Admonished thus, the sweet hour coming on.
A linnet warbled from those lofty elms,
A thrush sang loud, and other melodies,
At distance heard, peopled the milder air.
The old Man rose, and, with a sprightly mien 965
Of hopeful preparation, grasped his staff;
Together casting then a farewell look
Upon those silent walls, we left the shade;
And, ere the stars were visible, had reached
A village-inn, — our evening resting-place. 970

From THE RECLUSE

On Man, on Nature, and on Human Life,
Musing in solitude, I oft perceive   755
Fair trains of imagery before me rise,
Accompanied by feelings of delight
Pure, or with no unpleasing sadness mixed;
And I am conscious of affecting thoughts
And dear remembrances, whose presence soothes   760
Or elevates the Mind, intent to weigh
The good and evil of our mortal state.
— To these emotions, whencesoe'er they come,
Whether from breath of outward circumstance,
Or from the Soul — an impulse to herself —   765
I would give utterance in numerous verse.
Of Truth, of Grandeur, Beauty, Love, and Hope,
And melancholy Fear subdued by Faith;
Of blessed consolations in distress;
Of moral strength, and intellectual Power;   770
Of joy in widest commonalty spread;
Of the individual Mind that keeps her own
Inviolate retirement, subject there
To Conscience only, and the law supreme
Of that Intelligence which governs all —   775
I sing: — "fit audience let me find though few!"

So prayed, more gaining than he asked, the Bard —
In holiest mood. Urania, I shall need
Thy guidance, or a greater Muse, if such
Descend to earth or dwell in highest heaven!   780
For I must tread on shadowy ground, must sink
Deep — and, aloft ascending, breathe in worlds
To which the heaven of heavens is but a veil.
All strength — all terror, single or in bands,
That ever was put forth in personal form —   785
Jehovah — with his thunder, and the choir
Of shouting Angels, and the empyreal thrones —
I pass them unalarmed. Not Chaos, not
The darkest pit of lowest Erebus,
Nor aught of blinder vacancy, scooped out   790
By help of dreams — can breed such fear and awe
As fall upon us often when we look
Into our Minds, into the Mind of Man —
My haunt, and the main region of my song.
— Beauty — a living Presence of the earth,   795

Surpassing the most fair ideal Forms
Which craft of delicate Spirits hath composed
From earth's materials — waits upon my steps;
Pitches her tents before me as I move,
An hourly neighbour. Paradise, and groves   800
Elysian, Fortunate Fields — like those of old
Sought in the Atlantic Main — why should they be
A history only of departed things,
Or a mere fiction of what never was?
For the discerning intellect of Man,   805
When wedded to this goodly universe
In love and holy passion, shall find these
A simple produce of the common day.
— I, long before the blissful hour arrives,
Would chant, in lonely peace, the spousal verse   810
Of this great consummation: — and, by words
Which speak of nothing more than what we are,
Would I arouse the sensual from their sleep
Of Death, and win the vacant and the vain
To noble raptures; while my voice proclaims   815
How exquisitely the individual Mind
(And the progressive powers perhaps no less
Of the whole species) to the external World
Is fitted: — and how exquisitely, too —
Theme this but little heard of among men —   820
The external World is fitted to the Mind;
And the creation (by no lower name
Can it be called) which they with blended might
Accomplish: — this is our high argument.
— Such grateful haunts foregoing, if I oft   825
Must turn elsewhere — to travel near the tribes
And fellowships of men, and see ill sights
Of madding passions mutually inflamed;
Must hear Humanity in fields and groves
Pipe solitary anguish; or must hang   830
Brooding above the fierce confederate storm
Of sorrow, barricadoed evermore
Within the walls of cities — may these sounds
Have their authentic comment; that even these
Hearing, I be not downcast or forlorn! —   835
Descend, prophetic Spirit! that inspir'st
The human Soul of universal earth,
Dreaming on things to come; and dost possess
A metropolitan temple in the hearts
Of mighty Poets; upon me bestow   840
A gift of genuine insight; that my Song
With star-like virtue in its place may shine,

Shedding benignant influence, and secure,
Itself, from all malevolent effect
Of those mutations that extend their sway   845
Throughout the nether sphere! — And if with this
I mix more lowly matter; with the thing
Contemplated, describe the Mind and Man
Contemplating; and who, and what he was —
The transitory Being that beheld   850
This Vision; when and where, and how he lived; —
Be not this labour useless. If such theme
May sort with highest objects, then — dread Power!
Whose gracious favour is the primal source
Of all illumination — may my Life   855
Express the image of a better time,
More wise desires, and simpler manners; — nurse
My Heart in genuine freedom: — all pure thoughts
Be with me; — so shall thy unfailing love
Guide, and support, and cheer me to the end!   860

TO MY SISTER

IT is the first mild day of March:
Each minute sweeter than before,
The redbreast sings from the tall larch
That stands beside our door.

There is a blessing in the air,   5
Which seems a sense of joy to yield
To the bare trees, and mountains bare,
And grass in the green field.

My sister! ('tis a wish of mine)
Now that our morning meal is done,   10
Make haste, your morning task resign;
Come forth and feel the sun.

Edward will come with you; — and, pray,
Put on with speed your woodland dress;
And bring no book: for this one day   15
We'll give to idleness.

No joyless forms shall regulate
Our living calendar:
We from to-day, my Friend, will date
The opening of the year.   20

Love, now a universal birth,
From heart to heart is stealing,
From earth to man, from man to earth:
— It is the hour of feeling.

One moment now may give us more   25
Than years of toiling reason:
Our minds shall drink at every pore
The spirit of the season.

Some silent laws our hearts will make,
Which they shall long obey: 30
We for the year to come may take
Our temper from to-day.

And from the blessed power that rolls
About, below, above,
We'll frame the measure of our souls: 35
They shall be tuned to love.

Then come, my Sister! come, I pray,
With speed put on your woodland dress;
And bring no book: for this one day
We'll give to idleness.   40

LINES WRITTEN IN EARLY SPRING

I HEARD a thousand blended notes,
While in a grove I sate reclined,
In that sweet mood when pleasant thoughts
Bring sad thoughts to the mind.

To her fair works did Nature link   5
The human soul that through me ran;
And much it grieved my heart to think
What man has made of man.

Through primrose tufts, in that green bower,
The periwinkle trailed its wreaths;   10
And 'tis my faith that every flower
Enjoys the air it breathes.

The birds around me hopped and played,
Their thoughts I cannot measure: —
But the least motion which they made,   15
It seemed a thrill of pleasure.

The budding twigs spread out their fan,
To catch the breezy air;
And I must think, do all I can,
That there was pleasure there.　　　　　　　　　　20

If this belief from heaven be sent,
If such be Nature's holy plan,
Have I not reason to lament
What man has made of man?

WE ARE SEVEN

———— A SIMPLE Child,
That lightly draws its breath,
And feels its life in every limb,
What should it know of death?

I met a little cottage Girl:　　　　　　　　　　　5
She was eight years old, she said;
Her hair was thick with many a curl
That clustered round her head.

She had a rustic, woodland air,
And she was wildly clad:　　　　　　　　　　　10
Her eyes were fair, and very fair;
— Her beauty made me glad.

"Sisters and brothers, little Maid,
How many may you be?"
"How many? Seven in all," she said,　　　　　　15
And wondering looked at me.

"And where are they? I pray you tell."
She answered, "Seven are we;
And two of us at Conway dwell,
And two are gone to sea.　　　　　　　　　　　20

"Two of us in the church-yard lie,
My sister and my brother;
And, in the church-yard cottage, I
Dwell near them with my mother."

"You say that two at Conway dwell,　　　　　　25
And two are gone to sea,
Yet ye are seven! I pray you tell,
Sweet Maid, how this may be."

Then did the little Maid reply,
"Seven boys and girls are we;   30
Two of us in the church-yard lie,
Beneath the church-yard tree."

"You run about, my little Maid,
Your limbs they are alive;
If two are in the church-yard laid,   35
Then ye are only five."

"Their graves are green, they may be seen,"
The little Maid replied,
"Twelve steps or more from my mother's door,
And they are side by side.   40

"My stockings there I often knit,
My kerchief there I hem;
And there upon the ground I sit,
And sing a song to them.

"And often after sun-set, Sir,   45
When it is light and fair,
I take my little porringer,
And eat my supper there.

"The first that died was sister Jane;
In bed she moaning lay,   50
Till God released her of her pain;
And then she went away.

"So in the church-yard she was laid;
And, when the grass was dry,
Together round her grave we played,   55
My brother John and I.

"And when the ground was white with snow,
And I could run and slide,
My brother John was forced to go,
And he lies by her side."   60

"How many are you, then," said I,
"If they two are in heaven?"
Quick was the little Maid's reply,
"O Master! we are seven."

"But they are dead; those two are dead!   65
Their spirits are in heaven!"

'Twas throwing words away; for still
The little Maid would have her will,
And said, "Nay, we are seven!"

ANECDOTE FOR FATHERS

"Retine vim istam, falsa enim dicam, si coges."
EUSEBIUS.

I HAVE a boy of five years old;
His face is fair and fresh to see;
His limbs are cast in beauty's mould,
And dearly he loves me.

One morn we strolled on our dry walk,   5
Our quiet home all full in view,
And held such intermitted talk
As we are wont to do.

My thoughts on former pleasures ran;
I thought of Kilve's delightful shore,   10
Our pleasant home when spring began,
A long, long year before.

A day it was when I could bear
Some fond regrets to entertain;
With so much happiness to spare,   15
I could not feel a pain.

The green earth echoed to the feet
Of lambs that bounded through the glade,
From shade to sunshine, and as fleet
From sunshine back to shade.   20

Birds warbled round me — and each trace
Of inward sadness had its charm;
Kilve, thought I, was a favoured place,
And so is Liswyn farm.

My boy beside me tripped, so slim   25
And graceful in his rustic dress!
And, as we talked, I questioned him,
In very idleness.

"Now tell me, had you rather be,"
I said, and took him by the arm,   30

"On Kilve's smooth shore, by the green sea,
Or here at Liswyn farm?"

In careless mood he looked at me,
While still I held him by the arm,
And said, "At Kilve I'd rather be   35
Than here at Liswyn farm."

"Now, little Edward, say why so:
My little Edward, tell me why." —
"I cannot tell, I do not know." —
"Why, this is strange," said I;   40

"For, here are woods, hills smooth and warm:
There surely must some reason be
Why you would change sweet Liswyn farm
For Kilve by the green sea."

At this, my boy hung down his head,   45
He blushed with shame, nor made reply;
And three times to the child I said,
"Why, Edward, tell me why?"

His head he raised — there was in sight,
It caught his eye, he saw it plain —   50
Upon the house-top, glittering bright,
A broad and gilded vane.

Then did the boy his tongue unlock,
And eased his mind with this reply:
"At Kilve there was no weather-cock;   55
And that's the reason why."

O dearest, dearest boy! my heart
For better lore would seldom yearn,
Could I but teach the hundredth part
Of what from thee I learn.   60

A WHIRL-BLAST FROM BEHIND THE HILL

A WHIRL-BLAST from behind the hill
Rushed o'er the wood with startling sound;
Then — all at once the air was still,
And showers of hailstones pattered round.
Where leafless oaks towered high above,   5
I sat within an undergrove

Of tallest hollies, tall and green;
A fairer bower was never seen.
From year to year the spacious floor
With withered leaves is covered o'er,   10
And all the year the bower is green.
But see! where'er the hailstones drop
The withered leaves all skip and hop;
There's not a breeze — no breath of air —
Yet here, and there, and every where   15
Along the floor, beneath the shade
By those embowering hollies made,
The leaves in myriads jump and spring,
As if with pipes and music rare
Some Robin Good-fellow were there,   20
And all those leaves, in festive glee,
Were dancing to the minstrelsy.

SIMON LEE

THE OLD HUNTSMAN;
WITH AN INCIDENT IN WHICH HE WAS CONCERNED

In the sweet shire of Cardigan,
Not far from pleasant Ivor-hall,
An old Man dwells, a little man, —
'Tis said he once was tall.
Full five-and-thirty years he lived   5
A running huntsman merry;
And still the centre of his cheek
Is red as a ripe cherry.

No man like him the horn could sound,
And hill and valley rang with glee   10
When Echo bandied, round and round,
The halloo of Simon Lee.
In those proud days, he little cared
For husbandry or tillage;
To blither tasks did Simon rouse   15
The sleepers of the village.

He all the country could outrun,
Could leave both man and horse behind;
And often, ere the chase was done,
He reeled, and was stone-blind.   20
And still there's something in the world

At which his heart rejoices;
For when the chiming hounds are out,
He dearly loves their voices!

But, oh the heavy change! — bereft   25
Of health, strength, friends, and kindred, see!
Old Simon to the world is left
In liveried poverty.
His Master's dead, — and no one now
Dwells in the Hall of Ivor;   30
Men, dogs, and horses, all are dead;
He is the sole survivor.

And he is lean and he is sick;
His body, dwindled and awry,
Rests upon ankles swoln and thick;   35
His legs are thin and dry.
One prop he has, and only one,
His wife, an aged woman,
Lives with him, near the waterfall,
Upon the village Common.   40

Beside their moss-grown hut of clay,
Not twenty paces from the door,
A scrap of land they have, but they
Are poorest of the poor.
This scrap of land he from the heath   45
Enclosed when he was stronger;
But what to them avails the land
Which he can till no longer?

Oft, working by her Husband's side,
Ruth does what Simon cannot do;   50
For she, with scanty cause for pride,
Is stouter of the two.
And, though you with your utmost skill
From labour could not wean them,
'Tis little, very little — all   55
That they can do between them.

Few months of life has he in store
As he to you will tell,
For still, the more he works, the more
Do his weak ankles swell.   80
My gentle Reader, I perceive
How patiently you've waited,
And now I fear that you expect
Some tale will be related.

O Reader! had you in your mind   65
Such stores as silent thought can bring,
O gentle Reader! you would find
A tale in every thing.
What more I have to say is short,
And you must kindly take it: 70
It is no tale; but, should you think,
Perhaps a tale you'll make it.

One summer-day I chanced to see
This old Man doing all he could
To unearth the root of an old tree,   75
A stump of rotten wood.
The mattock tottered in his hand;
So vain was his endeavour,
That at the root of the old tree
He might have worked for ever.   80

"You're overtasked, good Simon Lee,
Give me your tool," to him I said;
And at the word right gladly he
Received my proffered aid.
I struck, and with a single blow   85
The tangled root I severed,
At which the poor old Man so long
And vainly had endeavoured.

The tears into his eyes were brought,
And thanks and praises seemed to run   90
So fast out of his heart, I thought
They never would have done.
— I've heard of hearts unkind, kind deeds
With coldness still returning;
Alas! the gratitude of men   95
Hath oftener left me mourning.

HER EYES ARE WILD

I

HER eyes are wild, her head is bare,
The sun has burnt her coal-black hair;
Her eyebrows have a rusty stain,
And she came far from over the main.
She has a baby on her arm,
Or else she were alone:
And underneath the hay-stack warm,

And on the greenwood stone,
She talked and sung the woods among,
And it was in the English tongue. 10

II

"Sweet babe! they say that I am mad,
But nay, my heart is far too glad;
And I am happy when I sing
Full many a sad and doleful thing:
Then, lovely baby, do not fear! 15
I pray thee have no fear of me;
But safe as in a cradle, here
My lovely baby! thou shalt be:
To thee I know too much I owe;
I cannot work thee any woe. 20

III

"A fire was once within my brain;
And in my head a dull, dull pain;
And fiendish faces, one, two, three,
Hung at my breast, and pulled at me;
But then there came a sight of joy; 25
It came at once to do me good;
I waked, and saw my little boy,
My little boy of flesh and blood;
Oh joy for me that sight to see!
For he was here, and only he. 30

IV

"Suck, little babe, oh suck again!
It cools my blood; it cools my brain;
Thy lips I feel them, baby! they
Draw from my heart the pain away.
Oh! press me with thy little hand; 35
It loosens something at my chest;
About that tight and deadly band
I feel thy little fingers prest.
The breeze I see is in the tree:
It comes to cool my babe and me. 40

V

"Oh! love me, love me, little boy!
Thou art thy mother's only joy;

And do not dread the waves below,
When o'er the sea-rock's edge we go;
The high crag cannot work me harm, 45
Nor leaping torrents when they howl;
The babe I carry on my arm,
He saves for me my precious soul;
Then happy lie; for blest am I;
Without me my sweet babe would die. 50

VI

"Then do not fear, my boy! for thee
Bold as a lion will I be;
And I will always be thy guide,
Through hollow snows and rivers wide.
I'll build an Indian bower; I know 55
The leaves that make the softest bed:
And, if from me thou wilt not go,
But still be true till I am dead,
My pretty thing! then thou shalt sing
As merry as the birds in spring. 60

VII

"Thy father cares not for my breast,
'Tis thine, sweet baby, there to rest;
'Tis all thine own! — and, if its hue
Be changed, that was so fair to view,
'Tis fair enough for thee, my dove! 65
My beauty, little child, is flown,
But thou wilt live with me in love;
And what if my poor cheek be brown?
'Tis well for me, thou canst not see
How pale and wan it else would be. 70

VIII

"Dread not their taunts, my little Life;
I am thy father's wedded wife;
And underneath the spreading tree
We two will live in honesty.
If his sweet boy he could forsake, 75
With me he never would have stayed:
From him no harm my babe can take;
But he, poor man! is wretched made;
And every day we two will pray
For him that's gone and far away. 80

IX

"I'll teach my boy the sweetest things:
I'll teach him how the owlet sings.
My little babe! thy lips are still,
And thou hast almost sucked thy fill.
— Where art thou gone, my own dear child? 85
What wicked looks are those I see?
Alas! alas! that look so wild,
It never, never came from me:
If thou art mad, my pretty lad,
Then I must be for ever sad. 90

X

"Oh! smile on me, my little lamb!
For I thy own dear mother am:
My love for thee has well been tried:
I've sought thy father far and wide.
I know the poisons of the shade; 95
I know the earth-nuts fit for food:
Then, pretty dear, be not afraid:
We'll find thy father in the wood.
Now laugh and be gay, to the woods away!
And there, my babe, we'll live for aye." 100

THE IDIOT BOY

'Tis eight o'clock, — a clear March night,
The moon is up, — the sky is blue,
The owlet, in the moonlight air,
Shouts from nobody knows where;
He lengthens out his lonely shout, 5
Halloo! halloo! a long halloo!

— Why bustle thus about your door,
What means this bustle, Betty Foy?
Why are you in this mighty fret?
And why on horseback have you set 10
Him whom you love, your Idiot Boy?

Scarcely a soul is out of bed;
Good Betty, put him down again;
His lips with joy they burr at you;
But, Betty! what has he to do 15
With stirrup, saddle, or with rein?

But Betty's bent on her intent;
For her good neighbour, Susan Gale,
Old Susan, she who dwells alone,
Is sick, and makes a piteous moan,   20
As if her very life would fail.

There's not a house within a mile,
No hand to help them in distress;
Old Susan lies a-bed in pain,
And sorely puzzled are the twain,   25
For what she ails they cannot guess.

And Betty's husband's at the wood,
Where by the week he doth abide,
A woodman in the distant vale;
There's none to help poor Susan Gale;   30
What must be done? what will betide?

And Betty from the lane has fetched
Her Pony, that is mild and good;
Whether he be in joy or pain,
Feeding at will along the lane,   35
Or bringing faggots from the wood.

And he is all in travelling trim, —
And, by the moonlight, Betty Foy
Has on the well-girt saddle set
(The like was never heard of yet)   40
Him whom she loves, her Idiot Boy.

And he must post without delay
Across the bridge and through the dale,
And by the church, and o'er the down,
To bring a Doctor from the town,   45
Or she will die, old Susan Gale.

There is no need of boot or spur,
There is no need of whip or wand;
For Johnny has his holly-bough,
And with a *hurly-burly* now   50
He shakes the green bough in his hand.

And Betty o'er and o'er has told
The Boy, who is her best delight,
Both what to follow, what to shun,
What do, and what to leave undone,   55
How turn to left, and how to right.

And Betty's most especial charge,
Was, "Johnny! Johnny! mind that you
Come home again, nor stop at all, —
Come home again, whate'er befal,   60
My Johnny, do, I pray you do."

To this did Johnny answer make,
Both with his head and with his hand,
And proudly shook the bridle too;
And then! his words were not a few,   65
Which Betty well could understand.

And now that Johnny is just going,
Though Betty's in a mighty flurry,
She gently pats the Pony's side,
On which her Idiot Boy must ride,   70
And seems no longer in a hurry.

But when the Pony moved his legs,
Oh! then for the poor Idiot Boy!
For joy he cannot hold the bridle,
For joy his head and heels are idle,   75
He's idle all for very joy.

And while the Pony moves his legs,
In Johnny's left hand you may see
The green bough motionless and dead:
The Moon that shines above his head   80
Is not more still and mute than he.

His heart it was so full of glee,
That till full fifty yards were gone,
He quite forgot his holly whip,
And all his skill in horsemanship: 85
Oh! happy, happy, happy John.

And while the Mother, at the door,
Stands fixed, her face with joy o'erflows,
Proud of herself, and proud of him,
She sees him in his travelling trim,   90
How quietly her Johnny goes.

The silence of her Idiot Boy,
What hopes it sends to Betty's heart!
He's at the guide-post — he turns right;
She watches till he's out of sight,   95
And Betty will not then depart.

Burr, burr — now Johnny's lips they burr,
As loud as any mill, or near it;
Meek as a lamb the Pony moves,
And Johnny makes the noise he loves,   100
And Betty listens, glad to hear it.

Away she hies to Susan Gale:
Her Messenger's in merry tune;
The owlets hoot, the owlets curr,
And Johnny's lips they burr, burr, burr,   105
As on he goes beneath the moon.

His steed and he right well agree;
For of this Pony there's a rumour,
That, should he lose his eyes and ears,
And should he live a thousand years,   110
He never will be out of humour.

But then he is a horse that thinks!
And when he thinks, his pace is slack;
Now, though he knows poor Johnny well,
Yet, for his life, he cannot tell   115
What he has got upon his back.

So through the moonlight lanes they go,
And far into the moonlight dale,
And by the church, and o'er the down,
To bring a Doctor from the town,   120
To comfort poor old Susan Gale.

And Betty, now at Susan's side,
Is in the middle of her story,
What speedy help her Boy will bring,
With many a most diverting thing,   125
Of Johnny's wit, and Johnny's glory.

And Betty, still at Susan's side,
By this time is not quite so flurried:
Demure with porringer and plate
She sits, as if in Susan's fate   130
Her life and soul were buried.

But Betty, poor good woman! she,
You plainly in her face may read it,
Could lend out of that moment's store
Five years of happiness or more   135
To any that might need it.

But yet I guess that now and then
With Betty all was not so well;
And to the road she turns her ears,
And thence full many a sound she hears,   140
Which she to Susan will not tell.

Poor Susan moans, poor Susan groans;
"As sure as there's a moon in heaven,"
Cries Betty, "he'll be back again;
They'll both be here — 'tis almost ten —   145
Both will be here before eleven."

Poor Susan moans, poor Susan groans;
The clock gives warning for eleven;
'Tis on the stroke — "He must be near,"
Quoth Betty, "and will soon be here,   150
As sure as there's a moon in heaven."

The clock is on the stroke of twelve,
And Johnny is not yet in sight:
— The Moon's in heaven, as Betty sees,
But Betty is not quite at ease;   155
And Susan has a dreadful night.

And Betty, half an hour ago,
On Johnny vile reflections cast:
"A little idle sauntering Thing!"
With other names, an endless string;   160
But now that time is gone and past.

And Betty's drooping at the heart,
That happy time all past and gone,
"How can it be he is so late?
The Doctor, he has made him wait;   165
Susan! they'll both be here anon."

And Susan's growing worse and worse,
And Betty's in a sad *quandary;*
And then there's nobody to say
If she must go, or she must stay!   170
— She's in a sad *quandary.*

The clock is on the stroke of one;
But neither Doctor nor his Guide
Appears along the moonlight road;
There's neither horse nor man abroad,   175
And Betty's still at Susan's side.

And Susan now begins to fear
Of sad mischances not a few,
That Johnny may perhaps be drowned;
Or lost, perhaps, and never found;   180
Which they must both for ever rue.

She prefaced half a hint of this
With, "God forbid it should be true!"
At the first word that Susan said
Cried Betty, rising from the bed,   185
"Susan, I'd gladly stay with you.

"I must be gone, I must away:
Consider, Johnny's but half-wise;
Susan, we must take care of him,
If he is hurt in life or limb" —   190
"Oh God forbid!" poor Susan cries.

"What can I do?" says Betty, going,
"What can I do to ease your pain?
Good Susan tell me, and I'll stay;
I fear you're in a dreadful way,   195
But I shall soon be back again."

"Nay, Betty, go! good Betty, go!
There's nothing that can ease my pain."
Then off she hies; but with a prayer
That God poor Susan's life would spare,   200
Till she comes back again.

So, through the moonlight lane she goes,
And far into the moonlight dale;
And how she ran, and how she walked,
And all that to herself she talked,   205
Would surely be a tedious tale.

In high and low, above, below,
In great and small, in round and square,
In tree and tower was Johnny seen,
In bush and brake, in black and green;   210
'Twas Johnny, Johnny, every where.

And while she crossed the bridge, there came
A thought with which her heart is sore —
Johnny perhaps his horse forsook,
To hunt the moon within the brook,   215
And never will be heard of more.

Now is she high upon the down,
Alone amid a prospect wide;
There's neither Johnny nor his Horse
Among the fern or in the gorse;   220
There's neither Doctor nor his Guide.

"Oh saints! what is become of him?
Perhaps he's climbed into an oak,
Where he will stay till he is dead;
Or, sadly he has been misled,   225
And joined the wandering gipsy-folk.

"Or him that wicked Pony's carried
To the dark cave, the goblin's hall;
Or in the castle he's pursuing
Among the ghosts his own undoing;   230
Or playing with the waterfall."

At poor old Susan then she railed,
While to the town she posts away;
"If Susan had not been so ill,
Alas! I should have had him still,   235
My Johnny, till my dying day."

Poor Betty, in this sad distemper,
The Doctor's self could hardly spare:
Unworthy things she talked, and wild;
Even he, of cattle the most mild,   240
The Pony had his share.

But now she's fairly in the town,
And to the Doctor's door she hies;
'Tis silence all on every side;
The town so long, the town so wide,   245
Is silent as the skies.

And now she's at the Doctor's door,
She lifts the knocker, rap, rap, rap;
The Doctor at the casement shows
His glimmering eyes that peep and doze!   250
And one hand rubs his old night-cap.

"O Doctor! Doctor! where's my Johnny?"
"I'm here, what is 't you want with me?"
"O Sir! you know I'm Betty Foy,
And I have lost my poor dear Boy,   255
You know him — him you often see;

"He's not so wise as some folks be:"
"The devil take his wisdom!" said
The Doctor, looking somewhat grim,
"What, Woman! should I know of him?"   260
And, grumbling, he went back to bed!

"O woe is me! O woe is me!
Here will I die; here will I die;
I thought to find my lost one here,
But he is neither far nor near,   265
Oh! what a wretched Mother I!"

She stops, she stands, she looks about;
Which way to turn she cannot tell.
Poor Betty! it would ease her pain
If she had heart to knock again;   270
— The clock strikes three — a dismal knell!

Then up along the town she hies,
No wonder if her senses fail;
This piteous news so much it shocked her,
She quite forgot to send the Doctor,   275
To comfort poor old Susan Gale.

And now she's high upon the down,
And she can see a mile of road:
"O cruel! I'm almost threescore;
Such night as this was ne'er before,   280
There's not a single soul abroad."

She listens, but she cannot hear
The foot of horse, the voice of man;
The streams with softest sound are flowing,
The grass you almost hear it growing,   285
You hear it now, if e'er you can.

The owlets through the long blue night
Are shouting to each other still;
Fond lovers! yet not quite hob nob,
They lengthen out the tremulous sob,   290
That echoes far from hill to hill.

Poor Betty now has lost all hope,
Her thoughts are bent on deadly sin,
A green-grown pond she just has past,
And from the brink she hurries fast,   295
Lest she should drown herself therein.

And now she sits her down and weeps;
Such tears she never shed before;
"Oh dear, dear Pony! my sweet joy!
Oh carry back my Idiot Boy!   300
And we will ne'er o'erload thee more."

A thought is come into her head:
The Pony he is mild and good,
And we have always used him well;
Perhaps he's gone along the dell,   305
And carried Johnny to the wood.

Then up she springs as if on wings;
She thinks no more of deadly sin;
If Betty fifty ponds should see,
The last of all her thoughts would be   310
To drown herself therein.

O Reader! now that I might tell
What Johnny and his Horse are doing!
What they've been doing all this time,
Oh could I put it into rhyme,   315
A most delightful tale pursuing!

Perhaps, and no unlikely thought!
He with his Pony now doth roam
The cliffs and peaks so high that are,
To lay his hands upon a star,   320
And in his pocket bring it home.

Perhaps he's turned himself about,
His face unto his horse's tail,
And, still and mute, in wonder lost,
All silent as a horseman-ghost,   325
He travels slowly down the vale.

And now, perhaps, is hunting sheep,
A fierce and dreadful hunter he;
Yon valley, now so trim and green,
In five months' time, should he be seen,   330
A desert wilderness will be!

Perhaps, with head and heels on fire,
And like the very soul of evil,
He's galloping away, away,
And so will gallop on for aye,   335
The bane of all that dread the devil!

I to the Muses have been bound
These fourteen years, by strong indentures:
O gentle Muses! let me tell
But half of what to him befel;   340
He surely met with strange adventures.

O gentle Muses! is this kind?
Why will ye thus my suit repel?
Why of your further aid bereave me?
And can ye thus unfriended leave me;   345
Ye Muses! whom I love so well?

Who's yon, that, near the waterfall,
Which thunders down with headlong force,
Beneath the moon, yet shining fair,
As careless as if nothing were,   350
Sits upright on a feeding horse?

Unto his horse — there feeding free,
He seems, I think, the rein to give;
Of moon or stars he takes no heed;
Of such we in romances read: 355
— 'Tis Johnny! Johnny! as I live.

And that's the very Pony, too!
Where is she, where is Betty Foy?
She hardly can sustain her fears;
The roaring waterfall she hears,   360
And cannot find her Idiot Boy.

Your Pony's worth his weight in gold:
Then calm your terrors, Betty Foy!
She's coming from among the trees,
And now all full in view she sees   365
Him whom she loves, her Idiot Boy.

And Betty sees the Pony too:
Why stand you thus, good Betty Foy?
It is no goblin, 'tis no ghost,
'Tis he whom you so long have lost,   370
He whom you love, your Idiot Boy.

She looks again — her arms are up —
She screams — she cannot move for joy;
She darts, as with a torrent's force,
She almost has o'erturned the Horse,   375
And fast she holds her Idiot Boy.

And Johnny burrs, and laughs aloud;
Whether in cunning or in joy
I cannot tell; but while he laughs,
Betty a drunken pleasure quaffs   380
To hear again her Idiot Boy.

And now she's at the Pony's tail,
And now is at the Pony's head, —
On that side now, and now on this;
And, almost stifled with her bliss,   385
A few sad tears does Betty shed.

She kisses o'er and o'er again
Him whom she loves, her Idiot Boy;
She's happy here, is happy there,
She is uneasy every where;   390
Her limbs are all alive with joy.

She pats the Pony, where or when
She knows not, happy Betty Foy!
The little Pony glad may be,
But he is milder far than she,   395
You hardly can perceive his joy.

"Oh! Johnny, never mind the Doctor;
You've done your best, and that is all:"
She took the reins, when this was said,
And gently turned the Pony's head   400
From the loud waterfall.

By this the stars were almost gone,
The moon was setting on the hill,
So pale you scarcely looked at her:
The little birds began to stir,   405
Though yet their tongues were still.

The Pony, Betty, and her Boy,
Wind slowly through the woody dale;
And who is she, betimes abroad,
That hobbles up the steep rough road?   410
Who is it, but old Susan Gale?

Long time lay Susan lost in thought;
And many dreadful fears beset her,
Both for her Messenger and Nurse;
And, as her mind grew worse and worse,   415
Her body — it grew better.

She turned, she tossed herself in bed,
On all sides doubts and terrors met her;
Point after point did she discuss;
And, while her mind was fighting thus,   420
Her body still grew better.

"Alas! what is become of them?
These fears can never be endured;
I'll to the wood." — The word scarce said,
Did Susan rise up from her bed,   425
As if by magic cured.

Away she goes up hill and down,
And to the wood at length is come;
She spies her Friends, she shouts a greeting;
Oh me! it is a merry meeting   430
As ever was in Christendom.

The owls have hardly sung their last,
While our four travellers homeward wend;
The owls have hooted all night long,
And with the owls began my song,   435
And with the owls must end.

For while they all were travelling home,
Cried Betty, "Tell us, Johnny, do,
Where all this long night you have been,
What you have heard, what you have seen: 440
And, Johnny, mind you tell us true."

Now Johnny all night long had heard
The owls in tuneful concert strive;
No doubt too he the moon had seen;
For in the moonlight he had been   445
From eight o'clock till five.

And thus, to Betty's question, he
Made answer, like a traveller bold,
(His very words I give to you,)
"The cocks did crow to-whoo, to-whoo,   450
And the sun did shine so cold!"
— Thus answered Johnny in his glory,
And that was all his travel's story.

THE THORN

I

"THERE is a Thorn — it looks so old,
In truth, you'd find it hard to say
How it could ever have been young,
It looks so old and grey.
Not higher than a two years' child   5
It stands erect, this aged Thorn;
No leaves it has, no prickly points;
It is a mass of knotted joints,
A wretched thing forlorn.
It stands erect, and like a stone   10
With lichens is it overgrown.

II

"Like rock or stone, it is o'ergrown,
With lichens to the very top,
And hung with heavy tufts of moss,
A melancholy crop: 15
Up from the earth these mosses creep,
And this poor Thorn they clasp it round
So close, you'd say that they are bent
With plain and manifest intent
To drag it to the ground;   20
And all have joined in one endeavour
To bury this poor Thorn for ever.

III

"High on a mountain's highest ridge,
Where oft the stormy winter gale
Cuts like a scythe, while through the clouds 25
It sweeps from vale to vale;
Not five yards from the mountain path,
This Thorn you on your left espy;
And to the left, three yards beyond,
You see a little muddy pond   30
Of water — never dry
Though but of compass small, and bare
To thirsty suns and parching air.

IV

"And, close beside this aged Thorn,
There is a fresh and lovely sight,   35
A beauteous heap, a hill of moss,
Just half a foot in height.
All lovely colours there you see,
All colours that were ever seen;
And mossy network too is there,   40
As if by hand of lady fair
The work had woven been;
And cups, the darlings of the eye,
So deep is their vermilion dye.

V

"Ah me! what lovely tints are there   45
Of olive green and scarlet bright,
In spikes, in branches, and in stars,
Green, red, and pearly white!
This heap of earth o'ergrown with moss,
Which close beside the Thorn you see,   50
So fresh in all its beauteous dyes,
Is like an infant's grave in size,
As like as like can be:
But never, never any where,
An infant's grave was half so fair.   55

VI

"Now would you see this aged Thorn,
This pond, and beauteous hill of moss,
You must take care and choose your time
The mountain when to cross.
For oft there sits between the heap   60
So like an infant's grave in size,
And that same pond of which I spoke,
A Woman in a scarlet cloak,
And to herself she cries,
'Oh misery! oh misery!   65
Oh woe is me! oh misery!'

VII

"At all times of the day and night
This wretched Woman thither goes;

And she is known to every star,
And every wind that blows;   **70**
And there, beside the Thorn, she sits
When the blue daylight's in the skies,
And when the whirlwind's on the hill,
Or frosty air is keen and still,
And to herself she cries,   **75**
Oh misery! oh misery!
Oh woe is me! oh misery!' "

VIII

"Now wherefore, thus, by day and night,
In rain, in tempest, and in snow,
Thus to the dreary mountain-top   **80**
Does this poor Woman go?
And why sits she beside the Thorn
When the blue daylight's in the sky
Or when the whirlwind's on the hill,
Or frosty air is keen and still,   **85**
And wherefore does she cry? —
O wherefore? wherefore? tell me why
Does she repeat that doleful cry?"

IX

"I cannot tell; I wish I could;
For the true reason no one knows: **90**
But would you gladly view the spot,
The spot to which she goes;
The hillock like an infant's grave,
The pond — and Thorn, so old and grey;
Pass by her door — 'tis seldom shut —   **95**
And, if you see her in her hut —
Then to the spot away!
I never heard of such as dare
Approach the spot when she is there."

X

"But wherefore to the mountain-top   **100**
Can this unhappy Woman go,
Whatever star is in the skies,
Whatever wind may blow?"
"Full twenty years are past and gone
Since she (her name is Martha Ray)   **105**
Gave with a maiden's true good-will

Her company to Stephen Hill;
And she was blithe and gay,
While friends and kindred all approved
Of him whom tenderly she loved.   110

XI

"And they had fixed the wedding day,
The morning that must wed them both;
But Stephen to another Maid
Had sworn another oath;
And, with this other Maid, to church   115
Unthinking Stephen went —
Poor Martha! on that woeful day
A pang of pitiless dismay
Into her soul was sent;
A fire was kindled in her breast,   120
Which might not burn itself to rest.

XII

"They say, full six months after this,
While yet the summer leaves were green,
She to the mountain-top would go,
And there was often seen.   125
What could she seek? — or wish to hide?
Her state to any eye was plain;
She was with child, and she was mad;
Yet often was she sober sad
From her exceeding pain.   130
O guilty Father — would that death
Had saved him from that breach of faith!

XIII

"Sad case for such a brain to hold
Communion with a stirring child!
Sad case, as you may think, for one   135
Who had a brain so wild!
Last Christmas-eve we talked of this,
And grey-haired Wilfred of the glen
Held that the unborn infant wrought
About its mother's heart, and brought   140
Her senses back again:
And, when at last her time drew near,
Her looks were calm, her senses clear.

XIV

"More know I not, I wish I did,
And it should all be told to you;   145
For what became of this poor child
No mortal ever knew;
Nay — if a child to her was born
No earthly tongue could ever tell;
And if 'twas born alive or dead,   150
Far less could this with proof be said;
But some remember well,
That Martha Ray about this time
Would up the mountain often climb.

XV

"And all that winter, when at night   155
The wind blew from the mountain-peak,
'Twas worth your while, though in the dark,
The churchyard path to seek:
For many a time and oft were heard
Cries coming from the mountain head: 160
Some plainly living voices were;
And others, I've heard many swear,
Were voices of the dead:
I cannot think, whate'er they say,
They had to do with Martha Ray.   165

XVI

"But that she goes to this old Thorn,
The Thorn which I described to you,
And there sits in a scarlet cloak,
I will be sworn is true.
For one day with my telescope,   170
To view the ocean wide and bright,
When to this country first I came,
Ere I had heard of Martha's name,
I climbed the mountain's height: —
A storm came on, and I could see   175
No object higher than my knee.

XVII

" 'Twas mist and rain, and storm and rain:
No screen, no fence could I discover;
And then the wind! in sooth, it was

A wind full ten times over. 180
I looked around, I thought I saw
A jutting crag, — and off I ran,
Head-foremost, through the driving rain,
The shelter of the crag to gain;
And, as I am a man, 185
Instead of jutting crag, I found
A Woman seated on the ground.

XVIII

"I did not speak — I saw her face;
Her face! — it was enough for me;
I turned about and heard her cry, 190
'Oh misery! oh misery!'
And there she sits, until the moon
Through half the clear blue sky will go;
And, when the little breezes make
The waters of the pond to shake, 195
As all the country know,
She shudders, and you hear her cry,
'Oh misery! oh misery!' "

XIX

"But what's the Thorn? and what the pond?
And what the hill of moss to her? 200
And what the creeping breeze that comes
The little pond to stir?"
"I cannot tell; but some will say
She hanged her baby on the tree;
Some say she drowned it in the pond, 205
Which is a little step beyond:
But all and each agree,
The little Babe was buried there,
Beneath that hill of moss so fair.

XX

"I've heard, the moss is spotted red 210
With drops of that poor infant's blood;
But kill a new-born infant thus,
I do not think she could!
Some say, if to the pond you go,
And fix on it a steady view, 215
The shadow of a babe you trace,
A baby and a baby's face,

And that it looks at you;
Whene'er you look on it, 'tis plain
The baby looks at you again.

220

XXI

"And some had sworn an oath that she
Should be to public justice brought;
And for the little infant's bones
With spades they would have sought.
But instantly the hill of moss
Before their eyes began to stir!
And, for full fifty yards around,
The grass — it shook upon the ground!
Yet all do still aver
The little Babe lies buried there,
Beneath that hill of moss so fair.

225

230

XXII

"I cannot tell how this may be,
But plain it is the Thorn is bound
With heavy tufts of moss that strive
To drag it to the ground;
And this I know, full many a time,
When she was on the mountain high,
By day, and in the silent night,
When all the stars shone clear and bright,
That I have heard her cry,
'Oh misery! oh misery!
Oh woe is me! oh misery!'"

235

240

PETER BELL

A TALE

What's in a *Name?*

    ◦   ◦   ◦   ◦   ◦

Brutus will start a Spirit as soon as Cæsar!

PROLOGUE

THERE's something in a flying horse,
There's something in a huge balloon;
But through the clouds I'll never float
Until I have a little Boat,
Shaped like the crescent-moon.   5

And now I *have* a little Boat,
In shape a very crescent-moon:
Fast through the clouds my Boat can sail;
But if perchance your faith should fail,
Look up — and you shall see me soon!   10

The woods, my Friends, are round you roaring,
Rocking and roaring like a sea;
The noise of danger's in your ears,
And ye have all a thousand fears
Both for my little Boat and me!   15

Meanwhile untroubled I admire
The pointed horns of my canoe;
And, did not pity touch my breast,
To see how ye are all distrest,
Till my ribs ached, I'd laugh at you!   20

Away we go, my Boat and I —
Frail man ne'er sate in such another;
Whether among the winds we strive,
Or deep into the clouds we dive,
Each is contented with the other.   25

Away we go — and what care we
For treasons, tumults, and for wars?
We are as calm in our delight
As is the crescent-moon so bright
Among the scattered stars.   30

Up goes my Boat among the stars
Through many a breathless field of light,
Through many a long blue field of ether,
Leaving ten thousand stars beneath her:
Up goes my little Boat so bright!   35

The Crab, the Scorpion, and the Bull —
We pry among them all; have shot
High o'er the red-haired race of Mars,
Covered from top to toe with scars;
Such company I like it not!   40

The towns in Saturn are decayed,
And melancholy Spectres throng them; —
The Pleiads, that appear to kiss
Each other in the vast abyss,
With joy I sail among them.   45

Swift Mercury resounds with mirth,
Great Jove is full of stately bowers;
But these, and all that they contain,
What are they to that tiny grain,
That little Earth of ours?   50

Then back to Earth, the dear green Earth: —
Whole ages if I here should roam,
The world for my remarks and me
Would not a whit the better be;
I've left my heart at home.   55

See! there she is, the matchless Earth!
There spreads the famed Pacific Ocean!
Old Andes thrusts yon craggy spear
Through the grey clouds; the Alps are here,
Like waters in commotion!   60

Yon tawny slip is Libya's sands;
That silver thread the river Dnieper;
And look, where clothed in brightest green
Is a sweet Isle, of isles the Queen;
Ye fairies, from all evil keep her!   65

And see the town where I was born!
Around those happy fields we span
In boyish gambols; — I was lost
Where I have been, but on this coast
I feel I am a man.   70

Never did fifty things at once
Appear so lovely, never, never; —
How tunefully the forests ring!
To hear the earth's soft murmuring
Thus could I hang for ever!   75

"Shame on you!" cried my little Boat,
"Was ever such a homesick Loon,
Within a living Boat to sit,
And make no better use of it;
A Boat twin-sister of the crescent-moon!   80

"Ne'er in the breast of full-grown Poet
Fluttered so faint a heart before; —
Was it the music of the spheres
That overpowered your mortal ears?
— Such din shall trouble them no more.   85

"These nether precincts do not lack
Charms of their own; — then come with me;
I want a comrade, and for you
There's nothing that I would not do;
Nought is there that you shall not see.   90

"Haste! and above Siberian snows
We'll sport amid the boreal morning;
Will mingle with her lustres gliding
Among the stars, the stars now hiding,
And now the stars adorning.   95

"I know the secrets of a land
Where human foot did never stray;
Fair is that land as evening skies,
And cool, though in the depth it lies
Of burning Africa.   100

"Or we'll into the realm of Faery,
Among the lovely shades of things;
The shadowy forms of mountains bare,
And streams, and bowers, and ladies fair,
The shades of palaces and kings!   105

"Or, if you thirst with hardy zeal
Less quiet regions to explore,
Prompt voyage shall to you reveal
How earth and heaven are taught to feel
The might of magic lore!"   110

"My little vagrant Form of light,
My gay and beautiful Canoe,
Well have you played your friendly part;
As kindly take what from my heart
Experience forces — then adieu!   115

"Temptation lurks among your words;
But, while these pleasures you're pursuing
Without impediment or let,
No wonder if you quite forget
What on the earth is doing.   120

"There was a time when all mankind
Did listen with a faith sincere
To tuneful tongues in mystery versed;
Then Poets fearlessly rehearsed
The wonders of a wild career.   125

"Go — (but the world's a sleepy world,
And 'tis, I fear, an age too late)
Take with you some ambitious Youth!
For, restless Wanderer! I, in truth,
Am all unfit to be your mate.   130

"Long have I loved what I behold,
The night that calms, the day that cheers;
The common growth of mother-earth
Suffices me — her tears, her mirth,
Her humblest mirth and tears.   135

"The dragon's wing, the magic ring,
I shall not covet for my dower,
If I along that lowly way
With sympathetic heart may stray,
And with a soul of power.   140

"These given, what more need I desire
To stir, to soothe, or elevate?
What nobler marvels than the mind
May in life's daily prospect find,
May find or there create?   145

"A potent wand doth Sorrow wield;
What spell so strong as guilty Fear!
Repentance is a tender Sprite;
If aught on earth have heavenly might,
'Tis lodged within her silent tear.   150

"But grant my wishes, — let us now
Descend from this ethereal height;
Then take thy way, adventurous Skiff,
More daring far than Hippogriff,
And be thy own delight!   155

"To the stone-table in my garden,
Loved haunt of many a summer hour,
The Squire is come: his daughter Bess
Beside him in the cool recess
Sits blooming like a flower.   160

"With these are many more convened;
They know not I have been so far; —
I see them there, in number nine,
Beneath the spreading Weymouth-pine!
I see them — there they are!   165

"There sits the Vicar and his Dame;
And there my good friend, Stephen Otter;
And, ere the light of evening fail,
To them I must relate the Tale
Of Peter Bell the Potter."   170

Off flew the Boat — away she flees,
Spurning her freight with indignation!
And I, as well as I was able,
On two poor legs, toward my stone-table
Limped on with sore vexation.   175

"O, here he is!" cried little Bess —
She saw me at the garden-door;
"We've waited anxiously and long,"
They cried, and all around me throng,
Full nine of them or more!   180

"Reproach me not — your fears be still —
Be thankful we again have met; —
Resume, my Friends! within the shade
Your seats, and quickly shall be paid
The well-remembered debt."   185

I spake with faltering voice, like one
Not wholly rescued from the pale
Of a wild dream, or worse illusion;
But, straight, to cover my confusion,
Began the promised Tale.   190

PART FIRST

ALL by the moonlight river side
Groaned the poor Beast — alas! in vain;
The staff was raised to loftier height,
And the blows fell with heavier weight
As Peter struck — and struck again.   195

"Hold!" cried the Squire, "against the rules
Of common sense you're surely sinning;
This leap is for us all too bold;
Who Peter was, let that be told,
And start from the beginning."   200

——— "A Potter, Sir, he was by trade,"
Said I, becoming quite collected;
"And wheresoever he appeared,
Full twenty times was Peter feared
For once that Peter was respected.   205

"He two-and-thirty years or more,
Had been a wild and woodland rover;
Had heard the Atlantic surges roar
On farthest Cornwall's rocky shore,
And trod the cliffs of Dover.   210

"And he had seen Caernarvon's towers,
And well he knew the spire of Sarum;
And he had been where Lincoln bell
Flings o'er the fen that ponderous knell —
A far-renowned alarum.   215

"At Doncaster, at York, and Leeds,
And merry Carlisle had he been;
And all along the Lowlands fair,
All through the bonny shire of Ayr;
And far as Aberdeen.   220

"And he had been at Inverness;
And Peter, by the mountain-rills,
Had danced his round with Highland lasses;
And he had lain beside his asses
On lofty Cheviot Hills: 225

"And he had trudged through Yorkshire dales,
Among the rocks and winding *scars;*
Where deep and low the hamlets lie

Beneath their little patch of sky
And little lot of stars: 230

"And all along the indented coast,
Bespattered with the salt-sea foam;
Where'er a knot of houses lay
On headland, or in hollow bay; —
Sure never man like him did roam!   235

"As well might Peter, in the Fleet,
Have been fast bound, a begging debtor; —
He travelled here, he travelled there; —
But not the value of a hair
Was heart or head the better.   240

"He roved among the vales and streams,
In the green wood and hollow dell;
They were his dwellings night and day, —
But nature ne'er could find the way
Into the heart of Peter Bell.   245

"In vain, through every changeful year,
Did Nature lead him as before;
A primrose by a river's brim
A yellow primrose was to him,
And it was nothing more.   250

"Small change it made in Peter's heart
To see his gentle panniered train
With more than vernal pleasure feeding,
Where'er the tender grass was leading
Its earliest green along the lane.   255

"In vain, through water, earth, and air,
The soul of happy sound was spread,
When Peter on some April morn,
Beneath the broom or budding thorn,
Made the warm earth his lazy bed.   260

"At noon, when, by the forest's edge
He lay beneath the branches high,
The soft blue sky did never melt
Into his heart; he never felt
The witchery of the soft blue sky!   265

"On a fair prospect some have looked
And felt, as I have heard them say,
As if the moving time had been

A thing as steadfast as the scene
On which they gazed themselves away.   270

"Within the breast of Peter Bell
These silent raptures found no place;
He was a Carl as wild and rude
As ever hue-and-cry pursued,
As ever ran a felon's race.   275

"Of all that lead a lawless life,
Of all that love their lawless lives,
In city or in village small,
He was the wildest far of all; —
He had a dozen wedded wives.   280

"Nay, start not! — wedded wives — and twelve!
But how one wife could e'er come near him,
In simple truth I cannot tell;
For, be it said of Peter Bell,
To see him was to fear him.   285

"Though Nature could not touch his heart
By lovely forms, and silent weather,
And tender sounds, yet you might see
At once, that Peter Bell and she
Had often been together.   290

"A savage wildness round him hung
As of a dweller out of doors;
In his whole figure and his mien
A savage character was seen
Of mountains and of dreary moors.   295

"To all the unshaped half-human thoughts
Which solitary Nature feeds
'Mid summer storms or winter's ice,
Had Peter joined whatever vice
The cruel city breeds.   300

"His face was keen as is the wind
That cuts along the hawthorn-fence;
Of courage you saw little there,
But, in its stead, a medley air
Of cunning and of impudence.   305

"He had a dark and sidelong walk,
And long and slouching was his gait;

Beneath his looks so bare and bold,
You might perceive, his spirit cold
Was playing with some inward bait. 310

"His forehead wrinkled was and furred;
A work, one half of which was done
By thinking of his '*whens*' and '*hows*;'
And half, by knitting of his brows
Beneath the glaring sun. 315

"There was a hardness in his cheek,
There was a hardness in his eye,
As if the man had fixed his face,
In many a solitary place,
Against the wind and open sky!" 320

ONE NIGHT, (and now my little Bess!
We've reached at last the promised Tale;)
One beautiful November night,
When the full moon was shining bright
Upon the rapid river Swale, 325

Along the river's winding banks
Peter was travelling all alone; —
Whether to buy or sell, or led
By pleasure running in his head,
To me was never known. 330

He trudged along through copse and brake,
He trudged along o'er hill and dale;
Nor for the moon cared he a tittle,
And for the stars he cared as little,
And for the murmuring river Swale. 335

But, chancing to espy a path
That promised to cut short the way;
As many a wiser man hath done,
He left a trusty guide for one
That might his steps betray. 340

To a thick wood he soon is brought
Where cheerily his course he weaves,
And whistling loud may yet be heard,
Though often buried, like a bird
Darkling, among the boughs and leaves. 345

But quickly Peter's mood is changed,
And on he drives with cheeks that burn
In downright fury and in wrath; —
There's little sign the treacherous path
Will to the road return!   350

The path grows dim, and dimmer still;
Now up, now down, the Rover wends,
With all the sail that he can carry,
Till brought to a deserted quarry —
And there the pathway ends.   355

He paused — for shadows of strange shape,
Massy and black, before him lay;
But through the dark, and through the cold,
And through the yawning fissures old,
Did Peter boldly press his way   360

Right through the quarry; — and behold
A scene of soft and lovely hue!
Where blue and grey, and tender green,
Together make as sweet a scene
As ever human eye did view.   365

Beneath the clear blue sky he saw
A little field of meadow ground;
But field or meadow name it not;
Call it of earth a small green plot,
With rocks encompassed round.   370

The Swale flowed under the grey rocks,
But he flowed quiet and unseen; —
You need a strong and stormy gale
To bring the noises of the Swale
To that green spot, so calm and green!   375

And is there no one dwelling here,
No hermit with his beads and glass?
And does no little cottage look
Upon this soft and fertile nook?
Does no one live near this green grass?   380

Across the deep and quiet spot
Is Peter driving through the grass —
And now has reached the skirting trees;
When, turning round his head, he sees
A solitary Ass.   385

"A prize!" cries Peter — but he first
Must spy about him far and near:
There's not a single house in sight,
No woodman's hut, no cottage light —
Peter, you need not fear!   390

There's nothing to be seen but woods,
And rocks that spread a hoary gleam,
And this one Beast, that from the bed
Of the green meadow hangs his head
Over the silent stream.   395

His head is with a halter bound;
The halter seizing, Peter leapt
Upon the Creature's back, and plied
With ready heels his shaggy side;
But still the Ass his station kept.   400

Then Peter gave a sudden jerk,
A jerk that from a dungeon-floor
Would have pulled up an iron ring;
But still the heavy-headed Thing
Stood just as he had stood before!   405

Quoth Peter, leaping from his seat,
"There is some plot against me laid;"
Once more the little meadow-ground
And all the hoary cliffs around
He cautiously surveyed.   410

All, all is silent — rocks and woods,
All still and silent — far and near!
Only the Ass, with motion dull,
Upon the pivot of his skull
Turns round his long left ear.   415

Thought Peter, What can mean all this?
Some ugly witchcraft must be here!
— Once more the Ass, with motion dull,
Upon the pivot of his skull
Turned round his long left ear.   420

Suspicion ripened into dread;
Yet with deliberate action slow,
His staff high-raising, in the pride
Of skill, upon the sounding hide,
He dealt a sturdy blow.   425

The poor Ass staggered with the shock;
And then, as if to take his ease,
In quiet uncomplaining mood,
Upon the spot where he had stood,
Dropped gently down upon his knees;   430

As gently on his side he fell;
And by the river's brink did lie;
And, while he lay like one that mourned,
The patient Beast on Peter turned
His shining hazel eye.   435

'Twas but one mild, reproachful look,
A look more tender than severe;
And straight in sorrow, not in dread,
He turned the eye-ball in his head
Towards the smooth river deep and clear.   440

Upon the Beast the sapling rings;
His lank sides heaved, his limbs they stirred;
He gave a groan, and then another,
Of that which went before the brother,
And then he gave a third.   445

All by the moonlight river side
He gave three miserable groans;
And not till now hath Peter seen
How gaunt the Creature is, — how lean
And sharp his staring bones!   450

With legs stretched out and stiff he lay: —
No word of kind commiseration
Fell at the sight from Peter's tongue;
With hard contempt his heart was wrung,
With hatred and vexation.   455

The meagre beast lay still as death;
And Peter's lips with fury quiver;
Quoth he, "You little mulish dog,
I'll fling your carcass like a log
Head-foremost down the river!"   460

An impious oath confirmed the threat —
Whereat from the earth on which he lay
To all the echoes, south and north,
And east and west, the Ass sent forth
A long and clamorous bray!   465

This outcry, on the heart of Peter,
Seems like a note of joy to strike, —
Joy at the heart of Peter knocks;
But in the echo of the rocks
Was something Peter did not like.   470

Whether to cheer his coward breast,
Or that he could not break the chain,
In this serene and solemn hour,
Twined round him by demoniac power,
To the blind work he turned again.   475

Among the rocks and winding crags;
Among the mountains far away;
Once more the Ass did lengthen out
More ruefully a deep-drawn shout,
The hard dry see-saw of his horrible bray!   480

What is there now in Peter's heart?
Or whence the might of this strange sound?
The moon uneasy looked and dimmer,
The broad blue heavens appeared to glimmer,
And the rocks staggered all around —   485

From Peter's hand the sapling dropped!
Threat has he none to execute;
"If any one should come and see
That I am here, they'll think," quoth he,
"I'm helping this poor dying brute."   490

He scans the Ass from limb to limb,
And ventures now to uplift his eyes;
More steady looks the moon, and clear,
More like themselves the rocks appear
And touch more quiet skies.   495

His scorn returns — his hate revives;
He stoops the Ass's neck to seize
With malice — that again takes flight;
For in the pool a startling sight
Meets him, among the inverted trees.   500

Is it the moon's distorted face?
The ghost-like image of a cloud?
Is it a gallows there portrayed?
Is Peter of himself afraid?
Is it a coffin, — or a shroud?   505

A grisly idol hewn in stone?
Or imp from witch's lap let fall?
Perhaps a ring of shining fairies?
Such as pursue their feared vagaries
In sylvan bower, or haunted hall?   510

Is it a fiend that to a stake
Of fire his desperate self is tethering?
Or stubborn spirit doomed to yell
In solitary ward or cell,
Ten thousand miles from all his brethren?   515

Never did pulse so quickly throb,
And never heart so loudly panted;
He looks, he cannot choose but look;
Like some one reading in a book —
A book that is enchanted.   520

Ah, well-a-day for Peter Bell!
He will be turned to iron soon,
Meet Statue for the court of Fear!
His hat is up — and every hair
Bristles, and whitens in the moon!   525

He looks, he ponders, looks again;
He sees a motion — hears a groan;
His eyes will burst — his heart will break —
He gives a loud and frightful shriek,
And back he falls, as if his life were flown!   530

PART SECOND

WE left our Hero in a trance,
Beneath the alders, near the river;
The Ass is by the river-side,
And, where the feeble breezes glide,
Upon the stream the moonbeams quiver.   535

A happy respite! but at length
He feels the glimmering of the moon;
Wakes with glazed eye, and feebly sighing —
To sink, perhaps, where he is lying,
Into a second swoon!   540

He lifts his head, he sees his staff;
He touches — 'tis to him a treasure!
Faint recollection seems to tell

That he is yet where mortals dwell —
A thought received with languid pleasure!   545

His head upon his elbow propped,
Becoming less and less perplexed,
Sky-ward he looks — to rock and wood —
And then — upon the glassy flood
His wandering eye is fixed.   550

Thought he, that is the face of one
In his last sleep securely bound!
So toward the stream his head he bent,
And downward thrust his staff, intent
The river's depth to sound.   555

Now — like a tempest-shattered bark,
That overwhelmed and prostrate lies,
And in a moment to the verge
Is lifted of a foaming surge —
Full suddenly the Ass doth rise!   560

His staring bones all shake with joy,
And close by Peter's side he stands:
While Peter o'er the river bends,
The little Ass his neck extends,
And fondly licks his hands.   565

Such life is in the Ass's eyes,
Such life is in his limbs and ears;
That Peter Bell, if he had been
The veriest coward ever seen,
Must now have thrown aside his fears.   570

The Ass looks on — and to his work
Is Peter quietly resigned;
He touches here — he touches there —
And now among the dead man's hair
His sapling Peter has entwined.   575

He pulls — and looks — and pulls again;
And he whom the poor Ass had lost,
The man who had been four days dead,
Head-foremost from the river's bed
Uprises like a ghost!   580

And Peter draws him to dry land;
And through the brain of Peter pass
Some poignant twitches, fast and faster;

"No doubt," quoth he, "he is the Master
Of this poor miserable Ass!"   585

The meagre shadow that looks on —
What would he now? what is he doing?
His sudden fit of joy is flown, —
He on his knees hath laid him down,
As if he were his grief renewing;   590

But no — that Peter on his back
Must mount, he shows well as he can:
Thought Peter then, come weal or woe,
I'll do what he would have me do,
In pity to this poor drowned man.   595

With that resolve he boldly mounts
Upon the pleased and thankful Ass;
And then, without a moment's stay,
That earnest Creature turned away,
Leaving the body on the grass.   600

Intent upon his faithful watch,
The Beast four days and nights had past;
A sweeter meadow ne'er was seen,
And there the Ass four days had been,
Nor ever once did break his fast: 605

Yet firm his step, and stout his heart;
The mead is crossed — the quarry's mouth
Is reached; but there the trusty guide
Into a thicket turns aside,
And deftly ambles towards the south.   610

When hark a burst of doleful sound!
And Peter honestly might say,
The like came never to his ears,
Though he has been, full thirty years,
A rover — night and day!   615

'Tis not a plover of the moors,
'Tis not a bittern of the fen;
Nor can it be a barking fox,
Nor night-bird chambered in the rocks,
Nor wild-cat in a woody glen!   620

The Ass is startled — and stops short
Right in the middle of the thicket;
And Peter, wont to whistle loud

Whether alone or in a crowd,
Is silent as a silent cricket.   625

What ails you now, my little Bess?
Well may you tremble and look grave!
This cry — that rings along the wood,
This cry — that floats adown the flood,
Comes from the entrance of a cave: 630

I see a blooming Wood-boy there,
And if I had the power to say
How sorrowful the wanderer is,
Your heart would be as sad as his
Till you had kissed his tears away!   635

Grasping a hawthorn branch in hand,
All bright with berries ripe and red,
Into the cavern's mouth he peeps;
Thence back into the moonlight creeps;
Whom seeks he — whom? — the silent dead: 640

His father! — Him doth he require —
Him hath he sought with fruitless pains,
Among the rocks, behind the trees;
Now creeping on his hands and knees,
Now running o'er the open plains.   645

And hither is he come at last,
When he through such a day has gone,
By this dark cave to be distrest
Like a poor bird — her plundered nest
Hovering around with dolorous moan!   650

Of that intense and piercing cry
The listening Ass conjectures well;
Wild as it is, he there can read
Some intermingled notes that plead
With touches irresistible.   655

But Peter — when he saw the Ass
Not only stop but turn, and change
The cherished tenor of his pace
That lamentable cry to chase —
It wrought in him conviction strange;   660

A faith that, for the dead man's sake
And this poor slave who loved him well,
Vengeance upon his head will fall,

Some visitation worse than all
Which ever till this night befel.   665

Meanwhile the Ass to reach his home,
Is striving stoutly as he may;
But, while he climbs the woody hill,
The cry grows weak — and weaker still;
And now at last it dies away.   670

So with his freight the Creature turns
Into a gloomy grove of beech,
Along the shade with footsteps true
Descending slowly, till the two
The open moonlight reach.   675

And there, along the narrow dell,
A fair smooth pathway you discern,
A length of green and open road —
As if it from a fountain flowed —
Winding away between the fern.   680

The rocks that tower on either side
Build up a wild fantastic scene;
Temples like those among the Hindoos,
And mosques, and spires, and abbey-windows,
And castles all with ivy green!   685

And, while the Ass pursues his way,
Along this solitary dell,
As pensively his steps advance,
The mosques and spires change countenance,
And look at Peter Bell!   690

That unintelligible cry
Hath left him high in preparation, —
Convinced that he, or soon or late,
This very night will meet his fate —
And so he sits in expectation!   695

The strenuous Animal hath clomb
With the green path; and now he wends
Where, shining like the smoothest sea,
In undisturbed immensity
A level plain extends.   700

But whence this faintly-rustling sound
By which the journeying pair are chased?

— A withered leaf is close behind,
Light plaything for the sportive wind
Upon that solitary waste. 705

When Peter spied the moving thing,
It only doubled his distress;
"Where there is not a bush or tree,
The very leaves they follow me —
So huge hath been my wickedness!" 710

To a close lane they now are come,
Where, as before, the enduring Ass
Moves on without a moment's stop,
Nor once turns round his head to crop
A bramble-leaf or blade of grass. 715

Between the hedges as they go,
The white dust sleeps upon the lane;
And Peter, ever and anon
Back-looking, sees, upon a stone,
Or in the dust, a crimson stain. 720

A stain — as of a drop of blood
By moonlight made more faint and wan;
Ha! why these sinkings of despair?
He knows not how the blood comes there —
And Peter is a wicked man. 725

At length he spies a bleeding wound,
Where he had struck the Ass's head;
He sees the blood, knows what it is, —
A glimpse of sudden joy was his,
But then it quickly fled; 730

Of him whom sudden death had seized
He thought, — of thee, O faithful Ass!
And once again those ghastly pains,
Shoot to and fro through heart and reins,
And through his brain like lightning pass. 735

PART THIRD

I'VE heard of one, a gentle Soul,
Though given to sadness and to gloom,
And for the fact will vouch, — one night
It chanced that by a taper's light
This man was reading in his room; 740

Bending, as you or I might bend
At night o'er any pious book,
When sudden blackness overspread
The snow-white page on which he read,
And made the good man round him look.   745

The chamber walls were dark all round, —
And to his book he turned again;
— The light had left the lonely taper,
And formed itself upon the paper
Into large letters — bright and plain!   750

The godly book was in his hand —
And, on the page, more black than coal,
Appeared, set forth in strange array,
A *word* — which to his dying day
Perplexed the good man's gentle soul.   755

The ghostly word, thus plainly seen,
Did never from his lips depart;
But he hath said, poor gentle wight!
It brought full many a sin to light
Out of the bottom of his heart.   760

Dread Spirits! to confound the meek
Why wander from your course so far,
Disordering colour, form, and stature!
— Let good men feel the soul of nature,
And see things as they are.   765

Yet, potent Spirits! well I know,
How ye, that play with soul and sense,
Are not unused to trouble friends
Of goodness, for most gracious ends —
And this I speak in reverence!   770

But might I give advice to you,
Whom in my fear I love so well;
From men of pensive virtue go,
Dread Beings! and your empire show
On hearts like that of Peter Bell.   775

Your presence often have I felt
In darkness and the stormy night;
And, with like force, if need there be,
Ye can put forth your agency
When earth is calm, and heaven is bright.   780

Then, coming from the wayward world,
That powerful world in which ye dwell,
Come, Spirits of the Mind! and try,
To-night, beneath the moonlight sky,
What may be done with Peter Bell!   785

— O, would that some more skilful voice
My further labour might prevent!
Kind Listeners, that around me sit,
I feel that I am all unfit
For such high argument.   790

I've played, I've danced, with my narration;
I loitered long ere I began:
Ye waited then on my good pleasure;
Pour out indulgence still, in measure
As liberal as ye can!   795

Our Travellers, ye remember well,
Are thridding a sequestered lane;
And Peter many tricks is trying,
And many anodynes applying,
To ease his conscience of its pain.   800

By this his heart is lighter far;
And, finding that he can account
So snugly for that crimson stain,
His evil spirit up again
Does like an empty bucket mount.   805

And Peter is a deep logician
Who hath no lack of wit mercurial;
"Blood drops — leaves rustle — yet," quoth he,
"This poor man never, but for me,
Could have had Christian burial.   810

"And, say the best you can, 'tis plain,
That here has been some wicked dealing;
No doubt the devil in me wrought;
I'm not the man who could have thought
An Ass like this was worth the stealing!"   815

So from his pocket Peter takes
His shining horn tobacco-box;
And, in a light and careless way,
As men who with their purpose play,
Upon the lid he knocks.   820

Let them whose voice can stop the clouds,
Whose cunning eye can see the wind,
Tell to a curious world the cause
Why, making here a sudden pause,
The Ass turned round his head, and *grinned.*   825

Appalling process! I have marked
The like on heath, in lonely wood;
And, verily, have seldom met
A spectacle more hideous — yet
It suited Peter's present mood.   830

And, grinning in his turn, his teeth
He in jocose defiance showed —
When, to upset his spiteful mirth,
A murmur, pent within the earth,
In the dead earth beneath the road,   835

Rolled audibly! it swept along,
A muffled noise — a rumbling sound! —
'Twas by a troop of miners made,
Plying with gunpowder their trade,
Some twenty fathoms underground.   840

Small cause of dire effect! for, surely,
If ever mortal, King or Cotter,
Believed that earth was charged to quake
And yawn for his unworthy sake,
'Twas Peter Bell the Potter.   845

But, as an oak in breathless air
Will stand though to the centre hewn;
Or as the weakest things, if frost
Have stiffened them, maintain their post;
So he, beneath the gazing moon! —   850

The Beast bestriding thus, he reached
A spot where, in a sheltering cove,
A little chapel stands alone,
With greenest ivy overgrown,
And tufted with an ivy grove;   855

Dying insensibly away
From human thoughts and purposes,
It seemed — wall, window, roof and tower —
To bow to some transforming power,
And blend with the surrounding trees.   860

As ruinous a place it was,
Thought Peter, in the shire of Fife
That served my turn, when following still
From land to land a reckless will
I married my sixth wife!   865

The unheeding Ass moves slowly on,
And now is passing by an inn
Brim-full of a carousing crew,
That make, with curses not a few,
An uproar and a drunken din.   870

I cannot well express the thoughts
Which Peter in those noises found; —
A stifling power compressed his frame,
While-as a swimming darkness came
Over that dull and dreary sound.   875

For well did Peter know the sound;
The language of those drunken joys
To him, a jovial soul, I ween,
But a few hours ago, had been
A gladsome and a welcome noise.   880

Now, turned adrift into the past,
He finds no solace in his course;
Like planet-stricken men of yore,
He trembles, smitten to the core
By strong compunction and remorse.   885

But, more than all, his heart is stung
To think of one, almost a child;
A sweet and playful Highland girl,
As light and beauteous as a squirrel,
As beauteous and as wild!   890

Her dwelling was a lonely house,
A cottage in a heathy dell;
And she put on her gown of green,
And left her mother at sixteen,
And followed Peter Bell.   895

But many good and pious thoughts
Had she; and, in the kirk to pray,
Two long Scotch miles, through rain or snow,
To kirk she had been used to go,
Twice every Sabbath-day.   900

And, when she followed Peter Bell,
It was to lead an honest life;
For he, with tongue not used to falter,
Had pledged his troth before the altar
To love her as his wedded wife.   905

A mother's hope is hers; — but soon
She drooped and pined like one forlorn;
From Scripture she a name did borrow;
Benoni, or the child of sorrow,
She called her babe unborn.   910

For she had learned how Peter lived,
And took it in most grievous part;
She to the very bone was worn,
And, ere that little child was born,
Died of a broken heart.   915

And now the Spirits of the Mind
Are busy with poor Peter Bell;
Upon the rights of visual sense
Usurping, with a prevalence
More terrible than magic spell.   920

Close by a brake of flowering furze
(Above it shivering aspens play)
He sees an unsubstantial creature,
His very self in form and feature,
Not four yards from the broad highway: 925

And stretched beneath the furze he sees
The Highland girl — it is no other;
And hears her crying as she cried,
The very moment that she died,
"My mother! oh my mother!"   930

The sweat pours down from Peter's face,
So grievous is his heart's contrition;
With agony his eye-balls ache
While he beholds by the furze-brake
This miserable vision!   935

Calm is the well-deserving brute,
His peace hath no offence betrayed;
But now, while down that slope he wends,
A voice to Peter's ear ascends,
Resounding from the woody glade: 940

The voice, though clamorous as a horn
Re-echoed by a naked rock,
Comes from that tabernacle — List!
Within, a fervent Methodist
Is preaching to no heedless flock!   945

"Repent! repent!" he cries aloud,
"While yet ye may find mercy; — strive
To love the Lord with all your might;
Turn to him, seek him day and night,
And save your souls alive!   950

"Repent! repent! though ye have gone,
Through paths of wickedness and woe,
After the Babylonian harlot;
And, though your sins be red as scarlet,
They shall be white as snow!"   955

Even as he passed the door, these words
Did plainly come to Peter's ears;
And they such joyful tidings were,
The joy was more than he could bear! —
He melted into tears.   960

Sweet tears of hope and tenderness!
And fast they fell, a plenteous shower!
His nerves, his sinews seemed to melt;
Through all his iron frame was felt
A gentle, a relaxing, power!   965

Each fibre of his frame was weak;
Weak all the animal within;
But, in its helplessness, grew mild
And gentle as an infant child,
An infant that has known no sin.   970

'Tis said, meek Beast! that, through Heaven's grace,
He not unmoved did notice now
The cross upon thy shoulder scored,
For lasting impress, by the Lord
To whom all human-kind shall bow;   975

Memorial of his touch — that day
When Jesus humbly deigned to ride,
Entering the proud Jerusalem,
By an immeasurable stream
Of shouting people deified!   980

Meanwhile the persevering Ass,
Turned towards a gate that hung in view
Across a shady lane; his chest
Against the yielding gate he pressed
And quietly passed through.   985

And up the stony lane he goes;
No ghost more softly ever trod;
Among the stones and pebbles, he
Sets down his hoofs inaudibly,
As if with felt his hoofs were shod.   990

Along the lane the trusty Ass
Went twice two hundred yards or more,
And no one could have guessed his aim, —
Till to a lonely house he came,
And stopped beside the door.   995

Thought Peter, 'tis the poor man's home!
He listens — not a sound is heard
Save from the trickling household rill;
But, stepping o'er the cottage-sill,
Forthwith a little Girl appeared.   1000

She to the Meeting-house was bound
In hopes some tidings there to gather:
No glimpse it is, no doubtful gleam;
She saw — and uttered with a scream,
"My father! here's my father!"   1005

The very word was plainly heard,
Heard plainly by the wretched Mother —
Her joy was like a deep affright:
And forth she rushed into the light,
And saw it was another!   1010

And, instantly, upon the earth,
Beneath the full moon shining bright,
Close to the Ass's feet she fell;
At the same moment Peter Bell
Dismounts in most unhappy plight.   1015

As he beheld the Woman lie
Breathless and motionless, the mind
Of Peter sadly was confused;
But, though to such demands unused,
And helpless almost as the blind,   1020

He raised her up; and, while he held
Her body propped against his knee,
The Woman waked — and when she spied
The poor Ass standing by her side,
She moaned most bitterly.   1025

"Oh! God be praised — my heart's at ease —
For he is dead — I know it well!"
— At this she wept a bitter flood;
And, in the best way that he could,
His tale did Peter tell.   1030

He trembles — he is pale as death;
His voice is weak with perturbation;
He turns aside his head, he pauses;
Poor Peter from a thousand causes,
Is crippled sore in his narration.   1035

At length she learned how he espied
The Ass in that small meadow-ground;
And that her Husband now lay dead,
Beside that luckless river's bed
In which he had been drowned.   1040

A piercing look the Widow cast
Upon the Beast that near her stands;
She sees 'tis he, that 'tis the same;
She calls the poor Ass by his name,
And wrings, and wrings her hands.   1045

"O wretched loss — untimely stroke!
If he had died upon his bed!
He knew not one forewarning pain;
He never will come home again —
Is dead, for ever dead!"   1050

Beside the woman Peter stands;
His heart is opening more and more;
A holy sense pervades his mind;
He feels what he for human-kind
Had never felt before.   1055

At length, by Peter's arm sustained,
The Woman rises from the ground —
"Oh, mercy! something must be done,
  y little Rachel, you must run, —
ɔome willing neighbour must be found.   1060

"Make haste — my little Rachel — do,
The first you meet with — bid him come,
Ask him to lend his horse to-night,
And this good Man, whom Heaven requite,
Will help to bring the body home." 1065

Away goes Rachel weeping loud; —
An Infant, waked by her distress,
Makes in the house a piteous cry;
And Peter hears the Mother sigh,
"Seven are they, and all fatherless!" 1070

And now is Peter taught to feel
That man's heart is a holy thing;
And Nature, through a world of death,
Breathes into him a second breath,
More searching than the breath of spring. 1075

Upon a stone the Woman sits
In agony of silent grief —
From his own thoughts did Peter start;
He longs to press her to his heart,
From love that cannot find relief. 1080

But roused, as if through every limb
Had past a sudden shock of dread,
The Mother o'er the threshold flies,
And up the cottage stairs she hies,
And on her pillow lays her burning head. 1085

And Peter turns his steps aside
Into a shade of darksome trees,
Where he sits down, he knows not how,
With his hands pressed against his brow,
His elbows on his tremulous knees. 1090

There, self-involved, does Peter sit
Until no sign of life he makes,
As if his mind were sinking deep
Through years that have been long asleep!
The trance is passed away — he wakes; 1095

He lifts his head — and sees the Ass
Yet standing in the clear moonshine;
"When shall I be as good as thou?
Oh! would, poor beast, that I had now
A heart but half as good as thine!" 1100

But *He* — who deviously hath sought
His Father through the lonesome woods,
Hath sought, proclaiming to the ear
Of night his grief and sorrowful fear —
He comes, escaped from fields and floods; —   1105

With weary pace is drawing nigh;
He sees the Ass — and nothing living
Had ever such a fit of joy
As hath this little orphan Boy,
For he has no misgiving!   1110

Forth to the gentle Ass he springs,
And up about his neck he climbs;
In loving words he talks to him,
He kisses, kisses face and limb, —
He kisses him a thousand times!   1115

This Peter sees, while in the shade
He stood beside the cottage-door;
And Peter Bell, the ruffian wild,
Sobs loud, he sobs even like a child,
"Oh! God, I can endure no more!"   1120

— Here ends my Tale: for in a trice
Arrived a neighbour with his horse;
Peter went forth with him straightway;
And, with due care, ere break of day,
Together they brought back the Corse.   1125

And many years did this poor Ass,
Whom once it was my luck to see
Cropping the shrubs of Leming-Lane,
Help by his labour to maintain
The Widow and her family.   1130

And Peter Bell, who, till that night,
Had been the wildest of his clan,
Forsook his crimes, renounced his folly,
And, after ten months' melancholy,
Became a good and honest man.   1135

EXPOSTULATION AND REPLY

"Why, William, on that old grey stone,
Thus for the length of half a day,
Why, William, sit you thus alone,
And dream your time away?

"Where are your books? — that light bequeathed   5
To Beings else forlorn and blind!
Up! up! and drink the spirit breathed
From dead men to their kind.

"You look round on your Mother Earth,
As if she for no purpose bore you;   10
As if you were her first-born birth,
And none had lived before you!"

One morning thus, by Esthwaite lake,
When life was sweet, I knew not why,
To me my good friend Matthew spake,   15
And thus I made reply.

"The eye — it cannot choose but see;
We cannot bid the ear be still;
Our bodies feel, where'er they be,
Against or with our will.   20

"Nor less I deem that there are Powers
Which of themselves our minds impress;
That we can feed this mind of ours
In a wise passiveness.

"Think you, 'mid all this mighty sum   25
Of things for ever speaking,
That nothing of itself will come,
But we must still be seeking?

"— Then ask not wherefore, here, alone,
Conversing as I may,   30
I sit upon this old grey stone,
And dream my time away."

THE TABLES TURNED

AN EVENING SCENE ON THE SAME SUBJECT

Up! up! my Friend, and quit your books;
Or surely you'll grow double:
Up! up! my Friend, and clear your looks;
Why all this toil and trouble?

The sun, above the mountain's head,   5
A freshening lustre mellow
Through all the long green fields has spread,
His first sweet evening yellow.

Books! 'tis a dull and endless strife:
Come, hear the woodland linnet,   10
How sweet his music! on my life,
There's more of wisdom in it.

And hark! how blithe the throstle sings!
He, too, is no mean preacher:
Come forth into the light of things,   15
Let Nature be your Teacher.

She has a world of ready wealth,
Our minds and hearts to bless —
Spontaneous wisdom breathed by health,
Truth breathed by cheerfulness.   20

One impulse from a vernal wood
May teach you more of man,
Of moral evil and of good,
Than all the sages can.

Sweet is the lore which Nature brings;   25
Our meddling intellect
Mis-shapes the beauteous forms of things: —
We murder to dissect.

Enough of Science and of Art;
Close up those barren leaves;   30
Come forth, and bring with you a heart
That watches and receives.

LINES

COMPOSED A FEW MILES ABOVE TINTERN ABBEY,
ON REVISITING THE BANKS OF THE WYE DURING
A TOUR, JULY 13, 1798

FIVE years have past; five summers, with the length
Of five long winters! and again I hear
These waters, rolling from their mountain-springs
With a soft inland murmur. — Once again
Do I behold these steep and lofty cliffs,   5
That on a wild secluded scene impress
Thoughts of more deep seclusion; and connect
The landscape with the quiet of the sky.
The day is come when I again repose
Here, under this dark sycamore, and view   10
These plots of cottage-ground, these orchard-tufts,
Which at this season, with their unripe fruits,
Are clad in one green hue, and lose themselves
'Mid groves and copses. Once again I see
These hedge-rows, hardly hedge-rows, little lines   15
Of sportive wood run wild: these pastoral farms,
Green to the very door; and wreaths of smoke
Sent up, in silence, from among the trees!
With some uncertain notice, as might seem
Of vagrant dwellers in the houseless woods,   20
Or of some Hermit's cave, where by his fire
The Hermit sits alone.

            These beauteous forms,
Through a long absence, have not been to me
As is a landscape to a blind man's eye:
But oft, in lonely rooms, and 'mid the din   25
Of towns and cities, I have owed to them
In hours of weariness, sensations sweet,
Felt in the blood, and felt along the heart;
And passing even into my purer mind,
With tranquil restoration: — feelings too   30
Of unremembered pleasure: such, perhaps,
As have no slight or trivial influence
On that best portion of a good man's life,
His little, nameless, unremembered, acts
Of kindness and of love. Nor less, I trust,   35
To them I may have owed another gift,
Of aspect more sublime; that blessed mood,

In which the burthen of the mystery,
In which the heavy and the weary weight
Of all this unintelligible world, 40
Is lightened: — that serene and blessed mood,
In which the affections gently lead us on, —
Until, the breath of this corporeal frame
And even the motion of our human blood
Almost suspended, we are laid asleep 45
In body, and become a living soul:
While with an eye made quiet by the power
Of harmony, and the deep power of joy,
We see into the life of things.

                                            If this
Be but a vain belief, yet, oh! how oft — 50
In darkness and amid the many shapes
Of joyless daylight; when the fretful stir
Unprofitable, and the fever of the world,
Have hung upon the beatings of my heart —
How oft, in spirit, have I turned to thee, 55
O sylvan Wye! thou wanderer thro' the woods,
How often has my spirit turned to thee!

    And now, with gleams of half-extinguished thought,
With many recognitions dim and faint,
And somewhat of a sad perplexity, 60
The picture of the mind revives again:
While here I stand, not only with the sense
Of present pleasure, but with pleasing thoughts
That in this moment there is life and food
For future years. And so I dare to hope, 65
Though changed, no doubt, from what I was when first
I came among these hills; when like a roe
I bounded o'er the mountains, by the sides
Of the deep rivers, and the lonely streams,
Wherever nature led: more like a man 70
Flying from something that he dreads, than one
Who sought the thing he loved. For nature then
(The coarser pleasures of my boyish days,
And their glad animal movements all gone by)
To me was all in all. — I cannot paint 75
What then I was. The sounding cataract
Haunted me like a passion: the tall rock,
The mountain, and the deep and gloomy wood,
Their colours and their forms, were then to me
An appetite; a feeling and a love, 80
That had no need of a remoter charm,
By thought supplied, nor any interest

Unborrowed from the eye. — That time is past,
And all its aching joys are now no more,
And all its dizzy raptures. Not for this   85
Faint I, nor mourn nor murmur; other gifts
Have followed; for such loss, I would believe,
Abundant recompense. For I have learned
To look on nature, not as in the hour
Of thoughtless youth; but hearing oftentimes   90
The still, sad music of humanity,
Nor harsh nor grating, though of ample power
To chasten and subdue. And I have felt
A presence that disturbs me with the joy
Of elevated thoughts; a sense sublime   95
Of something far more deeply interfused,
Whose dwelling is the light of setting suns,
And the round ocean and the living air,
And the blue sky, and in the mind of man:
A motion and a spirit, that impels   100
All thinking things, all objects of all thought,
And rolls through all things. Therefore am I still
A lover of the meadows and the woods,
And mountains; and of all that we behold
From this green earth; of all the mighty world   105
Of eye, and ear, — both what they half create,
And what perceive; well pleased to recognise
In nature and the language of the sense,
The anchor of my purest thoughts, the nurse,
The guide, the guardian of my heart, and soul   110
Of all my moral being.
                                   Nor perchance,
If I were not thus taught, should I the more
Suffer my genial spirits to decay:
For thou art with me here upon the banks
Of this fair river; thou my dearest Friend,   115
My dear, dear Friend; and in thy voice I catch
The language of my former heart, and read
My former pleasures in the shooting lights
Of thy wild eyes. Oh! yet a little while
May I behold in thee what I was once,   120
My dear, dear Sister! and this prayer I make,
Knowing that Nature never did betray
The heart that loved her; 'tis her privilege,
Through all the years of this our life, to lead
From joy to joy: for she can so inform   125
The mind that is within us, so impress
With quietness and beauty, and so feed
With lofty thoughts, that neither evil tongues,

Rash judgments, nor the sneers of selfish men,
Nor greetings where no kindness is, nor all   130
The dreary intercourse of daily life,
Shall e'er prevail against us, or disturb
Our cheerful faith, that all which we behold
Is full of blessings. Therefore let the moon
Shine on thee in thy solitary walk;   135
And let the misty mountain-winds be free
To blow against thee: and, in after years,
When these wild ecstasies shall be matured
Into a sober pleasure; when thy mind
Shall be a mansion for all lovely forms,   140
Thy memory be as a dwelling-place
For all sweet sounds and harmonies; oh! then,
If solitude, or fear, or pain, or grief,
Should be thy portion, with what healing thoughts
Of tender joy wilt thou remember me,   145
And these my exhortations! Nor, perchance —
If I should be where I no more can hear
Thy voice, nor catch from thy wild eyes these gleams
Of past existence — wilt thou then forget
That on the banks of this delightful stream   150
We stood together; and that I, so long
A worshipper of Nature, hither came
Unwearied in that service; rather say
With warmer love — oh! with far deeper zeal
Of holier love. Nor wilt thou then forget,   155
That after many wanderings, many years
Of absence, these steep woods and lofty cliffs,
And this green pastoral landscape, were to me
More dear, both for themselves and for thy sake!

NUTTING

——————————— It seems a day
(I speak of one from many singled out)
One of those heavenly days that cannot die;
When, in the eagerness of boyish hope,
I left our cottage-threshold, sallying forth   5
With a huge wallet o'er my shoulder slung,
A nutting-crook in hand; and turned my steps
Tow'rd some far-distant wood, a Figure quaint,
Tricked out in proud disguise of cast-off weeds
Which for that service had been husbanded,   10
By exhortation of my frugal Dame —
Motley accoutrement, of power to smile

At thorns, and brakes, and brambles, — and, in truth,
More raggèd than need was! O'er pathless rocks,
Through beds of matted fern, and tangled thickets,   15
Forcing my way, I came to one dear nook
Unvisited, where not a broken bough
Drooped with its withered leaves, ungracious sign
Of devastation; but the hazels rose
Tall and erect, with tempting clusters hung,   20
A virgin scene! — A little while I stood,
Breathing with such suppression of the heart
As joy delights in; and, with wise restraint
Voluptuous, fearless of a rival, eyed
The banquet; — or beneath the trees I sate   25
Among the flowers, and with the flowers I played;
A temper known to those, who, after long
And weary expectation, have been blest
With sudden happiness beyond all hope.
Perhaps it was a bower beneath whose leaves   30
The violets of five seasons re-appear
And fade, unseen by any human eye;
Where fairy water-breaks do murmur on
For ever; and I saw the sparkling foam,
And — with my cheek on one of those green stones   35
That, fleeced with moss, under the shady trees,
Lay round me, scattered like a flock of sheep —
I heard the murmur and the murmuring sound,
In that sweet mood when pleasure loves to pay
Tribute to ease; and, of its joy secure,   40
The heart luxuriates with indifferent things,
Wasting its kindliness on stocks and stones,
And on the vacant air. Then up I rose,
And dragged to earth both branch and bough, with crash
And merciless ravage: and the shady nook   45
Of hazels, and the green and mossy bower,
Deformed and sullied, patiently gave up
Their quiet being: and, unless I now
Confound my present feelings with the past;
Ere from the mutilated bower I turned   50
Exulting, rich beyond the wealth of kings,
I felt a sense of pain when I beheld
The silent trees, and saw the intruding sky. —
Then, dearest Maiden, move along these shades
In gentleness of heart; with gentle hand   55
Touch — for there is a spirit in the woods.

STRANGE FITS OF PASSION HAVE I KNOWN

STRANGE fits of passion have I known:
And I will dare to tell,
But in the Lover's ear alone,
What once to me befel.

When she I loved looked every day   5
Fresh as a rose in June,
I to her cottage bent my way,
Beneath an evening moon.

Upon the moon I fixed my eye,
All over the wide lea;   10
With quickening pace my horse drew nigh
Those paths so dear to me.

And now we reached the orchard-plot;
And, as we climbed the hill,
The sinking moon to Lucy's cot   15
Came near, and nearer still.

In one of those sweet dreams I slept,
Kind Nature's gentlest boon!
And all the while my eyes I kept
On the descending moon.   20

My horse moved on; hoof after hoof
He raised, and never stopped:
When down behind the cottage roof,
At once, the bright moon dropped.

What fond and wayward thoughts will slide   25
Into a Lover's head!
"O mercy!" to myself I cried,
"If Lucy should be dead!"

SHE DWELT AMONG THE UNTRODDEN WAYS

SHE dwelt among the untrodden ways
    Beside the springs of Dove,
A Maid whom there were none to praise
    And very few to love:

A violet by a mossy stone 5
   Half hidden from the eye!
— Fair as a star, when only one
   Is shining in the sky.

She lived unknown, and few could know
   When Lucy ceased to be; 10
But she is in her grave, and, oh,
   The difference to me!

THREE YEARS SHE GREW IN SUN AND SHOWER

THREE years she grew in sun and shower,
Then Nature said, "A lovelier flower
On earth was never sown;
This Child I to myself will take;
She shall be mine, and I will make 5
A Lady of my own.

"Myself will to my darling be
Both law and impulse: and with me
The Girl, in rock and plain,
In earth and heaven, in glade and bower, 10
Shall feel an overseeing power
To kindle or restrain.

"She shall be sportive as the fawn
That wild with glee across the lawn
Or up the mountain springs; 15
And hers shall be the breathing balm,
And hers the silence and the calm
Of mute insensate things.

"The floating clouds their state shall lend
To her; for her the willow bend; 20
Nor shall she fail to see
Even in the motions of the Storm
Grace that shall mould the Maiden's form
By silent sympathy.

"The stars of midnight shall be dear 25
To her; and she shall lean her ear
In many a secret place
Where rivulets dance their wayward round,
And beauty born of murmuring sound
Shall pass into her face. 30

"And vital feelings of delight
Shall rear her form to stately height,
Her virgin bosom swell;
Such thoughts to Lucy I will give
While she and I together live   35
Here in this happy dell."

Thus Nature spake — The work was done —
How soon my Lucy's race was run!
She died, and left to me
This heath, this calm, and quiet scene;   40
The memory of what has been,
And never more will be.

A SLUMBER DID MY SPIRIT SEAL

A SLUMBER did my spirit seal;
    I had no human fears:
She seemed a thing that could not feel
    The touch of earthly years.

No motion has she now, no force;   5
    She neither hears nor sees;
Rolled round in earth's diurnal course,
    With rocks, and stones, and trees.

LUCY GRAY

OR, SOLITUDE

OFT I had heard of Lucy Gray:
And, when I crossed the wild,
I chanced to see at break of day
The solitary child.

No mate, no comrade Lucy knew;   5
She dwelt on a wide moor,
— The sweetest thing that ever grew
Beside a human door!

You yet may spy the fawn at play,
The hare upon the green;   10
But the sweet face of Lucy Gray
Will never more be seen.

"To-night will be a stormy night —
You to the town must go;
And take a lantern, Child, to light   15
Your mother through the snow."

"That, Father! will I gladly do:
'Tis scarcely afternoon —
The minster-clock has just struck two,
And yonder is the moon!"   20

At this the Father raised his hook,
And snapped a faggot-band;
He plied his work; — and Lucy took
The lantern in her hand.

Not blither is the mountain roe: 25
With many a wanton stroke
Her feet disperse the powdery snow,
That rises up like smoke.

The storm came on before its time:
She wandered up and down;   30
And many a hill did Lucy climb:
But never reached the town.

The wretched parents all that night
Went shouting far and wide;
But there was neither sound nor sight   35
To serve them for a guide.

At day-break on a hill they stood
That overlooked the moor;
And thence they saw the bridge of wood,
A furlong from their door.   40

They wept — and, turning homeward, cried,
"In heaven we all shall meet;"
— When in the snow the mother spied
The print of Lucy's feet.

Then downwards from the steep hill's edge   45
They tracked the footmarks small;
And through the broken hawthorn hedge,
And by the long stone-wall;

And then an open field they crossed:
The marks were still the same;   50

They tracked them on, nor ever lost;
And to the bridge they came.

They followed from the snowy bank
Those footmarks, one by one,
Into the middle of the plank;   55
And further there were none!

— Yet some maintain that to this day
She is a living child;
That you may see sweet Lucy Gray
Upon the lonesome wild.   60

O'er rough and smooth she trips along,
And never looks behind;
And sings a solitary song
That whistles in the wind.

THE DANISH BOY

A FRAGMENT

I

BETWEEN two sister moorland rills
There is a spot that seems to lie
Sacred to flowerets of the hills,
And sacred to the sky.
And in this smooth and open dell   5
There is a tempest-stricken tree;
A corner-stone by lightning cut,
The last stone of a lonely hut;
And in this dell you see
A thing no storm can e'er destroy,   10
The shadow of a Danish Boy.

II

In clouds above, the lark is heard,
But drops not here to earth for rest;
Within this lonesome nook the bird
Did never build her nest.   15
No beast, no bird hath here his home;
Bees, wafted on the breezy air,
Pass high above those fragrant bells.
To other flowers: — to other dells

Their burthens do they bear; 20
The Danish Boy walks here alone:
The lovely dell is all his own.

III

A Spirit of noon-day is he;
Yet seems a form of flesh and blood;
Nor piping shepherd shall he be, 25
Nor herd-boy of the wood.
A regal vest of fur he wears,
In colour like a raven's wing;
It fears not rain, nor wind, nor dew;
But in the storm 'tis fresh and blue 30
As budding pines in spring;
His helmet has a vernal grace,
Fresh as the bloom upon his face.

IV

A harp is from his shoulder slung;
Resting the harp upon his knee, 35
To words of a forgotten tongue,
He suits its melody.
Of flocks upon the neighbouring hill
He is the darling and the joy;
And often, when no cause appears, 40
The mountain-ponies prick their ears,
— They hear the Danish Boy,
While in the dell he sings alone
Beside the tree and corner-stone.

V

There sits he; in his face you spy 45
No trace of a ferocious air,
Nor ever was a cloudless sky
So steady or so fair.
The lovely Danish Boy is blest
And happy in his flowery cove: 50
From bloody deeds his thoughts are far;
And yet he warbles songs of war,
That seem like songs of love,
For calm and gentle is his mien;
Like a dead Boy he is serene. 55

A POET'S EPITAPH

Art thou a Statist in the van
Of public conflicts trained and bred?
— First learn to love one living man;
Then may'st thou think upon the dead.

A Lawyer art thou? — draw not nigh!   5
Go, carry to some fitter place
The keenness of that practised eye,
The hardness of that sallow face.

Art thou a Man of purple cheer?
A rosy Man, right plump to see?   10
Approach; yet, Doctor, not too near,
This grave no cushion is for thee.

Or art thou one of gallant pride,
A Soldier and no man of chaff?
Welcome! — but lay thy sword aside,   15
And lean upon a peasant's staff.

Physician art thou? — one, all eyes,
Philosopher! — a fingering slave,
One that would peep and botanize
Upon his mother's grave?   20

Wrapt closely in thy sensual fleece,
O turn aside, — and take, I pray,
That he below may rest in peace,
Thy ever-dwindling soul, away!

A Moralist perchance appears;   25
Led, Heaven knows how! to this poor sod:
And he has neither eyes nor ears;
Himself his world, and his own God;

One to whose smooth-rubbed soul can cling
Nor form, nor feeling, great or small;   30
A reasoning, self-sufficing thing,
An intellectual All-in-all!

Shut close the door; press down the latch;
Sleep in thy intellectual crust;
Nor lose ten tickings of thy watch   35
Near this unprofitable dust.

But who is He, with modest looks,
And clad in homely russet brown?
He murmurs near the running brooks
A music sweeter than their own. 40

He is retired as noontide dew,
Or fountain in a noon-day grove;
And you must love him, ere to you
He will seem worthy of your love.

The outward shows of sky and earth, 45
Of hill and valley, he has viewed;
And impulses of deeper birth
Have come to him in solitude.

In common things that round us lie
Some random truths he can impart, — 50
The harvest of a quiet eye
That broods and sleeps on his own heart.

But he is weak; both Man and Boy,
Hath been an idler in the land;
Contented if he might enjoy 55
The things which others understand.

— Come hither in thy hour of strength;
Come, weak as is a breaking wave!
Here stretch thy body at full length;
Or build thy house upon this grave. 60

THE TWO APRIL MORNINGS

WE walked along, while bright and red
Uprose the morning sun;
And Matthew stopped, he looked, and said,
"The will of God be done!"

A village schoolmaster was he, 5
With hair of glittering grey;
As blithe a man as you could see
On a spring holiday.

And on that morning, through the grass,
And by the steaming rills,
We travelled merrily, to pass 10
A day among the hills.

"Our work," said I, "was well begun,
Then, from thy breast what thought,
Beneath so beautiful a sun,   15
So sad a sigh has brought?"

A second time did Matthew stop;
And fixing still his eye
Upon the eastern mountain-top,
To me he made reply: 20

"Yon cloud with that long purple cleft
Brings fresh into my mind
A day like this which I have left
Full thirty years behind.

"And just above yon slope of corn   25
Such colours, and no other,
Were in the sky, that April morn,
Of this the very brother.

"With rod and line I sued the sport
Which that sweet season gave,   30
And, to the church-yard come, stopped short
Beside my daughter's grave.

"Nine summers had she scarcely seen,
The pride of all the vale;
And then she sang; — she would have been   35
A very nightingale.

"Six feet in earth my Emma lay;
And yet I loved her more,
For so it seemed, than till that day
I e'er had loved before.   40

"And, turning from her grave, I met,
Beside the churchyard yew,
A blooming Girl, whose hair was wet
With points of morning dew.

"A basket on her head she bare;   45
Her brow was smooth and white:
To see a child so very fair,
It was a pure delight!

"No fountain from its rocky cave
E'er tripped with foot so free;   50

She seemed as happy as a wave
That dances on the sea.

"There came from me a sigh of pain
Which I could ill confine;
I looked at her, and looked again: 55
And did not wish her mine!"

Matthew is in his grave, yet now,
Methinks, I see him stand,
As at that moment, with a bough
Of wilding in his hand.   60

THE FOUNTAIN

A CONVERSATION

WE talked with open heart, and tongue
Affectionate and true,
A pair of friends, though I was young,
And Matthew seventy-two.

We lay beneath a spreading oak,   5
Beside a mossy seat;
And from the turf a fountain broke,
And gurgled at our feet.

"Now, Matthew!" said I, "let us match
This water's pleasant tune
With some old border-song, or catch   10
That suits a summer's noon;

"Or of the church-clock and the chimes
Sing here beneath the shade,
That half-mad thing of witty rhymes   15
Which you last April made!"

In silence Matthew lay, and eyed
The spring beneath the tree;
And thus the dear old Man replied,
The grey-haired man of glee: 20

"No check, no stay, this Streamlet fears;
How merrily it goes!
'Twill murmur on a thousand years,
And flow as now it flows.

"And here, on this delightful day,   25
I cannot choose but think
How oft, a vigorous man, I lay
Beside this fountain's brink.

"My eyes are dim with childish tears,
My heart is idly stirred,   30
For the same sound is in my ears
Which in those days I heard.

"Thus fares it still in our decay:
And yet the wiser mind
Mourns less for what age takes away   35
Than what it leaves behind.

"The blackbird amid leafy trees,
The lark above the hill,
Let loose their carols when they please,
Are quiet when they will.   40

"With Nature never do *they* wage
A foolish strife; they see
A happy youth, and their old age
Is beautiful and free:

"But we are pressed by heavy laws;   45
And often, glad no more,
We wear a face of joy, because
We have been glad of yore.

"If there be one who need bemoan
His kindred laid in earth,   50
The household hearts that were his own;
It is the man of mirth.

"My days, my Friend, are almost gone,
My life has been approved,
And many love me; but by none   55
Am I enough beloved."

"Now both himself and me he wrongs,
The man who thus complains!
I live and sing my idle songs
Upon these happy plains;   60

"And, Matthew, for thy children dead
I'll be a son to thee!"

At this he grasped my hand, and said,
"Alas! that cannot be."

We rose up from the fountain-side;   65
And down the smooth descent
Of the green sheep-track did we glide;
And through the wood we went;

And, ere we came to Leonard's rock,
He sang those witty rhymes   70
About the crazy old church-clock,
And the bewildered chimes.

TO M. H.

OUR walk was far among the ancient trees:
There was no road, nor any woodman's path;
But a thick umbrage — checking the wild growth
Of weed and sapling, along soft green turf
Beneath the branches — of itself had made   5
A track, that brought us to a slip of lawn,
And a small bed of water in the woods.
All round this pool both flocks and herds might drink
On its firm margin, even as from a well,
Or some stone-basin which the herdsman's hand   10
Had shaped for their refreshment; nor did sun,
Or wind from any quarter, ever come,
But as a blessing to this calm recess,
This glade of water and this one green field.
The spot was made by Nature for herself;   15
The travellers know it not, and 'twill remain
Unknown to them; but it is beautiful;
And if a man should plant his cottage near,
Should sleep beneath the shelter of its trees,
And blend its waters with his daily meal,   20
He would so love it, that in his death-hour
Its image would survive among his thoughts:
And therefore, my sweet MARY, this still Nook,
With all its beeches, we have named from You!

HART-LEAP WELL

Hart-Leap Well is a small spring of water, about five miles from Richmond in Yorkshire, and near the side of the road that leads from Richmond to Askrigg. Its name is derived from a remarkable Chase, the memory of which is preserved by the monuments spoken of in the second Part of the following Poem, which monuments do now exist as I have there described them.

PART FIRST

THE Knight had ridden down from Wensley Moor
With the slow motion of a summer's cloud,
And now, as he approached a vassal's door,
"Bring forth another horse!" he cried aloud.

"Another horse!" — That shout the vassal heard   5
And saddled his best Steed, a comely grey;
Sir Walter mounted him; he was the third
Which he had mounted on that glorious day.

Joy sparkled in the prancing courser's eyes;
The horse and horseman are a happy pair;   10
But, though Sir Walter like a falcon flies,
There is a doleful silence in the air.

A rout this morning left Sir Walter's Hall,
That as they galloped made the echoes roar;
But horse and man are vanished, one and all;   15
Such race, I think, was never seen before.

Sir Walter, restless as a veering wind,
Calls to the few tired dogs that yet remain:
Blanch, Swift, and Music, noblest of their kind,
Follow, and up the weary mountain strain.   20

The Knight hallooed, he cheered and chid them on
With suppliant gestures and upbraidings stern;
But breath and eyesight fail; and, one by one,
The dogs are stretched among the mountain fern.

Where is the throng, the tumult of the race?   25
The bugles that so joyfully were blown?
— This chase it looks not like an earthly chase;
Sir Walter and the Hart are left alone.

The poor Hart toils along the mountain-side;
I will not stop to tell how far he fled,
Nor will I mention by what death he died;
But now the Knight beholds him lying dead.   30

Dismounting, then, he leaned against a thorn;
He had no follower, dog, nor man, nor boy:
He neither cracked his whip, nor blew his horn,   35
But gazed upon the spoil with silent joy.

Close to the thorn on which Sir Walter leaned,
Stood his dumb partner in this glorious feat;
Weak as a lamb the hour that it is yeaned;
And white with foam as if with cleaving sleet.   40

Upon his side the Hart was lying stretched:
His nostril touched a spring beneath a hill,
And with the last deep groan his breath had fetched
The waters of the spring were trembling still.

And now, too happy for repose or rest,   45
(Never had living man such joyful lot!)
Sir Walter walked all round, north, south, and west,
And gazed and gazed upon that darling spot.

And climbing up the hill — (it was at least
Four roods of sheer ascent) Sir Walter found   50
Three several hoof-marks which the hunted Beast
Had left imprinted on the grassy ground.

Sir Walter wiped his face, and cried, "Till now
Such sight was never seen by human eyes:
Three leaps have borne him from this lofty brow,   55
Down to the very fountain where he lies.

"I'll build a pleasure-house upon this spot,
And a small arbour, made for rural joy;
'Twill be the traveller's shed, the pilgrim's cot,
A place of love for damsels that are coy.   60

"A cunning artist will I have to frame
A basin for that fountain in the dell!
And they who do make mention of the same,
From this day forth, shall call it Hart-leap Well.

"And, gallant Stag! to make thy praises known,   65
Another monument shall here be raised;

Three several pillars, each a rough-hewn stone,
And planted where thy hoofs the turf have grazed.

"And, in the summer-time when days are long,
I will come hither with my Paramour;   70
And with the dancers and the minstrel's song
We will make merry in that pleasant bower.

"Till the foundations of the mountains fail
My mansion with its arbour shall endure; —
The joy of them who till the fields of Swale,   75
And them who dwell among the woods of Ure!"

Then home he went, and left the Hart, stone-dead,
With breathless nostrils stretched above the spring.
— Soon did the Knight perform what he had said;
And far and wide the fame thereof did ring.   80

Ere thrice the Moon into her port had steered,
A cup of stone received the living well;
Three pillars of rude stone Sir Walter reared,
And built a house of pleasure in the dell.

And near the fountain, flowers of stature tall   85
With trailing plants and trees were intertwined, —
Which soon composed a little sylvan hall,
A leafy shelter from the sun and wind.

And thither, when the summer days were long,
Sir Walter led his wondering Paramour;   90
And with the dancers and the minstrel's song
Made merriment within that pleasant bower.

The Knight, Sir Walter, died in course of time,
And his bones lie in his paternal vale. —
But there is matter for a second rhyme,   95
And I to this would add another tale.

PART SECOND

The moving accident is not my trade;
To freeze the blood I have no ready arts:
'Tis my delight, alone in summer shade,
To pipe a simple song for thinking hearts.   100

As I from Hawes to Richmond did repair,
It chanced that I saw standing in a dell

Three aspens at three corners of a square;
And one, not four yards distant, near a well.

What this imported I could ill divine: 105
And, pulling now the rein my horse to stop,
I saw three pillars standing in a line, —
The last stone-pillar on a dark hill-top.

The trees were grey, with neither arms nor head;
Half wasted the square mound of tawny green;   110
So that you just might say, as then I said,
"Here in old time the hand of man hath been."

I looked upon the hill both far and near,
More doleful place did never eye survey;
It seemed as if the spring-time came not here,   115
And Nature here were willing to decay.

I stood in various thoughts and fancies lost,
When one, who was in shepherd's garb attired,
Came up the hollow: — him did I accost,
And what this place might be I then inquired.   120

The Shepherd stopped, and that same story told
Which in my former rhyme I have rehearsed.
"A jolly place," said he, "in times of old!
But something ails it now: the spot is curst.

"You see these lifeless stumps of aspen wood —   125
Some say that they are beeches, others elms —
These were the bower; and here a mansion stood,
The finest palace of a hundred realms!

"The arbour does its own condition tell;
You see the stones, the fountain, and the stream;   130
But as to the great Lodge! you might as well
Hunt half a day for a forgotten dream.

"There's neither dog nor heifer, horse nor sheep,
Will wet his lips within that cup of stone;
And oftentimes, when all are fast asleep,   135
This water doth send forth a dolorous groan.

"Some say that here a murder has been done,
And blood cries out for blood: but, for my part,

I've guessed, when I've been sitting in the sun,
That it was all for that unhappy Hart.   140

"What thoughts must through the creature's brain have past!
Even from the topmost stone, upon the steep,
Are but three bounds — and look, Sir, at this last —
O Master! it has been a cruel leap.

"For thirteen hours he ran a desperate race;   145
And in my simple mind we cannot tell
What cause the Hart might have to love this place,
And come and make his death-bed near the well.

"Here on the grass perhaps asleep he sank,
Lulled by the fountain in the summer-tide;   150
This water was perhaps the first he drank
When he had wandered from his mother's side.

"In April here beneath the flowering thorn
He heard the birds their morning carols sing;
And he, perhaps, for aught we know, was born   155
Not half a furlong from that self-same spring.

"Now, here is neither grass nor pleasant shade;
The sun on drearier hollow never shone;
So will it be, as I have often said,
Till trees, and stones, and fountain, all are gone."   160

"Grey-headed Shepherd, thou hast spoken well;
Small difference lies between thy creed and mine:
This Beast not unobserved by Nature fell;
His death was mourned by sympathy divine.

"The Being, that is in the clouds and air,   165
That is in the green leaves among the groves,
Maintains a deep and reverential care
For the unoffending creatures whom he loves.

"The pleasure-house is dust: — behind, before,
This is no common waste, no common gloom;   170
But Nature, in due course of time, once more
Shall here put on her beauty and her bloom.

"She leaves these objects to a slow decay,
That what we are, and have been, may be known;
But at the coming of the milder day,   175
These monuments shall all be overgrown.

"One lesson, Shepherd, let us two divide,
Taught both by what she shows, and what conceals;
Never to blend our pleasure or our pride
With sorrow of the meanest thing that feels."   180

THE BROTHERS

"THESE Tourists, heaven preserve us! needs must live
A profitable life: some glance along,
Rapid and gay, as if the earth were air,
And they were butterflies to wheel about
Long as the summer lasted: some, as wise,   5
Perched on the forehead of a jutting crag,
Pencil in hand and book upon the knee,
Will look and scribble, scribble on and look,
Until a man might travel twelve stout miles,
Or reap an acre of his neighbour's corn.   10
But, for that moping Son of Idleness,
Why can he tarry *yonder*? — In our church-yard
Is neither epitaph nor monument,
Tombstone nor name — only the turf we tread
And a few natural graves."

                              To Jane, his wife,   15
Thus spake the homely Priest of Ennerdale.
It was a July evening; and he sate
Upon the long stone-seat beneath the eaves
Of his old cottage, — as it chanced, that day,
Employed in winter's work. Upon the stone   20
His wife sate near him, teasing matted wool,
While, from the twin cards toothed with glittering wire,
He fed the spindle of his youngest child,
Who, in the open air, with due accord
Of busy hands and back-and-forward steps,   25
Her large round wheel was turning. Towards the field
In which the Parish Chapel stood alone,
Girt round with a bare ring of mossy wall,
While half an hour went by, the Priest had sent
Many a long look of wonder: and at last,   30
Risen from his seat, beside the snow-white ridge
Of carded wool which the old man had piled
He laid his implements with gentle care,
Each in the other locked; and, down the path
That from his cottage to the church-yard led,   35
He took his way, impatient to accost
The Stranger, whom he saw still lingering there.

'Twas one well known to him in former days,
A Shepherd-lad; who ere his sixteenth year
Had left that calling, tempted to entrust   40
His expectations to the fickle winds
And perilous waters; with the mariners
A fellow-mariner; — and so had fared
Through twenty seasons; but he had been reared
Among the mountains, and he in his heart   45
Was half a shepherd on the stormy seas.
Oft in the piping shrouds had Leonard heard
The tones of waterfalls, and inland sounds
Of caves and trees: — and, when the regular wind
Between the tropics filled the steady sail,   50
And blew with the same breath through days and weeks,
Lengthening invisibly its weary line
Along the cloudless Main, he, in those hours
Of tiresome indolence, would often hang
Over the vessel's side, and gaze and gaze;   55
And, while the broad blue wave and sparkling foam
Flashed round him images and hues that wrought
In union with the employment of his heart,
He, thus by feverish passion overcome,
Even with the organs of his bodily eye,   60
Below him, in the bosom of the deep,
Saw mountains; saw the forms of sheep that grazed
On verdant hills — with dwellings among trees,
And shepherds clad in the same country grey
Which he himself had worn.

                              And now, at last,   65
From perils manifold, with some small wealth
Acquired by traffic 'mid the Indian Isles,
To his paternal home he is returned,
With a determined purpose to resume
The life he had lived there; both for the sake   70
Of many darling pleasures, and the love
Which to an only brother he has borne
In all his hardships, since that happy time
When, whether it blew foul or fair, they two
Were brother-shepherds on their native hills.   75
— They were the last of all their race: and now,
When Leonard had approached his home, his heart
Failed in him; and, not venturing to enquire
Tidings of one so long and dearly loved,
He to the solitary church-yard turned;   80
That, as he knew in what particular spot
His family were laid, he thence might learn

If still his Brother lived, or to the file
Another grave was added. — He had found
Another grave, — near which a full half-hour   85
He had remained; but, as he gazed, there grew
Such a confusion in his memory,
That he began to doubt; and even to hope
That he had seen this heap of turf before, —
That it was not another grave; but one   90
He had forgotten. He had lost his path,
As up the vale, that afternoon, he walked
Through fields which once had been well known to him:
And oh what joy this recollection now
Sent to his heart! he lifted up his eyes,   95
And, looking round, imagined that he saw
Strange alteration wrought on every side
Among the woods and fields, and that the rocks,
And everlasting hills themselves were changed.

By this the Priest, who down the field had come,   100
Unseen by Leonard, at the church-yard gate
Stopped short, — and thence, at leisure, limb by limb
Perused him with a gay complacency.
Ay, thought the Vicar, smiling to himself,
'Tis one of those who needs must leave the path   105
Of the world's business to go wild alone:
His arms have a perpetual holiday;
The happy man will creep about the fields,
Following his fancies by the hour, to bring
Tears down his cheek, or solitary smiles   110
Into his face, until the setting sun
Write fool upon his forehead. — Planted thus
Beneath a shed that over-arched the gate
Of this rude church-yard, till the stars appeared
The good Man might have communed with himself,   115
But that the Stranger, who had left the grave,
Approached; he recognised the Priest at once,
And, after greetings interchanged, and given
By Leonard to the Vicar as to one
Unknown to him, this dialogue ensued.   120
    Leonard. You live, Sir, in these dales, a quiet life:
Your years make up one peaceful family;
And who would grieve and fret, if, welcome come
And welcome gone, they are so like each other,
They cannot be remembered? Scarce a funeral   125
Comes to this church-yard once in eighteen months;
And yet, some changes must take place among you:
And you, who dwell here, even among these rocks,
Can trace the finger of mortality,

And see, that with our threescore years and ten 130
We are not all that perish. —— I remember,
(For many years ago I passed this road)
There was a foot-way all along the fields
By the brook-side — 'tis gone — and that dark cleft!
To me it does not seem to wear the face 135
Which then it had!
  Priest.   Nay, Sir, for aught I know,
That chasm is much the same —
  Leonard.   But, surely, yonder —
  Priest. Ay, there, indeed, your memory is a friend
That does not play you false. — On that tall pike
(It is the loneliest place of all these hills) 140
There were two springs which bubbled side by side,
As if they had been made that they might be
Companions for each other: the huge crag
Was rent with lightning — one hath disappeared;
The other, left behind, is flowing still. 145
For accidents and changes such as these,
We want not store of them; — a water-spout
Will bring down half a mountain; what a feast
For folks that wander up and down like you,
To see an acre's breadth of that wide cliff 150
One roaring cataract! a sharp May-storm
Will come with loads of January snow,
And in one night send twenty score of sheep
To feed the ravens; or a shepherd dies
By some untoward death among the rocks: 155
The ice breaks up and sweeps away a bridge;
A wood is felled: — and then for our own homes!
A child is born or christened, a field ploughed,
A daughter sent to service, a web spun,
The old house-clock is decked with a new face; 160
And hence, so far from wanting facts or dates
To chronicle the time, we all have here
A pair of diaries, — one serving, Sir,
For the whole dale, and one for each fire-side —
Yours was a stranger's judgment: for historians, 165
Commend me to these valleys!
  Leonard.   Yet your Church-yard
Seems, if such freedom may be used with you,
To say that you are heedless of the past:
An orphan could not find his mother's grave:
Here's neither head nor foot-stone, plate of brass, 170
Cross-bones nor skull, — type of our earthly state
Nor emblem of our hopes: the dead man's home
Is but a fellow to that pasture-field.
  Priest. Why, there, Sir, is a thought that's new to me!

The stone-cutters, 'tis true, might beg their bread   175
If every English church-yard were like ours;
Yet your conclusion wanders from the truth:
We have no need of names and epitaphs;
We talk about the dead by our fire-sides.
And then, for our immortal part! *we* want   180
No symbols, Sir, to tell us that plain tale:
The thought of death sits easy on the man
Who has been born and dies among the mountains.
    Leonard. Your Dalesmen, then, do in each other's thoughts
Possess a kind of second life: no doubt   185
You, Sir, could help me to the history
Of half these graves?
    Priest.   For eight-score winters past,
With what I've witnessed, and with what I've heard,
Perhaps I might; and, on a winter-evening,
If you were seated at my chimney's nook,   190
By turning o'er these hillocks one by one,
We two could travel, Sir, through a strange round;
Yet all in the broad highway of the world.
Now there's a grave — your foot is half upon it, —
It looks just like the rest; and yet that man   195
Died broken-hearted.
    Leonard.   'Tis a common case.
We'll take another: who is he that lies
Beneath yon ridge, the last of those three graves?
It touches on that piece of native rock
Left in the church-yard wall.
    Priest.   That's Walter Ewbank.   200
He had as white a head and fresh a cheek
As ever were produced by youth and age
Engendering in the blood of hale fourscore.
Through five long generations had the heart
Of Walter's forefathers o'erflowed the bounds   205
Of their inheritance, that single cottage —
You see it yonder! and those few green fields.
They toiled and wrought, and still, from sire to son,
Each struggled, and each yielded as before
A little — yet a little, — and old Walter,   210
They left to him the family heart, and land
With other burthens than the crop it bore.
Year after year the old man still kept up
A cheerful mind, — and buffeted with bond,
Interest, and mortgages; at last he sank,   215
And went into his grave before his time.
Poor Walter! whether it was care that spurred him
God only knows, but to the very last

He had the lightest foot in Ennerdale:
His pace was never that of an old man: 220
I almost see him tripping down the path
With his two grandsons after him: — but you,
Unless our Landlord be your host to-night,
Have far to travel, — and on these rough paths
Even in the longest day of midsummer — 225
  Leonard. But those two Orphans!
   Priest.   Orphans! — Such they were —
Yet not while Walter lived: — for, though their parents
Lay buried side by side as now they lie,
The old man was a father to the boys,
Two fathers in one father: and if tears, 230
Shed when he talked of them where they were not,
And hauntings from the infirmity of love,
Are aught of what makes up a mother's heart,
This old Man, in the day of his old age,
Was half a mother to them. — If you weep, Sir, 235
To hear a stranger talking about strangers,
Heaven bless you when you are among your kindred!
Ay — you may turn that way — it is a grave
Which will bear looking at.
  Leonard.   These boys — I hope
They loved this good old Man? —
   Priest.   They did — and truly: 240
But that was what we almost overlooked,
They were such darlings of each other. Yes,
Though from the cradle they had lived with Walter,
The only kinsman near them, and though he
Inclined to both by reason of his age, 245
With a more fond, familiar, tenderness;
They, notwithstanding, had much love to spare,
And it all went into each other's hearts.
Leonard, the elder by just eighteen months,
Was two years taller: 'twas a joy to see, 250
To hear, to meet them! — From their house the school
Is distant three short miles, and in the time
Of storm and thaw, when every water-course
And unbridged stream, such as you may have noticed
Crossing our roads at every hundred steps, 255
Was swoln into a noisy rivulet,
Would Leonard then, when elder boys remained
At home, go staggering through the slippery fords,
Bearing his brother on his back. I have seen him,
On windy days, in one of those stray brooks, 260
Ay, more than once I have seen him, mid-leg deep,
Their two books lying both on a dry stone,

Upon the hither side: and once I said,
As I remember, looking round these rocks
And hills on which we all of us were born,   265
That God who made the great book of the world
Would bless such piety —
    Leonard.   It may be then —
    Priest. Never did worthier lads break English bread;
The very brightest Sunday Autumn saw
With all its mealy clusters of ripe nuts,   270
Could never keep those boys away from church,
Or tempt them to an hour of sabbath breach.
Leonard and James! I warrant, every corner
Among these rocks, and every hollow place
That venturous foot could reach, to one or both   275
Was known as well as to the flowers that grow there.
Like roe-bucks they went bounding o'er the hills;
They played like two young ravens on the crags:
Then they could write, ay and speak too, as well
As many of their betters — and for Leonard!   280
The very night before he went away,
In my own house I put into his hand
A bible, and I'd wager house and field
That, if he be alive, he has it yet.
    Leonard. It seems, these Brothers have not lived to be   285
A comfort to each other —
    Priest.   That they might
Live to such end is what both old and young
In this our valley all of us have wished,
And what, for my part, I have often prayed:
But Leonard —
    Leonard. Then James still is left among you!   290
    Priest. 'Tis of the elder brother I am speaking:
They had an uncle; — he was at that time
A thriving man, and trafficked on the seas:
And, but for that same uncle, to this hour
Leonard had never handled rope or shroud: 295
For the boy loved the life which we lead here;
And though of unripe years, a stripling only,
His soul was knit to this his native soil.
But, as I said, old Walter was too weak
To strive with such a torrent; when he died,   300
The estate and house were sold; and all their sheep,
A pretty flock, and which, for aught I know,
Had clothed the Ewbanks for a thousand years: —
Well — all was gone, and they were destitute,
And Leonard, chiefly for his Brother's sake,   305
Resolved to try his fortune on the seas.

Twelve years are past since we had tidings from him.
If there were one among us who had heard
That Leonard Ewbank was come home again,
From the Great Gavel, down by Leeza's banks,   310
And down the Enna, far as Egremont,
The day would be a joyous festival;
And those two bells of ours, which there you see —
Hanging in the open air — but, O good Sir!
This is sad talk — they'll never sound for him —   315
Living or dead. — When last we heard of him,
He was in slavery among the Moors
Upon the Barbary coast. — 'Twas not a little
That would bring down his spirit; and no doubt,
Before it ended in his death, the Youth   320
Was sadly crossed. — Poor Leonard! when we parted,
He took me by the hand, and said to me,
If e'er he should grow rich, he would return,
To live in peace upon his father's land,
And lay his bones among us.

    Leonard.   If that day   325
Should come, 'twould needs be a glad day for him;
He would himself, no doubt, be happy then
As any that should meet him —

    Priest.   Happy! Sir —

    Leonard. You said his kindred all were in their graves,
And that he had one Brother —

    Priest.   That is but   330
A fellow-tale of sorrow. From his youth
James, though not sickly, yet was delicate;
And Leonard being always by his side
Had done so many offices about him,
That, though he was not of a timid nature,   335
Yet still the spirit of a mountain-boy
In him was somewhat checked; and, when his Brother
Was gone to sea, and he was left alone,
The little colour that he had was soon
Stolen from his cheek; he drooped, and pined, and pined —   340

    Leonard. But these are all the graves of full-grown men!

    Priest. Ay, Sir, that passed away: we took him to us;
He was the child of all the dale — he lived
Three months with one, and six months with another;
And wanted neither food, nor clothes, nor love: 345
And many, many happy days were his.
But, whether blithe or sad, 'tis my belief
His absent Brother still was at his heart.
And, when he dwelt beneath our roof, we found
(A practice till this time unknown to him)   350

That often, rising from his bed at night,
He in his sleep would walk about, and sleeping
He sought his brother Leonard. — You are moved!
Forgive me, Sir: before I spoke to you,
I judged you most unkindly.

  Leonard.   But this Youth, 355
How did he die at last?
  Priest.   One sweet May-morning,
(It will be twelve years since when Spring returns)
He had gone forth among the new-dropped lambs,
With two or three companions, whom their course
Of occupation led from height to height 360
Under a cloudless sun — till he, at length,
Through weariness, or, haply, to indulge
The humour of the moment, lagged behind.
You see yon precipice; — it wears the shape
Of a vast building made of many crags; 365
And in the midst is one particular rock
That rises like a column from the vale,
Whence by our shepherds it is called, THE PILLAR.
Upon its aëry summit crowned with heath,
The loiterer, not unnoticed by his comrades, 370
Lay stretched at ease; but, passing by the place
On their return, they found that he was gone.
No ill was feared; till one of them by chance
Entering, when evening was far spent, the house
Which at that time was James's home, there learned 375
That nobody had seen him all that day:
The morning came, and still he was unheard of:
The neighbours were alarmed, and to the brook
Some hastened; some ran to the lake: ere noon
They found him at the foot of that same rock 380
Dead, and with mangled limbs. The third day after
I buried him, poor Youth, and there he lies!
  Leonard. And that then *is* his grave! — Before his death
You say that he saw many happy years?
  Priest. Ay, that he did —
  Leonard.   And all went well with him? — 385
  Priest. If he had one, the Youth had twenty homes.
  Leonard. And you believe, then, that his mind was easy? —
  Priest. Yes, long before he died, he found that time
Is a true friend to sorrow; and unless
His thoughts were turned on Leonard's luckless fortune, 390
He talked about him with a cheerful love.
  Leonard. He could not come to an unhallowed end!
  Priest. Nay, God forbid! — You recollect I mentioned
A habit which disquietude and grief

Had brought upon him; and we all conjectured   395
That, as the day was warm, he had lain down
On the soft heath, — and, waiting for his comrades,
He there had fallen asleep; that in his sleep
He to the margin of the precipice
Had walked, and from the summit had fallen headlong: 400
And so no doubt he perished.. When the Youth
Fell, in his hand he must have grasp'd, we think,
His shepherd's staff; for on that Pillar of rock
It had been caught mid-way; and there for years
It hung; — and mouldered there.

                         The Priest here ended —   405
The Stranger would have thanked him, but he felt
A gushing from his heart, that took away
The power of speech. Both left the spot in silence;
And Leonard, when they reached the church-yard gate,
As the Priest lifted up the latch, turned round, —   410
And, looking at the grave, he said, "My Brother!"
The Vicar did not hear the words: and now,
He pointed towards his dwelling-place, entreating
That Leonard would partake his homely fare:
The other thanked him with an earnest voice;   415
But added, that, the evening being calm,
He would pursue his journey. So they parted.

  It was not long ere Leonard reached a grove
That overhung the road: he there stopped short,
And, sitting down beneath the trees, reviewed   420
All that the Priest had said: his early years
Were with him: — his long absence, cherished hopes,
And thoughts which had been his an hour before,
All pressed on him with such a weight, that now,
This vale, where he had been so happy, seemed   425
A place in which he could not bear to live:
So he relinquished all his purposes.
He travelled back to Egremont: and thence,
That night, he wrote a letter to the Priest,
Reminding him of what had passed between them;   430
And adding, with a hope to be forgiven,
That it was from the weakness of his heart
He had not dared to tell him who he was.
This done, he went on shipboard, and is now
A Seaman, a grey-headed Mariner.   435

IT WAS AN APRIL MORNING

IT was an April morning: fresh and clear
The Rivulet, delighting in its strength,
Ran with a young man's speed; and yet the voice
Of waters which the winter had supplied
Was softened down into a vernal tone.   5
The spirit of enjoyment and desire,
And hopes and wishes, from all living things
Went circling, like a multitude of sounds.
The budding groves seemed eager to urge on
The steps of June; as if their various hues   10
Were only hindrances that stood between
Them and their object: but, meanwhile, prevailed
Such an entire contentment in the air
That every naked ash, and tardy tree
Yet leafless, showed as if the countenance   15
With which it looked on this delightful day
Were native to the summer. — Up the brook
I roamed in the confusion of my heart,
Alive to all things and forgetting all.
At length I to a sudden turning came   20
In this continuous glen, where down a rock
The Stream, so ardent in its course before,
Sent forth such sallies of glad sound, that all
Which I till then had heard, appeared the voice
Of common pleasure: beast and bird, the lamb,   25
The shepherd's dog, the linnet and the thrush
Vied with this waterfall, and made a song,
Which, while I listened, seemed like the wild growth
Or like some natural produce of the air,
That could not cease to be. Green leaves were here;   30
But 'twas the foliage of the rocks — the birch,
The yew, the holly, and the bright green thorn,
With hanging islands of resplendent furze:
And, on a summit, distant a short space,
By any who should look beyond the dell,   35
A single mountain-cottage might be seen.
I gazed and gazed, and to myself I said,
"Our thoughts at least are ours; and this wild nook,
My EMMA, I will dedicate to thee."
—— Soon did the spot become my other home,   40
My dwelling, and my out-of-doors abode.
And, of the Shepherds who have seen me there,

To whom I sometimes in our idle talk
Have told this fancy, two or three, perhaps,
Years after we are gone and in our graves,   45
When they have cause to speak of this wild place,
May call it by the name of EMMA'S DELL.

TO JOANNA

AMID the smoke of cities did you pass
The time of early youth; and there you learned,
From years of quiet industry, to love
The living Beings by your own fire-side,
With such a strong devotion, that your heart   5
Is slow to meet the sympathies of them
Who look upon the hills with tenderness,
And make dear friendships with the streams and groves.
Yet we, who are transgressors in this kind,
Dwelling retired in our simplicity   10
Among the woods and fields, we love you well,
Joanna! and I guess, since you have been
So distant from us now for two long years,
That you will gladly listen to discourse,
However trivial, if you thence be taught   15
That they, with whom you once were happy, talk
Familiarly of you and of old times.

    While I was seated, now some ten days past,
Beneath those lofty firs, that overtop
Their ancient neighbour, the old steeple-tower,   20
The Vicar from his gloomy house hard by
Came forth to greet me; and when he had asked,
"How fares Joanna, that wild-hearted Maid!
And when will she return to us?" he paused;
And, after short exchange of village news,   25
He with grave looks demanded, for what cause,
Reviving obsolete idolatry,
I, like a Runic Priest, in characters
Of formidable size had chiselled out
Some uncouth name upon the native rock,   30
Above the Rotha, by the forest-side.
— Now, by those dear immunities of heart
Engendered between malice and true love,
I was not loth to be so catechised,
And this was my reply: — "As it befel,   35

One summer morning we had walked abroad
At break of day, Joanna and myself.
— 'Twas that delightful season when the broom,
Full-flowered, and visible on every steep,
Along the copses runs in veins of gold.   40
Our pathway led us on to Rotha's banks;
And when we came in front of that tall rock
That eastward looks, I there stopped short — and stood
Tracing the lofty barrier with my eye
From base to summit; such delight I found   45
To note in shrub and tree, in stone and flower
That intermixture of delicious hues,
Along so vast a surface, all at once,
In one impression, by connecting force
Of their own beauty, imaged in the heart.   50
— When I had gazed perhaps two minutes' space,
Joanna, looking in my eyes, beheld
That ravishment of mine, and laughed aloud.
The Rock, like something starting from a sleep,
Took up the Lady's voice, and laughed again;   55
That ancient Woman seated on Helm-crag
Was ready with her cavern; Hammar-scar,
And the tall Steep of Silver-how, sent forth
A noise of laughter; southern Loughrigg heard,
And Fairfield answered with a mountain tone;   60
Helvellyn far into the clear blue sky
Carried the Lady's voice, — old Skiddaw blew
His speaking-trumpet; — back out of the clouds
Of Glaramara southward came the voice;
And Kirkstone tossed it from his misty head.   65
— Now whether (said I to our cordial Friend,
Who in the hey-day of astonishment
Smiled in my face) this were in simple truth
A work accomplished by the brotherhood
Of ancient mountains, or my ear was touched   70
With dreams and visionary impulses
To me alone imparted, sure I am
That there was a loud uproar in the hills.
And, while we both were listening, to my side
The fair Joanna drew, as if she wished   75
To shelter from some object of her fear.
— And hence, long afterwards, when eighteen moons
Were wasted, as I chanced to walk alone
Beneath this rock, at sunrise, on a calm
And silent morning, I sat down, and there,   80
In memory of affections old and true,

I chiselled out in those rude characters
Joanna's name deep in the living stone: —
And I, and all who dwell by my fireside,
Have called the lovely rock, JOANNA'S ROCK."   85

THERE IS AN EMINENCE

THERE is an Eminence, — of these our hills
The last that parleys with the setting sun;
We can behold it from our orchard-seat;
And, when at evening we pursue our walk
Along the public way, this Peak, so high   5
Above us, and so distant in its height,
Is visible; and often seems to send
Its own deep quiet to restore our hearts.
The meteors make of it a favourite haunt:
The star of Jove, so beautiful and large   10
In the mid heavens, is never half so fair
As when he shines above it. 'Tis in truth
The loneliest place we have among the clouds.
And She who dwells with me, whom I have loved
With such communion, that no place on earth   15
Can ever be a solitude to me,
Hath to this lonely Summit given my Name.

A NARROW GIRDLE OF ROUGH STONES

A NARROW girdle of rough stones and crags,
A rude and natural causeway, interposed
Between the water and a winding slope
Of copse and thicket, leaves the eastern shore
Of Grasmere safe in its own privacy: 5
And there myself and two beloved Friends,
One calm September morning, ere the mist
Had altogether yielded to the sun,
Sauntered on this retired and difficult way.
—— Ill suits the road with one in haste; but we   10
Played with our time; and, as we strolled along,
It was our occupation to observe
Such objects as the waves had tossed ashore —
Feather, or leaf, or weed, or withered bough,
Each on the other heaped, along the line   15

Of the dry wreck. And, in our vacant mood,
Not seldom did we stop to watch some tuft
Of dandelion seed or thistle's beard,
That skimmed the surface of the dead calm lake,
Suddenly halting now — a lifeless stand!   20
And starting off again with freak as sudden;
In all its sportive wanderings, all the while,
Making report of an invisible breeze
That was its wings, its chariot, and its horse,
Its playmate, rather say, its moving soul.   25
—— And often, trifling with a privilege
Alike indulged to all, we paused, one now,
And now the other, to point out, perchance
To pluck, some flower or water-weed, too fair
Either to be divided from the place   30
On which it grew, or to be left alone
To its own beauty. Many such there are,
Fair ferns and flowers, and chiefly that tall fern,
So stately, of the queen Osmunda named;
Plant lovelier, in its own retired abode   35
On Grasmere's beach, than Naiad by the side
Of Grecian brook, or Lady of the Mere,
Sole-sitting by the shores of old romance.
— So fared we that bright morning: from the fields,
Meanwhile, a noise was heard, the busy mirth   40
Of reapers, men and women, boys and girls.
Delighted much to listen to those sounds,
And feeding thus our fancies, we advanced
Along the indented shore; when suddenly,
Through a thin veil of glittering haze was seen   45
Before us, on a point of jutting land,
The tall and upright figure of a Man
Attired in peasant's garb, who stood alone,
Angling beside the margin of the lake.
"Improvident and reckless," we exclaimed,   50
"The Man must be, who thus can lose a day
Of the mid harvest, when the labourer's hire
Is ample, and some little might be stored
Wherewith to cheer him in the winter time."
Thus talking of that Peasant, we approached   55
Close to the spot where with his rod and line
He stood alone; whereat he turned his head
To greet us — and we saw a Man worn down
By sickness, gaunt and lean, with sunken cheeks
And wasted limbs, his legs so long and lean   60
That for my single self I looked at them,

Forgetful of the body they sustained. —
Too weak to labour in the harvest field,
The Man was using his best skill to gain
A pittance from the dead unfeeling lake   65
That knew not of his wants. I will not say
What thoughts immediately were ours, nor how
The happy idleness of that sweet morn,
With all its lovely images, was changed
To serious musing and to self-reproach.   70
Nor did we fail to see within ourselves
What need there is to be reserved in speech,
And temper all our thoughts with charity.
— Therefore, unwilling to forget that day,
My Friend, Myself, and She who then received 75
The same admonishment, have called the place
By a memorial name, uncouth indeed
As e'er by mariner was given to bay
Or foreland, on a new-discovered coast;
And POINT RASH-JUDGMENT is the name it bears.   80

MICHAEL

A PASTORAL POEM

IF from the public way you turn your steps
Up the tumultuous brook of Green-head Ghyll,
You will suppose that with an upright path
Your feet must struggle; in such bold ascent
The pastoral mountains front you, face to face.   5
But, courage! for around that boisterous brook
The mountains have all opened out themselves,
And made a hidden valley of their own.
No habitation can be seen; but they
Who journey thither find themselves alone   10
With a few sheep, with rocks and stones, and kites
That overhead are sailing in the sky.
It is in truth an utter solitude;
Nor should I have made mention of this Dell
But for one object which you might pass by,   15
Might see and notice not. Beside the brook
Appears a straggling heap of unhewn stones!
And to that simple object appertains
A story — unenriched with strange events,
Yet not unfit, I deem, for the fireside,   20
Or for the summer shade. It was the first
Of those domestic tales that spake to me
Of Shepherds, dwellers in the valleys, men
Whom I already loved; — not verily
For their own sakes, but for the fields and hills   25
Where was their occupation and abode.
And hence this Tale, while I was yet a Boy
Careless of books, yet having felt the power
Of Nature, by the gentle agency
Of natural objects, led me on to feel   30
For passions that were not my own, and think
(At random and imperfectly indeed)
On man, the heart of man, and human life.
Therefore, although it be a history
Homely and rude, I will relate the same   35
For the delight of a few natural hearts;
And, with yet fonder feeling, for the sake
Of youthful Poets, who among these hills
Will be my second self when I am gone.

UPON the forest-side in Grasmere Vale 40
There dwelt a Shepherd, Michael was his name;
An old man, stout of heart, and strong of limb.
His bodily frame had been from youth to age
Of an unusual strength: his mind was keen,
Intense, and frugal, apt for all affairs, 45
And in his shepherd's calling he was prompt
And watchful more than ordinary men.
Hence had he learned the meaning of all winds,
Of blasts of every tone; and, oftentimes,
When others heeded not, He heard the South 50
Make subterraneous music, like the noise
Of bagpipers on distant Highland hills.
The Shepherd, at such warning, of his flock
Bethought him, and he to himself would say,
"The winds are now devising work for me!" 55
And, truly, at all times, the storm, that drives
The traveller to a shelter, summoned him
Up to the mountains: he had been alone
Amid the heart of many thousand mists,
That came to him, and left him, on the heights. 60
So lived he till his eightieth year was past.
And grossly that man errs, who should suppose
That the green valleys, and the streams and rocks,
Were things indifferent to the Shepherd's thoughts.
Fields, where with cheerful spirits he had breathed 65
The common air; hills, which with vigorous step
He had so often climbed; which had impressed
So many incidents upon his mind
Of hardship, skill or courage, joy or fear;
Which, like a book, preserved the memory 70
Of the dumb animals, whom he had saved,
Had fed or sheltered, linking to such acts
The certainty of honourable gain;
Those fields, those hills — what could they less? had laid
Strong hold on his affections, were to him 75
A pleasurable feeling of blind love,
The pleasure which there is in life itself.

His days had not been passed in singleness.
His Helpmate was a comely matron, old —
Though younger than himself full twenty years. 80
She was a woman of a stirring life,
Whose heart was in her house: two wheels she had
Of antique form; this large, for spinning wool;
That small, for flax; and if one wheel had rest,
It was because the other was at work. 85

The Pair had but one inmate in their house,
An only Child, who had been born to them
When Michael, telling o'er his years, began
To deem that he was old, — in shepherd's phrase,
With one foot in the grave. This only Son,   90
With two brave sheep-dogs tried in many a storm,
The one of an inestimable worth,
Made all their household. I may truly say,
That they were as a proverb in the vale
For endless industry. When day was gone,   95
And from their occupations out of doors
The Son and Father were come home, even then,
Their labour did not cease; unless when all
Turned to the cleanly supper-board, and there,
Each with a mess of pottage and skimmed milk,   100
Sat round the basket piled with oaten cakes,
And their plain home-made cheese. Yet when the meal
Was ended, Luke (for so the Son was named)
And his old Father both betook themselves
To such convenient work as might employ   105
Their hands by the fire-side; perhaps to card
Wool for the Housewife's spindle, or repair
Some injury done to sickle, flail, or scythe,
Or other implement of house or field.

Down from the ceiling, by the chimney's edge,   110
That in our ancient uncouth country style
With huge and black projection overbrowed
Large space beneath, as duly as the light
Of day grew dim the Housewife hung a lamp;
An aged utensil, which had performed   115
Service beyond all others of its kind.
Early at evening did it burn — and late,
Surviving comrade of uncounted hours,
Which, going by from year to year, had found,
And left the couple neither gay perhaps   120
Nor cheerful, yet with objects and with hopes,
Living a life of eager industry.
And now, when Luke had reached his eighteenth year,
There by the light of this old lamp they sate,
Father and Son, while far into the night   125
The Housewife plied her own peculiar work,
Making the cottage through the silent hours
Murmur as with the sound of summer flies.
This light was famous in its neighbourhood,
And was a public symbol of the life   130
That thrifty Pair had lived. For, as it chanced,

Their cottage on a plot of rising ground
Stood single, with large prospect, north and south,
High into Easedale, up to Dunmail-Raise,
And westward to the village near the lake;   135
And from this constant light, so regular
And so far seen, the House itself, by all
Who dwelt within the limits of the vale,
Both old and young, was named THE EVENING STAR.

   Thus living on through such a length of years,   140
The Shepherd, if he loved himself, must needs
Have loved his Helpmate; but to Michael's heart
This son of his old age was yet more dear —
Less from instinctive tenderness, the same
Fond spirit that blindly works in the blood of all —   145
Than that a child, more than all other gifts
That earth can offer to declining man,
Brings hope with it, and forward-looking thoughts,
And stirrings of inquietude, when they
By tendency of nature needs must fail.   150
Exceeding was the love he bare to him,
His heart and his heart's joy! For oftentimes
Old Michael, while he was a babe in arms,
Had done him female service, not alone
For pastime and delight, as is the use   155
Of fathers, but with patient mind enforced
To acts of tenderness; and he had rocked
His cradle, as with a woman's gentle hand.

   And, in a later time, ere yet the Boy
Had put on boy's attire, did Michael love,   160
Albeit of a stern unbending mind,
To have the Young-one in his sight, when he
Wrought in the field, or on his shepherd's stool
Sate with a fettered sheep before him stretched
Under the large old oak, that near his door   165
Stood single, and, from matchless depth of shade,
Chosen for the Shearer's covert from the sun,
Thence in our rustic dialect was called
The CLIPPING TREE, a name which yet it bears.
There, while they two were sitting in the shade,   170
With others round them, earnest all and blithe,
Would Michael exercise his heart with looks
Of fond correction and reproof bestowed
Upon the Child, if he disturbed the sheep
By catching at their legs, or with his shouts   175
Scared them, while they lay still beneath the shears.

And when by Heaven's good grace the boy grew up
A healthy Lad, and carried in his cheek
Two steady roses that were five years old;
Then Michael from a winter coppice cut   180
With his own hand a sapling, which he hooped
With iron, making it throughout in all
Due requisites a perfect shepherd's staff,
And gave it to the Boy; wherewith equipt
He as a watchman oftentimes was placed   185
At gate or gap, to stem or turn the flock;
And, to his office prematurely called,
There stood the urchin, as you will divine,
Something between a hindrance and a help;
And for this cause not always, I believe,   190
Receiving from his Father hire of praise;
Though nought was left undone which staff, or voice,
Or looks, or threatening gestures, could perform.

But soon as Luke, full ten years old, could stand
Against the mountain blasts; and to the heights,   195
Not fearing toil, nor length of weary ways,
He with his Father daily went, and they
Were as companions, why should I relate
That objects which the Shepherd loved before
Were dearer now? that from the Boy there came   200
Feelings and emanations — things which were
Light to the sun and music to the wind;
And that the old Man's heart seemed born again?

Thus in his Father's sight the Boy grew up:
And now, when he had reached his eighteenth year,   205
He was his comfort and his daily hope.

While in this sort the simple household lived
From day to day, to Michael's ear there came
Distressful tidings. Long before the time
Of which I speak, the Shepherd had been bound   210
In surety for his brother's son, a man
Of an industrious life, and ample means;
But unforeseen misfortunes suddenly
Had prest upon him; and old Michael now
Was summoned to discharge the forfeiture,   215
A grievous penalty, but little less
Than half his substance. This unlooked-for claim,
At the first hearing, for a moment took
More hope out of his life than he supposed
That any old man ever could have lost.   220

As soon as he had armed himself with strength
To look his trouble in the face, it seemed
The Shepherd's sole resource to sell at once
A portion of his patrimonial fields.
Such was his first resolve; he thought again,   225
And his heart failed him. "Isabel," said he,
Two evenings after he had heard the news,
"I have been toiling more than seventy years,
And in the open sunshine of God's love
Have we all lived; yet if these fields of ours   230
Should pass into a stranger's hand, I think
That I could not lie quiet in my grave.
Our lot is a hard lot; the sun himself
Has scarcely been more diligent than I;
And I have lived to be a fool at last   235
To my own family. An evil man
That was, and made an evil choice, if he
Were false to us; and if he were not false,
There are ten thousand to whom loss like this
Had been no sorrow. I forgive him; — but   240
'Twere better to be dumb than to talk thus.

"When I began, my purpose was to speak
Of remedies and of a cheerful hope.
Our Luke shall leave us, Isabel; the land
Shall not go from us, and it shall be free;   245
He shall possess it, free as is the wind
That passes over it. We have, thou know'st,
Another kinsman — he will be our friend
In this distress. He is a prosperous man,
Thriving in trade — and Luke to him shall go,   250
And with his kinsman's help and his own thrift
He quickly will repair this loss, and then
He may return to us. If here he stay,
What can be done? Where every one is poor,
What can be gained?"
               At this the old Man paused,   255
And Isabel sat silent, for her mind
Was busy, looking back into past times.
There's Richard Bateman, thought she to herself,
He was a parish-boy — at the church-door
They made a gathering for him, shillings, pence   260
And halfpennies, wherewith the neighbours bought
A basket, which they filled with pedlar's wares;
And, with this basket on his arm, the lad
Went up to London, found a master there,
Who, out of many, chose the trusty boy   265

To go and overlook his merchandise
Beyond the seas; where he grew wondrous rich,
And left estates and monies to the poor,
And, at his birth-place, built a chapel floored
With marble, which he sent from foreign lands.   270
These thoughts, and many others of like sort,
Passed quickly through the mind of Isabel,
And her face brightened. The old Man was glad,
And thus resumed: — "Well, Isabel! this scheme
These two days, has been meat and drink to me.   275
Far more than we have lost is left us yet.
— We have enough — I wish indeed that I
Were younger; — but this hope is a good hope.
Make ready Luke's best garments, of the best
Buy for him more, and let us send him forth   280
To-morrow, or the next day, or to-night:
— If he *could* go, the Boy should go to-night."

Here Michael ceased, and to the fields went forth
With a light heart. The Housewife for five days
Was restless morn and night, and all day long   285
Wrought on with her best fingers to prepare
Things needful for the journey of her son.
But Isabel was glad when Sunday came
To stop her in her work: for, when she lay
By Michael's side, she through the last two nights   290
Heard him, how he was troubled in his sleep:
And when they rose at morning she could see
That all his hopes were gone. That day at noon
She said to Luke, while they two by themselves
Were sitting at the door, "Thou must not go: 295
We have no other Child but thee to lose,
None to remember — do not go away,
For if thou leave thy Father he will die."
The Youth made answer with a jocund voice;
And Isabel, when she had told her fears,   300
Recovered heart. That evening her best fare
Did she bring forth, and all together sat
Like happy people round a Christmas fire.

With daylight Isabel resumed her work;
And all the ensuing week the house appeared   305
As cheerful as a grove in Spring: at length
The expected letter from their kinsman came,
With kind assurances that he would do
His utmost for the welfare of the Boy;
To which, requests were added, that forthwith   310

He might be sent to him. Ten times or more
The letter was read over; Isabel
Went forth to show it to the neighbours round;
Nor was there at that time on English land
A prouder heart than Luke's. When Isabel   315
Had to her house returned, the old Man said,
"He shall depart to-morrow." To this word
The Housewife answered, talking much of things
Which, if at such short notice he should go,
Would surely be forgotten. But at length   320
She gave consent, and Michael was at ease.

Near the tumultuous brook of Green-head Ghyll,
In that deep valley, Michael had designed
To build a Sheep-fold; and, before he heard
The tidings of his melancholy loss,   325
For this same purpose he had gathered up
A heap of stones, which by the streamlet's edge
Lay thrown together, ready for the work.
With Luke that evening thitherward he walked:
And soon as they had reached the place he stopped,   330
And thus the old Man spake to him: — "My Son,
To-morrow thou wilt leave me: with full heart
I look upon thee, for thou art the same
That wert a promise to me ere thy birth,
And all thy life hast been my daily joy.   335
I will relate to thee some little part
Of our two histories; 'twill do thee good
When thou art from me, even if I should touch
On things thou canst not know of. —— After thou
First cam'st into the world — as oft befals   340
To new-born infants — thou didst sleep away
Two days, and blessings from thy Father's tongue
Then fell upon thee. Day by day passed on,
And still I loved thee with increasing love.
Never to living ear came sweeter sounds   345
Than when I heard thee by our own fire-side
First uttering, without words, a natural tune;
While thou, a feeding babe, didst in thy joy
Sing at thy Mother's breast. Month followed month,
And in the open fields my life was passed   350
And on the mountains; else I think that thou
Hadst been brought up upon thy Father's knees.
But we were playmates, Luke: among these hills,
As well thou knowest, in us the old and young
Have played together, nor with me didst thou   355
Lack any pleasure which a boy can know."

Luke had a manly heart; but at these words
He sobbed aloud. The old Man grasped his hand,
And said, "Nay, do not take it so — I see
That these are things of which I need not speak.   360
— Even to the utmost I have been to thee
A kind and a good Father: and herein
I but repay a gift which I myself
Received at others' hands; for, though now old
Beyond the common life of man, I still   365
Remember them who loved me in my youth.
Both of them sleep together: here they lived,
As all their Forefathers had done; and when
At length their time was come, they were not loth
To give their bodies to the family mould.   370
I wished that thou should'st live the life they lived:
But, 'tis a long time to look back, my Son,
And see so little gain from threescore years.
These fields were burthened when they came to me;
Till I was forty years of age, not more   375
Than half of my inheritance was mine.
I toiled and toiled; God blessed me in my work,
And till these three weeks past the land was free.
— It looks as if it never could endure
Another Master. Heaven forgive me, Luke,   380
If I judge ill for thee, but it seems good
That thou should'st go."
                            At this the old Man paused;
Then, pointing to the stones near which they stood,
Thus, after a short silence, he resumed:
"This was a work for us; and now, my Son,   385
It is a work for me. But, lay one stone —
Here, lay it for me, Luke, with thine own hands.
Nay, Boy, be of good hope; — we both may live
To see a better day. At eighty-four
I still am strong and hale; — do thou thy part;   390
I will do mine. — I will begin again
With many tasks that were resigned to thee:
Up to the heights, and in among the storms,
Will I without thee go again, and do
All works which I was wont to do alone,   395
Before I knew thy face. — Heaven bless thee, Boy!
Thy heart these two weeks has been beating fast
With many hopes; it should be so — yes — yes —
I knew that thou could'st never have a wish
To leave me, Luke: thou hast been bound to me   400
Only by links of love: when thou art gone,
What will be left to us! — But, I forget

My purposes. Lay now the corner-stone,
As I requested; and hereafter, Luke,
When thou art gone away, should evil men   405
Be thy companions, think of me, my Son,
And of this moment; hither turn thy thoughts,
And God will strengthen thee: amid all fear
And all temptation, Luke, I pray that thou
May'st bear in mind the life thy Fathers lived,   410
Who, being innocent, did for that cause
Bestir them in good deeds. Now, fare thee well —
When thou return'st, thou in this place wilt see
A work which is not here: a covenant
'Twill be between us; but, whatever fate   415
Befal thee, I shall love thee to the last,
And bear thy memory with me to the grave."

   The Shepherd ended here; and Luke stooped down,
And, as his Father had requested, laid
The first stone of the Sheep-fold. At the sight   420
The old Man's grief broke from him; to his heart
He pressed his Son, he kissèd him and wept;
And to the house together they returned.
— Hushed was that House in peace, or seeming peace,
Ere the night fell: — with morrow's dawn the Boy   425
Began his journey, and when he had reached
The public way, he put on a bold face;
And all the neighbours, as he passed their doors,
Came forth with wishes and with farewell prayers,
That followed him till he was out of sight.   430

   A good report did from their Kinsman come,
Of Luke and his well-doing: and the Boy
Wrote loving letters, full of wondrous news,
Which, as the Housewife phrased it, were throughout
"The prettiest letters that were ever seen."   435
Both parents read them with rejoicing hearts.
So, many months passed on: and once again
The Shepherd went about his daily work
With confident and cheerful thoughts; and now
Sometimes when he could find a leisure hour   440
He to that valley took his way, and there
Wrought at the Sheep-fold. Meantime Luke began
To slacken in his duty; and, at length,
He in the dissolute city gave himself
To evil courses: ignominy and shame   445
Fell on him, so that he was driven at last
To seek a hiding-place beyond the seas.

There is a comfort in the strength of love;
'Twill make a thing endurable, which else
Would overset the brain, or break the heart: 450
I have conversed with more than one who well
Remember the old Man, and what he was
Years after he had heard this heavy news.
His bodily frame had been from youth to age
Of an unusual strength. Among the rocks   455
He went, and still looked up to sun and cloud,
And listened to the wind; and, as before,
Performed all kinds of labour for his sheep,
And for the land, his small inheritance.
And to that hollow dell from time to time   460
Did he repair, to build the Fold of which
His flock had need. 'Tis not forgotten yet
The pity which was then in every heart
For the old Man — and 'tis believed by all
That many and many a day he thither went,   465
And never lifted up a single stone.

There, by the Sheep-fold, sometimes was he seen
Sitting alone, or with his faithful Dog,
Then old, beside him, lying at his feet.
The length of full seven years, from time to time,   470
He at the building of this Sheep-fold wrought,
And left the work unfinished when he died.
Three years, or little more, did Isabel
Survive her Husband: at her death the estate
Was sold, and went into a stranger's hand.   475
The Cottage which was named the EVENING STAR
Is gone — the ploughshare has been through the ground
On which it stood; great changes have been wrought
In all the neighbourhood: — yet the oak is left
That grew beside their door; and the remains   480
Of the unfinished Sheep-fold may be seen
Beside the boisterous brook of Green-head Ghyll.

I TRAVELLED AMONG UNKNOWN MEN

I TRAVELLED among unknown men,
  In lands beyond the sea;
Nor, England! did I know till then
  What love I bore to thee.

'Tis past, that melancholy dream!   5
  Nor will I quit thy shore
A second time; for still I seem
  To love thee more and more.

Among thy mountains did I feel
  The joy of my desire;   10
And she I cherished turned her wheel
  Beside an English fire.

Thy mornings showed, thy nights concealed
  The bowers where Lucy played;
And thine too is the last green field   15
  That Lucy's eyes surveyed.

TO A YOUNG LADY

WHO HAD BEEN REPROACHED FOR TAKING LONG WALKS IN THE COUNTRY

DEAR Child of Nature, let them rail!
— There is a nest in a green dale,
  A harbour and a hold;
Where thou, a Wife and Friend, shalt see
Thy own heart-stirring days, and be   5
  A light to young and old.

There, healthy as a shepherd boy,
And treading among flowers of joy
  Which at no season fade,
Thou, while thy babes around thee cling,   10
Shalt show us how divine a thing
  A Woman may be made.

Thy thoughts and feelings shall not die,
Nor leave thee, when grey hairs are nigh,

A melancholy slave;   15
But an old age serene and bright,
And lovely as a Lapland night,
Shall lead thee to thy grave.

THE SPARROW'S NEST

BEHOLD, within the leafy shade,
Those bright blue eggs together laid!
On me the chance-discovered sight
Gleamed like a vision of delight.
I started — seeming to espy   5
The home and sheltered bed,
The Sparrow's dwelling, which, hard by
My Father's house, in wet or dry
My sister Emmeline and I
     Together visited.   10

She looked at it and seemed to fear it;
Dreading, tho' wishing, to be near it:
Such heart was in her, being then
A little Prattler among men.
The Blessing of my later years   15
Was with me when a boy:
She gave me eyes, she gave me ears;
And humble cares, and delicate fears;
A heart, the fountain of sweet tears;
     And love, and thought, and joy.   20

TO A BUTTERFLY

STAY near me — do not take thy flight!
A little longer stay in sight!
Much converse do I find in thee,
Historian of my infancy!
Float near me; do not yet depart!   5
Dead times revive in thee:
Thou bring'st, gay creature as thou art!
A solemn image to my heart,
My father's family!

Oh! pleasant, pleasant were the days,   10
The time, when, in our childish plays,
My sister Emmeline and I
Together chased the butterfly!

A very hunter did I rush
Upon the prey: — with leaps and springs   15
I followed on from brake to bush;
But she, God love her! feared to brush
The dust from off its wings.

TO THE CUCKOO

O BLITHE New-comer! I have heard,
I hear thee and rejoice.
O Cuckoo! shall I call thee Bird,
Or but a wandering Voice?

While I am lying on the grass   5
Thy twofold shout I hear,
From hill to hill it seems to pass,
At once far off, and near.

Though babbling only to the Vale,
Of sunshine and of flowers,   10
Thou bringest unto me a tale
Of visionary hours.

Thrice welcome, darling of the Spring!
Even yet thou art to me
No bird, but an invisible thing,   15
A voice, a mystery;

The same whom in my school-boy days
I listened to; that Cry
Which made me look a thousand ways
In bush, and tree, and sky.   20

To seek thee did I often rove
Through woods and on the green;
And thou wert still a hope, a love;
Still longed for, never seen.

And I can listen to thee yet;   25
Can lie upon the plain
And listen, till I do beget
That golden time again.

O blessed Bird! the earth we pace
Again appears to be   30
An unsubstantial, faery place;
That is fit home for Thee!

MY HEART LEAPS UP

My heart leaps up when I behold
    A rainbow in the sky:
So was it when my life began;
So is it now I am a man;
So be it when I shall grow old,   5
    Or let me die!
The Child is father of the Man;
And I could wish my days to be
Bound each to each by natural piety.

WHEN, TO THE ATTRACTIONS OF
THE BUSY WORLD

When, to the attractions of the busy world,
Preferring studious leisure, I had chosen
A habitation in this peaceful Vale,
Sharp season followed of continual storm
In deepest winter; and, from week to week,   5
Pathway, and lane, and public road, were clogged
With frequent showers of snow. Upon a hill
At a short distance from my cottage, stands
A stately Fir-grove, whither I was wont
To hasten, for I found, beneath the roof   10
Of that perennial shade, a cloistral place
Of refuge, with an unincumbered floor.
Here, in safe covert, on the shallow snow,
And, sometimes, on a speck of visible earth,
The redbreast near me hopped; nor was I loth   15
To sympathise with vulgar coppice birds
That, for protection from the nipping blast,
Hither repaired. — A single beech-tree grew
Within this grove of firs! and, on the fork
Of that one beech, appeared a thrush's nest;   20
A last year's nest, conspicuously built
At such small elevation from the ground
As gave sure sign that they, who in that house
Of nature and of love had made their home
Amid the fir-trees, all the summer long   25
Dwelt in a tranquil spot. And oftentimes,
A few sheep, stragglers from some mountain-flock,
Would watch my motions with suspicious stare,

From the remotest outskirts of the grove, —
Some nook where they had made their final stand,   30
Huddling together from two fears — the fear
Of me and of the storm. Full many an hour
Here did I lose. But in this grove the trees
Had been so thickly planted, and had thriven
In such perplexed and intricate array;   35
That vainly did I seek, beneath their stems
A length of open space, where to and fro
My feet might move without concern or care;
And, baffled thus, though earth from day to day
Was fettered, and the air by storm disturbed,   40
I ceased the shelter to frequent, — and prized,
Less than I wished to prize, that calm recess.

The snows dissolved, and genial Spring returned
To clothe the fields with verdure. Other haunts
Meanwhile were mine; till, one bright April day,   45
By chance retiring from the glare of noon
To this forsaken covert, there I found
A hoary pathway traced between the trees,
And winding on with such an easy line
Along a natural opening, that I stood   50
Much wondering how I could have sought in vain
For what was now so obvious. To abide,
For an allotted interval of ease,
Under my cottage-roof, had gladly come
From the wild sea a cherished Visitant;   55
And with the sight of this same path — begun,
Begun and ended, in the shady grove,
Pleasant conviction flashed upon my mind
That, to this opportune recess allured,
He had surveyed it with a finer eye,   60
A heart more wakeful; and had worn the track
By pacing here, unwearied and alone,
In that habitual restlessness of foot
That haunts the Sailor measuring o'er and o'er
His short domain upon the vessel's deck,   65
While she pursues her course through the dreary sea.

When thou hadst quitted Esthwaite's pleasant shore,
And taken thy first leave of those green hills
And rocks that were the play-ground of thy youth,
Year followed year, my Brother! and we two,   70
Conversing not, knew little in what mould
Each other's mind was fashioned; and at length,
When once again we met in Grasmere Vale,

Between us there was little other bond
Than common feelings of fraternal love.   75
But thou, a School-boy, to the sea hadst carried
Undying recollections; Nature there
Was with thee; she, who loved us both, she still
Was with thee; and even so didst thou become
A *silent* Poet; from the solitude   80
Of the vast sea didst bring a watchful heart
Still couchant, an inevitable ear,
And an eye practised like a blind man's touch.
— Back to the joyless Ocean thou art gone;
Nor from this vestige of thy musing hours   85
Could I withhold thy honoured name, — and now
I love the fir-grove with a perfect love.
Thither do I withdraw when cloudless suns
Shine hot, or wind blows troublesome and strong;
And there I sit at evening, when the steep   90
Of Silver-how, and Grasmere's peaceful lake,
And one green island, gleam between the stems
Of the dark firs, a visionary scene!
And, while I gaze upon the spectacle
Of clouded splendour, on this dream-like sight   95
Of solemn loveliness, I think on thee,
My Brother, and on all which thou hast lost.
Nor seldom, if I rightly guess, while Thou,
Muttering the verses which I muttered first
Among the mountains, through the midnight watch   100
Art pacing thoughtfully the vessel's deck
In some far region, here, while o'er my head,
At every impulse of the moving breeze,
The fir-grove murmurs with a sea-like sound,
Alone I tread this path; — for aught I know,   105
Timing my steps to thine; and, with a store
Of undistinguishable sympathies,
Mingling most earnest wishes for the day
When we, and others whom we love, shall meet
A second time, in Grasmere's happy Vale.   110

TO A BUTTERFLY

I'VE watched you now a full half-hour,
Self-poised upon that yellow flower;
And, little Butterfly! indeed
I know not if you sleep or feed.
How motionless! — not frozen seas   5

More motionless! and then
What joy awaits you, when the breeze
Hath found you out among the trees,
And calls you forth again!

This plot of orchard-ground is ours;   10
My trees they are, my Sister's flowers;
Here rest your wings when they are weary;
Here lodge as in a sanctuary!
Come often to us, fear no wrong;
Sit near us on the bough!   15
We'll talk of sunshine and of song,
And summer days, when we were young;
Sweet childish days, that were as long
As twenty days are now.

STANZAS

WRITTEN IN MY POCKET-COPY OF THOMSON'S
CASTLE OF INDOLENCE

WITHIN our happy Castle there dwelt One
Whom without blame I may not overlook;
For never sun on living creature shone
Who more devout enjoyment with us took:
Here on his hours he hung as on a book,   5
On his own time here would he float away,
As doth a fly upon a summer brook;
But go to-morrow, or belike to-day,
Seek for him, — he is fled; and whither none can say.

Thus often would he leave our peaceful home,   10
And find elsewhere his business or delight;
Out of our Valley's limits did he roam:
Full many a time, upon a stormy night,
His voice came to us from the neighbouring height:
Oft could we see him driving full in view   15
At mid-day when the sun was shining bright;
What ill was on him, what he had to do,
A mighty wonder bred among our quiet crew.

Ah! piteous sight it was to see this Man
When he came back to us, a withered flower, —   20
Or like a sinful creature, pale and wan.
Down would he sit; and without strength or power
Look at the common grass from hour to hour:

And oftentimes, how long I fear to say,
Where apple-trees in blossom made a bower,   25
Retired in that sunshiny shade he lay;
And, like a naked Indian, slept himself away.

Great wonder to our gentle tribe it was
Whenever from our Valley he withdrew;
For happier soul no living creature has   30
Than he had, being here the long day through.
Some thought he was a lover, and did woo:
Some thought far worse of him, and judged him wrong;
But verse was what he had been wedded to;
And his own mind did like a tempest strong   35
Come to him thus, and drove the weary Wight along.

With him there often walked in friendly guise,
Or lay upon the moss by brook or tree,
A noticeable Man with large grey eyes,
And a pale face that seemed undoubtedly   40
As if a blooming face it ought to be;
Heavy his low-hung lip did oft appear,
Deprest by weight of musing Phantasy;
Profound his forehead was, though not severe;
Yet some did think that he had little business here: 45

Sweet heaven forefend! his was a lawful right;
Noisy he was, and gamesome as a boy;
His limbs would toss about him with delight
Like branches when strong winds the trees annoy.
Nor lacked his calmer hours device or toy   50
To banish listlessness and irksome care;
He would have taught you how you might employ
Yourself; and many did to him repair, —
And certes not in vain; he had inventions rare.

Expedients, too, of simplest sort he tried: 55
Long blades of grass, plucked round him as he lay,
Made, to his ear attentively applied,
A pipe on which the wind would deftly play;
Glasses he had, that little things display,
The beetle panoplied in gems and gold,   60
A mailèd angel on a battle-day;
The mysteries that cups of flowers enfold,
And all the gorgeous sights which fairies do behold.

He would entice that other Man to hear
His music, and to view his imagery: 65

And, sooth, these two were each to the other dear:
No livelier love in such a place could be:
There did they dwell — from earthly labour free,
As happy spirits as were ever seen;
If but a bird, to keep them company,   70
Or butterfly sate down, they were, I ween,
As pleased as if the same had been a Maiden-queen.

1801

I GRIEVED for Buonaparté, with a vain
And an unthinking grief! The tenderest mood
Of that Man's mind — what can it be? what food
Fed his first hopes? what knowledge could *he* gain?
'Tis not in battles that from youth we train   5
The Governor who must be wise and good,
And temper with the sternness of the brain
Thoughts motherly, and meek as womanhood.
Wisdom doth live with children round her knees:
Books, leisure, perfect freedom, and the talk   10
Man holds with week-day man in the hourly walk
Of the mind's business: these are the degrees
By which true Sway doth mount; this is the stalk
True Power doth grow on; and her rights are these.

RESOLUTION AND INDEPENDENCE

I

THERE was a roaring in the wind all night;
The rain came heavily and fell in floods;
But now the sun is rising calm and bright;
The birds are singing in the distant woods;
Over his own sweet voice the Stock-dove broods;   5
The Jay makes answer as the Magpie chatters;
And all the air is filled with pleasant noise of waters.

II

All things that love the sun are out of doors;
The sky rejoices in the morning's birth;
The grass is bright with rain-drops; — on the moors   10
The hare is running races in her mirth;
And with her feet she from the plashy earth

Raises a mist; that, glittering in the sun,
Runs with her all the way, wherever she doth run.

III

I was a Traveller then upon the moor;   15
I saw the hare that raced about with joy;
I heard the woods and distant waters roar;
Or heard them not, as happy as a boy:
The pleasant season did my heart employ:
My old remembrances went from me wholly;   20
And all the ways of men, so vain and melancholy.

IV

But, as it sometimes chanceth, from the might
Of joy in minds that can no further go,
As high as we have mounted in delight
In our dejection do we sink as low;   25
To me that morning did it happen so;
And fears and fancies thick upon me came;
Dim sadness — and blind thoughts, I knew not, nor could name.

V

I heard the sky-lark warbling in the sky;
And I bethought me of the playful hare: 30
Even such a happy Child of earth am I;
Even as these blissful creatures do I fare;
Far from the world I walk, and from all care;
But there may come another day to me —
Solitude, pain of heart, distress, and poverty.   35

VI

My whole life I have lived in pleasant thought,
As if life's business were a summer mood;
As if all needful things would come unsought
To genial faith, still rich in genial good;
But how can He expect that others should   40
Build for him, sow for him, and at his call
Love him, who for himself will take no heed at all?

VII

I thought of Chatterton, the marvellous Boy,
The sleepless Soul that perished in his pride;

Of Him who walked in glory and in joy   45
Following his plough, along the mountain-side:
By our own spirits are we deified:
We Poets in our youth begin in gladness;
But thereof come in the end despondency and madness.

VIII

Now, whether it were by peculiar grace,   50
A leading from above, a something given,
Yet it befel, that, in this lonely place,
When I with these untoward thoughts had striven,
Beside a pool bare to the eye of heaven
I saw a Man before me unawares: 55
The oldest man he seemed that ever wore grey hairs.

IX

As a huge stone is sometimes seen to lie
Couched on the bald top of an eminence;
Wonder to all who do the same espy,
By what means it could thither come, and whence;   60
So that it seems a thing endued with sense:
Like a sea-beast crawled forth, that on a shelf
Of rock or sand reposeth, there to sun itself;

X

Such seemed this Man, not all alive nor dead,
Nor all asleep — in his extreme old age: 65
His body was bent double, feet and head
Coming together in life's pilgrimage;
As if some dire constraint of pain, or rage
Of sickness felt by him in times long past,
A more than human weight upon his frame had cast.   70

XI

Himself he propped, limbs, body, and pale face,
Upon a long grey staff of shaven wood:
And, still as I drew near with gentle pace,
Upon the margin of that moorish flood
Motionless as a cloud the old Man stood,   75
That heareth not the loud winds when they call;
And moveth all together, if it move at all.

XII

At length, himself unsettling, he the pond
Stirred with his staff, and fixedly did look
Upon the muddy water, which he conned,   80
As if he had been reading in a book:
And now a stranger's privilege I took;
And, drawing to his side, to him did say,
"This morning gives us promise of a glorious day."

XIII

A gentle answer did the old Man make,   85
In courteous speech which forth he slowly drew:
And him with further words I thus bespake,
"What occupation do you there pursue?
This is a lonesome place for one like you."
Ere he replied, a flash of mild surprise   90
Broke from the sable orbs of his yet-vivid eyes.

XIV

His words came feebly, from a feeble chest,
But each in solemn order followed each,
With something of a lofty utterance drest —
Choice word and measured phrase, above the reach   95
Of ordinary men; a stately speech;
Such as grave Livers do in Scotland use,
Religious men, who give to God and man their dues.

XV

He told, that to these waters he had come
To gather leeches, being old and poor: 100
Employment hazardous and wearisome!
And he had many hardships to endure:
From pond to pond he roamed, from moor to moor;
Housing, with God's good help, by choice or chance;
And in this way he gained an honest maintenance.   105

XVI

The old Man still stood talking by my side;
But now his voice to me was like a stream
Scarce heard; nor word from word could I divide;
And the whole body of the Man did seem
Like one whom I had met with in a dream;   110

Or like a man from some far region sent,
To give me human strength, by apt admonishment.

XVII

My former thoughts returned: the fear that kills;
And hope that is unwilling to be fed;
Cold, pain, and labour, and all fleshly ills;   115
And mighty Poets in their misery dead.
— Perplexed, and longing to be comforted,
My question eagerly did I renew,
"How is it that you live, and what is it you do?"

XVIII

He with a smile did then his words repeat;   120
And said, that, gathering leeches, far and wide
He travelled; stirring thus about his feet
The waters of the pools where they abide.
"Once I could meet with them on every side;
But they have dwindled long by slow decay;   125
Yet still I persevere, and find them where I may."

XIX

While he was talking thus, the lonely place,
The old Man's shape, and speech — all troubled me:
In my mind's eye I seemed to see him pace
About the weary moors continually,   130
Wandering about alone and silently.
While I these thoughts within myself pursued,
He, having made a pause, the same discourse renewed.

XX

And soon with this he other matter blended,
Cheerfully uttered, with demeanour kind,   135
But stately in the main; and when he ended,
I could have laughed myself to scorn to find
In that decrepit Man so firm a mind.
"God," said I, "be my help and stay secure;
I'll think of the Leech-gatherer on the lonely moor!"   140

COMPOSED UPON WESTMINSTER BRIDGE, SEPTEMBER 3, 1802

EARTH has not any thing to show more fair:
Dull would he be of soul who could pass by
A sight so touching in its majesty:
This City now doth, like a garment, wear
The beauty of the morning; silent, bare,   5
Ships, towers, domes, theatres, and temples lie
Open unto the fields, and to the sky;
All bright and glittering in the smokeless air.
Never did sun more beautifully steep
In his first splendour, valley, rock, or hill;   10
Ne'er saw I, never felt, a calm so deep!
The river glideth at his own sweet will:
Dear God! the very houses seem asleep;
And all that mighty heart is lying still!

IT IS A BEAUTEOUS EVENING, CALM AND FREE

IT is a beauteous evening, calm and free,
The holy time is quiet as a Nun
Breathless with adoration; the broad sun
Is sinking down in its tranquillity;
The gentleness of heaven broods o'er the Sea: 5
Listen! the mighty Being is awake,
And doth with his eternal motion make
A sound like thunder — everlastingly.
Dear Child! dear Girl! that walkest with me here,
If thou appear untouched by solemn thought,   10
Thy nature is not therefore less divine:
Thou liest in Abraham's bosom all the year;
And worshipp'st at the Temple's inner shrine,
God being with thee when we know it not.

COMPOSED BY THE SEA-SIDE, NEAR CALAIS, AUGUST, 1802

FAIR Star of evening, Splendour of the west,
Star of my Country! — on the horizon's brink
Thou hangest, stooping, as might seem, to sink
On England's bosom; yet well pleased to rest,

Meanwhile, and be to her a glorious crest   5
Conspicuous to the Nations. Thou, I think,
Should'st be my Country's emblem; and should'st wink,
Bright Star! with laughter on her banners, drest
In thy fresh beauty. There! that dusky spot
Beneath thee, that is England; there she lies.   10
Blessings be on you both! one hope, one lot,
One life, one glory! — I, with many a fear
For my dear Country, many heartfelt sighs,
Among men who do not love her, linger here.

COMPOSED IN THE VALLEY NEAR DOVER, ON THE DAY OF LANDING

HERE, on our native soil, we breathe once more.
The cock that crows, the smoke that curls, that sound
Of bells; — those boys who in yon meadow-ground
In white-sleeved shirts are playing; and the roar
Of the waves breaking on the chalky shore; —   5
All, all are English. Oft have I looked round
With joy in Kent's green vales; but never found
Myself so satisfied in heart before.
Europe is yet in bonds; but let that pass,
Thought for another moment. Thou art free,   10
My Country! and 'tis joy enough and pride
For one hour's perfect bliss, to tread the grass
Of England once again, and hear and see,
With such a dear Companion at my side.

SEPTEMBER, 1802, NEAR DOVER

INLAND, within a hollow vale, I stood;
And saw, while sea was calm and air was clear,
The coast of France — the coast of France how near!
Drawn almost into frightful neighbourhood.
I shrunk; for verily the barrier flood   5
Was like a lake, or river bright and fair,
A span of waters; yet what power is there!
What mightiness for evil and for good!
Even so doth God protect us if we be
Virtuous and wise. Winds blow, and waters roll,   10
Strength to the brave, and Power, and Deity;
Yet in themselves are nothing! One decree
Spake laws to *them*, and said that by the soul
Only, the Nations shall be great and free.

WRITTEN IN LONDON, SEPTEMBER, 1802

O FRIEND! I know not which way I must look
For comfort, being, as I am, opprest,
To think that now our life is only drest
For show; mean handy-work of craftsman, cook,
Or groom! — We must run glittering like a brook   5
In the open sunshine, or we are unblest:
The wealthiest man among us is the best:
No grandeur now in nature or in book
Delights us. Rapine, avarice, expense,
This is idolatry; and these we adore: 10
Plain living and high thinking are no more:
The homely beauty of the good old cause
Is gone; our peace, our fearful innocence,
And pure religion breathing household laws.

LONDON, 1802

MILTON! thou should'st be living at this hour:
England hath need of thee: she is a fen
Of stagnant waters: altar, sword, and pen,
Fireside, the heroic wealth of hall and bower,
Have forfeited their ancient English dower   5
Of inward happiness. We are selfish men;
Oh! raise us up, return to us again;
And give us manners, virtue, freedom, power.
Thy soul was like a Star, and dwelt apart:
Thou hadst a voice whose sound was like the sea: 10
Pure as the naked heavens, majestic, free,
So didst thou travel on life's common way,
In cheerful godliness; and yet thy heart
The lowliest duties on herself did lay.

COMPOSED AFTER A JOURNEY ACROSS THE HAMBLETON HILLS, YORKSHIRE

DARK and more dark the shades of evening fell;
The wished-for point was reached — but at an hour
When little could be gained from that rich dower
Of prospect, whereof many thousands tell.
Yet did the glowing west with marvellous power   5
Salute us: there stood Indian citadel,

Temple of Greece, and minster with its tower
Substantially expressed — a place for bell
Or clock to toll from! Many a tempting isle,
With groves that never were imagined, lay   10
'Mid seas how steadfast! objects all for the eye
Of silent rapture; but we felt the while
We should forget them; they are of the sky,
And from our earthly memory fade away.

THOSE WORDS WERE UTTERED

————"they are of the sky,
And from our earthly memory fade away."

THOSE words were uttered as in pensive mood
We turned, departing from that solemn sight:
A contrast and reproach to gross delight,
And life's unspiritual pleasures daily wooed!
But now upon this thought I cannot brood;   5
It is unstable as a dream of night;
Nor will I praise a cloud, however bright,
Disparaging Man's gifts, and proper food.
Grove, isle, with every shape of sky-built dome,
Though clad in colours beautiful and pure,   10
Find in the heart of man no natural home:
The immortal Mind craves objects that endure:
These cleave to it; from these it cannot roam,
Nor they from it: their fellowship is secure.

THERE IS A LITTLE UNPRETENDING RILL

THERE is a little unpretending Rill
Of limpid water, humbler far than aught
That ever among Men or Naiads sought
Notice or name! — It quivers down the hill,
Furrowing its shallow way with dubious will;   5
Yet to my mind this scanty Stream is brought
Oftener than Ganges or the Nile; a thought
Of private recollection sweet and still!
Months perish with their moons; year treads on year;
But, faithful Emma! thou with me canst say   10
That, while ten thousand pleasures disappear,
And flies their memory fast almost as they;
The immortal Spirit of one happy day
Lingers beside that Rill, in vision clear.

TO TOUSSAINT L'OUVERTURE

TOUSSAINT, the most unhappy man of men!
Whether the whistling Rustic tend his plough
Within thy hearing, or thy head be now
Pillowed in some deep dungeon's earless den; —
O miserable Chieftain! where and when   5
Wilt thou find patience? Yet die not; do thou
Wear rather in thy bonds a cheerful brow:
Though fallen thyself, never to rise again,
Live, and take comfort. Thou hast left behind
Powers that will work for thee; air, earth, and skies;   10
There's not a breathing of the common wind
That will forget thee; thou hast great allies;
Thy friends are exultations, agonies,
And love, and man's unconquerable mind.

ON THE EXTINCTION OF THE
VENETIAN REPUBLIC

ONCE did She hold the gorgeous east in fee;
And was the safeguard of the west: the worth
Of Venice did not fall below her birth,
Venice, the eldest Child of Liberty.
She was a maiden City, bright and free;   5
No guile seduced, no force could violate;
And, when she took unto herself a Mate,
She must espouse the everlasting Sea.
And what if she had seen those glories fade,
Those titles vanish, and that strength decay;   10
Yet shall some tribute of regret be paid
When her long life hath reached its final day:
Men are we, and must grieve when even the Shade
Of that which once was great, is passed away.

IT IS NOT TO BE THOUGHT OF
THAT THE FLOOD

IT is not to be thought of that the Flood
Of British freedom, which, to the open sea
Of the world's praise, from dark antiquity
Hath flowed, "with pomp of waters, unwithstood,"
Roused though it be full often to a mood   5
Which spurns the check of salutary bands,

That this most famous Stream in bogs and sands
Should perish; and to evil and to good
Be lost for ever. In our halls is hung
Armoury of the invincible Knights of old: 10
We must be free or die, who speak the tongue
That Shakspeare spake; the faith and morals hold
Which Milton held. — In every thing we are sprung
Of Earth's first blood, have titles manifold.

TO H. C.

SIX YEARS OLD

O THOU! whose fancies from afar are brought;
Who of thy words dost make a mock apparel,
And fittest to unutterable thought
The breeze-like motion and the self-born carol;
Thou faery voyager! that dost float   5
In such clear water, that thy boat
May rather seem
To brood on air than on an earthly stream;
Suspended in a stream as clear as sky,
Where earth and heaven do make one imagery;   10
O blessed vision! happy child!
Thou art so exquisitely wild,
I think of thee with many fears
For what may be thy lot in future years.

I thought of times when Pain might be thy guest,   15
Lord of thy house and hospitality;
And Grief, uneasy lover! never rest
But when she sate within the touch of thee.
O too industrious folly!
O vain and causeless melancholy!   20
Nature will either end thee quite;
Or, lengthening out thy season of delight,
Preserve for thee, by individual right,
A young lamb's heart among the full-grown flocks.
What hast thou to do with sorrow,   25
Or the injuries of to-morrow?
Thou art a dew-drop, which the morn brings forth,
Ill fitted to sustain unkindly shocks,
Or to be trailed along the soiling earth;
A gem that glitters while it lives,   30
And no forewarning gives;
But, at the touch of wrong, without a strife
Slips in a moment out of life.

TO A HIGHLAND GIRL

(AT INVERSNEYDE, UPON LOCH LOMOND)

SWEET Highland Girl, a very shower
Of beauty is thy earthly dower!
Twice seven consenting years have shed
Their utmost bounty on thy head:
And these grey rocks; that household lawn;⁣   5
Those trees, a veil just half withdrawn;
This fall of water that doth make
A murmur near the silent lake;
This little bay; a quiet road
That holds in shelter thy Abode —   10
In truth together do ye seem
Like something fashioned in a dream;
Such Forms as from their covert peep
When earthly cares are laid asleep!
But, O fair Creature! in the light   15
Of common day, so heavenly bright,
I bless Thee, Vision as thou art,
I bless thee with a human heart;
God shield thee to thy latest years!
Thee, neither know I, nor thy peers;   20
And yet my eyes are filled with tears.

With earnest feeling I shall pray
For thee when I am far away:
For never saw I mien, or face,
In which more plainly I could trace   25
Benignity and home-bred sense
Ripening in perfect innocence.
Here scattered, like a random seed,
Remote from men, Thou dost not need
The embarrassed look of shy distress,   30
And maidenly shamefacedness:
Thou wear'st upon thy forehead clear
The freedom of a Mountaineer:
A face with gladness overspread!
Soft smiles, by human kindness bred!   35
And seemliness complete, that sways
Thy courtesies, about thee plays;
With no restraint, but such as springs
From quick and eager visitings
Of thoughts that lie beyond the reach   40

Of thy few words of English speech:
A bondage sweetly brooked, a strife
That gives thy gestures grace and life!
So have I, not unmoved in mind,
Seen birds of tempest-loving kind —   45
Thus beating up against the wind.

    What hand but would a garland cull
For thee who art so beautiful?
O happy pleasure! here to dwell
Beside thee in some heathy dell;   50
Adopt your homely ways, and dress,
A Shepherd, thou a Shepherdess!
But I could frame a wish for thee
More like a grave reality:
Thou art to me but as a wave   55
Of the wild sea; and I would have
Some claim upon thee, if I could,
Though but of common neighbourhood.
What joy to hear thee, and to see!
Thy elder Brother I would be,   60
Thy Father — anything to thee!

    Now thanks to Heaven! that of its grace
Hath led me to this lonely place.
Joy have I had; and going hence
I bear away my recompense.   65
In spots like these it is we prize
Our Memory, feel that she hath eyes:
Then, why should I be loth to stir?
I feel this place was made for her;
To give new pleasure like the past,   70
Continued long as life shall last.
Nor am I loth, though pleased at heart,
Sweet Highland Girl! from thee to part;
For I, methinks, till I grow old,
As fair before me shall behold,   75
As I do now, the cabin small,
The lake, the bay, the waterfall;
And Thee, the Spirit of them all!

YARROW UNVISITED

See the various Poems the scene of which is laid upon the banks of the
Yarrow; in particular, the exquisite Ballad of Hamilton beginning
        "Busk ye, busk ye, my bonny, bonny Bride,
        Busk ye, busk ye, my winsome Marrow!" —

FROM Stirling castle we had seen
The mazy Forth unravelled;
Had trod the banks of Clyde, and Tay,
And with the Tweed had travelled;
And when we came to Clovenford,   5
Then said my *"winsome Marrow,"*
"Whate'er betide, we'll turn aside,
And see the Braes of Yarrow."

"Let Yarrow folk, *frae* Selkirk town,
Who have been buying, selling,   10
Go back to Yarrow, 'tis their own;
Each maiden to her dwelling!
On Yarrow's banks let herons feed,
Hares couch, and rabbits burrow!
But we will downward with the Tweed,   15
Nor turn aside to Yarrow.

"There's Galla Water, Leader Haughs,
Both lying right before us;
And Dryborough, where with chiming Tweed
The lintwhites sing in chorus;   20
There's pleasant Tiviot-dale, a land
Made blithe with plough and harrow:
Why throw away a needful day
To go in search of Yarrow?

"What's Yarrow but a river bare,   25
That glides the dark hills under?
There are a thousand such elsewhere
As worthy of your wonder."
— Strange words they seemed of slight and scorn;
My True-love sighed for sorrow;   30
And looked me in the face, to think
I thus could speak of Yarrow!

"Oh! green," said I, "are Yarrow's holms,
And sweet is Yarrow flowing!

Fair hangs the apple frae the rock,   35
But we will leave it growing.
O'er hilly path, and open strath,
We'll wander Scotland thorough;
But, though so near, we will not turn
Into the dale of Yarrow.   40

"Let beeves and home-bred kine partake
The sweets of Burn-mill meadow;
The swan on still St. Mary's Lake
Float double, swan and shadow!
We will not see them; will not go,   45
To-day, nor yet to-morrow;
Enough if in our hearts we know
There's such a place as Yarrow.

"Be Yarrow stream unseen, unknown!
It must, or we shall rue it: 50
We have a vision of our own;
Ah! why should we undo it?
The treasured dreams of times long past,
We'll keep them, winsome Marrow!
For when we're there, although 'tis fair,   55
'Twill be another Yarrow!

"If Care with freezing years should come,
And wandering seem but folly, —
Should we be loth to stir from home,
And yet be melancholy;   60
Should life be dull, and spirits low,
'Twill soothe us in our sorrow,
That earth has something yet to show,
The bonny holms of Yarrow!"

TO THE MEN OF KENT, OCTOBER, 1803

VANGUARD of Liberty, ye men of Kent,
Ye children of a Soil that doth advance
Her haughty brow against the coast of France,
Now is the time to prove your hardiment!
To France be words of invitation sent!   5
They from their fields can see the countenance
Of your fierce war, may ken the glittering lance
And hear you shouting forth your brave intent.
Left single, in bold parley, ye, of yore,
Did from the Norman win a gallant wreath;   10

Confirmed the charters that were yours before; —
No parleying now! In Britain is one breath;
We all are with you now from shore to shore: —
Ye men of Kent, 'tis victory or death!

YEW-TREES

THERE is a Yew-tree, pride of Lorton Vale,
Which to this day stands single, in the midst
Of its own darkness, as it stood of yore:
Not loth to furnish weapons for the bands
Of Umfraville or Percy ere they marched   5
To Scotland's heaths; or those that crossed the sea
And drew their sounding bows at Azincour,
Perhaps at earlier Crecy, or Poictiers.
Of vast circumference and gloom profound
This solitary Tree! a living thing   10
Produced too slowly ever to decay;
Of form and aspect too magnificent
To be destroyed. But worthier still of note
Are those fraternal Four of Borrowdale,
Joined in one solemn and capacious grove;   15
Huge trunks! and each particular trunk a growth
Of intertwisted fibres serpentine
Up-coiling, and inveterately convolved;
Nor uninformed with Phantasy, and looks
That threaten the profane; — a pillared shade,   20
Upon whose grassless floor of red-brown hue,
By sheddings from the pining umbrage tinged
Perennially — beneath whose sable roof
Of boughs, as if for festal purpose, decked
With unrejoicing berries — ghostly Shapes   25
May meet at noontide; Fear and trembling Hope,
Silence and Foresight; Death the Skeleton
And Time the Shadow; — there to celebrate,
As in a natural temple scattered o'er
With altars undisturbed of mossy stone,   30
United worship; or in mute repose
To lie, and listen to the mountain flood
Murmuring from Glaramara's inmost caves.

NUNS FRET NOT AT THEIR CONVENT'S
NARROW ROOM

Nuns fret not at their convent's narrow room;
And hermits are contented with their cells;
And students with their pensive citadels;
Maids at the wheel, the weaver at his loom,
Sit blithe and happy; bees that soar for bloom,   5
High as the highest Peak of Furness-fells,
Will murmur by the hour in foxglove bells:
In truth the prison, unto which we doom
Ourselves, no prison is: and hence for me,
In sundry moods, 'twas pastime to be bound   10
Within the Sonnet's scanty plot of ground;
Pleased if some Souls (for such there needs must be)
Who have felt the weight of too much liberty,
Should find brief solace there, as I have found.

METHOUGHT I SAW THE FOOTSTEPS
OF A THRONE

Methought I saw the footsteps of a throne
Which mists and vapours from mine eyes did shroud —
Nor view of who might sit thereon allowed;
But all the steps and ground about were strown
With sights the ruefullest that flesh and bone   5
Ever put on; a miserable crowd,
Sick, hale, old, young, who cried before that cloud,
"Thou art our king, O Death! to thee we groan."
Those steps I clomb; the mists before me gave
Smooth way; and I beheld the face of one   10
Sleeping alone within a mossy cave,
With her face up to heaven; that seemed to have
Pleasing remembrance of a thought foregone;
A lovely Beauty in a summer grave!

WHERE LIES THE LAND TO WHICH YON
SHIP MUST GO?

Where lies the Land to which yon Ship must go?
Fresh as a lark mounting at break of day,
Festively she puts forth in trim array;
Is she for tropic suns, or polar snow?

What boots the inquiry? — Neither friend nor foe   5
She cares for; let her travel where she may,
She finds familiar names, a beaten way
Ever before her, and a wind to blow.
Yet still I ask, what haven is her mark?
And, almost as it was when ships were rare,   10
(From time to time, like Pilgrims, here and there
Crossing the waters) doubt, and something dark,
Of the old Sea some reverential fear,
Is with me at thy farewell, joyous Bark!

WITH SHIPS THE SEA WAS SPRINKLED FAR AND NIGH

WITH Ships the sea was sprinkled far and nigh,
Like stars in heaven, and joyously it showed;
Some lying fast at anchor in the road,
Some veering up and down, one knew not why.
A goodly Vessel did I then espy   5
Come like a giant from a haven broad;
And lustily along the bay she strode,
Her tackling rich, and of apparel high.
This Ship was nought to me, nor I to her,
Yet I pursued her with a Lover's look;   10
This Ship to all the rest did I prefer:
When will she turn, and whither? She will brook
No tarrying; where She comes the winds must stir:
On went She, and due north her journey took.

THE WORLD IS TOO MUCH WITH US

THE world is too much with us; late and soon,
Getting and spending, we lay waste our powers:
Little we see in Nature that is ours;
We have given our hearts away, a sordid boon!
This Sea that bares her bosom to the moon;   5
The winds that will be howling at all hours,
And are up-gathered now like sleeping flowers;
For this, for every thing, we are out of tune;
It moves us not. — Great God! I'd rather be
A Pagan suckled in a creed outworn;   10
So might I, standing on this pleasant lea,
Have glimpses that would make me less forlorn;
Have sight of Proteus rising from the sea;
Or hear old Triton blow his wreathèd horn.

PERSONAL TALK

I

I AM not One who much or oft delight
To season my fireside with personal talk, —
Of friends, who live within an easy walk,
Or neighbours, daily, weekly, in my sight:
And, for my chance-acquaintance, ladies bright,   **5**
Sons, mothers, maidens withering on the stalk,
These all wear out of me, like Forms, with chalk
Painted on rich men's floors, for one feast-night.
Better than such discourse doth silence long,
Long, barren silence, square with my desire;   **10**
To sit without emotion, hope, or aim,
In the loved presence of my cottage-fire,
And listen to the flapping of the flame,
Or kettle whispering its faint undersong.

II

"Yet life," you say, "is life; we have seen and see,   **15**
And with a living pleasure we describe;
And fits of sprightly malice do but bribe
The languid mind into activity.
Sound sense, and love itself, and mirth and glee
Are fostered by the comment and the gibe."   **20**
Even be it so: yet still among your tribe,
Our daily world's true Worldlings, rank not me!
Children are blest, and powerful; their world lies
More justly balanced; partly at their feet,
And part far from them: — sweetest melodies   **25**
Are those that are by distance made more sweet;
Whose mind is but the mind of his own eyes,
He is a Slave; the meanest we can meet!

III

Wings have we, — and as far as we can go
We may find pleasure: wilderness and wood,   **30**
Blank ocean and mere sky, support that mood
Which with the lofty sanctifies the low.
Dreams, books, are each a world; and books, we know,
Are a substantial world, both pure and good:
Round these, with tendrils strong as flesh and blood,   **35**

Our pastime and our happiness will grow.
There find I personal themes, a plenteous store,
Matter wherein right voluble I am,
To which I listen with a ready ear;
Two shall be named, pre-eminently dear, —   40
The gentle Lady married to the Moor;
And heavenly Una with her milk-white Lamb.

IV

Nor can I not believe but that hereby
Great gains are mine; for thus I live remote
From evil-speaking; rancour, never sought,   45
Comes to me not; malignant truth, or lie.
Hence have I genial seasons, hence have I
Smooth passions, smooth discourse, and joyous thought:
And thus from day to day my little boat
Rocks in its harbour, lodging peaceably.   50
Blessings be with them — and eternal praise,
Who gave us nobler loves, and nobler cares —
The Poets, who on earth have made us heirs
Of truth and pure delight by heavenly lays!
Oh! might my name be numbered among theirs,   55
Then gladly would I end my mortal days.

ODE TO DUTY

"Jam non consilio bonus, sed more eò perductus, ut non tantum rectè facere possim, sed nisi rectè facere non possim."

STERN Daughter of the Voice of God!
O Duty! if that name thou love
Who art a light to guide, a rod
To check the erring, and reprove;
Thou, who art victory and law   5
When empty terrors overawe;
From vain temptations dost set free;
And calm'st the weary strife of frail humanity!

There are who ask not if thine eye
Be on them; who, in love and truth,   10
Where no misgiving is, rely
Upon the genial sense of youth:
Glad Hearts! without reproach or blot;
Who do thy work, and know it not:
Oh! if through confidence misplaced   15
They fail, thy saving arms, dread Power! around them cast.

Serene will be our days and bright,
And happy will our nature be,
When love is an unerring light,
And joy its own security. 20
And they a blissful course may hold
Even now, who, not unwisely bold,
Live in the spirit of this creed;
Yet seek thy firm support, according to their need.

I, loving freedom, and untried; 25
No sport of every random gust,
Yet being to myself a guide,
Too blindly have reposed my trust:
And oft, when in my heart was heard
Thy timely mandate, I deferred 30
The task, in smoother walks to stray;
But thee I now would serve more strictly, if I may.

Through no disturbance of my soul,
Or strong compunction in me wrought,
I supplicate for thy control; 35
But in the quietness of thought:
Me this unchartered freedom tires;
I feel the weight of chance-desires:
My hopes no more must change their name,
I long for a repose that ever is the same. 40

Stern Lawgiver! yet thou dost wear
The Godhead's most benignant grace;
Nor know we any thing so fair
As is the smile upon thy face:
Flowers laugh before thee on their beds 45
And fragrance in thy footing treads;
Thou dost preserve the stars from wrong;
And the most ancient heavens, through Thee, are fresh and
    strong.

To humbler functions, awful Power!
I call thee: I myself commend 50
Unto thy guidance from this hour;
Oh, let my weakness have an end!
Give unto me, made lowly wise,
The spirit of self-sacrifice;
The confidence of reason give; 55
And in the light of truth thy Bondman let me live!

ODE

INTIMATIONS OF IMMORTALITY FROM RECOLLECTIONS
OF EARLY CHILDHOOD

The Child is Father of the Man;
And I could wish my days to be
Bound each to each by natural piety.

I

THERE was a time when meadow, grove, and stream,
The earth, and every common sight,
    To me did seem
    Apparelled in celestial light,
The glory and the freshness of a dream.   5
It is not now as it hath been of yore; —
    Turn wheresoe'er I may,
    By night or day,
The things which I have seen I now can see no more.

II

    The Rainbow comes and goes,   10
    And lovely is the Rose,
    The Moon doth with delight
Look round her when the heavens are bare,
    Waters on a starry night
    Are beautiful and fair;   15
    The sunshine is a glorious birth;
    But yet I know, where'er I go,
That there hath past away a glory from the earth.

III

Now, while the birds thus sing a joyous song,
    And while the young lambs bound   20
    As to the tabor's sound,
To me alone there came a thought of grief:
A timely utterance gave that thought relief,
    And I again am strong:
The cataracts blow their trumpets from the steep;   25
No more shall grief of mine the season wrong;
I hear the Echoes through the mountains throng,

The Winds come to me from the fields of sleep,
  And all the earth is gay;
    Land and sea   30
  Give themselves up to jollity,
    And with the heart of May
  Doth every Beast keep holiday; —
    Thou Child of Joy,
Shout round me, let me hear thy shouts, thou happy Shepherd-boy! 35

                    IV

Ye blessed Creatures, I have heard the call
  Ye to each other make; I see
The heavens laugh with you in your jubilee;
  My heart is at your festival,
    My head hath its coronal,   40
The fulness of your bliss, I feel — I feel it all.
    Oh evil day! if I were sullen
    While Earth herself is adorning,
      This sweet May-morning,
    And the Children are culling   45
      On every side,
    In a thousand valleys far and wide,
    Fresh flowers; while the sun shines warm,
And the Babe leaps up on his Mother's arm: —
    I hear, I hear, with joy I hear!   50
    — But there's a Tree, of many, one,
A single Field which I have looked upon,
Both of them speak of something that is gone:
      The Pansy at my feet
      Doth the same tale repeat: 55
Whither is fled the visionary gleam?
Where is it now, the glory and the dream?

                    V

Our birth is but a sleep and a forgetting:
The Soul that rises with us, our life's Star,
    Hath had elsewhere its setting,   60
      And cometh from afar:
    Not in entire forgetfulness,
    And not in utter nakedness,
But trailing clouds of glory do we come
    From God, who is our home: 65
Heaven lies about us in our infancy!
Shades of the prison-house begin to close
      Upon the growing Boy,

But He beholds the light, and whence it flows,
    He sees it in his joy;   **70**
The Youth, who daily farther from the east
    Must travel, still is Nature's Priest,
    And by the vision splendid
    Is on his way attended;
At length the Man perceives it die away,   **75**
And fade into the light of common day.

VI

Earth fills her lap with pleasures of her own;
Yearnings she hath in her own natural kind,
And, even with something of a Mother's mind,
    And no unworthy aim,   **80**
    The homely Nurse doth all she can
To make her Foster-child, her Inmate Man,
    Forget the glories he hath known,
And that imperial palace whence he came.

VII

Behold the Child among his new-born blisses,   **85**
A six years' Darling of a pigmy size!
See, where 'mid work of his own hand he lies,
Fretted by sallies of his mother's kisses,
With light upon him from his father's eyes!
See, at his feet, some little plan or chart,   **90**
Some fragment from his dream of human life,
Shaped by himself with newly-learned art;
    A wedding or a festival,
    A mourning or a funeral;
      And this hath now his heart,   **95**
    And unto this he frames his song:
      Then will he fit his tongue
To dialogues of business, love, or strife;
    But it will not be long
    Ere this be thrown aside,   **100**
    And with new joy and pride
The little Actor cons another part;
Filling from time to time his "humorous stage"
With all the Persons, down to palsied Age,
That Life brings with her in her equipage;   **105**
    As if his whole vocation
    Were endless imitation.

VIII

Thou, whose exterior semblance doth belie
    Thy Soul's immensity;
Thou best Philosopher, who yet dost keep   110
Thy heritage, thou Eye among the blind,
That, deaf and silent, read'st the eternal deep,
Haunted for ever by the eternal mind, —
    Mighty Prophet! Seer blest!
    On whom those truths do rest,   115
Which we are toiling all our lives to find,
In darkness lost, the darkness of the grave;
Thou, over whom thy Immortality
Broods like the Day, a Master o'er a Slave,
A Presence which is not to be put by;   120
Thou little Child, yet glorious in the might
Of heaven-born freedom on thy being's height,
Why with such earnest pains dost thou provoke
The years to bring the inevitable yoke,
Thus blindly with thy blessedness at strife?   125
Full soon thy Soul shall have her earthly freight,
And custom lie upon thee with a weight,
Heavy as frost, and deep almost as life!

IX

    O joy! that in our embers
    Is something that doth live,   130
    That nature yet remembers
    What was so fugitive!
The thought of our past years in me doth breed
Perpetual benediction: not indeed
For that which is most worthy to be blest;   135
Delight and liberty, the simple creed
Of Childhood, whether busy or at rest,
With new-fledged hope still fluttering in his breast: —
    Not for these I raise
    The song of thanks and praise;   140
    But for those obstinate questionings
    Of sense and outward things,
    Fallings from us, vanishings;
    Blank misgivings of a Creature
Moving about in worlds not realised,   145
High instincts before which our mortal Nature
Did tremble like a guilty Thing surprised:
    But for those first affections,

Those shadowy recollections,
　　Which, be they what they may, 　　　　　　　　　　　150
Are yet the fountain light of all our day,
Are yet a master light of all our seeing;
　　Uphold us, cherish, and have power to make
Our noisy years seem moments in the being
Of the eternal Silence: truths that wake, 　　　　　　　155
　　To perish never;
Which neither listlessness, nor mad endeavour,
　　Nor Man nor Boy,
Nor all that is at enmity with joy,
Can utterly abolish or destroy! 　　　　　　　　　　160
　Hence in a season of calm weather
　　Though inland far we be,
Our Souls have sight of that immortal sea
　　Which brought us hither,
　Can in a moment travel thither, 　　　　　　　　165
And see the Children sport upon the shore,
And hear the mighty waters rolling evermore.

X

Then sing, ye Birds, sing, sing a joyous song!
　　And let the young Lambs bound
　　As to the tabor's sound! 　　　　　　　　　　　170
We in thought will join your throng,
　　Ye that pipe and ye that play,
　　Ye that through your hearts to-day
　　Feel the gladness of the May!
What though the radiance which was once so bright 　175
Be now for ever taken from my sight,
　　Though nothing can bring back the hour
Of splendour in the grass, of glory in the flower;
　　We will grieve not, rather find
　　Strength in what remains behind; 　　　　　　　180
　　In the primal sympathy
　　Which having been must ever be;
　　In the soothing thoughts that spring
　　Out of human suffering;
　　In the faith that looks through death, 　　　　　185
In years that bring the philosophic mind.

XI

And O, ye Fountains, Meadows, Hills, and Groves,
Forebode not any severing of our loves!
Yet in my heart of hearts I feel your might;

I only have relinquished one delight 190
To live beneath your more habitual sway.
I love the Brooks which down their channels fret,
Even more than when I tripped lightly as they;
The innocent brightness of a new-born Day
        Is lovely yet; 195
The Clouds that gather round the setting sun
Do take a sober colouring from an eye
That hath kept watch o'er man's mortality;
Another race hath been, and other palms are won.
Thanks to the human heart by which we live, 200
Thanks to its tenderness, its joys, and fears,
To me the meanest flower that blows can give
Thoughts that do often lie too deep for tears.

I WANDERED LONELY AS A CLOUD

    I WANDERED lonely as a cloud
    That floats on high o'er vales and hills,
    When all at once I saw a crowd,
    A host, of golden daffodils;
    Beside the lake, beneath the trees, 5
    Fluttering and dancing in the breeze.

    Continuous as the stars that shine
    And twinkle on the milky way,
    They stretched in never-ending line
    Along the margin of a bay: 10
    Ten thousand saw I at a glance,
    Tossing their heads in sprightly dance.

    The waves beside them danced; but they
    Out-did the sparkling waves in glee:
    A poet could not but be gay, 15
    In such a jocund company:
    I gazed — and gazed — but little thought
    What wealth the show to me had brought:

    For oft, when on my couch I lie
    In vacant or in pensive mood, 20
    They flash upon that inward eye
    Which is the bliss of solitude;
    And then my heart with pleasure fills,
    And dances with the daffodils.

SHE WAS A PHANTOM OF DELIGHT

SHE was a Phantom of delight
When first she gleamed upon my sight;
A lovely Apparition, sent
To be a moment's ornament;
Her eyes as stars of Twilight fair;   5
Like Twilight's, too, her dusky hair;
But all things else about her drawn
From May-time and the cheerful Dawn;
A dancing Shape, an Image gay,
To haunt, to startle, and way-lay.   10

I saw her upon nearer view,
A Spirit, yet a Woman too!
Her household motions light and free,
And steps of virgin-liberty;
A countenance in which did meet   15
Sweet records, promises as sweet;
A Creature not too bright or good
For human nature's daily food;
For transient sorrows, simple wiles,
Praise, blame, love, kisses, tears, and smiles.   20

And now I see with eye serene
The very pulse of the machine;
A Being breathing thoughtful breath,
A Traveller between life and death;
The reason firm, the temperate will,   25
Endurance, foresight, strength, and skill;
A perfect Woman, nobly planned,
To warn, to comfort, and command;
And yet a Spirit still, and bright
With something of angelic light.   30

THE PRELUDE
OR, GROWTH OF A POET'S MIND

AN AUTOBIOGRAPHICAL POEM

BOOK FIRST

INTRODUCTION — CHILDHOOD AND SCHOOL-TIME

O THERE is blessing in this gentle breeze,
A visitant that while it fans my cheek
Doth seem half-conscious of the joy it brings
From the green fields, and from yon azure sky.
Whate'er its mission, the soft breeze can come　　　　5
To none more grateful than to me; escaped
From the vast city, where I long had pined
A discontented sojourner: now free,
Free as a bird to settle where I will.
What dwelling shall receive me? in what vale　　　　10
Shall be my harbour? underneath what grove
Shall I take up my home? and what clear stream
Shall with its murmur lull me into rest?
The earth is all before me. With a heart
Joyous, nor scared at its own liberty,　　　　15
I look about; and should the chosen guide
Be nothing better than a wandering cloud,
I cannot miss my way. I breathe again!
Trances of thought and mountings of the mind
Come fast upon me: it is shaken off,　　　　20
That burthen of my own unnatural self,
The heavy weight of many a weary day
Not mine, and such as were not made for me.
Long months of peace (if such bold word accord
With any promises of human life),　　　　25
Long months of ease and undisturbed delight
Are mine in prospect; whither shall I turn,
By road or pathway, or through trackless field,
Up hill or down, or shall some floating thing
Upon the river point me out my course?　　　　30

　　Dear Liberty! Yet what would it avail
But for a gift that consecrates the joy?
For I, methought, while the sweet breath of heaven
Was blowing on my body, felt within
A correspondent breeze, that gently moved　　　　35

With quickening virtue, but is now become
A tempest, a redundant energy,
Vexing its own creation. Thanks to both,
And their congenial powers, that, while they join
In breaking up a long-continued frost,   40
Bring with them vernal promises, the hope
Of active days urged on by flying hours, —
Days of sweet leisure, taxed with patient thought
Abstruse, nor wanting punctual service high,
Matins and vespers of harmonious verse!   45

Thus far, O Friend! did I, not used to make
A present joy the matter of a song,
Pour forth that day my soul in measured strains
That would not be forgotten, and are here
Recorded: to the open fields I told   50
A prophecy: poetic numbers came
Spontaneously to clothe in priestly robe
A renovated spirit singled out,
Such hope was mine, for holy services.
My own voice cheered me, and, far more, the mind's   55
Internal echo of the imperfect sound;
To both I listened, drawing from them both
A cheerful confidence in things to come.

Content and not unwilling now to give
A respite to this passion, I paced on   60
With brisk and eager steps; and came, at length,
To a green shady place, where down I sate
Beneath a tree, slackening my thoughts by choice,
And settling into gentler happiness.
'Twas autumn, and a clear and placid day,   65
With warmth, as much as needed, from a sun
Two hours declined towards the west; a day
With silver clouds, and sunshine on the grass,
And in the sheltered and the sheltering grove
A perfect stillness. Many were the thoughts   70
Encouraged and dismissed, till choice was made
Of a known Vale, whither my feet should turn,
Nor rest till they had reached the very door
Of the one cottage which methought I saw.
No picture of mere memory ever looked   75
So fair; and while upon the fancied scene
I gazed with growing love, a higher power
Than Fancy gave assurance of some work
Of glory there forthwith to be begun,
Perhaps too there performed. Thus long I mused,   80

Nor e'er lost sight of what I mused upon,
Save when, amid the stately grove of oaks,
Now here, now there, an acorn, from its cup
Dislodged, through sere leaves rustled, or at once
To the bare earth dropped with a startling sound.   85
From that soft couch I rose not, till the sun
Had almost touched the horizon; casting then
A backward glance upon the curling cloud
Of city smoke, by distance ruralised;
Keen as a Truant or a Fugitive,   90
But as a Pilgrim resolute, I took,
Even with the chance equipment of that hour,
The road that pointed toward the chosen Vale.
It was a splendid evening, and my soul
Once more made trial of her strength, nor lacked   95
Æolian visitations; but the harp
Was soon defrauded, and the banded host
Of harmony dispersed in straggling sounds,
And lastly utter silence! "Be it so;
Why think of any thing but present good?"   100
So, like a home-bound labourer I pursued
My way beneath the mellowing sun, that shed
Mild influence; nor left in me one wish
Again to bend the Sabbath of that time
To a servile yoke. What need of many words?   105
A pleasant loitering journey, through three days
Continued, brought me to my hermitage.
I spare to tell of what ensued, the life
In common things — the endless store of things,
Rare, or at least so seeming, every day   110
Found all about me in one neighbourhood —
The self-congratulation, and, from morn
To night, unbroken cheerfulness serene.
But speedily an earnest longing rose
To brace myself to some determined aim,   115
Reading or thinking; either to lay up
New stores, or rescue from decay the old
By timely interference: and therewith
Came hopes still higher, that with outward life
I might endue some airy phantasies   120
That had been floating loose about for years,
And to such beings temperately deal forth
The many feelings that oppressed my heart.
That hope hath been discouraged; welcome light
Dawns from the east, but dawns to disappear   125
And mock me with a sky that ripens not
Into a steady morning: if my mind,

Remembering the bold promise of the past,
Would gladly grapple with some noble theme,
Vain is her wish; where'er she turns she finds   130
Impediments from day to day renewed.

   And now it would content me to yield up
Those lofty hopes awhile, for present gifts
Of humbler industry. But, oh, dear Friend!
The Poet, gentle creature as he is,   135
Hath, like the Lover, his unruly times;
His fits when he is neither sick nor well,
Though no distress be near him but his own
Unmanageable thoughts: his mind, best pleased
While she as duteous as the mother dove   140
Sits brooding, lives not always to that end,
But like the innocent bird, hath goadings on
That drive her as in trouble through the groves;
With me is now such passion, to be blamed
No otherwise than as it lasts too long.   145

   When, as becomes a man who would prepare
For such an arduous work, I through myself
Make rigorous inquisition, the report
Is often cheering; for I neither seem
To lack that first great gift, the vital soul,   150
Nor general Truths, which are themselves a sort
Of Elements and Agents, Under-powers,
Subordinate helpers of the living mind:
Nor am I naked of external things,
Forms, images, nor numerous other aids   155
Of less regard, though won perhaps with toil
And needful to build up a Poet's praise.
Time, place, and manners do I seek, and these
Are found in plenteous store, but nowhere such
As may be singled out with steady choice;   160
No little band of yet remembered names
Whom I, in perfect confidence, might hope
To summon back from lonesome banishment,
And make them dwellers in the hearts of men
Now living, or to live in future years.   165
Sometimes the ambitious Power of choice, mistaking
Proud spring-tide swellings for a regular sea,
Will settle on some British theme, some old
Romantic tale by Milton left unsung;
More often turning to some gentle place   170
Within the groves of Chivalry, I pipe
To shepherd swains, or seated harp in hand,

Amid reposing knights by a river side
Or fountain, listen to the grave reports
Of dire enchantments faced and overcome   1754
By the strong mind, and tales of warlike feats,
Where spear encountered spear, and sword with sword
Fought, as if conscious of the blazonry
That the shield bore, so glorious was the strife;
Whence inspiration for a song that winds   180
Through ever changing scenes of votive quest
Wrongs to redress, harmonious tribute paid
To patient courage and unblemished truth,
To firm devotion, zeal unquenchable,
And Christian meekness hallowing faithful loves.   185
Sometimes, more sternly moved, I would relate
How vanquished Mithridates northward passed,
And, hidden in the cloud of years, became
Odin, the Father of a race by whom
Perished the Roman Empire: how the friends   190
And followers of Sertorius, out of Spain
Flying, found shelter in the Fortunate Isles,
And left their usages, their arts and laws,
To disappear by a slow gradual death,
To dwindle and to perish one by one,   195
Starved in those narrow bounds: but not the soul
Of Liberty, which fifteen hundred years
Survived, and, when the European came
With skill and power that might not be withstood,
Did, like a pestilence, maintain its hold   200
And wasted down by glorious death that race
Of natural heroes: or I would record
How, in tyrannic times, some high-souled man,
Unnamed among the chronicles of kings,
Suffered in silence for Truth's sake: or tell,   205
How that one Frenchman, through continued force
Of meditation on the inhuman deeds
Of those who conquered first the Indian Isles,
Went single in his ministry across
The Ocean; not to comfort the oppressed,   210
But, like a thirsty wind, to roam about
Withering the Oppressor: how Gustavus sought
Help at his need in Dalecarlia's mines:
How Wallace fought for Scotland; left the name
Of Wallace to be found, like a wild flower,   215
All over his dear Country; left the deeds
Of Wallace, like a family of Ghosts,
To people the steep rocks and river banks,
Her natural sanctuaries, with a local soul

Of independence and stern liberty.   220
Sometimes it suits me better to invent
A tale from my own heart, more near akin
To my own passions and habitual thoughts;
Some variegated story, in the main
Lofty, but the unsubstantial structure melts   225
Before the very sun that brightens it,
Mist into air dissolving! Then a wish,
My best and favourite aspiration, mounts
With yearning toward some philosophic song
Of Truth that cherishes our daily life;   230
With meditations passionate from deep
Recesses in man's heart, immortal verse
Thoughtfully fitted to the Orphean lyre;
But from this awful burthen I full soon
Take refuge and beguile myself with trust   235
That mellower years will bring a riper mind
And clearer insight. Thus my days are past
In contradiction; with no skill to part
Vague longing, haply bred by want of power,
From paramount impulse not to be withstood,   240
A timorous capacity from prudence,
From circumspection, infinite delay.
Humility and modest awe themselves
Betray me, serving often for a cloak
To a more subtle selfishness; that now   245
Locks every function up in blank reserve,
Now dupes me, trusting to an anxious eye
That with intrusive restlessness beats off
Simplicity and self-presented truth.
Ah! better far than this, to stray about   250
Voluptuously through fields and rural walks,
And ask no record of the hours, resigned
To vacant musing, unreproved neglect
Of all things, and deliberate holiday
Far better never to have heard the name   255
Of zeal and just ambition, than to live
Baffled and plagued by a mind that every hour
Turns recreant to her task; takes heart again,
Then feels immediately some hollow thought
Hang like an interdict upon her hopes.   260
This is my lot; for either still I find
Some imperfection in the chosen theme,
Or see of absolute accomplishment
Much wanting, so much wanting, in myself,
That I recoil and droop, and seek repose   265
In listlessness from vain perplexity,

Unprofitably travelling toward the grave,
Like a false steward who hath much received
And renders nothing back.
              Was it for this
That one, the fairest of all rivers, loved   270
To blend his murmurs with my nurse's song,
And, from his alder shades and rocky falls,
And from his fords and shallows, sent a voice
That flowed along my dreams? For this, didst thou,
O Derwent! winding among grassy holms   275
Where I was looking on, a babe in arms,
Make ceaseless music that composed my thoughts
To more than infant softness, giving me
Amid the fretful dwellings of mankind
A foretaste, a dim earnest, of the calm   280
That Nature breathes among the hills and groves.
When he had left the mountains and received
On his smooth breast the shadow of those towers
That yet survive, a shattered monument
Of feudal sway, the bright blue river passed   285
Along the margin of our terrace walk;
A tempting playmate whom we dearly loved.
Oh, many a time have I, a five years' child,
In a small mill-race severed from his stream,
Made one long bathing of a summer's day;   290
Basked in the sun, and plunged and basked again
Alternate, all a summer's day, or scoured
The sandy fields, leaping through flowery groves
Of yellow ragwort; or when rock and hill,
The woods, and distant Skiddaw's lofty height,   295
Were bronzed with deepest radiance, stood alone
Beneath the sky, as if I had been born
On Indian plains, and from my mother's hut
Had run abroad in wantonness, to sport
A naked savage, in the thunder shower.   300

    Fair seed-time had my soul, and I grew up
Fostered alike by beauty and by fear:
Much favoured in my birth-place, and no less
In that beloved Vale to which erelong
We were transplanted — there were we let loose   305
For sports of wider range. Ere I had told
Ten birth-days, when among the mountain slopes
Frost, and the breath of frosty wind, had snapped
The last autumnal crocus, 'twas my joy
With store of springes o'er my shoulder hung   310
To range the open heights where woodcocks run

Along the smooth green turf. Through half the night,
Scudding away from snare to snare, I plied
That anxious visitation; — moon and stars
Were shining o'er my head. I was alone,   315
And seemed to be a trouble to the peace
That dwelt among them. Sometimes it befel
In these night wanderings, that a strong desire
O'erpowered my better reason, and the bird
Which was the captive of another's toil   320
Became my prey; and when the deed was done
I heard among the solitary hills
Low breathings coming after me, and sounds
Of undistinguishable motion, steps
Almost as silent as the turf they trod.   325

Nor less when spring had warmed the cultured Vale,
Roved we as plunderers where the mother-bird
Had in high places built her lodge; though mean
Our object and inglorious, yet the end
Was not ignoble. Oh! when I have hung   330
Above the raven's nest, by knots of grass
And half-inch fissures in the slippery rock
But ill sustained, and almost (so it seemed)
Suspended by the blast that blew amain,
Shouldering the naked crag, oh, at that time   335
While on the perilous ridge I hung alone,
With what strange utterance did the loud dry wind
Blow through my ear! the sky seemed not a sky
Of earth — and with what motion moved the clouds!

Dust as we are, the immortal spirit grows   340
Like harmony in music; there is a dark
Inscrutable workmanship that reconciles
Discordant elements, makes them cling together
In one society. How strange that all
The terrors, pains, and early miseries,   345
Regrets, vexations, lassitudes interfused
Within my mind, should e'er have borne a part,
And that a needful part, in making up
The calm existence that is mine when I
Am worthy of myself! Praise to the end!   350
Thanks to the means which Nature deigned to employ;
Whether her fearless visitings, or those
That came with soft alarm, like hurtless light
Opening the peaceful clouds; or she may use
Severer interventions, ministry   355
More palpable, as best might suit her aim.

One summer evening (led by her) I found
A little boat tied to a willow tree
Within a rocky cave, its usual home.
Straight I unloosed her chain, and stepping in   360
Pushed from the shore. It was an act of stealth
And troubled pleasure, nor without the voice
Of mountain-echoes did my boat move on;
Leaving behind her still, on either side,
Small circles glittering idly in the moon,   365
Until they melted all into one track
Of sparkling light. But now, like one who rows,
Proud of his skill, to reach a chosen point
With an unswerving line, I fixed my view
Upon the summit of a craggy ridge,   370
The horizon's utmost boundary; for above
Was nothing but the stars and the grey sky.
She was an elfin pinnace; lustily
I dipped my oars into the silent lake,
And, as I rose upon the stroke, my boat   375
Went heaving through the water like a swan;
When, from behind that craggy steep till then
The horizon's bound, a huge peak, black and huge,
As if with voluntary power instinct
Upreared its head. I struck and struck again,   380
And growing still in stature the grim shape
Towered up between me and the stars, and still,
For so it seemed, with purpose of its own
And measured motion like a living thing,
Strode after me. With trembling oars I turned,   385
And through the silent water stole my way
Back to the covert of the willow tree;
There in her mooring-place I left my bark, —
And through the meadows homeward went, in grave
And serious mood; but after I had seen   390
That spectacle, for many days, my brain
Worked with a dim and undetermined sense
Of unknown modes of being; o'er my thoughts
There hung a darkness, call it solitude
Or blank desertion. No familiar shapes   395
Remained, no pleasant images of trees,
Of sea or sky, no colours of green fields;
But huge and mighty forms, that do not live
Like living men, moved slowly through the mind
By day, and were a trouble to my dreams.   400

Wisdom and Spirit of the universe!
Thou Soul that art the eternity of thought,

That givest to forms and images a breath
And everlasting motion, not in vain
By day or star-light thus from my first dawn   405
Of childhood didst thou intertwine for me
The passions that build up our human soul;
Not with the mean and vulgar works of man,
But with high objects, with enduring things —
With life and nature, purifying thus   410
The elements of feeling and of thought,
And sanctifying, by such discipline,
Both pain and fear, until we recognise
A grandeur in the beatings of the heart.
Nor was this fellowship vouchsafed to me   415
With stinted kindness. In November days,
When vapours rolling down the valley made
A lonely scene more lonesome, among woods,
At noon and 'mid the calm of summer nights,
When, by the margin of the trembling lake,   420
Beneath the gloomy hills homeward I went
In solitude, such intercourse was mine;
Mine was it in the fields both day and night,
And by the waters, all the summer long.

And in the frosty season, when the sun   425
Was set, and visible for many a mile
The cottage windows blazed through twilight gloom,
I heeded not their summons: happy time
It was indeed for all of us — for me
It was a time of rapture! Clear and loud   430
The village clock tolled six, — I wheeled about,
Proud and exulting like an untired horse
That cares not for his home. All shod with steel,
We hissed along the polished ice in games
Confederate, imitative of the chase   435
And woodland pleasures, — the resounding horn,
The pack loud chiming, and the hunted hare.
So through the darkness and the cold we flew,
And not a voice was idle; with the din
Smitten, the precipices rang aloud;   440
The leafless trees and every icy crag
Tinkled like iron; while far distant hills
Into the tumult sent an alien sound
Of melancholy not unnoticed, while the stars
Eastward were sparkling clear, and in the west   445
The orange sky of evening died away.
Not seldom from the uproar I retired
Into a silent bay, or sportively

Glanced sideway, leaving the tumultuous throng,
To cut across the reflex of a star   450
That fled, and, flying still before me, gleamed
Upon the glassy plain; and oftentimes,
When we had given our bodies to the wind,
And all the shadowy banks on either side
Came sweeping through the darkness, spinning still   455
The rapid line of motion, then at once
Have I, reclining back upon my heels,
Stopped short; yet still the solitary cliffs
Wheeled by me — even as if the earth had rolled
With visible motion her diurnal round!   460
Behind me did they stretch in solemn train,
Feebler and feebler, and I stood and watched
Till all was tranquil as a dreamless sleep.

    Ye Presences of Nature in the sky
And on the earth! Ye Visions of the hills!   465
And Souls of lonely places! can I think
A vulgar hope was yours when ye employed
Such ministry, when ye through many a year
Haunting me thus among my boyish sports,
On caves and trees, upon the woods and hills,   470
Impressed upon all forms the characters
Of danger or desire; and thus did make
The surface of the universal earth
With triumph and delight, with hope and fear,
Work like a sea?
                            Not uselessly employed,   475
Might I pursue this theme through every change
Of exercise and play, to which the year
Did summon us in his delightful round.

    We were a noisy crew; the sun in heaven
Beheld not vales more beautiful than ours;   480
Nor saw a band in happiness and joy
Richer, or worthier of the ground they trod.
I could record with no reluctant voice
The woods of autumn, and their hazel bowers
With milk-white clusters hung; the rod and line,   485
True symbol of hope's foolishness, whose strong
And unreproved enchantment led us on
By rocks and pools shut out from every star,
All the green summer, to forlorn cascades
Among the windings hid of mountain brooks.   490
— Unfading recollections! at this hour
The heart is almost mine with which I felt

From some hill-top on sunny afternoons,
The paper kite high among fleecy clouds
Pull at her rein like an impetuous courser;   495
Or, from the meadows sent on gusty days,
Beheld her breast the wind, then suddenly
Dashed headlong, and rejected by the storm.

    Ye lowly cottages wherein we dwelt,
A ministration of your own was yours;   500
Can I forget you, being as you were
So beautiful among the pleasant fields
In which ye stood? or can I here forget
The plain and seemly countenance with which
Ye dealt out your plain comforts? Yet had ye   505
Delights and exultations of your own.
Eager and never weary we pursued
Our home-amusements by the warm peat-fire
At evening, when with pencil, and smooth slate
In square divisions parcelled out and all   510
With crosses and with cyphers scribbled o'er,
We schemed and puzzled, head opposed to head
In strife too humble to be named in verse:
Or round the naked table, snow-white deal,
Cherry or maple, sate in close array,   515
And to the combat, Loo or Whist, led on
A thick-ribbed army; not, as in the world,
Neglected and ungratefully thrown by
Even for the very service they had wrought,
But husbanded through many a long campaign.   520
Uncouth assemblage was it, where no few
Had changed their functions; some, plebeian cards
Which Fate, beyond the promise of their birth,
Had dignified, and called to represent
The persons of departed potentates.   525
Oh, with what echoes on the board they fell!
Ironic diamonds, — clubs, hearts, diamonds, spades,
A congregation piteously akin!
Cheap matter offered they to boyish wit,
Those sooty knaves, precipitated down   530
With scoffs and taunts, like Vulcan out of heaven:
The paramount ace, a moon in her eclipse,
Queens gleaming through their splendour's last decay,
And monarchs surly at the wrongs sustained
By royal visages. Meanwhile abroad   535
Incessant rain was falling, or the frost
Raged bitterly, with keen and silent tooth;
And, interrupting oft that eager game
From under Esthwaite's splitting fields of ice

The pent-up air, struggling to free itself, 540
Gave out to meadow grounds and hills a loud
Protracted yelling, like the noise of wolves
Howling in troops along the Bothnic Main.

Nor, sedulous as I have been to trace
How Nature by extrinsic passion first 545
Peopled the mind with forms sublime or fair,
And made me love them, may I here omit
How other pleasures have been mine, and joys
Of subtler origin; how I have felt,
Not seldom even in that tempestuous time, 550
Those hallowed and pure motions of the sense
Which seem, in their simplicity, to own
An intellectual charm; that calm delight
Which, if I err not, surely must belong
To those first-born affinities that fit 555
Our new existence to existing things,
And, in our dawn of being, constitute
The bond of union between life and joy.

Yes, I remember when the changeful earth,
And twice five summers on my mind had stamped 560
The faces of the moving year, even then
I held unconscious intercourse with beauty
Old as creation, drinking in a pure
Organic pleasure from the silver wreaths
Of curling mist, or from the level plain 565
Of waters coloured by impending clouds.

The sands of Westmoreland, the creeks and bays
Of Cumbria's rocky limits, they can tell
How, when the Sea threw off his evening shade,
And to the shepherd's hut on distant hills 570
Sent welcome notice of the rising moon,
How I have stood, to fancies such as these
A stranger, linking with the spectacle
No conscious memory of a kindred sight,
And bringing with me no peculiar sense 575
Of quietness or peace; yet have I stood,
Even while mine eye hath moved o'er many a league
Of shining water, gathering as it seemed
Through every hair-breadth in that field of light
New pleasure like a bee among the flowers. 580

Thus oft amid those fits of vulgar joy
Which, through all seasons, on a child's pursuits
Are prompt attendants, 'mid that giddy bliss

Which, like a tempest, works along the blood
And is forgotten; even then I felt   585
Gleams like the flashing of a shield; — the earth
And common face of Nature spake to me
Rememberable things; sometimes, 'tis true,
By chance collisions and quaint accidents
(Like those ill-sorted unions, work supposed   590
Of evil-minded fairies), yet not vain
Nor profitless, if haply they impressed
Collateral objects and appearances,
Albeit lifeless then, and doomed to sleep
Until maturer seasons called them forth   595
To impregnate and to elevate the mind.
— And if the vulgar joy by its own weight
Wearied itself out of the memory,
The scenes which were a witness of that joy
Remained in their substantial lineaments   600
Depicted on the brain, and to the eye
Were visible, a daily sight; and thus
By the impressive discipline of fear,
By pleasure and repeated happiness,
So frequently repeated, and by force   605
Of obscure feelings representative
Of things forgotten, these same scenes so bright,
So beautiful, so majestic in themselves,
Though yet the day was distant, did become
Habitually dear, and all their forms   610
And changeful colours by invisible links
Were fastened to the affections.
                                   I began
My story early — not misled, I trust,
By an infirmity of love for days
Disowned by memory — fancying flowers where none   615
Not even the sweetest do or can survive
For him at least whose dawning day they cheered.
Nor will it seem to thee, O Friend! so prompt
In sympathy, that I have lengthened out
With fond and feeble tongue a tedious tale.   620
Meanwhile, my hope has been, that I might fetch
Invigorating thoughts from former years;
Might fix the wavering balance of my mind,
And haply meet reproaches too, whose power
May spur me on, in manhood now mature,   625
To honourable toil. Yet should these hopes
Prove vain, and thus should neither I be taught
To understand myself, nor thou to know
With better knowledge how the heart was framed
Of him thou lovest; need I dread from thee   630

Harsh judgments, if the song be loth to quit
Those recollected hours that have the charm
Of visionary things, those lovely forms
And sweet sensations that throw back our life,
And almost make remotest infancy   635
A visible scene, on which the sun is shining?

   One end at least hath been attained; my mind
Hath been revived, and if this genial mood
Desert me not, forthwith shall be brought down
Through later years the story of my life.   640
The road lies plain before me; — 'tis a theme
Single and of determined bounds; and hence
I choose it rather at this time, than work
Of ampler or more varied argument,
Where I might be discomfited and lost: 645
And certain hopes are with me, that to thee
This labour will be welcome, honoured Friend!

BOOK SECOND

SCHOOL-TIME (CONTINUED)

Thus far, O Friend! have we, though leaving much
Unvisited, endeavoured to retrace
The simple ways in which my childhood walked;
Those chiefly that first led me to the love
Of rivers, woods, and fields. The passion yet   5
Was in its birth, sustained as might befal
By nourishment that came unsought; for still
From week to week, from month to month, we lived
A round of tumult. Duly were our games
Prolonged in summer till the day-light failed: 10
No chair remained before the doors; the bench
And threshold steps were empty; fast asleep
The labourer, and the old man who had sate
A later lingerer; yet the revelry
Continued and the loud uproar: at last,   15
When all the ground was dark, and twinkling stars
Edged the black clouds, home and to bed we went,
Feverish with weary joints and beating minds.
Ah! is there one who ever has been young,
Nor needs a warning voice to tame the pride   20
Of intellect and virtue's self-esteem?
One is there, though the wisest and the best
Of all mankind, who covets not at times
Union that cannot be; — who would not give,

If so he might, to duty and to truth   25
The eagerness of infantine desire?
A tranquillising spirit presses now
On my corporeal frame, so wide appears
The vacancy between me and those days
Which yet have such self-presence in my mind,   30
That, musing on them, often do I seem
Two consciousnesses, conscious of myself
And of some other Being. A rude mass
Of native rock, left midway in the square
Of our small market village, was the goal   35
Or centre of these sports; and when, returned
After long absence, thither I repaired,
Gone was the old grey stone, and in its place
A smart Assembly-room usurped the ground
That had been ours. There let the fiddle scream,   40
And be ye happy! Yet, my Friends! I know
That more than one of you will think with me
Of those soft starry nights, and that old Dame
From whom the stone was named, who there had sate,
And watched her table with its huckster's wares   45
Assiduous, through the length of sixty years.

We ran a boisterous course; the year span round
With giddy motion. But the time approached
That brought with it a regular desire
For calmer pleasures, when the winning forms   50
Of Nature were collaterally attached
To every scheme of holiday delight
And every boyish sport, less grateful else
And languidly pursued.

                              When summer came,
Our pastime was, on bright half-holidays,   55
To sweep along the plain of Windermere
With rival oars; and the selected bourne
Was now an Island musical with birds
That sang and ceased not; now a Sister Isle
Beneath the oaks' umbrageous covert, sown   60
With lilies of the valley like a field;
And now a third small Island, where survived
In solitude the ruins of a shrine
Once to Our Lady dedicate, and served
Daily with chaunted rites. In such a race   65
So ended, disappointment could be none,
Uneasiness, or pain, or jealousy:
We rested in the shade, all pleased alike,
Conquered and conqueror. Thus the pride of strength,
And the vain-glory of superior skill,   70

Were tempered; thus was gradually produced
A quiet independence of the heart;
And to my Friend who knows me I may add,
Fearless of blame, that hence for future days
Ensued a diffidence and modesty,   75
And I was taught to feel, perhaps too much,
The self-sufficing power of Solitude.

    Our daily meals were frugal, Sabine fare!
More than we wished we knew the blessing then
Of vigorous hunger — hence corporeal strength   80
Unsapped by delicate viands; for, exclude
A little weekly stipend, and we lived
Through three divisions of the quartered year
In penniless poverty. But now to school
From the half-yearly holidays returned,   85
We came with weightier purses, that sufficed
To furnish treats more costly than the Dame
Of the old grey stone, from her scant board, supplied.
Hence rustic dinners on the cool green ground,
Or in the woods, or by a river side   90
Or shady fountain, while among the leaves
Soft airs were stirring, and the mid-day sun
Unfelt shone brightly round us in our joy.
Nor is my aim neglected if I tell
How sometimes, in the length of those half-years,   95
We from our funds drew largely; — proud to curb,
And eager to spur on, the galloping steed;
And with the cautious inn-keeper, whose stud
Supplied our want, we haply might employ
Sly subterfuge, if the adventure's bound   100
Were distant: some famed temple where of yore
The Druids worshipped, or the antique walls
Of that large abbey, where within the Vale
Of Nightshade, to St. Mary's honour built,
Stands yet a mouldering pile with fractured arch,   105
Belfry, and images, and living trees,
A holy scene! Along the smooth green turf
Our horses grazed. To more than inland peace
Left by the west wind sweeping overhead
From a tumultuous ocean, trees and towers   110
In that sequestered valley may be seen,
Both silent and both motionless alike;
Such the deep shelter that is there, and such
The safeguard for repose and quietness.

    Our steeds remounted and the summons given,   115
With whip and spur we through the chauntry flew

In uncouth race, and left the cross-legged knight,
And the stone-abbot, and that single wren
Which one day sang so sweetly in the nave
Of the old church, that — though from recent showers   120
The earth was comfortless, and touched by faint
Internal breezes, sobbings of the place
And respirations, from the roofless walls
The shuddering ivy dripped large drops — yet still
So sweetly 'mid the gloom the invisible bird   125
Sang to herself, that there I could have made
My dwelling-place, and lived for ever there
To hear such music. Through the walls we flew
And down the valley, and, a circuit made
In wantonness of heart, through rough and smooth   130
We scampered homewards. Oh, ye rocks and streams,
And that still spirit shed from evening air!
Even in this joyous time I sometimes felt
Your presence, when with slackened step we breathed
Along the sides of the steep hills, or when   135
Lighted by gleams of moonlight from the sea
We beat with thundering hoofs the level sand.

Midway on long Winander's eastern shore,
Within the crescent of a pleasant bay,
A tavern stood; no homely-featured house,   140
Primeval like its neighbouring cottages,
But 'twas a splendid place, the door beset
With chaises, grooms, and liveries, and within
Decanters, glasses, and the blood-red wine.
In ancient times, or ere the Hall was built   145
On the large island, had this dwelling been
More worthy of a poet's love, a hut,
Proud of its one bright fire and sycamore shade.
But — though the rhymes were gone that once inscribed
The threshold, and large golden characters,   150
Spread o'er the spangled sign-board, had dislodged
The old Lion and usurped his place, in slight
And mockery of the rustic painter's hand —
Yet, to this hour, the spot to me is dear
With all its foolish pomp. The garden lay   155
Upon a slope surmounted by a plain
Of a small bowling-green; beneath us stood
A grove, with gleams of water through the trees
And over the tree-tops; nor did we want
Refreshment, strawberries and mellow cream.   160
There, while through half an afternoon we played
On the smooth platform, whether skill prevailed

Or happy blunder triumphed, bursts of glee
Made all the mountains ring. But, ere night-fall,
When in our pinnace we returned at leisure   165
Over the shadowy lake, and to the beach
Of some small island steered our course with one,
The Minstrel of the Troop, and left him there,
And rowed off gently, while he blew his flute
Alone upon the rock — oh, then, the calm   170
And dead still water lay upon my mind
Even with a weight of pleasure, and the sky,
Never before so beautiful, sank down
Into my heart, and held me like a dream!
Thus were my sympathies enlarged, and thus   175
Daily the common range of visible things
Grew dear to me: already I began
To love the sun; a boy I loved the sun,
Not as I since have loved him, as a pledge
And surety of our earthly life, a light   180
Which we behold and feel we are alive;
Nor for his bounty to so many worlds —
But for this cause, that I had seen him lay
His beauty on the morning hills, had seen
The western mountain touch his setting orb,   185
In many a thoughtless hour, when, from excess
Of happiness, my blood appeared to flow
For its own pleasure, and I breathed with joy.
And, from like feelings, humble though intense,
To patriotic and domestic love   190
Analogous, the moon to me was dear;
For I could dream away my purposes,
Standing to gaze upon her while she hung
Midway between the hills, as if she knew
No other region, but belonged to thee,   195
Yea, appertained by a peculiar right
To thee and thy grey huts, thou one dear Vale!

   Those incidental charms which first attached
My heart to rural objects, day by day
Grew weaker, and I hasten on to tell   200
How Nature, intervenient till this time
And secondary, now at length was sought
For her own sake. But who shall parcel out
His intellect by geometric rules,
Split like a province into round and square?   205
Who knows the individual hour in which
His habits were first sown, even as a seed?
Who that shall point as with a wand and say

"This portion of the river of my mind
Came from yon fountain?" Thou, my Friend! art one   210
More deeply read in thy own thoughts; to thee
Science appears but what in truth she is,
Not as our glory and our absolute boast,
But as a succedaneum, and a prop
To our infirmity. No officious slave   215
Art thou of that false secondary power
By which we multiply distinctions, then
Deem that our puny boundaries are things
That we perceive, and not that we have made.
To thee, unblinded by these formal arts,   220
The unity of all hath been revealed,
And thou wilt doubt with me, less aptly skilled
Than many are to range the faculties
In scale and order, class the cabinet
Of their sensations, and in voluble phrase   225
Run through the history and birth of each
As of a single independent thing.
Hard task, vain hope, to analyse the mind,
If each most obvious and particular thought,
Not in a mystical and idle sense,   230
But in the words of Reason deeply weighed,
Hath no beginning.

                       Blest the infant Babe,
(For with my best conjecture I would trace
Our Being's earthly progress,) blest the Babe,
Nursed in his Mother's arms, who sinks to sleep   235
Rocked on his Mother's breast; who with his soul
Drinks in the feelings of his Mother's eye!
For him, in one dear Presence, there exists
A virtue which irradiates and exalts
Objects through widest intercourse of sense.   240
No outcast he, bewildered and depressed:
Along his infant veins are interfused
The gravitation and the filial bond
Of nature that connect him with the world.
Is there a flower, to which he points with hand   245
Too weak to gather it, already love
Drawn from love's purest earthly fount for him
Hath beautified that flower; already shades
Of pity cast from inward tenderness
Do fall around him upon aught that bears   250
Unsightly marks of violence or harm.
Emphatically such a Being lives,
Frail creature as he is, helpless as frail,
An inmate of this active universe.

For feeling has to him imparted power 255
That through the growing faculties of sense
Doth like an agent of the one great Mind
Create, creator and receiver both,
Working but in alliance with the works
Which it beholds. — Such, verily, is the first 260
Poetic spirit of our human life,
By uniform control of after years,
In most, abated or suppressed; in some,
Through every change of growth and of decay,
Pre-eminent till death.
                    From early days, 265
Beginning not long after that first time
In which, a Babe, by intercourse of touch
I held mute dialogues with my Mother's heart,
I have endeavoured to display the means
Whereby this infant sensibility, 270
Great birthright of our being, was in me
Augmented and sustained. Yet is a path
More difficult before me; and I fear
That in its broken windings we shall need
The chamois' sinews, and the eagle's wing: 275
For now a trouble came into my mind
From unknown causes. I was left alone
Seeking the visible world, nor knowing why.
The props of my affections were removed,
And yet the building stood, as if sustained 280
By its own spirit! All that I beheld
Was dear, and hence to finer influxes
The mind lay open to a more exact
And close communion. Many are our joys
In youth, but oh! what happiness to live 285
When every hour brings palpable access
Of knowledge, when all knowledge is delight,
And sorrow is not there! The seasons came,
And every season wheresoe'er I moved
Unfolded transitory qualities, 290
Which, but for this most watchful power of love,
Had been neglected; left a register
Of permanent relations, else unknown.
Hence life, and change, and beauty, solitude
More active even than "best society" — 295
Society made sweet as solitude
By inward concords, silent, inobtrusive,
And gentle agitations of the mind
From manifold distinctions, difference
Perceived in things, where, to the unwatchful eye, 300

No difference is, and hence, from the same source,
Sublimer joy; for I would walk alone,
Under the quiet stars, and at that time
Have felt whate'er there is of power in sound
To breathe an elevated mood, by form   305
Or image unprofaned; and I would stand,
If the night blackened with a coming storm,
Beneath some rock, listening to notes that are
The ghostly language of the ancient earth,
Or make their dim abode in distant winds.   310
Thence did I drink the visionary power;
And deem not profitless those fleeting moods
Of shadowy exultation: not for this,
That they are kindred to our purer mind
And intellectual life; but that the soul,   315
Remembering how she felt, but what she felt
Remembering not, retains an obscure sense
Of possible sublimity, whereto
With growing faculties she doth aspire,
With faculties still growing, feeling still   320
That whatsoever point they gain, they yet
Have something to pursue.
                                    And not alone,
'Mid gloom and tumult, but no less 'mid fair
And tranquil scenes, that universal power
And fitness in the latent qualities   325
And essences of things, by which the mind
Is moved with feelings of delight, to me
Came, strengthened with a superadded soul,
A virtue not its own. My morning walks
Were early; — oft before the hours of school   330
I travelled round our little lake, five miles
Of pleasant wandering. Happy time! more dear
For this, that one was by my side, a Friend,
Then passionately loved; with heart how full
Would he peruse these lines! For many years   335
Have since flowed in between us, and, our minds
Both silent to each other, at this time
We live as if those hours had never been.
Nor seldom did I lift our cottage latch
Far earlier, ere one smoke-wreath had risen   340
From human dwelling, or the thrush, high-perched,
Piped to the woods his shrill reveillé, sate
Alone upon some jutting eminence,
At the first gleam of dawn-light, when the Vale,
Yet slumbering, lay in utter solitude.   345
How shall I seek the origin? where find
Faith in the marvellous things which then I felt?

Oft in these moments such a holy calm
Would overspread my soul, that bodily eyes
Were utterly forgotten, and what I saw   350
Appeared like something in myself, a dream,
A prospect in the mind.
              'Twere long to tell
What spring and autumn, what the winter snows,
And what the summer shade, what day and night,
Evening and morning, sleep and waking thought   355
From sources inexhaustible, poured forth
To feed the spirit of religious love
In which I walked with Nature. But let this
Be not forgotten, that I still retained
My first creative sensibility;   360
That by the regular action of the world
My soul was unsubdued. A plastic power
Abode with me; a forming hand, at times
Rebellious, acting in a devious mood;
A local spirit of his own, at war   365
With general tendency, but, for the most,
Subservient strictly to external things
With which it communed. An auxiliar light
Came from my mind, which on the setting sun
Bestowed new splendour; the melodious birds,   370
The fluttering breezes, fountains that run on
Murmuring so sweetly in themselves, obeyed
A like dominion, and the midnight storm
Grew darker in the presence of my eye:
Hence my obeisance, my devotion hence,   375
And hence my transport.
               Nor should this, perchance,
Pass unrecorded, that I still had loved
The exercise and produce of a toil,
Than analytic industry to me
More pleasing, and whose character I deem   380
Is more poetic as resembling more
Creative agency. The song would speak
Of that interminable building reared
By observation of affinities
In objects where no brotherhood exists   385
To passive minds. My seventeenth year was come;
And, whether from this habit rooted now
So deeply in my mind, or from excess
In the great social principle of life
Coercing all things into sympathy,   390
To unorganic natures were transferred
My own enjoyments; or the power of truth
Coming in revelation, did converse

With things that really are; I, at this time,
Saw blessings spread around me like a sea.   395
Thus while the days flew by, and years passed on,
From Nature overflowing in my soul,
I had received so much, that all my thoughts
Were steeped in feeling; I was only then
Contented, when with bliss ineffable   400
I felt the sentiment of Being spread
O'er all that moves and all that seemeth still;
O'er all that, lost beyond the reach of thought
And human knowledge, to the human eye
Invisible, yet liveth to the heart;   405
O'er all that leaps and runs, and shouts and sings,
Or beats the gladsome air; o'er all that glides
Beneath the wave, yea, in the wave itself,
And mighty depth of waters. Wonder not
If high the transport, great the joy I felt,   410
Communing in this sort through earth and heaven
With every form of creature, as it looked
Towards the Uncreated with a countenance
Of adoration, with an eye of love.
One song they sang, and it was audible,   415
Most audible, then, when the fleshly ear,
O'ercome by humblest prelude of that strain,
Forgot her functions, and slept undisturbed.

    If this be error, and another faith
Find easier access to the pious mind,   420
Yet were I grossly destitute of all
Those human sentiments that make this earth
So dear, if I should fail with grateful voice
To speak of you, ye mountains, and ye lakes
And sounding cataracts, ye mists and winds   425
That dwell among the hills where I was born.
If in my youth I have been pure in heart,
If, mingling with the world, I am content
With my own modest pleasures, and have lived
With God and Nature communing, removed   430
From little enmities and low desires,
The gift is yours; if in these times of fear,
This melancholy waste of hopes o'erthrown,
If, 'mid indifference and apathy,
And wicked exultation when good men   435
On every side fall off, we know not how,
To selfishness, disguised in gentle names
Of peace and quiet and domestic love,
Yet mingled not unwillingly with sneers

On visionary minds; if, in this time 440
Of dereliction and dismay, I yet
Despair not of our nature, but retain
A more than Roman confidence, a faith
That fails not, in all sorrow my support,
The blessing of my life; the gift is yours, 445
Ye winds and sounding cataracts! 'tis yours,
Ye mountains! thine, O Nature! Thou hast fed
My lofty speculations; and in thee,
For this uneasy heart of ours, I find
A never-failing principle of joy 450
And purest passion.
        Thou, my Friend! wert reared
In the great city, 'mid far other scenes;
But we, by different roads, at length have gained
The self-same bourne. And for this cause to thee
I speak, unapprehensive of contempt, 455
The insinuated scoff of coward tongues,
And all that silent language which so oft
In conversation between man and man
Blots from the human countenance all trace
Of beauty and of love. For thou hast sought 460
The truth in solitude, and, since the days
That gave thee liberty, full long desired,
To serve in Nature's temple, thou hast been
The most assiduous of her ministers;
In many things my brother, chiefly here 465
In this our deep devotion.
        Fare thee well!
Health and the quiet of a healthful mind
Attend thee! seeking oft the haunts of men,
And yet more often living with thyself,
And for thyself, so haply shall thy days 470
Be many, and a blessing to mankind.

BOOK THIRD

RESIDENCE AT CAMBRIDGE

It was a dreary morning when the wheels
Rolled over a wide plain o'erhung with clouds,
And nothing cheered our way till first we saw
The long-roofed chapel of King's College lift
Turrets and pinnacles in answering files, 5
Extended high above a dusky grove.

Advancing, we espied upon the road
A student clothed in gown and tasselled cap,
Striding along as if o'ertasked by Time,
Or covetous of exercise and air;   10
He passed — nor was I master of my eyes
Till he was left an arrow's flight behind.
As near and nearer to the spot we drew,
It seemed to suck us in with an eddy's force.
Onward we drove beneath the Castle; caught,   15
While crossing Magdalene Bridge, a glimpse of Cam;
And at the *Hoop* alighted, famous Inn.

My spirit was up, my thoughts were full of hope;
Some friends I had, acquaintances who there
Seemed friends, poor simple school-boys, now hung round   20
With honour and importance: in a world
Of welcome faces up and down I roved;
Questions, directions, warnings and advice,
Flowed in upon me, from all sides; fresh day
Of pride and pleasure! to myself I seemed   25
A man of business and expense, and went
From shop to shop about my own affairs,
To Tutor or to Tailor, as befel,
From street to street with loose and careless mind.

I was the Dreamer, they the Dream; I roamed   30
Delighted through the motley spectacle;
Gowns grave, or gaudy, doctors, students, streets,
Courts, cloisters, flocks of churches, gateways, towers:
Migration strange for a stripling of the hills,
A northern villager.
                     As if the change   35
Had waited on some Fairy's wand, at once
Behold me rich in monies, and attired
In splendid garb, with hose of silk, and hair
Powdered like rimy trees, when frost is keen.
My lordly dressing-gown, I pass it by,   40
With other signs of manhood that supplied
The lack of beard. — The weeks went roundly on,
With invitations, suppers, wine and fruit,
Smooth housekeeping within, and all without
Liberal, and suiting gentleman's array.   45

The Evangelist St. John my patron was:
Three Gothic courts are his, and in the first
Was my abiding-place, a nook obscure;
Right underneath, the College kitchens made

A humming sound, less tuneable than bees,   50
But hardly less industrious; with shrill notes
Of sharp command and scolding intermixed.
Near me hung Trinity's loquacious clock,
Who never let the quarters, night or day,
Slip by him unproclaimed, and told the hours   55
Twice over with a male and female voice.
Her pealing organ was my neighbour too;
And from my pillow, looking forth by light
Of moon or favouring stars, I could behold
The antechapel where the statue stood   60
Of Newton with his prism and silent face,
The marble index of a mind for ever
Voyaging through strange seas of Thought, alone.

  Of College labours, of the Lecturer's room
All studded round, as thick as chairs could stand,   65
With loyal students faithful to their books,
Half-and-half idlers, hardy recusants,
And honest dunces — of important days,
Examinations, when the man was weighed
As in a balance! of excessive hopes,   70
Tremblings withal and commendable fears,
Small jealousies, and triumphs good or bad,
Let others that know more speak as they know.
Such glory was but little sought by me,
And little won. Yet from the first crude days   75
Of settling time in this untried abode,
I was disturbed at times by prudent thoughts,
Wishing to hope without a hope, some fears
About my future worldly maintenance,
And, more than all, a strangeness in the mind,   80
A feeling that I was not for that hour,
Nor for that place. But wherefore be cast down?
For (not to speak of Reason and her pure
Reflective acts to fix the moral law
Deep in the conscience, nor of Christian Hope,   85
Bowing her head before her sister Faith
As one far mightier), hither I had come,
Bear witness Truth, endowed with holy powers
And faculties, whether to work or feel.
Oft when the dazzling show no longer new   90
Had ceased to dazzle, ofttimes did I quit
My comrades, leave the crowd, buildings and groves,
And as I paced alone the level fields
Far from those lovely sights and sounds sublime
With which I had been conversant, the mind   95

Drooped not; but there into herself returning,
With prompt rebound seemed fresh as heretofore.
At least I more distinctly recognised
Her native instincts: let me dare to speak
A higher language, say that now I felt   100
What independent solaces were mine,
To mitigate the injurious sway of place
Or circumstance, how far soever changed
In youth, or *to* be changed in manhood's prime;
Or for the few who shall be called to look   105
On the long shadows in our evening years,
Ordained precursors to the night of death.
As if awakened, summoned, roused, constrained,
I looked for universal things; perused
The common countenance of earth and sky: 110
Earth, nowhere unembellished by some trace
Of that first Paradise whence man was driven;
And sky, whose beauty and bounty are expressed
By the proud name she bears — the name of Heaven.
I called on both to teach me what they might;   115
Or turning the mind in upon herself
Pored, watched, expected, listened, spread my thoughts
And spread them with a wider creeping; felt
Incumbencies more awful, visitings
Of the Upholder of the tranquil soul,   120
That tolerates the indignities of Time,
And, from the centre of Eternity
All finite motions overruling, lives
In glory immutable. But peace! enough
Here to record I had ascended now   125
To such community with highest truth —
A track pursuing, not untrod before,
From strict analogies by thought supplied
Or consciousnesses not to be subdued.
To every natural form, rock, fruit or flower,   130
Even the loose stones that cover the high-way,
I gave a moral life: I saw them feel,
Or linked them to some feeling: the great mass
Lay bedded in a quickening soul, and all
That I beheld respired with inward meaning.   135
Add that whate'er of Terror or of Love
Or Beauty, Nature's daily face put on
From transitory passion, unto this
I was as sensitive as waters are
To the sky's influence, in a kindred mood   140
Of passion was obedient as a lute
That waits upon the touches of the wind.
Unknown, unthought of, yet I was most rich —

I had a world about me — 'twas my own;
I made it, for it only lived to me,   145
And to the God who sees into the heart.
Such sympathies, though rarely, were betrayed
By outward gestures and by visible looks:
Some called it madness — so indeed it was,
If child-like fruitfulness in passing joy,   150
If steady moods of thoughtfulness matured
To inspiration, sort with such a name;
If prophecy be madness; if things viewed
By poets in old time, and higher up
By the first men, earth's first inhabitants,   155
May in these tutored days no more be seen
With undisordered sight. But leaving this,
It was no madness, for the bodily eye
Amid my strongest workings evermore
Was searching out the lines of difference   160
As they lie hid in all external forms,
Near or remote, minute or vast, an eye
Which from a tree, a stone, a withered leaf,
To the broad ocean and the azure heavens
Spangled with kindred multitudes of stars,   165
Could find no surface where its power might sleep;
Which spake perpetual logic to my soul,
And by an unrelenting agency
Did bind my feelings even as in a chain.

And here, O Friend! have I retraced my life   170
Up to an eminence, and told a tale
Of matters which not falsely may be called
The glory of my youth. Of genius, power,
Creation and divinity itself
I have been speaking, for my theme has been   175
What passed within me. Not of outward things
Done visibly for other minds, words, signs,
Symbols or actions, but of my own heart
Have I been speaking, and my youthful mind.
O Heavens! how awful is the might of souls,   180
And what they do within themselves while yet
The yoke of earth is new to them, the world
Nothing but a wild field where they were sown.
This is, in truth, heroic argument,
This genuine prowess, which I wished to touch   185
With hand however weak, but in the main
It lies far hidden from the reach of words.
Points have we all of us within our souls
Where all stand single; this I feel, and make
Breathings for incommunicable powers;   190

But is not each a memory to himself?
And, therefore, now that we must quit this theme,
I am not heartless, for there's not a man
That lives who hath not known his god-like hours,
And feels not what an empire we inherit   195
As natural beings in the strength of Nature.

   No more: for now into a populous plain
We must descend. A Traveller I am,
Whose tale is only of himself; even so,
So be it, if the pure of heart be prompt   200
To follow, and if thou, my honoured Friend!
Who in these thoughts art ever at my side,
Support, as heretofore, my fainting steps.

   It hath been told, that when the first delight
That flashed upon me from this novel show   205
Had failed, the mind returned into herself;
Yet true it is, that I had made a change
In climate, and my nature's outward coat
Changed also slowly and insensibly.
Full oft the quiet and exalted thoughts   210
Of loneliness gave way to empty noise
And superficial pastimes; now and then
Forced labour, and more frequently forced hopes;
And, worst of all, a treasonable growth
Of indecisive judgments, that impaired   215
And shook the mind's simplicity. — And yet
This was a gladsome time. Could I behold —
Who, less insensible than sodden clay
In a sea-river's bed at ebb of tide,
Could have beheld, — with undelighted heart,   220
So many happy youths, so wide and fair
A congregation in its budding-time
Of health, and hope, and beauty, all at once
So many divers samples from the growth
Of life's sweet season — could have seen unmoved   225
That miscellaneous garland of wild flowers
Decking the matron temples of a place
So famous through the world? To me, at least,
It was a goodly prospect: for, in sooth,
Though I had learnt betimes to stand unpropped,   230
And independent musings pleased me so
That spells seemed on me when I was alone,
Yet could I only cleave to solitude
In lonely places; if a throng was near
That way I leaned by nature; for my heart   235
Was social, and loved idleness and joy.

    Not seeking those who might participate
My deeper pleasures (nay, I had not once,
Though not unused to mutter lonesome songs,
Even with myself divided such delight,   240
Or looked that way for aught that might be clothed
In human language), easily I passed
From the remembrances of better things,
And slipped into the ordinary works
Of careless youth, unburthened, unalarmed.   245
Caverns there were within my mind which sun
Could never penetrate, yet did there not
Want store of leafy *arbours* where the light
Might enter in at will. Companionships,
Friendships, acquaintances, were welcome all.   250
We sauntered, played, or rioted; we talked
Unprofitable talk at morning hours;
Drifted about along the streets and walks,
Read lazily in trivial books, went forth
To gallop through the country in blind zeal   255
Of senseless horsemanship, or on the breast
Of Cam sailed boisterously, and let the stars
Come forth, perhaps without one quiet thought.

    Such was the tenor of the second act
In this new life. Imagination slept,   260
And yet not utterly. I could not print
Ground where the grass had yielded to the steps
Of generations of illustrious men,
Unmoved. I could not always lightly pass
Through the same gateways, sleep where they had slept, 265
Wake where they waked, range that inclosure old,
That garden of great intellects, undisturbed.
Place also by the side of this dark sense
Of nobler feeling, that those spiritual men,
Even the great Newton's own ethereal self,   270
Seemed humbled in these precincts, thence to be
The more endeared. Their several memories here
(Even like their persons in their portraits clothed
With the accustomed garb of daily life)
Put on a lowly and a touching grace   275
Of more distinct humanity, that left
All genuine admiration unimpaired.

    Beside the pleasant Mill of Trompington
I laughed with Chaucer, in the hawthorn shade
Heard him, while birds were warbling, tell his tales 280
Of amorous passion. And that gentle Bard,
Chosen by the Muses for their Page of State —

Sweet Spenser, moving through his clouded heaven
With the moon's beauty and the moon's soft pace,
I called him Brother, Englishman, and Friend! 285
Yea, our blind Poet, who, in his later day,
Stood almost single; uttering odious truth —
Darkness before, and danger's voice behind,
Soul awful — if the earth has ever lodged
An awful soul — I seemed to see him here 290
Familiarly, and in his scholar's dress
Bounding before me, yet a stripling youth —
A boy, no better, with his rosy cheeks
Angelical, keen eye, courageous look,
And conscious step of purity and pride. 295
Among the band of my compeers was one
Whom chance had stationed in the very room
Honoured by Milton's name. O temperate Bard!
Be it confest that, for the first time, seated
Within thy innocent lodge and oratory, 300
One of a festive circle, I poured out
Libations, to thy memory drank, till pride
And gratitude grew dizzy in a brain
Never excited by the fumes of wine
Before that hour, or since. Then, forth I ran 305
From the assembly; through a length of streets,
Ran, ostrich-like, to reach our chapel door
In not a desperate or opprobrious time,
Albeit long after the importunate bell
Had stopped, with wearisome Cassandra voice 310
No longer haunting the dark winter night.
Call back, O Friend! a moment to thy mind
The place itself and fashion of the rites.
With careless ostentation shouldering up
My surplice, through the inferior throng I clove 315
Of the plain Burghers, who in audience stood
On the last skirts of their permitted ground,
Under the pealing organ. Empty thoughts!
I am ashamed of them: and that great Bard,
And thou, O Friend! who in thy ample mind 320
Hast placed me high above my best deserts,
Ye will forgive the weakness of that hour,
In some of its unworthy vanities,
Brother to many more.

           In this mixed sort
The months passed on, remissly, not given up 325
To wilful alienation from the right,
Or walks of open scandal, but in vague
And loose indifference, easy likings, aims
Of a low pitch — duty and zeal dismissed,

Yet Nature, or a happy course of things   330
Not doing in their stead the needful work.
The memory languidly revolved, the heart
Reposed in noontide rest, the inner pulse
Of contemplation almost failed to beat.
Such life might not inaptly be compared   335
To a floating island, an amphibious spot
Unsound, of spongy texture, yet withal
Not wanting a fair face of water weeds
And pleasant flowers. The thirst of living praise,
Fit reverence for the glorious Dead, the sight   340
Of those long vistas, sacred catacombs,
Where mighty *minds* lie visibly entombed,
Have often stirred the heart of youth, and bred
A fervent love of rigorous discipline. —
Alas! such high emotion touched not me.   345
Look was there none within these walls to shame
My easy spirits, and discountenance
Their light composure, far less to instil
A calm resolve of mind, firmly addressed
To puissant efforts. Nor was this the blame   350
Of others but my own; I should, in truth,
As far as doth concern my single self,
Misdeem most widely, lodging it elsewhere:
For I, bred up 'mid Nature's luxuries,
Was a spoiled child, and rambling like the wind,   355
As I had done in daily intercourse
With those crystalline rivers, solemn heights,
And mountains, ranging like a fowl of the air,
I was ill-tutored for captivity;
To quit my pleasure, and, from month to month,   360
Take up a station calmly on the perch
Of sedentary peace. Those lovely forms
Had also left less space within my mind,
Which, wrought upon instinctively, had found
A freshness in those objects of her love,   365
A winning power, beyond all other power.
Not that I slighted books, — that were to lack
All sense, — but other passions in me ruled,
Passions more fervent, making me less prompt
To in-door study than was wise or well,   370
Or suited to those years. Yet I, though used
In magisterial liberty to rove,
Culling such flowers of learning as might tempt
A random choice, could shadow forth a place
(If now I yield not to a flattering dream)   375
Whose studious aspect should have bent me down
To instantaneous service; should at once

Have made me pay to science and to arts
And written lore, acknowledged my liege lord,
A homage frankly offered up, like that   380
Which I had paid to Nature. Toil and pains
In this recess, by thoughtful Fancy built,
Should spread from heart to heart; and stately groves,
Majestic edifices, should not want
A corresponding dignity within.   385
The congregating temper that pervades
Our unripe years, not wasted, should be taught
To minister to works of high attempt —
Works which the enthusiast would perform with love.
Youth should be awed, religiously possessed   390
With a conviction of the power that waits
On knowledge, when sincerely sought and prized
For its own sake, on glory and on praise
If but by labour won, and fit to endure.
The passing day should learn to put aside   395
Her trappings here, should strip them off abashed
Before antiquity and stedfast truth
And strong book-mindedness; and over all
A healthy sound simplicity should reign,
A seemly plainness, name it what you will,   400
Republican or pious.

                           If these thoughts
Are a gratuitous emblazonry
That mocks the recreant age *we* live in, then
Be Folly and False-seeming free to affect
Whatever formal gait of discipline   405
Shall raise them highest in their own esteem —
Let them parade among the Schools at will,
But spare the House of God. Was ever known
The witless shepherd who persists to drive
A flock that thirsts not to a pool disliked?   410
A weight must surely hang on days begun
And ended with such mockery. Be wise,
Ye Presidents and Deans, and, till the spirit
Of ancient times revive, and youth be trained
At home in pious service, to your bells   415
Give seasonable rest, for 'tis a sound
Hollow as ever vexed the tranquil air;
And your officious doings bring disgrace
On the plain steeples of our English Church,
Whose worship, 'mid remotest village trees,   420
Suffers for this. Even Science, too, at hand
In daily sight of this irreverence,
Is smitten thence with an unnatural taint,
Loses her just authority, falls beneath

Collateral suspicion, else unknown.   425
This truth escaped me not, and I confess,
That having 'mid my native hills given loose
To a schoolboy's vision, I had raised a pile
Upon the basis of the coming time,
That fell in ruins round me. Oh, what joy   430
To see a sanctuary for our country's youth
Informed with such a spirit as might be
Its own protection; a primeval grove,
Where, though the shades with cheerfulness were filled,
Nor indigent of songs warbled from crowds   435
In under-coverts, yet the countenance
Of the whole place should bear a stamp of awe;
A habitation sober and demure
For ruminating creatures; a domain
For quiet things to wander in; a haunt   440
In which the heron should delight to feed
By the shy rivers, and the pelican
Upon the cypress spire in lonely thought
Might sit and sun himself. — Alas! Alas!
In vain for such solemnity I looked;   445
Mine eyes were crossed by butterflies, ears vexed
By chattering popinjays; the inner heart
Seemed trivial, and the impresses without
Of a too gaudy region.
                                        Different sight
Those venerable Doctors saw of old,   450
When all who dwelt within these famous walls
Led in abstemiousness a studious life;
When, in forlorn and naked chambers cooped
And crowded, o'er the ponderous books they hung
Like caterpillars eating out their way   455
In silence, or with keen devouring noise
Not to be tracked or fathered. Princes then
At matins froze, and couched at curfew-time,
Trained up through piety and zeal to prize
Spare diet, patient labour, and plain weeds.   460
O seat of Arts! renowned throughout the world!
Far different service in those homely days
The Muses' modest nurslings underwent
From their first childhood: in that glorious time
When Learning, like a stranger come from far,   465
Sounding through Christian lands her trumpet, roused
Peasant and king; when boys and youths, the growth
Of ragged villages and crazy huts,
Forsook their homes, and, errant in the quest
Of Patron, famous school or friendly nook,   470
Where, pensioned, they in shelter might sit down,

From town to town and through wide scattered realms
Journeyed with ponderous folios in their hands;
And often, starting from some covert place,
Saluted the chance comer on the road,   475
Crying, "An obolus, a penny give
To a poor scholar!" — when illustrious men,
Lovers of truth, by penury constrained,
Bucer, Erasmus, or Melancthon, read
Before the doors or windows of their cells   480
By moonshine through mere lack of taper light.

But peace to vain regrets! We see but darkly
Even when we look behind us, and best things
Are not so pure by nature that they needs
Must keep to all, as fondly all believe,   485
Their highest promise. If the mariner,
When at reluctant distance he hath passed
Some tempting island, could but know the ills
That must have fallen upon him had he brought
His bark to land upon the wished-for shore,   490
Good cause would oft be his to thank the surf
Whose white belt scared him thence, or wind that blew
Inexorably adverse: for myself
I grieve not; happy is the gownèd youth,
Who only misses what I missed, who falls   495
No lower than I fell.

                            I did not love,
Judging not ill perhaps, the timid course
Of our scholastic studies; could have wished
To see the river flow with ampler range
And freer pace; but more, far more, I grieved   500
To see displayed among an eager few,
Who in the field of contest persevered,
Passions unworthy of youth's generous heart
And mounting spirit, pitiably repaid,
When so disturbed, whatever palms are won.   505
From these I turned to travel with the shoal
Of more unthinking natures, easy minds
And pillowy; yet not wanting love that makes
The day pass lightly on, when foresight sleeps,
And wisdom and the pledges interchanged   510
With our own inner being are forgot.

Yet was this deep vacation not given up
To utter waste. Hitherto I had stood
In my own mind remote from social life,
(At least from what we commonly so name,)   515

Like a lone shepherd on a promontory
Who lacking occupation looks far forth
Into the boundless sea, and rather makes
Than finds what he beholds. And sure it is,
That this first transit from the smooth delights   520
And wild outlandish walks of simple youth
To something that resembles an approach
Towards human business, to a privileged world
Within a world, a midway residence
With all its intervenient imagery,   525
Did better suit my visionary mind,
Far better, than to have been bolted forth,
Thrust out abruptly into Fortune's way
Among the conflicts of substantial life;
By a more just gradation did lead on   530
To higher things; more naturally matured,
For permanent possession, better fruits,
Whether of truth or virtue, to ensue.
In serious mood, but oftener, I confess,
With playful zest of fancy did we note   535
(How could we less?) the manners and the ways
Of those who lived distinguished by the badge
Of good or ill report; or those with whom
By frame of Academic discipline
We were perforce connected, men whose sway   540
And known authority of office served
To set our minds on edge, and did no more.
Nor wanted we rich pastime of this kind,
Found everywhere, but chiefly in the ring
Of the grave Elders, men unscoured, grotesque   545
In character, tricked out like aged trees
Which through the lapse of their infirmity
Give ready place to any random seed
That chooses to be reared upon their trunks.

Here on my view, confronting vividly   550
Those shepherd swains whom I had lately left,
Appeared a different aspect of old age;
How different! yet both distinctly marked,
Objects embossed to catch the general eye,
Or portraitures for special use designed,   555
As some might seem, so aptly do they serve
To illustrate Nature's book of rudiments —
That book upheld as with maternal care
When she would enter on her tender scheme
Of teaching comprehension with delight,   560
And mingling playful with pathetic thoughts.

The surfaces of artificial life
And manners finely wrought, the delicate race
Of colours, lurking, gleaming up and down
Through that state arras woven with silk and gold;   565
This wily interchange of snaky hues,
Willingly or unwillingly revealed,
I neither knew nor cared for; and as such
Were wanting here, I took what might be found
Of less elaborate fabric. At this day   570
I smile, in many a mountain solitude
Conjuring up scenes as obsolete in freaks
Of character, in points of wit as broad,
As aught by wooden images performed
For entertainment of the gaping crowd   575
At wake or fair. And oftentimes do flit
Remembrances before me of old men —
Old humourists, who have been long in their graves,
And having almost in my mind put off
Their human names, have into phantoms passed   580
Of texture midway between life and books.

I play the loiterer: 'tis enough to note
That here in dwarf proportions were expressed
The limbs of the great world; its eager strifes
Collaterally pourtrayed, as in mock fight,   585
A tournament of blows, some hardly dealt
Though short of mortal combat; and whate'er
Might in this pageant be supposed to hit
An artless rustic's notice, this way less,
More that way, was not wasted upon me —   590
And yet the spectacle may well demand
A more substantial name, no mimic show,
Itself a living part of a live whole,
A creek in the vast sea; for, all degrees
And shapes of spurious fame and short-lived praise   595
Here sate in state, and fed 'with daily alms
Retainers won away from solid good;
And here was Labour, his own bond-slave; Hope,
That never set the pains against the prize;
Idleness halting with his weary clog,   600
And poor misguided Shame, and witless Fear,
And simple Pleasure foraging for Death;
Honour misplaced, and Dignity astray;
Feuds, factions, flatteries, enmity, and guile;
Murmuring submission, and bald government,   605
(The idol weak as the idolator,)
And Decency and Custom starving Truth,
And blind Authority beating with his staff

The child that might have led him; Emptiness
Followed as of good omen, and meek Worth   610
Left to herself unheard of and unknown.

   Of these and other kindred notices
I cannot say what portion is in truth
The naked recollection of that time,
And what may rather have been called to life   615
By after-meditation. But delight
That, in an easy temper lulled asleep,
Is still with Innocence its own reward,
This was not wanting. Carelessly I roamed
As through a wide museum from whose stores   620
A casual rarity is singled out
And has its brief perusal, then gives way
To others, all supplanted in their turn;
Till 'mid this crowded neighbourhood of things
That are by nature most unneighbourly,   625
The head turns round and cannot right itself;
And though an aching and a barren sense
Of gay confusion still be uppermost,
With few wise longings and but little love,
Yet to the memory something cleaves at last, ·   630
Whence profit may be drawn in times to come.

   Thus in submissive idleness, my Friend!
The labouring time of autumn, winter, spring,
Eight months! rolled pleasingly away; the ninth
Came and returned me to my native hills.   635

BOOK FOURTH

SUMMER VACATION

BRIGHT was the summer's noon when quickening steps
Followed each other till a dreary moor
Was crossed, a bare ridge clomb, upon whose top
Standing alone, as from a rampart's edge,
I overlooked the bed of Windermere,   5
Like a vast river, stretching in the sun.
With exultation, at my feet I saw
Lake, islands, promontories, gleaming bays,
A universe of Nature's fairest forms
Proudly revealed with instantaneous burst,   10
Magnificent, and beautiful, and gay.
I bounded down the hill shouting amain

For the old Ferryman; to the shout the rocks
Replied, and when the Charon of the flood
Had staid his oars, and touched the jutting pier,   15
I did not step into the well-known boat
Without a cordial greeting. Thence with speed
Up the familiar hill I took my way
Towards that sweet Valley where I had been reared;
'Twas but a short hour's walk, ere veering round   20
I saw the snow-white church upon her hill
Sit like a thronèd Lady, sending out
A gracious look all over her domain.
Yon azure smoke betrays the lurking town;
With eager footsteps I advance and reach   25
The cottage threshold where my journey closed.
Glad welcome had I, with some tears, perhaps,
From my old Dame, so kind and motherly,
While she perused me with a parent's pride.
The thoughts of gratitude shall fall like dew   30
Upon thy grave, good creature! While my heart
Can beat never will I forget thy name.
Heaven's blessing be upon thee where thou liest
After thy innocent and busy stir
In narrow cares, thy little daily growth   35
Of calm enjoyments, after eighty years,
And more than eighty, of untroubled life,
Childless, yet by the strangers to thy blood
Honoured with little less than filial love.
What joy was mine to see thee once again,   40
Thee and thy dwelling, and a crowd of things
About its narrow precincts all beloved,
And many of them seeming yet my own!
Why should I speak of what a thousand hearts
Have felt, and every man alive can guess?   45
The rooms, the court, the garden were not left
Long unsaluted, nor the sunny seat
Round the stone table under the dark pine,
Friendly to studious or to festive hours;
Nor that unruly child of mountain birth,   50
The froward brook, who, soon as he was boxed
Within our garden, found himself at once,
As if by trick insidious and unkind,
Stripped of his voice and left to dimple down
(Without an effort and without a will)   55
A channel paved by man's officious care.
I looked at him and smiled, and smiled again,
And in the press of twenty thousand thoughts,
"Ha," quoth I, "pretty prisoner, are you there!"
Well might sarcastic Fancy then have whispered,   60

"An emblem here behold of thy own life;
In its late course of even days with all
Their smooth enthralment;" but the heart was full,
Too full for that reproach. My aged Dame
Walked proudly at my side: she guided me;   65
I willing, nay — nay, wishing to be led.
— The face of every neighbour whom I met
Was like a volume to me; some were hailed
Upon the road, some busy at their work,
Unceremonious greetings interchanged   70
With half the length of a long field between.
Among my schoolfellows I scattered round
Like recognitions, but with some constraint
Attended, doubtless, with a little pride,
But with more shame, for my habiliments,   75
The transformation wrought by gay attire.
Not less delighted did I take my place
At our domestic table: and, dear Friend!
In this endeavour simply to relate
A Poet's history, may I leave untold   80
The thankfulness with which I laid me down
In my accustomed bed, more welcome now
Perhaps than if it had been more desired
Or been more often thought of with regret;
That lowly bed whence I had heard the wind   85
Roar and the rain beat hard, where I so oft
Had lain awake on summer nights to watch
The moon in splendour couched among the leaves
Of a tall ash, that near our cottage stood;
Had watched her with fixed eyes while to and fro   90
In the dark summit of the waving tree
She rocked with every impulse of the breeze.

    Among the favourites whom it pleased me well
To see again, was one by ancient right
Our inmate, a rough terrier of the hills;   95
By birth and call of nature pre-ordained
To hunt the badger and unearth the fox
Among the impervious crags, but having been
From youth our own adopted, he had passed
Into a gentler service. And when first   100
The boyish spirit flagged, and day by day
Along my veins I kindled with the stir,
The fermentation, and the vernal heat
Of poesy, affecting private shades
Like a sick Lover, then this dog was used   105
To watch me, an attendant and a friend,
Obsequious to my steps early and late,

Though often of such dilatory walk
Tired, and uneasy at the halts I made.
A hundred times when, roving high and low, 110
I have been harassed with the toil of verse,
Much pains and little progress, and at once
Some lovely Image in the song rose up
Full-formed, like Venus rising from the sea;
Then have I darted forwards to let loose 115
My hand upon his back with stormy joy,
Caressing him again and yet again.
And when at evening on the public way
I sauntered, like a river murmuring
And talking to itself when all things else 120
Are still, the creature trotted on before;
Such was his custom; but whene'er he met
A passenger approaching, he would turn
To give me timely notice, and straightway,
Grateful for that admonishment, I hushed 125
My voice, composed my gait, and, with the air
And mien of one whose thoughts are free, advanced
To give and take a greeting that might save
My name from piteous rumours, such as wait
On men suspected to be crazed in brain. 130

Those walks well worthy to be prized and loved —
Regretted! — that word, too, was on my tongue,
But they were richly laden with all good,
And cannot be remembered but with thanks
And gratitude, and perfect joy of heart — 135
Those walks in all their freshness now came back
Like a returning Spring. When first I made
Once more the circuit of our little lake,
If ever happiness hath lodged with man,
That day consummate happiness was mine, 140
Wide-spreading, steady, calm, contemplative.
The sun was set, or setting, when I left
Our cottage door, and evening soon brought on
A sober hour, not winning or serene,
For cold and raw the air was, and untuned: 145
But as a face we love is sweetest then
When sorrow damps it, or, whatever look
It chance to wear, is sweetest if the heart
Have fulness in herself; even so with me
It fared that evening. Gently did my soul 150
Put off her veil, and, self-transmuted, stood
Naked, as in the presence of her God.
While on I walked, a comfort seemed to touch
A heart that had not been disconsolate:

Strength came where weakness was not known to be,   155
At least not felt; and restoration came
Like an intruder knocking at the door
Of unacknowledged weariness. I took
The balance, and with firm hand weighed myself.
— Of that external scene which round me lay,   160
Little, in this abstraction, did I see;
Remembered less; but I had inward hopes
And swellings of the spirit, was rapt and soothed,
Conversed with promises, had glimmering views
How life pervades the undecaying mind;   165
How the immortal soul with God-like power
Informs, creates, and thaws the deepest sleep
That time can lay upon her; how on earth,
Man, if he do but live within the light
Of high endeavours, daily spreads abroad   170
His being armed with strength that cannot fail.
Nor was there want of milder thoughts, of love,
Of innocence, and holiday repose;
And more than pastoral quiet, 'mid the stir
Of boldest projects, and a peaceful end   175
At last, or glorious, by endurance won.
Thus musing, in a wood I sate me down
Alone, continuing there to muse: the slopes
And heights meanwhile were slowly overspread
With darkness, and before a rippling breeze   180
The long lake lengthened out its hoary line,
And in the sheltered coppice where I sate,
Around me from among the hazel leaves,
Now here, now there, moved by the straggling wind,
Came ever and anon a breath-like sound,   185
Quick as the pantings of the faithful dog,
The off and on companion of my walk;
And such, at times, believing them to be,
I turned my head to look if he were there;
Then into solemn thought I passed once more.   190

    A freshness also found I at this time
In human Life, the daily life of those
Whose occupations really I loved;
The peaceful scene oft filled me with surprise,
Changed like a garden in the heat of spring   195
After an eight-days' absence. For (to omit
The things which were the same and yet appeared
Far otherwise) amid this rural solitude,
A narrow Vale where each was known to all,
'Twas not indifferent to a youthful mind   200
To mark some sheltering bower or sunny nook,

Where an old man had used to sit alone,
Now vacant; pale-faced babes whom I had left
In arms, now rosy prattlers at the feet
Of a pleased grandame tottering up and down;   205
And growing girls whose beauty, filched away
With all its pleasant promises, was gone
To deck some slighted playmate's homely cheek.

　　Yes, I had something of a subtler sense,
And often looking round was moved to smiles   210
Such as a delicate work of humour breeds;
I read, without design, the opinions, thoughts,
Of those plain-living people now observed
With clearer knowledge; with another eye
I saw the quiet woodman in the woods,   215
The shepherd roam the hills. With new delight,
This chiefly, did I note my grey-haired Dame;
Saw her go forth to church or other work
Of state, equipped in monumental trim;
Short velvet cloak, (her bonnet of the like),   220
A mantle such as Spanish Cavaliers
Wore in old time. Her smooth domestic life,
Affectionate without disquietude,
Her talk, her business, pleased me; and no less
Her clear though shallow stream of piety   225
That ran on Sabbath days a fresher course;
With thoughts unfelt till now I saw her read
Her Bible on hot Sunday afternoons,
And loved the book, when she had dropped asleep
And made of it a pillow for her head.   230

　　Nor less do I remember to have felt,
Distinctly manifested at this time,
A human-heartedness about my love
For objects hitherto the absolute wealth
Of my own private being and no more: 235
Which I had loved, even as a blessed spirit
Or Angel, if he were to dwell on earth,
Might love in individual happiness.
But now there opened on me other thoughts,
Of change, congratulation or regret,   240
A pensive feeling! It spread far and wide;
The trees, the mountains shared it, and the brooks,
The stars of Heaven, now seen in their old haunts —
White Sirius glittering o'er the southern crags,
Orion with his belt, and those fair Seven,   245
Acquaintances of every little child,
And Jupiter, my own beloved star!

Whatever shadings of mortality,
Whatever imports from the world of death
Had come among these objects heretofore,   250
Were, in the main, of mood less tender: strong,
Deep, gloomy were they, and severe; the scatterings
Of awe or tremulous dread, that had given way
In later youth to yearnings of a love
Enthusiastic, to delight and hope.   255

    As one who hangs down-bending from the side
Of a slow-moving boat, upon the breast
Of a still water, solacing himself
With such discoveries as his eye can make
Beneath him in the bottom of the deep,   260
Sees many beauteous sights — weeds, fishes, flowers,
Grots, pebbles, roots of trees, and fancies more,
Yet often is perplexed and cannot part
The shadow from the substance, rocks and sky,
Mountains and clouds, reflected in the depth   265
Of the clear flood, from things which there abide
In their true dwelling; now is crossed by gleam
Of his own image, by a sun-beam now,
And wavering motions sent he knows not whence,
Impediments that make his task more sweet;   270
Such pleasant office have we long pursued
Incumbent o'er the surface of past time
With like success, nor often have appeared
Shapes fairer or less doubtfully discerned
Than these to which the Tale, indulgent Friend!   275
Would now direct thy notice. Yet in spite
Of pleasure won, and knowledge not withheld,
There was an inner falling off — I loved,
Loved deeply all that had been loved before,
More deeply even than ever: but a swarm   280
Of heady schemes jostling each other, gawds,
And feast and dance, and public revelry,
And sports and games (too grateful in themselves,
Yet in themselves less grateful, I believe,
Than as they were a badge glossy and fresh   285
Of manliness and freedom) all conspired
To lure my mind from firm habitual quest
Of feeding pleasures, to depress the zeal
And damp those daily yearnings which had once been mine —
A wild, unworldly-minded youth, given up   290
To his own eager thoughts. It would demand
Some skill, and longer time than may be spared,
To paint these vanities, and how they wrought
In haunts where they, till now, had been unknown.

It seemed the very garments that I wore   295
Preyed on my strength, and stopped the quiet stream
Of self-forgetfulness.
                                    Yes, that heartless chase
Of trivial pleasures was a poor exchange
For books and nature at that early age.
'Tis true, some casual knowledge might be gained   300
Of character or life; but at that time,
Of manners put to school I took small note,
And all my deeper passions lay elsewhere.
Far better had it been to exalt the mind
By solitary study, to uphold   305
Intense desire through meditative peace;
And yet, for chastisement of these regrets,
The memory of one particular hour
Doth here rise up against me. 'Mid a throng
Of maids and youths, old men, and matrons staid,   310
A medley of all tempers, I had passed
The night in dancing, gaiety, and mirth,
With din of instruments and shuffling feet,
And glancing forms, and tapers glittering,
And unaimed prattle flying up and down;   315
Spirits upon the stretch, and here and there
Slight shocks of young love-liking interspersed,
Whose transient pleasure mounted to the head,
And tingled through the veins. Ere we retired,
The cock had crowed, and now the eastern sky   320
Was kindling, not unseen, from humble copse
And open field, through which the pathway wound,
And homeward led my steps. Magnificent
The morning rose, in memorable pomp,
Glorious as e'er I had beheld — in front,   325
The sea lay laughing at a distance; near,
The solid mountains shone, bright as the clouds,
Grain-tinctured, drenched in empyrean light;
And in the meadows and the lower grounds
Was all the sweetness of a common dawn —   330
Dews, vapours, and the melody of birds,
And labourers going forth to till the fields.
Ah! need I say, dear Friend! that to the brim
My heart was full; I made no vows, but vows
Were then made for me; bond unknown to me   335
Was given, that I should be, else sinning greatly,
A dedicated Spirit. On I walked
In thankful blessedness, which yet survives.

    Strange rendezvous my mind was at that time,
A parti-coloured show of grave and gay,   340

Solid and light, short-sighted and profound;
Of inconsiderate habits and sedate,
Consorting in one mansion unreproved.
The worth I knew of powers that I possessed,
Though slighted and too oft misused. Besides,   345
That summer, swarming as it did with thoughts
Transient and idle, lacked not intervals
When Folly from the frown of fleeting Time
Shrunk, and the mind experienced in herself
Conformity as just as that of old   350
To the end and written spirit of God's works,
Whether held forth in Nature or in Man,
Through pregnant vision, separate or conjoined.

    When from our better selves we have too long
Been parted by the hurrying world, and droop,   355
Sick of its business, of its pleasures tired,
How gracious, how benign, is Solitude;
How potent a mere image of her sway;
Most potent when impressed upon the mind
With an appropriate human centre — hermit,   360
Deep in the bosom of the wilderness;
Votary (in vast cathèdral, where no foot
Is treading, where no other face is seen)
Kneeling at prayers; or watchman on the top
Of lighthouse, beaten by Atlantic waves;   365
Or as the soul of that great Power is met
Sometimes embodied on a public road,
When, for the night deserted, it assumes
A character of quiet more profound
Than pathless wastes.
                    Once, when those summer months 370
Were flown, and autumn brought its annual show
Of oars with oars contending, sails with sails,
Upon Winander's spacious breast, it chanced
That — after I had left a flower-decked room
(Whose in-door pastime, lighted up, survived   375
To a late hour), and spirits overwrought
Were making night do penance for a day
Spent in a round of strenuous idleness —
My homeward course led up a long ascent,
Where the road's watery surface, to the top   380
Of that sharp rising, glittered to the moon
And bore the semblance of another stream
Stealing with silent lapse to join the brook
That murmured in the vale. All else was still;
No living thing appeared in earth or air,   385
And, save the flowing water's peaceful voice,

Sound there was none — but, lo! an uncouth shape,
Shown by a sudden turning of the road,
So near that, slipping back into the shade
Of a thick hawthorn, I could mark him well,   390
Myself unseen. He was of stature tall,
A span above man's common measure, tall,
Stiff, lank, and upright; a more meagre man
Was never seen before by night or day.
Long were his arms, pallid his hands; his mouth   395
Looked ghastly in the moonlight: from behind,
A mile-stone propped him; I could also ken
That he was clothed in military garb,
Though faded, yet entire. Companionless,
No dog attending, by no staff sustained,   400
He stood, and in his very dress appeared
A desolation, a simplicity,
To which the trappings of a gaudy world
Make a strange back-ground. From his lips, ere long,
Issued low muttered sounds, as if of pain   405
Or some uneasy thought; yet still his form
Kept the same awful steadiness — at his feet
His shadow lay, and moved not. From self-blame
Not wholly free, I watched him thus; at length
Subduing my heart's specious cowardice,   410
I left the shady nook where I had stood
And hailed him. Slowly from his resting-place
He rose, and with a lean and wasted arm
In measured gesture lifted to his head
Returned my salutation; then resumed   415
His station as before; and when I asked
His history, the veteran, in reply,
Was neither slow nor eager; but, unmoved,
And with a quiet uncomplaining voice,
A stately air of mild indifference,   420
He told in few plain words a soldier's tale —
That in the Tropic Islands he had served,
Whence he had landed scarcely three weeks past;
That on his landing he had been dismissed,
And now was travelling towards his native home.   425
This heard, I said, in pity, "Come with me."
He stooped, and straightway from the ground took up
An oaken staff by me yet unobserved —
A staff which must have dropt from his slack hand
And lay till now neglected in the grass.   430
Though weak his step and cautious, he appeared
To travel without pain, and I beheld,
With an astonishment but ill suppressed,
His ghastly figure moving at my side;

Nor could I, while we journeyed thus, forbear   435
To turn from present hardships to the past,
And speak of war, battle, and pestilence,
Sprinkling this talk with questions, better spared,
On what he might himself have seen or felt.
He all the while was in demeanour calm,   440
Concise in answer; solemn and sublime
He might have seemed, but that in all he said
There was a strange half-absence, as of one
Knowing too well the importance of his theme,
But feeling it no longer. Our discourse   445
Soon ended, and together on we passed
In silence through a wood gloomy and still.
Up-turning, then, along an open field,
We reached a cottage. At the door I knocked,
And earnestly to charitable care   450
Commended him as a poor friendless man,
Belated and by sickness overcome.
Assured that now the traveller would repose
In comfort, I entreated that henceforth
He would not linger in the public ways,   455
But ask for timely furtherance and help
Such as his state required. At this reproof,
With the same ghastly mildness in his look,
He said, "My trust is in the God of Heaven,
And in the eye of him who passes me!"   460

   The cottage door was speedily unbarred,
And now the soldier touched his hat once more
With his lean hand, and in a faltering voice,
Whose tone bespake reviving interests
Till then unfelt, he thanked me; I returned   465
The farewell blessing of the patient man,
And so we parted. Back I cast a look,
And lingered near the door a little space,
Then sought with quiet heart my distant home.

BOOK FIFTH

BOOKS

WHEN Contemplation, like the night-calm felt
Through earth and sky, spreads widely, and sends deep
Into the soul its tranquillising power,
Even then I sometimes grieve for thee, O Man,
Earth's paramount Creature! not so much for woes   5
That thou endurest; heavy though that weight be,

Cloud-like it mounts, or touched with light divine
Doth melt away; but for those palms achieved,
Through length of time, by patient exercise
Of study and hard thought; there, there, it is   10
That sadness finds its fuel. Hitherto,
In progress through this Verse, my mind hath looked
Upon the speaking face of earth and heaven
As her prime teacher, intercourse with man
Established by the sovereign Intellect,   15
Who through that bodily image hath diffused,
As might appear to the eye of fleeting time,
A deathless spirit. Thou also, man! hast wrought,
For commerce of thy nature with herself,
Things that aspire to unconquerable life;   20
And yet we feel — we cannot choose but feel —
That they must perish. Tremblings of the heart
It gives, to think that our immortal being
No more shall need such garments; and yet man,
As long as he shall be the child of earth,   25
Might almost "weep to have" what he may lose,
Nor be himself extinguished, but survive,
Abject, depressed, forlorn, disconsolate.
A thought is with me sometimes, and I say, —
Should the whole frame of earth by inward throes   30
Be wrenched, or fire come down from far to scorch
Her pleasant habitations, and dry up
Old Ocean, in his bed left singed and bare,
Yet would the living Presence still subsist
Victorious, and composure would ensue,   35
And kindlings like the morning — presage sure
Of day returning and of life revived.
But all the meditations of mankind,
Yea, all the adamantine holds of truth
By reason built, or passion, which itself   40
Is highest reason in a soul sublime;
The consecrated works of Bard and Sage,
Sensuous or intellectual, wrought by men,
Twin labourers and heirs of the same hopes;
Where would they be? Oh! why hath not the Mind   45
Some element to stamp her image on
In nature somewhat nearer to her own?
Why, gifted with such powers to send abroad
Her spirit, must it lodge in shrines so frail?

One day, when from my lips a like complaint   50
Had fallen in presence of a studious friend,
He with a smile made answer, that in truth

'Twas going far to seek disquietude;
But on the front of his reproof confessed
That he himself had oftentimes given way   55
To kindred hauntings. Whereupon I told,
That once in the stillness of a summer's noon,
While I was seated in a rocky cave
By the sea-side, perusing, so it chanced,
The famous history of the errant knight   60
Recorded by Cervantes, these same thoughts
Beset me, and to height unusual rose,
While listlessly I sate, and, having closed
The book, had turned my eyes toward the wide sea.
On poetry and geometric truth,   65
And their high privilege of lasting life,
From all internal injury exempt,
I mused, upon these chiefly: and at length,
My senses yielding to the sultry air,
Sleep seized me, and I passed into a dream.   70
I saw before me stretched a boundless plain
Of sandy wilderness, all black and void,
And as I looked around, distress and fear
Came creeping over me, when at my side,
Close at my side, an uncouth shape appeared   75
Upon a dromedary, mounted high.
He seemed an Arab of the Bedouin tribes:
A lance he bore, and underneath one arm
A stone, and in the opposite hand a shell
Of a surpassing brightness. At the sight   80
Much I rejoiced, not doubting but a guide
Was present, one who with unerring skill
Would through the desert lead me; and while yet
I looked and looked, self-questioned what this freight
Which the new-comer carried through the waste   85
Could mean, the Arab told me that the stone
(To give it in the language of the dream)
Was "Euclid's Elements;" and "This," said he,
"Is something of more worth;" and at the word
Stretched forth the shell, so beautiful in shape,   90
In colour so resplendent, with command
That I should hold it to my ear. I did so,
And heard that instant in an unknown tongue,
Which yet I understood, articulate sounds,
A loud prophetic blast of harmony;   95
An Ode, in passion uttered, which foretold
Destruction to the children of the earth
By deluge, now at hand. No sooner ceased
The song, than the Arab with calm look declared

That all would come to pass of which the voice 100
Had given forewarning, and that he himself
Was going then to bury those two books:
The one that held acquaintance with the stars,
And wedded soul to soul in purest bond
Of reason, undisturbed by space or time; 105
The other that was a god, yea many gods,
Had voices more than all the winds, with power
To exhilarate the spirit, and to soothe,
Through every clime, the heart of human kind.
While this was uttering, strange as it may seem, 110
I wondered not, although I plainly saw
The one to be a stone, the other a shell;
Nor doubted once but that they both were books,
Having a perfect faith in all that passed.
Far stronger, now, grew the desire I felt 115
To cleave unto this man; but when I prayed
To share his enterprise, he hurried on
Reckless of me: I followed, not unseen,
For oftentimes he cast a backward look,
Grasping his twofold treasure. — Lance in rest, 120
He rode, I keeping pace with him; and now
He, to my fancy, had become the knight
Whose tale Cervantes tells; yet not the knight,
But was an Arab of the desert too;
Of these was neither, and was both at once. 125
His countenance, meanwhile, grew more disturbed;
And, looking backwards when he looked, mine eyes
Saw, over half the wilderness diffused,
A bed of glittering light: I asked the cause:
"It is," said he, "the waters of the deep 130
Gathering upon us;" quickening then the pace
Of the unwieldly creature he bestrode,
He left me: I called after him aloud;
He heeded not; but, with his twofold charge
Still in his grasp, before me, full in view, 135
Went hurrying o'er the illimitable waste,
With the fleet waters of a drowning world
In chase of him; whereat I waked in terror,
And saw the sea before me, and the book,
In which I had been reading, at my side. 140

Full often, taking from the world of sleep
This Arab phantom, which I thus beheld,
This semi-Quixote, I to him have given
A substance, fancied him a living man,
A gentle dweller in the desert. crazed 145

By love and feeling, and internal thought
Protracted among endless solitudes;
Have shaped him wandering upon this quest!
Nor have I pitied him; but rather felt
Reverence was due to a being thus employed;   150
And thought that, in the blind and awful lair
Of such a madness, reason did lie couched.
Enow there are on earth to take in charge
Their wives, their children, and their virgin loves,
Or whatsoever else the heart holds dear;   155
Enow to stir for these; yea, will I say,
Contemplating in soberness the approach
Of an event so dire, by signs in earth
Or heaven made manifest, that I could share
That maniac's fond anxiety, and go   160
Upon like errand. Oftentimes at least
Me hath such strong entrancement overcome,
When I have held a volume in my hand,
Poor earthly casket of immortal verse,
Shakespeare, or Milton, labourers divine!   165

   Great and benign, indeed, must be the power
Of living nature, which could thus so long
Detain me from the best of other guides
And dearest helpers, left unthanked, unpraised.
Even in the time of lisping infancy,   170
And later down, in prattling childhood, even
While I was travelling back among those days,
How could I ever play an ingrate's part?
Once more should I have made those bowers resound,
By intermingling strains of thankfulness   175
With their own thoughtless melodies; at least
It might have well beseemed me to repeat
Some simply fashioned tale, to tell again,
In slender accents of sweet verse, some tale
That did bewitch me then, and soothes me now.   180
O Friend! O Poet! brother of my soul,
Think not that I could pass along untouched
By these remembrances. Yet wherefore speak?
Why call upon a few weak words to say
What is already written in the hearts   185
Of all that breathe? — what in the path of all
Drops daily from the tongue of every child,
Wherever man is found? The trickling tear
Upon the cheek of listening Infancy
Proclaims it, and the insuperable look   190
That drinks as if it never could be full.

That portion of my story I shall leave
There registered: whatever else of power
Or pleasure, sown or fostered thus, may be
Peculiar to myself, let that remain   195
Where still it works, though hidden from all search
Among the depths of time. Yet is it just
That here, in memory of all books which lay
Their sure foundations in the heart of man,
Whether by native prose, or numerous verse,   200
That in the name of all inspirèd souls,
From Homer the great Thunderer, from the voice
That roars along the bed of Jewish song,
And that more varied and elaborate,
Those trumpet-tones of harmony that shake   205
Our shores in England, — from those loftiest notes
Down to the low and wren-like warblings, made
For cottagers and spinners at the wheel,
And sun-burnt travellers resting their tired limbs,
Stretched under wayside hedge-rows, ballad tunes,   210
Food for the hungry ears of little ones,
And of old men who have survived their joys:
'Tis just that in behalf of these, the works,
And of the men that framed them, whether known,
Or sleeping nameless in their scattered graves,   215
That I should here assert their rights, attest
Their honours, and should, once for all, pronounce
Their benediction; speak of them as Powers
For ever to be hallowed; only less,
For what we are and what we may become,   220
Than Nature's self, which is the breath of God,
Or His pure Word by miracle revealed.

    Rarely and with reluctance would I stoop
To transitory themes; yet I rejoice,
And, by these thoughts admonished, will pour out   225
Thanks with uplifted heart, that I was reared
Safe from an evil which these days have laid
Upon the children of the land, a pest
That might have dried me up, body and soul.
This verse is dedicate to Nature's self,   230
And things that teach as Nature teaches: then,
Oh! where had been the Man, the Poet where,
Where had we been, we two, beloved Friend!
If in the season of unperilous choice,
In lieu of wandering, as we did, through vales   235
Rich with indigenous produce, open ground
Of Fancy, happy pastures ranged at will,

We had been followed, hourly watched, and noosed,
Each in his several melancholy walk
Stringed like a poor man's heifer at its feed,   240
Led through the lanes in forlorn servitude;
Or rather like a stallèd ox debarred
From touch of growing grass, that may not taste
A flower till it have yielded up its sweets
A prelibation to the mower's scythe.   245

   Behold the parent hen amid her brood,
Though fledged and feathered, and well pleased to part
And straggle from her presence, still a brood,
And she herself from the maternal bond
Still undischarged; yet doth she little more   250
Than move with them in tenderness and love,
A centre to the circle which they make;
And now and then, alike from need of theirs
And call of her own natural appetites,
She scratches, ransacks up the earth for food,   255
Which they partake at pleasure. Early died
My honoured Mother, she who was the heart
And hinge of all our learnings and our loves:
She left us destitute, and, as we might,
Trooping together. Little suits it me   260
To break upon the sabbath of her rest
With any thought that looks at others' blame;
Nor would I praise her but in perfect love.
Hence am I checked: but let me boldly say,
In gratitude, and for the sake of truth,   265
Unheard by her, that she, not falsely taught,
Fetching her goodness rather from times past,
Than shaping novelties for times to come,
Had no presumption, no such jealousy,
Nor did by habit of her thoughts mistrust   270
Our nature, but had virtual faith that He
Who fills the mother's breast with innocent milk,
Doth also for our nobler part provide,
Under His great correction and control,
As innocent instincts, and as innocent food;   275
Or draws for minds that are left free to trust
In the simplicities of opening life
Sweet honey out of spurned or dreaded weeds.
This was her creed, and therefore she was pure
From anxious fear of error or mishap,   280
And evil, overweeningly so called;
Was not puffed up by false unnatural hopes,
Nor selfish with unnecessary cares,

Nor with impatience from the season asked
More than its timely produce; rather loved   285
The hours for what they are, than from regard
Glanced on their promises in restless pride.
Such was she — not from faculties more strong
Than others have, but from the times, perhaps,
And spot in which she lived, and through a grace   290
Of modest meekness, simple-mindedness,
A heart that found benignity and hope,
Being itself benign.

              My drift I fear
Is scarcely obvious; but, that common sense
May try this modern system by its fruits,   295
Leave let me take to place before her sight
A specimen pourtrayed with faithful hand.
Full early trained to worship seemliness,
This model of a child is never known
To mix in quarrels; that were far beneath   300
Its dignity; with gifts he bubbles o'er
As generous as a fountain; selfishness
May not come near him, nor the little throng
Of flitting pleasures tempt him from his path;
The wandering beggars propagate his name,   305
Dumb creatures find him tender as a nun,
And natural or supernatural fear,
Unless it leap upon him in a dream,
Touches him not. To enhance the wonder, see
How arch his notices, how nice his sense   310
Of the ridiculous; not blind is he
To the broad follies of the licensed world,
Yet innocent himself withal, though shrewd,
And can read lectures upon innocence;
A miracle of scientific lore,   315
Ships he can guide across the pathless sea,
And tell you all their cunning; he can read
The inside of the earth, and spell the stars;
He knows the policies of foreign lands;
Can string you names of districts, cities, towns,   320
The whole world over, tight as beads of dew
Upon a gossamer thread; he sifts, he weighs;
All things are put to question; he must live
Knowing that he grows wiser every day
Or else not live at all, and seeing too   325
Each little drop of wisdom as it falls
Into the dimpling cistern of his heart:
For this unnatural growth the trainer blame,
Pity the tree. — Poor human vanity,

Wert thou extinguished, little would be left   330
Which he could truly love; but how escape?
For, ever as a thought of purer birth
Rises to lead him toward a better clime,
Some intermeddler still is on the watch
To drive him back, and pound him, like a stray,   335
Within the pinfold of his own conceit.
Meanwhile old grandame earth is grieved to find
The playthings, which her love designed for him,
Unthought of: in their woodland beds the flowers
Weep, and the river sides are all forlorn.   340
Oh! give us once again the wishing cap
Of Fortunatus, and the invisible coat
Of Jack the Giant-killer, Robin Hood,
And Sabra in the forest with St. George!
The child, whose love is here, at least, doth reap   345
One precious gain, that he forgets himself.

    These mighty workmen of our later age,
Who, with a broad highway, have overbridged
The froward chaos of futurity,
Tamed to their bidding; they who have the skill   350
To manage books, and things, and make them act
On infant minds as surely as the sun
Deals with a flower; the keepers of our time,
The guides and wardens of our faculties,
Sages who in their prescience would control   355
All accidents, and to the very road
Which they have fashioned would confine us down,
Like engines; when will their presumption learn,
That in the unreasoning progress of the world
A wiser spirit is at work for us,   360
A better eye than theirs, most prodigal
Of blessings, and most studious of our good,
Even in what seem our most unfruitful hours?

    There was a Boy: ye knew him well, ye cliffs
And islands of Winander! — many a time   365
At evening, when the earliest stars began
To move along the edges of the hills,
Rising or setting, would he stand alone
Beneath the trees or by the glimmering lake,
And there, with fingers interwoven, both hands   370
Pressed closely palm to palm, and to his mouth
Uplifted, he, as through an instrument,
Blew mimic hootings to the silent owls,
That they might answer him; and they would shout

Across the watery vale, and shout again, 375
Responsive to his call, with quivering peals,
And long halloos and screams, and echoes loud,
Redoubled and redoubled, concourse wild
Of jocund din; and, when a lengthened pause
Of silence came and baffled his best skill, 380
Then sometimes, in that silence while he hung
Listening, a gentle shock of mild surprise
Has carried far into his heart the voice
Of mountain torrents; or the visible scene
Would enter unawares into his mind, 385
With all its solemn imagery, its rocks,
Its woods, and that uncertain heaven, received
Into the bosom of the steady lake.

This Boy was taken from his mates, and died
In childhood, ere he was full twelve years old. 390
Fair is the spot, most beautiful the vale
Where he was born; the grassy churchyard hangs
Upon a slope above the village school,
And through that churchyard when my way has led
On summer evenings, I believe that there 395
A long half hour together I have stood
Mute, looking at the grave in which he lies!
Even now appears before the mind's clear eye
That self-same village church; I see her sit
(The thronèd Lady whom erewhile we hailed) 400
On her green hill, forgetful of this Boy
Who slumbers at her feet, — forgetful, too,
Of all her silent neighbourhood of graves,
And listening only to the gladsome sounds
That, from the rural school ascending, play 405
Beneath her and about her. May she long
Behold a race of young ones like to those
With whom I herded! — (easily, indeed,
We might have fed upon a fatter soil
Of arts and letters — but be that forgiven) — 410
A race of real children; not too wise,
Too learned, or too good; but wanton, fresh,
And bandied up and down by love and hate;
Not unresentful where self-justified;
Fierce, moody, patient, venturous, modest, shy; 415
Mad at their sports like withered leaves in winds;
Though doing wrong and suffering, and full oft
Bending beneath our life's mysterious weight
Of pain, and doubt, and fear, yet yielding not
In happiness to the happiest upon earth. 420

Simplicity in habit, truth in speech,
Be these the daily strengtheners of their minds;
May books and Nature be their early joy!
And knowledge, rightly honoured with that name —
Knowledge not purchased by the loss of power!   425

   Well do I call to mind the very week
When I was first intrusted to the care
Of that sweet Valley; when its paths, its shores,
And brooks were like a dream of novelty
To my half-infant thoughts; that very week,   430
While I was roving up and down alone,
Seeking I knew not what, I chanced to cross
One of those open fields, which, shaped like ears,
Make green peninsulas on Esthwaite's Lake:
Twilight was coming on, yet through the gloom   435
Appeared distinctly on the opposite shore
A heap of garments, as if left by one
Who might have there been bathing. Long I watched,
But no one owned them; meanwhile the calm lake
Grew dark with all the shadows on its breast,   440
And, now and then, a fish up-leaping snapped
The breathless stillness. The succeeding day,
Those unclaimed garments telling a plain tale
Drew to the spot an anxious crowd; some looked
In passive expectation from the shore,   445
While from a boat others hung o'er the deep,
Sounding with grappling irons and long poles.
At last, the dead man, 'mid that beauteous scene
Of trees and hills and water, bolt upright
Rose, with his ghastly face, a spectre shape   450
Of terror; yet no soul-debasing fear,
Young as I was, a child not nine years old,
Possessed me, for my inner eye had seen
Such sights before, among the shining streams
Of faëry land, the forest of romance.   455
Their spirit hallowed the sad spectacle
With decoration of ideal grace;
A dignity, a smoothness, like the works
Of Grecian art, and purest poesy.

   A precious treasure had I long possessed,   460
A little yellow, canvas-covered book,
A slender abstract of the Arabian tales;
And, from companions in a new abode,
When first I learnt, that this dear prize of mine
Was but a block hewn from a mighty quarry —   465

That there were four large volumes, laden all
With kindred matter, 'twas to me, in truth,
A promise scarcely earthly. Instantly,
With one not richer than myself, I made
A covenant that each should lay aside   470
The moneys he possessed, and hoard up more,
Till our joint savings had amassed enough
To make this book our own. Through several months,
In spite of all temptation, we preserved
Religiously that vow; but firmness failed,   475
Nor were we ever masters of our wish.

    And when thereafter to my father's house
The holidays returned me, there to find
That golden store of books which I had left,
What joy was mine! How often in the course   480
Of those glad respites, though a soft west wind
Ruffled the waters to the angler's wish
For a whole day together, have I lain
Down by thy side, O Derwent! murmuring stream,
On the hot stones, and in the glaring sun,   485
And there have read, devouring as I read,
Defrauding the day's glory, desperate!
Till with a sudden bound of smart reproach,
Such as an idler deals with in his shame,
I to the sport betook myself again.   490

    A gracious spirit o'er this earth presides,
And o'er the heart of man: invisibly
It comes, to works of unreproved delight,
And tendency benign, directing those
Who care not, know not, think not what they do.   495
The tales that charm away the wakeful night
In Araby; romances; legends penned
For solace by dim light of monkish lamps;
Fictions, for ladies of their love, devised
By youthful squires; adventures endless, spun   500
By the dismantled warrior in old age,
Out of the bowels of those very schemes
In which his youth did first extravagate;
These spread like day, and something in the shape
Of these will live till man shall be no more.   505
Dumb yearnings, hidden appetites, are ours,
And *they must* have their food. Our childhood sits,
Our simple childhood, sits upon a throne
That hath more power than all the elements.
I guess not what this tells of Being past.   510

Nor what it augurs of the life to come;
But so it is, and, in that dubious hour,
That twilight when we first begin to see
This dawning earth, to recognise, expect,
And in the long probation that ensues,   515
The time of trial, ere we learn to live
In reconcilement with our stinted powers;
To endure this state of meagre vassalage,
Unwilling to forego, confess, submit,
Uneasy and unsettled, yoke-fellows   520
To custom, mettlesome, and not yet tamed
And humbled down; oh! then we feel, we feel,
We know where we have friends. Ye dreamers, then,
Forgers of daring tales! we bless you then,
Impostors, drivellers, dotards, as the ape   525
Philosophy will call you: *then* we feel
With what, and how great might ye are in league,
Who make our wish our power, our thought a deed,
An empire, a possession, — ye whom time
And seasons serve; all Faculties; to whom   530
Earth crouches, the elements are potter's clay,
Space like a heaven filled up with northern lights,
Here, nowhere, there, and everywhere at once.

    Relinquishing this lofty eminence
For ground, though humbler, not the less a tract   535
Of the same isthmus, which our spirits cross
In progress from their native continent
To earth and human life, the Song might dwell
On that delightful time of growing youth,
When craving for the marvellous gives way   540
To strengthening love for things that we have seen;
When sober truth and steady sympathies,
Offered to notice by less daring pens,
Take firmer hold of us, and words themselves
Move us with conscious pleasure.   I am sad   545
At thought of raptures now for ever flown;
Almost to tears I sometimes could be sad
To think of, to read over, many a page,
Poems withal of name, which at that time
Did never fail to entrance me, and are now   550
Dead in my eyes, dead as a theatre
Fresh emptied of spectators. Twice five years
Or less I might have seen, when first my mind
With conscious pleasure opened to the charm
Of words in tuneful order, found them sweet   555

For their own *sakes,* a passion, and a power;
And phrases pleased me chosen for delight,
For pomp, or love. Oft, in the public roads
Yet unfrequented, while the morning light
Was yellowing the hill tops, I went abroad   560
With a dear friend, and for the better part
Of two delightful hours we strolled along
By the still borders of the misty lake,
Repeating favourite verses with one voice,
Or conning more, as happy as the birds   565
That round us chaunted. Well might we be glad,
Lifted above the ground by airy fancies,
More bright than madness or the dreams of wine;
And, though full oft the objects of our love
Were false, and in their splendour overwrought,   570
Yet was there surely then no vulgar power
Working within us, — nothing less, in truth,
Than that most noble attribute of man,
Though yet untutored and inordinate,
That wish for something loftier, more adorned,   575
Than is the common aspect, daily garb,
Of human life. What wonder, then, if sounds
Of exultation echoed through the groves!
For, images, and sentiments, and words,
And everything encountered or pursued   580
In that delicious world of poesy,
Kept holiday, a never-ending show,
With music, incense, festival, and flowers!

    Here must we pause: this only let me add,
From heart-experience, and in humblest sense   585
Of modesty, that he, who in his youth
A daily wanderer among woods and fields
With living Nature hath been intimate,
Not only in that raw unpractised time
Is stirred to extasy, as others are,   590
By glittering verse; but further, doth receive,
In measure only dealt out to himself,
Knowledge and increase of enduring joy
From the great Nature that exists in works
Of mighty Poets. Visionary power   595
Attends the motions of the viewless winds,
Embodied in the mystery of words:
There, darkness makes abode, and all the host
Of shadowy things work endless changes, — there,
As in a mansion like their proper home,   600
Even forms and substances are circumfused

By that transparent veil with light divine,
And, through the turnings intricate of verse,
Present themselves as objects recognised,
In flashes, and with glory not their own.   605

   Thus far a scanty record is deduced
Of what I owed to Books in early life;
Their later influence yet remains untold;
But as this work was taking in my thoughts
Proportions that seem'd larger than had first   610
Been meditated, I was indisposed
To any further progress at a time
When these acknowledgements were left unpaid.

BOOK SIXTH

CAMBRIDGE AND THE ALPS

THE leaves were fading when to Esthwaite's banks
And the simplicities of cottage life
I bade farewell; and, one among the youth
Who, summoned by that season, reunite
As scattered birds troop to the fowler's lure,   5
Went back to Granta's cloisters, not so prompt
Or eager, though as gay and undepressed
In mind, as when I thence had taken flight
A few short months before. I turned my face
Without repining from the coves and heights   10
Clothed in the sunshine of the withering fern;
Quitted, not loth, the mild magnificence
Of calmer lakes and louder streams; and you,
Frank-hearted maids of rocky Cumberland,
You and your not unwelcome days of mirth,   15
Relinquished, and your nights of revelry,
And in my own unlovely cell sate down
In lightsome mood — such privilege has youth
That cannot take long leave of pleasant thoughts.

   The bonds of indolent society   20
Relaxing in their hold, henceforth I lived
More to myself. Two winters may be passed
Without a separate notice: many books
Were skimmed, devoured, or studiously perused,
But with no settled plan. I was detached   25
Internally from academic cares;
Yet independent study seemed a course

Of hardy disobedience toward friends
And kindred, proud rebellion and unkind.
This spurious virtue, rather let it bear   30
A name it more deserves, this cowardice,
Gave treacherous sanction to that over-love
Of freedom which encouraged me to turn
From regulations even of my own
As from restraints and bonds. Yet who can tell —   35
Who knows what thus may have been gained, both then
And at a later season, or preserved;
What love of nature, what original strength
Of contemplation, what intuitive truths,
The deepest and the best, what keen research,   40
Unbiassed, unbewildered, and unawed?

     The Poet's soul was with me at that time;
Sweet meditations, the still overflow
Of present happiness, while future years
Lacked not anticipations, tender dreams,   45
No few of which have since been realised;
And some remain, hopes for my future life.
Four years and thirty, told this very week,
Have I been now a sojourner on earth,
By sorrow not unsmitten; yet for me   50
Life's morning radiance hath not left the hills,
Her dew is on the flowers. Those were the days
Which also first emboldened me to trust
With firmness, hitherto but lightly touched
By such a daring thought, that I might leave   55
Some monument behind me which pure hearts
Should reverence. The instinctive humbleness,
Maintained even by the very name and thought
Of printed books and authorship, began
To melt away; and further, the dread awe   60
Of mighty names was softened down and seemed
Approachable, admitting fellowship
Of modest sympathy. Such aspect now,
Though not familiarly, my mind put on,
Content to observe, to admire, and to enjoy.   65

     All winter long, whenever free to choose,
Did I by night frequent the College groves
And tributary walks; the last, and oft
The only one, who had been lingering there
Through hours of silence, till the porter's bell,   70
A punctual follower on the stroke of nine,
Rang with its blunt unceremonious voice,

Inexorable summons! Lofty elms,
Inviting shades of opportune recess,
Bestowed composure on a neighbourhood   75
Unpeaceful in itself. A single tree
With sinuous trunk, boughs exquisitely wreathed,
Grew there; an ash which Winter for himself
Decked as in pride, and with outlandish grace:
Up from the ground, and almost to the top,   80
The trunk and every master branch were green
With clustering ivy, and the lightsome twigs
And outer spray profusely tipped with seeds
That hung in yellow tassels, while the air
Stirred them, not voiceless. Often have I stood   85
Foot-bound uplooking at this lovely tree
Beneath a frosty moon. The hemisphere
Of magic fiction, verse of mine perchance
May never tread; but scarcely Spenser's self
Could have more tranquil visions in his youth,   90
Or could more bright appearances create
Of human forms with superhuman powers,
Than I beheld loitering on calm clear nights
Alone, beneath this fairy work of earth.

   On the vague reading of a truant youth   95
'Twere idle to descant. My inner judgment
Not seldom differed from my taste in books,
As if it appertained to another mind,
And yet the books which then I valued most
Are dearest to me *now;* for, having scanned,   100
Not heedlessly, the laws, and watched the forms
Of Nature, in that knowledge I possessed
A standard, often usefully applied,
Even when unconsciously, to things removed
From a familiar sympathy. — In fine,   105
I was a better judge of thoughts than words,
Misled in estimating words, not only
By common inexperience of youth,
But by the trade in classic niceties,
The dangerous craft of culling term and phrase   110
From languages that want the living voice
To carry meaning to the natural heart;
To tell us what is passion, what is truth,
What reason, what simplicity and sense.

   Yet may we not entirely overlook   115
The pleasure gathered from the rudiments
Of geometric science. Though advanced

In these inquiries, with regret I speak,
No farther than the threshold, there I found
Both elevation and composed delight: 120
With Indian awe and wonder, ignorance pleased
With its own struggles, did I meditate
On the relation those abstractions bear
To Nature's laws, and by what process led,
Those immaterial agents bowed their heads   125
Duly to serve the mind of earth-born man;
From star to star, from kindred sphere to sphere,
From system on to system without end.

More frequently from the same source I drew
A pleasure quiet and profound, a sense   130
Of permanent and universal sway,
And paramount belief; there, recognised
A type, for finite natures, of the one
Supreme Existence, the surpassing life
Which — to the boundaries of space and time,   135
Of melancholy space and doleful time,
Superior, and incapable of change,
Nor touched by welterings of passion — is,
And hath the name of, God. Transcendent peace
And silence did await upon these thoughts   140
That were a frequent comfort to my youth.

'Tis told by one whom stormy waters threw,
With fellow-sufferers by the shipwreck spared,
Upon a desert coast, that having brought
To land a single volume, saved by chance,   145
A treatise of Geometry, he wont,
Although of food and clothing destitute,
And beyond common wretchedness depressed,
To part from company and take this book
(Then first a self-taught pupil in its truths)   150
To spots remote, and draw his diagrams
With a long staff upon the sand, and thus
Did oft beguile his sorrow, and almost
Forget his feeling: so (if like effect
From the same cause produced, 'mid outward things   155
So different, may rightly be compared),
So was it then with me, and so will be
With Poets ever. Mighty is the charm
Of those abstractions to a mind beset
With images, and haunted by herself,   160
And specially delightful unto me
Was that clear synthesis built up aloft
So gracefully; even then when it appeared

Not more than a mere plaything, or a toy
To sense embodied: not the thing it is   165
In verity, an independent world,
Created out of pure intelligence.

Such dispositions then were mine unearned
By aught, I fear, of genuine desert —
Mine, through heaven's grace and inborn aptitudes.   170
And not to leave the story of that time
Imperfect, with these habits must be joined,
Moods melancholy, fits of spleen, that loved
A pensive sky, sad days, and piping winds,
The twilight more than dawn, autumn than spring;   175
A treasured and luxurious gloom of choice
And inclination mainly, and the mere
Redundancy of youth's contentedness.
— To time thus spent, add multitudes of hours
Pilfered away, by what the Bard who sang   180
Of the Enchanter Indolence hath called
"Good-natured lounging," and behold a map
Of my collegiate life — far less intense
Than duty called for, or, without regard
To duty, *might* have sprung up of itself   185
By change of accidents, or even, to speak
Without unkindness, in another place.
Yet why take refuge in that plea? — the fault,
This I repeat, was mine; mine be the blame.

In summer, making quest for works of art,   190
Or scenes renowned for beauty, I explored
That streamlet whose blue current works its way
Between romantic Dovedale's spiry rocks;
Pried into Yorkshire dales, or hidden tracts
Of my own native region, and was blest   195
Between these sundry wanderings with a joy
Above all joys, that seemed another morn
Risen on mid noon; blest with the presence, Friend!
Of that sole Sister, she who hath been long
Dear to thee also, thy true friend and mine,   200
Now, after separation desolate,
Restored to me — such absence that she seemed
A gift then first bestowed. The varied banks
Of Emont, hitherto unnamed in song,
And that monastic castle, 'mid tall trees,   205
Low-standing by the margin of the stream,
A mansion visited (as fame reports)
By Sidney, where, in sight of our Helvellyn,
Or stormy Cross-fell, snatches he might pen

Of his Arcadia, by fraternal love   210
Inspired; — that river and those mouldering towers
Have seen us side by side, when, having clomb
The darksome windings of a broken stair,
And crept along a ridge of fractured wall,
Not without trembling, we in safety looked   215
Forth, through some Gothic window's open space,
And gathered with one mind a rich reward
From the far-stretching landscape, by the light
Of morning beautified, or purple eve;
Or, not less pleased, lay on some turret's head,   220
Catching from tufts of grass and hare-bell flowers
Their faintest whisper to the passing breeze,
Given out while mid-day heat oppressed the plains.

　　Another maid there was, who also shed
A gladness o'er that season, then to me,   225
By her exulting outside look of youth
And placid under-countenance, first endeared;
That other spirit, Coleridge! who is now
So near to us, that meek confiding heart,
So reverenced by us both. O'er paths and fields   230
In all that neighbourhood, through narrow lanes
Of eglantine, and through the shady woods,
And o'er the Border Beacon, and the waste
Of naked pools, and common crags that lay
Exposed on the bare fell, were scattered love,   235
The spirit of pleasure, and youth's golden gleam.
O Friend! we had not seen thee at that time,
And yet a power is on me, and a strong
Confusion, and I seem to plant thee there.
Far art thou wandered now in search of health   240
And milder breezes, — melancholy lot!
But thou art with us, with us in the past,
The present, with us in the times to come.
There is no grief, no sorrow, no despair,
No languor, no dejection, no dismay,   245
No absence scarcely can there be, for those
Who love as we do. Speed thee well! divide
With us thy pleasure; thy returning strength,
Receive it daily as a joy of ours;
Share with us thy fresh spirits, whether gift   250
Of gales Etesian or of tender thoughts.

　　I, too, have been a wanderer; but, alas!
How different the fate of different men.
Though mutually unknown, yea nursed and reared

As if in several elements, we were framed   255
To bend at last to the same discipline,
Predestined, if two beings ever were,
To seek the same delights, and have one health,
One happiness. Throughout this narrative,
Else sooner ended, I have borne in mind   260
For whom it registers the birth, and marks the growth,
Of gentleness, simplicity, and truth,
And joyous loves, that hallow innocent days
Of peace and self-command. Of rivers, fields,
And groves I speak to thee, my Friend! to thee,   265
Who, yet a liveried schoolboy, in the depths
Of the huge city, on the leaded roof
Of that wide edifice, thy school and home,
Wert used to lie and gaze upon the clouds
Moving in heaven; or, of that pleasure tired,   270
To shut thine eyes, and by internal light
See trees, and meadows, and thy native stream,
Far distant, thus beheld from year to year
Of a long exile. Nor could I forget,
In this late portion of my argument,   275
That scarcely, as my term of pupilage
Ceased, had I left those academic bowers
When thou wert thither guided. From the heart
Of London, and from cloisters there, thou camest,
And didst sit down in temperance and peace,   280
A rigorous student. What a stormy course
Then followed. Oh! it is a pang that calls
For utterance, to think what easy change
Of circumstances might to thee have spared
A world of pain, ripened a thousand hopes,   285
For ever withered. Through this retrospect
Of my collegiate life I still have had
Thy after-sojourn in the self-same place
Present before my eyes, have played with times
And accidents as children do with cards,   290
Or as a man, who, when his house is built,
A frame locked up in wood and stone, doth still,
As impotent fancy prompts, by his fireside,
Rebuild it to his liking. I have thought
Of thee, thy learning, gorgeous eloquence,   295
And all the strength and plumage of thy youth,
Thy subtle speculations, toils abstruse
Among the schoolmen, and Platonic forms
Of wild ideal pageantry, shaped out
From things well-matched or ill, and words for things,   300
The self-created sustenance of a mind

Debarred from Nature's living images,
Compelled to be a life unto herself,
And unrelentingly possessed by thirst
Of greatness, love, and beauty. Not alone,   305
Ah! surely not in singleness of heart
Should I have seen the light of evening fade
From smooth Cam's silent waters: had we met,
Even at that early time, needs must I trust
In the belief, that my maturer age,   310
My calmer habits, and more steady voice,
Would with an influence benign have soothed,
Or chased away, the airy wretchedness
That battened on thy youth. But thou hast trod
A march of glory, which doth put to shame   315
These vain regrets; health suffers in thee, else
Such grief for thee would be the weakest thought
That ever harboured in the breast of man.

   A passing word erewhile did lightly touch
On wanderings of my own, that now embraced   320
With livelier hope a region wider far.

   When the third summer freed us from restraint,
A youthful friend, he too a mountaineer,
Not slow to share my wishes, took his staff,
And sallying forth, we journeyed side by side,   325
Bound to the distant Alps. A hardy slight
Did this unprecedented course imply
Of college studies and their set rewards;
Nor had, in truth, the scheme been formed by me
Without uneasy forethought of the pain,   330
The censures, and ill-omening of those
To whom my worldly interests were dear.
But Nature then was sovereign in my mind,
And mighty forms, seizing a youthful fancy,
Had given a charter to irregular hopes.   335
In any age of uneventful calm
Among the nations, surely would my heart
Have been possessed by similar desire;
But Europe at that time was thrilled with joy,
France standing on the top of golden hours,   340
And human nature seeming born again.

   Lightly equipped, and but a few brief looks
Cast on the white cliffs of our native shore
From the receding vessel's deck, we chanced
To land at Calais on the very eve   345

Of that great federal day; and there we saw,
In a mean city, and among a few,
How bright a face is worn when joy of one
Is joy for tens of millions. Southward thence
We held our way, direct through hamlets, towns,   350
Gaudy with reliques of that festival,
Flowers left to wither on triumphal arcs,
And window-garlands. On the public roads,
And, once, three days successively, through paths
By which our toilsome journey was abridged,   355
Among sequestered villages we walked
And found benevolence and blessedness
Spread like a fragrance everywhere, when spring
Hath left no corner of the land untouched:
Where elms for many and many a league in files   360
With their thin umbrage, on the stately roads
Of that great kingdom, rustled o'er our heads,
For ever near us as we paced along:
How sweet at such a time, with such delight
On every side, in prime of youthful strength,   365
To feed a Poet's tender melancholy
And fond conceit of sadness, with the sound
Of undulations varying as might please
The wind that swayed them; once, and more than once,
Unhoused beneath the evening star we saw   370
Dances of liberty, and, in late hours
Of darkness, dances in the open air
Deftly prolonged, though grey-haired lookers on
Might waste their breath in chiding.
                                        Under hills —
The vine-clad hills and slopes of Burgundy,   375
Upon the bosom of the gentle Saone
We glided forward with the flowing stream.
Swift Rhone! thou wert the *wings* on which we cut
A winding passage with majestic ease
Between thy lofty rocks. Enchanting show   380
Those woods and farms and orchards did present,
And single cottages and lurking towns,
Reach after reach, succession without end
Of deep and stately vales! A lonely pair
Of strangers, till day closed, we sailed along,   385
Clustered together with a merry crowd
Of those emancipated, a blithe host
Of travellers, chiefly delegates returning
From the great spousals newly solemnised
At their chief city, in the sight of Heaven.   390
Like bees they swarmed, gaudy and gay as bees;

Some vapoured in the unruliness of joy,
And with their swords flourished as if to fight
The saucy air. In this proud company
We landed — took with them our evening meal,   395
Guests welcome almost as the angels were
To Abraham of old. The supper done,
With flowing cups elate and happy thoughts
We rose at signal given, and formed a ring
And, hand in hand, danced round and round the board;   400
All hearts were open, every tongue was loud
With amity and glee; we bore a name
Honoured in France, the name of Englishmen,
And hospitably did they give us hail,
As their forerunners in a glorious course;   405
And round and round the board we danced again.
With these blithe friends our voyage we renewed
At early dawn. The monastery bells
Made a sweet jingling in our youthful ears;
The rapid river flowing without noise,   410
And each uprising or receding spire
Spake with a sense of peace, at intervals
Touching the heart amid the boisterous crew
By whom we were encompassed. Taking leave
Of this glad throng, foot-travellers side by side,   415
Measuring our steps in quiet, we pursued
Our journey, and ere twice the sun had set
Beheld the Convent of Chartreuse, and there
Rested within an awful *solitude*:
Yes, for even then no other than a place   420
Of soul-affecting *solitude* appeared
That far-famed region, though our eyes had seen,
As toward the sacred mansion we advanced,
Arms flashing, and a military glare
Of riotous men commissioned to expel   425
The blameless inmates, and belike subvert
That frame of social being, which so long
Had bodied forth the ghostliness of things
In silence visible and perpetual calm.
— "Stay, stay your sacrilegious hands!" — The voice   430
Was Nature's, uttered from her Alpine throne;
I heard it then and seem to hear it now —
"Your impious work forbear, perish what may,
Let this one temple last, be this one spot
Of earth devoted to eternity!"   435
She ceased to speak, but while St. Bruno's pines
Waved their dark tops, not silent as they waved,
And while below, along their several beds,

Murmured the sister streams of Life and Death,
Thus by conflicting passions pressed, my heart   440
Responded; "Honour to the patriot's zeal!
Glory and hope to new-born Liberty!
Hail to the mighty projects of the time!
Discerning sword that Justice wields, do thou
Go forth and prosper; and, ye purging fires,   445
Up to the loftiest towers of Pride ascend,
Fanned by the breath of angry Providence.
But oh! if Past and Future be the wings
On whose support harmoniously conjoined
Moves the great spirit of human knowledge, spare   450
These courts of mystery, where a step advanced
Between the portals of the shadowy rocks
Leaves far behind life's treacherous vanities,
For penitential tears and trembling hopes
Exchanged — to equalise in God's pure sight   455
Monarch and peasant: be the house redeemed
With its unworldly votaries, for the sake
Of conquest over sense, hourly achieved
Through faith and meditative reason, resting
Upon the word of heaven-imparted truth,   460
Calmly triumphant; and for humbler claim
Of that imaginative impulse sent
From these majestic floods, yon shining cliffs,
The untransmuted shapes of many worlds,
Cerulean ether's pure inhabitants,   465
These forests unapproachable by death,
That shall endure as long as man endures,
To think, to hope, to worship, and to feel,
To struggle, to be lost within himself
In trepidation, from the blank abyss   470
To look with bodily eyes, and be consoled."
Not seldom since that moment have I wished
That thou, O Friend! the trouble or the calm
Hadst shared, when, from profane regards apart,
In sympathetic reverence we trod   475
The floors of those dim cloisters, till that hour,
From their foundation, strangers to the presence
Of unrestricted and unthinking man.
Abroad, how cheeringly the sunshine lay
Upon the open lawns! Vallombre's groves   480
Entering, we fed the soul with darkness; thence
Issued, and with uplifted eyes beheld,
In different quarters of the bending sky,
The cross of Jesus stand erect, as if
Hands of angelic powers had fixed it there,   485

Memorial reverenced by a thousand storms;
Yet then, from the undiscriminating sweep
And rage of one State-whirlwind, insecure.

   'Tis not my present purpose to retrace
That variegated journey step by step. 490
A march it was of military speed,
And Earth did change her images and forms
Before us, fast as clouds are changed in heaven.
Day after day, up early and down late,
From hill to vale we dropped, from vale to hill 495
Mounted — from province on to province swept,
Keen hunters in a chase of fourteen weeks,
Eager as birds of prey, or as a ship
Upon the stretch, when winds are blowing fair:
Sweet coverts did we cross of pastoral life, 500
Enticing valleys, greeted them and left
Too soon, while yet the very flash and gleam
Of salutation were not passed away.
Oh! sorrow for the youth who could have seen
Unchastened, unsubdued, unawed, unraised 505
To patriarchal dignity of mind,
And pure simplicity of wish and will,
Those sanctified abodes of peaceful man,
Pleased (though to hardship born, and compassed round
With danger, varying as the seasons change), 510
Pleased with his daily task, or, if not pleased,
Contented, from the moment that the dawn
(Ah! surely not without attendant gleams
Of soul-illumination) calls him forth
To industry, by glistenings flung on rocks, 515
Whose evening shadows lead him to repose.

   Well might a stranger look with bounding heart
Down on a green recess, the first I saw
Of those deep haunts, an aboriginal vale,
Quiet and lorded over and possessed 520
By naked huts, wood-built, and sown like tents
Or Indian cabins over the fresh lawns
And by the river side.
                That very day,
From a bare ridge we also first beheld
Unveiled the summit of Mont Blanc, and grieved 525
To have a soulless image on the eye
That had usurped upon a living thought
That never more could be. The wondrous Vale
Of Chamouny stretched far below, and soon

With its dumb cataracts and streams of ice,   530
A motionless array of mighty waves,
Five rivers broad and vast, made rich amends,
And reconciled us to realities;
There small birds warble from the leafy trees,
The eagle soars high in the element,   535
There doth the reaper bind the yellow sheaf,
The maiden spread the haycock in the sun,
While Winter like a well-tamed lion walks,
Descending from the mountain to make sport
Among the cottages by beds of flowers.   540

   Whate'er in this wide circuit we beheld,
Or heard, was fitted to our unripe state
Of intellect and heart. With such a book
Before our eyes, we could not choose but read
Lessons of genuine brotherhood, the plain   545
And universal reason of mankind,
The truths of young and old. Nor, side by side
Pacing, two social pilgrims, or alone
Each with his humour, could we fail to abound
In dreams and fictions, pensively composed: 550
Dejection taken up for pleasure's sake,
And gilded sympathies, the willow wreath,
And sober posies of funereal flowers,
Gathered among those solitudes sublime
From formal gardens of the lady Sorrow,   555
Did sweeten many a meditative hour.

   Yet still in me with those soft luxuries
Mixed something of stern mood, an under-thirst
Of vigour seldom utterly allayed.
And from that source how different a sadness   560
Would issue, let one incident make known.
When from the Vallais we had turned, and clomb
Along the Simplon's steep and rugged road,
Following a band of muleteers, we reached
A halting-place, where all together took   565
Their noon-tide meal. Hastily rose our guide,
Leaving us at the board; awhile we lingered,
Then paced the beaten downward way that led
Right to a rough stream's edge, and there broke off;
The only track now visible was one   570
That from the torrent's further brink held forth
Conspicuous invitation to ascend
A lofty mountain. After brief delay
Crossing the unbridged stream, that road we took,

And clomb with eagerness, till anxious fears   575
Intruded, for we failed to overtake
Our comrades gone before. By fortunate chance,
While every moment added doubt to doubt,
A peasant met us, from whose mouth we learned
That to the spot which had perplexed us first   580
We must descend, and there should find the road,
Which in the stony channel of the stream
Lay a few steps, and then along its banks;
And, that our future course, all plain to sight,
Was downwards, with the current of that stream.   585
Loth to believe what we so grieved to hear,
For still we had hopes that pointed to the clouds,
We questioned him again, and yet again;
But every word that from the peasant's lips
Came in reply, translated by our feelings,   590
Ended in this, — *that we had crossed the Alps.*

    Imagination — here the Power so called
Through sad incompetence of human speech,
That awful Power rose from the mind's abyss
Like an unfathered vapour that enwraps,   595
At once, some lonely traveller. I was lost;
Halted without an effort to break through;
But to my conscious soul I now can say —
"I recognise thy glory:" in such strength
Of usurpation, when the light of sense   600
Goes out, but with a flash that has revealed
The invisible world, doth greatness make abode,
There harbours whether we be young or old.
Our destiny, our being's heart and home,
Is with infinitude, and only there;   605
With hope it is, hope that can never die,
Effort, and expectation, and desire,
And something evermore about to be.
Under such banners militant, the soul
Seeks for no trophies, struggles for no spoils   610
That may attest her prowess, blest in thoughts
That are their own perfection and reward,
Strong in herself and in beatitude
That hides her, like the mighty flood of Nile
Poured from his fount of Abyssinian clouds   615
To fertilise the whole Egyptian plain.

    The melancholy slackening that ensued
Upon those tidings by the peasant given
Was soon dislodged. Downwards we hurried fast,

And, with the half-shaped road which we had missed, 620
Entered a narrow chasm. The brook and road
Were fellow-travellers in this gloomy strait,
And with them did we journey several hours
At a slow pace. The immeasurable height
Of woods decaying, never to be decayed, 625
The stationary blasts of waterfalls,
And in the narrow rent at every turn
Winds thwarting winds, bewildered and forlorn,
The torrents shooting from the clear blue sky,
The rocks that muttered close upon our ears, 630
Black drizzling crags that spake by the way-side
As if a voice were in them, the sick sight
And giddy prospect of the raving stream,
The unfettered clouds and region of the Heavens,
Tumult and peace, the darkness and the light — 635
Were all like workings of one mind, the features
Of the same face, blossoms upon one tree;
Characters of the great Apocalypse,
The types and symbols of Eternity,
Of first, and last, and midst, and without end. 640

    That night our lodging was a house that stood
Alone within the valley, at a point
Where, tumbling from aloft, a torrent swelled
The rapid stream whose margin we had trod;
A dreary mansion, large beyond all need, 645
With high and spacious rooms, deafened and stunned
By noise of waters, making innocent sleep
Lie melancholy among weary bones.

    Uprisen betimes, our journey we renewed,
Led by the stream, ere noon-day magnified 650
Into a lordly river, broad and deep,
Dimpling along in silent majesty,
With mountains for its neighbours, and in view
Of distant mountains and their snowy tops,
And thus proceeding to Locarno's Lake, 655
Fit resting-place for such a visitant.
Locarno! spreading out in width like Heaven,
How dost thou cleave to the poetic heart,
Bask in the sunshine of the memory;
And Como! thou, a treasure whom the earth 660
Keeps to herself, confined as in a depth
Of Abyssinian privacy. I spake
Of thee, thy chestnut woods, and garden plots
Of Indian corn tended by dark-eyed maids;

Thy lofty steeps, and pathways roofed with vines,   665
Winding from house to house, from town to town,
Sole link that binds them to each other; walks,
League after league, and cloistral avenues,
Where silence dwells if music be not there:
While yet a youth undisciplined in verse,   670
Through fond ambition of that hour, I strove
To chant your praise; nor can approach you now
Ungreeted by a more melodious Song,
Where tones of Nature smoothed by learned Art
May flow in lasting current. Like a breeze   675
Or sunbeam over your domain I passed
In motion without pause; but ye have left
Your beauty with me, a serene accord
Of forms and colours, passive, yet endowed
In their submissiveness with power as sweet   680
And gracious, almost might I dare to say,
As virtue is, or goodness; sweet as love,
Or the remembrance of a generous deed,
Or mildest visitations of pure thought,
When God, the giver of all joy, is thanked   685
Religiously, in silent blessedness;
Sweet as this last herself, for such it is.

With those delightful pathways we advanced,
For two days' space, in presence of the Lake,
That, stretching far among the Alps, assumed   690
A character more stern. The second night,
From sleep awakened, and misled by sound
Of the church clock telling the hours with strokes
Whose import then we had not learned, we rose
By moonlight, doubting not that day was nigh,   695
And that meanwhile, by no uncertain path,
Along the winding margin of the lake,
Led, as before, we should behold the scene
Hushed in profound repose. We left the town
Of Gravedona with this hope; but soon   700
Were lost, bewildered among woods immense,
And on a rock sate down, to wait for day.
An open place it was, and overlooked,
From high, the sullen water far beneath,
On which a dull red image of the moon   705
Lay bedded, changing oftentimes its form
Like an uneasy snake. From hour to hour
We sate and sate, wondering, as if the night
Had been ensnared by witchcraft. On the rock
At last we stretched our weary limbs for sleep,   710

But *could not* sleep, tormented by the stings
Of insects, which, with noise like that of noon,
Filled all the woods; the cry of unknown birds;
The mountains more by blackness visible
And their own size, than any outward light;   715
The breathless wilderness of clouds; the clock
That told, with unintelligible voice,
The widely parted hours; the noise of streams,
And sometimes rustling motions nigh at hand,
That did not leave us free from personal fear;   720
And, lastly, the withdrawing moon, that set
Before us, while she still was high in heaven; —
These were our food; and such a summer's night
Followed that pair of golden days that shed
On Como's Lake, and all that round it lay,   725
Their fairest, softest, happiest influence.

But here I must break off, and bid farewell
To days, each offering some new sight, or fraught
With some untried adventure, in a course
Prolonged till sprinklings of autumnal snow   730
Checked our unwearied steps. Let this alone
Be mentioned as a parting word, that not
In hollow exultation, dealing out
Hyperboles of praise comparative;
Not rich one moment to be poor for ever;   735
Not prostrate, overborne, as if the mind
Herself were nothing, a mean pensioner
On outward forms — did we in presence stand
Of that magnificent region. On the front
Of this whole Song is written that my heart   740
Must, in such Temple, needs have offered up
A different worship. Finally, whate'er
I saw, or heard, or felt, was but a stream
That flowed into a kindred stream; a gale,
Confederate with the current of the soul,   745
To speed my voyage; every sound or sight,
In its degree of power, administered
To grandeur or to tenderness, — to the one
Directly, but to tender thoughts by means
Less often instantaneous in effect;   750
Led me to these by paths that, in the main,
Were more circuitous, but not less sure
Duly to reach the point marked out by Heaven.

Oh, most belovèd Friend! a glorious time,
A happy time that was; triumphant looks   755

Were then the common language of all eyes;
As if awaked from sleep, the Nations hailed
Their great expectancy: the fife of war
Was then a spirit-stirring sound indeed,
A black-bird's whistle in a budding grove.   760
We left the Swiss exulting in the fate
Of their near neighbours; and, when shortening fast
Our pilgrimage, nor distant far from home,
We crossed the Brabant armies on the fret
For battle in the cause of Liberty.   765
A stripling, scarcely of the household then
Of social life, I looked upon these things
As from a distance; heard, and saw, and felt,
Was touched, but with no intimate concern;
I seemed to move along them, as a bird   770
Moves through the air, or as a fish pursues
Its sport, or feeds in its proper element;
I wanted not that joy, I did not need
Such help; the ever-living universe,
Turn where I might, was opening out its glories,   775
And the independent spirit of pure youth
Called forth, at every season, new delights
Spread round my steps like sunshine o'er green fields.

BOOK SEVENTH

RESIDENCE IN LONDON

SIX changeful years have vanished since I first
Poured out (saluted by that quickening breeze
Which met me issuing from the City's walls)
A glad preamble to this Verse: I sang
Aloud, with fervour irresistible   5
Of short-lived transport, like a torrent bursting,
From a black thunder-cloud, down Scafell's side
To rush and disappear. But soon broke forth
(So willed the Muse) a less impetuous stream,
That flowed awhile with unabating strength,   10
Then stopped for years; not audible again
Before last primrose-time. Beloved Friend!
The assurance which then cheered some heavy thoughts
On thy departure to a foreign land
Has failed; too slowly moves the promised work.   15
Through the whole summer have I been at rest,
Partly from voluntary holiday,
And part through outward hindrance. But I heard,

After the hour of sunset yester-even,
Sitting within doors between light and dark, 20
A choir of redbreasts gathered somewhere near
My threshold, — minstrels from the distant woods
Sent in on Winter's service, to announce,
With preparation artful and benign,
That the rough lord had left the surly North 25
On his accustomed journey. The delight,
Due to this timely notice, unawares
Smote me, and, listening, I in whispers said,
"Ye heartsome Choristers, ye and I will be
Associates, and, unscared by blustering winds, 30
Will chant together." Thereafter, as the shades
Of twilight deepened, going forth, I spied
A glow-worm underneath a dusky plume
Or canopy of yet unwithered fern,
Clear-shining, like a hermit's taper seen 35
Through a thick forest. Silence touched me here
No less than sound had done before; the child
Of Summer, lingering, shining, by herself,
The voiceless worm on the unfrequented hills,
Seemed sent on the same errand with the choir 40
Of Winter that had warbled at my door,
And the whole year breathed tenderness and love.

The last night's genial feeling overflowed
Upon this morning, and my favourite grove,
Tossing in sunshine its dark boughs aloft, 45
As if to make the strong wind visible,
Wakes in me agitations like its own,
A spirit friendly to the Poet's task,
Which we will now resume with lively hope,
Nor checked by aught of tamer argument 50
That lies before us, needful to be told.

Returned from that excursion, soon I bade
Farewell for ever to the sheltered seats
Of gownèd students, quitted hall and bower,
And every comfort of that privileged ground, 55
Well pleased to pitch a vagrant tent among
The unfenced regions of society.

Yet undetermined to what course of life
I should adhere, and seeming to possess
A little space of intermediate time 60
At full command, to London first I turned,
In no disturbance of excessive hope,

By personal ambition unenslaved,
Frugal as there was need, and, though self-willed,
From dangerous passions free. Three years had flown   65
Since I had felt in heart and soul the shock
Of the huge town's first presence, and had paced
Her endless streets, a transient visitant:
Now, fixed amid that concourse of mankind
Where Pleasure whirls about incessantly,   70
And life and labour seem but one, I filled
An idler's place; an idler well content
To have a house (what matter for a home?)
That owned him; living cheerfully abroad
With unchecked fancy ever on the stir,   75
And all my young affections out of doors.

    There was a time when whatsoe'er is feigned
Of airy palaces, and gardens built
By Genii of romance; or hath in grave
Authentic history been set forth of Rome,   80
Alcairo, Babylon, or Persepolis;
Or given upon report by pilgrim friars,
Of golden cities ten months' journey deep
Among Tartarian wilds — fell short, far short,
Of what my fond simplicity believed   85
And thought of London — held me by a chain
Less strong of wonder and obscure delight.
Whether the bolt of childhood's Fancy shot
For me beyond its ordinary mark,
'Twere vain to ask; but in our flock of boys   90
Was One, a cripple from his birth, whom chance
Summoned from school to London; fortunate
And envied traveller! When the Boy returned,
After short absence, curiously I scanned
His mien and person, nor was free, in sooth,   95
From disappointment, not to find some change
In look and air, from that new region brought,
As if from Fairy-land. Much I questioned him;
And every word he uttered, on my ears
Fell flatter than a cagèd parrot's note,   100
That answers unexpectedly awry,
And mocks the prompter's listening. Marvellous things
Had vanity (quick Spirit that appears
Almost as deeply seated and as strong
In a Child's heart as fear itself) conceived   105
For my enjoyment. Would that I could now
Recall what then I pictured to myself,
Of mitred Prelates, Lords in ermine clad,

The King, and the King's Palace, and, not last,
Nor least, Heaven bless him! the renowned Lord Mayor: 110
Dreams not unlike to those which once begat
A change of purpose in young Whittington,
When he, a friendless and a drooping boy,
Sate on a stone, and heard the bells speak out
Articulate music. Above all, one thought   115
Baffled my understanding: how men lived
Even next-door neighbours, as we say, yet still
Strangers, nor knowing each the other's name.

O, wond'rous power of words, by simple faith
Licensed to take the meaning that we love!   120
Vauxhall and Ranelagh! I then had heard
Of your green groves, and wilderness of lamps
Dimming the stars, and fireworks magical,
And gorgeous ladies, under splendid domes,
Floating in dance, or warbling high in air   125
The songs of spirits! Nor had Fancy fed
With less delight upon that other class
Of marvels, broad-day wonders permanent:
The River proudly bridged; the dizzy top
And Whispering Gallery of St. Paul's; the tombs   130
Of Westminster; the Giants of Guildhall;
Bedlam, and those carved maniacs at the gates,
Perpetually recumbent; Statues — man,
And the horse under him — in gilded pomp
Adorning flowery gardens, 'mid vast squares;   135
The Monument, and that Chamber of the Tower
Where England's sovereigns sit in long array,
Their steeds bestriding, — every mimic shape
Cased in the gleaming mail the monarch wore,
Whether for gorgeous tournament addressed,   140
Or life or death upon the battle-field.
Those bold imaginations in due time
Had vanished, leaving others in their stead:
And now I looked upon the living scene;
Familiarly perused it; oftentimes,   145
In spite of strongest disappointment, pleased
Through courteous self-submission, as a tax
Paid to the object by prescriptive right.

Rise up, thou monstrous ant-hill on the plain
Of a too busy world! Before me flow,   150
Thou endless stream of men and moving things!
Thy every-day appearance, as it strikes —
With wonder heightened, or sublimed by awe —

On strangers, of all ages; the quick dance
Of colours, lights, and forms; the deafening din;   155
The comers and the goers face to face,
Face after face; the string of dazzling wares,
Shop after shop, with symbols, blazoned names,
And all the tradesman's honours overhead:
Here, fronts of houses, like a title-page,   160
With letters huge inscribed from top to toe;
Stationed above the door, like guardian saints,
There, allegoric shapes, female or male,
Or physiognomies of real men,
Land-warriors, kings, or admirals of the sea,   165
Boyle, Shakspeare, Newton, or the attractive head
Of some quack-doctor, famous in his day.

　　Meanwhile the roar continues, till at length,
Escaped as from an enemy, we turn
Abruptly into some sequestered nook,   170
Still as a sheltered place when winds blow loud!
At leisure, thence, through tracts of thin resort,
And sights and sounds that come at intervals,
We take our way. A raree-show is here,
With children gathered round; another street   175
Presents a company of dancing dogs,
Or dromedary, with an antic pair
Of monkeys on his back; a minstrel band
Of Savoyards; or, single and alone,
An English ballad-singer. Private courts,   180
Gloomy as coffins, and unsightly lanes
Thrilled by some female vendor's scream, belike
The very shrillest of all London cries,
May then entangle our impatient steps;
Conducted through those labyrinths, unawares,   185
To privileged regions and inviolate,
Where from their airy lodges studious lawyers
Look out on waters, walks, and gardens green.

　　Thence back into the throng, until we reach,
Following the tide that slackens by degrees,   190
Some half-frequented scene, where wider streets
Bring straggling breezes of suburban air.
Here files of ballads dangle from dead walls;
Advertisements, of giant-size, from high
Press forward, in all colours, on the sight;   195
These, bold in conscious merit; lower down,
That, fronted with a most imposing word,
Is, peradventure, one in masquerade.
As on the broadening causeway we advance,

Behold, turned upwards, a face hard and strong   200
In lineaments, and red with over-toil.
'Tis one encountered here and everywhere;
A travelling cripple, by the trunk cut short,
And stumping on his arms. In sailor's garb
Another lies at length, beside a range   205
Of well-formed characters, with chalk inscribed
Upon the smooth flat stones: the Nurse is here,
The Bachelor, that loves to sun himself,
The military Idler, and the Dame,
That field-ward takes her walk with decent steps.   210

    Now homeward through the thickening hubbub, where
See, among less distinguishable shapes,
The begging scavenger, with hat in hand;
The Italian, as he thrids his way with care,
Steadying, far-seen, a frame of images   215
Upon his head; with basket at his breast
The Jew; the stately and slow-moving Turk,
With freight of slippers piled beneath his arm!

    Enough; — the mighty concourse I surveyed
With no unthinking mind, well pleased to note   220
Among the crowd all specimens of man,
Through all the colours which the sun bestows,
And every character of form and face:
The Swede, the Russian; from the genial south,
The Frenchman and the Spaniard; from remote   225
America, the Hunter-Indian; Moors,
Malays, Lascars, the Tartar, the Chinese,
And Negro Ladies in white muslin gowns.

    At leisure, then, I viewed, from day to day,
The spectacles within doors, — birds and beasts   230
Of every nature, and strange plants convened
From every clime; and, next, those sights that ape
The absolute presence of reality,
Expressing, as in mirror, sea and land,
And what earth is, and what she has to shew.   235
I do not here allude to subtlest craft,
By means refined attaining purest ends,
But imitations, fondly made in plain
Confession of man's weakness and his loves.
Whether the Painter, whose ambitious skill   240
Submits to nothing less than taking in
A whole horizon's circuit, do with power,
Like that of angels or commissioned spirits,
Fix us upon some lofty pinnacle,

Or in a ship on waters, with a world   245
Of life, and life-like mockery, beneath,
Above, behind, far stretching and before;
Or more mechanic artist represent
By scale exact, in model, wood or clay,
From blended colours also borrowing help,   250
Some miniature of famous spots or things, —
St. Peter's Church; or, more aspiring aim,
In microscopic vision, Rome herself;
Or, haply, some choice rural haunt, — the Falls
Of Tivoli; and, high upon that steep,   255
The Sibyl's mouldering Temple! every tree,
Villa, or cottage, lurking among rocks
Throughout the landscape; tuft, stone scratch minute —
All that the traveller sees when he is there.

  Add to these exhibitions, mute and still,   260
Others of wider scope, where living men,
Music, and shifting pantomimic scenes,
Diversified the allurement. Need I fear
To mention by its name, as in degree,
Lowest of these and humblest in attempt,   265
Yet richly graced with honours of her own,
Half-rural Sadler's Wells? Though at that time
Intolerant, as is the way of youth
Unless itself be pleased, here more than once
Taking my seat, I saw (nor blush to add,   270
With ample recompense) giants and dwarfs,
Clowns, conjurors, posture-masters, harlequins,
Amid the uproar of the rabblement,
Perform their feats. Nor was it mean delight
To watch crude Nature work in untaught minds;   275
To note the laws and progress of belief;
Though obstinate on this way, yet on that
How willingly we travel, and how far!
To have, for instance, brought upon the scene
The champion, Jack the Giant-killer: Lo!   280
He dons his coat of darkness; on the stage
Walks, and achieves his wonders, from the eye
Of living Mortal covert, "as the moon
Hid in her vacant interlunar cave."
Delusion bold! and how can it be wrought?   285
The garb he wears is black as death, the word
"*Invisible*" flames forth upon his chest.

  Here, too, were "forms and pressures of the time,"
Rough, bold, as Grecian comedy displayed
When Art was young; dramas of living men,   290

And recent things yet warm with life; a sea-fight,
Shipwreck, or some domestic incident
Divulged by Truth and magnified by Fame,
Such as the daring brotherhood of late
Set forth, too serious theme for that light place —   295
I mean, O distant Friend! a story drawn
From our own ground, — the Maid of Buttermere, —
And how, unfaithful to a virtuous wife
Deserted and deceived, the spoiler came
And wooed the artless daughter of the hills,   300
And wedded her, in cruel mockery
Of love and marriage bonds. These words to thee
Must needs bring back the moment when we first,
Ere the broad world rang with the maiden's name,
Beheld her serving at the cottage inn,   305
Both stricken, as she entered or withdrew,
With admiration of her modest mien
And carriage, marked by unexampled grace.
Not unfamiliarly we since that time
Have seen her, — her discretion have observed,   310
Her just opinions, delicate reserve,
Her patience, and humility of mind
Unspoiled by commendation and the excess
Of public notice — an offensive light
To a meek spirit suffering inwardly.   315

    From this memorial tribute to my theme
I was returning, when, with sundry forms
Commingled — shapes which met me in the way
That we must tread — thy image rose again,
Maiden of Buttermere! She lives in peace   320
Upon the spot where she was born and reared;
Without contamination doth she live
In quietness, without anxiety:
Beside the mountain chapel, sleeps in earth
Her new-born infant, fearless as a lamb   325
That, thither driven from some unsheltered place,
Rests underneath the little rock-like pile
When storms are raging. Happy are they both —
Mother and child! — These feelings, in themselves
Trite, do yet scarcely seem so when I think   330
On those ingenuous moments of our youth
Ere we have learnt by use to slight the crimes
And sorrows of the world. Those simple days
Are now my theme; and, foremost of the scenes,
Which yet survive in memory, appears   335
One, at whose centre sate a lovely Boy,
A sportive infant, who, for six months' space,

Not more, had been of age to deal about
Articulate prattle — Child as beautiful
As ever clung around a mother's neck,   340
Or father fondly gazed upon with pride.
There, too, conspicuous for stature tall
And large dark eyes, beside her infant stood
The mother; but, upon her cheeks diffused,
False tints too well accorded with the glare   345
From play-house lustres thrown without reserve
On every object near. The Boy had been
The pride and pleasure of all lookers-on
In whatsoever place, but seemed in this
A sort of alien scattered from the clouds.   350
Of lusty vigour, more than infantine
He was in limb, in cheek a summer rose
Just three parts blown — a cottage-child — if e'er,
By cottage-door on breezy mountain side,
Or in some sheltering vale, was seen a babe   355
By Nature's gifts so favoured. Upon a board
Decked with refreshments had this child been placed,
His little stage in the vast theatre,
And there he sate surrounded with a throng
Of chance spectators, chiefly dissolute men   360
And shameless women, treated and caressed;
Ate, drank, and with the fruit and glasses played,
While oaths and laughter and indecent speech
Were rife about him as the songs of birds
Contending after showers. The mother now   365
Is fading out of memory, but I see
The lovely Boy as I beheld him then
Among the wretched and the falsely gay,
Like one of those who walked with hair unsinged
Amid the fiery furnace. Charms and spells   370
Muttered on black and spiteful instigation
Have stopped, as some believe, the kindliest growths.
Ah, with how different spirit might a prayer
Have been preferred, that this fair creature, checked
By special privilege of Nature's love,   375
Should in his childhood be detained for ever!
But with its universal freight the tide
Hath rolled along, and this bright innocent,
Mary! may now have lived till he could look
With envy on thy nameless babe that sleeps,   380
Beside the mountain chapel, undisturbed.

Four rapid years had scarcely then been told
Since, travelling southward from our pastoral hills,

I heard, and for the first time in my life,
The voice of woman utter blasphemy —   385
Saw woman as she is, to open shame
Abandoned, and the pride of public vice;
I shuddered, for a barrier seemed at once
Thrown in, that from humanity divorced
Humanity, splitting the race of man   390
In twain, yet leaving the same outward form.
Distress of mind ensued upon the sight
And ardent meditation. Later years
Brought to such spectacle a milder sadness,
Feelings of pure commiseration, grief   395
For the individual and the overthrow
Of her soul's beauty; farther I was then
But seldom led, or wished to go; in truth
The sorrow of the passion stopped me there.

   But let me now, less moved, in order take   400
Our argument. Enough is said to show
How casual incidents of real life,
Observed where pastime only had been sought,
Outweighed, or put to flight, the set events
And measured passions of the stage, albeit   405
By Siddons trod in the fulness of her power.
Yet was the theatre my dear delight;
The very gilding, lamps and painted scrolls,
And all the mean upholstery of the place,
Wanted not animation, when the tide   410
Of pleasure ebbed but to return as fast
With the ever-shifting figures of the scene,
Solemn or gay: whether some beauteous dame
Advanced in radiance through a deep recess
Of thick entangled forest, like the moon   415
Opening the clouds; or sovereign king, announced
With flourishing trumpet, came in full-blown state
Of the world's greatness, winding round with train
Of courtiers, banners, and a length of guards;
Or captive led in abject weeds, and jingling   420
His slender manacles; or romping girl
Bounced, leapt, and pawed the air; or mumbling sire,
A scare-crow pattern of old age dressed up
In all the tatters of infirmity
All loosely put together, hobbled in,   425
Stumping upon a cane with which he smites,
From time to time, the solid boards, and makes them
Prate somewhat loudly of the whereabout
Of one so overloaded with his years.

But what of this! the laugh, the grin, grimace,   430
The antics striving to outstrip each other,
Were all received, the least of them not lost,
With an unmeasured welcome. Through the night,
Between the show, and many-headed mass
Of the spectators, and each several nook   435
Filled with its fray or brawl, how eagerly
And with what flashes, as it were, the mind
Turned this way — that way! sportive and alert
And watchful, as a kitten when at play,
While winds are eddying round her, among straws   440
And rustling leaves. Enchanting age and sweet!
Romantic almost, looked at through a space,
How small, of intervening years! For then,
Though surely no mean progress had been made
In meditations holy and sublime,   445
Yet something of a girlish child-like gloss
Of novelty survived for scenes like these;
Enjoyment haply handed down from times
When at a country-playhouse, some rude barn
Tricked out for that proud use, if I perchance   450
Caught, on a summer evening through a chink
In the old wall, an unexpected glimpse
Of daylight, the bare thought of where I was
Gladdened me more than if I had been led
Into a dazzling cavern of romance,   455
Crowded with Genii busy among works
Not to be looked at by the common sun.

    The matter that detains us now may seem,
To many, neither dignified enough
Nor arduous, yet will not be scorned by them,   460
Who, looking inward, have observed the ties
That bind the perishable hours of life
Each to the other, and the curious props
By which the world of memory and thought
Exists and is sustained. More lofty themes,   465
Such as at least do wear a prouder face,
Solicit our regard; but when I think
Of these, I feel the imaginative power
Languish within me; even then it slept,
When, pressed by tragic sufferings, the heart   470
Was more than full; amid my sobs and tears
It slept, even in the pregnant season of youth.
For though I was most passionately moved
And yielded to all changes of the scene
With an obsequious promptness, yet the storm   475

Passed not beyond the suburbs of the mind;
Save when realities of act and mien,
The incarnation of the spirits that move
In harmony amid the Poet's world,
Rose to ideal grandeur, or, called forth   480
By power of contrast, made me recognise,
As at a glance, the things which I had shaped,
And yet not shaped, had seen and scarcely seen,
When, having closed the mighty Shakspeare's page,
I mused, and thought, and felt, in solitude.   485

    Pass we from entertainments, that are such
Professedly, to others titled higher,
Yet, in the estimate of youth at least,
More near akin to those than names imply, —
I mean the brawls of lawyers in their courts   490
Before the ermined judge, or that great stage
Where senators, tongue-favoured men, perform,
Admired and envied. Oh! the beating heart,
When one among the prime of these rose up, —
One, of whose name from childhood we had heard   495
Familiarly, a household term, like those,
The Bedfords, Glosters, Salsburys, of old
Whom the fifth Harry talks of. Silence! hush!
This is no trifler, no short-flighted wit,
No stammerer of a minute, painfully   500
Delivered. No! the Orator hath yoked
The Hours, like young Aurora, to his car:
Thrice welcome Presence! how can patience e'er
Grow weary of attending on a track
That kindles with such glory! All are charmed,   505
Astonished; like a hero in romance,
He winds away his never-ending horn;
Words follow words, sense seems to follow sense:
What memory and what logic! till the strain
Transcendent, superhuman as it seemed,   510
Grows tedious even in a young man's ear.

    Genius of Burke! forgive the pen seduced
By specious wonders, and too slow to tell
Of what the ingenuous, what bewildered men,
Beginning to mistrust their boastful guides,   515
And wise men, willing to grow wiser, caught,
Rapt auditors! from thy most eloquent tongue —
Now mute, for ever mute in the cold grave.
I see him, — old, but vigorous in age, —
Stand like an oak whose stag-horn branches start   520

Out of its leafy brow, the more to awe
The younger brethren of the grove. But some —
While he forewarns, denounces, launches forth,
Against all systems built on abstract rights,
Keen ridicule; the majesty proclaims   525
Of Institutes and Laws, hallowed by time;
Declares the vital power of social ties
Endeared by Custom; and with high disdain,
Exploding upstart Theory, insists
Upon the allegiance to which men are born —   530
Some — say at once a froward multitude —
Murmur (for truth is hated, where not loved)
As the winds fret within the Æolian cave,
Galled by their monarch's chain. The times were big
With ominous change, which, night by night, provoked   535
Keen struggles, and black clouds of passion raised;
But memorable moments intervened,
When Wisdom, like the Goddess from Jove's brain,
Broke forth in armour of resplendent words,
Startling the Synod. Could a youth, and one   540
In ancient story versed, whose breast had heaved
Under the weight of classic eloquence,
Sit, see, and hear, unthankful, uninspired?

   Nor did the Pulpit's oratory fail
To achieve its higher triumphs. Not unfelt   545
Were its admonishments, nor lightly heard
The awful truths delivered thence by tongues
Endowed with various power to search the soul;
Yet ostentation, domineering, oft
Poured forth harangues, how sadly out of place! —   550
There have I seen a comely bachelor,
Fresh from a toilette of two hours, ascend
His rostrum, with seraphic glance look up,
And, in a tone elaborately low
Beginning, lead his voice through many a maze   555
A minuet course; and, winding up his mouth,
From time to time, into an orifice
Most delicate, a lurking eyelet, small,
And only not invisible, again
Open it out, diffusing thence a smile   560
Of rapt irradiation, exquisite.
Meanwhile the Evangelists, Isaiah, Job,
Moses, and he who penned, the other day,
The Death of Abel, Shakspeare, and the Bard
Whose genius spangled o'er a gloomy theme   565
With fancies thick as his inspiring stars,

And Ossian (doubt not, 'tis the naked truth)
Summoned from streamy Morven — each and all
Would, in their turns, lend ornaments and flowers
To entwine the crook of eloquence that helped   570
This pretty Shepherd, pride of all the plains,
To rule and guide his captivated flock.

    I glance but at a few conspicuous marks,
Leaving a thousand others, that, in hall,
Court, theatre, conventicle, or shop,   575
In public room or private, park or street,
Each fondly reared on his own pedestal,
Looked out for admiration. Folly, vice,
Extravagance in gesture, mien, and dress,
And all the strife of singularity,   580
Lies to the ear, and lies to every sense —
Of these, and of the living shapes they wear,
There is no end. Such candidates for regard,
Although well pleased to be where they were found,
I did not hunt after, nor greatly prize,   585
Nor made unto myself a secret boast
Of reading them with quick and curious eye;
But, as a common produce, things that are
To-day, to-morrow will be, took of them
Such willing note, as, on some errand bound   590
That asks not speed, a Traveller might bestow
On sea-shells that bestrew the sandy beach,
Or daisies swarming through the fields of June.

    But foolishness and madness in parade,
Though most at home in this their dear domain,   595
Are scattered everywhere, no rarities,
Even to the rudest novice of the Schools.
Me, rather, it employed, to note, and keep
In memory, those individual sights
Of courage, or integrity, or truth,   600
Or tenderness, which there, set off by foil,
Appeared more touching. One will I select;
A Father — for he bore that sacred name —
Him saw I, sitting in an open square,
Upon a corner-stone of that low wall,   605
Wherein were fixed the iron pales that fenced
A spacious grass-plot; there, in silence, sate
This One Man, with a sickly babe outstretched
Upon his knee, whom he had thither brought
For sunshine, and to breathe the fresher air.   610
Of those who passed, and me who looked at him.

He took no heed; but in his brawny arms
(The Artificer was to the elbow bare,
And from his work this moment had been stolen)
He held the child, and, bending over it,   615
As if he were afraid both of the sun
And of the air, which he had come to seek,
Eyed the poor babe with love unutterable.

    As the black storm upon the mountain top
Sets off the sunbeam in the valley, so   620
That huge fermenting mass of human-kind
Serves as a solemn back-ground, or relief,
To single forms and objects, whence they draw,
For feeling and contemplative regard,
More than inherent liveliness and power.   625
How oft, amid those overflowing streets,
Have I gone forward with the crowd, and said
Unto myself, "The face of every one
That passes by me is a mystery!"
Thus have I looked, nor ceased to look, oppressed   630
By thoughts of what and whither, when and how,
Until the shapes before my eyes became
A second-sight procession, such as glides
Over still mountains, or appears in dreams;
And once, far-travelled in such mood, beyond   635
The reach of common indication, lost
Amid the moving pageant, I was smitten
Abruptly, with the view (a sight not rare)
Of a blind Beggar, who, with upright face,
Stood, propped against a wall, upon his chest   640
Wearing a written paper, to explain
His story, whence he came, and who he was.
Caught by the spectacle my mind turned round
As with the might of waters; an apt type
This label seemed of the utmost we can know,   645
Both of ourselves and of the universe;
And, on the shape of that unmoving man,
His steadfast face and sightless eyes, I gazed,
As if admonished from another world.

    Though reared upon the base of outward things,   650
Structures like these the excited spirit mainly
Builds for herself; scenes different there are,
Full-formed, that take, with small internal help,
Possession of the faculties, — the peace
That comes with night; the deep solemnity   655
Of nature's intermediate hours of rest,

When the great tide of human life stands still;
The business of the day to come, unborn,
Of that gone by, locked up, as in the grave;
The blended calmness of the heavens and earth,   660
Moonlight and stars, and empty streets, and sounds
Unfrequent as in deserts; at late hours
Of winter evenings, when unwholesome rains
Are falling hard, with people yet astir,
The feeble salutation from the voice   665
Of some unhappy woman, now and then
Heard as we pass, when no one looks about,
Nothing is listened to. But these, I fear,
Are falsely catalogued; things that are, are not,
As the mind answers to them, or the heart   670
Is prompt, or slow, to feel. What say you, then,
To times, when half the city shall break out
Full of one passion, vengeance, rage, or fear?
To executions, to a street on fire,
Mobs, riots, or rejoicings? From these sights   675
Take one, — that ancient festival, the Fair,
Holden where martyrs suffered in past time,
And named of St. Bartholomew; there, see
A work completed to our hands, that lays,
If any spectacle on earth can do,   680
The whole creative powers of man asleep! —
For once, the Muse's help will we implore,
And she shall lodge us, wafted on her wings,
Above the press and danger of the crowd,
Upon some showman's platform. What a shock   685
For eyes and ears! what anarchy and din,
Barbarian and infernal, — a phantasma,
Monstrous in colour, motion, shape, sight, sound!
Below, the open space, through every nook
Of the wide area, twinkles, is alive   690
With heads; the midway region, and above,
Is thronged with staring pictures and huge scrolls,
Dumb proclamations of the Prodigies;
With chattering monkeys dangling from their poles,
And children whirling in their roundabouts;   695
With those that stretch the neck and strain the eyes,
And crack the voice in rivalship, the crowd
Inviting; with buffoons against buffoons
Grimacing, writhing, screaming, — him who grinds
The hurdy-gurdy, at the fiddle weaves,   700
Rattles the salt-box, thumps the kettle-drum,
And him who at the trumpet puffs his cheeks,
The silver-collared Negro with his timbrel,

Equestrians, tumblers, women, girls, and boys,
Blue-breeched, pink-vested, with high-towering plumes. — 705
All moveables of wonder, from all parts,
Are here — Albinos, painted Indians, Dwarfs,
The Horse of knowledge, and the learned Pig,
The Stone-eater, the man that swallows fire,
Giants, Ventriloquists, the Invisible Girl, 710
The Bust that speaks and moves its goggling eyes,
The Wax-work, Clock-work, all the marvellous craft
Of modern Merlins, Wild Beasts, Puppet-shows,
All out-o'-the-way, far-fetched, perverted things,
All freaks of nature, all Promethean thoughts 715
Of man, his dullness, madness, and their feats
All jumbled up together, to compose
A Parliament of Monsters. Tents and Booths
Meanwhile, as if the whole were one vast mill,
Are vomiting, receiving on all sides, 720
Men, Women, three-years' Children, Babes in arms.

Oh, blank confusion! true epitome
Of what the mighty City is herself,
To thousands upon thousands of her sons,
Living amid the same perpetual whirl 725
Of trivial objects, melted and reduced
To one identity, by differences
That have no law, no meaning, and no end —
Oppression, under which even highest minds
Must labour, whence the strongest are not free. 730
But though the picture weary out the eye,
By nature an unmanageable sight,
It is not wholly so to him who looks
In steadiness, who hath among least things
An under-sense of greatest; sees the parts 735
As parts, but with a feeling of the whole.
This, of all acquisitions first, awaits
On sundry and most widely different modes
Of education, nor with least delight
On that through which I passed. Attention springs, 740
And comprehensiveness and memory flow,
From early converse with the works of God
Among all regions; chiefly where appear
Most obviously simplicity and power.
Think, how the everlasting streams and woods, 745
Stretched and still stretching far and wide, exalt
The roving Indian. On his desert sands
What grandeur not unfelt, what pregnant show
Of beauty, meets the sun-burnt Arab's eye:
And, as the sea propels, from zone to zone, 750

Its currents; magnifies its shoals of life
Beyond all compass; spreads, and sends aloft
Armies of clouds, — even so, its powers and aspects
Shape for mankind, by principles as fixed,
The views and aspirations of the soul   755
To majesty. Like virtue have the forms
Perennial of the ancient hills; nor less
The changeful language of their countenances
Quickens the slumbering mind, and aids the thoughts,
However multitudinous, to move   760
With order and relation. This, if still,
As hitherto, in freedom I may speak,
Not violating any just restraint,
As may be hoped, of real modesty, —
This did I feel, in London's vast domain.   765
The Spirit of Nature was upon me there;
The soul of Beauty and enduring Life
Vouchsafed her inspiration, and diffused,
Through meagre lines and colours, and the press
Of self-destroying, transitory things,   770
Composure, and ennobling Harmony.

BOOK EIGHTH

RETROSPECT — LOVE OF NATURE LEADING TO LOVE OF MAN

WHAT sounds are those, Helvellyn, that are heard
Up to thy summit, through the depth of air
Ascending, as if distance had the power
To make the sounds more audible? What crowd
Covers, or sprinkles o'er, yon village green?   5
Crowd seems it, solitary hill! to thee,
Though but a little family of men,
Shepherds and tillers of the ground — betimes
Assembled with their children and their wives,
And here and there a stranger interspersed.   10
They hold a rustic fair — a festival,
Such as, on this side now, and now on that,
Repeated through his tributary vales,
Helvellyn, in the silence of his rest,
Sees annually, if clouds towards either ocean   15
Blown from their favourite resting-place, or mists
Dissolved, have left him an unshrouded head.
Delightful day it is for all who dwell
In this secluded glen, and eagerly
They give it welcome. Long ere heat of noon,   20
From byre or field the kine were brought; the sheep

Are penned in cotes; the chaffering is begun.
The heifer lows, uneasy at the voice
Of a new master; bleat the flocks aloud.
Booths are there none; a stall or two is here;   25
A lame man or a blind, the one to beg,
The other to make music; hither, too,
From far, with basket, slung upon her arm,
Of hawker's wares — books, pictures, combs, and pins —
Some aged woman finds her way again,   30
Year after year, a punctual visitant!
There also stands a speech-maker by rote,
Pulling the strings of his boxed raree-show;
And in the lapse of many years may come
Prouder itinerant, mountebank, or he   35
Whose wonders in a covered wain lie hid.
But one there is, the loveliest of them all,
Some sweet lass of the valley, looking out
For gains, and who that sees her would not buy?
Fruits of her father's orchard are her wares,   40
And with the ruddy produce she walks round
Among the crowd, half pleased with, half ashamed
Of her new office, blushing restlessly.
The children now are rich, for the old to-day
Are generous as the young; and, if content   45
With looking on, some ancient wedded pair
Sit in the shade together, while they gaze,
"A cheerful smile unbends the wrinkled brow,
The days departed start again to life,
And all the scenes of childhood reappear,   50
Faint, but more tranquil, like the changing sun
To him who slept at noon and wakes at eve."
Thus gaiety and cheerfulness prevail,
Spreading from young to old, from old to young,
And no one seems to want his share. — Immense   55
Is the recess, the circumambient world
Magnificent, by which they are embraced:
They move about upon the soft green turf:
How little they, they and their doings, seem,
And all that they can further or obstruct!   60
Through utter weakness pitiably dear,
As tender infants are: and yet how great!
For all things serve them: them the morning light
Loves, as it glistens on the silent rocks;
And them the silent rocks, which now from high   65
Look down upon them; the reposing clouds;
The wild brooks prattling from invisible haunts;
And old Helvellyn, conscious of the stir
Which animates this day their calm abode.

With deep devotion, Nature, did I feel,　　　　70
In that enormous City's turbulent world
Of men and things, what benefit I owed
To thee, and those domains of rural peace,
Where to the sense of beauty first my heart
Was opened; tract more exquisitely fair　　　75
Than that famed paradise of ten thousand trees,
Or Gehol's matchless gardens, for delight
Of the Tartarian dynasty composed
(Beyond that mighty wall, not fabulous,
China's stupendous mound) by patient toil　　80
Of myriads and boon nature's lavish help;
There, in a clime from widest empire chosen,
Fulfilling (could enchantment have done more?)
A sumptuous dream of flowery lawns, with domes
Of pleasure sprinkled over, shady dells　　　85
For eastern monasteries, sunny mounts
With temples crested, bridges, gondolas,
Rocks, dens, and groves of foliage taught to melt
Into each other their obsequious hues,
Vanished and vanishing in subtle chase,　　　90
Too fine to be pursued; or standing forth
In no discordant opposition, strong
And gorgeous as the colours side by side
Bedded among rich plumes of tropic birds;
And mountains over all, embracing all;　　　95
And all the landscape, endlessly enriched
With waters running, falling, or asleep.

But lovelier far than this, the paradise
Where I was reared; in Nature's primitive gifts
Favoured no less, and more to every sense　　100
Delicious, seeing that the sun and sky,
The elements, and seasons as they change,
Do find a worthy fellow-labourer there —
Man free, man working for himself, with choice
Of time, and place, and object; by his wants,　105
His comforts, native occupations, cares,
Cheerfully led to individual ends
Or social, and still followed by a train
Unwooed, unthought-of even — simplicity,
And beauty, and inevitable grace.　　　　110

Yea, when a glimpse of those imperial bowers
Would to a child be transport over-great,
When but a half-hour's roam through such a place
Would leave behind a dance of images,
That shall break in upon his sleep for weeks;　115

Even then the common haunts of the green earth,
And ordinary interests of man,
Which they embosom, all without regard
As both may seem, are fastening on the heart
Insensibly, each with the other's help. 120
For me, when my affections first were led
From kindred, friends, and playmates, to partake
Love for the human creature's absolute self,
That noticeable kindliness of heart
Sprang out of fountains, there abounding most 125
Where sovereign Nature dictated the tasks
And occupations which her beauty adorned,
And Shepherds were the men that pleased me first;
Not such as Saturn ruled 'mid Latian wilds,
With arts and laws so tempered, that their lives 130
Left, even to us toiling in this late day,
A bright tradition of the golden age;
Not such as, 'mid Arcadian fastnesses
Sequestered, handed down among themselves
Felicity, in Grecian song renowned; 135
Nor such as, when an adverse fate had driven,
From house and home, the courtly band whose fortunes
Entered, with Shakspeare's genius, the wild woods
Of Arden, amid sunshine or in shade,
Culled the best fruits of Time's uncounted hours, 140
Ere Phœbe sighed for the false Ganymede;
Or there where Perdita and Florizel
Together danced, Queen of the feast, and King;
Nor such as Spenser fabled. True it is,
That I had heard (what he perhaps had seen) 145
Of maids at sunrise bringing in from far
Their May-bush, and along the street in flocks
Parading with a song of taunting rhymes,
Aimed at the laggards slumbering within doors;
Had also heard, from those who yet remembered, 150
Tales of the May-pole dance, and wreaths that decked
Porch, door-way, or kirk-pillar; and of youths,
Each with his maid, before the sun was up,
By annual custom, issuing forth in troops,
To drink the waters of some sainted well, 155
And hang it round with garlands. Love survives;
But, for such purpose, flowers no longer grow:
The times, too sage, perhaps too proud, have dropped
These lighter graces; and the rural ways
And manners which my childhood looked upon 160
Were the unluxuriant produce of a life
Intent on little but substantial needs,

Yet rich in beauty, beauty that was felt.
But images of danger and distress,
Man suffering among awful Powers and Forms;   165
Of this I heard, and saw enough to make
Imagination restless; nor was free
Myself from frequent perils; nor were tales
Wanting, — the tragedies of former times,
Hazards and strange escapes, of which the rocks   170
Immutable and everflowing streams,
Where'er I roamed, were speaking monuments.

    Smooth life had flock and shepherd in old time,
Long springs and tepid winters, on the banks
Of delicate Galesus; and no less   175
Those scattered along Adria's myrtle shores:
Smooth life had herdsman, and his snow-white herd
To triumphs and to sacrificial rites
Devoted, on the inviolable stream
Of rich Clitumnus; and the goat-herd lived   180
As calmly, underneath the pleasant brows
Of cool Lucretilis, where the pipe was heard
Of Pan, Invisible God, thrilling the rocks
With tutelary music, from all harm
The fold protecting. I myself, mature   185
In manhood then, have seen a pastoral tract
Like one of these, where Fancy might run wild,
Though under skies less generous, less serene:
There, for her own delight had Nature framed
A pleasure-ground, diffused a fair expanse   190
Of level pasture, islanded with groves
And banked with woody risings; but the Plain
Endless, here opening widely out, and there
Shut up in lesser lakes or beds of lawn
And intricate recesses, creek or bay   195
Sheltered within a shelter, where at large
The shepherd strays, a rolling hut his home.
Thither he comes with spring-time, there abides
All summer, and at sunrise ye may hear
His flageolet to liquid notes of love   200
Attuned, or sprightly fife resounding far.
Nook is there none, nor tract of that vast space
Where passage opens, but the same shall have
In turn its visitant, telling there his hours
In unlaborious pleasure, with no task   205
More toilsome than to carve a beechen bowl
For spring or fountain, which the traveller finds,
When through the region he pursues at will

His devious course. A glimpse of such sweet life
I saw when, from the melancholy walls   210
Of Goslar, once imperial, I renewed
My daily walk along that wide champaign,
That, reaching to her gates, spreads east and west,
And northwards, from beneath the mountainous verge
Of the Hercynian forest. Yet, hail to you   215
Moors, mountains, headlands, and ye hollow vales,
Ye long deep channels for the Atlantic's voice,
Powers of my native region! Ye that seize
The heart with firmer grasp! Your snows and streams
Ungovernable, and your terrifying winds,   220
That howl so dismally for him who treads
Companionless your awful solitudes!
There, 'tis the shepherd's task the winter long
To wait upon the storms: of their approach
Sagacious, into sheltering coves he drives   225
His flock, and thither from the homestead bears
A toilsome burden up the craggy ways,
And deals it out, their regular nourishment
Strewn on the frozen snow. And when the spring
Looks out, and all the pastures dance with lambs,   230
And when the flock, with warmer weather, climbs
Higher and higher, him his office leads
To watch their goings, whatsoever track
The wanderers choose. For this he quits his home
At day-spring, and no sooner doth the sun   235
Begin to strike him with a fire-like heat,
Than he lies down upon some shining rock,
And breakfasts with his dog. When they have stolen,
As is their wont, a pittance from strict time,
For rest not needed or exchange of love,   240
Then from his couch he starts; and now his feet
Crush out a livelier fragrance from the flowers
Of lowly thyme, by Nature's skill enwrought
In the wild turf: the lingering dews of morn
Smoke round him, as from hill to hill he hies,   245
His staff protending like a hunter's spear,
Or by its aid leaping from crag to crag,
And o'er the brawling beds of unbridged streams.
Philosophy, methinks, at Fancy's call,
Might deign to follow him through what he does   250
Or sees in his day's march; himself he feels,
In those vast regions where his service lies,
A freeman, wedded to his life of hope
And hazard, and hard labour interchanged
With that majestic indolence so dear   255
To native man. A rambling school-boy, thus

I felt his presence in his own domain,
As of a lord and master, or a power,
Or genius, under Nature, under God,
Presiding; and severest solitude 260
Had more commanding looks when he was there.
When up the lonely brooks on rainy days
Angling I went, or trod the trackless hills
By mists bewildered, suddenly mine eyes
Have glanced upon him distant a few steps, 265
In size a giant, stalking through thick fog,
His sheep like Greenland bears; or, as he stepped
Beyond the boundary line of some hill-shadow,
His form hath flashed upon me, glorified
By the deep radiance of the setting sun: 270
Or him have I descried in distant sky,
A solitary object and sublime,
Above all height! like an aerial cross
Stationed alone upon a spiry rock
Of the Chartreuse, for worship. Thus was man 275
Ennobled outwardly before my sight,
And thus my heart was early introduced
To an unconscious love and reverence
Of human nature; hence the human form
To me became an index of delight, 280
Of grace and honour, power and worthiness.
Meanwhile this creature — spiritual almost
As those of books, but more exalted far;
Far more of an imaginative form
Than the gay Corin of the groves, who lives 285
For his own fancies, or to dance by the hour,
In coronal, with Phyllis in the midst —
Was, for the purposes of kind, a man
With the most common; husband, father; learned,
Could teach, admonish; suffered with the rest 290
From vice and folly, wretchedness and fear;
Of this I little saw, cared less for it,
But something must have felt.
       Call ye these appearances —
Which I beheld of shepherds in my youth,
This sanctity of Nature given to man — 295
A shadow, a delusion, ye who pore
On the dead letter, miss the spirit of things;
Whose truth is not a motion or a shape
Instinct with vital functions, but a block
Or waxen image which yourselves have made, 300
And ye adore! But blessed be the God
Of Nature and of Man that this was so;
That men before my inexperienced eyes

Did first present themselves thus purified,
Removed, and to a distance that was fit: 305
And so we all of us in some degree
Are led to knowledge, whencesoever led,
And howsoever; were it otherwise,
And we found evil fast as we find good
In our first years, or think that it is found,   310
How could the innocent heart bear up and live!
But doubly fortunate my lot; not here
Alone, that something of a better life
Perhaps was round me than it is the privilege
Of most to move in, but that first I looked   315
At Man through objects that were great or fair;
First communed with him by their help. And thus
Was founded a sure safeguard and defence
Against the weight of meanness, selfish cares,
Coarse manners, vulgar passions, that beat in   320
On all sides from the ordinary world
In which we traffic. Starting from this point
I had my face turned toward the truth, began
With an advantage furnished by that kind
Of prepossession, without which the soul   325
Receives no knowledge that can bring forth good,
No genuine insight ever comes to her.
From the restraint of over-watchful eyes
Preserved, I moved about, year after year,
Happy, and now most thankful that my walk   330
Was guarded from too early intercourse
With the deformities of crowded life,
And those ensuing laughters and contempts,
Self-pleasing, which, if we would wish to think
With a due reverence on earth's rightful lord,   335
Here placed to be the inheritor of heaven,
Will not permit us; but pursue the mind,
That to devotion willingly would rise,
Into the temple and the temple's heart.

Yet deem not, Friend! that human kind with me   340
Thus early took a place pre-eminent;
Nature herself was, at this unripe time,
But secondary to my own pursuits
And animal activities, and all
Their trivial pleasures; and when these had drooped   345
And gradually expired, and Nature, prized
For her own sake, became my joy, even then —
And upwards through late youth, until not less
Than two-and-twenty summers had been told —
Was Man in my affections and regards   350

Subordinate to her, her visible forms
And viewless agencies: a passion, she,
A rapture often, and immediate love
Ever at hand; he, only a delight
Occasional, an accidental grace,   355
His hour being not yet come. Far less had then
The inferior creatures, beast or bird, attuned
My spirit to that gentleness of love
(Though they had long been carefully observed),
Won from me those minute obeisances   360
Of tenderness, which I may number now
With my first blessings. Nevertheless, on these
The light of beauty did not fall in vain,
Or grandeur circumfuse them to no end.

   But when that first poetic faculty   365
Of plain Imagination and severe,
No longer a mute influence of the soul,
Ventured, at some rash Muse's earnest call,
To try her strength among harmonious words;
And to book-notions and the rules of art   370
Did knowingly conform itself; there came
Among the simple shapes of human life
A wilfulness of fancy and conceit;
And Nature and her objects beautified
These fictions, as in some sort, in their turn,   375
They burnished her. From touch of this new power
Nothing was safe: the elder-tree that grew
Beside the well-known charnel-house had then
A dismal look: the yew-tree had its ghost,
That took his station there for ornament: 380
The dignities of plain occurrence then
Were tasteless, and truth's golden mean, a point
Where no sufficient pleasure could be found.
Then, if a widow, staggering with the blow
Of her distress, was known to have turned her steps   385
To the cold grave in which her husband slept,
One night, or haply more than one, through pain
Or half-insensate impotence of mind,
The fact was caught at greedily, and there
She must be visitant the whole year through,   390
Wetting the turf with never-ending tears.

   Through quaint obliquities I might pursue
These cravings; when the fox-glove, one by one,
Upwards through every stage of the tall stem,
Had shed beside the public way its bells,   395
And stood of all dismantled, save the last

Left at the tapering ladder's top, that seemed
To bend as doth a slender blade of grass
Tipped with a rain-drop, Fancy loved to seat,
Beneath the plant despoiled, but crested still   400
With this last relic, soon itself to fall,
Some vagrant mother, whose arch little ones,
All unconcerned by her dejected plight,
Laughed as with rival eagerness their hands
Gathered the purple cups that round them lay,   405
Strewing the turf's green slope.

                    A diamond light
(Whene'er the summer sun, declining, smote
A smooth rock wet with constant springs) was seen
Sparkling from out a copse-clad bank that rose
Fronting our cottage. Oft beside the hearth   410
Seated, with open door, often and long
Upon this restless lustre have I gazed,
That made my fancy restless as itself.
'Twas now for me a burnished silver shield
Suspended over a knight's tomb, who lay   415
Inglorious, buried in the dusky wood:
An entrance now into some magic cave
Or palace built by fairies of the rock;
Nor could I have been bribed to disenchant
The spectacle, by visiting the spot.   420
Thus wilful Fancy, in no hurtful mood,
Engrafted far-fetched shapes on feelings bred
By pure Imagination: busy Power
She was, and with her ready pupil turned
Instinctively to human passions, then   425
Least understood. Yet, 'mid the fervent swarm
Of these vagaries, with an eye so rich
As mine was through the bounty of a grand
And lovely region, I had forms distinct
To steady me: each airy thought revolved   430
Round a substantial centre, which at once
Incited it to motion, and controlled.
I did not pine like one in cities bred,
As was thy melancholy lot, dear Friend!
Great Spirit as thou art, in endless dreams   435
Of sickliness, disjoining, joining, things
Without the light of knowledge. Where the harm,
If, when the woodman languished with disease
Induced by sleeping nightly on the ground
Within his sod-built cabin, Indian-wise,   440
I called the pangs of disappointed love,
And all the sad etcetera of the wrong,
To help him to his grave? Meanwhile the man,

If not already from the woods retired
To die at home, was haply, as I knew,   445
Withering by slow degrees, 'mid gentle airs,
Birds, running streams, and hills so beautiful
On golden evenings, while the charcoal pile
Breathed up its smoke, an image of his ghost
Or spirit that full soon must take her flight.   450
Nor shall we not be tending towards that point
Of sound humanity to which our Tale
Leads, though by sinuous ways, if here I shew
How Fancy, in a season when she wove
Those slender cords, to guide the unconscious Boy   455
For the Man's sake, could feed at Nature's call
Some pensive musings which might well beseem
Maturer years.
        A grove there is whose boughs
Stretch from the western marge of Thurston-mere,
With length of shade so thick, that whoso glides   460
Along the line of low-roofed water, moves
As in a cloister. Once — while, in that shade
Loitering, I watched the golden beams of light
Flung from the setting sun, as they reposed
In silent beauty on the naked ridge   465
Of a high eastern hill — thus flowed my thoughts
In a pure stream of words fresh from the heart:
Dear native Regions, wheresoe'er shall close
My mortal course, there will I think on you;
Dying, will cast on you a backward look;   470
Even as this setting sun (albeit the Vale
Is no where touched by one memorial gleam)
Doth with the fond remains of his last power
Still linger, and a farewell lustre sheds
On the dear mountain-tops where first he rose.   475

  Enough of humble arguments; recall,
My Song! those high emotions which thy voice
Has heretofore made known; that bursting forth
Of sympathy, inspiring and inspired,
When everywhere a vital pulse was felt,   480
And all the several frames of things, like stars,
Through every magnitude distinguishable,
Shone mutually indebted, or half lost
Each in the other's blaze, a galaxy
Of life and glory. In the midst stood Man,   485
Outwardly, inwardly contemplated,
As, of all visible natures, crown, though born
Of dust, and kindred to the worm; a Being,
Both in perception and discernment, first

In every capability of rapture, 490
Through the divine effect of power and love;
As, more than anything we know, instinct
With godhead, and, by reason and by will,
Acknowledging dependency sublime.

Ere long, the lonely mountains left, I moved, 495
Begirt, from day to day, with temporal shapes
Of vice and folly thrust upon my view,
Objects of sport, and ridicule, and scorn,
Manners and characters discriminate,
And little bustling passions that eclipsed, 500
As well they might, the impersonated thought,
The idea, or abstraction of the kind.

An idler among academic bowers,
Such was my new condition, as at large
Has been set forth; yet here the vulgar light 505
Of present, actual, superficial life,
Gleaming through colouring of other times,
Old usages and local privilege,
Was welcome, softened, if not solemnised.
This notwithstanding, being brought more near 510
To vice and guilt, forerunning wretchedness,
I trembled, — thought, at times, of human life
With an indefinite terror and dismay,
Such as the storms and angry elements
Had bred in me; but gloomier far, a dim 515
Analogy to uproar and misrule,
Disquiet, danger, and obscurity.

It might be told (but wherefore speak of things
Common to all?) that, seeing, I was led
Gravely to ponder — judging between good 520
And evil, not as for the mind's delight
But for her guidance — one who was to *act*,
As sometimes to the best of feeble means
I did, by human sympathy impelled:
And, through dislike and most offensive pain, 525
Was to the truth conducted; of this faith
Never forsaken, that, by acting well,
And understanding, I should learn to love
The end of life, and every thing we know.

Grave Teacher, stern Preceptress! for at times 530
Thou canst put on an aspect most severe;
London, to thee I willingly return.
Erewhile my verse played idly with the flowers

Enwrought upon thy mantle; satisfied
With that amusement, and a simple look   535
Of child-like inquisition now and then
Cast upwards on thy countenance, to detect
Some inner meanings which might harbour there.
But how could I in mood so light indulge,
Keeping such fresh remembrance of the day,   540
When, having thridded the long labyrinth
Of the suburban villages, I first
Entered thy vast dominion? On the roof
Of an itinerant vehicle I sate,
With vulgar men about me, trivial forms   545
Of houses, pavement, streets, of men and things, —
Mean shapes on every side: but, at the instant,
When to myself it fairly might be said,
The threshold now is overpast, (how strange
That aught external to the living mind   550
Should have such mighty sway! yet so it was),
A weight of ages did at once descend
Upon my heart; no thought embodied, no
Distinct remembrances, but weight and power, —
Power growing under weight: alas! I feel   555
That I am trifling: 'twas a moment's pause, —
All that took place within me came and went
As in a moment; yet with Time it dwells,
And grateful memory, as a thing divine.

The curious traveller, who, from open day,   560
Hath passed with torches into some huge cave,
The Grotto of Antiparos, or the Den
In old time haunted by that Danish Witch,
Yordas; he looks around and sees the vault
Widening on all sides; sees, or thinks he sees,   565
Erelong, the massy roof above his head,
That instantly unsettles and recedes, —
Substance and shadow, light and darkness, all
Commingled, making up a canopy
Of shapes and forms and tendencies to shape   570
That shift and vanish, change and interchange
Like spectres, — ferment silent and sublime!
That after a short space works less and less,
Till, every effort, every motion gone,
The scene before him stands in perfect view   575
Exposed, and lifeless as a written book! —
But let him pause awhile, and look again,
And a new quickening shall succeed, at first
Beginning timidly, then creeping fast,
Till the whole cave, so late a senseless mass,   580

Busies the eye with images and forms
Boldly assembled, — here is shadowed forth
From the projections, wrinkles, cavities,
A variegated landscape, — there the shape
Of some gigantic warrior clad in mail,   585
The ghostly semblance of a hooded monk,
Veiled nun, or pilgrim resting on his staff:
Strange congregation! yet not slow to meet
Eyes that perceive through minds that can inspire.

    Even in such sort had I at first been moved,   590
Nor otherwise continued to be moved,
As I explored the vast metropolis,
Fount of my country's destiny and the world's;
That great emporium, chronicle at once
And burial-place of passions, and their home   595
Imperial, their chief living residence.

    With strong sensations teeming as it did
Of past and present, such a place must needs
Have pleased me, seeking knowledge at that time
Far less than craving power; yet knowledge came,   600
Sought or unsought, and influxes of power
Came, of themselves, or at her call derived
In fits of kindliest apprehensiveness,
From all sides, when whate'er was in itself
Capacious found, or seemed to find, in me   605
A correspondent amplitude of mind;
Such is the strength and glory of our youth!
The human nature unto which I felt
That I belonged, and reverenced with love,
Was not a punctual presence, but a spirit   610
Diffused through time and space, with aid derived
Of evidence from monuments, erect,
Prostrate, or leaning towards their common rest
In earth, the widely scattered wreck sublime
Of vanished nations, or more clearly drawn   615
From books and what they picture and record.

    'Tis true, the history of our native land,
With those of Greece compared and popular Rome,
And in our high-wrought modern narratives
Stript of their harmonising soul, the life   620
Of manners and familiar incidents,
Had never much delighted me. And less
Than other intellects had mine been used
To lean upon extrinsic circumstance
Of record or tradition; but a sense   625

Of what in the Great City had been done
And suffered, and was doing, suffering, still,
Weighed with me, could support the test of thought;
And, in despite of all that had gone by,
Or was departing never to return,   630
There I conversed with majesty and power
Like independent natures. Hence the place
Was thronged with impregnations like the Wilds
In which my early feelings had been nursed —
Bare hills and valleys, full of caverns, rocks,   635
And audible seclusions, dashing lakes,
Echoes and waterfalls, and pointed crags
That into music touch the passing wind.
Here then my young imagination found
No uncongenial element; could here   640
Among new objects serve or give command,
Even as the heart's occasions might require,
To forward reason's else too scrupulous march.
The effect was, still more elevated views
Of human nature. Neither vice nor guilt,   645
Debasement undergone by body or mind,
Nor all the misery forced upon my sight,
Misery not lightly passed, but sometimes scanned
Most feelingly, could overthrow my trust
In what we *may* become; induce belief   650
That I was ignorant, had been falsely taught,
A solitary, who with vain conceits
Had been inspired, and walked about in dreams.
From those sad scenes when meditation turned,
Lo! every thing that was indeed divine   655
Retained its purity inviolate,
Nay brighter shone, by this portentous gloom
Set off; such opposition as aroused
The mind of Adam, yet in Paradise
Though fallen from bliss, when in the East he saw   660
Darkness ere day's mid course, and morning light
More orient in the western cloud, that drew
O'er the blue firmament a radiant white,
Descending slow with something heavenly fraught.

    Add also, that among the multitudes   665
Of that huge city, oftentimes was seen
Affectingly set forth, more than elsewhere
Is possible, the unity of man,
One spirit over ignorance and vice
Predominant, in good and evil hearts;   670
One sense for moral judgments, as one eye
For the sun's light. The soul when smitten thus

By a sublime *idea*, whencesoe'er
Vouchsafed for union or communion, feeds
On the pure bliss, and takes her rest with God.   675

Thus from a very early age, O Friend!
My thoughts by slow gradations had been drawn
To human-kind, and to the good and ill
Of human life: Nature had led me on;
And oft amid the "busy hum" I seemed   680
To travel independent of her help,
As if I had forgotten her; but no,
The world of human-kind outweighed not hers
In my habitual thoughts; the scale of love,
Though filling daily, still was light, compared   685
With that in which *her* mighty objects lay.

BOOK NINTH

RESIDENCE IN FRANCE

EVEN as a river, — partly (it might seem)
Yielding to old remembrances, and swayed
In part by fear to shape a way direct,
That would engulph him soon in the ravenous sea —
Turns, and will measure back his course, far back,   5
Seeking the very regions which he crossed
In his first outset; so have we, my Friend!
Turned and returned with intricate delay.
Or as a traveller, who has gained the brow
Of some aerial Down, while there he halts   10
For breathing-time, is tempted to review
The region left behind him; and, if aught
Deserving notice have escaped regard,
Or been regarded with too careless eye,
Strives, from that height, with one and yet one more   15
Last look, to make the best amends he may:
So have we lingered. Now we start afresh
With courage, and new hope risen on our toil.
Fair greetings to this shapeless eagerness,
Whene'er it comes! needful in work so long,   20
Thrice needful to the argument which now
Awaits us! Oh, how much unlike the past!

Free as a colt at pasture on the hill,
I ranged at large, through London's wide domain,
Month after month. Obscurely did I live,   25

Not seeking frequent intercourse with men,
By literature, or elegance, or rank,
Distinguished. Scarcely was a year thus spent
Ere I forsook the crowded solitude,
With less regret for its luxurious pomp,   30
And all the nicely-guarded shows of art,
Than for the humble book-stalls in the streets,
Exposed to eye and hand where'er I turned.

France lured me forth; the realm that I had crossed
So lately, journeying toward the snow-clad Alps.   35
But now, relinquishing the scrip and staff,
And all enjoyment which the summer sun
Sheds round the steps of those who meet the day
With motion constant as his own, I went
Prepared to sojourn in a pleasant town,   40
Washed by the current of the stately Loire.

Through Paris lay my readiest course, and there
Sojourning a few days, I visited,
In haste, each spot of old or recent fame,
The latter chiefly; from the field of Mars   45
Down to the suburbs of St. Antony,
And from Mont Martyr southward to the Dome
Of Geneviève. In both her clamorous Halls,
The National Synod and the Jacobins,
I saw the Revolutionary Power   50
Toss like a ship at anchor, rocked by storms;
The Arcades I traversed, in the Palace huge
Of Orleans; coasted round and round the line
Of Tavern, Brothel, Gaming-house, and Shop,
Great rendezvous of worst and best, the walk   55
Of all who had a purpose, or had not;
I stared and listened, with a stranger's ears,
To Hawkers and Haranguers, hubbub wild!
And hissing Factionists with ardent eyes,
In knots, or pairs, or single. Not a look   60
Hope takes, or Doubt or Fear is forced to wear,
But seemed there present; and I scanned them all,
Watched every gesture uncontrollable,
Of anger, and vexation, and despite,
All side by side, and struggling face to face,   65
With gaiety and dissolute idleness.

Where silent zephyrs sported with the dust
Of the Bastille, I sate in the open sun,
And from the rubbish gathered up a stone,

And pocketed the relic, in the guise   70
Of an enthusiast; yet, in honest truth,
I looked for something that I could not find,
Affecting more emotion than I felt;
For 'tis most certain, that these various sights,
However potent their first shock, with me   75
Appeared to recompense the traveller's pains
Less than the painted Magdalene of Le Brun,
A beauty exquisitely wrought, with hair
Dishevelled, gleaming eyes, and rueful cheek
Pale and bedropped with everflowing tears.   80

    But hence to my more permanent abode
I hasten; there, by novelties in speech,
Domestic manners, customs, gestures, looks,
And all the attire of ordinary life,
Attention was engrossed; and, thus amused,   85
I stood, 'mid those concussions, unconcerned,
Tranquil almost, and careless as a flower
Glassed in a green-house, or a parlour shrub
That spreads its leaves in unmolested peace,
While every bush and tree, the country through,   90
Is shaking to the roots: indifference this
Which may seem strange: but I was unprepared
With needful knowledge, had abruptly passed
Into a theatre, whose stage was filled
And busy with an action far advanced.   95
Like others, I had skimmed, and sometimes read
With care, the master pamphlets of the day;
Nor wanted such half-insight as grew wild
Upon that meagre soil, helped out by talk
And public news; but having never seen   100
A chronicle that might suffice to show
Whence the main organs of the public power
Had sprung, their transmigrations, when and how
Accomplished, giving thus unto events
A form and body; all things were to me   105
Loose and disjointed, and the affections left
Without a vital interest. At that time,
Moreover, the first storm was overblown,
And the strong hand of outward violence
Locked up in quiet. For myself, I fear   110
Now in connection with so great a theme
To speak (as I must be compelled to do)
Of one so unimportant; night by night
Did I frequent the formal haunts of men,
Whom, in the city, privilege of birth   115

Sequestered from the rest, societies
Polished in arts, and in punctilio versed;
Whence, and from deeper causes, all discourse
Of good and evil of the time was shunned
With scrupulous care; but these restrictions soon   120
Proved tedious, and I gradually withdrew
Into a noisier world, and thus ere long
Became a patriot; and my heart was all
Given to the people, and my love was theirs.

   A band of military Officers,   125
Then stationed in the city, were the chief
Of my associates: some of these wore swords
That had been seasoned in the wars, and all
Were men well-born; the chivalry of France.
In age and temper differing, they had yet   130
One spirit ruling in each heart; alike
(Save only one, hereafter to be named)
Were bent upon undoing what was done:
This was their rest and only hope; therewith
No fear had they of bad becoming worse,   135
For worst to them was come; nor would have stirred,
Or deemed it worth a moment's thought to stir,
In any thing, save only as the act
Looked thitherward. One, reckoning by years,
Was in the prime of manhood, and erewhile   140
He had sate lord in many tender hearts;
Though heedless of such honours now, and changed:
His temper was quite mastered by the times,
And they had blighted him, had eat away
The beauty of his person, doing wrong   145
Alike to body and to mind: his port,
Which once had been erect and open, now
Was stooping and contracted, and a face,
Endowed by Nature with her fairest gifts
Of symmetry and light and bloom, expressed,   150
As much as any that was ever seen,
A ravage out of season, made by thoughts
Unhealthy and vexatious. With the hour,
That from the press of Paris duly brought
Its freight of public news, the fever came,   155
A punctual visitant, to shake this man,
Disarmed his voice and fanned his yellow cheek
Into a thousand colours; while he read,
Or mused, his sword was haunted by his touch
Continually, like an uneasy place   160
In his own body. 'Twas in truth an hour

Of universal ferment; mildest men
Were agitated; and commotions, strife
Of passion and opinion, filled the walls
Of peaceful houses with unquiet sounds.
The soil of common life was, at that time,   165
Too hot to tread upon. Oft said I then,
And not then only, "What a mockery this
Of history, the past and that to come!
Now do I feel how all men are deceived,   170
Reading of nations and their works, in faith,
Faith given to vanity and emptiness;
Oh! laughter for the page that would reflect
To future times the face of what now is!"
The land all swarmed with passion, like a plain   175
Devoured by locusts, — Carra, Gorsas, — add
A hundred other names, forgotten now,
Nor to be heard of more; yet, they were powers,
Like earthquakes, shocks repeated day by day,
And felt through every nook of town and field.   180

   Such was the state of things. Meanwhile the chief
Of my associates stood prepared for flight
To augment the band of emigrants in arms
Upon the borders of the Rhine, and leagued
With foreign foes mustered for instant war.   185
This was their undisguised intent, and they
Were waiting with the whole of their desires
The moment to depart.
                     An Englishman,
Born in a land whose very name appeared
To license some unruliness of mind;   190
A stranger, with youth's further privilege,
And the indulgence that a half-learnt speech
Wins from the courteous; I, who had been else
Shunned and not tolerated, freely lived
With these defenders of the Crown, and talked,   195
And heard their notions; nor did they disdain
The wish to bring me over to their cause.

   But though untaught by thinking or by books
To reason well of polity or law,
And nice distinctions, then on every tongue,   200
Of natural rights and civil; and to acts
Of nations and their passing interests
(If with unworldly ends and aims compared)
Almost indifferent, even the historian's tale
Prizing but little otherwise than I prized   205

Tales of the poets, as it made the heart
Beat high, and filled the fancy with fair forms,
Old heroes and their sufferings and their deeds;
Yet in the regal sceptre, and the pomp
Of orders and degrees, I nothing found   210
Then, or had ever, even in crudest youth,
That dazzled me, but rather what I mourned
And ill could brook, beholding that the best
Ruled not, and feeling that they ought to rule.

    For, born in a poor district, and which yet   215
Retaineth more of ancient homeliness,
Than any other nook of English ground,
It was my fortune scarcely to have seen,
Through the whole tenor of my school-day time,
The face of one, who, whether boy or man,   220
Was vested with attention or respect
Through claims of wealth or blood; nor was it least
Of many benefits, in later years
Derived from academic institutes
And rules, that they held something up to view   225
Of a Republic, where all stood thus far
Upon equal ground; that we were brothers all
In honour, as in one community,
Scholars and gentlemen; where, furthermore,
Distinction lay open to all that came,   230
And wealth and titles were in less esteem
Than talents, worth, and prosperous industry.
Add unto this, subservience from the first
To presences of God's mysterious power
Made manifest in Nature's sovereignty,   235
And fellowship with venerable books,
To sanction the proud workings of the soul,
And mountain liberty. It could not be
But that one tutored thus should look with awe
Upon the faculties of man, receive   240
Gladly the highest promises, and hail,
As best, the government of equal rights
And individual worth. And hence, O Friend!
If at the first great outbreak I rejoiced
Less than might well befit my youth, the cause   245
In part lay here, that unto me the events
Seemed nothing out of nature's certain course,
A gift that was come rather late than soon.
No wonder, then, if advocates like these,
Inflamed by passion, blind with prejudice,   250
And stung with injury, at this riper day,

Were impotent to make my hopes put on
The shape of theirs, my understanding bend
In honour to their honour: zeal, which yet
Had slumbered, now in opposition burst   255
Forth like a Polar summer: every word
They uttered was a dart, by counter-winds
Blown back upon themselves; their reason seemed
Confusion-stricken by a higher power
Than human understanding, their discourse   260
Maimed, spiritless; and, in their weakness strong,
I triumphed.
                Meantime, day by day, the roads
Were crowded with the bravest youth of France,
And all the promptest of her spirits, linked
In gallant soldiership, and posting on   265
To meet the war upon her frontier bounds.
Yet at this very moment do tears start
Into mine eyes: I do not say I weep —
I wept not then, — but tears have dimmed my sight,
In memory of the farewells of that time,   270
Domestic severings, female fortitude
At dearest separation, patriot love
And self-devotion, and terrestrial hope,
Encouraged with a martyr's confidence;
Even files of strangers merely seen but once,   275
And for a moment, men from far with sound
Of music, martial tunes, and banners spread,
Entering the city, here and there a face,
Or person singled out among the rest,
Yet still a stranger and beloved as such;   280
Even by these passing spectacles my heart
Was oftentimes uplifted, and they seemed
Arguments sent from Heaven to prove the cause
Good, pure, which no one could stand up against,
Who was not lost, abandoned, selfish, proud,   285
Mean, miserable, wilfully depraved,
Hater perverse of equity and truth.

    Among that band of Officers was one,
Already hinted at, of other mould —
A patriot, thence rejected by the rest,   290
And with an oriental loathing spurned,
As of a different caste. A meeker man
Than this lived never, nor a more benign,
Meek though enthusiastic. Injuries
Made *him* more gracious, and his nature then   295
Did breathe its sweetness out most sensibly,

As aromatic flowers on Alpine turf,
When foot hath crushed them. He through the events
Of that great change wandered in perfect faith,
As through a book, an old romance, or tale   300
Of Fairy, or some dream of actions wrought
Behind the summer clouds. By birth he ranked
With the most noble, but unto the poor
Among mankind he was in service bound,
As by some tie invisible, oaths professed   305
To a religious order. Man he loved
As man; and, to the mean and the obscure,
And all the homely in their homely works,
Transferred a courtesy which had no air
Of condescension; but did rather seem   310
A passion and a gallantry, like that
Which he, a soldier, in his idler day
Had paid to woman: somewhat vain he was,
Or seemed so, yet it was not vanity,
But fondness, and a kind of radiant joy   315
Diffused around him, while he was intent
On works of love or freedom, or revolved
Complacently the progress of a cause,
Whereof he was a part: yet this was meek
And placid, and took nothing from the man   320
That was delightful. Oft in solitude
With him did I discourse about the end
Of civil government, and its wisest forms;
Of ancient loyalty, and chartered rights,
Custom and habit, novelty and change;   325
Of self-respect, and virtue in the few
For patrimonial honour set apart,
And ignorance in the labouring multitude.
For he, to all intolerance indisposed,
Balanced these contemplations in his mind;   330
And I, who at that time was scarcely dipped
Into the turmoil, bore a sounder judgment
Than later days allowed; carried about me,
With less alloy to its integrity,
The experience of past ages, as, through help   335
Of books and common life, it makes sure way
To youthful minds, by objects over near
Not pressed upon, nor dazzled or misled
By struggling with the crowd for present ends.

    But though not deaf, nor obstinate to find   340
Error without excuse upon the side
Of them who strove against us, more delight

We took, and let this freely be confessed,
In painting to ourselves the miseries
Of royal courts, and that voluptuous life   345
Unfeeling, where the man who is of soul
The meanest thrives the most; where dignity,
True personal dignity, abideth not;
A light, a cruel, and vain world cut off
From the natural inlets of just sentiment,   350
From lowly sympathy and chastening truth;
Where good and evil interchange their names,
And thirst for bloody spoils abroad is paired
With vice at home. We added dearest themes —
Man and his noble nature, as it is   355
The gift which God has placed within his power,
His blind desires and steady faculties
Capable of clear truth, the one to break
Bondage, the other to build liberty
On firm foundations, making social life,   360
Through knowledge spreading and imperishable,
As just in regulation, and as pure
As individual in the wise and good.

    We summoned up the honourable deeds
Of ancient Story, thought of each bright spot,   365
That could be found in all recorded time,
Of truth preserved and error passed away;
Of single spirits that catch the flame from Heaven,
And how the multitudes of men will feed
And fan each other; thought of sects, how keen   370
They are to put the appropriate nature on,
Triumphant over every obstacle
Of custom, language, country, love, or hate,
And what they do and suffer for their creed;
How far they travel, and how long endure;   375
How quickly mighty Nations have been formed,
From least beginnings; how, together locked
By new opinions, scattered tribes have made
One body, spreading wide as clouds in heaven.
To aspirations then of our own minds   380
Did we appeal; and, finally, beheld
A living confirmation of the whole
Before us, in a people from the depth
Of shameful imbecility uprisen,
Fresh as the morning star. Elate we looked   385
Upon their virtues; saw, in rudest men,
Self-sacrifice the firmest; generous love,
And continence of mind, and sense of right,
Uppermost in the midst of fiercest strife.

Oh, sweet it is, in academic groves,   390
Or such retirement, Friend! as we have known
In the green dales beside our Rotha's stream,
Greta, or Derwent, or some nameless rill,
To ruminate, with interchange of talk,
On rational liberty, and hope in man,   395
Justice and peace. But far more sweet such toil —
Toil, say I, for it leads to thoughts abstruse —
If nature then be standing on the brink
Of some great trial, and we hear the voice
Of one devoted, — one whom circumstance   400
Hath called upon to embody his deep sense
In action, give it outwardly a shape,
And that of benediction, to the world.
Then doubt is not, and truth is more than truth, —
A hope it is, and a desire; a creed   405
Of zeal, by an authority Divine
Sanctioned, of danger, difficulty, or death.
Such conversation, under Attic shades,
Did Dion hold with Plato; ripened thus
For a Deliverer's glorious task, — and such   410
He, on that ministry already bound,
Held with Eudemus and Timonides,
Surrounded by adventurers in arms,
When those two vessels with their daring freight,
For the Sicilian Tyrant's overthrow,   415
Sailed from Zacynthus, — philosophic war,
Led by Philosophers. With harder fate,
Though like ambition, such was he, O Friend!
Of whom I speak. So Beaupuis (let the name
Stand near the worthiest of Antiquity)   420
Fashioned his life; and many a long discourse,
With like persuasion honoured, we maintained:
He, on his part, accoutred for the worst.
He perished fighting, in supreme command,
Upon the borders of the unhappy Loire,   425
For liberty, against deluded men,
His fellow country-men; and yet most blessed
In this, that he the fate of later times
Lived not to see, nor what we now behold,
Who have as ardent hearts as he had then.   430

Along that very Loire, with festal mirth
Resounding at all hours, and innocent yet
Of civil slaughter, was our frequent walk;
Or in wide forests of continuous shade,
Lofty and over-arched, with open space   435
Beneath the trees, clear footing many a mile —

A solemn region. Oft amid those haunts,
From earnest dialogues I slipped in thought,
And let remembrance steal to other times,
When, o'er those interwoven roots, moss-clad,   440
And smooth as marble or a waveless sea,
Some Hermit, from his cell forth-strayed, might pace
In sylvan meditation undisturbed;
As on the pavement of a Gothic church
Walks a lone Monk, when service hath expired,   445
In peace and silence. But if e'er was heard, —
Heard, though unseen, — a devious traveller,
Retiring or approaching from afar
With speed and echoes loud of trampling hoofs
From the hard floor reverberated, then   450
It was Angelica thundering through the woods
Upon her palfrey, or that gentle maid
Erminia, fugitive as fair as she.
Sometimes methought I saw a pair of knights
Joust underneath the trees, that as in storm   455
Rocked high above their heads; anon, the din
Of boisterous merriment, and music's roar,
In sudden proclamation, burst from haunt
Of Satyrs in some viewless glade, with dance
Rejoicing o'er a female in the midst,   460
A mortal beauty, their unhappy thrall.
The width of those huge forests, unto me
A novel scene, did often in this way
Master my fancy while I wandered on
With that revered companion. And sometimes —   465
When to a convent in a meadow green,
By a brook-side, we came, a roofless pile,
And not by reverential touch of Time
Dismantled, but by violence abrupt —
In spite of those heart-bracing colloquies,   470
In spite of real fervour, and of that
Less genuine and wrought up within myself —
I could not but bewail a wrong so harsh,
And for the Matin-bell to sound no more
Grieved, and the twilight taper, and the cross   475
High on the topmost pinnacle, a sign
(How welcome to the weary traveller's eyes!)
Of hospitality and peaceful rest.
And when the partner of those varied walks
Pointed upon occasion to the site   480
Of Romorentin, home of ancient kings,
To the imperial edifice of Blois,
Or to that rural castle, name now slipped
From my remembrance, where a lady lodged,

By the first Francis wooed, and bound to him   485
In chains of mutual passion, from the tower,
As a tradition of the country tells,
Practised to commune with her royal knight
By cressets and love-beacons, intercourse
'Twixt her high-seated residence and his   490
Far off at Chambord on the plain beneath;
Even here, though less than with the peaceful house
Religious, 'mid those frequent monuments
Of Kings, their vices and their better deeds,
Imagination, potent to inflame   495
At times with virtuous wrath and noble scorn,
Did also often mitigate the force
Of civic prejudice, the bigotry,
So call it, of a youthful patriot's mind;
And on these spots with many gleams I looked   500
Of chivalrous delight. Yet not the less,
Hatred of absolute rule, where will of one
Is law for all, and of that barren pride
In them who, by immunities unjust,
Between the sovereign and the people stand,   505
His helper and not theirs, laid stronger hold
Daily upon me, mixed with pity too
And love; for where hope is, there love will be
For the abject multitude. And when we chanced
One day to meet a hunger-bitten girl,   510
Who crept along fitting her languid gait
Unto a heifer's motion, by a cord
Tied to her arm, and picking thus from the lane
Its sustenance, while the girl with pallid hands
Was busy knitting in a heartless mood   515
Of solitude, and at the sight my friend
In agitation said, " 'Tis against *that*
That we are fighting," I with him believed
That a benignant spirit was abroad
Which might not be withstood, that poverty   520
Abject as this would in a little time
Be found no more, that we should see the earth
Unthwarted in her wish to recompense
The meek, the lowly, patient child of toil,
All institutes for ever blotted out   525
That legalised exclusion, empty pomp
Abolished, sensual state and cruel power,
Whether by edict of the one or few;
And finally, as sum and crown of all,
Should see the people having a strong hand   530
In framing their own laws; whence better days
To all mankind. But, these things set apart,

Was not this single confidence enough
To animate the mind that ever turned
A thought to human welfare? That henceforth   535
Captivity by mandate without law
Should cease; and open accusation lead
To sentence in the hearing of the world,
And open punishment, if not the air
Be free to breathe in, and the heart of man   540
Dread nothing. From this height I shall not stoop
To humbler matter that detained us oft
In thought or conversation, public acts,
And public persons, and emotions wrought
Within the breast, as ever-varying winds   545
Of record or report swept over us;
But I might here, instead, repeat a tale,
Told by my Patriot friend, of sad events,
That prove to what low depth had struck the roots,
How widely spread the boughs, of that old tree   550
Which, as a deadly mischief, and a foul
And black dishonour, France was weary of.

    Oh, happy time of youthful lovers, (thus
The story might begin). Oh, balmy time,
In which a love-knot, on a lady's brow,   555
Is fairer than the fairest star in Heaven!
So might — and with that prelude *did* begin
The record; and, in faithful verse, was given
The doleful sequel.

              But our little bark
On a strong river boldly hath been launched;   560
And from the driving current should we turn
To loiter wilfully within a creek,
Howe'er attractive, Fellow voyager!
Would'st thou not chide? Yet deem not my pains lost:
For Vaudracour and Julia (so were named   565
The ill-fated pair) in that plain tale will draw
Tears from the hearts of others, when their own
Shall beat no more. Thou, also, there mayst read,
At leisure, how the enamoured youth was driven,
By public power abased, to fatal crime,   570
Nature's rebellion against monstrous law;
How, between heart and heart, oppression thrust
Her mandates, severing whom true love had joined,
Harassing both; until he sank and pressed
The couch his fate had made for him; supine,   575
Save when the stings of viperous remorse,
Trying their strength, enforced him to start up,
Aghast and prayerless. Into a deep wood

He fled, to shun the haunts of human kind;
There dwelt, weakened in spirit more and more;   580
Nor could the voice of Freedom, which through France
Full speedily resounded, public hope,
Or personal memory of his own worst wrongs,
Rouse him; but, hidden in those gloomy shades,
His days he wasted, — an imbecile mind.   585

BOOK TENTH

RESIDENCE IN FRANCE (CONTINUED)

It was a beautiful and silent day
That overspread the countenance of earth,
Then fading with unusual quietness, —
A day as beautiful as e'er was given
To soothe regret, though deepening what it soothed,   5
When by the gliding Loire I paused, and cast
Upon his rich domains, vineyard and tilth,
Green meadow-ground, and many-coloured woods,
Again, and yet again, a farewell look;
Then from the quiet of that scene passed on,   10
Bound to the fierce Metropolis. From his throne
The King had fallen, and that invading host —
Presumptuous cloud, on whose black front was written
The tender mercies of the dismal wind
That bore it — on the plains of Liberty   15
Had burst innocuous. Say in bolder words,
They — who had come elate as eastern hunters
Banded beneath the Great Mogul, when he
Erewhile went forth from Agra or Lahore,
Rajahs and Omrahs in his train, intent   20
To drive their prey enclosed within a ring
Wide as a province, but, the signal given,
Before the point of the life-threatening spear
Narrowing itself by moments — they, rash men,
Had seen the anticipated quarry turned   25
Into avengers, from whose wrath they fled
In terror. Disappointment and dismay
Remained for all whose fancies had run wild
With evil expectations; confidence
And perfect triumph for the better cause.   30

The State, as if to stamp the final seal
On her security, and to the world
Show what she was, a high and fearless soul,
Exulting in defiance, or heart-stung

By sharp resentment, or belike to taunt   35
With spiteful gratitude the baffled League,
That had stirred up her slackening faculties
To a new transition, when the King was crushed,
Spared not the empty throne, and in proud haste
Assumed the body and venerable name   40
Of a Republic. Lamentable crimes,
'Tis true, had gone before this hour, dire work
Of massacre, in which the senseless sword
Was prayed to as a judge; but these were past,
Earth free from them for ever, as was thought, —   45
Ephemeral monsters, to be seen but once!
Things that could only show themselves and die.

    Cheered with this hope, to Paris I returned,
And ranged, with ardour heretofore unfelt,
The spacious city, and in progress passed   50
The prison where the unhappy Monarch lay,
Associate with his children and his wife
In bondage; and the palace, lately stormed
With roar of cannon by a furious host.
I crossed the square (an empty area then!)   55
Of the Carrousel, where so late had lain
The dead, upon the dying heaped, and gazed
On this and other spots, as doth a man
Upon a volume whose contents he knows
Are memorable, but from him locked up,   60
Being written in a tongue he cannot read,
So that he questions the mute leaves with pain,
And half upbraids their silence. But that night
I felt most deeply in what world I was,
What ground I trod on, and what air I breathed.   65
High was my room and lonely, near the roof
Of a large mansion or hotel, a lodge
That would have pleased me in more quiet times;
Nor was it wholly without pleasure then.
With unextinguished taper I kept watch,   70
Reading at intervals; the fear gone by
Pressed on me almost like a fear to come.
I thought of those September massacres,
Divided from me by one little month,
Saw them and touched: the rest was conjured up   75
From tragic fictions or true history,
Remembrances and dim admonishments.
The horse is taught his manage, and no star
Of wildest course but treads back his own steps;
For the spent hurricane the air provides   80

As fierce a successor; the tide retreats
But to return out of its hiding-place
In the great deep; all things have second birth;
The earthquake is not satisfied at once;
And in this way I wrought upon myself,   85
Until I seemed to hear a voice that cried,
To the whole city, "Sleep no more." The trance
Fled with the voice to which it had given birth;
But vainly comments of a calmer mind
Promised soft peace and sweet forgetfulness.   90
The place, all hushed and silent as it was,
Appeared unfit for the repose of night,
Defenceless as a wood where tigers roam.

　　With early morning towards the Palace-walk
Of Orleans eagerly I turned; as yet   95
The streets were still; not so those long Arcades;
There, 'mid a peal of ill-matched sounds and cries,
That greeted me on entering, I could hear
Shrill voices from the hawkers in the throng,
Bawling, "Denunciation of the Crimes   100
Of Maximilian Robespierre;" the hand,
Prompt as the voice, held forth a printed speech,
The same that had been recently pronounced,
When Robespierre, not ignorant for what mark
Some words of indirect reproof had been   105
Intended, rose in hardihood, and dared
The man who had an ill surmise of him
To bring his charge in openness; whereat,
When a dead pause ensued, and no one stirred,
In silence of all present, from his seat   110
Louvet walked single through the avenue,
And took his station in the Tribune, saying,
"I, Robespierre, accuse thee!" Well is known
The inglorious issue of that charge, and how
He, who had launched the startling thunderbolt,   115
The one bold man, whose voice the attack had sounded,
Was left without a follower to discharge
His perilous duty, and retire lamenting
That Heaven's best aid is wasted upon men
Who to themselves are false.   120
　　　　　　　　　　　But these are things
Of which I speak, only as they were storm
Or sunshine to my individual mind,
No further. Let me then relate that now —
In some sort seeing with my proper eyes
That Liberty, and Life, and Death would soon   125

To the remotest corners of the land
Lie in the arbitrement of those who ruled
The capital City; what was struggled for,
And by what combatants victory must be won;
The indecision on their part whose aim   130
Seemed best, and the straightforward path of those
Who in attack or in defence were strong
Through their impiety — my inmost soul
Was agitated; yea, I could almost
Have prayed that throughout earth upon all men,   135
By patient exercise of reason made
Worthy of liberty, all spirits filled
With zeal expanding in Truth's holy light,
The gift of tongues might fall, and power arrive
From the four quarters of the winds to do   140
For France, what without help she could not do,
A work of honour; think not that to this
I added, work of safety: from all doubt
Or trepidation for the end of things
Far was I, far as angels are from guilt.   145

    Yet did I grieve, nor only grieved, but thought
Of opposition and of remedies:
An insignificant stranger and obscure,
And one, moreover, little graced with power
Of eloquence even in my native speech,   150
And all unfit for tumult or intrigue,
Yet would I at this time with willing heart
Have undertaken for a cause so great
Service however dangerous. I revolved,
How much the destiny of Man had still   155
Hung upon single persons; that there was,
Transcendent to all local patrimony,
One nature, as there is one sun in heaven;
That objects, even as they are great, thereby
Do come within the reach of humblest eyes;   160
That Man is only weak through his mistrust
And want of hope where evidence divine
Proclaims to him that hope should be most sure;
Nor did the inexperience of my youth
Preclude conviction, that a spirit strong   165
In hope, and trained to noble aspirations,
A spirit thoroughly faithful to itself,
Is for Society's unreasoning herd
A domineering instinct, serves at once
For way and guide, a fluent receptacle   170
That gathers up each petty straggling rill

And vein of water, glad to be rolled on
In safe obedience; that a mind, whose rest
Is where it ought to be, in self-restraint,
In circumspection and simplicity,   175
Falls rarely in entire discomfiture
Below its aim, or meets with, from without,
A treachery that foils it or defeats;
And, lastly, if the means on human will,
Frail human will, dependent should betray   180
Him who too boldly trusted them, I felt
That 'mid the loud distractions of the world
A sovereign voice subsists within the soul,
Arbiter undisturbed of right and wrong,
Of life and death, in majesty severe   185
Enjoining, as may best promote the aims
Of truth and justice, either sacrifice,
From whatsoever region of our cares
Or our infirm affections Nature pleads,
Earnest and blind, against the stern decree.   190

On the other side, I called to mind those truths
That are the common-places of the schools —
(A theme for boys, too hackneyed for their sires,)
Yet, with a revelation's liveliness,
In all their comprehensive bearings known   195
And visible to philosophers of old,
Men who, to business of the world untrained,
Lived in the shade; and to Harmodius known
And his compeer Aristogiton, known
To Brutus — that tyrannic power is weak,   200
Hath neither gratitude, nor faith, nor love,
Nor the support of good or evil men
To trust in; that the godhead which is ours
Can never utterly be charmed or stilled;
That nothing hath a natural right to last   205
But equity and reason; that all else
Meets foes irreconcilable, and at best
Lives only by variety of disease.

Well might my wishes be intense, my thoughts
Strong and perturbed, not doubting at that time   210
But that the virtue of one paramount mind
Would have abashed those impious crests — have quelled
Outrage and bloody power, and, in despite
Of what the People long had been and were
Through ignorance and false teaching, sadder proof   215
Of immaturity, and in the teeth

Of desperate opposition from without —
Have cleared a passage for just government,
And left a solid birthright to the State,
Redeemed, according to example given   220
By ancient lawgivers.
                In this frame of mind,
Dragged by a chain of harsh necessity,
So seemed it, — now I thankfully acknowledge,
Forced by the gracious providence of Heaven, —
To England I returned, else (though assured   225
That I both was and must be of small weight,
No better than a landsman on the deck
Of a ship struggling with a hideous storm)
Doubtless, I should have then made common cause
With some who perished; haply perished too,   230
A poor mistaken and bewildered offering, —
Should to the breast of Nature have gone back,
With all my resolutions, all my hopes,
A Poet only to myself, to men
Useless, and even, beloved Friend! a soul   235
To thee unknown!
                Twice had the trees let fall
Their leaves, as often Winter had put on
His hoary crown, since I had seen the surge
Beat against Albion's shore, since ear of mine
Had caught the accents of my native speech   240
Upon our native country's sacred ground.
A patriot of the world, how could I glide
Into communion with her sylvan shades,
Erewhile my tuneful haunt? It pleased me more
To abide in the great City, where I found   245
The general air still busy with the stir
Of that first memorable onset made
By a strong levy of humanity
Upon the traffickers in Negro blood;
Effort which, though defeated, had recalled   250
To notice old forgotten principles,
And through the nation spread a novel heat
Of virtuous feeling. For myself, I own
That this particular strife had wanted power
To rivet my affections; nor did now   255
Its unsuccessful issue much excite
My sorrow; for I brought with me the faith
That, if France prospered, good men would not long
Pay fruitless worship to humanity,
And this most rotten branch of human shame,   260
Object, so seemed it, of superfluous pains,

Would fall together with its parent tree.
What, then, were my emotions, when in arms
Britain put forth her free-born strength in league,
Oh, pity and shame! with those confederate Powers!   265
Not in my single self alone I found,
But in the minds of all ingenuous youth,
Change and subversion from that hour. No shock
Given to my moral nature had I known
Down to that very moment; neither lapse   270
Nor turn of sentiment that might be named
A revolution, save at this one time;
All else was progress on the self-same path
On which, with a diversity of pace,
I had been travelling: this a stride at once   275
Into another region. As a light
And pliant harebell, swinging in the breeze
On some grey rock — its birth-place — so had I
Wantoned, fast rooted on the ancient tower
Of my beloved country, wishing not   280
A happier fortune than to wither there:
Now was I from that pleasant station torn
And tossed about in whirlwind. I rejoiced,
Yea, afterwards — truth most painful to record! —
Exulted, in the triumph of my soul,   285
When Englishmen by thousands were o'erthrown,
Left without glory on the field, or driven,
Brave hearts! to shameful flight. It was a grief, —
Grief call it not, 'twas anything but that, —
A conflict of sensations without name,   290
Of which *he* only, who may love the sight
Of a village steeple, as I do, can judge,
When, in the congregation bending all
To their great Father, prayers were offered up,
Or praises for our country's victories;   295
And, 'mid the simple worshippers, perchance
I only, like an uninvited guest
Whom no one owned, sate silent, shall I add,
Fed on the day of vengeance yet to come.

    Oh! much have they to account for, who could tear,   300
By violence, at one decisive rent,
From the best youth in England their dear pride,
Their joy, in England; this, too, at a time
In which worst losses easily might wear
The best of names, when patriotic love   305
Did of itself in modesty give way,
Like the Precursor when the Deity

Is come Whose harbinger he was; a time
In which apostasy from ancient faith
Seemed but conversion to a higher creed;   310
Withal a season dangerous and wild,
A time when sage Experience would have snatched
Flowers out of any hedge-row to compose
A chaplet in contempt of his grey locks.

When the proud fleet that bears the red-cross flag   315
In that unworthy service was prepared
To mingle, I beheld the vessels lie,
A brood of gallant creatures, on the deep;
I saw them in their rest, a sojourner
Through a whole month of calm and glassy days   320
In that delightful island which protects
Their place of convocation — there I heard,
Each evening, pacing by the still sea-shore,
A monitory sound that never failed, —
The sunset cannon. While the orb went down   325
In the tranquillity of nature, came
That voice, ill requiem! seldom heard by me
Without a spirit overcast by dark
Imaginations, sense of woes to come,
Sorrow for human kind, and pain of heart.   330

In France, the men, who, for their desperate ends,
Had plucked up mercy by the roots, were glad
Of this new enemy. Tyrants, strong before
In wicked pleas, were strong as demons now;
And thus, on every side beset with foes,   335
The goaded land waxed mad; the crimes of few
Spread into madness of the many; blasts
From hell came sanctified like airs from heaven.
The sternness of the just, the faith of those
Who doubted not that Providence had times   340
Of vengeful retribution, theirs who throned
The human Understanding paramount
And made of that their God, the hopes of men
Who were content to barter short-lived pangs
For a paradise of ages, the blind rage   345
Of insolent tempers, the light vanity
Of intermeddlers, steady purposes
Of the suspicious, slips of the indiscreet,
And all the accidents of life were pressed
Into one service, busy with one work.   350
The Senate stood aghast, her prudence quenched,
Her wisdom stifled, and her justice scared,

Her frenzy only active to extol
Past outrages, and shape the way for new,
Which no one dared to oppose or mitigate.   355

   Domestic carnage now filled the whole year
With feast-days; old men from the chimney-nook,
The maiden from the bosom of her love,
The mother from the cradle of her babe,
The warrior from the field — all perished, all —   360
Friends, enemies, of all parties, ages, ranks,
Head after head, and never heads enough
For those that bade them fall. They found their joy,
They made it proudly, eager as a child,
(If light desires of innocent little ones   365
May with such heinous appetites be compared),
Pleased in some open field to exercise
A toy that mimics with revolving wings
The motion of a wind-mill; though the air
Do of itself blow fresh, and make the vanes   370
Spin in his eyesight, *that* contents him not,
But, with the plaything at arm's length, he sets
His front against the blast, and runs amain,
That it may whirl the faster.
                   Amid the depth
Of those enormities, even thinking minds   375
Forgot, at seasons, whence they had their being;
Forgot that such a sound was ever heard
As Liberty upon earth: yet all beneath
Her innocent authority was wrought,
Nor could have been, without her blessed name.   380
The illustrious wife of Roland, in the hour
Of her composure, felt that agony,
And gave it vent in her last words. O Friend!
It was a lamentable time for man,
Whether a hope had e'er been his or not;   385
A woful time for them whose hopes survived
The shock; most woful for those few who still
Were flattered, and had trust in human kind:
They had the deepest feeling of the grief.
Meanwhile the Invaders fared as they deserved: 390
The Herculean Commonwealth had put forth her arms,
And throttled with an infant godhead's might
The snakes about her cradle; that was well,
And as it should be; yet no cure for them
Whose souls were sick with pain of what would be   395
Hereafter brought in charge against mankind.
Most melancholy at that time, O Friend!

Were my day-thoughts, — my nights were miserable;
Through months, through years, long after the last beat
Of those atrocities, the hour of sleep   400
To me came rarely charged with natural gifts,
Such ghastly visions had I of despair
And tyranny, and implements of death;
And innocent victims sinking under fear,
And momentary hope, and worn-out prayer,   405
Each in his separate cell, or penned in crowds
For sacrifice, and struggling with forced mirth
And levity in dungeons, where the dust
Was laid with tears. Then suddenly the scene
Changed, and the unbroken dream entangled me   410
In long orations, which I strove to plead
Before unjust tribunals, — with a voice
Labouring, a brain confounded, and a sense,
Death-like, of treacherous desertion, felt
In the last place of refuge — my own soul.   415

When I began in youth's delightful prime
To yield myself to Nature, when that strong
And holy passion overcame me first,
Nor day nor night, evening or morn, was free
From its oppression. But, O Power Supreme!   420
Without Whose care this world would cease to breathe,
Who from the fountain of Thy grace dost fill
The veins that branch through every frame of life,
Making man what he is, creature divine,
In single or in social eminence,   425
Above the rest raised infinite ascents
When reason that enables him to be
Is not sequestered — what a change is here!
How different ritual for this after-worship,
What countenance to promote this second love!   430
The first was service paid to things which lie
Guarded within the bosom of Thy will.
Therefore to serve was high beatitude;
Tumult was therefore gladness, and the fear
Ennobling, venerable; sleep secure,   435
And waking thoughts more rich than happiest dreams.

But as the ancient Prophets, borne aloft
In vision, yet constrained by natural laws
With them to take a troubled human heart,
Wanted not consolations, nor a creed   440
Of reconcilement, then when they denounced,
On towns and cities, wallowing in the abyss

Of their offences, punishment to come;
Or saw, like other men, with bodily eyes,
Before them, in some desolated place,   445
The wrath consummate and the threat fulfilled;
So, with devout humility be it said,
So did a portion of that spirit fall
On me uplifted from the vantage-ground
Of pity and sorrow to a state of being   450
That through the time's exceeding fierceness saw
Glimpses of retribution, terrible,
And in the order of sublime behests:
But, even if that were not, amid the awe
Of unintelligible chastisement,   455
Not only acquiescences of faith
Survived, but daring sympathies with power,
Motions not treacherous or profane, else why
Within the folds of no ungentle breast
Their dread vibration to this hour prolonged?   460
Wild blasts of music thus could find their way
Into the midst of turbulent events;
So that worst tempests might be listened to.
Then was the truth received into my heart,
That, under heaviest sorrow earth can bring,   465
If from the affliction somewhere do not grow
Honour which could not else have been, a faith,
An elevation and a sanctity,
If new strength be not given nor old restored,
The blame is ours, not Nature's. When a taunt   470
Was taken up by scoffers in their pride,
Saying, "Behold the harvest that we reap
From popular government and equality,"
I clearly saw that neither these nor aught
Of wild belief engrafted on their names   475
By false philosophy had caused the woe,
But a terrific reservoir of guilt
And ignorance filled up from age to age,
That could no longer hold its loathsome charge,
But burst and spread in deluge through the land.   480

  And as the desert hath green spots, the sea
Small islands scattered amid stormy waves,
So *that* disastrous period did not want
Bright sprinklings of all human excellence,
To which the silver wands of saints in Heaven   485
Might point with rapturous joy. Yet not the less,
For those examples in no age surpassed
Of fortitude and energy and love,

And human nature faithful to herself
Under worst trials, was I driven to think   490
Of the glad times when first I traversed France
A youthful pilgrim; above all reviewed
That eventide, when under windows bright
With happy faces and with garlands hung,
And through a rainbow-arch that spanned the street,   495
Triumphal pomp for liberty confirmed,
I paced, a dear companion at my side,
The town of Arras, whence with promise high
Issued, on delegation to sustain
Humanity and right, *that* Robespierre,   500
He who thereafter, and in how short time!
Wielded the sceptre of the Atheist crew.
When the calamity spread far and wide —
And this same city, that did then appear
To outrun the rest in exultation, groaned   505
Under the vengeance of her cruel son,
As Lear reproached the winds — I could almost
Have quarrelled with that blameless spectacle
For lingering yet an image in my mind
To mock me under such a strange reverse.   510

O Friend! few happier moments have been mine
Than that which told the downfall of this Tribe
So dreaded, so abhorred. The day deserves
A separate record. Over the smooth sands
Of Leven's ample estuary lay   515
My journey, and beneath a genial sun,
With distant prospect among gleams of sky
And clouds, and intermingling mountain tops,
In one inseparable glory clad,
Creatures of one ethereal substance met   520
In consistory, like a diadem
Or crown of burning seraphs as they sit
In the empyrean. Underneath that pomp
Celestial, lay unseen the pastoral vales
Among whose happy fields I had grown up   525
From childhood. On the fulgent spectacle,
That neither passed away nor changed, I gazed
Enrapt; but brightest things are wont to draw
Sad opposites out of the inner heart,
As even their pensive influence drew from mine.   530
How could it otherwise? for not in vain
That very morning had I turned aside
To seek the ground where, 'mid a throng of graves,
An honoured teacher of my youth was laid,

And on the stone were graven by his desire   535
Lines from the churchyard elegy of Gray.
This faithful guide, speaking from his death-bed,
Added no farewell to his parting counsel,
But said to me, "My head will soon lie low;"
And when I saw the turf that covered him,   540
After the lapse of full eight years, those words,
With sound of voice and countenance of the Man,
Came back upon me, so that some few tears
Fell from me in my own despite. But now
I thought, still traversing that widespread plain,   545
With tender pleasure of the verses graven
Upon his tombstone, whispering to myself:
He loved the Poets, and, if now alive,
Would have loved me, as one not destitute
Of promise, nor belying the kind hope   550
That he had formed, when I, at his command,
Began to spin, with toil, my earliest songs.

As I advanced, all that I saw or felt
Was gentleness and peace. Upon a small
And rocky island near, a fragment stood   555
(Itself like a sea rock) the low remains
(With shells encrusted, dark with briny weeds)
Of a dilapidated structure, once
A Romish chapel, where the vested priest
Said matins at the hour that suited those   560
Who crossed the sands with ebb of morning tide.
Not far from that still ruin all the plain
Lay spotted with a variegated crowd
Of vehicles and travellers, horse and foot,
Wading beneath the conduct of their guide   565
In loose procession through the shallow stream
Of inland waters; the great sea meanwhile
Heaved at safe distance, far retired. I paused,
Longing for skill to paint a scene so bright
And cheerful, but the foremost of the band   570
As he approached, no salutation given
In the familiar language of the day,
Cried, "Robespierre is dead!" — nor was a doubt,
After strict question, left within my mind
That he and his supporters all were fallen.   575

Great was my transport, deep my gratitude
To everlasting Justice, by this fiat
Made manifest. "Come now, ye golden times,"
Said I forth-pouring on those open sands

A hymn of triumph: "as the morning comes,   580
From out the bosom of the night, come ye:
Thus far our trust is verified; behold!
They who with clumsy desperation brought
A river of Blood, and preached that nothing else
Could cleanse the Augean stable, by the might   585
Of their own helper have been swept away;
Their madness stands declared and visible;
Elsewhere will safety now be sought, and earth
March firmly towards righteousness and peace." —
Then schemes I framed more calmly, when and how   590
The madding factions might be tranquillised,
And how through hardships manifold and long
The glorious renovation would proceed.
Thus interrupted by uneasy bursts
Of exultation, I pursued my way   595
Along that very shore which I had skimmed
In former days, when — spurring from the Vale
Of Nightshade, and St. Mary's mouldering fane,
And the stone abbot, after circuit made
In wantonness of heart, a joyous band   600
Of school-boys hastening to their distant home
Along the margin of the moonlight sea —
We beat with thundering hoofs the level sand.

BOOK ELEVENTH

FRANCE (CONCLUDED)

FROM that time forth, Authority in France
Put on a milder face; Terror had ceased,
Yet every thing was wanting that might give
Courage to them who looked for good by light
Of rational Experience, for the shoots
And hopeful blossoms of a second spring:
Yet, in me, confidence was unimpaired;
The Senate's language, and the public acts
And measures of the Government, though both
Weak, and of heartless omen, had not power   10
To daunt me; in the People was my trust,
And in the virtues which mine eyes had seen;
I knew that wound external could not take
Life from the young Republic; that new foes
Would only follow, in the path of shame,   15
Their brethren, and her triumphs be in the end
Great, universal, irresistible.

This intuition led me to confound
One victory with another, higher far, —
Triumphs of unambitious peace at home,   20
And noiseless fortitude. Beholding still
Resistance strong as heretofore, I thought
That what was in degree the same was likewise
The same in quality, — that, as the worse
Of the two spirits then at strife remained   25
Untired, the better, surely, would preserve
The heart that first had roused him. Youth maintains,
In all conditions of society,
Communion more direct and intimate
With Nature, — hence, ofttimes, with reason too —   30
Than age or manhood, even. To Nature, then,
Power had reverted: habit, custom, law,
Had left an interregnum's open space
For *her* to move about in, uncontrolled.
Hence could I see how Babel-like their task,   35
Who, by the recent deluge stupified,
With their whole souls went culling from the day
Its petty promises, to build a tower
For their own safety; laughed with my compeers
At gravest heads, by enmity to France   40
Distempered, till they found, in every blast
Forced from the street-disturbing newsman's horn,
For her great cause record or prophecy
Of utter ruin. How might we believe
That wisdom could, in any shape, come near   45
Men clinging to delusions so insane?
And thus, experience proving that no few
Of our opinions had been just, we took
Like credit to ourselves where less was due,
And thought that other notions were as sound,   50
Yea, could not but be right, because we saw
That foolish men opposed them.
                                   To a strain
More animated I might here give way,
And tell, since juvenile errors are my theme,
What in those days, through Britain, was performed   55
To turn *all* judgments out of their right course;
But this is passion over-near ourselves,
Reality too close and too intense,
And intermixed with something, in my mind,
Of scorn and condemnation personal,   60
That would profane the sanctity of verse.
Our Shepherds, this say merely, at that time
Acted, or seemed at least to act, like men

Thirsting to make the guardian crook of law
A tool of murder; they who ruled the State,   65
Though with such awful proof before their eyes
That he, who would sow death, reaps death, or worse,
And can reap nothing better, child-like longed
To imitate, not wise enough to avoid;
Or left (by mere timidity betrayed)   70
The plain straight road, for one no better chosen
Than if their wish had been to undermine
Justice, and make an end of Liberty.

But from these bitter truths I must return
To my own history. It hath been told   75
That I was led to take an eager part
In arguments of civil polity,
Abruptly, and indeed before my time:
I had approached, like other youths, the shield
Of human nature from the golden side,   80
And would have fought, even to the death, to attest
The quality of the metal which I saw.
What there is best in individual man,
Of wise in passion, and sublime in power,
Benevolent in small societies,   85
And great in large ones, I had oft revolved,
Felt deeply, but not thoroughly understood
By reason: nay, far from it; they were yet,
As cause was given me afterwards to learn,
Not proof against the injuries of the day;   90
Lodged only at the sanctuary's door,
Not safe within its bosom. Thus prepared,
And with such general insight into evil,
And of the bounds which sever it from good,
As books and common intercourse with life   95
Must needs have given — to the inexperienced mind,
When the world travels in a beaten road,
Guide faithful as is needed — I began
To meditate with ardour on the rule
And management of nations; what it is   100
And ought to be; and strove to learn how far
Their power or weakness, wealth or poverty,
Their happiness or misery, depends
Upon their laws, and fashion of the State.

O pleasant exercise of hope and joy!   105
For mighty were the auxiliars which then stood
Upon our side, we who were strong in love!
Bliss was it in that dawn to be alive,
But to be young was very Heaven! O times,

In which the meagre, stale, forbidding ways   110
Of custom, law, and statute, took at once
The attraction of a country in romance!
When Reason seemed the most to assert her rights
When most intent on making of herself
A prime enchantress — to assist the work,   115
Which then was going forward in her name!
Not favoured spots alone, but the whole Earth,
The beauty wore of promise — that which sets
(As at some moments might not be unfelt
Among the bowers of Paradise itself)   120
The budding rose above the rose full blown.
What temper at the prospect did not wake
To happiness unthought of? The inert
Were roused, and lively natures rapt away!
They who had fed their childhood upon dreams,   125
The play-fellows of fancy, who had made
All powers of swiftness, subtilty, and strength
Their ministers, — who in lordly wise had stirred
Among the grandest objects of the sense,
And dealt with whatsoever they found there   130
As if they had within some lurking right
To wield it; — they, too, who of gentle mood
Had watched all gentle motions, and to these
Had fitted their own thoughts, schemers more mild,
And in the region of their peaceful selves; —   135
Now was it that *both* found, the meek and lofty
Did both find helpers to their hearts' desire,
And stuff at hand, plastic as they could wish, —
Were called upon to exercise their skill,
Not in Utopia, — subterranean fields, —   140
Or some secreted island, Heaven knows where!
But in the very world, which is the world
Of all of us, — the place where, in the end,
We find our happiness, or not at all!

Why should I not confess that Earth was then   145
To me, what an inheritance, new-fallen,
Seems, when the first time visited, to one
Who thither comes to find in it his home?
He walks about and looks upon the spot
With cordial transport, moulds it and remoulds,   150
And is half pleased with things that are amiss,
'Twill be such joy to see them disappear.

An active partisan, I thus convoked
From every object pleasant circumstance
To suit my ends; I moved among mankind   155

With genial feelings still predominant;
When erring, erring on the better part,
And in the kinder spirit; placable,
Indulgent, as not uninformed that men
See as they have been taught, and that Antiquity   160
Gives rights to error; and aware, no less,
That throwing off oppression must be work
As well of License as of Liberty;
And above all — for this was more than all —
Not caring if the wind did now and then   165
Blow keen upon an eminence that gave
Prospect so large into futurity;
In brief, a child of Nature, as at first,
Diffusing only those affections wider
That from the cradle had grown up with me,   170
And losing, in no other way than light
Is lost in light, the weak in the more strong.

    In the main outline, such it might be said
Was my condition, till with open war
Britain opposed the liberties of France.   175
This threw me first out of the pale of love;
Soured and corrupted, upwards to the source,
My sentiments; was not, as hitherto,
A swallowing up of lesser things in great,
But change of them into their contraries;   180
And thus a way was opened for mistakes
And false conclusions, in degree as gross,
In kind more dangerous. What had been a pride,
Was now a shame; my likings and my loves
Ran in new channels, leaving old ones dry;   185
And hence a blow that, in maturer age,
Would but have touched the judgment, struck more deep
Into sensations near the heart: meantime,
As from the first, wild theories were afloat,
To whose pretensions, sedulously urged,   190
I had but lent a careless ear, assured
That time was ready to set all things right,
And that the multitude, so long oppressed,
Would be oppressed no more.
                              But when events
Brought less encouragement, and unto these   195
The immediate proof of principles no more
Could be entrusted, while the events themselves,
Worn out in greatness, stripped of novelty,
Less occupied the mind, and sentiments
Could through my understanding's natural growth   200
No longer keep their ground, by faith maintained

Of inward consciousness, and hope that laid
Her hand upon her object — evidence
Safer, of universal application, such
As could not be impeached, was sought elsewhere.   205

   But now, become oppressors in their turn,
Frenchmen had changed a war of self-defence
For one of conquest, losing sight of all
Which they had struggled for: and mounted up,
Openly in the eye of earth and heaven,   210
The scale of liberty. I read her doom,
With anger vexed, with disappointment sore,
But not dismayed, nor taking to the shame
Of a false prophet. While resentment rose
Striving to hide, what nought could heal, the wounds   215
Of mortified presumption, I adhered
More firmly to old tenets, and, to prove
Their temper, strained them more; and thus, in heat
Of contest, did opinions every day
Grow into consequence, till round my mind   220
They clung, as if they were its life, nay more,
The very being of the immortal soul.

   This was the time, when, all things tending fast
To depravation, speculative schemes —
That promised to abstract the hopes of Man   225
Out of his feelings, to be fixed thenceforth
For ever in a purer element —
Found ready welcome. Tempting region *that*
For Zeal to enter and refresh herself,
Where passions had the privilege to work,   230
And never hear the sound of their own names.
But, speaking more in charity, the dream
Flattered the young, pleased with extremes, nor least
With that which makes our Reason's naked self
The object of its fervour. What delight!   235
How glorious! in self-knowledge and self-rule,
To look through all the frailties of the world,
And, with a resolute mastery shaking off
Infirmities of nature, time, and place,
Build social upon personal Liberty,   240
Which, to the blind restraints of general laws
Superior, magisterially adopts
One guide, the light of circumstances, flashed
Upon an independent intellect.
Thus expectation rose again; thus hope,   245
From her first ground expelled, grew proud once more.
Oft, as my thoughts were turned to human kind,

I scorned indifference; but, inflamed with thirst
Of a secure intelligence, and sick
Of other longing, I pursued what seemed   250
A more exalted nature; wished that Man
Should start out of his earthy, worm-like state,
And spread abroad the wings of Liberty,
Lord of himself, in undisturbed delight —
A noble aspiration! *yet* I feel   255
(Sustained by worthier as by wiser thoughts)
The aspiration, nor shall ever cease
To feel it; — but return we to our course.

Enough, 'tis true — could such a plea excuse
Those aberrations — had the clamorous friends   260
Of ancient Institutions said and done
To bring disgrace upon their very names;
Disgrace, of which, custom and written law,
And sundry moral sentiments as props
Or emanations of those institutes,   265
Too justly bore a part. A veil had been
Uplifted; why deceive ourselves? in sooth,
'Twas even so; and sorrow for the man
Who either had not eyes wherewith to see,
Or, seeing, had forgotten! A strong shock   270
Was given to old opinions; all men's minds
Had felt its power, and mine was both let loose,
Let loose and goaded. After what hath been
Already said of patriotic love,
Suffice it here to add, that, somewhat stern   275
In temperament, withal a happy man,
And therefore bold to look on painful things,
Free likewise of the world, and thence more bold,
I summoned my best skill, and toiled, intent
To anatomise the frame of social life,   280
Yea, the whole body of society
Searched to its heart. Share with me, Friend! the wish
That some dramatic tale, endued with shapes
Livelier, and flinging out less guarded words
Than suit the work we fashion, might set forth   285
What then I learned, or think I learned, of truth,
And the errors into which I fell, betrayed
By present objects, and by reasonings false
From their beginnings, inasmuch as drawn
Out of a heart that had been turned aside   290
From Nature's way by outward accidents,
And which was thus confounded, more and more
Misguided, and misguiding. So I fared,
Dragging all precepts, judgments, maxims, creeds,

Like culprits to the bar; calling the mind,   295
Suspiciously, to establish in plain day
Her titles and her honours; now believing,
Now disbelieving; endlessly perplexed
With impulse, motive, right and wrong, the ground
Of obligation, what the rule and whence   300
The sanction; till, demanding formal *proof,*
And seeking it in every thing, I lost
All feeling of conviction, and, in fine,
Sick, wearied out with contrarieties,
Yielded up moral questions in despair.   305

    This was the crisis of that strong disease,
This the soul's last and lowest ebb; I drooped,
Deeming our blessed reason of least use
Where wanted most: "The lordly attributes
Of will and choice," I bitterly exclaimed,   310
"What are they but a mockery of a Being
Who hath in no concerns of his a test
Of good and evil; knows not what to fear
Or hope for, what to covet or to shun;
And who, if those could be discerned, would yet   315
Be little profited, would see, and ask
Where is the obligation to enforce?
And, to acknowledged law rebellious, still,
As selfish passion urged, would act amiss;
The dupe of folly, or the slave of crime."   320

    Depressed, bewildered thus, I did not walk
With scoffers, seeking light and gay revenge
From indiscriminate laughter, nor sate down
In reconcilement with an utter waste
Of intellect; such sloth I could not brook,   325
(Too well I loved, in that my spring of life,
Pains-taking thoughts, and truth, their dear **reward)**
But turned to abstract science, and there sought
Work for the reasoning faculty enthroned
Where the disturbances of space and time —   330
Whether in matter's various properties
Inherent, or from human will and power
Derived — find no admission. Then it was —
Thanks to the bounteous Giver of all good! —
That the beloved Sister in whose sight   335
Those days were passed, now speaking **in a voice**
Of sudden admonition — like a brook
That did but *cross* a lonely road, and now
Is seen, heard, felt, and caught at every turn,
Companion never lost through many a league —   340

Maintained for me a saving intercourse
With my true self; for, though bedimmed and changed
Much, as it seemed, I was no further changed
Than as a clouded and a waning moon:
She whispered still that brightness would return,⁣   345
She, in the midst of all, preserved me still
A Poet, made me seek beneath that name,
And that alone, my office upon earth;
And, lastly, as hereafter will be shown,
If willing audience fail not, Nature's self,   350
By all varieties of human love
Assisted, led me back through opening day
To those sweet counsels between head and heart
Whence grew that genuine knowledge, fraught with peace,
Which, through the later sinkings of this cause,   355
Hath still upheld me, and upholds me now
In the catastrophe (for so they dream,
And nothing less), when, finally to close
And rivet down the gains of France, a Pope
Is summoned in, to crown an Emperor —   360
This last opprobrium, when we see a people,
That once looked up in faith, as if to Heaven
For manna, take a lesson from the dog
Returning to his vomit; when the sun
That rose in splendour, was alive, and moved   365
In exultation with a living pomp
Of clouds — his glory's natural retinue —
Hath dropped all functions by the gods bestowed,
And, turned into a gewgaw, a machine,
Sets like an Opera phantom.
                    Thus, O Friend!   370
Through times of honour and through times of shame
Descending, have I faithfully retraced
The perturbations of a youthful mind
Under a long-lived storm of great events —
A story destined for thy ear, who now,   375
Among the fallen of nations, dost abide
Where Etna, over hill and valley, casts
His shadow stretching towards Syracuse,
The city of Timoleon! Righteous Heaven!
How are the mighty prostrated! They first,   380
They first of all that breathe should have awaked
When the great voice was heard from out the tombs
Of ancient heroes. If I suffered grief
For ill-requited France, by many deemed
A trifler only in her proudest day;   385
Have been distressed to think of what she once
Promised, now is; a far more sober cause

Thine eyes must see of sorrow in a land,
Though with the wreck of loftier years bestrewn —
To the reanimating influence lost   390
Of memory, to virtue lost and hope.

    But indignation works where hope is not,
And thou, O Friend! wilt be refreshed. There is
One great society alone on earth:
The noble Living and the noble Dead.   395

    Thine be such converse strong and sanative,
A ladder for thy spirit to reascend
To health and joy and pure contentedness;
To me the grief confined, that thou art gone
From this last spot of earth, where Freedom now   400
Stands single in her only sanctuary;
A lonely wanderer art gone, by pain
Compelled and sickness, at this latter day,
This sorrowful reverse for all mankind.
I feel for thee, must utter what I feel: 405
The sympathies erewhile in part discharged,
Gather afresh, and will have vent again:
My own delights do scarcely seem to me
My own delights; the lordly Alps themselves,
Those rosy peaks, from which the Morning looks   410
Abroad on many nations, are no more
For me that image of pure gladsomeness
Which they were wont to be. Through kindred scenes,
For purpose, at a time, how different!
Thou tak'st thy way, carrying the heart and soul   415
That Nature gives to Poets, now by thought
Matured, and in the summer of their strength.
Oh! wrap him in your shades, ye giant woods,
On Etna's side; and thou, O flowery field
Of Enna! is there not some nook of thine,   420
From the first play-time of the infant world
Kept sacred to restorative delight,
When from afar invoked by anxious love?

    Child of the mountains, among shepherds reared,
Ere yet familiar with the classic page,   425
I learnt to dream of Sicily; and lo,
The gloom, that, but a moment past, was deepened
At thy command, at her command gives way;
A pleasant promise, wafted from her shores,
Comes o'er my heart: in fancy I behold   430
Her seas yet smiling, her once happy vales;
Nor can my tongue give utterance to a name

Of note belonging to that honoured isle,
Philosopher or Bard, Empedocles,
Or Archimedes, pure abstracted soul!   435
That doth not yield a solace to my grief:
And, O Theocritus, so far have some
Prevailed among the powers of heaven and earth,
By their endowments, good or great, that they
Have had, as thou reportest, miracles   440
Wrought for them in old time: yea, not unmoved,
When thinking on my own beloved friend,
I hear thee tell how bees with honey fed
Divine Comates, by his impious lord
Within a chest imprisoned; how they came   445
Laden from blooming grove or flowery field,
And fed him there, alive, month after month,
Because the goatherd, blessed man! had lips
Wet with the Muses' nectar.
                            Thus I soothe
The pensive moments by this calm fire-side,   450
And find a thousand bounteous images
To cheer the thoughts of those I love, and mine.
Our prayers have been accepted; thou wilt stand
On Etna's summit, above earth and sea,
Triumphant, winning from the invaded heavens   455
Thoughts without bound, magnificent designs,
Worthy of poets who attuned their harps
In wood or echoing cave, for discipline
Of heroes; or, in reverence to the gods,
'Mid temples, served by sapient priests, and choirs   460
Of virgins crowned with roses. Not in vain
Those temples, where they in their ruins yet
Survive for inspiration, shall attract
Thy solitary steps: and on the brink
Thou wilt recline of pastoral Arethuse;   465
Or, if that fountain be in truth no more,
Then, near some other spring, which, by the name
Thou gratulatest, willingly deceived,
I see thee linger a glad votary,
And not a captive pining for his home.   470

BOOK TWELFTH

IMAGINATION AND TASTE, HOW IMPAIRED AND RESTORED

Long time have human ignorance and guilt
Detained us, on what spectacles of woe
Compelled to look, and inwardly oppressed

With sorrow, disappointment, vexing thoughts,
Confusion of the judgment, zeal decayed, 5
And, lastly, utter loss of hope itself
And things to hope for! Not with these began
Our song, and not with these our song must end. —
Ye motions of delight, that haunt the sides
Of the green hills; ye breezes and soft airs, 10
Whose subtle intercourse with breathing flowers,
Feelingly watched, might teach Man's haughty race
How without injury to take, to give
Without offence; ye who, as if to show
The wondrous influence of power gently used, 15
Bend the complying heads of lordly pines,
And, with a touch, shift the stupendous clouds
Through the whole compass of the sky; ye brooks,
Muttering along the stones, a busy noise
By day, a quiet sound in silent night; 20
Ye waves, that out of the great deep steal forth
In a calm hour to kiss the pebbly shore,
Not mute, and then retire, fearing no storm;
And you, ye groves, whose ministry it is
To interpose the covert of your shades, 25
Even as a sleep, between the heart of man
And outward troubles, between man himself,
Not seldom, and his own uneasy heart:
Oh! that I had a music and a voice
Harmonious as your own, that I might tell 30
What ye have done for me. The morning shines,
Nor heedeth Man's perverseness; Spring returns, —
I saw the Spring return, and could rejoice,
In common with the children of her love,
Piping on boughs, or sporting on fresh fields, 35
Or boldly seeking pleasure nearer heaven
On wings that navigate cerulean skies.
So neither were complacency, nor peace,
Nor tender yearnings, wanting for my good
Through these distracted times; in Nature still 40
Glorying, I found a counterpoise in her,
Which, when the spirit of evil reached its height,
Maintained for me a secret happiness.

    This narrative, my Friend! hath chiefly told
Of intellectual power, fostering love, 45
Dispensing truth, and, over men and things,
Where reason yet might hesitate, diffusing
Prophetic sympathies of genial faith:
So was I favoured — such my happy lot —
Until that natural graciousness of mind 50

Gave way to overpressure from the times
And their disastrous issues. What availed,
When spells forbade the voyager to land,
That fragrant notice of a pleasant shore
Wafted, at intervals, from many a bower   55
Of blissful gratitude and fearless love?
Dare I avow that wish was mine to see,
And hope that future times *would* surely see,
The man to come, parted, as by a gulph,
From him who had been; that I could no more   60
Trust the elevation which had made me one
With the great family that still survives
To illuminate the abyss of ages past,
Sage, warrior, patriot, hero; for it seemed
That their best virtues were not free from taint   65
Of something false and weak, that could not stand
The open eye of Reason. Then I said,
"Go to the Poets, they will speak to thee
More perfectly of purer creatures; — yet
If reason be nobility in man,   70
Can aught be more ignoble than the man
Whom they delight in, blinded as he is
By prejudice, the miserable slave
Of low ambition or distempered love?"

In such strange passion, if I may once more   75
Review the past, I warred against myself —
A bigot to a new idolatry —
Like a cowled monk who hath forsworn the world,
Zealously laboured to cut off my heart
From all the sources of her former strength;   80
And as, by simple waving of a wand,
The wizard instantaneously dissolves
Palace or grove, even so could I unsoul
As readily by syllogistic words
Those mysteries of being which have made,   85
And shall continue evermore to make,
Of the whole human race one brotherhood.

What wonder, then, if, to a mind so far
Perverted, even the visible Universe
Fell under the dominion of a taste   90
Less spiritual, with microscopic view
Was scanned, as I had scanned the moral world?

O Soul of Nature! excellent and fair!
That didst rejoice with me, with whom I, too,

Rejoiced through early youth, before the winds   95
And roaring waters, and in lights and shades
That marched and countermarched about the hills
In glorious apparition, Powers on whom
I daily waited, now all eye and now
All ear; but never long without the heart   100
Employed, and man's unfolding intellect:
O Soul of Nature! that, by laws divine
Sustained and governed, still dost overflow
With an impassioned life, what feeble ones
Walk on this earth! how feeble have I been   105
When thou wert in thy strength! Nor this through stroke
Of human suffering, such as justifies
Remissness and inaptitude of mind,
But through presumption; even in pleasure pleased
Unworthily, disliking here, and there   110
Liking; by rules of mimic art transferred
To things above all art; but more, — for this,
Although a strong infection of the age,
Was never much my habit — giving way
To a comparison of scene with scene,   115
Bent overmuch on superficial things,
Pampering myself with meagre novelties
Of colour and proportion; to the moods
Of time and season, to the moral power,
The affections and the spirit of the place,   120
Insensible. Nor only did the love
Of sitting thus in judgment interrupt
My deeper feelings, but another cause,
More subtle and less easily explained,
That almost seems inherent in the creature,   125
A twofold frame of body and of mind.
I speak in recollection of a time
When the bodily eye, in every stage of life
The most despotic of our senses, gained
Such strength in *me* as often held my mind   130
In absolute dominion. Gladly here,
Entering upon abstruser argument,
Could I endeavour to unfold the means
Which Nature studiously employs to thwart
This tyranny, summons all the senses each   135
To counteract the other, and themselves,
And makes them all, and the objects with which all
Are conversant, subservient in their turn
To the great ends of Liberty and Power.
But leave we this: enough that my delights   140
(Such as they were) were sought insatiably.

Vivid the transport, vivid though not profound;
I roamed from hill to hill, from rock to rock,
Still craving combinations of new forms,
New pleasure, wider empire for the sight, 145
Proud of her own endowments, and rejoiced
To lay the inner faculties asleep.
Amid the turns and counterturns, the strife
And various trials of our complex being,
As we grow up, such thraldom of that sense 150
Seems hard to shun. And yet I knew a maid,
A young enthusiast, who escaped these bonds;
Her eye was not the mistress of her heart;
Far less did rules prescribed by passive taste,
Or barren intermeddling subtleties, 155
Perplex her mind; but, wise as women are
When genial circumstance hath favoured them,
She welcomed what was given, and craved no more;
Whate'er the scene presented to her view,
That was the best, to that she was attuned 160
By her benign simplicity of life,
And through a perfect happiness of soul,
Whose variegated feelings were in this
Sisters, that they were each some new delight.
Birds in the bower, and lambs in the green field, 165
Could they have known her, would have loved; methought
Her very presence such a sweetness breathed,
That flowers, and trees, and even the silent hills,
And every thing she looked on, should have had
An intimation how she bore herself 170
Towards them and to all creatures. God delights
In such a being; for her common thoughts
Are piety, her life is gratitude.

Even like this maid, before I was called forth
From the retirement of my native hills, 175
I loved whate'er I saw: nor lightly loved,
But most intensely; never dreamt of aught
More grand, more fair, more exquisitely framed
Than those few nooks to which my happy feet
Were limited. I had not at that time 180
Lived long enough, nor in the least survived
The first diviner influence of this world,
As it appears to unaccustomed eyes.
Worshipping then among the depth of things,
As piety ordained, could I submit 185
To measured admiration, or to aught
That should preclude humility and love?

I felt, observed, and pondered; did not judge,
Yea, never thought of judging; with the gift
Of all this glory filled and satisfied.   190
And afterwards, when through the gorgeous **Alps**
Roaming, I carried with me the same heart:
In truth, the degradation — howsoe'er
Induced, effect, in whatsoe'er degree,
Of custom that prepares a partial scale   195
In which the little oft outweighs the great;
Or any other cause that hath been named;
Or lastly, aggravated by the times
And their impassioned sounds, which well **might make**
The milder minstrelsies of rural scenes   200
Inaudible — was transient; I had known
Too forcibly, too early in my life,
Visitings of imaginative power
For this to last: I shook the habit off
Entirely and for ever, and again   205
In Nature's presence stood, as now I stand,
A sensitive being, a *creative* soul.

There are in our existence spots of time,
That with distinct pre-eminence retain
A renovating virtue, whence, depressed   210
By false opinion and contentious thought,
Or aught of heavier or more deadly weight,
In trivial occupations, and the round
Of ordinary intercourse, our minds
Are nourished and invisibly repaired;   215
A virtue, by which pleasure is enhanced,
That penetrates, enables us to mount,
When high, more high, and lifts us up when fallen.
This efficacious spirit chiefly lurks
Among those passages of life that give   220
Profoundest knowledge to what point, and how,
The mind is lord and master — outward sense
The obedient servant of her will. Such moments
Are scattered everywhere, taking their date
From our first childhood. I remember well,   225
That once, while yet my inexperienced hand
Could scarcely hold a bridle, with proud hopes
I mounted, and we journeyed towards the hills:
An ancient servant of my father's house
Was with me, my encourager and guide: 230
We had not travelled long, ere some mischance
Disjoined me from my comrade; and, through fear
Dismounting, down the rough and stony moor

I led my horse, and, stumbling on, at length
Came to a bottom, where in former times   235
A murderer had been hung in iron chains.
The gibbet-mast had mouldered down, the bones
And iron case were gone; but on the turf,
Hard by, soon after that fell deed was wrought,
Some unknown hand had carved the murderer's name.   240
The monumental letters were inscribed
In times long past; but still, from year to year,
By superstition of the neighbourhood,
The grass is cleared away, and to this hour
The characters are fresh and visible: 245
A casual glance had shown them, and I fled,
Faltering and faint, and ignorant of the road:
Then, reascending the bare common, saw
A naked pool that lay beneath the hills,
The beacon on the summit, and, more near,   250
A girl, who bore a pitcher on her head,
And seemed with difficult steps to force her way
Against the blowing wind. It was, in truth,
An ordinary sight; but I should need
Colours and words that are unknown to man,   255
To paint the visionary dreariness
Which, while I looked all round for my lost guide,
Invested moorland waste, and naked pool,
The beacon crowning the lone eminence,
The female and her garments vexed and tossed   260
By the strong wind. When, in the blessed hours
Of early love, the loved one at my side,
I roamed, in daily presence of this scene,
Upon the naked pool and dreary crags,
And on the melancholy beacon, fell   265
A spirit of pleasure and youth's golden gleam;
And think ye not with radiance more sublime
For these remembrances, and for the power
They had left behind? So feeling comes in aid
Of feeling, and diversity of strength   270
Attends us, if but once we have been strong.
Oh! mystery of man, from what a depth
Proceed thy honours. I am lost, but see
In simple childhood something of the base
On which thy greatness stands; but this I feel,   275
That from thyself it comes, that thou must give,
Else never canst receive. The days gone by
Return upon me almost from the dawn
Of life: the hiding-places of man's power
Open; I would approach them, but they close.   280

I see by glimpses now; when age comes on,
May scarcely see at all; and I would give,
While yet we may, as far as words can give,
Substance and life to what I feel, enshrining,
Such is my hope, the spirit of the Past   285
For future restoration. — Yet another
Of these memorials: —
                              One Christmas-time,
On the glad eve of its dear holidays,
Feverish, and tired, and restless, I went forth
Into the fields, impatient for the sight   290
Of those led palfreys that should bear us home;
My brothers and myself. There rose a crag,
That, from the meeting-point of two highways
Ascending, overlooked them both, far stretched;
Thither, uncertain on which road to fix   295
My expectation, thither I repaired,
Scout-like, and gained the summit; 'twas a day
Tempestuous, dark, and wild, and on the grass
I sate half-sheltered by a naked wall;
Upon my right hand couched a single sheep,   300
Upon my left a blasted hawthorn stood;
With those companions at my side, I watched,
Straining my eyes intensely, as the mist
Gave intermitting prospect of the copse
And plain beneath. Ere we to school returned, —   305
That dreary time, — ere we had been ten days
Sojourners in my father's house, he died,
And I and my three brothers, orphans then,
Followed his body to the grave. The event,
With all the sorrow that it brought, appeared   310
A chastisement; and when I called to mind
That day so lately past, when from the crag
I looked in such anxiety of hope;
With trite reflections of morality,
Yet in the deepest passion, I bowed low   315
To God, Who thus corrected my desires;
And, afterwards, the wind and sleety rain,
And all the business of the elements,
The single sheep, and the one blasted tree,
And the bleak music from that old stone wall,   320
The noise of wood and water, and the mist
That on the line of each of those two roads
Advanced in such indisputable shapes;
All these were kindred spectacles and sounds
To which I oft repaired, and thence would drink,   325
As at a fountain; and on winter nights,

Down to this very time, when storm and rain
Beat on my roof, or, haply, at noon-day,
While in a grove I walk, whose lofty trees,
Laden with summer's thickest foliage, rock   330
In a strong wind, some working of the spirit,
Some inward agitations thence are brought,
Whate'er their office, whether to beguile
Thoughts over busy in the course they took,
Or animate an hour of vacant ease.   335

BOOK THIRTEENTH

IMAGINATION AND TASTE, HOW IMPAIRED AND RESTORED (CONCLUDED)

FROM Nature doth emotion come, and moods
Of calmness equally are Nature's gift:
This is her glory; these two attributes
Are sister horns that constitute her strength.
Hence Genius, born to thrive by interchange   5
Of peace and excitation, finds in her
His best and purest friend; from her receives
That energy by which he seeks the truth,
From her that happy stillness of the mind
Which fits him to receive it when unsought.   10

Such benefit the humblest intellects
Partake of, each in their degree; 'tis mine
To speak, what I myself have known and felt;
Smooth task! for words find easy way, inspired
By gratitude, and confidence in truth.   15
Long time in search of knowledge did I range
The field of human life, in heart and mind
Benighted; but, the dawn beginning now
To re-appear, 'twas proved that not in vain
I had been taught to reverence a Power   20
That is the visible quality and shape
And image of right reason; that matures
Her processes by steadfast laws; gives birth
To no impatient or fallacious hopes,
No heat of passion or excessive zeal,   25
No vain conceits; provokes to no quick turns
Of self-applauding intellect; but trains
To meekness, and exalts by humble faith;
Holds up before the mind intoxicate
With present objects, and the busy dance   30
Of things that pass away, a temperate show

Of objects that endure; and by this course
Disposes her, when over-fondly set
On throwing off incumbrances, to seek
In man, and in the frame of social life,   35
Whate'er there is desirable and good
Of kindred permanence, unchanged in form
And function, or, through strict vicissitude
Of life and death, revolving. Above all
Were re-established now those watchful thoughts   40
Which, seeing little worthy or sublime
In what the Historian's pen so much delights
To blazon — power and energy detached
From moral purpose — early tutored me
To look with feelings of fraternal love   45
Upon the unassuming things that hold
A silent station in this beauteous world.

   Thus moderated, thus composed, I found
Once more in Man an object of delight,
Of pure imagination, and of love;   50
And, as the horizon of my mind enlarged,
Again I took the intellectual eye
For my instructor, studious more to see
Great truths, than touch and handle little ones.
Knowledge was given accordingly; my trust   55
Became more firm in feelings that had stood
The test of such a trial; clearer far
My sense of excellence — of right and wrong:
The promise of the present time retired
Into its true proportion; sanguine schemes,   60
Ambitious projects, pleased me less; I sought
For present good in life's familiar face,
And built thereon my hopes of good to come.

   With settling judgments now of what would last
And what would disappear; prepared to find   65
Presumption, folly, madness, in the men
Who thrust themselves upon the passive world
As Rulers of the world; to see in these,
Even when the public welfare is their aim,
Plans without thought, or built on theories   70
Vague and unsound; and having brought the books
Of modern statists to their proper test,
Life, human life, with all its sacred claims
Of sex and age, and heaven-descended rights,
Mortal, or those beyond the reach of death;   75
And having thus discerned how dire a thing

Is worshipped in that idol proudly named
"The Wealth of Nations," *where* alone that wealth
Is lodged, and how increased; and having gained
A more judicious knowledge of the worth   80
And dignity of individual man,
No composition of the brain, but man
Of whom we read, the man whom we behold
With our own eyes — I could not but inquire —
Not with less interest than heretofore,   85
But greater, though in spirit more subdued —
Why is this glorious creature to be found
One only in ten thousand? What one is,
Why may not millions be? What bars are thrown
By Nature in the way of such a hope?   90
Our animal appetites and daily wants,
Are these obstructions insurmountable?
If not, then others vanish into air.
"Inspect the basis of the social pile:
Inquire," said I, "how much of mental power   95
And genuine virtue they possess who live
By bodily toil, labour exceeding far
Their due proportion, under all the weight
Of that injustice which upon ourselves
Ourselves entail." Such estimate to frame   100
I chiefly looked (what need to look beyond?)
Among the natural abodes of men,
Fields with their rural works; recalled to mind
My earliest notices; with these compared
The observations made in later youth,   105
And to that day continued. — For, the time
Had never been when throes of mighty Nations
And the world's tumult unto me could yield,
How far soe'er transported and possessed,
Full measure of content; but still I craved   110
An intermingling of distinct regards
And truths of individual sympathy
Nearer ourselves. Such often might be gleaned
From the great City, else it must have proved
To me a heart-depressing wilderness;   115
But much was wanting: therefore did I turn
To you, ye pathways, and ye lonely roads;
Sought you enriched with everything I prized,
With human kindnesses and simple joys.

Oh! next to one dear state of bliss, vouchsafed   120
Alas! to few in this untoward world,
The bliss of walking daily in life's prime.

Through field or forest with the maid we love,
While yet our hearts are young, while yet we breathe
Nothing but happiness, in some lone nook,   125
Deep vale, or any where, the home of both,
From which it would be misery to stir:
Oh! next to such enjoyment of our youth,
In my esteem, next to such dear delight,
Was that of wandering on from day to day   130
Where I could meditate in peace, and cull
Knowledge that step by step might lead me on
To wisdom; or, as lightsome as a bird
Wafted upon the wind from distant lands,
Sing notes of greeting to strange fields or groves,   135
Which lacked not voice to welcome me in turn;
And, when that pleasant toil had ceased to please,
Converse with men, where if we meet a face
We almost meet a friend, on naked heaths
With long long ways before, by cottage bench,   140
Or well-spring where the weary traveller rests.

   Who doth not love to follow with his eye
The windings of a public way? the sight,
Familiar object as it is, hath wrought
On my imagination since the morn   145
Of childhood, when a disappearing line,
One daily present to my eyes, that crossed
The naked summit of a far-off hill
Beyond the limits that my feet had trod,
Was like an invitation into space   150
Boundless, or guide into eternity.
Yes, something of the grandeur which invests
The mariner who sails the roaring sea
Through storm and darkness, early in my mind
Surrounded, too, the wanderers of the earth;   155
Grandeur as much, and loveliness far more.
Awed have I been by strolling Bedlamites;
From many other uncouth vagrants (passed
In fear) have walked with quicker step; but why
Take note of this? When I began to enquire,   160
To watch and question those I met, and speak
Without reserve to them, the lonely roads
Were open schools in which I daily read
With most delight the passions of mankind,
Whether by words, looks, sighs, or tears, revealed;   165
There saw into the depth of human souls,
Souls that appear to have no depth at all
To careless eyes. And — now convinced at heart

How little those formalities, to which
With overweening trust alone we give   170
The name of Education, have to do
With real feeling and just sense; how vain
A correspondence with the talking world
Proves to the most; and called to make good search
If man's estate, by doom of Nature yoked   175
With toil, be therefore yoked with ignorance;
If virtue be indeed so hard to rear,
And intellectual strength so rare a boon —
I prized such walks still more, for there I found
Hope to my hope, and to my pleasure peace   180
And steadiness, and healing and repose
To every angry passion. There I heard,
From mouths of men obscure and lowly, truths
Replete with honour; sounds in unison
With loftiest promises of good and fair.   185

　　There are who think that strong affection, love
Known by whatever name, is falsely deemed
A gift, to use a term which they would use,
Of vulgar nature; that its growth requires
Retirement, leisure, language purified   190
By manners studied and elaborate;
That whoso feels such passion in its strength
Must live within the very light and air
Of courteous usages refined by art.
True is it, where oppression worse than death   195
Salutes the being at his birth, where grace
Of culture hath been utterly unknown,
And poverty and labour in excess
From day to day pre-occupy the ground
Of the affections, and to Nature's self   200
Oppose a deeper nature; there, indeed,
Love cannot be; nor does it thrive with ease
Among the close and overcrowded haunts
Of cities, where the human heart is sick,
And the eye feeds it not, and cannot feed.   205
　— Yes, in those wanderings deeply did I feel
How we mislead each other; above all,
How books mislead us, seeking their reward
From judgments of the wealthy Few, who see
By artificial lights; how they debase   210
The Many for the pleasure of those Few;
Effeminately level down the truth
To certain general notions, for the sake
Of being understood at once, or else

Through want of better knowledge in the heads   215
That framed them; flattering self-conceit with words,
That, while they most ambitiously set forth
Extrinsic differences, the outward marks
Whereby society has parted man
From man, neglect the universal heart.   220

Here, calling up to mind what then I saw,
A youthful traveller, and see daily now
In the familiar circuit of my home,
Here might I pause, and bend in reverence
To Nature, and the power of human minds,   225
To men as they are men within themselves.
How oft high service is performed within,
When all the external man is rude in show, —
Not like a temple rich with pomp and gold,
But a mere mountain chapel, that protects   230
Its simple worshippers from sun and shower.
Of these, said I, shall be my song; of these,
If future years mature me for the task,
Will I record the praises, making verse
Deal boldly with substantial things; in truth   235
And sanctity of passion, speak of these,
That justice may be done, obeisance paid
Where it is due: thus haply shall I teach,
Inspire, through unadulterated ears
Pour rapture, tenderness, and hope, — my theme   240
No other than the very heart of man,
As found among the best of those who live,
Not unexalted by religious faith,
Nor uninformed by books, good books, though few,
In Nature's presence: thence may I select   245
Sorrow, that is not sorrow, but delight;
And miserable love, that is not pain
To hear of, for the glory that redounds
Therefrom to human kind, and what we are.
Be mine to follow with no timid step   250
Where knowledge leads me: it shall be my pride
That I have dared to tread this holy ground,
Speaking no dream, but things oracular;
Matter not lightly to be heard by those
Who to the letter of the outward promise   255
Do read the invisible soul; by men adroit
In speech, and for communion with the world
Accomplished; minds whose faculties are then
Most active when they are most eloquent,
And elevated most when most admired.   260

Men may be found of other mould than these,
Who are their own upholders, to themselves
Encouragement, and energy, and will,
Expressing liveliest thoughts in lively words
As native passion dictates. Others, too,   265
There are among the walks of homely life
Still higher, men for contemplation framed,
Shy, and unpractised in the strife of phrase;
Meek men, whose very souls perhaps would sink
Beneath them, summoned to such intercourse: 270
Theirs is the language of the heavens, the power,
The thought, the image, and the silent joy:
Words are but under-agents in their souls;
When they are grasping with their greatest strength,
They do not breathe among them: this I speak   275
In gratitude to God, Who feeds our hearts
For His own service; knoweth, loveth us,
When we are unregarded by the world.

    Also, about this time did I receive
Convictions still more strong than heretofore,   280
Not only that the inner frame is good,
And graciously composed, but that, no less,
Nature for all conditions wants not power
To consecrate, if we have eyes to see,
The outside of her creatures, and to breathe   285
Grandeur upon the very humblest face
Of human life. I felt that the array
Of act and circumstance, and visible form,
Is mainly to the pleasure of the mind
What passion makes them; that meanwhile the forms   290
Of Nature have a passion in themselves,
That intermingles with those works of man
To which she summons him; although the works
Be mean, have nothing lofty of their own;
And that the Genius of the Poet hence   295
May boldly take his way among mankind
Wherever Nature leads; that he hath stood
By Nature's side among the men of old,
And so shall stand for ever. Dearest Friend!
If thou partake the animating faith   300
That Poets, even as Prophets, each with each
Connected in a mighty scheme of truth,
Have each his own peculiar faculty,
Heaven's gift, a sense that fits him to perceive
Objects unseen before, thou wilt not blame   305
The humblest of this band who dares to hope
That unto him hath also been vouchsafed

An insight that in some sort he possesses,
A privilege whereby a work of his,
Proceeding from a source of untaught things,   310
Creative and enduring, may become
A power like one of Nature's. To a hope
Not less ambitious once among the wilds
Of Sarum's Plain, my youthful spirit was raised;
There, as I ranged at will the pastoral downs   315
Trackless and smooth, or paced the bare white roads
Lengthening in solitude their dreary line,
Time with his retinue of ages fled
Backwards, nor checked his flight until I saw
Our dim ancestral Past in vision clear;   320
Saw multitudes of men, and, here and there,
A single Briton clothed in wolf-skin vest,
With shield and stone-axe, stride across the wold;
The voice of spears was heard, the rattling spear
Shaken by arms of mighty bone, in strength,   325
Long mouldered, of barbaric majesty.
I called on Darkness — but before the word
Was uttered, midnight darkness seemed to take
All objects from my sight; and lo! again
The Desert visible by dismal flames;   330
It is the sacrificial altar, fed
With living men — how deep the groans! the voice
Of those that crowd the giant wicker thrills
The monumental hillocks, and the pomp
Is for both worlds, the living and the dead.   335
At other moments (for through that wide waste
Three summer days I roamed) where'er the Plain
Was figured o'er with circles, lines, or mounds,
That yet survive, a work, as some divine,
Shaped by the Druids, so to represent   340
Their knowledge of the heavens, and image forth
The constellations; gently was I charmed
Into a waking dream, a reverie
That, with believing eyes, where'er I turned,
Beheld long-bearded teachers, with white wands   345
Uplifted, pointing to the starry sky,
Alternately, and plain below, while breath
Of music swayed their motions, and the waste
Rejoiced with them and me in those sweet sounds.

This for the past, and things that may be viewed   350
Or fancied in the obscurity of years
From monumental hints: and thou, O Friend!
Pleased with some unpremeditated strains
That served those wanderings to beguile, hast said

That then and there my mind had exercised   355
Upon the vulgar forms of present things,
The actual world of our familiar days,
Yet higher power; had caught from them a tone,
An image, and a character, by books
Not hitherto reflected. Call we this   360
A partial judgment — and yet why? for *then*
We were as strangers; and I may not speak
Thus wrongfully of verse, however rude,
Which on thy young imagination, trained
In the great City, broke like light from far.   365
Moreover, each man's Mind is to herself
Witness and judge; and I remember well
That in life's every-day appearances
I seemed about this time to gain clear sight
Of a new world — a world, too, that was fit   370
To be transmitted, and to other eyes
Made visible; as ruled by those fixed laws
Whence spiritual dignity originates,
Which do both give it being and maintain
A balance, an ennobling interchange   375
Of action from without and from within;
The excellence, pure function, and best power
Both of the object seen, and eye that sees.

BOOK FOURTEENTH

CONCLUSION

IN one of those excursions (may they ne'er
Fade from remembrance!) through the Northern tracts
Of Cambria ranging with a youthful friend,
I left Bethgelert's huts at couching-time,
And westward took my way, to see the sun   5
Rise from the top of Snowdon. To the door
Of a rude cottage at the mountain's base
We came, and roused the shepherd who attends
The adventurous stranger's steps, a trusty guide;
Then, cheered by short refreshment, sallied forth.   10

    It was a close, warm, breezeless summer night,
Wan, dull, and glaring, with a dripping fog
Low-hung and thick that covered all the sky;
But, undiscouraged, we began to climb
The mountain-side. The mist soon girt us round,   15
And, after ordinary travellers' talk
With our conductor, pensively we sank

Each into commerce with his private thoughts:
Thus did we breast the ascent, and by myself
Was nothing either seen or heard that checked   20
Those musings or diverted, save that once
The shepherd's lurcher, who, among the crags,
Had to his joy unearthed a hedgehog, teased
His coiled-up prey with barkings turbulent.
This small adventure, for even such it seemed   25
In that wild place and at the dead of night,
Being over and forgotten, on we wound
In silence as before. With forehead bent
Earthward, as if in opposition set
Against an enemy, I panted up   30
With eager pace, and no less eager thoughts.
Thus might we wear a midnight hour away,
Ascending at loose distance each from each,
And I, as chanced, the foremost of the band;
When at my feet the ground appeared to brighten,   35
And with a step or two seemed brighter still;
Nor was time given to ask or learn the cause,
For instantly a light upon the turf
Fell like a flash, and lo! as I looked up,
The Moon hung naked in a firmament   40
Of azure without cloud, and at my feet
Rested a silent sea of hoary mist.
A hundred hills their dusky backs upheaved
All over this still ocean; and beyond,
Far, far beyond, the solid vapours stretched,   45
In headlands, tongues, and promontory shapes,
Into the main Atlantic, that appeared
To dwindle, and give up his majesty,
Usurped upon far as the sight could reach.
Not so the ethereal vault; encroachment none   50
Was there, nor loss; only the inferior stars
Had disappeared, or shed a fainter light
In the clear presence of the full-orbed Moon,
Who, from her sovereign elevation, gazed
Upon the billowy ocean, as it lay   55
All meek and silent, save that through a rift —
Not distant from the shore whereon we stood,
A fixed, abysmal, gloomy, breathing-place —
Mounted the roar of waters, torrents, streams
Innumerable, roaring with one voice!   60
Heard over earth and sea, and, in that hour,
For so it seemed, felt by the starry heavens.

When into air had partially dissolved
That vision, given to spirits of the night

And three chance human wanderers, in calm thought   65
Reflected, it appeared to me the type
Of a majestic intellect, its acts
And its possessions, what it has and craves,
What in itself it is, and would become.
There I beheld the emblem of a mind   70
That feeds upon infinity, that broods
Over the dark abyss, intent to hear
Its voices issuing forth to silent light
In one continuous stream; a mind sustained
By recognitions of transcendent power,   75
In sense conducting to ideal form,
In soul of more than mortal privilege.
One function, above all, of such a mind
Had Nature shadowed there, by putting forth,
'Mid circumstances awful and sublime,   80
That mutual domination which she loves
To exert upon the face of outward things,
So moulded, joined, abstracted, so endowed
With interchangeable supremacy,
That men, least sensitive, see, hear, perceive,   85
And cannot choose but feel. The power, which all
Acknowledge when thus moved, which Nature thus
To bodily sense exhibits, is the express
Resemblance of that glorious faculty
That higher minds bear with them as their own.   90
This is the very spirit in which they deal
With the whole compass of the universe:
They from their native selves can send abroad
Kindred mutations; for themselves create
A like existence; and, whene'er it dawns   95
Created for them, catch it, or are caught
By its inevitable mastery,
Like angels stopped upon the wing by sound
Of harmony from Heaven's remotest spheres.
Them the enduring and the transient both   100
Serve to exalt; they build up greatest things
From least suggestions; ever on the watch,
Willing to work and to be wrought upon,
They need not extraordinary calls
To rouse them; in a world of life they live,   105
By sensible impressions not enthralled,
But by their quickening impulse made more prompt
To hold fit converse with the spiritual world,
And with the generations of mankind
Spread over time, past, present, and to come,   110
Age after age, till Time shall be no more.

Such minds are truly from the Deity,
For they are Powers; and hence the highest bliss
That flesh can know is theirs — the consciousness
Of Whom they are, habitually infused   115
Through every image and through every thought,
And all affections by communion raised
From earth to heaven, from human to divine;
Hence endless occupation for the Soul,
Whether discursive or intuitive;   120
Hence cheerfulness for acts of daily life,
Emotions which best foresight need not fear,
Most worthy then of trust when most intense.
Hence, amid ills that vex and wrongs that crush
Our hearts — if here the words of Holy Writ   125
May with fit reverence be applied — that peace
Which passeth understanding, that repose
In moral judgments which from this pure source
Must come, or will by man be sought in vain.

Oh! who is he that hath his whole life long   130
Preserved, enlarged, this freedom in himself?
For this alone is genuine liberty:
Where is the favoured being who hath held
That course unchecked, unerring, and untired,
In one perpetual progress smooth and bright? —   135
A humbler destiny have we retraced,
And told of lapse and hesitating choice,
And backward wanderings along thorny ways:
Yet — compassed round by mountain solitudes,
Within whose solemn temple I received   140
My earliest visitations, careless then
Of what was given me; and which now I range,
A meditative, oft a suffering man —
Do I declare — in accents which, from truth
Deriving cheerful confidence, shall blend   145
Their modulation with these vocal streams —
That, whatsoever falls my better mind,
Revolving with the accidents of life,
May have sustained, that, howsoe'er misled,
Never did I, in quest of right and wrong,   150
Tamper with conscience from a private aim;
Nor was in any public hope the dupe
Of selfish passions; nor did ever yield
Wilfully to mean cares or low pursuits,
But shrunk with apprehensive jealousy   155
From every combination which might aid
The tendency, too potent in itself,

Of use and custom to bow down the soul
Under a growing weight of vulgar sense,
And substitute a universe of death   160
For that which moves with light and life informed,
Actual, divine, and true. To fear and love,
To love as prime and chief, for there fear ends,
Be this ascribed; to early intercourse,
In presence of sublime or beautiful forms,   165
With the adverse principles of pain and joy —
Evil as one is rashly named by men
Who know not what they speak. By love subsists
All lasting grandeur, by pervading love;
That gone, we are as dust. — Behold the fields   170
In balmy spring-time full of rising flowers
And joyous creatures; see that pair, the lamb
And the lamb's mother, and their tender ways
Shall touch thee to the heart; thou callest this love,
And not inaptly so, for love it is,   175
Far as it carries thee. In some green bower
Rest, and be not alone, but have thou there
The One who is thy choice of all the world:
There linger, listening, gazing, with delight
Impassioned, but delight how pitiable!   180
Unless this love by a still higher love
Be hallowed, love that breathes not without awe;
Love that adores, but on the knees of prayer,
By heaven inspired; that frees from chains the soul,
Bearing in union with the purest best   185
Of earthborn passions on the wings of praise
A mutual tribute to the Almighty's Throne.

    This spiritual Love acts not nor can exist
Without Imagination, which, in truth,
Is but another name for absolute power   190
And clearest insight, amplitude of mind,
And Reason in her most exalted mood.
This faculty hath been the feeding source
Of our long labour: we have traced the stream
From the blind cavern whence is faintly heard   195
Its natal murmur; followed it to light
And open day; accompanied its course
Among the ways of Nature, for a time
Lost sight of it bewildered and engulphed:
Then given it greeting as it rose once more   200
In strength, reflecting from its placid breast
The works of man and face of human life;
And lastly, from its progress have we drawn

Faith in life endless, the sustaining thought
Of human Being, Eternity, and God.   205

   Imagination having been our theme,
So also hath that intellectual Love,
For they are each in each, and cannot stand
Dividually. — Here must thou be, O Man!
Power to thyself; no Helper hast thou here;   210
Here keepest thou in singleness thy state:
No other can divide with thee this work:
No secondary hand can intervene
To fashion this ability; 'tis thine,
The prime and vital principle is thine   215
In the recesses of thy nature, far
From any reach of outward fellowship,
Else is not thine at all. But joy to him,
Oh, joy to him who here hath sown, hath laid
Here, the foundation of his future years!   220
For all that friendship, all that love can do,
All that a darling countenance can look
Or dear voice utter, to complete the man,
Perfect him, made imperfect in himself,
All shall be his: and he whose soul hath risen   225
Up to the height of feeling intellect
Shall want no humbler tenderness; his heart
Be tender as a nursing mother's heart;
Of female softness shall his life be full,
Of humble cares and delicate desires,   230
Mild interests and gentlest sympathies.

   Child of my parents! Sister of my soul!
Thanks in sincerest verse have been elsewhere
Poured out for all the early tenderness
Which I from thee imbibed: and 'tis most true   235
That later seasons owed to thee no less;
For, spite of thy sweet influence and the touch
Of kindred hands that opened out the springs
Of genial thought in childhood, and in spite
Of all that unassisted I had marked   240
In life or nature of those charms minute
That win their way into the heart by stealth,
Still to the very going-out of youth
I too exclusively esteemed *that* love,
And sought *that* beauty, which, as Milton sings,   245
Hath terror in it. Thou didst soften down
This over-sternness; but for thee, dear Friend!
My soul, too reckless of mild grace, had stood

In her original self too confident,
Retained too long a countenance severe;   250
A rock with torrents roaring, with the clouds
Familiar, and a favourite of the stars:
But thou didst plant its crevices with flowers,
Hang it with shrubs that twinkle in the breeze,
And teach the little birds to build their nests   255
And warble in its chambers. At a time
When Nature, destined to remain so long
Foremost in my affections, had fallen back
Into a second place, pleased to become
A handmaid to a nobler than herself,   260
When every day brought with it some new sense
Of exquisite regard for common things,
And all the earth was budding with these gifts
Of more refined humanity, thy breath,
Dear Sister! was a kind of gentler spring   265
That went before my steps. Thereafter came
One whom with thee friendship had early paired;
She came, no more a phantom to adorn
A moment, but an inmate of the heart,
And yet a spirit, there for me enshrined   270
To penetrate the lofty and the low;
Even as one essence of pervading light
Shines in the brightest of ten thousand stars
And the meek worm that feeds her lonely lamp
Couched in the dewy grass.

           With such a theme,   275
Coleridge! with this my argument, of thee
Shall I be silent? O capacious Soul!
Placed on this earth to love and understand,
And from thy presence shed the light of love,
Shall I be mute, ere thou be spoken of?   280
Thy kindred influence to my heart of hearts
Did also find its way. Thus fear relaxed
Her overweening grasp; thus thoughts and things
In the self-haunting spirit learned to take
More rational proportions; mystery,   285
The incumbent mystery of sense and soul,
Of life and death, time and eternity,
Admitted more habitually a mild
Interposition — a serene delight
In closelier gathering cares, such as become   290
A human creature, howsoe'er endowed,
Poet, or destined for a humbler name;
And so the deep enthusiastic joy,
The rapture of the hallelujah sent

From all that breathes and is, was chastened, stemmed 295
And balanced by pathetic truth, by trust
In hopeful reason, leaning on the stay
Of Providence; and in reverence for duty,
Here, if need be, struggling with storms, and there
Strewing in peace life's humblest ground with herbs, 300
At every season green, sweet at all hours.

And now, O Friend! this history is brought
To its appointed close: the discipline
And consummation of a Poet's mind,
In everything that stood most prominent, 305
Have faithfully been pictured; we have reached
The time (our guiding object from the first)
When we may, not presumptuously, I hope,
Suppose my powers so far confirmed, and such
My knowledge, as to make me capable 310
Of building up a Work that shall endure.
Yet much hath been omitted, as need was;
Of books how much! and even of the other wealth
That is collected among woods and fields,
Far more: for Nature's secondary grace 315
Hath hitherto been barely touched upon,
The charm more superficial that attends
Her works, as they present to Fancy's choice
Apt illustrations of the moral world,
Caught at a glance, or traced with curious pains. 320

Finally, and above all, O Friend! (I speak
With due regret) how much is overlooked
In human nature and her subtle ways,
As studied first in our own hearts, and then
In life among the passions of mankind, 325
Varying their composition and their hue,
Where'er we move, under the diverse shapes
That individual character presents
To an attentive eye. For progress meet,
Along this intricate and difficult path, 330
Whate'er was wanting, something had I gained,
As one of many schoolfellows compelled,
In hardy independence, to stand up
Amid conflicting interests, and the shock
Of various tempers; to endure and note 335
What was not understood, though known to be;
Among the mysteries of love and hate,
Honour and shame, looking to right and left,
Unchecked by innocence too delicate,

And moral notions too intolerant,   340
Sympathies too contracted. Hence, when called
To take a station among men, the step
Was easier, the transition more secure,
More profitable also; for, the mind
Learns from such timely exercise to keep   345
In wholesome separation the two natures,
The one that feels, the other that observes.

    Yet one word more of personal concern —
Since I withdrew unwillingly from France,
I led an undomestic wanderer's life,   350
In London chiefly harboured, whence I roamed,
Tarrying at will in many a pleasant spot
Of rural England's cultivated vales
Or Cambrian solitudes. A youth — (he bore
The name of Calvert — it shall live, if words   355
Of mine can give it life,) in firm belief
That by endowments not from me withheld
Good might be furthered — in his last decay
By a bequest sufficient for my needs
Enabled me to pause for choice, and walk   360
At large and unrestrained, nor damped too soon
By mortal cares. Himself no Poet, yet
Far less a common follower of the world,
He deemed that my pursuits and labours lay
Apart from all that leads to wealth, or even   365
A necessary maintenance insures,
Without some hazard to the finer sense;
He cleared a passage for me, and the stream
Flowed in the bent of Nature.
                      Having now
Told what best merits mention, further pains   370
Our present purpose seems not to require,
And I have other tasks. Recall to mind
The mood in which this labour was begun,
O Friend! The termination of my course
Is nearer now, much nearer; yet even then,   375
In that distraction and intense desire,
I said unto the life which I had lived,
Where art thou? Hear I not a voice from thee
Which 'tis reproach to hear? Anon I rose
As if on wings, and saw beneath me stretched   380
Vast prospect of the world which I had been
And was; and hence this Song, which like a lark
I have protracted, in the unwearied heavens
Singing, and often with more plaintive voice

To earth attempered and her deep-drawn sighs,   385
Yet centring all in love, and in the end
All gratulant, if rightly understood.

   Whether to me shall be allotted life,
And, with life, power to accomplish aught of worth,
That will be deemed no insufficient plea   390
For having given the story of myself,
Is all uncertain: but, beloved Friend!
When, looking back, thou seest, in clearer view
Than any liveliest sight of yesterday,
That summer, under whose indulgent skies,   395
Upon smooth Quantock's airy ridge we roved
Unchecked, or loitered 'mid her sylvan combs,
Thou in bewitching words, with happy heart,
Didst chaunt the vision of that Ancient Man,
The bright-eyed Mariner, and rueful woes   400
Didst utter of the Lady Christabel;
And I, associate with such labour, steeped
In soft forgetfulness the livelong hours,
Murmuring of him who, joyous hap, was found,
After the perils of his moonlight ride,   405
Near the loud waterfall; or her who sate
In misery near the miserable Thorn;
When thou dost to that summer turn thy thoughts,
And hast before thee all which then we were,
To thee, in memory of that happiness,   410
It will be known, by thee at least, my Friend!
Felt, that the history of a Poet's mind
Is labour not unworthy of regard:
To thee the work shall justify itself.

   The last and later portions of this gift   415
Have been prepared, not with the buoyant spirits
That were our daily portion when we first
Together wantoned in wild Poesy,
But, under pressure of a private grief,
Keen and enduring, which the mind and heart,   420
That in this meditative history
Have been laid open, needs must make me feel
More deeply, yet enable me to bear
More firmly; and a comfort now hath risen
From hope that thou art near, and wilt be soon   425
Restored to us in renovated health;
When, after the first mingling of our tears,
'Mong other consolations, we may draw
Some pleasure from this offering of my love.

Oh! yet a few short years of useful life,   430
And all will be complete, thy race be run,
Thy monument of glory will be raised;
Then, though (too weak to tread the ways of truth)
This age fall back to old idolatry,
Though men return to servitude as fast   435
As the tide ebbs, to ignominy and shame
By nations sink together, we shall still
Find solace — knowing what we have learnt to know,
Rich in true happiness if allowed to be
Faithful alike in forwarding a day   440
Of firmer trust, joint labourers in the work
(Should Providence such grace to us vouchsafe)
Of their deliverance, surely yet to come.
Prophets of Nature, we to them will speak
A lasting inspiration, sanctified   445
By reason, blest by faith: what we have loved,
Others will love, and we will teach them how;
Instruct them how the mind of man becomes
A thousand times more beautiful than the earth
On which he dwells, above this frame of things   450
(Which, 'mid all revolution in the hopes
And fears of men, doth still remain unchanged)
In beauty exalted, as it is itself
Of quality and fabric more divine.

STEPPING WESTWARD

While my Fellow-traveller and I were walking by the side of Loch Ket-
terine, one fine evening after sunset, in our road to a Hut where, in the
course of our Tour, we had been hospitably entertained some weeks before,
we met, in one of the loneliest parts of that solitary region, two well-dressed
Women, one of whom said to us, by way of greeting, "What, you are
stepping westward?"

"*What, you are stepping westward?*" — "*Yea.*"
— 'Twould be a *wildish* destiny,
If we, who thus together roam
In a strange Land, and far from home,
Were in this place the guests of Chance: 5
Yet who would stop, or fear to advance,
Though home or shelter he had none,
With such a sky to lead him on?

The dewy ground was dark and cold;
Behind, all gloomy to behold;   10
And stepping westward seemed to be
A kind of *heavenly* destiny:
I liked the greeting; 'twas a sound
Of something without place or bound;
And seemed to give me spiritual right   15
To travel through that region bright.

The voice was soft, and she who spake
Was walking by her native lake:
The salutation had to me
The very sound of courtesy: 20
Its power was felt; and while my eye
Was fixed upon the glowing Sky,
The echo of the voice enwrought
A human sweetness with the thought
Of travelling through the world that lay   25
Before me in my endless way.

THE SOLITARY REAPER

BEHOLD her, single in the field,
Yon solitary Highland Lass!
Reaping and singing by herself;
Stop here, or gently pass!

Alone she cuts and binds the grain,   5
And sings a melancholy strain;
O listen! for the Vale profound
Is overflowing with the sound.

No Nightingale did ever chaunt
More welcome notes to weary bands   10
Of travellers in some shady haunt,
Among Arabian sands:
A voice so thrilling ne'er was heard
In spring-time from the Cuckoo-bird,
Breaking the silence of the seas   15
Among the farthest Hebrides.

Will no one tell me what she sings? —
Perhaps the plaintive numbers flow
For old, unhappy, far-off things,
And battles long ago: 20
Or is it some more humble lay,
Familiar matter of to-day?
Some natural sorrow, loss, or pain,
That has been, and may be again?

Whate'er the theme, the Maiden sang   25
As if her song could have no ending;
I saw her singing at her work,
And o'er the sickle bending; —
I listened, motionless and still;
And, as I mounted up the hill,   30
The music in my heart I bore,
Long after it was heard no more.

CHARACTER OF THE HAPPY WARRIOR

WHO is the happy Warrior? Who is he
That every man in arms should wish to be?
— It is the generous Spirit, who, when brought
Among the tasks of real life, hath wrought
Upon the plan that pleased his boyish thought: 5
Whose high endeavours are an inward light
That makes the path before him always bright:
Who, with a natural instinct to discern
What knowledge can perform, is diligent to learn;
Abides by this resolve, and stops not there,   10
But makes his moral being his prime care;
Who, doomed to go in company with Pain,

And Fear, and Bloodshed, miserable train!
Turns his necessity to glorious gain;
In face of these doth exercise a power   15
Which is our human nature's highest dower;
Controls them and subdues, transmutes, bereaves
Of their bad influence, and their good receives:
By objects, which might force the soul to abate
Her feeling, rendered more compassionate;   20
Is placable — because occasions rise
So often that demand such sacrifice;
More skilful in self-knowledge, even more pure,
As tempted more; more able to endure,
As more exposed to suffering and distress;   25
Thence, also, more alive to tenderness.
— 'Tis he whose law is reason; who depends
Upon that law as on the best of friends;
Whence, in a state where men are tempted still
To evil for a guard against worse ill,   30
And what in quality or act is best
Doth seldom on a right foundation rest,
He labours good on good to fix, and owes
To virtue every triumph that he knows:
— Who, if he rise to station of command,   35
Rises by open means; and there will stand
On honourable terms, or else retire,
And in himself possess his own desire;
Who comprehends his trust, and to the same
Keeps faithful with a singleness of aim;   40
And therefore does not stoop, nor lie in wait
For wealth, or honours, or for worldly state;
Whom they must follow; on whose head must fall,
Like showers of manna, if they come at all:
Whose powers shed round him in the common strife,   45
Or mild concerns of ordinary life,
A constant influence, a peculiar grace;
But who, if he be called upon to face
Some awful moment to which Heaven has joined
Great issues, good or bad for human kind,   50
Is happy as a Lover; and attired
With sudden brightness, like a Man inspired;
And, through the heat of conflict, keeps the law
In calmness made, and sees what he foresaw;
Or if an unexpected call succeed,   55
Come when it will, is equal to the need:
— He who, though thus endued as with a sense
And faculty for storm and turbulence,
Is yet a Soul whose master-bias leans

To homefelt pleasures and to gentle scenes; 60
Sweet images! which, wheresoe'er he be,
Are at his heart; and such fidelity
It is his darling passion to approve;
More brave for this, that he hath much to love: —
'Tis, finally, the Man, who, lifted high, 65
Conspicuous object in a Nation's eye,
Or left unthought-of in obscurity, —
Who, with a toward or untoward lot,
Prosperous or adverse, to his wish or not —
Plays, in the many games of life, that one 70
Where what he most doth value must be won:
Whom neither shape of danger can dismay,
Nor thought of tender happiness betray;
Who, not content that former worth stand fast,
Looks forward, persevering to the last, 75
From well to better, daily self-surpast:
Who, whether praise of him must walk the earth
For ever, and to noble deeds give birth,
Or he must fall, to sleep without his fame,
And leave a dead unprofitable name — 80
Finds comfort in himself and in his cause;
And, while the mortal mist is gathering, draws
His breath in confidence of Heaven's applause:
This is the happy Warrior; this is He
That every Man in arms should wish to be. 85

POWER OF MUSIC

An Orpheus! an Orpheus! yes, Faith may grow bold,
And take to herself all the wonders of old; —
Near the stately Pantheon you'll meet with the same
In the street that from Oxford hath borrowed its name.

His station is there; and he works on the crowd, 5
He sways them with harmony merry and loud;
He fills with his power all their hearts to the brim —
Was aught ever heard like his fiddle and him?

What an eager assembly! what an empire is this!
The weary have life, and the hungry have bliss; 10
The mourner is cheered, and the anxious have rest;
And the guilt-burthened soul is no longer opprest.

As the Moon brightens round her the clouds of the night,
So He, where he stands, is a centre of light;
It gleams on the face, there, of dusky-browed Jack, 15
And the pale-visaged Baker's, with basket on back.

That errand-bound 'Prentice was passing in haste —
What matter! he's caught — and his time runs to waste;
The Newsman is stopped, though he stops on the fret;
And the half-breathless Lamplighter — he's in the net!   20

The Porter sits down on the weight which he bore;
The Lass with her barrow wheels hither her store; —
If a thief could be here he might pilfer at ease;
She sees the Musician, 'tis all that she sees!

He stands, backed by the wall; — he abates not his din;   25
His hat gives him vigour, with boons dropping in,
From the old and the young, from the poorest; and there!
The one-pennied Boy has his penny to spare.

O blest are the hearers, and proud be the hand
Of the pleasure it spreads through so thankful a band;   30
I am glad for him, blind as he is! — all the while
If they speak 'tis to praise, and they praise with a smile.

That tall Man, a giant in bulk and in height,
Not an inch of his body is free from delight;
Can he keep himself still, if he would? oh, not he!   35
The music stirs in him like wind through a tree.

Mark that Cripple who leans on his crutch; like a tower
That long has leaned forward, leans hour after hour! —
That Mother, whose spirit in fetters is bound,
While she dandles the Babe in her arms to the sound.   40

Now, coaches and chariots! roar on like a stream;
Here are twenty souls happy as souls in a dream:
They are deaf to your murmurs — they care not for you,
Nor what ye are flying, nor what ye pursue!

STAR-GAZERS

WHAT crowd is this? what have we here! we must not pass it by;
A Telescope upon its frame, and pointed to the sky:
Long is it as a barber's pole, or mast of little boat,
Some little pleasure-skiff, that doth on Thames's waters float.

The Show-man chooses well his place, 'tis Leicester's busy Square;   5
And is as happy in his night, for the heavens are blue and fair;
Calm, though impatient, is the crowd; each stands ready with the
     fee,
And envies him that's looking; — what an insight must it be!

Yet, Show-man, where can lie the cause? Shall thy Implement have
  blame,
A boaster, that when he is tried, fails, and is put to shame? 10
Or is it good as others are, and be their eyes in fault?
Their eyes, or minds? or, finally, is yon resplendent vault?

Is nothing of that radiant pomp so good as we have here?
Or gives a thing but small delight that never can be dear?
The silver moon with all her vales, and hills of mightiest fame, 15
Doth she betray us when they're seen? or are they but a name?

Or is it rather that Conceit rapacious is and strong,
And bounty never yields so much but it seems to do her wrong?
Or is it, that when human Souls a journey long have had
And are returned into themselves, they cannot but be sad? 20

Or must we be constrained to think that these Spectators rude,
Poor in estate, of manners base, men of the multitude,
Have souls which never yet have risen, and therefore prostrate lie?
No, no, this cannot be; — men thirst for power and majesty!

Does, then, a deep and earnest thought the blissful mind employ 25
Of him who gazes, or has gazed? a grave and steady joy,
That doth reject all show of pride, admits no outward sign,
Because not of this noisy world, but silent and divine!

Whatever be the cause, 'tis sure that they who pry and pore
Seem to meet with little gain, seem less happy than before: 30
One after One they take their turn, nor have I one espied
That doth not slackly go away, as if dissatisfied.

YES, IT WAS THE MOUNTAIN ECHO

Yes, it was the mountain Echo,
Solitary, clear, profound,
Answering to the shouting Cuckoo,
Giving to her sound for sound!

Unsolicited reply 5
To a babbling wanderer sent;
Like her ordinary cry,
Like — but oh, how different!

Hears not also mortal Life?
Hear not we, unthinking Creatures! 10
Slaves of folly, love, or strife —
Voices of two different natures?

Have not *we* too? — yes, we have
Answers, and we know not whence;
Echoes from beyond the grave,   15
Recognised intelligence!

Such rebounds our inward ear
Catches sometimes from afar —
Listen, ponder, hold them dear;
For of God, — of God they are.   20

ELEGIAC STANZAS

SUGGESTED BY A PICTURE OF PEELE CASTLE, IN A STORM,
PAINTED BY SIR GEORGE BEAUMONT

I WAS thy neighbour once, thou rugged Pile!
Four summer weeks I dwelt in sight of thee:
I saw thee every day; and all the while
Thy Form was sleeping on a glassy sea.

So pure the sky, so quiet was the air!   5
So like, so very like, was day to day!
Whene'er I looked, thy Image still was there;
It trembled, but it never passed away.

How perfect was the calm! it seemed no sleep;
No mood, which season takes away, or brings: 10
I could have fancied that the mighty Deep
Was even the gentlest of all gentle Things.

Ah! THEN, if mine had been the Painter's hand,
To express what then I saw; and add the gleam,
The light that never was, on sea or land,   15
The consecration, and the Poet's dream;

I would have planted thee, thou hoary Pile
Amid a world how different from this!
Beside a sea that could not cease to smile;
On tranquil land, beneath a sky of bliss.   20

Thou shouldst have seemed a treasure-house divine
Of peaceful years; a chronicle of heaven; —
Of all the sunbeams that did ever shine
The very sweetest had to thee been given.

A Picture had it been of lasting ease,   25
Elysian quiet, without toil or strife;

No motion but the moving tide, a breeze,
Or merely silent Nature's breathing life.

Such, in the fond illusion of my heart,
Such Picture would I at that time have made: 30
And seen the soul of truth in every part,
A stedfast peace that might not be betrayed.

So once it would have been, — 'tis so no more;
I have submitted to a new control:
A power is gone, which nothing can restore; 35
A deep distress hath humanised my Soul.

Not for a moment could I now behold
A smiling sea, and be what I have been:
The feeling of my loss will ne'er be old;
This, which I know, I speak with mind serene. 40

Then, Beaumont, Friend! who would have been the Friend,
If he had lived, of Him whom I deplore,
This work of thine I blame not, but commend;
This sea in anger, and that dismal shore.

O 'tis a passionate Work! — yet wise and well, 45
Well chosen is the spirit that is here;
That Hulk which labours in the deadly swell,
This rueful sky, this pageantry of fear!

And this huge Castle, standing here sublime,
I love to see the look with which it braves, 50
Cased in the unfeeling armour of old time,
The lightning, the fierce wind, and trampling waves.

Farewell, farewell the heart that lives alone,
Housed in a dream, at distance from the Kind!
Such happiness, wherever it be known, 55
Is to be pitied; for 'tis surely blind.

But welcome fortitude, and patient cheer,
And frequent sights of what is to be borne!
Such sights, or worse, as are before me here. —
Not without hope we suffer and we mourn. 60

THOUGHT OF A BRITON ON THE
SUBJUGATION OF SWITZERLAND

Two Voices are there; one is of the sea,
One of the mountains; each a mighty Voice:
In both from age to age thou didst rejoice,
They were thy chosen music, Liberty!
There came a Tyrant, and with holy glee   5
Thou fought'st against him; but hast vainly striven:
Thou from thy Alpine holds at length art driven,
Where not a torrent murmurs heard by thee.
Of one deep bliss thine ear hath been bereft:
Then cleave, O cleave to that which still is left;   10
For, high-souled Maid, what sorrow would it be
That Mountain floods should thunder as before,
And Ocean bellow from his rocky shore,
And neither awful Voice be heard by thee!

THE WHITE DOE OF RYLSTONE

OR, THE FATE OF THE NORTONS

"Action is transitory — a step, a blow,
The motion of a muscle — this way or that —
'Tis done; and in the after-vacancy
We wonder at ourselves like men betrayed:
Suffering is permanent, obscure and dark,
And has the nature of infinity.
Yet through that darkness (infinite though it seem
And irremoveable) gracious openings lie,
By which the soul — with patient steps of thought
Now toiling, wafted now on wings of prayer —
May pass in hope, and, though from mortal bonds
Yet undelivered, rise with sure ascent
Even to the fountain-head of peace divine."

"They that deny a God, destroy Man's nobility: for certainly Man is of kinn
to the Beast by his Body; and if he be not of kinn to God by his Spirit, he
is a base ignoble Creature. It destroys likewise Magnanimity, and the raising
of humane Nature: for take an example of a Dogg, and mark what a
generosity and courage he will put on, when he finds himself maintained
by a Man, who to him is instead of a God, or Melior Natura. Which courage
is manifestly such, as that Creature without that confidence of a better
Nature than his own could never attain. So Man, when he resteth and
assureth himself upon Divine protection and favour, gathereth a force and
faith which human Nature in itself could not obtain."

LORD BACON.

CANTO FIRST

FROM Bolton's old monastic tower
The bells ring loud with gladsome power;
The sun shines bright; the fields are gay
With people in their best array
Of stole and doublet, hood and scarf,   5
Along the banks of crystal Wharf,
Through the Vale retired and lowly,
Trooping to that summons holy.
And, up among the moorlands, see
What sprinklings of blithe company!   10
Of lasses and of shepherd grooms,
That down the steep hills force their way,
Like cattle through the budded brooms;
Path, or no path, what care they?

And thus in joyous mood they hie   15
To Bolton's mouldering Priory.

   What would they there? — full fifty years
That sumptuous Pile, with all its peers,
Too harshly hath been doomed to taste
The bitterness of wrong and waste: 20
Its courts are ravaged; but the tower
Is standing with a voice of power,
That ancient voice which wont to call
To mass or some high festival;
And in the shattered fabric's heart   25
Remaineth one protected part;
A Chapel, like a wild-bird's nest,
Closely embowered and trimly drest;
And thither young and old repair,
This Sabbath-day, for praise and prayer.   30

   Fast the church-yard fills; — anon
Look again, and they all are gone;
The cluster round the porch, and the folk
Who sate in the shade of the Prior's Oak!
And scarcely have they disappeared   35
Ere the prelusive hymn is heard: —
With one consent the people rejoice,
Filling the church with a lofty voice!
They sing a service which they feel:
For 'tis the sunrise now of zeal;   40
Of a pure faith the vernal prime —
In great Eliza's golden time.

   A moment ends the fervent din,
And all is hushed, without and within;
For though the priest, more tranquilly,   45
Recites the holy liturgy,
The only voice which you can hear
Is the river murmuring near.
— When soft! — the dusky trees between,
And down the path through the open green,   50
Where is no living thing to be seen;
And through yon gateway, where is found,
Beneath the arch with ivy bound,
Free entrance to the church-yard ground —
Comes gliding in with lovely gleam,   55
Comes gliding in serene and slow,
Soft and silent as a dream,
A solitary Doe!

White she is as lily of June,
And beauteous as the silver moon   60
When out of sight the clouds are driven
And she is left alone in heaven;
Or like a ship some gentle day
In sunshine sailing far away,
A glittering ship, that hath the plain   65
Of ocean for her own domain.

Lie silent in your graves, ye dead!
Lie quiet in your church-yard bed!
Ye living, tend your holy cares;
Ye multitude, pursue your prayers;   70
And blame not me if my heart and sight
Are occupied with one delight!
'Tis a work for sabbath hours
If I with this bright Creature go:
Whether she be of forest bowers,   75
From the bowers of earth below;
Or a Spirit for one day given,
A pledge of grace from purest heaven.

What harmonious pensive changes
Wait upon her as she ranges   80
Round and through this Pile of state
Overthrown and desolate!
Now a step or two her way
Leads through space of open day,
Where the enamoured sunny light   85
Brightens her that was so bright;
Now doth a delicate shadow fall,
Falls upon her like a breath,
From some lofty arch or wall,
As she passes underneath: 90
Now some gloomy nook partakes
Of the glory that she makes, —
High-ribbed vault of stone, or cell,
With perfect cunning framed as well
Of stone, and ivy, and the spread   95
Of the elder's bushy head;
Some jealous and forbidding cell,
That doth the living stars repel,
And where no flower hath leave to dwell.

The presence of this wandering Doe   100
Fills many a damp obscure recess
With lustre of a saintly show;
And, reappearing, she no less

Sheds on the flowers that round her blow
A more than sunny liveliness. 105
But say, among these holy places,
Which thus assiduously she paces,
Comes she with a votary's task,
Rite to perform, or boon to ask?
Fair Pilgrim! harbours she a sense 110
Of sorrow, or of reverence?
Can she be grieved for quire or shrine,
Crushed as if by wrath divine?
For what survives of house where God
Was worshipped, or where Man abode; 115
For old magnificence undone;
Or for the gentler work begun
By Nature, softening and concealing,
And busy with a hand of healing?
Mourns she for lordly chamber's hearth 120
That to the sapling ash gives birth;
For dormitory's length laid bare
Where the wild rose blossoms fair;
Or altar, whence the cross was rent,
Now rich with mossy ornament? 125
— She sees a warrior carved in stone,
Among the thick weeds, stretched alone;
A warrior, with his shield of pride
Cleaving humbly to his side,
And hands in resignation prest, 130
Palm to palm, on his tranquil breast;
As little she regards the sight
As a common creature might:
If she be doomed to inward care,
Or service, it must lie elsewhere. 135
— But hers are eyes serenely bright,
And on she moves — with pace how light!
Nor spares to stoop her head, and taste
The dewy turf with flowers bestrown;
And thus she fares, until at last 140
Beside the ridge of a grassy grave
In quietness she lays her down;
Gentle as a weary wave
Sinks, when the summer breeze hath died,
Against an anchored vessel's side; 145
Even so, without distress, doth she
Lie down in peace, and lovingly.

   The day is placid in its going,
To a lingering motion bound,
Like the crystal stream now flowing 150

With its softest summer sound:
So the balmy minutes pass,
While this radiant Creature lies
Couched upon the dewy grass,
Pensively with downcast eyes.   155
— But now again the people raise
With awful cheer a voice of praise;
It is the last, the parting song;
And from the temple forth they throng,
And quickly spread themselves abroad,   160
While each pursues his several road.
But some — a variegated band
Of middle-aged, and old, and young,
And little children by the hand
Upon their leading mothers hung —   165
With mute obeisance gladly paid
Turn towards the spot, where, full in view,
The white Doe, to her service true,
Her sabbath couch has made.

It was a solitary mound;   170
Which two spears' length of level ground
Did from all other graves divide:
As if in some respect of pride;
Or melancholy's sickly mood,
Still shy of human neighbourhood;   175
Or guilt, that humbly would express
A penitential loneliness.

"Look, there she is, my Child! draw near;
She fears not, wherefore should we fear?
She means no harm;" — but still the Boy,   180
To whom the words were softly said,
Hung back, and smiled, and blushed for joy,
A shame-faced blush of glowing red!
Again the Mother whispered low,
"Now you have seen the famous Doe;   185
From Rylstone she hath found her way
Over the hills this sabbath day;
Her work, whate'er it be, is done,
And she will depart when we are gone;
Thus doth she keep, from year to year,   190
Her sabbath morning, foul or fair."

Bright was the Creature, as in dreams
The Boy had seen her, yea, more bright;
But is she truly what she seems?
He asks with insecure delight,   195

Asks of himself, and doubts, — and still
The doubt returns against his will:
Though he, and all the standers-by,
Could tell a tragic history
Of facts divulged, wherein appear   200
Substantial motive, reason clear,
Why thus the milk-white Doe is found
Couchant beside that lonely mound;
And why she duly loves to pace
The circuit of this hallowed place.   205
Nor to the Child's inquiring mind
Is such perplexity confined:
For, spite of sober Truth that sees
A world of fixed remembrances
Which to this mystery belong,   210
If, undeceived, my skill can trace
The characters of every face,
There lack not strange delusion here,
Conjecture vague, and idle fear,
And superstitious fancies strong,   215
Which do the gentle Creature wrong.

   That bearded, staff-supported Sire —
Who in his boyhood often fed
Full cheerily on convent-bread
And heard old tales by the convent-fire,   220
And to his grave will go with scars,
Relics of long and distant wars —
That Old Man, studious to expound
The spectacle, is mounting high
To days of dim antiquity;   225
When Lady Aäliza mourned
Her Son, and felt in her despair
The pang of unavailing prayer;
Her Son in Wharf's abysses drowned,
The noble Boy of Egremound.   230
From which affliction — when the grace
Of God had in her heart found place —
A pious structure, fair to see,
Rose up, this stately Priory!
The Lady's work; — but now laid low;   235
To the grief of her soul that doth come and go,
In the beautiful form of this innocent Doe:
Which, though seemingly doomed in its breast to sustain
A softened remembrance of sorrow and pain,
Is spotless, and holy, and gentle, and bright;   240
And glides o'er the earth like an angel of light.

Pass, pass who will, yon chantry door;
And, through the chink in the fractured floor
Look down, and see a griesly sight;
A vault where the bodies are buried upright!   245
There, face by face, and hand by hand,
The Claphams and Mauleverers stand;
And, in his place, among son and sire,
Is John de Clapham, that fierce Esquire,
A valiant man, and a name of dread   250
In the ruthless wars of the White and Red;
Who dragged Earl Pembroke from Banbury church
And smote off his head on the stones of the porch!
Look down among them, if you dare;
Oft does the White Doe loiter there,   255
Prying into the darksome rent;
Nor can it be with good intent:
So thinks that Dame of haughty air,
Who hath a Page her book to hold,
And wears a frontlet edged with gold.   260
Harsh thoughts with her high mood agree —
Who counts among her ancestry
Earl Pembroke, slain so impiously!

That slender Youth, a scholar pale,
From Oxford come to his native vale,   265
He also hath his own conceit:
It is, thinks he, the gracious Fairy,
Who loved the Shepherd-lord to meet
In his wanderings solitary:
Wild notes she in his hearing sang,   270
A song of Nature's hidden powers;
That whistled like the wind, and rang
Among the rocks and holly bowers.
'Twas said that She all shapes could wear;
And oftentimes before him stood,   275
Amid the trees of some thick wood,
In semblance of a lady fair;
And taught him signs, and showed him sights,
In Craven's dens, on Cumbrian heights;
When under cloud of fear he lay,   280
A shepherd clad in homely grey;
Nor left him at his later day.
And hence, when he, with spear and shield,
Rode full of years to Flodden-field,
His eye could see the hidden spring,   285
And how the current was to flow;
The fatal end of Scotland's King,

And all that hopeless overthrow.
But not in wars did he delight,
This Clifford wished for worthier might;   290
Nor in broad pomp, or courtly state;
Him his own thoughts did elevate, —
Most happy in the shy recess
Of Barden's lowly quietness.
And choice of studious friends had he   295
Of Bolton's dear fraternity;
Who, standing on this old church tower,
In many a calm propitious hour,
Perused, with him, the starry sky;
Or, in their cells, with him did pry   300
For other lore, — by keen desire
Urged to close toil with chemic fire;
In quest belike of transmutations
Rich as the mine's most bright creations.
But they and their good works are fled,   305
And all is now disquieted —
And peace is none, for living or dead!

Ah, pensive Scholar, think not so,
But look again at the radiant Doe!
What quiet watch she seems to keep,   310
Alone, beside that grassy heap!
Why mention other thoughts unmeet
For vision so composed and sweet?
While stand the people in a ring,
Gazing, doubting, questioning;   315
Yea, many overcome in spite
Of recollections clear and bright;
Which yet do unto some impart
An undisturbed repose of heart.
And all the assembly own a law   320
Of orderly respect and awe;
But see — they vanish one by one,
And last, the Doe herself is gone.

Harp! we have been full long beguiled
By vague thoughts, lured by fancies wild;   325
To which, with no reluctant strings,
Thou hast attuned thy murmurings;
And now before this Pile we stand
In solitude, and utter peace:
But, Harp! thy murmurs may not cease —   330
A Spirit, with his angelic wings,
In soft and breeze-like visitings,

Has touched thee — and a Spirit's hand:
A voice is with us — a command
To chant, in strains of heavenly glory,   335
A tale of tears, a mortal story!

CANTO SECOND

THE Harp in lowliness obeyed;
And first we sang of the greenwood shade
And a solitary Maid;
Beginning, where the song must end,   340
With her, and with her sylvan Friend;
The Friend, who stood before her sight,
Her only unextinguished light;
Her last companion in a dearth
Of love, upon a hopeless earth.   345

   For She it was — this Maid, who wrought
Meekly, with foreboding thought,
In vermeil colours and in gold
An unblest work; which, standing by,
Her Father did with joy behold, —   350
Exulting in its imagery;
A Banner, fashioned to fulfil
Too perfectly his headstrong will:
For on this Banner had her hand
Embroidered (such her Sire's command)   355
The sacred Cross; and figured there
The five dear wounds our Lord did bear;
Full soon to be uplifted high,
And float in rueful company!

   It was the time when England's Queen   360
Twelve years had reigned, a Sovereign dread;
Nor yet the restless crown had been
Disturbed upon her virgin head;
But now the inly-working North
Was ripe to send its thousands forth,   365
A potent vassalage, to fight
In Percy's and in Neville's right,
Two Earls fast leagued in discontent,
Who gave their wishes open vent;
And boldly urged a general plea,   370
The rites of ancient piety
To be triumphantly restored,
By the stern justice of the sword!
And that same Banner on whose breast

The blameless Lady had exprest   375
Memorials chosen to give life
And sunshine to a dangerous strife;
That Banner, waiting for the Call,
Stood quietly in Rylstone-hall.

It came; and Francis Norton said,   380
"O Father! rise not in this fray —
The hairs are white upon your head;
Dear Father, hear me when I say
It is for you too late a day!
Bethink you of your own good name: 385
A just and gracious queen have we,
A pure religion, and the claim
Of peace on our humanity. —
'Tis meet that I endure your scorn;
I am your son, your eldest born;   390
But not for lordship or for land,
My Father, do I clasp your knees;
The Banner touch not, stay your hand,
This multitude of men disband,
And live at home in blameless ease;   395
For these my brethren's sake, for me;
And, most of all, for Emily!"

Tumultuous noises filled the hall;
And scarcely could the Father hear
That name — pronounced with a dying fall —   400
The name of his only Daughter dear,
As on the banner which stood near
He glanced a look of holy pride,
And his moist eyes were glorified;
Then did he seize the staff, and say;   405
"Thou, Richard, bear'st thy father's name,
Keep thou this ensign till the day
When I of thee require the same:
Thy place be on my better hand; —
And seven as true as thou, I see,   410
Will cleave to this good cause and me."
He spake, and eight brave sons straightway
All followed him, a gallant band!

Thus, with his sons, when forth he came
The sight was hailed with loud acclaim   415
And din of arms and minstrelsy,
From all his warlike tenantry,
All horsed and harnessed with him to ride, —
A voice to which the hills replied!

But Francis, in the vacant hall, 420
Stood silent under dreary weight, —
A phantasm, in which roof and wall
Shook, tottered, swam before his sight;
A phantasm like a dream of night!
Thus overwhelmed, and desolate, 425
He found his way to a postern-gate;
And, when he waked, his languid eye
Was on the calm and silent sky;
With air about him breathing sweet,
And earth's green grass beneath his feet; 430
Nor did he fail ere long to hear
A sound of military cheer,
Faint — but it reached that sheltered spot;
He heard, and it disturbed him not.

There stood he, leaning on a lance 435
Which he had grasped unknowingly,
Had blindly grasped in that strong trance,
That dimness of heart-agony;
There stood he, cleansed from the despair
And sorrow of his fruitless prayer. 440
The past he calmly hath reviewed:
But where will be the fortitude
Of this brave man, when he shall see
That Form beneath the spreading tree,
And know that it is Emily? 445

He saw her where in open view
She sate beneath the spreading yew —
Her head upon her lap, concealing
In solitude her bitter feeling:
"Might ever son *command* a sire, 450
The act were justified to-day."
This to himself — and to the Maid,
Whom now he had approached, he said —
"Gone are they, — they have their desire;
And I with thee one hour will stay, 455
To give thee comfort if I may."

She heard, but looked not up, nor spake;
And sorrow moved him to partake
Her silence; then his thoughts turned round,
And fervent words a passage found. 460

"Gone are they, bravely, though misled;
With a dear Father at their head!

The Sons obey a natural lord;
The Father had given solemn word
To noble Percy; and a force   465
Still stronger, bends him to his course.
This said, our tears to-day may fall
As at an innocent funeral.
In deep and awful channel runs
This sympathy of Sire and Sons;   470
Untried our Brothers have been loved
With heart by simple nature moved;
And now their faithfulness is proved:
For faithful we must call them, bearing
That soul of conscientious daring.   475
— There were they all in circle — there
Stood Richard, Ambrose, Christopher,
John with a sword that will not fail,
And Marmaduke in fearless mail,
And those bright Twins were side by side;   480
And there, by fresh hopes beautified,
Stood He, whose arm yet lacks the power
Of man, our youngest, fairest flower!
I, by the right of eldest born,
And in a second father's place,   485
Presumed to grapple with their scorn,
And meet their pity face to face;
Yea, trusting in God's holy aid,
I to my Father knelt and prayed;
And one, the pensive Marmaduke,   490
Methought, was yielding inwardly,
And would have laid his purpose by,
But for a glance of his Father's eye,
Which I myself could scarcely brook.

"Then be we, each and all, forgiven!   495
Thou, chiefly thou, my Sister dear,
Whose pangs are registered in heaven —
The stifled sigh, the hidden tear,
And smiles, that dared to take their place,
Meek filial smiles, upon thy face,   500
As that unhallowed Banner grew
Beneath a loving old Man's view.
Thy part is done — thy painful part;
Be thou then satisfied in heart!
A further, though far easier, task   505
Than thine hath been, my duties ask;
With theirs my efforts cannot blend,
I cannot for such cause contend;

Their aims I utterly forswear;
But I in body will be there.   510
Unarmed and naked will I go,
Be at their side, come weal or woe:
On kind occasions I may wait,
See, hear, obstruct, or mitigate.
Bare breast I take and an empty hand." —   515
Therewith he threw away the lance,
Which he had grasped in that strong trance;
Spurned it, like something that would stand
Between him and the pure intent
Of love on which his soul was bent.   520

  "For thee, for thee, is left the sense
Of trial past without offence
To God or man; such innocence,
Such consolation, and the excess
Of an unmerited distress;   525
In that thy very strength must lie.
— O Sister, I could prophesy!
The time is come that rings the knell
Of all we loved, and loved so well:
Hope nothing, if I thus may speak   530
To thee, a woman, and thence weak:
Hope nothing, I repeat; for we
Are doomed to perish utterly:
'Tis meet that thou with me divide
The thought while I am by thy side,   535
Acknowledging a grace in this,
A comfort in the dark abyss.
But look not for me when I am gone,
And be no farther wrought upon:
Farewell all wishes, all debate,   540
All prayers for this cause, or for that!
Weep, if that aid thee; but depend
Upon no help of outward friend;
Espouse thy doom at once, and cleave
To fortitude without reprieve.   545
For we must fall, both we and ours —
This Mansion and these pleasant bowers,
Walks, pools, and arbours, homestead, hall —
Our fate is theirs, will reach them all;
The young horse must forsake his manger,   550
And learn to glory in a Stranger;
The hawk forget his perch; the hound
Be parted from his ancient ground:
The blast will sweep us all away —

One desolation, one decay!   555
And even this Creature!" which words saying,
He pointed to a lovely Doe,
A few steps distant, feeding, straying;
Fair creature, and more white than snow!
"Even she will to her peaceful woods   560
Return, and to her murmuring floods,
And be in heart and soul the same
She was before she hither came;
Ere she had learned to love us all,
Herself beloved in Rylstone-hall.   565
— But thou, my Sister, doomed to be
The last leaf on a blasted tree;
If not in vain we breathed the breath
Together of a purer faith;
If hand in hand we have been led,   570
And thou, (O happy thought this day!)
Not seldom foremost in the way;
If on one thought our minds have fed,
And we have in one meaning read;
If, when at home our private weal   575
Hath suffered from the shock of zeal,
Together we have learned to prize
Forbearance and self-sacrifice;
If we like combatants have fared,
And for this issue been prepared;   580
If thou art beautiful, and youth
And thought endue thee with all truth —
Be strong; — be worthy of the grace
Of God, and fill thy destined place:
A Soul, by force of sorrows high,   585
Uplifted to the purest sky
Of undisturbed humanity!"

He ended, — or she heard no more;
He led her from the yew-tree shade,
And at the mansion's silent door,   590
He kissed the consecrated Maid;
And down the valley then pursued,
Alone, the armèd Multitude.

CANTO THIRD

Now joy for you who from the towers
Of Brancepeth look in doubt and fear,   595
Telling melancholy hours!

Proclaim it, let your Masters hear
That Norton with his band is near!
The watchmen from their station high
Pronounced the word, — and the Earls descry,   600
Well-pleased, the armèd Company
Marching down the banks of Were.

    Said fearless Norton to the pair
Gone forth to greet him on the plain —
"This meeting, noble Lords! looks fair,   605
I bring with me a goodly train;
Their hearts are with you: hill and dale
Have helped us: Ure we crossed, and Swale,
And horse and harness followed — see
The best part of their Yeomanry!   610
— Stand forth, my Sons! — these eight are mine,
Whom to this service I commend;
Which way soe'er our fate incline,
These will be faithful to the end;
They are my all" — voice failed him here —   615
"My all save one, a Daughter dear!
Whom I have left, Love's mildest birth,
The meekest Child on this blessed earth.
I had — but these are by my side,
These Eight, and this is a day of pride!   620
The time is ripe. With festive din
Lo! how the people are flocking in, —
Like hungry fowl to the feeder's hand
When snow lies heavy upon the land."

    He spake bare truth; for far and near   625
From every side came noisy swarms
Of Peasants in their homely gear;
And, mixed with these, to Brancepeth came
Grave Gentry of estate and name,
And Captains known for worth in arms;   630
And prayed the Earls in self-defence
To rise, and prove their innocence. —
"Rise, noble Earls, put forth your might
For holy Church, and the People's right!"

    The Norton fixed, at this demand,   635
His eye upon Northumberland,
And said; "The Minds of Men will own
No loyal rest while England's Crown
Remains without an Heir, the bait
Of strife and factions desperate;   640

Who, paying deadly hate in kind
Through all things else, in this can find
A mutual hope, a common mind;
And plot, and pant to overwhelm
All ancient honour in the realm.   645
— Brave Earls! to whose heroic veins
Our noblest blood is given in trust,
To you a suffering State complains,
And ye must raise her from the dust.
With wishes of still bolder scope   650
On you we look, with dearest hope;
Even for our Altars — for the prize
In Heaven, of life that never dies;
For the old and holy Church we mourn,
And must in joy to her return.   655
Behold!" — and from his Son whose stand
Was on his right, from that guardian hand
He took the Banner, and unfurled
The precious folds — "behold," said he,
"The ransom of a sinful world;   660
Let this your preservation be;
The wounds of hands and feet and side,
And the sacred Cross on which Jesus died!
— This bring I from an ancient hearth,
These Records wrought in pledge of love   665
By hands of no ignoble birth,
A Maid o'er whom the blessed Dove
Vouchsafed in gentleness to brood
While she the holy work pursued."
"Uplift the Standard!" was the cry   670
From all the listeners that stood round,
"Plant it, — by this we live or die."
The Norton ceased not for that sound,
But said; "The prayer which ye have heard,
Much injured Earls! by these preferred,   675
Is offered to the Saints, the sigh
Of tens of thousands, secretly."
"Uplift it!" cried once more the Band,
And then a thoughtful pause ensued:
"Uplift it!" said Northumberland —   680
Whereat, from all the multitude
Who saw the Banner reared on high
In all its dread emblazonry,
A voice of uttermost joy brake out:
The transport was rolled down the river of Were,   685
And Durham, the time-honoured Durham, did hear,
And the towers of Saint Cuthbert were stirred by the shout!

Now was the North in arms: — they shine
In warlike trim from Tweed to Tyne,
At Percy's voice: and Neville sees   690
His Followers gathering in from Tees,
From Were, and all the little rills
Concealed among the forkèd hills —
Seven hundred Knights, Retainers all
Of Neville, at their Master's call   695
Had sate together in Raby Hall!
Such strength that Earldom held of yore;
Nor wanted at this time rich store
Of well-appointed chivalry.
— Not loth the sleepy lance to wield,   700
And greet the old paternal shield,
They heard the summons; — and, furthermore,
Horsemen and Foot of each degree,
Unbound by pledge of fealty,
Appeared, with free and open hate   705
Of novelties in Church and State;
Knight, burgher, yeoman, and esquire;
And Romish priest, in priest's attire.
And thus, in arms, a zealous Band
Proceeding under joint command,   710
To Durham first their course they bear;
And in Saint Cuthbert's ancient seat
Sang mass, — and tore the book of prayer, —
And trod the bible beneath their feet.

Thence marching southward smooth and free   715
"They mustered their host at Wetherby,
Full sixteen thousand fair to see;"
The Choicest Warriors of the North!
But none for beauty and for worth
Like those eight Sons — who, in a ring,   720
(Ripe men, or blooming in life's spring)
Each with a lance, erect and tall,
A falchion, and a buckler small,
Stood by their Sire, on Clifford-moor,
To guard the Standard which he bore.   725
On foot they girt their Father round;
And so will keep the appointed ground
Where'er their march: no steed will he
Henceforth bestride; — triumphantly,
He stands upon the grassy sod,   730
Trusting himself to the earth, and God.
Rare sight to embolden and inspire!
Proud was the field of Sons and Sire;

Of him the most; and, sooth to say,
No shape of man in all the array   735
So graced the sunshine of that day.
The monumental pomp of age
Was with this goodly Personage;
A stature undepressed in size,
Unbent, which rather seemed to rise,   740
In open victory o'er the weight
Of seventy years, to loftier height;
Magnific limbs of withered state;
A face to fear and venerate;
Eyes dark and strong; and on his head   745
Bright locks of silver hair, thick spread,
Which a brown morion half-concealed,
Light as a hunter's of the field;
And thus, with girdle round his waist,
Whereon the Banner-staff might rest   750
At need, he stood, advancing high
The glittering, floating Pageantry.

   Who sees him? — thousands see, and One
With unparticipated gaze;
Who, 'mong those thousands, friend hath none,   755
And treads in solitary ways.
He, following wheresoe'er he might,
Hath watched the Banner from afar,
As shepherds watch a lonely star,
Or mariners the distant light   760
That guides them through a stormy night.
And now, upon a chosen plot
Of rising ground, yon heathy spot!
He takes alone his far-off stand,
With breast unmailed, unweaponed hand.   765
Bold is his aspect; but his eye
Is pregnant with anxiety,
While, like a tutelary Power,
He there stands fixed from hour to hour:
Yet sometimes in more humble guise,   770
Upon the turf-clad height he lies
Stretched, herdsman-like, as if to bask
In sunshine were his only task,
Or by his mantle's help to find
A shelter from the nipping wind: 775
And thus, with short oblivion blest,
His weary spirits gather rest.
Again he lifts his eyes; and lo!
The pageant glancing to and fro;

And hope is wakened by the sight,   78(
He thence may learn, ere fall of night,
Which way the tide is doomed to flow.

To London were the Chieftains bent;
But what avails the bold intent?
A Royal army is gone forth   785
To quell the RISING OF THE NORTH;
They march with Dudley at their head,
And, in seven days' space, will to York be led! —
Can such a mighty Host be raised
Thus suddenly, and brought so near?   790
The Earls upon each other gazed,
And Neville's cheek grew pale with fear;
For, with a high and valiant name,
He bore a heart of timid frame;
And bold if both had been, yet they   795
"Against so many may not stay."
Back therefore will they hie to seize
A strong Hold on the banks of Tees;
There wait a favourable hour,
Until Lord Dacre with his power   800
From Naworth come; and Howard's aid
Be with them openly displayed.

While through the Host, from man to man,
A rumour of this purpose ran,
The Standard trusting to the care   805
Of him who heretofore did bear
That charge, impatient Norton sought
The Chieftains to unfold his thought,
And thus abruptly spake; — "We yield
(And can it be?) an unfought field! —   810
How oft has strength, the strength of heaven,
To few triumphantly been given!
Still do our very children boast
Of mitred Thurston — what a Host
He conquered! — Saw we not the Plain   815
(And flying shall behold again)
Where faith was proved? — while to battle moved
The Standard, on the Sacred Wain
That bore it, compassed round by a bold
Fraternity of Barons old;   820
And with those grey-haired champions stood,
Under the saintly ensigns three,
The infant Heir of Mowbray's blood —
All confident of victory! —

Shall Percy blush, then, for his name? 825
Must Westmoreland be asked with shame
Whose were the numbers, where the loss,
In that other day of Neville's Cross?
When the Prior of Durham with holy hand
Raised, as the Vision gave command, 830
Saint Cuthbert's Relic — far and near
Kenned on the point of a lofty spear;
While the Monks prayed in Maiden's Bower
To God descending in his power.
Less would not at our need be due 835
To us, who war against the Untrue; —
The delegates of Heaven we rise,
Convoked the impious to chastise:
We, we, the sanctities of old
Would re-establish and uphold: 840
Be warned" — His zeal the Chiefs confounded,
But word was given, and the trumpet sounded:
Back through the melancholy Host
Went Norton, and resumed his post.
Alas! thought he, and have I borne 845
This Banner raised with joyful pride,
This hope of all posterity,
By those dread symbols sanctified;
Thus to become at once the scorn
Of babbling winds as they go by, 850
A spot of shame to the sun's bright eye,
To the light clouds a mockery!
— "Even these poor eight of mine would stem —"
Half to himself, and half to them
He spake — "would stem, or quell, a force 855
Ten times their number, man and horse;
This by their own unaided might,
Without their father in their sight,
Without the Cause for which they fight;
A Cause, which on a needful day 860
Would breed us thousands brave as they."
— So speaking, he his reverend head
Raised towards that Imagery once more:
But the familiar prospect shed
Despondency unfelt before: 865
A shock of intimations vain,
Dismay, and superstitious pain,
Fell on him, with the sudden thought
Of her by whom the work was wrought: —
Oh wherefore was her countenance bright 870
With love divine and gentle light?

She would not, could not, disobey,
But her Faith leaned another way.
Ill tears she wept; I saw them fall,
I overheard her as she spake   875
Sad words to that mute Animal,
The White Doe, in the hawthorn brake;
She steeped, but not for Jesu's sake,
This Cross in tears: by her, and One
Unworthier far we are undone —   880
Her recreant Brother — he prevailed
Over that tender Spirit — assailed
Too oft alas! by her whose head
In the cold grave hath long been laid:
She first, in reason's dawn beguiled   885
Her docile, unsuspecting Child:
Far back — far back my mind must go
To reach the well-spring of this woe!

    While thus he brooded, music sweet
Of border tunes was played to cheer   890
The footsteps of a quick retreat;
But Norton lingered in the rear,
Stung with sharp thoughts; and ere the last
From his distracted brain was cast,
Before his Father, Francis stood,   895
And spake in firm and earnest mood.

    "Though here I bend a suppliant knee
In reverence, and unarmed, I bear
In your indignant thoughts my share;
Am grieved this backward march to see   900
So careless and disorderly.
I scorn your Chiefs — men who would lead,
And yet want courage at their need:
Then look at them with open eyes!
Deserve they further sacrifice? —   905
If — when they shrink, nor dare oppose
In open field their gathering foes,
(And fast, from this decisive day,
Yon multitude must melt away;)
If now I ask a grace not claimed   910
While ground was left for hope; unblamed
Be an endeavour that can do
No injury to them or you.
My Father! I would help to find
A place of shelter, till the rage   915
Of cruel men do like the wind

Exhaust itself and sink to rest;
Be Brother now to Brother joined!
Admit me in the equipage
Of your misfortunes, that at least,   920
Whatever fate remain behind,
I may bear witness in my breast
To your nobility of mind!"

   "Thou Enemy, my bane and blight!
Oh! bold to fight the Coward's fight   925
Against all good" — but why declare,
At length, the issue of a prayer
Which love had prompted, yielding scope
Too free to one bright moment's hope?
Suffice it that the Son, who strove   930
With fruitless effort to allay
That passion, prudently gave way;
Nor did he turn aside to prove
His Brothers' wisdom or their love —
But calmly from the spot withdrew;   935
His best endeavours to renew,
Should e'er a kindlier time ensue.

CANTO FOURTH

'TIS night: in silence looking down,
The Moon, from cloudless ether, sees
A Camp, and a beleaguered Town,   940
And Castle like a stately crown
On the steep rocks of winding Tees; —
And southward far, with moor between,
Hill-top, and flood, and forest green,
The bright Moon sees that valley small   945
Where Rylstone's old sequestered Hall
A venerable image yields
Of quiet to the neighbouring fields;
While from one pillared chimney breathes
The smoke, and mounts in silver wreaths.   950
— The courts are hushed; — for timely sleep
The grey-hounds to their kennel creep;
The peacock in the broad ash tree
Aloft is roosted for the night,
He who in proud prosperity   955
Of colours manifold and bright
Walked round, affronting the daylight;
And higher still, above the bower

Where he is perched, from yon lone Tower
The hall-clock in the clear moonshine   960
With glittering finger points at nine.

    Ah! who could think that sadness here
Hath any sway? or pain, or fear?
A soft and lulling sound is heard
Of streams inaudible by day;   965
The garden pool's dark surface, stirred
By the night insects in their play,
Breaks into dimples small and bright;
A thousand, thousand rings of light
That shape themselves and disappear   970
Almost as soon as seen: — and lo!
Not distant far, the milk-white Doe —
The same who quietly was feeding
On the green herb, and nothing heeding,
When Francis, uttering to the Maid   975
His last words in the yew-tree shade,
Involved whate'er by love was brought
Out of his heart, or crossed his thought,
Or chance presented to his eye,
In one sad sweep of destiny —   980
The same fair Creature, who hath found
Her way into forbidden ground;
Where now — within this spacious plot
For pleasure made, a goodly spot,
With lawns and beds of flowers, and shades   985
Of trellis-work in long arcades,
And cirque and crescent framed by wall
Of close-clipt foliage green and tall,
Converging walks, and fountains gay,
And terraces in trim array —   990
Beneath yon cypress spiring high,
With pine and cedar spreading wide
Their darksome boughs on either side,
In open moonlight doth she lie;
Happy as others of her kind,   995
That, far from human neighbourhood,
Range unrestricted as the wind,
Through park, or chase, or savage wood.

    But see the consecrated Maid
Emerging from a cedar shade   1000
To open moonshine, where the Doe
Beneath the cypress-spire is laid;
Like a patch of April snow —

Upon a bed of herbage green,
Lingering in a woody glade   1005
Or behind a rocky screen —
Lonely relic! which, if seen
By the shepherd, is passed by
With an inattentive eye.
Nor more regard doth She bestow   1010
Upon the uncomplaining Doe
Now couched at ease, though oft this day
Not unperplexed nor free from pain,
When she had tried, and tried in vain,
Approaching in her gentle way,   1015
To win some look of love, or gain
Encouragement to sport or play;
Attempts which still the heart-sick Maid
Rejected, or with slight repaid.

Yet Emily is soothed; — the breeze   1020
Came fraught with kindly sympathies.
As she approached yon rustic Shed
Hung with late-flowering woodbine, spread
Along the walls and overhead,
The fragrance of the breathing flowers   1025
Revived a memory of those hours
When here, in this remote alcove,
(While from the pendent woodbine came
Like odours, sweet as if the same)
A fondly-anxious Mother strove   1030
To teach her salutary fears
And mysteries above her years.
Yes, she is soothed: an Image faint,
And yet not faint — a presence bright
Returns to her — that blessèd Saint   1035
Who with mild looks and language mild
Instructed here her darling Child,
While yet a prattler on the knee,
To worship in simplicity
The invisible God, and take for guide   1040
The faith reformed and purified.

'Tis flown — the Vision, and the sense
Of that beguiling influence;
"But oh! thou Angel from above,
Mute Spirit of maternal love,   1045
That stood'st before my eyes, more clear
Than ghosts are fabled to appear
Sent upon embassies of fear;

As thou thy presence hast to me
Vouchsafed, in radiant ministry   1050
Descend on Francis; nor forbear
To greet him with a voice, and say; —
'If hope be a rejected stay,
Do thou, my christian Son, beware
Of that most lamentable snare,   1055
The self-reliance of despair!' "

Then from within the embowered retreat
Where she had found a grateful seat
Perturbed she issues. She will go!
Herself will follow to the war,   1060
And clasp her Father's knees; — ah, no!
She meets the insuperable bar,
The injunction by her Brother laid;
His parting charge — but ill obeyed —
That interdicted all debate,   1065
All prayer for this cause or for that;
All efforts that would turn aside
The headstrong current of their fate:
Her duty is to stand and wait;
In resignation to abide   1070
The shock, AND FINALLY SECURE
O'ER PAIN AND GRIEF A TRIUMPH PURE.
— She feels it, and her pangs are checked.
But now, as silently she paced
The turf, and thought by thought was chased,   1075
Came One who, with sedate respect,
Approached, and, greeting her, thus spake;
"An old man's privilege I take:
Dark is the time — a woeful day!
Dear daughter of affliction, say   1080
How can I serve you? point the way."

"Rights have you, and may well be bold:
You with my Father have grown old
In friendship — strive — for his sake go —
Turn from us all the coming woe: 1085
This would I beg; but on my mind
A passive stillness is enjoined.
On you, if room for mortal aid
Be left, is no restriction laid;
You not forbidden to recline   1090
With hope upon the Will divine."

"Hope," said the old Man, "must abide
With all of us, whate'er betide.

In Craven's Wilds is many a den,
To shelter persecuted men: 1095
Far under ground is many a cave,
Where they might lie as in the grave,
Until this storm hath ceased to rave:
Or let them cross the River Tweed,
And be at once from peril freed!"   1100

    "Ah tempt me not!" she faintly sighed;
"I will not counsel nor exhort,
With my condition satisfied;
But you, at least, may make report
Of what befals; — be this your task —   1105
This may be done; — 'tis all I ask!"

    She spake — and from the Lady's sight
The Sire, unconscious of his age,
Departed promptly as a Page
Bound on some errand of delight.   1110
— The noble Francis — wise as brave,
Thought he, may want not skill to save.
With hopes in tenderness concealed,
Unarmed he followed to the field;
Him will I seek: the insurgent Powers   1115
Are now besieging Barnard's Towers, —
"Grant that the Moon which shines this night
May guide them in a prudent flight!"

    But quick the turns of chance and change,
And knowledge has a narrow range;   1120
Whence idle fears, and needless pain,
And wishes blind, and efforts vain. —
The Moon may shine, but cannot be
Their guide in flight — already she
Hath witnessed their captivity.   1125
She saw the desperate assault
Upon that hostile castle made; —
But dark and dismal is the vault
Where Norton and his sons are laid!
Disastrous issue! — he had said   1130
"This night yon faithless Towers must yield,
Or we for ever quit the field.
— Neville is utterly dismayed,
For promise fails of Howard's aid;
And Dacre to our call replies   1135
That *he* is unprepared to rise.
My heart is sick; — this weary pause
Must needs be fatal to our cause.

The breach is open — on the wall,
This night, — the Banner shall be planted!"   1140
— 'Twas done: his Sons were with him — all;
They belt him round with hearts undaunted
And others follow; — Sire and Son
Leap down into the court; — " 'Tis won" —
They shout aloud — but Heaven decreed   1145
That with their joyful shout should close
The triumph of a desperate deed
Which struck with terror friends and foes!
The friend shrinks back — the foe recoils
From Norton and his filial band;   1150
But they, now caught within the toils,
Against a thousand cannot stand; —
The foe from numbers courage drew,
And overpowered that gallant few.
"A rescue for the Standard!" cried   1155
The Father from within the walls;
But, see, the sacred Standard falls! —
Confusion through the Camp spread wide:
Some fled; and some their fears detained:
But ere the Moon had sunk to rest   1160
In her pale chambers of the west,
Of that rash levy nought remained.

CANTO FIFTH

HIGH on a point of rugged ground
Among the wastes of Rylstone Fell,
Above the loftiest ridge or mound   1165
Where foresters or shepherds dwell,
An edifice of warlike frame
Stands single — Norton Tower its name —
It fronts all quarters, and looks round
O'er path and road, and plain and dell,   1170
Dark moor, and gleam of pool and stream,
Upon a prospect without bound.

  The summit of this bold ascent —
Though bleak and bare, and seldom free
As Pendle-hill or Pennygent   1175
From wind, or frost, or vapours wet —
Had often heard the sound of glee
When there the youthful Nortons met,
To practise games and archery:
How proud and happy they! the crowd   1180
Of Lookers-on how pleased and proud!

And from the scorching noon-tide sun,
From showers, or when the prize was won,
They to the Tower withdrew, and there
Would mirth run round, with generous fare;   1185
And the stern old Lord of Rylstone-hall,
Was happiest, proudest, of them all!

But now, his Child, with anguish pale,
Upon the height walks to and fro;
'Tis well that she hath heard the tale,   1190
Received the bitterness of woe:
For she *had* hoped, had hoped and feared,
Such rights did feeble nature claim;
And oft her steps had hither steered,
Though not unconscious of self-blame;   1195
For she her brother's charge revered,
His farewell words; and by the same,
Yea by her brother's very name,
Had, in her solitude, been cheered.

Beside the lonely watch-tower stood   1200
That grey-haired Man of gentle blood,
Who with her Father had grown old
In friendship; rival hunters they,
And fellow warriors in their day;
To Rylstone he the tidings brought;   1205
Then on this height the Maid had sought,
And, gently as he could, had told
The end of that dire Tragedy,
Which it had been his lot to see.

To him the Lady turned; "You said   1210
That Francis lives, *he* is not dead?"

"Your noble brother hath been spared;
To take his life they have not dared;
On him and on his high endeavour
The light of praise shall shine for ever!   1215
Nor did he (such Heaven's will) in vain
His solitary course maintain;
Not vainly struggled in the might
Of duty, seeing with clear sight;
He was their comfort to the last,   1220
Their joy till every pang was past.

"I witnessed when to York they came —
What, Lady, if their feet were tied;
They might deserve a good Man's blame;

But marks of infamy and shame —   1225
These were their triumph, these their pride;
Nor wanted 'mid the pressing crowd
Deep feeling, that found utterance loud,
'Lo, Francis comes,' there were who cried,
'A Prisoner once, but now set free!   1230
'Tis well, for he the worst defied
Through force of natural piety;
He rose not in this quarrel, he,
For concord's sake and England's good,
Suit to his Brothers often made   1235
With tears, and of his Father prayed —
And when he had in vain withstood
Their purpose — then did he divide,
He parted from them; but at their side
Now walks in unanimity.   1240
Then peace to cruelty and scorn,
While to the prison they are borne,
Peace, peace to all indignity!'

   "And so in Prison were they laid —
Oh hear me, hear me, gentle Maid,   1245
For I am come with power to bless,
By scattering gleams, through your distress,
Of a redeeming happiness.
Me did a reverent pity move
And privilege of ancient love;   1250
And, in your service, making bold,
Entrance I gained to that strong-hold.

   "Your Father gave me cordial greeting;
But to his purposes, that burned
Within him, instantly returned: 1255
He was commanding and entreating,
And said — 'We need not stop, my Son!
Thoughts press, and time is hurrying on' —
And so to Francis he renewed
His words, more calmly thus pursued.   1260

   " 'Might this our enterprise have sped,
Change wide and deep the Land had seen,
A renovation from the dead,
A spring-tide of immortal green:
The darksome altars would have blazed   1265
Like stars when clouds are rolled away;
Salvation to all eyes that gazed,
Once more the Rood had been upraised
To spread its arms, and stand for aye.

Then, then — had I survived to see   1270
New life in Bolton Priory;
The voice restored, the eye of Truth
Re-opened that inspired my youth;
To see her in her pomp arrayed —
This Banner (for such vow I made)   1275
Should on the consecrated breast
Of that same Temple have found rest:
I would myself have hung it high,
Fit offering of glad victory!

      " 'A shadow of such thought remains   1280
To cheer this sad and pensive time;
A solemn fancy yet sustains
One feeble Being — bids me climb
Even to the last — one effort more
To attest my Faith, if not restore.   1285

      " 'Hear then,' said he, 'while I impart,
My Son, the last wish of my heart.
The Banner strive thou to regain;
And, if the endeavour prove not vain,
Bear it — to whom if not to thee   1290
Shall I this lonely thought consign? —
Bear it to Bolton Priory,
And lay it on Saint Mary's shrine;
To wither in the sun and breeze
'Mid those decaying sanctities.   1295
There let at least the gift be laid,
The testimony there displayed;
Bold proof that with no selfish aim,
But for lost Faith and Christ's dear name,
I helmeted a brow though white,   1300
And took a place in all men's sight;
Yea offered up this noble Brood,
This fair unrivalled Brotherhood,
And turned away from thee, my Son!
And left — but be the rest unsaid,   1305
The name untouched, the tear unshed; —
My wish is known, and I have done:
Now promise, grant this one request,
This dying prayer, and be thou blest!'

      "Then Francis answered — 'Trust thy Son   1310
For, with God's will, it shall be done!' —

      "The pledge obtained, the solemn word
Thus scarcely given, a noise was heard,

And Officers appeared in state
To lead the prisoners to their fate.   1315
They rose, oh! wherefore should I fear
To tell, or, Lady, you to hear?
They rose — embraces none were given —
They stood like trees when earth and heaven
Are calm; they knew each other's worth,   1320
And reverently the Band went forth.
They met, when they had reached the door,
One with profane and harsh intent
Placed there — that he might go before
And, with that rueful Banner borne   1325
Aloft in sign of taunting scorn,
Conduct them to their punishment:
So cruel Sussex, unrestrained
By human feeling, had ordained.
The unhappy Banner Francis saw,   1330
And, with a look of calm command
Inspiring universal awe,
He took it from the soldier's hand;
And all the people that stood round
Confirmed the deed in peace profound.   1335
— High transport did the Father shed
Upon his Son — and they were led,
Led on, and yielded up their breath;
Together died, a happy death! —
But Francis, soon as he had braved   1340
That insult, and the Banner saved,
Athwart the unresisting tide
Of the spectators occupied
In admiration or dismay,
Bore instantly his Charge away."   1345

These things, which thus had in the sight
And hearing passed of Him who stood
With Emily, on the Watch-tower height,
In Rylstone's woeful neighbourhood,
He told; and oftentimes with voice   1350
Of power to comfort or rejoice;
For deepest sorrows that aspire,
Go high, no transport ever higher.
"Yes — God is rich in mercy," said
The old Man to the silent Maid,   1355
"Yet, Lady! shines, through this black night,
One star of aspect heavenly bright;
Your Brother lives — he lives — is come
Perhaps already to his home;

Then let us leave this dreary place."   1360
She yielded, and with gentle pace,
Though without one uplifted look,
To Rylstone-hall her way she took.

CANTO SIXTH

WHY comes not Francis? — From the doleful City
He fled, — and, in his flight, could hear   1365
The death-sounds of the Minster-bell:
That sullen stroke pronounced farewell
To Marmaduke, cut off from pity!
To Ambrose that! and then a knell
For him, the sweet half-opened Flower!   1370
For all — all dying in one hour!
— Why comes not Francis? Thoughts of love
Should bear him to his Sister dear
With the fleet motion of a dove;
Yea, like a heavenly messenger   1375
Of speediest wing, should he appear.
Why comes he not? — for westward fast
Along the plain of York he past;
Reckless of what impels or leads,
Unchecked he hurries on; — nor heeds   1380
The sorrow, through the Villages,
Spread by triumphant cruelties
Of vengeful military force,
And punishment without remorse.
He marked not, heard not, as he fled;   1385
All but the suffering heart was dead
For him abandoned to blank awe,
To vacancy, and horror strong:
And the first object which he saw,
With conscious sight, as he swept along —   1390
It was the Banner in his hand!
He felt — and made a sudden stand.

   He looked about like one betrayed:
What hath he done? what promise made?
Oh weak, weak moment! to what end   1395
Can such a vain oblation tend,
And he the Bearer? — Can he go
Carrying this instrument of woe,
And find, find any where, a right
To excuse him in his Country's sight?   1400
No; will not all men deem the change

A downward course, perverse and strange?
Here is it; — but how? when? must she,
The unoffending Emily,
Again this piteous object see?   1405

    Such conflict long did he maintain,
Nor liberty nor rest could gain:
His own life into danger brought
By this sad burden — even that thought,
Exciting self-suspicion strong,   1410
Swayed the brave man to his wrong.
And how — unless it were the sense
Of all-disposing Providence,
Its will unquestionably shown —
How has the Banner clung so fast   1415
To a palsied, and unconscious hand;
Clung to the hand to which it passed
Without impediment? And why
But that Heaven's purpose might be known
Doth now no hindrance meet his eye,   1420
No intervention, to withstand
Fulfilment of a Father's prayer
Breathed to a Son forgiven, and blest
When all resentments were at rest,
And life in death laid the heart bare? —   1425
Then, like a spectre sweeping by,
Rushed through his mind the prophecy
Of utter desolation made
To Emily in the yew-tree shade:
He sighed, submitting will and power   1430
To the stern embrace of that grasping hour.
"No choice is left, the deed is mine —
Dead are they, dead! — and I will go,
And, for their sakes, come weal or woe,
Will lay the Relic on the shrine."   1435

    So forward with a steady will
He went, and traversed plain and hill;
And up the vale of Wharf his way
Pursued; — and, at the dawn of day,
Attained a summit whence his eyes   1440
Could see the Tower of Bolton rise.
There Francis for a moment's space
Made halt — but hark! a noise behind
Of horsemen at an eager pace!
He heard, and with misgiving mind.   1445
— 'Tis Sir George Bowes who leads the Band:

They come, by cruel Sussex sent;
Who, when the Nortons from the hand
Of death had drunk their punishment,
Bethought him, angry and ashamed,   1450
How Francis, with the Banner claimed
As his own charge, had disappeared,
By all the standers-by revered.
His whole bold carriage (which had quelled
Thus far the Opposer, and repelled   1455
All censure, enterprise so bright
That even bad men had vainly striven
Against that overcoming light)
Was then reviewed, and prompt word given,
That to what place soever fled   1460
He should be seized, alive or dead.

  The troop of horse have gained the height
Where Francis stood in open sight.
They hem him round — "Behold the proof,"
They cried, "the Ensign in his hand!   1465
He did not arm, he walked aloof!
For why? — to save his Father's land; —
Worst Traitor of them all is he,
A Traitor dark and cowardly!"

  "I am no Traitor," Francis said,   1470
"Though this unhappy freight I bear;
And must not part with. But beware; —
Err not, by hasty zeal misled,
Nor do a suffering Spirit wrong,
Whose self-reproaches are too strong!"   1475
At this he from the beaten road
Retreated towards a brake of thorn,
That like a place of vantage showed;
And there stood bravely, though forlorn.
In self-defence with warlike brow   1480
He stood, — nor weaponless was now;
He from a Soldier's hand had snatched
A spear, — and, so protected, watched
The Assailants, turning round and round;
But from behind with treacherous wound   1485
A Spearman brought him to the ground.
The guardian lance, as Francis fell,
Dropped from him; but his other hand
The Banner clenched; till, from out the Band,
One, the most eager for the prize,   1490
Rushed in; and — while, O grief to tell!

A glimmering sense still left, with eyes
Unclosed the noble Francis lay —
Seized it, as hunters seize their prey;
But not before the warm life-blood   1495
Had tinged more deeply, as it flowed,
The wounds the broidered Banner showed,
Thy fatal work, O Maiden, innocent as good!

Proudly the Horsemen bore away
The Standard; and where Francis lay   1500
There was he left alone, unwept,
And for two days unnoticed slept.
For at that time bewildering fear
Possessed the country, far and near;
But, on the third day, passing by   1505
One of the Norton Tenantry
Espied the uncovered Corse; the Man
Shrunk as he recognised the face,
And to the nearest homesteads ran
And called the people to the place.   1510
— How desolate is Rylstone-hall!
This was the instant thought of all;
And if the lonely Lady there
Should be; to her they cannot bear
This weight of anguish and despair.   1515
So, when upon sad thoughts had prest
Thoughts sadder still, they deemed it best
That, if the Priest should yield assent
And no one hinder their intent,
Then, they, for Christian pity's sake,   1520
In holy ground a grave would make;
And straightway buried he should be
In the Church-yard of the Priory.

Apart, some little space, was made
The grave where Francis must be laid.   1525
In no confusion or neglect
This did they, — but in pure respect
That he was born of gentle blood;
And that there was no neighbourhood
Of kindred for him in that ground: 1530
So to the Church-yard they are bound,
Bearing the body on a bier;
And psalms they sing — a holy sound
That hill and vale with sadness hear.

But Emily hath raised her head,   1535
And is again disquieted;

She must behold! — so many gone,
Where is the solitary One?
And forth from Rylstone-hall stepped she, —
To seek her Brother forth she went,   1540
And tremblingly her course she bent
Toward Bolton's ruined Priory.
She comes, and in the vale hath heard
The funeral dirge; — she sees the knot
Of people, sees them in one spot —   1545
And darting like a wounded bird
She reached the grave, and with her breast
Upon the ground received the rest, —
The consummation, the whole ruth
And sorrow of this final truth!   1550

CANTO SEVENTH

"Powers there are
That touch each other to the quick — in modes
Which the gross world no sense hath to perceive,
No soul to dream of."

THOU Spirit, whose angelic hand
Was to the harp a strong command,
Called the submissive strings to wake
In glory for this Maiden's sake,
Say, Spirit! whither hath she fled   1555
To hide her poor afflicted head?
What mighty forest in its gloom
Enfolds her? — is a rifted tomb
Within the wilderness her seat?
Some island which the wild waves beat —   1560
Is that the Sufferer's last retreat?
Or some aspiring rock, that shrouds
Its perilous front in mists and clouds?
High-climbing rock, low sunless dale,
Sea, desert, what do these avail?   1565
Oh take her anguish and her fears
Into a deep recess of years!

'Tis done; — despoil and desolation
O'er Rylstone's fair domain have blown;
Pools, terraces, and walks are sown   1570
With weeds; the bowers are overthrown,
Or have given way to slow mutation,
While, in their ancient habitation
The Norton name hath been unknown.

The lordly Mansion of its pride   1575
Is stripped; the ravage hath spread wide
Through park and field, a perishing
That mocks the gladness of the Spring!
And, with this silent gloom agreeing,
Appears a joyless human Being,   1580
Of aspect such as if the waste
Were under her dominion placed.
Upon a primrose bank, her throne
Of quietness, she sits alone;
Among the ruins of a wood,   1585
Erewhile a covert bright and green,
And where full many a brave tree stood,
That used to spread its boughs, and ring
With the sweet birds' carolling.
Behold her, like a virgin Queen,   1590
Neglecting in imperial state
These outward images of fate,
And carrying inward a serene
And perfect sway, through many a thought
Of chance and change, that hath been brought   1595
To the subjection of a holy,
Though stern and rigorous, melancholy!
The like authority, with grace
Of awfulness, is in her face, —
There hath she fixed it; yet it seems   1600
To o'ershadow by no native right
That face, which cannot lose the gleams,
Lose utterly the tender gleams,
Of gentleness and meek delight,
And loving-kindness ever bright: 1605
Such is her sovereign mien: — her dress
(A vest with woollen cincture tied,
A hood of mountain-wool undyed)
Is homely, — fashioned to express
A wandering Pilgrim's humbleness.   1610

  And she *hath* wandered, long and far,
Beneath the light of sun and star;
Hath roamed in trouble and in grief,
Driven forward like a withered leaf,
Yea like a ship at random blown   1615
To distant places and unknown.
But now she dares to seek a haven
Among her native wilds of Craven;
Hath seen again her Father's roof,
And put her fortitude to proof;   1620

The mighty sorrow hath been borne,
And she is thoroughly forlorn:
Her soul doth in itself stand fast,
Sustained by memory of the past
And strength of Reason; held above   1625
The infirmities of mortal love;
Undaunted, lofty, calm, and stable,
And awfully impenetrable.

   And so — beneath a mouldered tree,
A self-surviving leafless oak   1630
By unregarded age from stroke
Of ravage saved — sate Emily.
There did she rest, with head reclined,
Herself most like a stately flower,
(Such have I seen) whom chance of birth   1635
Hath separated from its kind,
To live and die in a shady bower,
Single on the gladsome earth.

   When, with a noise like distant thunder,
A troop of deer came sweeping by;   1640
And, suddenly, behold a wonder!
For One, among those rushing deer,
A single One, in mid career
Hath stopped, and fixed her large full eye
Upon the Lady Emily;   1645
A Doe most beautiful, clear-white,
A radiant creature, silver-bright!

   Thus checked, a little while it stayed;
A little thoughtful pause it made;
And then advanced with stealth-like pace, 1650
Drew softly near her, and more near —
Looked round — but saw no cause for fear;
So to her feet the Creature came,
And laid its head upon her knee,
And looked into the Lady's face,   1655
A look of pure benignity,
And fond unclouded memory.
It is, thought Emily, the same,
The very Doe of other years! —
The pleading look the Lady viewed,   1660
And, by her gushing thoughts subdued,
She melted into tears —
A flood of tears, that flowed apace,
Upon the happy Creature's face.

Oh, moment ever blest! O Pair   1665
Beloved of Heaven, Heaven's chosen care,
This was for you a precious greeting;
And may it prove a fruitful meeting!
Joined are they, and the sylvan Doe
Can she depart? can she forego   1670
The Lady, once her playful peer,
And now her sainted Mistress dear?
And will not Emily receive
This lovely chronicler of things
Long past, delights and sorrowings?   1675
Lone Sufferer! will not she believe
The promise in that speaking face;
And welcome, as a gift of grace,
The saddest thought the Creature brings?

That day, the first of a re-union   1680
Which was to teem with high communion,
That day of balmy April weather,
They tarried in the wood together.
And when, ere fall of evening dew,
She from her sylvan haunt withdrew,   1685
The White Doe tracked with faithful pace
The Lady to her dwelling-place;
That nook where, on paternal ground,
A habitation she had found,
The Master of whose humble board   1690
Once owned her Father for his Lord;
A hut, by tufted trees defended,
Where Rylstone brook with Wharf is blended.

When Emily by morning light
Went forth, the Doe stood there in sight.   1695
She shrunk: — with one frail shock of pain
Received and followed by a prayer,
She saw the Creature once again;
Shun will she not, she feels, will bear; —
But, wheresoever she looked round,   1700
All now was trouble-haunted ground;
And therefore now she deems it good
Once more this restless neighbourhood
To leave. — Unwooed, yet unforbidden,
The White Doe followed up the vale,   1705
Up to another cottage, hidden
In the deep fork of Amerdale;
And there may Emily restore
Herself, in spots unseen before.

— Why tell of mossy rock, or tree,   1710
By lurking Dernbrook's pathless side,
Haunts of a strengthening amity
That calmed her, cheered, and fortified?
For she hath ventured now to read
Of time, and place, and thought, and deed —   1715
Endless history that lies
In her silent Follower's eyes;
Who with a power like human reason
Discerns the favourable season,
Skilled to approach or to retire, —   1720
From looks conceiving her desire;
From look, deportment, voice, or mien,
That vary to the heart within.
If she too passionately wreathed
Her arms, or over-deeply breathed,   1725
Walked quick or slowly, every mood
In its degree was understood;
Then well may their accord be true,
And kindliest intercourse ensue.
— Oh! surely 'twas a gentle rousing   1730
When she by sudden glimpse espied
The White Doe on the mountain browsing,
Or in the meadow wandered wide!
How pleased, when down the Straggler sank
Beside her, on some sunny bank!   1735
How soothed, when in thick bower enclosed,
They, like a nested pair, reposed!
Fair Vision! when it crossed the Maid
Within some rocky cavern laid,
The dark cave's portal gliding by,   1740
White as whitest cloud on high
Floating through the azure sky.
— What now is left for pain or fear?
That Presence, dearer and more dear,
While they, side by side, were straying,   1745
And the shepherd's pipe was playing,
Did now a very gladness yield
At morning to the dewy field,
And with a deeper peace endued
The hour of moonlight solitude.   1750

   With her Companion, in such frame
Of mind, to Rylstone back she came;
And, ranging through the wasted groves,
Received the memory of old loves,
Undisturbed and undistrest,   1755

Into a soul which now was blest
With a soft spring-day of holy,
Mild, and grateful, melancholy:
Not sunless gloom or unenlightened,
But by tender fancies brightened.   1760

When the bells of Rylstone played
Their sabbath music — "𝕲𝖔𝖉 𝖚𝖘 𝖆𝖞𝖉𝖊!"
That was the sound they seemed to speak;
Inscriptive legend which I ween
May on those holy bells be seen,   1765
That legend and her Grandsire's name;
And oftentimes the Lady meek
Had in her childhood read the same;
Words which she slighted at that day;
But now, when such sad change was wrought,   1770
And of that lonely name she thought,
The bells of Rylstone seemed to say,
While she sate listening in the shade,
With vocal music, "𝕲𝖔𝖉 𝖚𝖘 𝖆𝖞𝖉𝖊;"
And all the hills were glad to bear   1775
Their part in this effectual prayer.

Nor lacked she Reason's firmest power;
But with the White Doe at her side
Up would she climb to Norton Tower,
And thence look round her far and wide,   1780
Her fate there measuring; — all is stilled, —
The weak One hath subdued her heart;
Behold the prophecy fulfilled,
Fulfilled, and she sustains her part!
But here her Brother's words have failed;   1785
Here hath a milder doom prevailed;
That she, of him and all bereft,
Hath yet this faithful Partner left;
This one Associate that disproves
His words, remains for her, and loves.   1790
If tears are shed, they do not fall
For loss of him — for one, or all;
Yet, sometimes, sometimes doth she weep
Moved gently in her soul's soft sleep;
A few tears down her cheek descend   1795
For this her last and living Friend.

Bless, tender Hearts, their mutual lot,
And bless for both this savage spot;
Which Emily doth sacred hold

For reasons dear and manifold — 1800
Here hath she, here before her sight,
Close to the summit of this height,
The grassy rock-encircled Pound
In which the Creature first was found.
So beautiful the timid Thrall 1805
(A spotless Youngling white as foam)
Her youngest Brother brought it home;
The youngest, then a lusty boy,
Bore it, or led, to Rylstone-hall
With heart brimful of pride and joy! 1810

But most to Bolton's sacred Pile,
On favouring nights, she loved to go;
There ranged through cloister, court, and aisle,
Attended by the soft-paced Doe;
Nor feared she in the still moonshine 1815
To look upon Saint Mary's shrine;
Nor on the lonely turf that showed
Where Francis slept in his last abode.
For that she came; there oft she sate
Forlorn, but not disconsolate: 1820
And, when she from the abyss returned
Of thought, she neither shrunk nor mourned;
Was happy that she lived to greet
Her mute Companion as it lay
In love and pity at her feet; 1825
How happy in its turn to meet
The recognition! the mild glance
Beamed from that gracious countenance;
Communication, like the ray
Of a new morning, to the nature 1830
And prospects of the inferior Creature!

A mortal Song we sing, by dower
Encouraged of celestial power;
Power which the viewless Spirit shed
By whom we were first visited; 1835
Whose voice we heard, whose hand and wings
Swept like a breeze the conscious strings,
When, left in solitude, erewhile
We stood before this ruined Pile,
And, quitting unsubstantial dreams, 1840
Sang in this Presence kindred themes;
Distress and desolation spread
Through human hearts, and pleasure dead, —
Dead — but to live again on earth,

A second and yet nobler birth;
Dire overthrow, and yet how high
The re-ascent in sanctity!
From fair to fairer; day by day
A more divine and loftier way!
Even such this blessèd Pilgrim trod,
By sorrow lifted towards her God;
Uplifted to the purest sky
Of undisturbed mortality.
Her own thoughts loved she; and could bend
A dear look to her lowly Friend;
There stopped; her thirst was satisfied
With what this innocent spring supplied:
Her sanction inwardly she bore,
And stood apart from human cares:
But to the world returned no more,
Although with no unwilling mind
Help did she give at need, and joined
The Wharfdale peasants in their prayers.
At length, thus faintly, faintly tied
To earth, she was set free, and died.
Thy soul, exalted Emily,
Maid of the blasted family,
Rose to the God from whom it came!
— In Rylstone Church her mortal frame
Was buried by her Mother's side.

Most glorious sunset! and a ray
Survives — the twilight of this day —
In that fair Creature whom the fields
Support, and whom the forest shields;
Who, having filled a holy place,
Partakes, in her degree, Heaven's grace;
And bears a memory and a mind
Raised far above the law of kind;
Haunting the spots with lonely cheer
Which her dear Mistress once held dear:
Loves most what Emily loved most —
The enclosure of this church-yard ground;
Here wanders like a gliding ghost,
And every sabbath here is found;
Comes with the people when the bells
Are heard among the moorland dells,
Finds entrance through yon arch, where way
Lies open on the sabbath-day;
Here walks amid the mournful waste
Of prostrate altars, shrines defaced,

1845

1850

1855

1860

1865

1870

1875

1880

1885

1890

And floors encumbered with rich show
Of fret-work imagery laid low;
Paces softly, or makes halt,
By fractured cell, or tomb, or vault;
By plate of monumental brass   **1895**
Dim-gleaming among weeds and grass,
And sculptured Forms of Warriors brave:
But chiefly by that single grave,
That one sequestered hillock green,
The pensive visitant is seen.   **1900**
There doth the gentle Creature lie
With those adversities unmoved;
Calm spectacle, by earth and sky
In their benignity approved!
And aye, methinks, this hoary Pile,   **1905**
Subdued by outrage and decay,
Looks down upon her with a smile,
A gracious smile, that seems to say —
"Thou, thou art not a Child of Time,
But Daughter of the Eternal Prime!"   **1910**

CHARACTERISTICS OF A CHILD
THREE YEARS OLD

LOVING she is, and tractable, though wild;
And Innocence hath privilege in her
To dignify arch looks and laughing eyes;
And feats of cunning; and the pretty round
Of trespasses, affected to provoke   5
Mock-chastisement and partnership in play.
And, as a faggot sparkles on the hearth,
Not less if unattended and alone
Than when both young and old sit gathered round
And take delight in its activity;   10
Even so this happy Creature of herself
Is all-sufficient; solitude to her
Is blithe society, who fills the air
With gladness and involuntary songs.
Light are her sallies as the tripping fawn's   15
Forth-startled from the fern where she lay couched;
Unthought-of, unexpected, as the stir
Of the soft breeze ruffling the meadow-flowers,
Or from before it chasing wantonly
The many-coloured images imprest   20
Upon the bosom of a placid lake.

SURPRISED BY JOY

SURPRISED by joy — impatient as the Wind
I turned to share the transport — Oh! with whom
But Thee, deep buried in the silent tomb,
That spot which no vicissitude can find?
Love, faithful love, recalled thee to my mind —   5
But how could I forget thee? Through what power,
Even for the least division of an hour,
Have I been so beguiled as to be blind
To my most grievous loss! — That thought's return
Was the worst pang that sorrow ever bore,   10
Save one, one only, when I stood forlorn,
Knowing my heart's best treasure was no more;
That neither present time, nor years unborn
Could to my sight that heavenly face restore.

THE SHEPHERD, LOOKING EASTWARD, SOFTLY SAID

THE Shepherd, looking eastward, softly said,
"Bright is thy veil, O Moon, as thou art bright!"
Forthwith, that little cloud, in ether spread
And penetrated all with tender light,
She cast away, and showed her fulgent head   5
Uncovered; dazzling the Beholder's sight
As if to vindicate her beauty's right,
Her beauty thoughtlessly disparagèd.
Meanwhile that veil, removed or thrown aside,
Went floating from her, darkening as it went;   10
And a huge mass, to bury or to hide,
Approached this glory of the firmament;
Who meekly yields, and is obscured — content
With one calm triumph of a modest pride.

YARROW VISITED

SEPTEMBER, 1814

AND is this — Yarrow? — *This* the Stream
Of which my fancy cherished,
So faithfully, a waking dream?
An image that hath perished!
O that some Minstrel's harp were near,   5
To utter notes of gladness,
And chase this silence from the air,
That fills my heart with sadness!

Yet why? — a silvery current flows
With uncontrolled meanderings;   10
Nor have these eyes by greener hills
Been soothed, in all my wanderings.
And, through her depths, Saint Mary's Lake
Is visibly delighted;
For not a feature of those hills   15
Is in the mirror slighted.

A blue sky bends o'er Yarrow vale,
Save where that pearly whiteness
Is round the rising sun diffused,
A tender hazy brightness;   20

Mild dawn of promise! that excludes
All profitless dejection;
Though not unwilling here to admit
A pensive recollection.

Where was it that the famous Flower   25
Of Yarrow Vale lay bleeding?
His bed perchance was yon smooth mound
On which the herd is feeding:
And haply from this crystal pool,
Now peaceful as the morning,   30
The Water-wraith ascended thrice —
And gave his doleful warning.

Delicious is the Lay that sings
The haunts of happy Lovers,
The path that leads them to the grove,   35
The leafy grove that covers:
And Pity sanctifies the Verse
That paints, by strength of sorrow,
The unconquerable strength of love;
Bear witness, rueful Yarrow!   40

But thou, that didst appear so fair
To fond imagination,
Dost rival in the light of day
Her delicate creation:
Meek loveliness is round thee spread,   45
A softness still and holy;
The grace of forest charms decayed,
And pastoral melancholy.

That region left, the vale unfolds
Rich groves of lofty stature,   50
With Yarrow winding through the pomp
Of cultivated nature;
And, rising from those lofty groves,
Behold a Ruin hoary!
The shattered front of Newark's Towers,   55
Renowned in Border story.

Fair scenes for childhood's opening bloom,
For sportive youth to stray in;
For manhood to enjoy his strength;
And age to wear away in!   60
Yon cottage seems a bower of bliss.
A covert for protection

Of tender thoughts, that nestle there —
The brood of chaste affection.

How sweet, on this autumnal day,   65
The wild-wood fruits to gather,
And on my True-love's forehead plant
A crest of blooming heather!
And what if I enwreathed my own!
'Twere no offence to reason;   70
The sober Hills thus deck their brows
To meet the wintry season.

I see — but not by sight alone,
Loved Yarrow, have I won thee;
A ray of fancy still survives —   75
Her sunshine plays upon thee!
Thy ever-youthful waters keep
A course of lively pleasure;
And gladsome notes my lips can breath,
Accordant to the measure.   80

The vapours linger round the Heights,
They melt, and soon must vanish;
One hour is theirs, nor more is mine —
Sad thought, which I would banish,
But that I know, where'er I go,   85
Thy genuine image, Yarrow!
Will dwell with me — to heighten joy,
And cheer my mind in sorrow.

LAODAMIA

"With sacrifice before the rising morn
Vows have I made by fruitless hope inspired;
And from the infernal Gods, 'mid shades forlorn
Of night, my slaughtered Lord have I required:
Celestial pity I again implore; —   5
Restore him to my sight — great Jove, restore!"

So speaking, and by fervent love endowed
With faith, the Suppliant heavenward lifts her hands;
While, like the sun emerging from a cloud,
Her countenance brightens — and her eye expands;   10
Her bosom heaves and spreads, her stature grows;
And she expects the issue in repose.

O terror! what hath she perceived? — O joy!
What doth she look on? — whom doth she behold?
Her Hero slain upon the beach of Troy?   15
His vital presence? his corporeal mould?
It is — if sense deceive her not — 'tis He!
And a God leads him, winged Mercury!

Mild Hermes spake — and touched her with his wand
That calms all fear; "Such grace hath crowned thy prayer,   20
Laodamía! that at Jove's command
Thy Husband walks the paths of upper air:
He comes to tarry with thee three hours' space;
Accept the gift, behold him face to face!"

Forth sprang the impassioned Queen her Lord to clasp;   25
Again that consummation she essayed;
But unsubstantial Form eludes her grasp
As often as that eager grasp was made.
The Phantom parts — but parts to re-unite,
And re-assume his place before her sight.   30

"Protesiláus, lo! thy guide is gone!
Confirm, I pray, the vision with thy voice:
This is our palace, — yonder is thy throne;
Speak, and the floor thou tread'st on will rejoice.
Not to appal me have the gods bestowed   35
This precious boon; and blest a sad abode."

"Great Jove, Laodamía! doth not leave
His gifts imperfect: — Spectre though I be,
I am not sent to scare thee or deceive;
But in reward of thy fidelity.   40
And something also did my worth obtain;
For fearless virtue bringeth boundless gain.

"Thou knowest, the Delphic oracle foretold
That the first Greek who touched the Trojan strand
Should die; but me the threat could not withhold: 45
A generous cause a victim did demand;
And forth I leapt upon the sandy plain;
A self-devoted chief — by Hector slain."

"Supreme of Heroes — bravest, noblest, best!
Thy matchless courage I bewail no more,   50
Which then, when tens of thousands were deprest
By doubt, propelled thee to the fatal shore;
Thou found'st — and I forgive thee — here thou art —
A nobler counsellor than my poor heart.

"But thou, though capable of sternest deed,   55
Wert kind as resolute, and good as brave;
And he, whose power restores thee, hath decreed
Thou should'st elude the malice of the grave:
Redundant are thy locks, thy lips as fair
As when their breath enriched Thessalian air.   60

"No Spectre greets me, — no vain Shadow this;
Come, blooming Hero, place thee by my side!
Give, on this well-known couch, one nuptial kiss
To me, this day, a second time thy bride!"
Jove frowned in heaven: the conscious Parcæ threw   65
Upon those roseate lips a Stygian hue.

"This visage tells thee that my doom is past:
Nor should the change be mourned, even if the joys
Of sense were able to return as fast
And surely as they vanish. Earth destroys   70
Those raptures duly — Erebus disdains:
Calm pleasures there abide — majestic pains.

"Be taught, O faithful Consort, to control
Rebellious passion: for the Gods approve
The depth, and not the tumult, of the soul;   75
A fervent, not ungovernable, love.
Thy transports moderate; and meekly mourn
When I depart, for brief is my sojourn —"

"Ah, wherefore? — Did not Hercules by force
Wrest from the guardian Monster of the tomb   80
Alcestis, a reanimated corse,
Given back to dwell on earth in vernal bloom?
Medea's spells dispersed the weight of years,
And Æson stood a youth 'mid youthful peers.

"The Gods to us are merciful — and they   85
Yet further may relent: for mightier far
Than strength of nerve and sinew, or the sway
Of magic potent over sun and star,
Is love, though oft to agony distrest,
And though his favourite seat be feeble woman's breast.   90

"But if thou goest, I follow — " "Peace!" he said, —
She looked upon him and was calmed and cheered;
The ghastly colour from his lips had fled;
In his deportment, shape, and mien, appeared
Elysian beauty, melancholy grace,   95
Brought from a pensive though a happy place.

He spake of love, such love·as Spirits feel
In worlds whose course is equable and pure;
No fears to beat away — no strife to heal —
The past unsighed for, and the future sure;   100
Spake of heroic arts in graver mood
Revived, with finer harmony pursued;

Of all that is most beauteous — imaged there
In happier beauty; more pellucid streams,
An ampler ether, a diviner air,   105
And fields invested with purpureal gleams;
Climes which the sun, who sheds the brightest day
Earth knows, is all unworthy to survey.

Yet there the Soul shall enter which hath earned
That privilege by virtue. — "Ill," said he,   110
"The end of man's existence I discerned,
Who from ignoble games and revelry
Could draw, when we had parted, vain delight,
While tears were thy best pastime, day and night;

"And while my youthful peers before my eyes   115
(Each hero following his peculiar bent)
Prepared themselves for glorious enterprise
By martial sports, — or, seated in the tent,
Chieftains and kings in council were detained;
What time the fleet at Aulis lay enchained.   120

"The wished-for wind was given: — I then revolved
The oracle, upon the silent sea;
And, if no worthier led the way, resolved
That, of a thousand vessels, mine should be
The foremost prow in pressing to the strand, —   125
Mine the first blood that tinged the Trojan sand.

"Yet bitter, oft-times bitter, was the pang
When of thy loss I thought, belovèd Wife!
On thee too fondly did my memory hang,
And on the joys we shared in mortal life, —   130
The paths which we had trod — these fountains, flowers;
My new-planned cities, and unfinished towers.

"But should suspense permit the Foe to cry,
'Behold they tremble! — haughty their array,
Yet of their number no one dares to die?'   135
In soul I swept the indignity away:
Old frailties then recurred: — but lofty thought,
In act embodied, my deliverance wrought.

"And Thou, though strong in love, art all too weak
In reason, in self-government too slow;   140
I counsel thee by fortitude to seek
Our blest re-union in the shades below.
The invisible world with thee hath sympathised;
Be thy affections raised and solemnised.

"Learn, by a mortal yearning, to ascend —   145
Seeking a higher object. Love was given,
Encouraged, sanctioned, chiefly for that end;
For this the passion to excess was driven —
That self might be annulled: her bondage prove
The fetters of a dream, opposed to love." —   150

Aloud she shrieked! for Hermes re-appears!
Round the dear Shade she would have clung — 'tis vain:
The hours are past — too brief had they been years;
And him no mortal effort can detain:
Swift, toward the realms that know not earthly day,   155
He through the portal takes his silent way,
And on the palace-floor a lifeless corse She lay.

Thus, all in vain exhorted and reproved,
She perished; and, as for a wilful crime,
By the just Gods whom no weak pity moved,   160
Was doomed to wear out her appointed time,
Apart from happy Ghosts, that gather flowers
Of blissful quiet 'mid unfading bowers.

— Yet tears to human suffering are due;
And mortal hopes defeated and o'erthrown   165
Are mourned by man, and not by man alone,
As fondly he believes. — Upon the side
Of Hellespont (such faith was entertained)
A knot of spiry trees for ages grew
From out the tomb of him for whom she died;   170
And ever, when such stature they had gained
That Ilium's walls were subject to their view,
The trees' tall summits withered at the sight;
A constant interchange of growth and blight!

"WEAK IS THE WILL OF MAN"

"WEAK is the will of Man, his judgment blind;
Remembrance persecutes, and Hope betrays;
Heavy is woe; — and joy, for human-kind,
A mournful thing, so transient is the blaze!"
Thus might *he* paint our lot of mortal days   5
Who wants the glorious faculty assigned
To elevate the more-than-reasoning Mind,
And colour life's dark cloud with orient rays.
Imagination is that sacred power,
Imagination lofty and refined: 10
'Tis hers to pluck the amaranthine flower
Of Faith, and round the Sufferer's temples bind
Wreaths that endure affliction's heaviest shower,
And do not shrink from sorrow's keenest wind.

NOVEMBER 1

How clear, how keen, how marvellously bright
The effluence from yon distant mountain's head,
Which, strewn with snow smooth as the sky can shed,
Shines like another sun — on mortal sight
Uprisen, as if to check approaching Night,   5
And all her twinkling stars. Who now would tread,
If so he might, yon mountain's glittering head —
Terrestrial, but a surface, by the flight
Of sad mortality's earth-sullying wing,
Unswept, unstained? Nor shall the aërial Powers   10
Dissolve that beauty, destined to endure,
White, radiant, spotless, exquisitely pure,
Through all vicissitudes, till genial Spring
Has filled the laughing vales with welcome flowers.

SEPTEMBER, 1815

WHILE not a leaf seems faded; while the fields,
With ripening harvest prodigally fair,
In brightest sunshine bask; this nipping air,
Sent from some distant clime where Winter wields
His icy scimitar, a foretaste yields   5
Of bitter change, and bids the flowers beware;
And whispers to the silent birds, "Prepare

Against the threatening foe your trustiest shields."
For me, who under kindlier laws belong
To Nature's tuneful quire, this rustling dry   10
Through leaves yet green, and yon crystalline sky,
Announce a season potent to renew,
'Mid frost and snow, the instinctive joys of song,
And nobler cares than listless summer knew.

COMPOSED UPON AN EVENING OF
EXTRAORDINARY SPLENDOUR AND BEAUTY

I

HAD this effulgence disappeared
With flying haste, I might have sent,
Among the speechless clouds, a look
Of blank astonishment;
But 'tis endued with power to stay,   5
And sanctify one closing day,
That frail Mortality may see —
What is? — ah no, but what *can* be!
Time was when field and watery cove
With modulated echoes rang,   10
While choirs of fervent Angels sang
Their vespers in the grove;
Or, crowning, star-like, each some sovereign height,
Warbled, for heaven above and earth below,
Strains suitable to both. — Such holy rite,   15
Methinks, if audibly repeated now
From hill or valley, could not move
Sublimer transport, purer love,
Than doth this silent spectacle — the gleam —
The shadow — and the peace supreme!   20

II

No sound is uttered, — but a deep
And solemn harmony pervades
The hollow vale from steep to steep,
And penetrates the glades.
Far-distant images draw nigh,   25
Called forth by wondrous potency
Of beamy radiance, that imbues,
Whate'er it strikes, with gem-like hues!
In vision exquisitely clear,

Herds range along the mountain side; 30
And glistening antlers are descried;
And gilded flocks appear.
Thine is the tranquil hour, purpureal Eve!
But long as god-like wish, or hope divine,
Informs my spirit, ne'er can I believe 35
That this magnificence is wholly thine!
— From worlds not quickened by the sun
A portion of the gift is won;
An intermingling of Heaven's pomp is spread
On ground which British shepherds tread! 40

III

And, if there be whom broken ties
Afflict, or injuries assail,
Yon hazy ridges to their eyes
Present a glorious scale,
Climbing suffused with sunny air, 45
To stop — no record hath told where!
And tempting Fancy to ascend,
And with immortal Spirits blend!
— Wings at my shoulders seem to play;
But, rooted here, I stand and gaze 50
On those bright steps that heaven-ward raise
Their practicable way.
Come forth, ye drooping old men, look abroad,
And see to what fair countries ye are bound!
And if some traveller, weary of his road, 55
Hath slept since noon-tide on the grassy ground,
Ye Genii! to his covert speed;
And wake him with such gentle heed
As may attune his soul to meet the dower
Bestowed on this transcendent hour! 60

IV

Such hues from their celestial Urn
Were wont to stream before mine eye,
Where'er it wandered in the morn
Of blissful infancy.
This glimpse of glory, why renewed? 65
Nay, rather speak with gratitude;
For, if a vestige of those gleams
Survived, 'twas only in my dreams.
Dread Power! whom peace and calmness serve
No less than Nature's threatening voice, 70

If aught unworthy be my choice,
From THEE if I would swerve;
Oh, let thy grace remind me of the light
Full early lost, and fruitlessly deplored;
Which, at this moment, on my waking sight   75
Appears to shine, by miracle restored;
My soul, though yet confined to earth,
Rejoices in a second birth!
— 'Tis past, the visionary splendour fades;
And night approaches with her shades.   80

SOLE LISTENER, DUDDON!

SOLE listener, Duddon! to the breeze that played
With thy clear voice, I caught the fitful sound
Wafted o'er sullen moss and craggy mound —
Unfruitful solitudes, that seemed to upbraid
The sun in heaven! — but now, to form a shade   5
For Thee, green alders have together wound
Their foliage; ashes flung their arms around;
And birch-trees risen in silver colonnade.
And thou hast also tempted here to rise,
'Mid sheltering pines, this Cottage rude and grey; 10
Whose ruddy children, by the mother's eyes
Carelessly watched, sport through the summer day,
Thy pleased associates: — light as endless May
On infant bosoms lonely Nature lies.

AFTER-THOUGHT

I THOUGHT of Thee, my partner and my guide,
As being past away. — Vain sympathies!
For, backward, Duddon! as I cast my eyes,
I see what was, and is, and will abide;
Still glides the Stream, and shall for ever glide; 5
The Form remains, the Function never dies;
While we, the brave, the mighty, and the wise,
We Men, who in our morn of youth defied
The elements, must vanish; — be it so!
Enough, if something from our hands have power   10
To live, and act, and serve the future hour;
And if, as toward the silent tomb we go,
Through love, through hope, and faith's transcendent dower,
We feel that we are greater than we know.

INSIDE OF KING'S COLLEGE CHAPEL,
CAMBRIDGE

Tax not the royal Saint with vain expense,
With ill-matched aims the Architect who planned —
Albeit labouring for a scanty band
Of white-robed Scholars only — this immense
And glorious Work of fine intelligence!   5
Give all thou canst; high Heaven rejects the lore
Of nicely-calculated less or more;
So deemed the man who fashioned for the sense
These lofty pillars, spread that branching roof
Self-poised, and scooped into ten thousand cells,   10
Where light and shade repose, where music dwells
Lingering — and wandering on as loth to die;
Like thoughts whose very sweetness yieldeth proof
That they were born for immortality.

MUTABILITY

From low to high doth dissolution climb,
And sink from high to low, along a scale
Of awful notes, whose concord shall not fail;
A musical but melancholy chime,
Which they can hear who meddle not with crime,   5
Nor avarice, nor over-anxious care.
Truth fails not; but her outward forms that bear
The longest date do melt like frosty rime,
That in the morning whitened hill and plain
And is no more; drop like the tower sublime   10
Of yesterday, which royally did wear
His crown of weeds, but could not even sustain
Some casual shout that broke the silent air,
Or the unimaginable touch of Time.

TO ——

Look at the fate of summer flowers,
Which blow at daybreak, droop ere even-song;
And, grieved for their brief date, confess that ours,
Measured by what we are and ought to be,
Measured by all that, trembling, we foresee,   5
    Is not so long!

If human Life do pass away,
Perishing yet more swiftly than the flower,
If we are creatures of a *winter's* day;
What space hath Virgin's beauty to disclose   10
Her sweets, and triumph o'er the breathing rose?
          Not even an hour!

The deepest grove whose foliage hid
The happiest lovers Arcady might boast,
Could not the entrance of this thought forbid: 15
O be thou wise as they, soul-gifted Maid!
Nor rate too high what must so quickly fade,
          So soon be lost.

Then shall love teach some virtuous Youth
"To draw, out of the object of his eyes,"   20
The while on thee they gaze in simple truth,
Hues more exalted, "a refinèd Form,"
That dreads not age, nor suffers from the worm,
          And never dies.

TO A SKY-LARK

ETHEREAL minstrel! pilgrim of the sky!
Dost thou despise the earth where cares abound?
Or, while the wings aspire, are heart and eye
Both with thy nest upon the dewy ground?
Thy nest which thou canst drop into at will,   5
Those quivering wings composed, that music still!

Leave to the nightingale her shady wood;
A privacy of glorious light is thine;
Whence thou dost pour upon the world a flood
Of harmony, with instinct more divine;   10
Type of the wise who soar, but never roam;
True to the kindred points of Heaven and Home!

SCORN NOT THE SONNET

SCORN not the Sonnet; Critic, you have frowned,
Mindless of its just honours; with this key
Shakspeare unlocked his heart; the melody
Of this small lute gave ease to Petrarch's wound;
A thousand times this pipe did Tasso sound;   5
With it Camöens soothed an exile's grief;

The Sonnet glittered a gay myrtle leaf
Amid the cypress with which Dante crowned
His visionary brow: a glow-worm lamp,
It cheered mild Spenser, called from Faery-land   10
To struggle through dark ways; and, when a damp
Fell round the path of Milton, in his hand
The Thing became a trumpet; whence he blew
Soul-animating strains — alas, too few!

IF THOU INDEED DERIVE THY LIGHT
FROM HEAVEN

IF thou indeed derive thy light from Heaven,
Then, to the measure of that heaven-born light,
Shine, Poet! in thy place, and be content: —
The stars pre-eminent in magnitude,
And they that from the zenith dart their beams,   5
(Visible though they be to half the earth,
Though half a sphere be conscious of their brightness)
Are yet of no diviner origin,
No purer essence, than the one that burns,
Like an untended watch-fire, on the ridge   10
Of some dark mountain; or than those which seem
Humbly to hang, like twinkling winter lamps,
Among the branches of the leafless trees;
All are the undying offspring of one Sire:
Then, to the measure of the light vouchsafed,   15
Shine, Poet! in thy place, and be content.

YARROW REVISITED

The following Stanzas are a memorial of a day passed with Sir Walter
Scott, and other Friends visiting the Banks of the Yarrow under his guidance,
immediately before his departure from Abbotsford, for Naples.

The title *Yarrow Revisited* will stand in no need of explanation, for
Readers acquainted with the Author's previous poems suggested by that
celebrated Stream.

THE gallant Youth, who may have gained,
    Or seeks, a "winsome Marrow,"
Was but an Infant in the lap
    When first I looked on Yarrow;
Once more, by Newark's Castle-gate   5
    Long left without a warder,
I stood, looked, listened, and with Thee,
    Great Minstrel of the Border!

Grave thoughts ruled wide on that sweet day,
　　Their dignity installing　　　　　　　　　　　　　10
In gentle bosoms, while sere leaves
　　Were on the bough, or falling;
But breezes played, and sunshine gleamed —
　　The forest to embolden;
Reddened the fiery hues, and shot　　　　　　　　　15
　　Transparence through the golden.

For busy thoughts the Stream flowed on
　　In foamy agitation;
And slept in many a crystal pool
　　For quiet contemplation:　　　　　　　　　　　　20
No public and no private care
　　The freeborn mind enthralling,
We made a day of happy hours,
　　Our happy days recalling.

Brisk Youth appeared, the Morn of youth,　　　　25
　　With freaks of graceful folly, —
Life's temperate Noon, her sober Eve,
　　Her Night not melancholy;
Past, present, future, all appeared
　　In harmony united,　　　　　　　　　　　　　　30
Like guests that meet, and some from far,
　　By cordial love invited.

And if, as Yarrow, through the woods
　　And down the meadow ranging,
Did meet us with unaltered face,　　　　　　　　　35
　　Though we were changed and changing;
If, *then,* some natural shadows spread
　　Our inward prospect over,
The soul's deep valley was not slow
　　Its brightness to recover.　　　　　　　　　　　40

Eternal blessings on the Muse,
　　And her divine employment!
The blameless Muse, who trains her Sons
　　For hope and calm enjoyment;
Albeit sickness, lingering yet,　　　　　　　　　　45
　　Has o'er their pillow brooded;
And Care waylays their steps — a Sprite
　　Not easily eluded.

For thee, O Scott! compelled to change
　　Green Eildon-hill and Cheviot　　　　　　　　　50
For warm Vesuvio's vine-clad slopes;

And leave thy Tweed and Tiviot
For mild Sorento's breezy waves;
  May classic Fancy, linking
With native Fancy her fresh aid,   55
  Preserve thy heart from sinking!

O! while they minister to thee,
  Each vying with the other,
May Health return to mellow Age,
  With Strength, her venturous brother;   60
And Tiber, and each brook and rill
  Renowned in song and story,
With unimagined beauty shine,
  Nor lose one ray of glory!

For Thou, upon a hundred streams,   65
  By tales of love and sorrow,
Of faithful love, undaunted truth,
  Hast shed the power of Yarrow;
And streams unknown, hills yet unseen,
  Wherever they invite Thee,   70
At parent Nature's grateful call,
  With gladness must requite Thee.

A gracious welcome shall be thine,
  Such looks of love and honour
As thy own Yarrow gave to me   75
  When first I gazed upon her;
Beheld what I had feared to see,
  Unwilling to surrender
Dreams treasured up from early days,
  The holy and the tender.   80

And what, for this frail world, were all
  That mortals do or suffer,
Did no responsive harp, no pen,
  Memorial tribute offer?
Yea, what were mighty Nature's self?   85
  Her features, could they win us,
Unhelped by the poetic voice
  That hourly speaks within us?

Nor deem that localised Romance
  Plays false with our affections;
Unsanctifies our tears — made sport   90
  For fanciful dejections:
Ah, no! the visions of the past

  Sustain the heart in feeling
Life as she is — our changeful Life,   95
  With friends and kindred dealing.

Bear witness, Ye, whose thoughts that day
  In Yarrow's groves were centred;
Who through the silent portal arch
  Of mouldering Newark enter'd;   100
And clomb the winding stair that once
  Too timidly was mounted
By the "last Minstrel," (not the last!)
  Ere he his Tale recounted.

Flow on for ever, Yarrow Stream!   105
  Fulfil thy pensive duty,
Well pleased that future Bards should chant
  For simple hearts thy beauty;
To dream-light dear while yet unseen,
  Dear to the common sunshine,   110
And dearer still, as now I feel,
  To memory's shadowy moonshine!

CALM IS THE FRAGRANT AIR

CALM is the fragrant air, and loth to lose
Day's grateful warmth, tho' moist with falling **dews**.
Look for the stars, you'll say that there are none;
Look up a second time, and, one by one,
You mark them twinkling out with silvery light,   5
And wonder how they could elude the sight!
The birds, of late so noisy in their bowers,
Warbled a while with faint and fainter powers,
But now are silent as the dim-seen flowers:
Nor does the village Church-clock's iron tone   10
The time's and season's influence disown;
Nine beats distinctly to each other bound
In drowsy sequence — how unlike the sound
That, in rough winter, oft inflicts a fear
On fireside listeners, doubting what they hear!   15
The shepherd, bent on rising with the sun,
Had closed his door before the day was done,
And now with thankful heart to bed doth creep,
And joins his little children in their sleep.
The bat, lured forth where trees the lane o'ershade,   20
Flits and reflits along the close arcade;

The busy dor-hawk chases the white moth
With burring note, which Industry and Sloth
Might both be pleased with, for it suits them both.
A stream is heard — I see it not, but know   25
By its soft music whence the waters flow:
Wheels and the tread of hoofs are heard no more;
One boat there was, but it will touch the shore
With the next dipping of its slackened oar;
Faint sound, that, for the gayest of the gay,   30
Might give to serious thought a moment's sway,
As a last token of man's toilsome day!

STEAMBOATS, VIADUCTS, AND RAILWAYS

Motions and Means, on land and sea at war
With old poetic feeling, not for this,
Shall ye, by Poets even, be judged amiss!
Nor shall your presence, howsoe'er it mar
The loveliness of Nature, prove a bar   5
To the Mind's gaining that prophetic sense
Of future change, that point of vision, whence
May be discovered what in soul ye are.
In spite of all that beauty may disown
In your harsh features, Nature doth embrace   10
Her lawful offspring in Man's art; and Time,
Pleased with your triumphs o'er his brother Space,
Accepts from your bold hands the proffered crown
Of hope, and smiles on you with cheer sublime.

MOST SWEET IT IS WITH UNUPLIFTED EYES

Most sweet it is with unuplifted eyes
To pace the ground, if path be there or none,
While a fair region round the traveller lies
Which he forbears again to look upon;
Pleased rather with some soft ideal scene,   5
The work of Fancy, or some happy tone
Of meditation, slipping in between
The beauty coming and the beauty gone.
If Thought and Love desert us, from that day
Let us break off all commerce with the Muse: 10
With Thought and Love companions of our way,
Whate'er the senses take or may refuse,
The Mind's internal heaven shall shed her dews
Of inspiration on the humblest lay.

EXTEMPORE EFFUSION UPON THE DEATH OF JAMES HOGG

WHEN first, descending from the moorlands,
I saw the Stream of Yarrow glide
Along a bare and open valley,
The Ettrick Shepherd was my guide.

When last along its banks I wandered,   5
Through groves that had begun to shed
Their golden leaves upon the pathways,
My steps the Border-minstrel led.

The mighty Minstrel breathes no longer,
'Mid mouldering ruins low he lies;   10
And death upon the braes of Yarrow,
Has closed the Shepherd-poet's eyes:

Nor has the rolling year twice measured,
From sign to sign, its stedfast course,
Since every mortal power of Coleridge   15
Was frozen at its marvellous source;

The rapt One, of the godlike forehead,
The heaven-eyed creature sleeps in earth:
And Lamb, the frolic and the gentle,
Has vanished from his lonely hearth.   20

Like clouds that rake the mountain-summits,
Or waves that own no curbing hand,
How fast has brother followed brother,
From sunshine to the sunless land!

Yet I, whose lids from infant slumber   25
Were earlier raised, remain to hear
A timid voice, that asks in whispers,
"Who next will drop and disappear?"

Our haughty life is crowned with darkness,
Like London with its own black wreath,   30
On which with thee, O Crabbe! forth-looking,
I gazed from Hampstead's breezy heath.

As if but yesterday departed,
Thou too art gone before; but why,

O'er ripe fruit, seasonably gathered,   35
Should frail survivors heave a sigh?

Mourn rather for that holy Spirit,
Sweet as the spring, as ocean deep;
For Her who, ere her summer faded,
Has sunk into a breathless sleep.   40

No more of old romantic sorrows,
For slaughtered Youth or love-lorn Maid!
With sharper grief is Yarrow smitten,
And Ettrick mourns with her their Poet dead.

PREFACES

ADVERTISEMENT TO *LYRICAL BALLADS* (1798)[1]

IT is the honourable characteristic of Poetry that its materials are to be found in every subject which can interest the human mind. The evidence of this fact is to be sought, not in the writings of Critics, but in those of Poets themselves.

The majority of the following poems are to be considered as experiments. They were written chiefly with a view to ascertain how far the language of conversation in the middle and lower classes of society is adapted to the purposes of poetic pleasure. Readers accustomed to the gaudiness and inane phraseology of many modern writers, if they persist in reading this book to its conclusion, will perhaps frequently have to struggle with feelings of strangeness and aukwardness: they will look round for poetry, and will be induced to enquire by what species of courtesy these attempts can be permitted to assume that title. It is desirable that such readers, for their own sakes, should not suffer the solitary word Poetry, a word of very disputed meaning, to stand in the way of their gratification; but that, while they are perusing this book, they should ask themselves if it contains a natural delineation of human passions, human characters, and human incidents; and if the answer be favorable to the author's wishes, that they should consent to be pleased in spite of that most dreadful enemy to our pleasures, our own pre-established codes of decision.

Readers of superior judgment may disapprove of the style in which many of these pieces are executed; it must be expected that many lines and phrases will not exactly suit their taste. It will perhaps appear to them, that wishing to avoid the prevalent fault of the day, the author has sometimes descended too low, and that many of his expressions are too familiar, and not of sufficient dignity. It is apprehended, that the more conversant the reader is with our elder writers, and with those in modern times who have been the most successful in painting manners and passions, the fewer complaints of this kind will he have to make.

An accurate taste in poetry, and in all the other arts, Sir Joshua Reynolds has observed, is an acquired talent, which can only be produced by severe thought, and a long continued intercourse with the best models of composition. This is mentioned not with so ridiculous

[1] Never reprinted by Wordsworth. The third sentence of the second paragraph and all of the fourth paragraph are repeated almost verbatim in the 1800 Preface.

443

a purpose as to prevent the most inexperienced reader from judging for himself; but merely to temper the rashness of decision, and to suggest that if poetry be a subject on which much time has not been bestowed, the judgment may be erroneous, and that in many cases it necessarily will be so.

The tale of Goody Blake and Harry Gill is founded on a well-authenticated fact which happened in Warwickshire. Of the other poems in the collection, it may be proper to say that they are either absolute inventions of the author, or facts which took place within his personal observation or that of his friends. The poem of the Thorn, as the reader will soon discover, is not supposed to be spoken in the author's own person: the character of the loquacious narrator will sufficiently shew itself in the course of the story. The Rime of the Ancyent Marinere was professedly written in imitation of the *style*, as well as of the spirit of the elder poets; but with a few exceptions, the Author believes that the language adopted in it has been equally intelligible for these three last centuries. The lines entitled Expostulation and Reply, and those which follow, arose out of conversation with a friend who was somewhat unreasonably attached to modern books of moral philosophy.

PREFACE TO THE SECOND EDITION
OF *LYRICAL BALLADS* (1800)[1]

THE first Volume of these Poems has already been submitted to general perusal. It was published, as an experiment, which, I hoped, might be of some use to ascertain, how far, by fitting to metrical arrangement a selection of the real language of men in a state of vivid sensation, that sort of pleasure and that quantity of pleasure may be imparted, which a Poet may rationally endeavour to impart.

I had formed no very inaccurate estimate of the probable effect of those Poems: I flattered myself that they who should be pleased with them would read them with more than common pleasure: and, on the other hand, I was well aware, that by those who should dislike them, they would be read with more than common dislike. The result has differed from my expectation in this only, that a greater number have been pleased than I ventured to hope I should please.

      ❖   ❖   ❖   ❖   ❖   ❖

Several of my Friends are anxious for the success of these Poems, from a belief, that, if the views with which they were composed were indeed realised, a class of Poetry would be produced, well adapted to interest mankind permanently, and not unimportant in the quality, and in the multiplicity of its moral relations: and on this account they have advised me to prefix a systematic defence of the theory upon which the Poems were written. But I was unwilling to undertake the task, knowing that on this occasion the Reader would look coldly upon my arguments, since I might be suspected of having been principally influenced by the selfish and foolish hope of *reasoning* him into an approbation of these particular Poems: and I was still more unwilling to undertake the task, because, adequately to display the opinions, and fully to enforce the arguments, would require a space wholly disproportionate to a preface. For, to treat the subject with the clearness and coherence of which it is susceptible, it would be necessary to give a full account of the present state of the public taste in this country, and to determine how far this taste is healthy or depraved; which, again, could not be determined, without pointing out

---

1 Written in September–October 1800; some substantial additions first appeared in 1802. For discussion of the main ideas and their sources see M. H. Abrams, *The Mirror and the Lamp* (1953), ch. V, and W. J. B. Owen, *Wordsworth's Preface to Lyrical Ballads* (*Anglista*, vol. IX, Copenhagen, 1957).

in what manner language and the human mind act and re-act on each other, and without retracing the revolutions, not of literature alone, but likewise of society itself. I have therefore altogether declined to enter regularly upon this defence; yet I am sensible, that there would be something like impropriety in abruptly obtruding upon the Public, without a few words of introduction, Poems so materially different from those upon which general approbation is at present bestowed.

It is supposed, that by the act of writing in verse an Author makes a formal engagement that he will gratify certain known habits of association; that he not only thus apprises the Reader that certain classes of ideas and expressions will be found in his book, but that others will be carefully excluded. This exponent or symbol held forth by metrical language must in different eras of literature have excited very different expectations: for example, in the age of Catullus, Terence, and Lucretius, and that of Statius or Claudian; and in our own country, in the age of Shakspeare and Beaumont and Fletcher, and that of Donne and Cowley, or Dryden, or Pope. I will not take upon me to determine the exact import of the promise which, by the act of writing in verse, an Author, in the present day makes to his reader: but it will undoubtedly appear to many persons that I have not fulfilled the terms of an engagement thus voluntarily contracted. They who have been accustomed to the gaudiness and inane phraseology of many modern writers, if they persist in reading this book to its conclusion, will, no doubt, frequently have to struggle with feelings of strangeness and awkwardness: they will look round for poetry, and will be induced to inquire by what species of courtesy these attempts can be permitted to assume that title. I hope therefore the reader will not censure me for attempting to state what I have proposed to myself to perform; and also (as far as the limits of a preface will permit) to explain some of the chief reasons which have determined me in the choice of my purpose: that at least he may be spared any unpleasant feeling of disappointment, and that I myself may be protected from one of the most dishonourable accusations which can be brought against an Author; namely, that of an indolence which prevents him from endeavouring to ascertain what is his duty, or, when his duty is ascertained, prevents him from performing it.

The principal object,[2] then, proposed in these Poems was to choose incidents and situations from common life, and to relate or describe them, throughout, as far as was possible in a selection of language really used by men, and, at the same time, to throw over them a certain colouring of imagination, whereby ordinary things should be

[2] Cf. Coleridge's explanation of "the two cardinal points of poetry" (*Biographia Literaria*, ch. XIV), quoted in the notes to *Peter Bell*.

presented to the mind in an unusual aspect; and, further, and above all, to make these incidents and situations interesting by tracing in them, truly though not ostentatiously, the primary laws of our nature: chiefly, as far as regards the manner in which we associate ideas in a state of excitement. Humble and rustic life was generally chosen, because, in that condition, the essential passions of the heart find a better soil in which they can attain their maturity, are less under restraint, and speak a plainer and more emphatic language; because in that condition of life our elementary feelings co-exist in a state of greater simplicity, and, consequently, may be more accurately contemplated, and more forcibly communicated; because the manners of rural life germinate from those elementary feelings, and, from the necessary character of rural occupations, are more easily comprehended, and are more durable; and, lastly, because in that condition the passions of men are incorporated with the beautiful and permanent forms of nature. The language, too, of these men has been adopted (purified indeed from what appear to be its real defects, from all lasting and rational causes of dislike or disgust) because such men hourly communicate with the best objects from which the best part of language is originally derived; and because, from their rank in society and the sameness and narrow circle of their intercourse, being less under the influence of social vanity, they convey their feelings and notions in simple and unelaborated expressions. Accordingly, such a language, arising out of repeated experience and regular feelings, is a more permanent, and a far more philosophical language, than that which is frequently substituted for it by Poets, who think that they are conferring honour upon themselves and their art, in proportion as they separate themselves from the sympathies of men, and indulge in arbitrary and capricious habits of expression, in order to furnish food for fickle tastes, and fickle appetites, of their own creation.[3]

I cannot, however, be insensible to the present outcry against the triviality and meanness, both of thought and language, which some of my contemporaries have occasionally introduced into their metrical compositions; and I acknowledge that this defect, where it exists, is more dishonourable to the Writer's own character than false refinement or arbitrary innovation, though I should contend at the same time, that it is far less pernicious in the sum of its consequences. From such verses the Poems in these volumes will be found distinguished at least by one mark of difference, that each of them has a worthy *purpose.* Not that I always began to write with a distinct purpose

---

3 "It is worth while here to observe, that the affecting parts of Chaucer are almost always expressed in language pure and universally intelligible even to this day" (Wordsworth's note).

formally conceived; but habits of meditation have, I trust, so prompted and regulated my feelings, that my descriptions of such objects as strongly excite those feelings, will be found to carry along with them a *purpose*. If this opinion be erroneous, I can have little right to the name of a Poet. For all good poetry is the spontaneous overflow of powerful feelings: and though this be true, Poems to which any value can be attached were never produced on any variety of subjects but by a man who, being possessed of more than usual organic sensibility, had also thought long and deeply. For our continued influxes of feeling are modified and directed by our thoughts, which are indeed the representatives of all our past feelings; and, as by contemplating the relation of these general representatives to each other, we discover what is really important to men, so, by the repetition and continuance of this act, our feelings will be connected with important subjects, till at length, if we be originally possessed of much sensibility, such habits of mind will be produced, that, by obeying blindly and mechanically the impulses of those habits, we shall describe objects, and utter sentiments, of such a nature, and in such connection with each other, that the understanding of the Reader must necessarily be in some degree enlightened, and his affections strengthened and purified.

It has been said that each of these poems has a purpose.[4] Another circumstance must be mentioned which distinguishes these Poems from the popular Poetry of the day; it is this, that the feeling therein developed gives importance to the action and situation, and not the action and situation to the feeling.

A sense of false modesty shall not prevent me from asserting, that the Reader's attention is pointed to this mark of distinction, far less for the sake of these particular Poems than from the general importance of the subject. The subject is indeed important! For the human

[4] Originally the text continued with a passage that reads, in part, "I have also informed my Reader what this purpose will be found principally to be: namely to illustrate the manner in which our feelings and ideas are associated in a state of excitement. But speaking in less general language, it is to follow the fluxes and refluxes of the mind when agitated by the great and simple affections of our nature. This object I have endeavoured in these short essays to attain by various means; by tracing the maternal passion through many of its more subtle windings, as in the poems of the IDIOT BOY and the MAD MOTHER ["Her Eyes Are Wild"]; . . . by shewing, as in the Stanzas entitled WE ARE SEVEN, the perplexity and obscurity which in childhood attend our notion of death, or rather our utter inability to admit that notion; or by displaying the strength of fraternal, or to speak more philosophically, of moral attachment when early associated with the great and beautiful objects of nature, as in THE BROTHERS; or, as in the Incident of SIMON LEE, by placing my Reader in the way of receiving from ordinary moral sensations another and more salutary impression than we are accustomed to receive from them . . ." (1800; slightly revised in 1802 and 1836; omitted in 1845).

mind is capable of being excited without the application of gross and violent stimulants; and he must have a very faint perception of its beauty and dignity who does not know this, and who does not further know, that one being is elevated above another, in proportion as he possesses this capability. It has therefore appeared to me, that to endeavour to produce or enlarge this capability is one of the best services in which, at any period, a Writer can be engaged; but this service, excellent at all times, is especially so at the present day. For a multitude of causes, unknown to former times, are now acting with a combined force to blunt the discriminating powers of the mind, and, unfitting it for all voluntary exertion, to reduce it to a state of almost savage torpor. The most effective of these causes are the great national events which are daily taking place, and the increasing accumulation of men in cities, where the uniformity of their occupations produces a craving for extraordinary incident, which the rapid communication of intelligence hourly gratifies. To this tendency of life and manners the literature and theatrical exhibitions of the country have conformed themselves. The invaluable works of our elder writers, I had almost said the works of Shakspeare and Milton, are driven into neglect by frantic novels, sickly and stupid German Tragedies, and deluges of idle and extravagant stories in verse. — When I think upon this degrading thirst after outrageous stimulation, I am almost ashamed to have spoken of the feeble endeavour made in these volumes to counteract it; and, reflecting upon the magnitude of the general evil, I should be oppressed with no dishonourable melancholy, had I not a deep impression of certain inherent and indestructible qualities of the human mind, and likewise of certain powers in the great and permanent objects that act upon it, which are equally inherent and indestructible; and were there not added to this impression a belief, that the time is approaching when the evil will be systematically opposed, by men of greater powers, and with far more distinguished success.

Having dwelt thus long on the subjects and aim of these Poems, I shall request the Reader's permission to apprise him of a few circumstances relating to their *style*, in order, among other reasons, that he may not censure me for not having performed what I never attempted. The Reader will find that personifications of abstract ideas rarely occur in these volumes; and are utterly rejected, as an ordinary device to elevate the style, and raise it above prose. My purpose was to imitate, and, as far as is possible, to adopt the very language of men; and assuredly such personifications do not make any natural or regular part of that language. They are, indeed, a figure of speech occasionally prompted by passion, and I have made use of them as such; but have endeavoured utterly to reject them as a mechanical device of style, or as a family language which Writers in metre seem to lay claim to by prescription. I have wished to keep the Reader in the company of flesh and blood, persuaded that by so doing I shall interest him. Others who pursue a different track will interest him likewise; I do not interfere with their claim, but wish to prefer a claim of my own. There will also be found in these volumes little of what is usually called poetic diction; as much pains has been taken to avoid it as is ordinarily taken to produce it; this has been done for the reason already alleged, to bring my language near to the language of men; and further, because the pleasure which I have proposed to myself to impart, is of a kind very different from that which is supposed by many persons to be the proper object of poetry. Without being culpably particular, I do not know how to give my Reader a more exact notion of the style in which it was my wish and intention to write, than by informing him that I have at all times endeavoured to look steadily at my subject; consequently, there is I hope in these Poems little falsehood of description, and my ideas are expressed in language fitted to their respective importance. Something must have been gained by this practice, as it is friendly to one property of all good poetry, namely, good sense: but it has necessarily cut me off from a large portion of phrases and figures of speech which from father to son have long been regarded as the common inheritance of Poets. I have also thought it expedient to restrict myself still further, having abstained from the use of many expressions, in themselves proper and beautiful, but which have been foolishly repeated by bad Poets, till such feelings of disgust are connected with them as it is scarcely possible by any art of association to overpower.

If in a poem there should be found a series of lines, or even a single line, in which the language, though naturally arranged, and according to the strict laws of metre, does not differ from that of prose, there is a numerous class of critics, who, when they stumble upon these prosaisms, as they call them, imagine that they have made a notable discovery, and exult over the Poet as over a man ignorant of his own profession. Now these men would establish a canon of criticism which the Reader will conclude he must utterly reject, if he wishes to be pleased with these volumes. And it would be a most easy task to prove to him, that not only the language of a large portion of every good poem, even of the most elevated character, must necessarily, except with reference to the metre, in no respect differ from that of good prose, but likewise that some of the most interesting parts of the best poems will be found to be strictly the language of prose when prose is well written. The truth of this assertion might be demonstrated by innumerable passages from almost all the poetical writings, even of Milton himself. To illustrate the subject in a general manner, I will here adduce a short composition of Gray, who was at the head of those who, by their reasonings, have attempted to widen the space of separation betwixt Prose and Metrical composition, and was more than any other man curiously elaborate in the structure of his own poetic diction.

> "In vain to me the smiling mornings shine,
> And reddening Phœbus lifts his golden fire:
> The birds in vain their amorous descant join,
> Or cheerful fields resume their green attire.
> These ears, alas! for other notes repine;
> *A different object do these eyes require;*
> *My lonely anguish melts no heart but mine;*
> *And in my breast the imperfect joys expire;*
> Yet morning smiles the busy race to cheer,
> And new-born pleasure brings to happier men;
> The fields to all their wonted tribute bear;
> To warm their little loves the birds complain.
> *I fruitless mourn to him that cannot hear,*
> *And weep the more because I weep in vain.*"[5]

It will easily be perceived, that the only part of this Sonnet which is of any value is the lines printed in Italics; it is equally obvious, that, except in the rhyme, and in the use of the single word "fruitless" for fruitlessly, which is so far a defect, the language of these lines does in no respect differ from that of prose.

By the foregoing quotation it has been shown that the language of Prose may yet be well adapted to Poetry; and it was previously asserted, that a large portion of the language of every good poem can in no respect differ from that of good Prose. We will go further. It may be safely affirmed, that there neither is, nor can be, any *essential* difference between the language of prose and metrical composition. We are fond of tracing the resemblance between Poetry and Painting, and, accordingly, we call them Sisters: but where shall we find bonds of connection sufficiently strict to typify the affinity betwixt metrical and prose composition? They both speak by and to the same organs; the bodies in which both of them are clothed may be said to be of the same substance, their affections are kindred, and almost identical, not necessarily differing even in degree; Poetry[6] sheds no tears "such as

5 Gray's "Sonnet on the Death of Richard West."

6 "I here use the word 'Poetry' (though against my own judgment) as opposed to the word Prose, and synonymous with metrical composition. But much confusion has been introduced into criticism by this contradistinction of Poetry and Prose, instead of the more philosophical one of Poetry and Matter of Fact, or Science. The only strict antithesis to Prose is Metre; nor is this, in truth, a *strict* antithesis, because lines and passages of metre so naturally occur in writing prose, that it would be scarcely possible to avoid them, even were it desirable" (Wordsworth's note).

Angels weep,"[7] but natural and human tears; she can boast of no celestial ichor that distinguishes her vital juices from those of prose; the same human blood circulates through the veins of them both.

If it be affirmed that rhyme and metrical arrangement of themselves constitute a distinction which overturns what has just been said on the strict affinity of metrical language with that of prose, and paves the way for other artificial distinctions which the mind voluntarily admits, I answer that[8] the language of such Poetry as is here recommended is, as far as is possible, a selection of the language really spoken by men; that this selection, wherever it is made with true taste and feeling, will of itself form a distinction far greater than would at first be imagined, and will entirely separate the composition from the vulgarity and meanness of ordinary life; and, if metre be superadded thereto, I believe that a dissimilitude will be produced altogether sufficient for the gratification of a rational mind. What other distinction would we have? Whence is it to come? And where is it to exist? Not, surely, where the Poet speaks through the mouths of his characters: it cannot be necessary here, either for elevation of style, or any of its supposed ornaments: for, if the Poet's subject be judiciously chosen, it will naturally, and upon fit occasion, lead him to passions the language of which, if selected truly and judiciously, must necessarily be dignified and variegated, and alive with metaphors and figures. I forbear to speak of an incongruity which would shock the intelligent Reader, should the Poet interweave any foreign splendour of his own with that which the passion naturally suggests: it is sufficient to say that such addition is unnecessary. And, surely, it is more probable that those passages, which with propriety abound with metaphors and figures, will have their due effect, if, upon other occasions where the passions are of a milder character, the style also be subdued and temperate.

But, as the pleasure which I hope to give by the Poems now presented to the Reader must depend entirely on just notions upon this subject, and, as it is in itself of high importance to our taste and moral feelings, I cannot content myself with these detached remarks. And if, in what I am about to say, it shall appear to some that my labour is unnecessary, and that I am like a man fighting a battle without enemies, such persons may be reminded, that, whatever be the language outwardly holden by men, a practical faith in the opinions which I am wishing to establish is almost unknown. If my conclusions are admitted, and carried as far as they must be carried if admitted at all,

---

[7] *Paradise Lost,* I.620.

[8] The rest of this paragraph, the next eight paragraphs, and most of the ninth were added in 1802 (see note 11).

our judgments concerning the works of the greatest Poets both ancient and modern will be far different from what they are at present, both when we praise, and when we censure: and our moral feelings influencing and influenced by these judgments will, I believe, be corrected and purified.

Taking up the subject, then, upon general grounds, let me ask, what is meant by the word Poet? What is a Poet? To whom does he address himself? And what language is to be expected from him? — He is a man speaking to men: a man, it is true, endowed with more lively sensibility, more enthusiasm and tenderness, who has a greater knowledge of human nature, and a more comprehensive soul, than are supposed to be common among mankind; a man pleased with his own passions and volitions, and who rejoices more than other men in the spirit of life that is in him; delighting to contemplate similar volitions and passions as manifested in the goings-on of the Universe, and habitually impelled to create them where he does not find them. To these qualities he has added a disposition to be affected more than other men by absent things as if they were present; an ability of conjuring up in himself passions, which are indeed far from being the same as those produced by real events, yet (especially in those parts of the general sympathy which are pleasing and delightful) do more nearly resemble the passions produced by real events, than anything which, from the motions of their own minds merely, other men are accustomed to feel in themselves: — whence, and from practice, he has acquired a greater readiness and power in expressing what he thinks and feels, and especially those thoughts and feelings which, by his own choice, or from the structure of his own mind, arise in him without immediate external excitement.

But whatever portion of this faculty we may suppose even the greatest Poet to possess, there cannot be a doubt that the language which it will suggest to him, must often, in liveliness and truth, fall short of that which is uttered by men in real life, under the actual pressure of those passions, certain shadows of which the Poet thus produces, or feels to be produced, in himself.

However exalted a notion we would wish to cherish of the character of a Poet, it is obvious, that while he describes and imitates passions, his employment is in some degree mechanical, compared with the freedom and power of real and substantial action and suffering. So that it will be the wish of the Poet to bring his feelings near to those of the persons whose feelings he describes, nay, for short spaces of time, perhaps, to let himself slip into an entire delusion, and even confound and identify his own feelings with theirs; modifying only the language which is thus suggested to him by a consideration that he describes for a particular purpose, that of giving pleasure. Here, then, he will apply the principle of selection which has been already insisted upon. He will depend upon this for removing what would otherwise be painful or disgusting in the passion; he will feel that there is no necessity to trick out or to elevate nature: and, the more industriously he applies this principle, the deeper will be his faith that no words, which *his* fancy or imagination can suggest, will be to be compared with those which are the emanations of reality and truth.

But it may be said by those who do not object to the general spirit of these remarks, that, as it is impossible for the Poet to produce upon all occasions language as exquisitely fitted for the passion as that which the real passion itself suggests, it is proper that he should consider himself as in the situation of a translator, who does not scruple to substitute excellencies of another kind for those which are unattainable by him; and endeavours occasionally to surpass his original, in order to make some amends for the general inferiority to which he feels that he must submit. But this would be to encourage idleness and unmanly despair. Further, it is the language of men who speak of what they do not understand; who talk of Poetry as of a matter of amusement and idle pleasure; who will converse with us as gravely about a *taste* for Poetry, as they express it, as if it were a thing as indifferent as a taste for rope-dancing, or Frontiniac or Sherry. Aristotle, I have been told, has said, that Poetry is the most philosophic of all writing:[9] it is so: its object is truth, not individual and local, but general, and operative; not standing upon external testimony, but carried alive into the heart by passion; truth which is its own testimony, which gives competence and confidence to the tribunal to which it appeals, and receives them from the same tribunal. Poetry is the image of man and nature. The obstacles which stand in the way of the fidelity of the Biographer and Historian, and of their consequent utility, are incalculably greater than those which are to be encountered by the Poet who comprehends the dignity of his art. The Poet writes under one restriction only, namely, the necessity of giving immediate pleasure to a human Being possessed of that information which may be expected from him, not as a lawyer, a physician, a mariner, an astronomer, or a natural philosopher, but as a Man. Except this one restriction, there is no object standing between the Poet and the image of things; between this, and the Biographer and Historian, there are a thousand.

Nor let this necessity of producing immediate pleasure be considered as a degradation of the Poet's art. It is far otherwise. It is an acknowledgment of the beauty of the universe, an acknowledgment

9 *Poetics*, IX.3.

the more sincere, because not formal, but indirect; it is a task light and easy to him who looks at the world in the spirit of love: further, it is a homage paid to the native and naked dignity of man, to the grand elementary principle of pleasure, by which he knows, and feels, and lives, and moves. We have no sympathy but what is propagated by pleasure: I would not be misunderstood; but wherever we sympathise with pain, it will be found that the sympathy is produced and carried on by subtle combinations with pleasure. We have no knowledge, that is, no general principles drawn from the contemplation of particular facts, but what has been built up by pleasure, and exists in us by pleasure alone. The Man of science, the Chemist and Mathematician, whatever difficulties and disgusts they may have had to struggle with, know and feel this. However painful may be the objects with which the Anatomist's knowledge is connected, he feels that his knowledge is pleasure; and where he has no pleasure he has no knowledge. What then does the Poet? He considers man and the objects that surround him as acting and re-acting upon each other, so as to produce an infinite complexity of pain and pleasure; he considers man in his own nature and in his ordinary life as contemplating this with a certain quantity of immediate knowledge, with certain convictions, intuitions, and deductions, which from habit acquire the quality of intuitions; he considers him as looking upon this complex scene of ideas and sensations, and finding every where objects that immediately excite in him sympathies which, from the necessities of his nature, are accompanied by an overbalance of enjoyment.

To this knowledge which all men carry about with them, and to these sympathies in which, without any other discipline than that of our daily life, we are fitted to take delight, the Poet principally directs his attention. He considers man and nature as essentially adapted to each other, and the mind of man as naturally the mirror of the fairest and most interesting properties of nature. And thus the Poet, prompted by this feeling of pleasure, which accompanies him through the whole course of his studies, converses with general nature, with affections akin to those, which, through labour and length of time, the Man of science has raised up in himself, by conversing with those particular parts of nature which are the objects of his studies. The knowledge both of the Poet and the Man of science is pleasure; but the knowledge of the one cleaves to us as a necessary part of our existence, our natural and unalienable inheritance; the other is a personal and individual acquisition, slow to come to us, and by no habitual and direct sympathy connecting us with our fellow-beings. The Man of science seeks truth as a remote and unknown benefactor; he cherishes and loves it in his solitude: the Poet, singing a song in which all human beings join with him, rejoices in the presence of truth as our visible friend and hourly companion. Poetry is the breath and finer spirit of all knowledge; it is the impassioned expression which is in the countenance of all Science. Emphatically may it be said of the Poet, as Shakspeare hath said of man, "that he looks before and after."[10] He is the rock of defence for human nature; an upholder and preserver, carrying everywhere with him relationship and love. In spite of difference of soil and climate, of language and manners, of laws and customs: in spite of things silently gone out of mind, and things violently destroyed; the Poet binds together by passion and knowledge the vast empire of human society, as it is spread over the whole earth, and over all time. The objects of the Poet's thoughts are every where; though the eyes and senses of man are, it is true, his favourite guides, yet he will follow wheresoever he can find an atmosphere of sensation in which to move his wings. Poetry is the first and last of all knowledge — it is as immortal as the heart of man. If the labours of Men of science should ever create any material revolution, direct or indirect, in our condition, and in the impressions which we habitually receive, the Poet will sleep then no more than at present; he will be ready to follow the steps of the Man of science, not only in those general indirect effects, but he will be at his side, carrying sensation into the midst of the objects of the science itself. The remotest discoveries of the Chemist, the Botanist, or Mineralogist, will be as proper objects of the Poet's art as any upon which it can be employed, if the time should ever come when these things shall be familiar to us, and the relations under which they are contemplated by the followers of these respective sciences shall be manifestly and palpably material to us as enjoying and suffering beings. If the time should ever come when what is now called science, thus familiarised to men, shall be ready to put on, as it were, a form of flesh and blood, the Poet will lend his divine spirit to aid the transfiguration, and will welcome the Being thus produced, as a dear and genuine inmate of the household of man. — It is not, then, to be supposed that any one, who holds that sublime notion of Poetry which I have attempted to convey, will break in upon the sanctity and truth of his pictures by transitory and accidental ornaments, and endeavour to excite admiration of himself by arts, the necessity of which must manifestly depend upon the assumed meanness of his subject.

What has been thus far said applies to Poetry in general; but especially to those parts of composition where the Poet speaks through the mouths of his characters; and upon this point it appears to authorise the conclusion that there are few persons of good sense, who would not allow that the dramatic parts of composition are defective,

10 *Hamlet,* IV.iv.37.

in proportion as they deviate from the real language of nature, and are coloured by a diction of the Poet's own, either peculiar to him as an individual Poet or belonging simply to Poets in general; to a body of men who, from the circumstance of their compositions being in metre, it is expected will employ a particular language.

It is not, then, in the dramatic parts of composition that we look for this distinction of language; but still it may be proper and necessary where the Poet speaks to us in his own person and character. To this I answer by referring the Reader to the description before given of a Poet. Among the qualities there enumerated as principally conducing to form a Poet, is implied nothing differing in kind from other men, but only in degree. The sum of what was said is, that the Poet is chiefly distinguished from other men by a greater promptness to think and feel without immediate external excitement, and a greater power in expressing such thoughts and feelings as are produced in him in that manner. But these passions and thoughts and feelings are the general passions and thoughts and feelings of men. And with what are they connected? Undoubtedly with our moral sentiments and animal sensations, and with the causes which excite these; with the operations of the elements, and the appearances of the visible universe; with storm and sunshine, with the revolutions of the seasons, with cold and heat, with loss of friends and kindred, with injuries and resentments, gratitude and hope, with fear and sorrow. These, and the like, are the sensations and objects which the Poet describes, as they are the sensations of other men, and the objects which interest them. The Poet thinks and feels in the spirit of human passions. How, then, can his language differ in any material degree from that of all other men who feel vividly and see clearly? It might be *proved* that it is impossible. But supposing that this were not the case, the Poet might then be allowed to use a peculiar language when expressing his feelings for his own gratification, or that of men like himself. But Poets do not write for Poets alone, but for men. Unless therefore we are advocates for that admiration which subsists upon ignorance, and that pleasure which arises from hearing what we do not understand, the Poet must descend from this supposed height; and, in order to excite rational sympathy, he must express himself as other men express themselves. To this it may be added, that while he is only selecting from the real language of men, or, which amounts to the same thing, composing accurately in the spirit of such selection, he is treading upon safe ground, and we know what we are to expect from him. Our feelings are the same with respect to metre; for, as it may be proper to remind the Reader,[11] the distinction of metre is regular and uniform, and not, like that which is produced by what is usually called POETIC

11 Here ends the addition of 1802 (see note 8).

DICTION, arbitrary, and subject to infinite caprices upon which no calculation whatever can be made. In the one case, the Reader is utterly at the mercy of the Poet, respecting what imagery or diction he may choose to connect with the passion; whereas, in the other, the metre obeys certain laws, to which the Poet and Reader both willingly submit because they are certain, and because no interference is made by them with the passion, but such as the concurring testimony of ages has shown to heighten and improve the pleasure which co-exists with it.

It will now be proper to answer an obvious question, namely, Why, professing these opinions, have I written in verse? To this, in addition to such answer as is included in what has been already said, I reply, in the first place, Because, however I may have restricted myself, there is still left open to me what confessedly constitutes the most valuable object of all writing, whether in prose or verse; the great and universal passions of men, the most general and interesting of their occupations, and the entire world of nature before me — to supply endless combinations of forms and imagery. Now, supposing for a moment that whatever is interesting in these objects may be as vividly described in prose, why should I be condemned for attempting to superadd to such description, the charm which, by the consent of all nations, is acknowledged to exist in metrical language? To this, by such as are yet unconvinced, it may be answered that a very small part of the pleasure given by Poetry depends upon the metre, and that it is injudicious to write in metre, unless it be accompanied with the other artificial distinctions of style with which metre is usually accompanied, and that, by such deviation, more will be lost from the shock which will thereby be given to the Reader's associations than will be counterbalanced by any pleasure which he can derive from the general power of numbers. In answer to those who still contend for the necessity of accompanying metre with certain appropriate colours of style in order to the accomplishment of its appropriate end, and who also, in my opinion, greatly under-rate the power of metre in itself, it might, perhaps, as far as relates to these Volumes, have been almost sufficient to observe, that poems are extant, written upon more humble subjects, and in a still more naked and simple style, which have continued to give pleasure from generation to generation. Now, if nakedness and simplicity be a defect, the fact here mentioned affords a strong presumption that poems somewhat less naked and simple are capable of affording pleasure at the present day; and, what I wished *chiefly* to attempt, at present, was to justify myself for having written under the impression of this belief.

But various causes might be pointed out why, when the style is manly, and the subject of some importance, words metrically arranged will long continue to impart such a pleasure to mankind as he who proves the extent of that pleasure will be desirous to impart. The end of Poetry is to produce excitement in co-existence with an overbalance of pleasure; but, by the supposition, excitement is an unusual and irregular state of the mind; ideas and feelings do not, in that state, succeed each other in accustomed order. If the words, however, by which this excitement is produced be in themselves powerful, or the images and feelings have an undue proportion of pain connected with them, there is some danger that the excitement may be carried beyond its proper bounds. Now the co-presence of something regular, something to which the mind has been accustomed in various moods and in a less excited state, cannot but have great efficacy in tempering and restraining the passion by an intertexture of ordinary feeling, and of feeling not strictly and necessarily connected with the passion. This is unquestionably true; and hence, though the opinion will at first appear paradoxical, from the tendency of metre to divest language, in a certain degree, of its reality, and thus to throw a sort of half-consciousness of unsubstantial existence over the whole composition, there can be little doubt but that more pathetic situations and sentiments, that is, those which have a greater proportion of pain connected with them, may be endured in metrical composition, especially in rhyme, than in prose. The metre of the old ballads is very artless; yet they contain many passages which would illustrate this opinion; and, I hope, if the following Poems be attentively perused, similar instances will be found in them. This opinion may be further illustrated by appealing to the Reader's own experience of the reluctance with which he comes to the re-perusal of the distressful parts of Clarissa Harlowe, or the Gamester;[12] while Shakspeare's writings, in the most pathetic scenes, never act upon us, as pathetic, beyond the bounds of pleasure — an effect which, in a much greater degree than might at first be imagined, is to be ascribed to small, but continual and regular impulses of pleasurable surprise from the metrical arrangement. — On the other hand (what it must be allowed will much more frequently happen) if the Poet's words should be incommensurate with the passion, and inadequate to raise the Reader to a height of desirable excitement, then, (unless the Poet's choice of his metre has been grossly injudicious) in the feelings of pleasure which the Reader has been accustomed to connect with metre in general, and in the feeling, whether cheerful or melancholy, which he has been accustomed to connect with that particular movement of metre, there will

12 Richardson's novel (1747–48) and a domestic tragedy by Edward Moore (1753).

be found something which will greatly contribute to impart passion to the words, and to effect the complex end which the Poet proposes to himself.

If I had undertaken a SYSTEMATIC defence of the theory here maintained, it would have been my duty to develope the various causes upon which the pleasure received from metrical language depends. Among the chief of these causes is to be reckoned a principle which must be well known to those who have made any of the Arts the object of accurate reflection; namely, the pleasure which the mind derives from the perception of similitude in dissimilitude. This principle is the great spring of the activity of our minds, and their chief feeder. From this principle the direction of the sexual appetite, and all the passions connected with it, take their origin: it is the life of our ordinary conversation; and upon the accuracy with which similitude in dissimilitude, and dissimilitude in similitude are perceived, depend our taste and our moral feelings. It would not be a useless employment to apply this principle to the consideration of metre, and to show that metre is hence enabled to afford much pleasure, and to point out in what manner that pleasure is produced. But my limits will not permit me to enter upon this subject, and I must content myself with a general summary.

I have said that poetry is the spontaneous overflow of powerful feelings: it takes its origin from emotion recollected in tranquillity: the emotion is contemplated till, by a species of re-action, the tranquillity gradually disappears, and an emotion, kindred to that which was before the subject of contemplation, is gradually produced, and does itself actually exist in the mind. In this mood successful composition generally begins, and in a mood similar to this it is carried on; but the emotion, of whatever kind, and in whatever degree, from various causes, is qualified by various pleasures, so that in describing any passions whatsoever, which are voluntarily described, the mind will, upon the whole, be in a state of enjoyment. If Nature be thus cautious to preserve in a state of enjoyment a being so employed, the Poet ought to profit by the lesson held forth to him, and ought especially to take care, that, whatever passions he communicates to his Reader, those passions, if his Reader's mind be sound and vigorous, should always be accompanied with an overbalance of pleasure. Now the music of harmonious metrical language, the sense of difficulty overcome, and the blind association of pleasure which has been previously received from works of rhyme or metre of the same or similar construction, an indistinct perception perpetually renewed of language closely resembling that of real life, and yet, in the circumstance of metre, differing from it so widely — all these imperceptibly make up a complex feeling of delight, which is of the most important use in tempering the painful feeling always found intermingled with powerful descriptions of the deeper passions. This effect is always produced in pathetic and impassioned poetry; while, in lighter compositions, the ease and gracefulness with which the Poet manages his numbers are themselves confessedly a principal source of the gratification of the Reader. All that it is *necessary* to say, however, upon this subject, may be effected by affirming, what few persons will deny, that, of two descriptions, either of passions, manners, or characters, each of them equally well executed, the one in prose and the other in verse, the verse will be read a hundred times where the prose is read once.[13]

Having thus explained a few of my reasons for writing in verse, and why I have chosen subjects from common life, and endeavoured to bring my language near to the real language of men, if I have been too minute in pleading my own cause, I have at the same time been treating a subject of general interest; and for this reason a few words shall be added with reference solely to these particular poems, and to some defects which will probably be found in them. I am sensible that my associations must have sometimes been particular instead of general, and that, consequently, giving to things a false importance, I may have sometimes written upon unworthy subjects; but I am less apprehensive on this account, than that my language may frequently have suffered from those arbitrary connections of feelings and ideas with particular words and phrases, from which no man can altogether protect himself. Hence I have no doubt, that, in some instances, feelings, even of the ludicrous, may be given to my Readers by expressions which appeared to me tender and pathetic. Such faulty expressions, were I convinced they were faulty at present, and that they must necessarily continue to be so, I would willingly take all reasonable pains to correct. But it is dangerous to make these alterations on the simple authority of a few individuals, or even of certain classes of men; for where the understanding of an Author is not convinced, or his feelings altered, this cannot be done without great injury to himself: for his own feelings

---

13 Originally (1800–36) the paragraph continued, "We see that Pope by the power of verse alone, has continued to render the plainest common sense interesting, and even frequently to invest it with the appearance of passion. In consequence of these convictions I related in metre the Tale of Goody Blake and Harry Gill, which is one of the rudest of this collection. I wished to draw attention to the truth that the power of the human imagination is sufficient to produce such changes even in our physical nature as might almost appear miraculous. The truth is an important one; the fact (for it is a *fact*) is a valuable illustration of it. And I have the satisfaction of knowing that it has been communicated to many hundreds of people who would never have heard of it, had it not been narrated as a Ballad, and in a more impressive metre than is usual in Ballads."

are his stay and support; and, if he set them aside in one instance, he may be induced to repeat this act till his mind shall lose all confidence in itself, and become utterly debilitated. To this it may be added, that the critic ought never to forget that he is himself exposed to the same errors as the Poet, and, perhaps, in a much greater degree: for there can be no presumption in saying of most readers, that it is not probable they will be so well acquainted with the various stages of meaning through which words have passed, or with the fickleness or stability of the relations of particular ideas to each other; and, above all, since they are so much less interested in the subject, they may decide lightly and carelessly.

Long as the Reader has been detained, I hope he will permit me to caution him against a mode of false criticism which has been applied to Poetry, in which the language closely resembles that of life and nature. Such verses have been triumphed over in parodies, of which Dr. Johnson's stanza is a fair specimen: —

> "I put my hat upon my head
> And walked into the Strand,
> And there I met another man
> Whose hat was in his hand."[14]

Immediately under these lines let us place one of the most justly-admired stanzas of the *"Babes in the Wood."*

> "These pretty Babes with hand in hand
> Went wandering up and down;
> But never more they saw the Man
> Approaching from the Town."

In both these stanzas the words, and the order of the words, in no respect differ from the most unimpassioned conversation. There are words in both, for example, "the Strand," and "the Town," connected with none but the most familiar ideas; yet the one stanza we admit as admirable, and the other as a fair example of the superlatively contemptible. Whence arises this difference? Not from the metre, not from the language, not from the order of the words; but the *matter* expressed in Dr. Johnson's stanza is contemptible. The proper method of treating trivial and simple verses, to which Dr. Johnson's stanza would be a fair parallelism, is not to say, this is a bad kind of poetry, or, this is not poetry; but, this wants sense; it is neither interesting in itself, nor can *lead* to any thing interesting; the images neither originate in that sane state of feeling which arises out of thought, nor can

[14] Johnson's stanza parodies Thomas Percy's *The Hermit of Warkworth* (1771).

excite thought or feeling in the Reader. This is the only sensible manner of dealing with such verses. Why trouble yourself about the species till you have previously decided upon the genus? Why take pains to prove that an ape is not a Newton, when it is self-evident that he is not a man?

One request I must make of my reader, which is, that in judging these Poems he would decide by his own feelings genuinely, and not by reflection upon what will probably be the judgment of others. How common is it to hear a person say, I myself do not object to this style of composition, or this or that expression, but, to such and such classes of people it will appear mean or ludicrous! This mode of criticism, so destructive of all sound unadulterated judgment, is almost universal: let the Reader then abide, independently, by his own feelings, and, if he finds himself affected, let him not suffer such conjectures to interfere with his pleasure.

If an Author, by any single composition, has impressed us with respect for his talents, it is useful to consider this as affording a presumption, that on other occasions where we have been displeased, he, nevertheless, may not have written ill or absurdly; and further, to give him so much credit for this one composition as may induce us to review what has displeased us, with more care than we should otherwise have bestowed upon it. This is not only an act of justice, but, in our decisions upon poetry especially, may conduce, in a high degree, to the improvement of our own taste; for an *accurate* taste in poetry, and in all the other arts, as Sir Joshua Reynolds has observed,[15] is an *acquired* talent, which can only be produced by thought and a long-continued intercourse with the best models of composition. This is mentioned, not with so ridiculous a purpose as to prevent the most inexperienced Reader from judging for himself, (I have already said that I wish him to judge for himself;) but merely to temper the rashness of decision, and to suggest, that, if Poetry be a subject on which much time has not been bestowed, the judgment may be erroneous; and that, in many cases, it necessarily will be so.

Nothing would, I know, have so effectually contributed to further the end which I have in view, as to have shown of what kind the pleasure is, and how that pleasure is produced, which is confessedly produced by metrical composition essentially different from that which I have here endeavoured to recommend: for the Reader will say that he has been pleased by such composition; and what more can be done for him? The power of any art is limited; and he will suspect, that, if it be proposed to furnish him with new friends, that can be only upon

15 In his presidential *Discourses* (1769–90) delivered to students of the Royal Academy, especially Discourses VI and VII.

condition of his abandoning his old friends. Besides, as I have said, the Reader is himself conscious of the pleasure which he has received from such composition, composition to which he has peculiarly attached the endearing name of Poetry; and all men feel an habitual gratitude, and something of an honourable bigotry, for the objects which have long continued to please them: we not only wish to be pleased, but to be pleased in that particular way in which we have been accustomed to be pleased. There is in these feelings enough to resist a host of arguments; and I should be the less able to combat them successfully, as I am willing to allow, that, in order entirely to enjoy the Poetry which I am recommending, it would be necessary to give up much of what is ordinarily enjoyed. But, would my limits have permitted me to point out how this pleasure is produced, many obstacles might have been removed, and the Reader assisted in perceiving that the powers of language are not so limited as he may suppose; and that it is possible for poetry to give other enjoyments, of a purer, more lasting, and more exquisite nature. This part of the subject has not been altogether neglected, but it has not been so much my present aim to prove, that the interest excited by some other kinds of poetry is less vivid, and less worthy of the nobler powers of the mind, as to offer reasons for presuming, that if my purpose were fulfilled, a species of poetry would be produced, which is genuine poetry; in its nature well adapted to interest mankind permanently, and likewise important in the multiplicity and quality of its moral relations.

From what has been said, and from a perusal of the Poems, the Reader will be able clearly to perceive the object which I had in view: he will determine how far it has been attained; and, what is a much more important question, whether it be worth attaining: and upon the decision of these two questions will rest my claim to the approbation of the Public.

APPENDIX TO THE PREFACE (1802)

See pages 457–58 — "by what is usually called POETIC DICTION."

PERHAPS, as I have no right to expect that attentive perusal, without which, confined, as I have been, to the narrow limits of a preface, my meaning cannot be thoroughly understood, I am anxious to give an exact notion of the sense in which the phrase poetic diction has been used; and for this purpose, a few words shall here be added, concerning the origin and characteristics of the phraseology, which I have condemned under that name.

The earliest poets of all nations generally wrote from passion excited by real events; they wrote naturally, and as men: feeling powerfully as they did, their language was daring, and figurative. In succeeding times, Poets, and Men ambitious of the fame of Poets, perceiving the influence of such language, and desirous of producing the same effect without being animated by the same passion, set themselves to a mechanical adoption of these figures of speech, and made use of them, sometimes with propriety, but much more frequently applied them to feelings and thoughts with which they had no natural connection whatsoever. A language was thus insensibly produced, differing materially from the real language of men in *any situation*. The Reader or Hearer of this distorted language found himself in a perturbed and unusual state of mind: when affected by the genuine language of passion he had been in a perturbed and unusual state of mind also: in both cases he was willing that his common judgment and understanding should be laid asleep, and he had no instinctive and infallible perception of the true to make him reject the false; the one served as a passport for the other. The emotion was in both cases delightful, and no wonder if he confounded the one with the other, and believed them both to be produced by the same, or similar causes. Besides, the Poet spake to him in the character of a man to be looked up to, a man of genius and authority. Thus, and from a variety of other causes, this distorted language was received with admiration; and Poets, it is probable, who had before contented themselves for the most part with misapplying only expressions which at first had been dictated by real passion, carried the abuse still further, and introduced phrases composed apparently in the spirit of the original figurative language of passion, yet altogether of their own invention, and characterised by various degrees of wanton deviation from good sense and nature.

It is indeed true, that the language of the earliest Poets was felt to differ materially from ordinary language, because it was the language of extraordinary occasions; but it was really spoken by men, language which the Poet himself had uttered when he had been affected by the events which he described, or which he had heard uttered by those around him. To this language it is probable that metre of some sort or other was early superadded. This separated the genuine language of Poetry still further from common life, so that whoever read or heard the poems of these earliest Poets felt himself moved in a way in which he had not been accustomed to be moved in real life, and by causes manifestly different from those which acted upon him in real life. This was the great temptation to all the corruptions which have followed: under the protection of this feeling succeeding Poets constructed a phraseology which had one thing, it is true, in common with the genuine language of poetry, namely, that it was not heard in ordinary conversation; that it was unusual. But the first Poets, as I have said, spake a language which, though unusual, was still the language of men. This circumstance, however, was disregarded by their successors; they found that they could please by easier means: they became proud of modes of expression which they themselves had invented, and which were uttered only by themselves. In process of time metre became a symbol or promise of this unusual language, and whoever took upon him to write in metre, according as he possessed more or less of true poetic genius, introduced less or more of this adulterated phraseology into his compositions, and the true and the false were inseparably interwoven until, the taste of men becoming gradually perverted, this language was received as a natural language: and at length, by the influence of books upon men, did to a certain degree really become so. Abuses of this kind were imported from one nation to another, and with the progress of refinement this diction became daily more and more corrupt, thrusting out of sight the plain humanities of nature by a motley masquerade of tricks, quaintnesses, hieroglyphics, and enigmas.

It would not be uninteresting to point out the causes of the pleasure given by this extravagant and absurd diction. It depends upon a great variety of causes, but upon none, perhaps, more than its influence in impressing a notion of the peculiarity and exaltation of the Poet's character, and in flattering the Reader's self-love by bringing him nearer to a sympathy with that character; an effect which is accomplished by unsettling ordinary habits of thinking, and thus assisting the Reader to approach to that perturbed and dizzy state of mind in which if he does not find himself, he imagines that he is *balked* of a peculiar enjoyment which poetry can and ought to bestow.

The sonnet quoted from Gray, in the Preface, except the lines printed in Italics, consists of little else but this diction, though not of the worst kind; and indeed, if one may be permitted to say so, it is far too common in the best writers both ancient and modern. Perhaps in no way, by positive example, could more easily be given a notion of what I mean by the phrase *poetic diction* than by referring to a comparison between the metrical paraphrases which we have of passages in the Old and New Testament, and those passages as they exist in our common Translation. See Pope's "Messiah" throughout; Prior's "Did sweeter sounds adorn my flowing tongue," &c. &c. "Though I speak with the tongues of men and of angels," &c. &c. 1st Corinthians, chap. xiii. By way of immediate example, take the following of Dr. Johnson:[1]

> "Turn on the prudent Ant thy heedless eyes,
> Observe her labours, Sluggard, and be wise;
> No stern command, no monitory voice,
> Prescribes her duties, or directs her choice;
> Yet, timely provident, she hastes away
> To snatch the blessings of a plenteous day;
> When fruitful Summer loads the teeming plain,
> She crops the harvest, and she stores the grain.
> How long shall sloth usurp thy useless hours,
> Unnerve thy vigour, and enchain thy powers?
> While artful shades thy downy couch enclose,
> And soft solicitation courts repose,
> Amidst the drowsy charms of dull delight,
> Year chases year with unremitted flight,
> Till Want now following, fraudulent and slow,
> Shall spring to seize thee, like an ambush'd foe."

From this hubbub of words pass to the original. "Go to the Ant, thou Sluggard, consider her ways, and be wise: which having no guide, overseer, or ruler, provideth her meat in the summer, and gathereth her food in the harvest. How long wilt thou sleep, O Sluggard? when wilt thou arise out of thy sleep? Yet a little sleep, a little slumber, a little folding of the hands to sleep. So shall thy poverty come as one that travelleth, and thy want as an armed man." Proverbs, chap. vi.

One more quotation, and I have done. It is from Cowper's *Verses supposed to be written by Alexander Selkirk:* —

[1] Pope's "Messiah" combines paraphrase of several passages of Isaiah with imitation of Virgil's fourth eclogue; Prior's "Charity" is a paraphrase of I Corinthians 13, and Johnson's "The Ant" a paraphrase of Proverbs 6:6–11.

"Religion! what treasure untold
Resides in that heavenly word!
More precious than silver and gold,
Or all that this earth can afford.
But the sound of the church-going bell
These valleys and rocks never heard,
Ne'er sighed at the sound of a knell,
Or smiled when a sabbath appeared.

"Ye winds, that have made me your sport
Convey to this desolate shore
Some cordial endearing report
Of a land I must visit no more.
My Friends, do they now and then send
A wish or a thought after me?
O tell me I yet have a friend,
Though a friend I am never to see."

This passage is quoted as an instance of three different styles of composition. The first four lines are poorly expressed; some Critics would call the language prosaic; the fact is, it would be bad prose, so bad, that it is scarcely worse in metre. The epithet "church-going" applied to a bell, and that by so chaste a writer as Cowper, is an instance of the strange abuses which Poets have introduced into their language, till they and their Readers take them as matters of course, if they do not single them out expressly as objects of admiration. The two lines "Ne'er sighed at the sound," &c., are, in my opinion, an instance of the language of passion wrested from its proper use, and, from the mere circumstance of the composition being in metre, applied upon an occasion that does not justify such violent expressions; and I should condemn the passage, though perhaps few Readers will agree with me, as vicious poetic diction. The last stanza is throughout admirably expressed: it would be equally good whether in prose or verse, except that the Reader has an exquisite pleasure in seeing such natural language so naturally connected with metre. The beauty of this stanza tempts me to conclude with a principle which ought never to be lost sight of, and which has been my chief guide in all I have said, — namely, that in works *of imagination and sentiment,* for of these only have I been treating, in proportion as ideas and feelings are valuable, whether the composition be in prose or in verse, they require and exact one and the same language. Metre is but adventitious to composition, and the phraseology for which that passport is necessary, even where it may be graceful at all, will be little valued by the judicious.

PREFACE TO *THE EXCURSION* (1814)

THE Title-page announces that this is only a portion of a poem;[1] and the Reader must be here apprised that it belongs to the second part of a long and laborious Work, which is to consist of three parts. — The Author will candidly acknowledge that, if the first of these had been completed, and in such a manner as to satisfy his own mind, he should have preferred the natural order of publication, and have given that to the world first; but, as the second division of the Work was designed to refer more to passing events, and to an existing state of things, than the others were meant to do, more continuous exertion was naturally bestowed upon it, and greater progress made here than in the rest of the poem; and as this part does not depend upon the preceding, to a degree which will materially injure its own peculiar interest, the Author, complying with the earnest entreaties of some valued Friends, presents the following pages to the Public.

It may be proper to state whence the poem, of which The Excursion is a part, derives its Title of THE RECLUSE. — Several years ago, when the Author retired to his native mountains, with the hope of being enabled to construct a literary Work that might live, it was a reasonable thing that he should take a review of his own mind, and examine how far Nature and Education had qualified him for such employment. As subsidiary to this preparation, he undertook to record, in verse, the origin and progress of his own powers, as far as he was acquainted with them. That Work, addressed to a dear Friend,[2] most distinguished for his knowledge and genius, and to whom the Author's Intellect is deeply indebted, has been long finished; and the result of the investigation which gave rise to it was a determination to compose a philosophical poem, containing views of Man, Nature, and Society; and to be entitled, The Recluse; as having for its principal subject the sensations and opinions of a poet living in retirement. — The preparatory poem is biographical, and conducts the history of the Author's mind to the point when he was emboldened to hope that his faculties were sufficiently matured for entering upon the arduous labour which he had proposed to himself; and the two Works have the same kind of relation to each other, if he may so express himself, as the ante-chapel has to the body of a gothic church. Continuing this allusion, he may

---

[1] The full title in 1814 was *The Excursion, Being a Portion of The Recluse, A Poem.* See the notes to the selection from "The Recluse."

[2] *The Prelude,* addressed to Coleridge.

be permitted to add, that his minor Pieces, which have been long before the Public, when they shall be properly arranged, will be found by the attentive Reader to have such connection with the main Work as may give them claim to be likened to the little cells, oratories, and sepulchral recesses, ordinarily included in those edifices.

The Author would not have deemed himself justified in saying, upon this occasion, so much of performances either unfinished, or unpublished, if he had not thought that the labour bestowed by him upon what he has heretofore and now laid before the Public, entitled him to candid attention for such a statement as he thinks necessary to throw light upon his endeavours to please and, he would hope, to benefit his countrymen. — Nothing further need be added, than that the first and third parts of The Recluse will consist chiefly of meditations in the Author's own person; and that in the intermediate part (The Excursion) the intervention of characters speaking is employed, and something of a dramatic form adopted.

It is not the Author's intention formally to announce a system: it was more animating to him to proceed in a different course; and if he shall succeed in conveying to the mind clear thoughts, lively images, and strong feelings, the Reader will have no difficulty in extracting the system for himself. And in the meantime the following passage, taken from the conclusion of the first book of The Recluse, may be acceptable as a kind of *Prospectus* of the design and scope of the whole Poem.[3]

[3] Here Wordsworth quotes the lines given above (pp. 45–47) from "The Recluse."

From ESSAY, SUPPLEMENTARY TO
THE PREFACE (1815)[1]

WITH the young of both sexes, Poetry is, like love, a passion; but, for much the greater part of those who have been proud of its power over their minds, a necessity soon arises of breaking the pleasing bondage; or it relaxes of itself; — the thoughts being occupied in domestic cares, or the time engrossed by business. Poetry then becomes only an occasional recreation; while to those whose existence passes away in a course of fashionable pleasure, it is a species of luxurious amusement. In middle and declining age, a scattered number of serious persons resort to poetry, as to religion, for a protection against the pressure of trivial employments, and as a consolation for the afflictions of life. And, lastly, there are many, who, having been enamoured of this art in their youth, have found leisure, after youth was spent, to cultivate general literature; in which poetry has continued to be comprehended *as a study.*

Into the above classes the Readers of poetry may be divided; Critics abound in them all; but from the last only can opinions be collected of absolute value, and worthy to be depended upon, as prophetic of the destiny of a new work. The young, who in nothing can escape delusion, are especially subject to it in their intercourse with Poetry. The cause, not so obvious as the fact is unquestionable, is the same as that from which erroneous judgments in this art, in the minds of men of all ages, chiefly proceed; but upon Youth it operates with peculiar force. The appropriate business of poetry, (which, nevertheless, if genuine, is as permanent as pure science,) her appropriate employment, her privilege and her *duty,* is to treat of things not as they *are,* but as they *appear;* not as they exist in themselves, but as they *seem* to exist to the *senses,* and to the *passions.* What a world of delusion does this acknowledged obligation prepare for the inexperienced! what temptations to go astray are here held forth for them whose thoughts have been little disciplined by the understanding, and whose feelings revolt from the sway of reason! — When a juvenile Reader is in the height of his rapture with some vicious passage, should experience throw in doubts, or common-sense suggest suspicions, a

[1] Originally the Essay was "supplementary to" the Preface of 1815 (which follows in the present volume); beginning with the edition of 1836-37, however, Wordsworth connected it instead with the Preface to *Lyrical Ballads.* Actually it supplements both prefaces.

471

lurking consciousness that the realities of the Muse are but shows, and that her liveliest excitements are raised by transient shocks of conflicting feeling and successive assemblages of contradictory thoughts — is ever at hand to justify extravagance, and to sanction absurdity. But, it may be asked, as these illusions are unavoidable, and, no doubt, eminently useful to the mind as a process, what good can be gained by making observations, the tendency of which is to diminish the confidence of youth in its feelings, and thus to abridge its innocent and even profitable pleasures? The reproach implied in the question could not be warded off, if Youth were incapable of being delighted with what is truly excellent; or, if these errors always terminated of themselves in due season. But, with the majority, though their force be abated, they continue through life. Moreover, the fire of youth is too vivacious an element to be extinguished or damped by a philosophical remark; and, while there is no danger that what has been said will be injurious or painful to the ardent and the confident, it may prove beneficial to those who, being enthusiastic, are, at the same time, modest and ingenuous. The intimation may unite with their own misgivings to regulate their sensibility, and to bring in, sooner than it would otherwise have arrived, a more discreet and sound judgment.

If it should excite wonder that men of ability, in later life, whose understandings have been rendered acute by practice in affairs, should be so easily and so far imposed upon when they happen to take up a new work in verse, this appears to be the cause; — that, having discontinued their attention to poetry, whatever progress may have been made in other departments of knowledge, they have not, as to this art, advanced in true discernment beyond the age of youth. If, then, a new poem fall in their way, whose attractions are of that kind which would have enraptured them during the heat of youth, the judgment not being improved to a degree that they shall be disgusted, they are dazzled; and prize and cherish the faults for having had power to make the present time vanish before them, and to throw the mind back, as by enchantment, into the happiest season of life. As they read, powers seem to be revived, passions are regenerated, and pleasures restored. The Book was probably taken up after an escape from the burden of business, and with a wish to forget the world, and all its vexations and anxieties. Having obtained this wish, and so much more, it is natural that they should make report as they have felt.

If Men of mature age, through want of practice, be thus easily beguiled into admiration of absurdities, extravagances, and misplaced ornaments, thinking it proper that their understandings should enjoy a holiday, while they are unbending their minds with verse, it may be expected that such Readers will resemble their former selves also in strength of prejudice, and an inaptitude to be moved by the unostentatious beauties of a pure style. In the higher poetry, an enlightened Critic chiefly looks for a reflection of the wisdom of the heart and the grandeur of the imagination. Wherever these appear, simplicity accompanies them; Magnificence herself, when legitimate, depending upon a simplicity of her own, to regulate her ornaments. But it is a well-known property of human nature, that our estimates are ever governed by comparisons, of which we are conscious with various degrees of distinctness. Is it not, then, inevitable (confining these observations to the effects of style merely) that an eye, accustomed to the glaring hues of diction by which such Readers are caught and excited, will for the most part be rather repelled than attracted by an original Work, the colouring of which is disposed according to a pure and refined scheme of harmony? It is in the fine arts as in the affairs of life, no man can *serve* (i.e. obey with zeal and fidelity) two Masters.

As Poetry is most just to its own divine origin when it administers the comforts and breathes the spirit of religion, they who have learned to perceive this truth, and who betake themselves to reading verse for sacred purposes, must be preserved from numerous illusions to which the two Classes of Readers, whom we have been considering, are liable. But, as the mind grows serious from the weight of life, the range of its passions is contracted accordingly; and its sympathies become so exclusive, that many species of high excellence wholly escape, or but languidly excite, its notice. Besides, men who read from religious or moral inclinations, even when the subject is of that kind which they approve, are beset with misconceptions and mistakes peculiar to themselves. Attaching so much importance to the truths which interest them, they are prone to over-rate the Authors by whom those truths are expressed and enforced. They come prepared to impart so much passion to the Poet's language, that they remain unconscious how little, in fact, they receive from it. And, on the other hand, religious faith is to him who holds it so momentous a thing, and error appears to be attended with such tremendous consequences, that, if opinions touching upon religion occur which the Reader condemns, he not only cannot sympathise with them, however animated the expression, but there is, for the most part, an end put to all satisfaction and enjoyment. Love, if it before existed, is converted into dislike; and the heart of the Reader is set against the Author and his book. — To these excesses, they, who from their professions ought to be the most guarded against them, are perhaps the most liable; I mean those sects whose religion, being from the calculating understanding, is cold and formal. For when Christianity, the religion of humility, is founded upon the proudest faculty of our nature, what can be expected but contradictions? Accordingly, believers of this cast are at one time contemptuous; at another, being troubled, as they are and must be, with inward misgivings, they are jealous and suspicious; — and at all seasons, they are under temptation to supply by the heat with which they defend their tenets, the animation which is wanting to the constitution of the religion itself.

Faith was given to man that his affections, detached from the treasures of time, might be inclined to settle upon those of eternity; — the elevation of his nature, which this habit produces on earth, being to him a presumptive evidence of a future state of existence; and giving him a title to partake of its holiness. The religious man values what he sees chiefly as an "imperfect shadowing forth" of what he is incapable of seeing. The concerns of religion refer to indefinite objects, and are too weighty for the mind to support them without relieving itself by resting a great part of the burthen upon words and symbols. The commerce between Man and his Maker cannot be carried on but by a process where much is represented in little, and the Infinite Being accommodates himself to a finite capacity. In all this may be perceived the affinity between religion and poetry; between religion — making up the deficiencies of reason by faith; and poetry — passionate for the instruction of reason; between religion — whose element is infinitude, and whose ultimate trust is the supreme of things, submitting herself to circumscription, and reconciled to substitutions; and poetry — ethereal and transcendent, yet incapable to sustain her existence without sensuous incarnation. In this community of nature may be perceived also the lurking incitements of kindred error; — so that we shall find that no poetry has been more subject to distortion, than that species, the argument and scope of which is religious; and no lovers of the art have gone farther astray than the pious and the devout.

Whither then shall we turn for that union of qualifications which must necessarily exist before the decisions of a critic can be of absolute value? For a mind at once poetical and philosophical; for a critic whose affections are as free and kindly as the spirit of society, and whose understanding is severe as that of dispassionate government? Where are we to look for that initiatory composure of mind which no selfishness can disturb? For a natural sensibility that has been tutored into correctness without losing anything of its quickness; and for active faculties, capable of answering the demands which an Author of original imagination shall make upon them, associated with a judgment that cannot be duped into admiration by aught that is unworthy of it? — among those and those only, who, never having suffered their youthful love of poetry to remit much of its force, have applied to the consideration of the laws of this art the best power of their understandings. At the same time it must be observed — that, as this Class comprehends the only judgments which are trust-worthy, so does it include the most erroneous and perverse. For to be mis-taught is worse than to be untaught; and no perverseness equals that which is supported by system, no errors are so difficult to root out as those which the understanding has pledged its credit to uphold. In this Class are contained censors, who, if they be pleased with what is good, are pleased with it only by imperfect glimpses, and upon false principles; who, should they generalise rightly, to a certain point, are sure to suffer for it in the end; who, if they stumble upon a sound rule, are fettered by misapplying it, or by straining it too far; being inca-pable of perceiving when it ought to yield to one of higher order. In it are found critics too petulant to be passive to a genuine poet, and too feeble to grapple with him; men, who take upon them to report of the course which *he* holds whom they are utterly unable to accom-pany, — confounded if he turn quick upon the wing, dismayed if he soar steadily "into the region;" — men of palsied imaginations and indurated hearts; in whose minds all healthy action is languid, who therefore feed as the many direct them, or, with the many, are greedy after vicious provocatives; — judges, whose censure is auspicious, and whose praise ominous! In this class meet together the two extremes of best and worst.

The observations presented in the foregoing series are of too un-gracious a nature to have been made without reluctance; and, were it only on this account, I would invite the reader to try them by the test of comprehensive experience. If the number of judges who can be confidently relied upon be in reality so small, it ought to follow that partial notice only, or neglect, perhaps long continued, or attention wholly inadequate to their merits — must have been the fate of most works in the higher departments of poetry; and that, on the other hand, numerous productions have blazed into popularity, and have passed away, leaving scarcely a trace behind them: it will be further found, that when Authors shall have at length raised themselves into general admiration and maintained their ground, errors and preju-dices have prevailed concerning their genius and their works, which the few who are conscious of those errors and prejudices would de-plore; if they were not recompensed by perceiving that there are select Spirits for whom it is ordained that their fame shall be in the world an existence like that of Virtue, which owes its being to the struggles it makes, and its vigour to the enemies whom it provokes; — a vivacious quality, ever doomed to meet with opposition, and still triumphing over it; and, from the nature of its dominion, incapable of being brought to the sad conclusion of Alexander, when he wept that there were no more worlds for him to conquer.

Let us take a hasty retrospect of the poetical literature of this Country for the greater part of the last two centuries, and see if the facts support these inferences. . . .[2]

As I do not mean to bring down this retrospect to our own times, it may with propriety be closed at the era of this distinguished event. From the literature of other ages and countries, proofs equally cogent might have been adduced, that the opinions announced in the former part of this Essay are founded upon truth. It was not an agreeable office, nor a prudent undertaking, to declare them; but their importance seemed to render it a duty. It may still be asked, where lies the particular relation of what has been said to these Volumes? — The question will be easily answered by the discerning Reader who is old enough to remember the taste that prevailed when some of these poems were first published, seventeen years ago; who has also observed to what degree the poetry of this Island has since that period been coloured by them; and who is further aware of the unremitting hostility with which, upon some principle or other, they have each and all been opposed. A sketch of my own notion of the constitution of Fame has been given; and, as far as concerns myself, I have cause to be satisfied. The love, the admiration, the indifference, the slight, the aversion, and even the contempt, with which these Poems have been received, knowing, as I do, the source within my own mind, from which they have proceeded, and the labour and pains, which, when labour and pains appeared needful, have been bestowed upon them, must all, if I think consistently, be received as pledges and tokens, bearing the same general impression, though widely different in value;

---

[2] Nineteen paragraphs are here omitted in which Wordsworth surveys the fortunes of Spenser, Shakespeare, Milton, Pope, Thomson, Collins, Percy's *Reliques,* Macpherson's *Ossian,* and discovers that the "facts" (neglect of genius, widespread popularity of the mediocre) do indeed support his inferences. The "distinguished event" mentioned in the next sentence printed here is the publication of Johnson's biographical prefaces (1779–81, later titled *The Lives of the English Poets*), in which, says Wordsworth, "to our astonishment the *first* name we find is that of Cowley! — What is become of the morning-star of English Poetry? Where . . . is the ever-to-be-honoured Chaucer? where is Spenser? where Sidney? and . . . where Shakspeare? — These, and a multitude of others not unworthy to be placed near them, their contemporaries and successors, we have *not*. But in their stead, we have . . . Roscommon, and Stepney, and Phillips, and Walsh, and Smith, and Duke, and King, and Spratt — Halifax, Granville, Sheffield, Congreve, Broome, and other reputed Magnates—metrical writers utterly worthless and useless, except for occasions like the present, when their productions are referred to as evidence what a small quantity of brain is necessary to procure a considerable stock of admiration, provided the aspirant will accommodate himself to the likings and fashions of his day."

— they are all proofs that for the present time I have not laboured in vain; and afford assurances, more or less authentic, that the products of my industry will endure.

If there be one conclusion more forcibly pressed upon us than another by the review which has been given of the fortunes and fate of poetical Works, it is this, — that every author, as far as he is great and at the same time *original*, has had the task of *creating* the taste by which he is to be enjoyed: so has it been, so will it continue to be. This remark was long since made to me by the philosophical Friend[3] for the separation of whose poems from my own I have previously expressed my regret. The predecessors of an original Genius of a high order will have smoothed the way for all that he has in common with them; — and much he will have in common; but, for what is peculiarly his own, he will be called upon to clear and often to shape his own road: — he will be in the condition of Hannibal among the Alps.

And where lies the real difficulty of creating that taste by which a truly original poet is to be relished? Is it in breaking the bonds of custom, in overcoming the prejudices of false refinement, and displacing the aversions of inexperience? Or, if he labour for an object which here and elsewhere I have proposed to myself, does it consist in divesting the reader of the pride that induces him to dwell upon those points wherein men differ from each other, to the exclusion of those in which all men are alike, or the same; and in making him ashamed of the vanity that renders him insensible of the appropriate excellence which civil arrangements, less unjust than might appear, and Nature illimitable in her bounty, have conferred on men who may stand below him in the scale of society? Finally, does it lie in establishing that dominion over the spirits of readers by which they are to be humbled and humanised, in order that they may be purified and exalted?

If these ends are to be attained by the mere communication of *knowledge,* it does *not* lie here. — Taste, I would remind the reader, like Imagination, is a word which has been forced to extend its services far beyond the point to which philosophy would have confined them. It is a metaphor, taken from a *passive* sense of the human body, and transferred to things which are in their essence *not* passive, — to intellectual *acts* and *operations*. The word, Imagination, has been overstrained, from impulses honourable to mankind, to meet the demands of the faculty which is perhaps the noblest of our nature. In the instance of Taste, the process has been reversed; and from the prevalence of dispositions at once injurious and discreditable, being no other than that selfishness which is the child of apathy, — which, as Nations decline in productive and creative power, makes them value

[3] Coleridge.

themselves upon a presumed refinement of judging. Poverty of language is the primary cause of the use which we make of the word, Imagination; but the word, Taste, has been stretched to the sense which it bears in modern Europe by habits of self-conceit, inducing that inversion in the order of things whereby a passive faculty is made paramount among the faculties conversant with the fine arts. Proportion and congruity, the requisite knowledge being supposed, are subjects upon which taste may be trusted; it is competent to this office; — for in its intercourse with these the mind is *passive,* and is affected painfully or pleasurably as by an instinct. But the profound and the exquisite in feeling, the lofty and universal in thought and imagination; or, in ordinary language, the pathetic and the sublime; — are neither of them, accurately speaking, objects of a faculty which could ever without a sinking in the spirit of Nations have been designated by the metaphor — *Taste.* And why? Because without the exertion of a co-operating *power* in the mind of the Reader, there can be no adequate sympathy with either of these emotions: without this auxiliary impulse, elevated or profound passion cannot exist.

Passion, it must be observed, is derived from a word which signifies *suffering;* but the connection which suffering has with effort, with exertion, and *action,* is immediate and inseparable. How strikingly is this property of human nature exhibited by the fact, that, in popular language, to be in a passion, is to be angry! — But,

> "Anger in hasty *words* or *blows*
> Itself discharges on its foes."

To be moved, then, by a passion, is to be excited, often to external, and always to internal, effort; whether for the continuance and strengthening of the passion, or for its suppression, accordingly as the course which it takes may be painful or pleasurable. If the latter, the soul must contribute to its support, or it never becomes vivid, — and soon languishes, and dies. And this brings us to the point. If every great poet with whose writings men are familiar, in the highest exercise of his genius, before he can be thoroughly enjoyed, has to call forth and to communicate *power,* this service, in a still greater degree, falls upon an original writer, at his first appearance in the world. — Of genius the only proof is, the act of doing well what is worthy to be done, and what was never done before: Of genius, in the fine arts, the only infallible sign is the widening the sphere of human sensibility, for the delight, honour, and benefit of human nature. Genius is the introduction of a new element into the intellectual universe: or, if that be not allowed, it is the application of powers to objects on which they had not before been exercised, or the employment of them in such a manner as to produce effects hitherto unknown. What is all this but an advance, or a conquest, made by the soul of the poet? Is it to be supposed that the reader can make progress of this kind, like an Indian prince or general — stretched on his palanquin, and borne by his slaves? No; he is invigorated and inspirited by his leader, in order that he may exert himself; for he cannot proceed in quiescence, he cannot be carried like a dead weight. Therefore to create taste is to call forth and bestow power, of which knowledge is the effect; and *there* lies the true difficulty.

As the pathetic participates of an *animal* sensation, it might seem — that, if the springs of this emotion were genuine, all men, possessed of competent knowledge of the facts and circumstances, would be instantaneously affected. And, doubtless, in the works of every true poet will be found passages of that species of excellence, which is proved by effects immediate and universal. But there are emotions of the pathetic that are simple and direct, and others — that are complex and revolutionary; some — to which the heart yields with gentleness; others — against which it struggles with pride; these varieties are infinite as the combinations of circumstance and the constitutions of character. Remember, also, that the medium through which, in poetry, the heart is to be affected, is language; a thing subject to endless fluctuations and arbitrary associations. The genius of the poet melts these down for his purpose; but they retain their shape and quality to him who is not capable of exerting, within his own mind, a corresponding energy. There is also a meditative, as well as a human, pathos; an enthusiastic, as well as an ordinary, sorrow; a sadness that has its seat in the depths of reason, to which the mind cannot sink gently of itself — but to which it must descend by treading the steps of thought. And for the sublime, — if we consider what are the cares that occupy the passing day, and how remote is the practice and the course of life from the sources of sublimity, in the soul of Man, can it be wondered that there is little existing preparation for a poet charged with a new mission to extend its kingdom, and to augment and spread its enjoyments?

Away, then, with the senseless iteration of the word, *popular,* applied to new works in poetry, as if there were no test of excellence in this first of the fine arts but that all men should run after its productions, as if urged by an appetite, or constrained by a spell! — The qualities of writing best fitted for eager reception are either such as startle the world into attention by their audacity and extravagance; or they are chiefly of a superficial kind, lying upon the surfaces of manners; or arising out of a selection and arrangement of incidents, by which the mind is kept upon the stretch of curiosity, and the fancy amused without the trouble of thought. But in everything which is to send the soul into herself, to be admonished of her weakness, or to be made conscious of her power; — wherever life and nature are described as operated upon by the creative or abstracting virtue of the imagination; wherever the instinctive wisdom of antiquity and her heroic passions uniting, in the heart of the poet, with the meditative wisdom of later ages, have produced that accord of sublimated humanity, which is at once a history of the remote past and a prophetic enunciation of the remotest future, *there,* the poet must reconcile himself for a season to few and scattered hearers. — Grand thoughts (and Shakspeare must often have sighed over this truth), as they are most naturally and most fitly conceived in solitude, so can they not be brought forth in the midst of plaudits, without some violation of their sanctity. Go to a silent exhibition of the productions of the sister Art, and be convinced that the qualities which dazzle at first sight, and kindle the admiration of the multitude, are essentially different from those by which permanent influence is secured. Let us not shrink from following up these principles as far as they will carry us, and conclude with observing — that there never has been a period, and perhaps never will be, in which vicious poetry, of some kind or other, has not excited more zealous admiration, and been far more generally read, than good; but this advantage attends the good, that the *individual,* as well as the species, survives from age to age; whereas, of the depraved, though the species be immortal, the individual quickly *perishes;* the object of present admiration vanishes, being supplanted by some other as easily produced; which, though no better, brings with it at least the irritation of novelty, — with adaptation, more or less skilful, to the changing humours of the majority of those who are most at leisure to regard poetical works when they first solicit their attention.

Is it the result of the whole, that, in the opinion of the Writer, the judgment of the People is not to be respected? The thought is most injurious; and, could the charge be brought against him, he would repel it with indignation. The People have already been justified, and their eulogium pronounced by implication, when it was said, above — that, of *good* poetry, the *individual,* as well as the species, *survives.* And how does it survive but through the People? What preserves it but their intellect and their wisdom?

> "—— Past and future, are the wings
> On whose support, harmoniously conjoined,
> Moves the great Spirit of human knowledge ——"[4]
>   MS.

4 *The Prelude,* VI.448–50.

The voice that issues from this Spirit, is that Vox Populi which the Deity inspires. Foolish must he be who can mistake for this a local acclamation, or a transitory outcry — transitory though it be for years, local though from a Nation. Still more lamentable is his error who can believe that there is any thing of divine infallibility in the clamour of that small though loud portion of the community, ever governed by factitious influence, which, under the name of the PUBLIC, passes itself, upon the unthinking, for the PEOPLE.[5] Towards the Public, the Writer hopes that he feels as much deference as it is entitled to: but to the People, philosophically characterised, and to the embodied spirit of their knowledge, so far as it exists and moves, at the present, faithfully supported by its two wings, the past and the future, his devout respect, his reverence, is due. He offers it willingly and readily; and, this done, takes leave of his Readers, by assuring them — that, if he were not persuaded that the contents of these Volumes, and the Work to which they are subsidiary, evince something of the "Vision and the Faculty divine;"[6] and that, both in words and things, they will operate in their degree, to extend the domain of sensibility for the delight, the honour, and the benefit of human nature, notwithstanding the many happy hours which he has employed in their composition, and the manifold comforts and enjoyments they have procured to him, he would not, if a wish could do it, save them from immediate destruction; — from becoming at this moment, to the world, as a thing that had never been.

5 Cf. Wordsworth's remark (cited in the notes to *Peter Bell*) that "The *People* would love the Poem of Peter Bell, but the *Public* (a very different Being) will never love it."

6 *The Excursion,* I.79.

From PREFACE TO THE EDITION OF 1815[1]

. . . Let us come now to the consideration of the words Fancy and Imagination, as employed in the classification of the following Poems. "A man," says an intelligent author, "has imagination in proportion as he can distinctly copy in idea the impressions of sense: it is the faculty which *images* within the mind the phenomena of sensation. A man has fancy in proportion as he can call up, connect, or associate, at pleasure, those internal images (φαντάζειν is to cause to appear) so as to complete ideal representations of absent objects. Imagination is the power of depicting, and fancy of evoking and combining. The imagination is formed by patient observation; the fancy by a voluntary activity in shifting the scenery of the mind. The more accurate the imagination, the more safely may a painter, or a poet, undertake a delineation, or a description, without the presence of the objects to be characterised. The more versatile the fancy, the more original and striking will be the decorations produced." — *British Synonyms discriminated, by W. Taylor*.[2]

Is not this as if a man should undertake to supply an account of a building, and be so intent upon what he had discovered of the foundation, as to conclude his task without once looking up at the superstructure? Here, as in other instances throughout the volume, the judicious Author's mind is enthralled by Etymology; he takes up the original word as his guide and escort, and too often does not perceive how soon he becomes its prisoner, without liberty to tread in any path but that to which it confines him. It is not easy to find out how imagination, thus explained, differs from distinct remembrance of images; or fancy from quick and vivid recollection of them: each is nothing more than a mode of memory. If the two words bear the above meaning, and no other, what term is left to designate that faculty of which the Poet is "all compact;" he whose eye glances from earth to heaven, whose spiritual attributes body forth what his pen is prompt in turning to shape;[3] or what is left to characterise Fancy, as insinuating herself into the heart of objects with creative activity? — Imagination,

[1] The first ten and final two paragraphs are here omitted. In the main body of the Preface Wordsworth attempts to explain the principles underlying his two most important classifications in the 1815 volume, "Poems of the Fancy" and "Poems of the Imagination." For his distinctions elsewhere between fancy and imagination, see the note to *The Prelude*, VIII.366, 373.

[2] William Taylor of Norwich, *English Synonyms Discriminated* (1813).

[3] *A Midsummer-Night's Dream*, V.i.8, 13–16.

in the sense of the word as giving title to a class of the following Poems, has no reference to images that are merely a faithful copy, existing in the mind, of absent external objects; but is a word of higher import, denoting operations of the mind upon those objects, and processes of creation or of composition, governed by certain fixed laws. I proceed to illustrate my meaning by instances. A parrot *hangs* from the wires of his cage by his beak or by his claws; or a monkey from the bough of a tree by his paws or his tail. Each creature does so literally and actually. In the first Eclogue of Virgil, the shepherd, thinking of the time when he is to take leave of his farm, thus addresses his goats: —

> "Non ego vos posthac viridi projectus in antro
> Dumosa *pendere* procul de rupe videbo."[4]

> ——— "half way down
> *Hangs* one who gathers samphire,"[5]

is the well-known expression of Shakspeare, delineating an ordinary image upon the cliffs of Dover. In these two instances is a slight exertion of the faculty which I denominate imagination, in the use of one word: neither the goats nor the samphire-gatherer do literally hang, as does the parrot or the monkey; but, presenting to the senses something of such an appearance, the mind in its activity, for its own gratification, contemplates them as hanging.

> "As when far off at sea a fleet descried
> *Hangs* in the clouds, by equinoctial winds
> Close sailing from Bengala, or the isles
> Of Ternate or Tidore, whence merchants bring
> Their spicy drugs; they on the trading flood
> Through the wide Ethiopian to the Cape
> Ply, stemming nightly toward the Pole: so seemed
> Far off the flying Fiend."[6]

Here is the full strength of the imagination involved in the word *hangs*, and exerted upon the whole image: First, the fleet, an aggregate of many ships, is represented as one mighty person, whose track, we know and feel, is upon the waters; but, taking advantage of its appearance to the senses, the Poet dares to represent it as *hanging in the clouds*, both for the gratification of the mind in contemplating the

---

4 *Eclogues*, I.75–76: "Never again, stretched out in some green hollow, shall I see you [the speaker's flock of goats] in the distance hang from a bushy cliff."
5 *King Lear*, IV.vi.15–16.
6 *Paradise Lost*, II.636–43.

image itself, and in reference to the motion and appearance of the sublime object to which it is compared.

From impressions of sight we will pass to those of sound; which, as they must necessarily be of a less definite character, shall be selected from these volumes:

> "Over his own sweet voice the Stock-dove *broods;*"[7]

of the same bird,

> "His voice was *buried* among trees,
> Yet to be come at by the breeze;"[8]

> "O, Cuckoo! shall I call thee *Bird,*
> Or but a wandering *Voice?*"[9]

The stock-dove is said to *coo,* a sound well imitating the note of the bird; but, by the intervention of the metaphor *broods,* the affections are called in by the imagination to assist in marking the manner in which the bird reiterates and prolongs her soft note, as if herself delighting to listen to it, and participating of a still and quiet satisfaction, like that which may be supposed inseparable from the continuous process of incubation. "His voice was buried among trees," a metaphor expressing the love of *seclusion* by which this Bird is marked; and characterising its note as not partaking of the shrill and the piercing, and therefore more easily deadened by the intervening shade; yet a note so peculiar and withal so pleasing, that the breeze, gifted with that love of the sound which the Poet feels, penetrates the shades in which it is entombed, and conveys it to the ear of the listener.

> "Shall I call thee Bird,
> Or but a wandering Voice?"

This concise interrogation characterises the seeming ubiquity of the voice of the cuckoo, and dispossesses the creature almost of a corporeal existence; the Imagination being tempted to this exertion of her power by a consciousness in the memory that the cuckoo is almost perpetually heard throughout the season of spring, but seldom becomes an object of sight.

Thus far of images independent of each other, and immediately endowed by the mind with properties that do not inhere in them, upon an incitement from properties and qualities the existence of which is inherent and obvious. These processes of imagination are carried on

---

[7] "Resolution and Independence," l. 5.
[8] "O Nightingale! Thou Surely Art" (omitted from this selection), ll. 13–14.
[9] "To the Cuckoo," ll. 3–4.

either by conferring additional properties upon an object, or abstracting from it some of those which it actually possesses, and thus enabling it to re-act upon the mind which hath performed the process, like a new existence.

I pass from the Imagination acting upon an individual image to a consideration of the same faculty employed upon images in a conjunction by which they modify each other. The Reader has already had a fine instance before him in the passage quoted from Virgil, where the apparently perilous situation of the goat, hanging upon the shaggy precipice, is contrasted with that of the shepherd contemplating it from the seclusion of the cavern in which he lies stretched at ease and in security. Take these images separately, and how unaffecting the picture compared with that produced by their being thus connected with, and opposed to, each other!

> "As a huge stone is sometimes seen to lie
> Couched on the bald top of an eminence,
> Wonder to all who do the same espy
> By what means it could thither come, and whence,
> So that it seems a thing endued with sense,
> Like a sea-beast crawled forth, which on a shelf
> Of rock or sand reposeth, there to sun himself.
>
> Such seemed this Man; not all alive or dead
> Nor all asleep, in his extreme old age.
>
>   ❄   ❄   ❄   ❄   ❄
>
> Motionless as a cloud the old Man stood,
> That heareth not the loud winds when they call,
> And moveth altogether if it move at all."[10]

In these images, the conferring, the abstracting, and the modifying powers of the Imagination, immediately and mediately acting, are all brought into conjunction. The stone is endowed with something of the power of life to approximate it to the sea-beast; and the sea-beast stripped of some of its vital qualities to assimilate it to the stone; which intermediate image is thus treated for the purpose of bringing the original image, that of the stone, to a nearer resemblance to the figure and condition of the aged Man; who is divested of so much of the indications of life and motion as to bring him to the point where the two objects unite and coalesce in just comparison. After what has been said, the image of the cloud need not be commented upon.

Thus far of an endowing or modifying power: but the Imagination also shapes and *creates;* and how? By innumerable processes; and in

[10] "Resolution and Independence," ll. 57–65, 75–77.

none does it more delight than in that of consolidating numbers into unity, and dissolving and separating unity into number, — alternations proceeding from, and governed by, a sublime consciousness of the soul in her own mighty and almost divine powers. Recur to the passage already cited from Milton. When the compact Fleet, as one Person, has been introduced "Sailing from Bengala," "They," *i.e.* the "merchants," representing the fleet resolved into a multitude of ships, "ply" their voyage towards the extremities of the earth: "So," (referring to the word "As" in the commencement) "seemed the flying Fiend;" the image of his Person acting to recombine the multitude of ships into one body, — the point from which the comparison set out. "So seemed," and to whom seemed? To the heavenly Muse who dictates the poem, to the eye of the Poet's mind, and to that of the Reader, present at one moment in the wide Ethiopian, and the next in the solitudes, then first broken in upon, of the infernal regions!

"Modo me Thebis, modo ponit Athenis."[11]

Hear again this mighty Poet, — speaking of the Messiah going forth to expel from heaven the rebellious angels,

"Attended by ten thousand thousand Saints
He onward came: far off his coming shone," —[12]

the retinue of Saints, and the Person of the Messiah himself, lost almost and merged in the splendour of that indefinite abstraction "His coming!"

As I do not mean here to treat this subject further than to throw some light upon the present Volumes, and especially upon one division of them, I shall spare myself and the Reader the trouble of considering the Imagination as it deals with thoughts and sentiments, as it regulates the composition of characters, and determines the course of actions: I will not consider it (more than I have already done by implication) as that power which, in the language of one of my most esteemed Friends, "draws all things to one; which makes things animate or inanimate, beings with their attributes, subjects with their accessaries, take one colour and serve to one effect."[13] The grand store-houses of enthusiastic and meditative Imagination, of poetical, as contradistinguished from human and dramatic Imagination, are the prophetic and lyrical parts of the Holy Scriptures, and the works of Milton; to which I cannot forbear to add those of Spenser. I select these writers in preference to those of ancient Greece and Rome, because the anthropomorphitism of the Pagan religion subjected the

---

11 Horace, *Epistles*, II.i.213: "He sets me down now at Thebes, now at Athens."
12 *Paradise Lost*, VI.767–68.
13 "Charles Lamb upon the genius of Hogarth" (Wordsworth's note).

minds of the greatest poets in those countries too much to the bondage of definite form; from which the Hebrews were preserved by their abhorrence of idolatry. This abhorrence was almost as strong in our great epic Poet, both from circumstances of his life, and from the constitution of his mind. However imbued the surface might be with classical literature, he was a Hebrew in soul; and all things tended in him towards the sublime. Spenser, of a gentler nature, maintained his freedom by aid of his allegorical spirit, at one time inciting him to create persons out of abstractions; and, at another, by a superior effort of genius, to give the universality and permanence of abstractions to his human beings, by means of attributes and emblems that belong to the highest moral truths and the purest sensations, — of which his character of Una is a glorious example. Of the human and dramatic Imagination the works of Shakspeare are an inexhaustible source.

> "I tax not you, ye Elements, with unkindness,
> I never gave you kingdoms, call'd you Daughters!"[14]

And if, bearing in mind the many Poets distinguished by this prime quality, whose names I omit to mention; yet justified by recollection of the insults which the ignorant, the incapable, and the presumptuous, have heaped upon these and my other writings, I may be permitted to anticipate the judgment of posterity upon myself, I shall declare (censurable, I grant, if the notoriety of the fact above stated does not justify me) that I have given in these unfavourable times, evidence of exertions of this faculty upon its worthiest objects, the external universe, the moral and religious sentiments of Man, his natural affections, and his acquired passions; which have the same ennobling tendency as the productions of men, in this kind, worthy to be holden in undying remembrance.[15]

To the mode in which Fancy has already been characterised as the

14 *King Lear*, III.ii.16–17.
15 Originally (1815–36) followed by an additional paragraph: "I dismiss this subject with observing — that, in the series of Poems placed under the head of Imagination, I have begun with one of the earliest processes of Nature in the development of this faculty ["There Was a Boy," incorporated into *The Prelude* as V.364–97]. Guided by one of my own primary consciousnesses, I have represented a commutation and transfer of internal feelings, co-operating with external accidents, to plant, for immortality, images of sound and sight, in the celestial soil of the Imagination. The Boy, there introduced, is listening, with something of a feverish and restless anxiety, for the recurrence of the riotous sounds which he had previously excited; and, at the moment when the intenseness of his mind is beginning to remit, he is surprised into a perception of the solemn and tranquillizing images which the Poem describes. — The Poems next in succession [e.g., "To the Cuckoo," "A Night-Piece," "Yew-Trees," "Nutting"] exhibit the faculty exerting itself upon various objects of the external universe; then follow others, where it is employed upon feelings, characters, and actions; and the Class is concluded with imaginative pictures of moral, political, and religious sentiments."

power of evoking and combining, or, as my friend Mr. Coleridge has styled it,[16] "the aggregative and associative power," my objection is only that the definition is too general. To aggregate and to associate, to evoke and to combine, belong as well to the Imagination as to the Fancy; but either the materials evoked and combined are different; or they are brought together under a different law, and for a different purpose. Fancy does not require that the materials which she makes use of should be susceptible of change in their constitution, from her touch; and, where they admit of modification, it is enough for her purpose if it be slight, limited, and evanescent. Directly the reverse of these, are the desires and demands of the Imagination. She recoils from every thing but the plastic, the pliant, and the indefinite. She leaves it to Fancy to describe Queen Mab as coming,

> "In shape no bigger than an agate-stone
> On the fore-finger of an alderman."[17]

Having to speak of stature, she does not tell you that her gigantic Angel was as tall as Pompey's Pillar; much less that he was twelve cubits, or twelve hundred cubits high; or that his dimensions equalled those of Teneriffe or Atlas; — because these, and if they were a million times as high it would be the same, are bounded: The expression is, "His stature reached the sky!"[18] the illimitable firmament! — When the Imagination frames a comparison, if it does not strike on the first presentation, a sense of the truth of the likeness, from the moment that it is perceived, grows — and continues to grow — upon the mind; the resemblance depending less upon outline of form and feature, than upon expression and effect; less upon casual and outstanding, than upon inherent and internal, properties: moreover, the images invariably modify each other. — The law under which the processes of Fancy are carried on is as capricious as the accidents of things, and the effects are surprising, playful, ludicrous, amusing, tender, or pathetic, as the objects happen to be appositely produced or fortunately combined. Fancy depends upon the rapidity and profusion with which she scatters her thoughts and images; trusting that their number, and the felicity with which they are linked together, will make amends for the want of individual value: or she prides herself upon the curious subtilty and the successful elaboration with which she can detect their lurking affinities. If she can win you over to her purpose, and impart to you her feelings, she cares not how unstable or transitory may be

[16] In an article contributed to Southey's *Omniana* (1812). Coleridge repeated the definition in *Biographia Literaria*, ch. XII.
[17] *Romeo and Juliet*, I.iv.56–57.
[18] *Paradise Lost*, IV.987–88.

her influence, knowing that it will not be out of her power to resume
it upon an apt occasion. But the Imagination is conscious of an indestructible dominion; — the Soul may fall away from it, not being
able to sustain its grandeur; but, if once felt and acknowledged, by no
act of any other faculty of the mind can it be relaxed, impaired, or
diminished. — Fancy is given to quicken and to beguile the temporal
part of our nature, Imagination to incite and to support the eternal. —
Yet is it not the less true that Fancy, as she is an active, is also, under
her own laws and in her own spirit, a creative faculty. In what manner
Fancy ambitiously aims at a rivalship with Imagination, and Imagination stoops to work with the materials of Fancy, might be illustrated
from the compositions of all eloquent writers, whether in prose or
verse; and chiefly from those of our own Country. Scarcely a page of
the impassioned parts of Bishop Taylor's[19] Works can be opened that
shall not afford examples. — Referring the Reader to those inestimable
volumes, I will content myself with placing a conceit (ascribed to Lord
Chesterfield) in contrast with a passage from the Paradise Lost: —

> "The dews of the evening most carefully shun,
> They are the tears of the sky for the loss of the sun."[20]

After the transgression of Adam, Milton, with other appearances of
sympathising Nature, thus marks the immediate consequence,

> "Sky lowered, and, muttering thunder, some sad drops
> Wept at completion of the mortal sin."[21]

The associating link is the same in each instance: Dew and rain, not
distinguishable from the liquid substance of tears, are employed as
indications of sorrow. A flash of surprise is the effect in the former
case; a flash of surprise, and nothing more; for the nature of things
does not sustain the combination. In the latter, the effects from the
act, of which there is this immediate consequence and visible sign, are
so momentous, that the mind acknowledges the justice and reason-
ableness of the sympathy in nature so manifested; and the sky weeps
drops of water as if with human eyes, as "Earth had before trembled
from her entrails, and Nature given a second groan." . . .

19 Jeremy Taylor (1613–67).
20 Chesterfield, "Advice to a Lady in Autumn," ll. 25–26.
21 These lines and the quotation at the end of the paragraph are from *Paradise Lost*, IX.1000–03.

SELECT BIBLIOGRAPHY

LIST OF ABBREVIATIONS

MAP OF THE LAKE DISTRICT

NOTES TO THE POEMS

INDEX OF TITLES

SELECT BIBLIOGRAPHY[1]

BIBLIOGRAPHICAL GUIDES

Bernbaum, Ernest, and James V. Logan, Jr. "Wordsworth." *The English Romantic Poets: A Review of Research*, ed. Thomas M. Raysor. Revised edn. New York, 1956.

Healey, George Harris. *The Cornell Wordsworth Collection: A Catalogue of Books and Manuscripts* . . . . Ithaca, 1957.

Henley, Elton F., and David H. Stam. *Wordsworthian Criticism, 1945–1964: An Annotated Bibliography*. New York, 1965.

Logan, James Venable. *Wordsworthian Criticism: A Guide and Bibliography*. Columbus, Ohio, 1947; reprinted 1961.

See also the annual bibliographies of research in *PMLA* (1922–), *ELH* (1937–49), *PQ* (1950–64), and *English Language Notes* (1965–).

EDITIONS: POEMS, PROSE, LETTERS

The Correspondence of Henry Crabb Robinson with the Wordsworth Circle (1808–1866), ed. Edith J. Morley. 2 vols. Oxford, 1927.

The Early Letters of William and Dorothy Wordsworth (1787–1805), ed. Ernest de Selincourt. Oxford, 1935. (*E.L.*)

The Letters of William and Dorothy Wordsworth: The Later Years, ed. Ernest de Selincourt. 3 vols. Oxford, 1939. (*L.Y.*)

The Letters of William and Dorothy Wordsworth: The Middle Years, ed. Ernest de Selincourt. 2 vols. Oxford, 1937. (*M.Y.*)

Lyrical Ballads, ed. Thomas Hutchinson. London, 1898.

Poems in Two Volumes, 1807, ed. Helen Darbishire. Oxford, 1914; 2nd edn., 1952.

The Poetical Works of William Wordsworth, ed. E. de Selincourt and Helen Darbishire. 5 vols. Oxford, 1940–49. (*P.W.*)

The Prelude, or Growth of a Poet's Mind, ed. Ernest de Selincourt. Oxford, 1926; 2nd edn., revised by Helen Darbishire, 1959.

The Prose Works of William Wordsworth, ed. Alexander B. Grosart. 3 vols. London, 1876.

Representative Poems, ed. Arthur Beatty. New York, 1937.

Wordsworth & Reed: The Poet's Correspondence with His American Editor: 1836–1850, ed. Leslie Nathan Broughton. Ithaca, 1933.

---

[1] Some abbreviations used in the notes are given in parentheses after various items. See also the List of Abbreviations following the Bibliography.

RELATED DOCUMENTS

Collected Letters of Samuel Taylor Coleridge, ed. Earl Leslie Griggs. 4 vols. (to date). Oxford, 1956–59.

Henry Crabb Robinson on Books and Their Writers, ed. Edith J. Morley. 3 vols. London, 1938. (*H.C.R.*)

Journals of Dorothy Wordsworth, ed. E. de Selincourt. 2 vols. London, 1941. (D.W., *Journals*)

BIOGRAPHY AND CRITICISM

Arnold, Matthew. "Wordsworth." *Essays in Criticism, Second Series.* London, 1888.

Bateson, F. W. *Wordsworth: A Re-Interpretation.* London, 1954; 2nd edn., 1956.

Batho, Edith C. *The Later Wordsworth.* Cambridge, 1933.

Beach, Joseph Warren. *The Concept of Nature in Nineteenth-Century English Poetry.* New York, 1936.

Beatty, Arthur. *William Wordsworth: His Doctrine and Art in Their Historical Relations.* Madison, Wis., 1922; 2nd edn., 1927, reprinted 1960.

Bloom, Harold. "William Wordsworth." *The Visionary Company: A Reading of English Romantic Poetry.* Garden City, N.Y., 1961.

Christensen, Francis. "Creative Sensibility in Wordsworth," *JEGP*, XLV (1946), 361–68.

Coleridge, S. T. *Biographia Literaria.* London, 1817; ed. J. Shawcross, 2 vols., Oxford, 1907. (*Biog. Lit.*)

Danby, John F. *The Simple Wordsworth: Studies in the Poems, 1797–1807.* London, 1960.

Darbishire, Helen. *The Poet Wordsworth: The Clark Lectures . . . 1949.* Oxford, 1950.

de Selincourt, Ernest. *Dorothy Wordsworth: A Biography.* Oxford, 1933.

Discussions of William Wordsworth, ed. Jack Davis. Boston, 1964.

Empson, William. "Sense in The Prelude." *The Structure of Complex Words.* London, 1951.

Ferry, David. *The Limits of Mortality: An Essay on Wordsworth's Major Poems.* Middletown, Conn., 1959.

Garrod, H. W. *Wordsworth: Lectures and Essays.* Oxford, 1923; 2nd edn., 1927.

Harper, George McLean. *William Wordsworth: His Life, Works, and Influence.* 2 vols. New York, 1916; revised edn., one vol., 1929.

Hartman, Geoffrey H. *Wordsworth's Poetry 1787–1814.* New Haven and London, 1964.

Havens, Raymond Dexter. *The Mind of a Poet: A Study of Wordsworth's Thought with Particular Reference to "The Prelude."* Baltimore, 1941.

Herford, C. H. *Wordsworth.* London, 1930.

Jones, John. *The Egotistical Sublime: A History of Wordsworth's Imagination.* London, 1954.

Jordan, John E. "Wordsworth's Humor," *PMLA*, LXXIII (1958), 81–93.

Leavis, F. R. "Wordsworth." *Revaluation: Tradition & Development in English Poetry.* London, 1936.

Legouis, Émile. *The Early Life of William Wordsworth, 1770–1798: A Study of "The Prelude,"* trans. J. W. Matthews. London, 1897.

Margoliouth, H. M. *Wordsworth and Coleridge, 1795–1834.* London, New York, Toronto, 1953.

Marsh, Florence. *Wordsworth's Imagery: A Study in Poetic Vision.* New Haven, 1952.

Mayo, Robert. "The Contemporaneity of the *Lyrical Ballads*," *PMLA*, LXIX (1954), 486–522.

Meyer, George Wilbur. *Wordsworth's Formative Years.* Ann Arbor, Mich., 1943.

Moorman, Mary. *William Wordsworth: A Biography. The Early Years, 1770–1803.* Oxford, 1957.

Parrish, Stephen Maxfield. "Dramatic Technique in the *Lyrical Ballads*," *PMLA*, LXXIV (1959), 85–97.

Parrish, Stephen Maxfield. "The Wordsworth-Coleridge Controversy," *PMLA*, LXXIII (1958), 367–74.

Perkins, David. *The Quest for Permanence: The Symbolism of Wordsworth, Shelley, and Keats.* Cambridge, Mass., 1959.

Perkins, David. *Wordsworth and the Poetry of Sincerity.* Cambridge, Mass., 1964.

Piper, H. W. *The Active Universe: Pantheism and the Concept of Imagination in the English Romantic Poets.* London, 1962.

Rader, Melvin M. *Presiding Ideas in Wordsworth's Poetry.* Seattle, 1931.

Smith, J. C. *A Study of Wordsworth.* Edinburgh, 1944.

Stallknecht, Newton P. *Strange Seas of Thought: Studies in William Wordsworth's Philosophy of Man and Nature.* Durham, N.C., 1945; 2nd edn., Bloomington, Ind., 1958.

Todd, F. M. *Politics and the Poet: A Study of Wordsworth.* London, 1957.

Weaver, Bennett. "Wordsworth's *Prelude*: The Poetic Function of Memory," *SP*, XXXIV (1937), 552–63.

Whitehead, Alfred North. *Science and the Modern World.* New York, 1925.

Willey, Basil. "On Wordsworth and the Locke Tradition." *The Seventeenth Century Background: Studies in the Thought of the Age in Relation to Poetry and Religion.* London, 1934.

Woodring, Carl. *Wordsworth.* Boston, 1965.

Wordsworth Centenary Studies, ed. Gilbert T. Dunklin. Princeton, 1951.

LIST OF ABBREVIATIONS[1]

Biog. Lit.	Coleridge, *Biographia Literaria*
D.W., *Journals*	Journals of Dorothy Wordsworth (1941)
E.L.	The Early Letters of William and Dorothy Wordsworth (1935)
ELH	ELH: A Journal of English Literary History
Exc.	Wordsworth, *The Excursion*
F.Q.	Spenser, *The Faerie Queene*
H.C.R.	Henry Crabb Robinson on Books and Their Writers (1938)
I.F.	Notes on the poems dictated by Wordsworth to Isabella Fenwick in 1843
JEGP	*Journal of English and Germanic Philology*
L.Y.	The Letters of William and Dorothy Wordsworth: The Later Years (1939)
MLN	*Modern Language Notes*
M.Y.	The Letters of William and Dorothy Wordsworth: The Middle Years (1937)
P.L.	Milton, *Paradise Lost*
PMLA	*Publications of the Modern Language Association of America*
PQ	*Philological Quarterly*
Prel.	Wordsworth, *The Prelude*
P.W.	The Poetical Works of William Wordsworth (1940–49)
SP	*Studies in Philology*
W.	Notes by Wordsworth published in various editions of his poems

[1] For more information on editions cited here, see the preceding Select Bibliography.

MAP OF THE LAKE DISTRICT

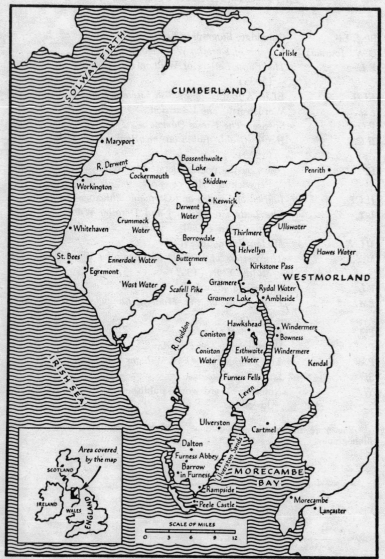

SOLWAY FIRTH

CUMBERLAND

Carlisle

Maryport

Bassenthwaite
Lake

R. Derwent

Cockermouth

Skiddaw

Penrith

Workington

Keswick

Derwent
Water

Whitehaven

Crummock
Water

Thirlmere

Ullswater

St. Bees

Ennerdale Water

Borrowdale

Helvellyn

Hawes Water

Egremont

Buttermere

Kirkstone Pass

Wast Water

Scafell Pike

Grasmere

WESTMORLAND

Rydal Water

Grasmere Lake

Ambleside

R. Duddon

Hawkshead

Windermere

Coniston

Bowness

Coniston
Water

Esthwaite
Water

Windermere

Kendal

Furness Fells

Leven

Ulverston

Cartmel

Dalton

Furness Abbey

Barrow
in Furness

Ulverston Sands

MORECAMBE
BAY

Rampside

Peele Castle

Morecambe

Lancaster

IRISH SEA

Area covered
by the map

SCOTLAND

IRELAND

WALES

ENGLAND

SCALE OF MILES

0   3   6   9   12

NOTES TO THE POEMS

An Evening Walk Page 3

Written c. 1787–89; published 1793.

> The young Lady to whom this was addressed was my Sister. It was composed at school, and during my two first College vacations. . . . [The image of ll. 214–15] is feebly and imperfectly expressed, but I recollect distinctly the very spot where this first struck me. It was in the way between Hawkshead and Ambleside, and gave me extreme pleasure. The moment was important in my poetical history; for I date from it my consciousness of the infinite variety of natural appearances which had been unnoticed by the poets of any age or country, so far as I was acquainted with them; and I made a resolution to supply, in some degree, the deficiency. I could not have been at that time above fourteen years of age. . . . [The plan of the poem] has not been confined to a particular walk or an individual place, — a proof (of which I was unconscious at the time) of my unwillingness to submit the poetic spirit to the chains of fact and real circumstance. The country is idealised rather than described in any one of its local aspects. (I.F.)

Wordsworth never published the considerable additions that he made in 1794 (see the apparatus in *P.W.*, I, esp. pp. 6–7, 9, 10, 12–13); the final text, more or less arrived at by 1820, though freer of literary borrowings and sixty-eight lines shorter, does not misrepresent the original of 1793. In 1801 he classed the poem with *Descriptive Sketches* (also published in 1793) as "juvenile productions, inflated and obscure, but . . . [containing] many new images, and vigorous lines" (*E.L.*, p. 270). It is included in the present selection principally to illustrate some of the stylistic characteristics of eighteenth-century topographical poetry that he soon outgrew.

3–11: Lodore is a waterfall at the foot of Derwent Water. For the lakes ("Winander[mere]" = Windermere), see the map on the opposite page. 15–16: These lines, recalling the tone of "Tintern Abbey" and the Intimations ode, were added after 1832. 39 embattled clouds: Beattie, *The Minstrel*, II.xii. 49 intake: "The word *intake* is local, and signifies a mountain-inclosure" (W.). 53–69: "The reader who has made the tour of this country, will recognise, in this description, the features which characterise the lower waterfall in the grounds of Rydal" (W.). 53 huddling rill: Cf. Milton, *Comus*, l. 495, "huddling brook." 66–67: Cf. *As You Like It*, II.i.31–32, "Under an oak whose antique root peeps out / Upon the brook that brawls along this wood." 72–73 Sabine . . . Blandusia: See Horace, *Odes*, III.xiii (in which "Blandusia" is a variant of the better-known "Bandusia"). 133 "green rings": Taken, as Wordsworth acknowledged, from an image in William Greenwood's *A Poem Written*

During a Shooting Excursion on the Moors (1787). **135:** In a note omitted from later editions Wordsworth cites *The Minstrel,* I.xxxix, "Down the rough slope the ponderous waggon rings." **141 thunders . . . remote:** *P.L.,* II.477. **146 Sweetly ferocious:** " 'Dolcemente feroce.' — TASSO [*Gerusalemme Liberata,* I.lviii]. In this description of the cock [146–55], I remembered a spirited one of the same animal in L'Agriculture . . . [1774, 1782, a poem by P. F. Rosset]" (W.). Modern readers will be reminded of Chaucer's Chauntecleer. **163 gulf profound:** *P.L.,* II.592. **175 "prospect . . . fire":** From Moses Browne, *Sunday Thoughts,* quoted in John Scott of Amwell's *Critical Essays* (1785). **190–91:** "From Thomson" (W.), a fairly close imitation of *The Seasons,* "Summer," ll. 1628–29, also quoted in Scott's *Critical Essays.* **196–211:** "See a description of an appearance of this kind in Clark's [James Clarke's] Survey of the Lakes [1787], accompanied by vouchers of its veracity, that may amuse the reader" (W.). **210 beacon:** Probably Penrith Beacon; see *Prel.,* VI.233 and note. **214–15:** See the I.F. note above. A recently discovered boyhood notebook contains in Wordsworth's hand an early version of this image: "As when the moon as she raises her orb above the Horizon rests upon the Branches of some tall Oak, which grows upon the summit of the Horizon" (see *The Early Wordsworthian Milieu,* ed. Z. S. Fink, 1958, p. 80, and cf. *Prel.,* IV.88–92). **237 "by . . . sweet":** Collins, "The Passions," l. 60. **250–78:** Much condensed from earlier versions. In 1794 Wordsworth explained in a note, "These verses relate the catastrophe of a poor woman who was found dead on Stanemoor two years ago with two children whom she had in vain attempted to protect from the storm in the manner described." **270 like . . . roars:** Pope, *An Essay on Criticism,* II.169. **279 Sweet . . . sounds:** Goldsmith, *The Deserted Village,* l. 113. **280 folding star:** Collins, "Ode to Evening," l. 21. **291:** In a note later omitted Wordsworth refers to *F.Q.,* I.iii.4. **306:** Cf. *The Tempest,* IV.i.155–56, "like this insubstantial pageant faded, / Leave not a rack behind." **359 silvery threads:** Cf. Milton, "Arcades," l. 16, "silver threds." **374:** Cf. *The Minstrel,* I.xxxix, "Through rustling corn the hare astonish'd springs." **377:** Gray, in his *Journal in the Lakes* (1775), under the date 9 October 1769, mentions "the thumping of huge hammers at an iron-forge not far distant."

Lines Left upon a Seat in a Yew-Tree   *Page 12*

Written mainly c. 1795–97; published 1798.

Composed in part at school at Hawkshead. . . . This spot was my favourite walk in the evenings during the latter part of my school-time. The individual whose habits and character are here given, was a gentleman of the neighbourhood, a man of talent and learning, who had been educated at one of our Universities, and returned to pass his time in seclusion on his own estate. He died a bachelor in middle age. Induced by the beauty of the prospect, he built a small summer-house

on the rocks above the peninsula on which the ferry-house stands. . . .
The site was long ago pointed out by Mr. West in his Guide, as the
pride of the lakes, and now goes by the name of "The Station." (I.F.)

The poem explicitly warns against pride, which is shown to have damaged
the solitary's view of human nature.

7 one . . . impulse: See "The Tables Turned," l. 21.   **35–36 gaze . . .
lovelier:** Creative sensibility at work. Cf. Coleridge's "This Lime-Tree
Bower My Prison" (written 1797), ll. 39–41, "gazing round / On the wide
landscape, gaze till all doth seem / Less gross than bodily," and D.W.,
Journals, I, 10 (26 February 1798), "We . . . gazed on the landscape till it
melted into more than natural loveliness."   **39–42 those . . . loveliness:**
I.e., others, less proud, who have learned to see beauty in "The world, and
human life"; they have progressed beyond the love of nature to the love of
man.   **52–54 he . . . used:** One statement of the "moral" of "The Rime
of the Ancient Mariner," which also first appeared in *Lyrical Ballads,* and
of *Peter Bell* and "Hart-Leap Well." Cf. Beattie, *The Minstrel,* I.xviii: "His
heart, from cruel sport estranged, would bleed / To work the woe of any
living thing."   **63:** I.e., can view himself as a representative of human
nature, with imperfections to be suspected and noble qualities to be revered.

The Reverie of Poor Susan   *Page 13*

Written according to Wordsworth in 1797; published 1800. "This arose out
of my observation of the affecting music of these birds hanging in this way
[i.e., in cages] in the London streets during the freshness and stillness of the
Spring morning" (I.F.). Susan's ailment is, of course, the homesickness
that gives rise to her visionary experience; like many of the succeeding
lyrical ballads, the poem illustrates "the manner in which we associate ideas
in a state of excitement" (see p. 447). In 1800 only, Wordsworth printed
a fifth stanza:

> Poor Outcast! return — to receive thee once more
> The house of thy Father will open its door,
> And thou once again, in thy plain russet gown,
> May'st hear the thrush sing from a tree of its own.

1 Wood Street: Like Lothbury (7) and Cheapside (8), a street in the
mercantile section of London, near the Thames.   **2 three years:** Presumably the length of time Susan has been (like the thrush, in a sense
imprisoned) in London.

The Old Cumberland Beggar   *Page 14*

Written 1797; published 1800. "Observed, and with great benefit to my
own heart, when I was a child [hence "Cumberland" in the title] . . . .
The political economists were about that time [when he wrote the poem]
beginning their war upon mendicity in all its forms, and by implication, if

not directly, on alms-giving also" (I.F.). In a letter of 14 January 1801, to the Whig statesman Charles James Fox, Wordsworth wrote that "the most calamitous effect . . . [of] the measures which have lately been pursued in this country, is a rapid decay of the domestic affections among the lower orders of society. . . . For many years past, the tendency of society amongst almost all the nations of Europe has been to produce it. But recently by the spreading of manufactures through every part of the country, by the heavy taxes upon postage, by workhouses, Houses of Industry, and the invention of Soup-shops &c. &c. . . . the bonds of domestic feeling among the poor, as far as the influence of these things has extended, have been weakened, and in innumerable instances entirely destroyed" (*E.L.*, pp. 260–61). The poem (explicitly beginning in l. 67) is addressed to "Statesmen," though ll. 68–72 show that Wordsworth had little faith in legislation as a means of curing social evils. With the description of the beggar cf. that of the old discharged soldier in *Prel.*, IV.387 ff.

61 cottage curs: Beattie, *The Minstrel*, I.xxxix.   **67–70 Statesmen . . . nuisances:** An early MS version reads, in part, "Not perhaps / Less useful than the smooth and portly squire / Who with his steady coachman, steady steeds / All slick and bright with comfortable gloss / Doth in his broad glass'd chariot drive along."   **73–83:** With "Nature's law" and the idea of benevolence, cf. "Lines Left upon a Seat in a Yew-Tree," esp. ll. 52 ff. **87–105:** The old beggar, as a recipient of the villagers' past charities and a reminder of them, is a kind of pedestrian objective correlative. Wordsworth manages to combine the ideas that men are naturally good (73–83, 147–53) and that they are naturally selfish and must be compelled (99) — almost tricked — into sympathy. With ll. 90–91, cf. "Tintern Abbey," ll. 30–35, a passage similarly based on association psychology.   **109–16:** One way in which the child is father of the man (see "My Heart Leaps Up").   **153:** Cf. *Prel.*, XIII.220, "the universal heart."   **179 HOUSE . . . INDUSTRY:** Workhouse or, as we would more commonly say, poorhouse.

Animal Tranquillity and Decay   *Page 18*

Written 1797; published 1798 (under the title "Old Man Travelling," with "Animal Tranquillity and Decay, A Sketch" as a subtitle). The lines represent "an overflowing" from "The Old Cumberland Beggar" (I.F.).

A Night-Piece   *Page 19*

Written 1798; published 1815. "Composed on the road between Nether Stowey and Alfoxden, extempore. I distinctly recollect the very moment when I was struck, as described, — 'He looks up — the clouds are split' &c." (I.F.). Dorothy Wordsworth provides a similar description in a journal entry for 25 January 1798: "The sky spread over with one continuous cloud, whitened by the light of the moon, which, though her dim shape was seen, did not throw forth so strong a light as to checquer the earth with shadows. At once the clouds seemed to cleave asunder, and left her in the centre of a black-blue vault. She sailed along, followed by multitudes of stars, small, and bright, and sharp. Their brightness seemed concentrated" (D.W., *Journals*, I, 4). In 1815 Henry Crabb Robinson recorded in his diary that Wordsworth "particularly recommended to me among his Poems of Imagination *Yew Trees* and a description of Night ["A Night-Piece"]. These, he says, are among the best for the imaginative power displayed in them" (*H.C.R.*, I, 166). On the images of the poem and their relation to those of the Mt. Snowdon episode of *Prel.*, XIV (esp. ll. 17–18, 35–41, 50–56), see James Kissane, *MLN*, LXXI (1956), 183–86.

   23 Vision: As in *An Evening Walk*, l. 319, and many places elsewhere, the word (even when capitalized) means primarily "thing actually seen." **24:** Cf. "Tintern Abbey," l. 94.

Goody Blake and Harry Gill   *Page 19*

Written and published 1798. The source is a "true" case history related in Erasmus Darwin's *Zoonomia; or, The Laws of Organic Life* (1794–96). Though the focus is different, the underlying idea is much the same as that of "The Rime of the Ancient Mariner"; in both poems a man is put under a curse (the "prayer" of ll. 95–102) for violating benevolence in nature. See Wordsworth's comment on the poem in the 1800 Preface to *Lyrical Ballads* (p. 461 n. in the present volume).

   34, 41 as . . . known, our streams: The narrator identifies himself with the locale of the poem. The ineptness of the simile of l. 116 may suggest that he is the apprentice poet-narrator of "The Idiot Boy."   **39 *canty:*** Italicized probably because it is a dialect word.   **124:** Cf. *King Lear*, III.iv.151 (and elsewhere), "Poor Tom's a-cold."

The Excursion, Book I   *Page 23*

Begun in 1795 and substantially completed (as an independent poem, "The Ruined Cottage") in the spring of 1798; revised (under a new title, "The Pedlar") in December 1801–March 1802; published as the first book of Wordsworth's longest poem in 1814. (For something of the character of that work and its relation to Wordsworth's scheme for the never-finished "The Recluse," see the notes to the next selection, and the Preface to *The Excursion*, pp. 469–70 in this volume.)

> The lines that were first written [871–916] . . . were composed in '95 at Racedown; and for several passages describing the employment and demeanour of Margaret during her affliction, I was indebted to observations made in Dorsetshire, and afterwards at Alfoxden . . . . [The character of the Wanderer] is chiefly an idea of what I fancied my own character might have become in his circumstances. Nevertheless, much of what he says and does had an external existence that fell under my own youthful and subsequent observation. . . . I was born too late to have a distinct remembrance of the origin of the American war, but the state in which I represent Robert's mind to be I had frequent opportunities of observing at the commencement of our rupture with France in '93. (I.F.)

The Wanderer's upbringing in nature (118 ff.) has a number of significant parallels with the poet's own experience as recounted in the early books of *The Prelude;* two passages originally describing the Wanderer were later incorporated into the autobiographical poem (see the notes to ll. 300, 347–433, below). The story of Margaret, which has been widely admired (e.g., by F. R. Leavis, *Revaluation*, p. 179: "It seems to me the finest thing that Wordsworth wrote, and it is certainly the most disturbingly poignant"), owes much of its success to the same slow piling up of detail that can be seen in "Michael."

12 twilight . . . own: Cf. *An Evening Walk,* l. 61. **53 market-village:** Hawkshead. **77–91:** Silent poets, who are endowed with the poetic imagination (here "The vision and the faculty divine") — a special way of viewing nature — but for various reasons do not or cannot *write* poetry. Cf. "When, to the Attractions of the Busy World," ll. 77–83, and *Prel.,* X.234–35, XIII.265–75. **108 Athol:** A mountainous district in N. Perthshire, Scotland. **113–14:** Cf. "Resolution and Independence," ll. 97–98. **132–62:** Both Hartleian association psychology and Wordsworthian creative sensibility (esp. in ll. 144–48, 153–62) are involved; the result is the creation of "an ebbing and a flowing mind" in external nature. With "Or . . . Or . . . Or" (157–59) cf. "whether . . . or . . . or" in *Prel.,* II.387–92. **133 not . . . free:** See the note to *Prel.,* I.302. **136–38 deep . . . substances:** See the note to *Prel.,* I.560. **166–69:** Cf. *Prel.,* III.130–35. **177–85:** On fairy tales and romances see *Prel.,* V.341–46, 496–507. **179 left half-told:** Milton, "Il Penseroso," l. 109. **197–218:** Cf. *Prel.,* II.386–418, IV.323–38. **212:** Between this line and the next, the 1798 MS adds, "He did not feel the God; he felt his works." **226–32:** On immortality and infinity see *Prel.,* II.319–22 (and note), VI.592–640, XIV.70–129. Wordsworth's italics (226, 232) emphasize the importance of sensory experience in the Wanderer's accession of faith. **239–41:** Cf. "Tintern Abbey," ll. 88–93. **252–57:** On Wordsworth's interest in mathematics see *Prel.,* VI.115–67 and note. **300:** Following this line, the 1798 MS contains a passage later incorporated into *The Prelude* as II.397–418. **341:** To this line Wordsworth appended a long note, consisting mainly of a quotation from Robert Heron's *Journey through the Western Counties of Scotland* (1793), in defense of pedlars — a "most useful class of men," says Heron, who "become eminently skilled in the knowledge of the world . . . *form habits of reflection and of sublime contemplation* . . . [and provide] in remote parts of the country, the best mirrors of fashion, and censors of manners . . . . It is not more than twenty or thirty years since a young man going from any part of Scotland to England, of purpose to *carry the pack,* was considered as going to lead the life and acquire the fortune of a gentleman." **343–47:** Cf. the fifth paragraph of the 1800 Preface to *Lyrical Ballads* (p. 447). **347–433 In . . . grave:** In place of these lines, the 1798 MS has a shorter passage that includes an early version of *Prel.,* III.130–69. **368 without:** John Jones, *The Egotistical Sublime*, p. 114, argues that the word should be "within," as in the early MS. **370–71 He . . . suffer:** Cf. *The Tempest,* I.ii.5–6, "I have suffer'd / With those

that I saw suffer." **441–43:** Cf. *Prel.*, IV.389–91. **471–74:** Cf. the
last seven lines of "Michael." **480–81 strong . . . passion:** A type of
creative sensibility; cf. *Prel.*, XIII.287–90. **500–502 the . . . socket:**
Quoted by Shelley at the end of his Preface to *Alastor* (1816). **546
And . . . not:** Cf. *P.L.*, VII.144, "whom thir place knows here no more."
703 'trotting brooks': Burns, "To William Simpson," l. 87, "trottin' burn
[= brook]." **708 bladed grass:** *A Midsummer-Night's Dream*, I.i.211.
922–30: See *Prel.*, XIII.246–49. **934–55:** Lines 934–39 and "the enlightened spirit . . . [reposing] Upon the breast of Faith" (953–55) were
added to the poem in 1845.

From The Recluse   *Page 45*

Early in 1798 Wordsworth began planning a long philosophical poem on
Man, Nature, and Society, to be called "The Recluse." His own account of
the enterprise is given in the Preface to *The Excursion* (pp. 469–70 in this
volume); Coleridge's, in his *Table Talk* for 21 July 1832, runs as follows:

> the plan laid out, and, I believe, partly suggested by me, was, that
> Wordsworth should assume the station of a man in mental repose,
> one whose principles were made up, and so prepared to deliver upon
> authority a system of philosophy. He was to treat man as man, — a
> subject of eye, ear, touch, and taste, in contact with external nature,
> and informing the senses from the mind, and not compounding a mind
> out of the senses; then he was to describe the pastoral and other
> states of society, assuming something of the Juvenalian spirit as he ap-
> proached the high civilization of cities and towns, and opening a
> melancholy picture of the present state of degeneracy and vice; thence
> he was to infer and reveal the proof of, and necessity for, the whole
> state of man and society being subject to, and illustrative of, a re-
> demptive process in operation, showing how this idea reconciled all
> the anomalies, and promised future glory and restoration. Something
> of this sort was, I think, agreed on.

Of the three parts that he projected, Wordsworth completed only the second
— *The Excursion* (1814), a sometimes heavily didactic nine-book-long
conversation between four principal characters, the Poet, the Wanderer, the
Solitary, and the Pastor, mainly intended to "correct" the Solitary's despondency over a number of things, from domestic afflictions and disappointment of his expectations from the French Revolution to a general
"want of faith in the great truths of Religion, and want of confidence in
the virtue of Mankind" (Argument to Book III). A single introductory book
of the first part, entitled "Home at Grasmere," was largely unpublished
until 1888. After 1805, a sizable obstacle to completion was the fact that
Wordsworth had already expressed most of his ideas on Man, Nature, and
Society in *The Prelude*, which, though originally conceived as a part of
"The Recluse," afterward became merely a "preparatory poem," as he calls
it in the Preface to *The Excursion*, examining "how far Nature and Education had qualified him" for the monumental task.

The passage given here, the final 107 lines of Part I, Book I ("Home at Grasmere"), was probably written in the spring of 1798; it was first published in 1814, at the end of the Preface to *The Excursion*, where it is quoted "as a kind of *Prospectus* of the design and scope of the whole Poem [i.e., "The Recluse"]." It states not only the theme of that large project, but Wordsworth's main concern in *The Prelude* and many of his shorter poems as well.

760–61 soothes . . . Mind: Cf. *Peter Bell*, l. 142. **765 Soul:** As frequently in Wordsworth's poems, the word is interchangeable with "mind" (see the note to ll. 793–94, below) and even "heart." **766 numerous verse:** *P.L.*, V.150. **768:** A later addition (the line does not appear in the earliest MSS). **776 "fit . . . few!":** *P.L.*, VII.31. Urania (778) is the muse invoked by Milton at the beginning of Book VII. **781–94:** Cf. *Prel.*, III.173–84, IX.238–40. **786–88 Jehovah . . . unalarmed:** In 1825 Crabb Robinson noted that "This '*pass them unalarmed*' greatly offended Blake. 'Does Mr. Wordsworth think his mind can surpass Jehovah?' I tried to twist this passage into a sense corresponding with Blake's own theories, but failed, and Wordsworth was finally set down as a Pagan" (*H.C.R.*, I, 327). **787 empyreal thrones:** *P.L.*, II.430. **793–94:** Cf. *Peter Bell*, ll. 143–45, *Prel.*, XIII.240–41, and see the Introduction. For l. 793 an early MS reads "Into my soul, into the soul of man." **806–807, 810–11:** Cf. the metaphors of marriage in Coleridge's "Dejection: An Ode," ll. 49, 68. **813 the sensual:** Those under the tyranny of the bodily eye (see *Prel.*, XII.127–51). With "sleep / Of Death" (813–14) cf. *Prel.*, XIV.160, "universe of death." **816–24:** The "ennobling interchange" of *Prel.*, XIII.375–78 (see note), exemplified in the Mt. Snowdon episode of Book XIV. **832 barricadoed:** *P.L.*, VIII.241. **836–38 Descend . . . come:** In a note Wordsworth cites Shakespeare's Sonnet 107, "Not mine own fears, nor the prophetic soul / Of the wide world dreaming on things to come." **842–43 star-like . . . influence:** Cf. *P.L.*, VII.374–75, "the *Pleiades* . . . Shedding sweet influence." **847–51:** Wordsworth's "more lowly matter" became *The Prelude*.

To My Sister   *Page 47*

Written and published 1798. The original title was "Lines Written at a Small Distance from My House, and Sent by My Little Boy to the Person to Whom They Are Addressed" (see the note to l. 13). Though the poem differs in tone from "Expostulation and Reply" and "The Tables Turned," with which it has several ideas in common, we ought not to treat it as a document in some peculiar Wordsworthian nature "philosophy"; the poet makes clear in ll. 15–16, 24, 39–40 that he is expressing the feelings of the moment.

5–8: Cf. *Prel.*, I.1–4 (and note "seem[s]" in both places). **13 Edward:** "My little boy-messenger on this occasion was the son of Basil Montagu" (I.F.). **26:** Originally (1798–1832) "Than fifty years of reason." **33–34:** Cf. "Tintern Abbey," ll. 93–102.

Lines Written in Early Spring   *Page 48*

Written and published 1798.

> Actually composed while I was sitting by the side of the brook that
> runs down from the Comb, in which stands the village of Alford,
> through the grounds of Alfoxden. It was a chosen resort of mine. The
> brook fell down a sloping rock so as to make a waterfall considerable
> for that country, and across the pool below, had fallen a tree, an ash
> if I rightly remember, from which rose perpendicularly, boughs in
> search of the light intercepted by the deep shade above. The boughs
> bore leaves of green that for want of sunshine had faded into almost
> lily-white; and from the underside of this natural sylvan bridge de-
> pended long and beautiful tresses of ivy which waved gently in the
> breeze that might poetically speaking be called the breath of the
> waterfall. (I.F. — cf. Coleridge's "This Lime-Tree Bower My Prison,"
> ll. 9–20)

The point of the poem (esp. in ll. 1–8, 21–24) is that everything in nature
is blended in harmony and pleasure, and only man is a cause of discord.
As in some parts of *The Prelude*, the poet is both a human participant in
this harmony (5–6) and a detached observer of man's follies (7–8). The
animistic tendencies of ll. 9–20, like the "what if" speculation of Coleridge's
"The Eolian Harp," ll. 44–48, are the product of momentary feeling (the
"sweet mood" of l. 3) rather than of any rationally conceived doctrine; l.
19 and the earlier version of ll. 21–22 (see note) suggest that reason is
opposed to such tendencies.

   3–4: See "Resolution and Independence," ll. 22–28 and note.   **5–6:**
On the linking of man's mind (here "human soul") and external nature,
see "The Recluse," ll. 805–24.   **11–12:** See *Prel.*, XII.11–12 and note,
and R. D. Havens' chapter on "Animism," *The Mind of a Poet*, pp. 68–87;
cf. "poetically speaking" at the end of the I.F. note above.   **21–22:**
Originally (1798–1815), "If I these thoughts may not prevent, / If such
be of my creed the plan."

We Are Seven   *Page 49*

Written and published 1798. "The little girl who is the heroine I met
within the area of Goodrich Castle [in the Wye Valley] in the year 1793.
. . . I composed it [the poem] while walking in the grove at Alfoxden.
My friends will not deem it too trifling to relate that while walking to and
fro I composed the last stanza.first, having begun with the last line" (I.F.).
See Wordsworth's explanation of the poem in the Preface to *Lyrical Ballads*
(p. 448 n. in this volume), and the comments by David Perkins, *The
Quest for Permanence*, pp. 69–71, and David Ferry, *The Limits of Mortality*, pp. 84–85. The poem presents an unresolved dramatic conflict —
between reason and imagination, or between two kinds of reason, the
analytic and the unifying — in which each side is valid. The adult speaker
makes a clear-cut distinction between a world of the living and another

world of the dead; the child refuses to give up her own (intuitive) view that the two realms are one (cf. "To H. C.," l. 10, "earth and heaven do make one imagery"). Because the child's position has a certain logic of its own (her six siblings are, after all, equally out of sight) and because the adult's mathematical precision and insistence on death become toward the end both comic and slightly unpleasant, we may say that the child has the poet's sympathy in this encounter — though it does not follow that he shares her simplicity of outlook. Cf. the next poem.

1–4: This stanza was contributed by Coleridge, and the first line was originally (1798–1805) "A simple child, dear brother Jim" ("Jim" being James Tobin, a friend who lived in Bristol). The fourth line may be interpreted as either "What can it be expected to know" or "What ought it to know." See Wordsworth's use of the stanza in the I.F. note to the Intimations ode. **19 Conway:** A seaport town in N. Wales. **65–69:** The final stanza combines despair (the child will never understand) with smugness (the adult knows better).

Anecdote for Fathers   Page 51

Written and published 1798 (with the subtitle "Shewing How the Art of Lying May Be Taught"). "This was suggested in front of Alfoxden. The Boy was a son of my friend, Basil Montagu, who had been two or three years under our care. The name of Kilve is from a village on the Bristol Channel, about a mile from Alfoxden; and the name of Liswyn Farm was taken from a beautiful spot on the Wye" (I.F.). Wordsworth's solemn explanation to one reader — "my intention was to point out the injurious effects of putting inconsiderate questions to Children, and urging them to give answers upon matters either uninteresting to them, or upon which they had no decided opinion" (*L.Y.*, I, 253) — is perhaps less helpful than the original ironic subtitle or the Latin epigraph that replaced it in 1845 (a translation from the Greek of Porphyry as quoted by Eusebius, *Preparatio Evangelica*, VI.v: "Restrain that force of yours, for I shall tell lies if you drive me to it"). Variants to ll. 14 ("To think, and think, and think again" 1798–1820) and 47 ("five times" 1798–1836) support the idea that we have here the same kind of conflict as in the preceding poem between an adult who questions on the basis of analytic reason and a child who responds intuitively. The last stanza, which was never altered after its first publication (cf. the deletion of original final lines in "The Reverie of Poor Susan," "A Whirl-Blast," and "Strange Fits of Passion"), presents a special problem: either the speaker has suddenly and unconvincingly awakened to a new understanding, or the lines represent a wooden attempt at sarcasm, in which, as at the end of "We Are Seven," the adult remains firm in his conviction that reason must prevail.

A Whirl-Blast from Behind the Hill   Page 52

Written in March 1798; published 1800. Though the poem was later classed with "Poems of the Fancy," it serves as a typical example of imagination at work on natural phenomena (with the last four lines especially, cf. "I Wandered Lonely as a Cloud," which Wordsworth included among "Poems of the Imagination"). Originally (1800–05) there were four additional lines after l. 22:

> Oh! grant me Heaven a heart at ease,
> That I may never cease to find,
> Even in appearances like these,
> Enough to nourish and to stir my mind!

Simon Lee   *Page 53*

Written and published 1798. "This old man had been huntsman to the squires of Alfoxden. . . . [The incident occurred] as mentioned in the poem . . . . The expression when the hounds were out, 'I dearly love their voice,' was word for word from his own lips" (I.F.). For an account of Wordsworth's many revisions from 1800 to 1845, mainly in the rearranging of stanzas and half-stanzas, see de Selincourt, *P.W.*, IV, 413; on the tone of the poem see John F. Danby, *The Simple Wordsworth*, pp. 38–47.

   1: Cardiganshire is a county in S. Wales.   **6 huntsman:** Manager of the hunt and the person in charge of the hounds. Simon's "ankles swoln and thick" (35) are the more impressive in connection with his former occupation.   **25 oh . . . change:** Milton, "Lycidas," l. 37.   **61 ff.:** Wordsworthian anticlimax; cf. "The Idiot Boy," ll. 312–46, the Prologue to *Peter Bell*, and "Hart-Leap Well," ll. 97–100.

Her Eyes Are Wild   *Page 55*

Written and published 1798. Originally (1798–1805) entitled "The Mad Mother," the poem is an example of Wordsworth's interest in abnormal psychology (see also the next poem, which is similarly concerned with maternal feelings); in madness, as in humble and rustic life, "our elementary feelings co-exist in a state of greater simplicity, and, consequently, may be more accurately contemplated, and more forcibly communicated" (see p. 447). It is also one of the many poems on the theme — very common at the time — of the deserted mother (see *An Evening Walk*, ll. 250–78, *Exc.*, I.502 ff., and "The Thorn"). Although "The subject was reported to me by a lady of Bristol, who had seen the poor creature" (I.F.), the poem has a number of details in common with "Lady Anne Bothwell's Lament," which Wordsworth read in Percy's *Reliques*.

The Idiot Boy   *Page 58*

Written and published 1798. "The last stanza . . . was the foundation of the whole. The words were reported to me by my dear friend, Thomas Poole; but I have since heard the same repeated of other Idiots. Let me add that this long poem was composed in the groves of Alfoxden, almost extempore; not a word, I believe, being corrected, though one stanza was omitted. I mention this in gratitude to those happy moments, for, in truth,

I never wrote anything with so much glee" (I.F.). To the young John Wilson's objections concerning the subject of the poem Wordsworth replied at length in a letter of June 1802:

> You begin what you say upon *The Idiot Boy* with this observation, that nothing is a fit subject for poetry which does not please. But here follows a question, Does not please whom? . . . [To the question of whom a poem ought to please] I answer, human nature, as it has been [and ever] will be. But where are we to find the best measure of this? I answer, [from with]in; by stripping our own hearts naked, and by looking out of ourselves to[wards men] who lead the simplest lives, and those most according to nature; men who have never known false refinements, wayward and artificial desires, false criticisms, effeminate habits of thinking and feeling, or who, having known these things, have outgrown them. . . . [Few people] ever consider books but with reference to their power of pleasing those persons and men of a higher rank; few descend lower, among cottages and fields, and among children. A man must have done this habitually before his judgment upon *The Idiot Boy* would be in any way decisive with me. I *know* I have done this myself habitually; I wrote the poem with exceeding delight and pleasure, and whenever I read it I read it with pleasure. You have given me praise for having reflected faithfully in my Poems the feelings of human nature. I would fain hope that I have done so. But a great Poet ought to do more than this: he ought, to a certain degree, to rectify men's feelings, to give them new compositions of feeling, to render their feelings more sane, pure, and permanent, in short, more consonant to nature, that is, to eternal nature, and the great moving spirit of things. He ought to travel before men occasionally as well as at their sides. . . . (*E.L.*, pp. 294–96; see the entire letter, pp. 292–98)

Though Southey praised the "excellence of its execution," the poem has been much ridiculed (e.g., by Byron in *English Bards and Scotch Reviewers*, ll. 247–54), and modern critics — with the exception of John E. Jordan, *PMLA*, LXXIII (1958), 88–89, and Danby, *The Simple Wordsworth*, pp. 48–57 — have been unable to reconcile Wordsworth's declared seriousness of purpose with the unquestionably intentional comic effects of his technique. We do well to keep in mind the experimental character of the lyrical ballads (see Wordsworth's plain statement in the second paragraph of the 1798 Advertisement, p. 443). Almost no subject in literature is more liable to sentimentality than maternal love, and where basic emotions are involved some kind of countering indirection is necessary. Here the chief indirection lies in the brisk manner of the fictitious narrator, a literal-minded apprentice poet who only half understands what is going on, who pleads with the Muses to be allowed some fanciful inventions, who is more surprised than we are upon the rediscovery of Johnny ("And that's the very Pony, too!"), and who enters fully into the silly, slapstick joyfulness of the reunion (the Pony, he notes, is "milder far" than the mother: "You hardly can perceive his joy"). Especially at the end, the grotesqueness of the humor tempers the sentiment, relieving the potential heaviness of the situation, and the simple tale of separation and reconciliation may move the sympathetic reader seemingly almost in spite of the obstacles that are put forth. For a suggestion of the principle involved, see the 1800 Preface to *Lyrical Ballads* (p. 459), where Wordsworth, in speaking of meter, mentions "tempering and restraining the passion by an intertexture of ordinary feeling, and of feeling not strictly and necessarily connected with the passion."

1 ff.: The bouncy meter, references to the time of night and the noise of the owl, and the narrator's questioning all are reminiscent of the opening of "Christabel," the first part of which was written probably in 1798. **26 what she ails:** I.e., what ails her. Despite ll. 21, 46 (further indications of the simplemindedness of the characters and the narrator), Susan's ailment is not very serious.   **168, 171 quandary:** Italicized probably for the same reason that Johnson in his *Dictionary* had called it a "low word." **312–46:** Wordsworthian anticlimax (see "Simon Lee," ll. 61 ff. and note). The narrator's romantic wishes (prefigured by Betty Foy's imaginings in ll. 222–31) are rejected by the tough-minded Muses of Coleridge's second cardinal point of poetry; see the dedicatory epistle and Prologue to *Peter Bell* and notes.   **338 fourteen years:** Since the normal term of apprenticeship was from five to seven years, the narrator is a slow learner, although ll. 435–36 show that he has gained something from his period of study.   **450:** Cf. "Christabel," ll. 2–3, "the owls have awakened the crowing cock; / Tu — whit! —— Tu — whoo!"

<h3 style="text-align:center">The Thorn   Page 70</h3>

Written (in March–April) and published 1798. "Arose out of my observing, on the ridge of Quantock Hill, on a stormy day, a thorn which I had often past, in calm and bright weather, without noticing it. I said to myself, 'Cannot I by some invention do as much to make this Thorn permanently an impressive object as the storm has made it to my eyes at this moment?' I began the poem accordingly, and composed it with great rapidity" (I.F.). For his brief explanation in the last paragraph of the 1798 Advertisement (see p. 444), Wordsworth in 1800–05 substituted a long note to the poem that reads, in part:

The character which I have here introduced speaking is sufficiently common. The Reader will perhaps have a general notion of it, if he has ever known a man, a Captain of a small trading vessel, for example, who, being past the middle age of life, had retired upon an annuity or small independent income to some village or country town of which he was not a native, or in which he had not been accustomed to live. Such men, having little to do, become credulous and talkative from indolence; and from the same cause, and other predisposing causes by which it is probable that such men may have been affected, they are prone to superstition. On which account it appeared to me proper to select a character like this to exhibit some of the general laws by which superstition acts upon the mind. Superstitious men are almost always men of slow faculties and deep feelings: their minds are not loose but adhesive; they have a reasonable share of imagination, by which word I mean the faculty which produces impressive effects out of simple elements; but they are utterly destitute of fancy, the power by which pleasure and surprise are excited by sudden varieties of situation and by accumulated imagery.

It was my wish in this poem to show the manner in which such men cleave to the same ideas; and to follow the turns of passion, always different, yet not palpably different, by which their conversation is swayed. I had two objects to attain; first, to represent a picture which should not be unimpressive, yet consistent with the character that should describe it; secondly, while I adhered to the style in which such persons describe, to take care that words, which in their minds are impregnated with passion, should likewise convey passion to Readers who are not accustomed to sympathize with men feeling in that manner or using such language. It seemed to me that this might be done by calling in the assistance of Lyrical and rapid Metre. It was necessary that the Poem, to be natural, should in reality move slowly; yet I hoped, that, by the aid of the metre, to those who should at all enter into the spirit of the Poem, it would appear to move quickly.

Like Wordsworth's contemporaries, most critics have discounted this statement of intention, preferring to read the poem as a study in social morality, with the main focus on the plight of Martha Ray (Helen Darbishire, *The Poet Wordsworth*, pp. 36–44, and Danby, *The Simple Wordsworth*, pp. 57–72, are recent examples); but S. M. Parrish, *ELH*, XXIV (1957), 153–63, has convincingly argued that Wordsworth did in fact know what he was doing:

> The manner in which the narrator associates ideas is precisely what "The Thorn" is about. The ideas themselves — that is, the "events" of the poem — are unimportant except as they reflect the working of the narrator's imagination. In fact, the point of the poem may very well be that its central "event" has no existence outside of the narrator's imagination — that there is no Martha Ray sitting in a scarlet cloak behind a crag on the mountain top, that the narrator has neither seen her nor heard her, that what he has seen is a gnarled old tree in a blinding storm, that what he has heard (besides the creaking of the branches, or the whistling of the mountain wind) is village superstition about a woman wronged years ago. (p. 155)

Cf. *Prel.*, VIII.365–406, esp. ll. 389–91. The poem shows only very general resemblances to the sources that have been suggested for it — William Taylor's translation of G. A. Bürger's "Des Pfarrers Tochter von Taubenhain" (*Monthly Magazine*, 1796), John Langhorne's *The Country Justice* (1774–77), and a Scottish ballad that Wordsworth could have read in David Herd's *Ancient and Modern Scottish Songs* (1776) or James Johnson's *The Scots Musical Museum* (1787–1803).

32–33: Originally (1798–1815), "I've measured it from side to side: / 'Tis three feet long, and two feet wide." Wordsworth altered these famous lines and some others (not noticed here) after Coleridge objected to them as "sudden and unpleasant sinkings" (*Biog. Lit.*, ch. XVII). **44, 46, 48 vermilion, scarlet, red:** Though the hill of moss is of "All colours," shades of red predominate — a fact that, in connection with Martha's scarlet cloak (63), may have a bearing on whether the narrator did actually see her (cf. l. 50 with 71, and see ll. 175–76, 187). **60, 67 For oft, At all times:** Cf. ll. 98–99, according to which no one (save possibly the narrator) has ever seen her there. **65–66:** The auditory similarity of "woe is me" and "misery" supports the idea that the narrator and others have heard merely the sounds of wind, storm, and breeze (mentioned many times in the poem). On the one occasion when he thinks he saw Martha, the narrator says he turned away (190) before he heard her cry. **89–90, 144–51:** Cf. the later reversal in ll. 203–31 (esp. 207, 229). The original version of ll. 144–51 (1798–1820) more strongly emphasizes the narrator's (and the townspeople's) ignorance of any facts: "No more I know, I wish I did, / And I would tell it all to you; / For what became of this poor child / There's none that ever knew: / And if a child was born or no, / There's no one that could ever tell; / And if 'twas born alive or dead, / There's no one knows, as I have said." **170–73:** See the second sentence of the 1800–05 note as quoted above. Possibly the narrator mentions his telescope (which he did not, of course, use after the storm came on) in an unconscious effort to bolster the truth (169) of his account. **175–91:** See the notes to ll. 44–48, 65–66. **203–31:** None of these very specific details of the local legend has been mentioned earlier; cf. ll. 89–90, 144–51.

Peter Bell   *Page 77*

Written in April–June 1798; revised in 1799 and subsequent years; published 1819 (for earlier readings from six MSS of the poem, see the apparatus in *P.W.*, II, 331–82).

> Founded upon an anecdote, which I read in a newspaper, of an ass being found hanging his head over a canal in a wretched posture. Upon examination a dead body was found in the water and proved to be the body of its master. The countenance, gait, and figure of Peter, were taken from a wild rover with whom I walked from Builth, on the river Wye, downwards nearly as far as the town of Hay. He told me strange stories. . . . The number of Peter's wives was taken from the trespasses in this way of a lawless creature who lived in the county of Durham . . . . Benoni, or the child of sorrow [909–10], I knew when I was a school-boy. His mother had been deserted by a gentleman in the neighbourhood, she herself being a gentlewoman by birth. The circumstances of her story were told me by my dear old Dame, Anne Tyson, who was her confidante. The Lady died broken-hearted. — In the woods of Alfoxden I used to take great delight in noticing the habits, tricks, and physiognomy of asses; and I have no doubt that I was thus put upon writing the poem out of liking for the creature that is so often dreadfully abused. — The crescent-moon, which makes such a figure in the prologue, assumed this

character one evening while I was watching its beauty in front of Alfoxden House. I intended this poem for the [1798] volume . . . but it was not published for more than twenty years afterwards. — The worship of the Methodists or Ranters is often heard during the stillness of the summer evening in the country with affecting accompaniments of rural beauty. In both the psalmody and the voice of the preacher there is, not unfrequently, much solemnity likely to impress the feelings of the rudest characters under favourable circumstances. (I.F.)

According to Wordsworth's 1819 dedicatory epistle (to Southey), "The Poem of Peter Bell, as the Prologue will shew, was composed under a belief that the Imagination not only does not require for its exercise the intervention of supernatural agency, but that, though such agency be excluded, the faculty may be called forth as imperiously, and for kindred results of pleasure, by incidents, within the compass of poetic probability, in the humblest departments of daily life." The statement has an important bearing on Coleridge's explanation (*Biog. Lit.*, ch. XIV) of "the two cardinal points of poetry" that he and Wordsworth intended to illustrate with "a series of poems . . . of two sorts" in *Lyrical Ballads:* "In the one [Coleridge's], the incidents and agents were to be, in part at least, supernatural; and the excellence aimed at was to consist in the interesting of the affections by the dramatic truth of such emotions, as would naturally accompany such situations, supposing them real. . . . Mr. Wordsworth, on the other hand, was . . . to give the charm of novelty to things of every day, and to excite a feeling analogous to the supernatural, by awakening the mind's attention from the lethargy of custom, and directing it to the loveliness and the wonders of the world before us." *Peter Bell* has frequently been compared with "The Ancient Mariner" (see Charles J. Smith, *SP*, LIV, 1957, 58–63, and earlier works cited there): both poems make use of a dramatic framework, a plot of crime, punishment, and redemption, a journey filled with torments for the hero, a union with society at the end; and they have a similar theme (though Coleridge stresses the sanctity of all things in nature, Wordsworth the sanctity of the human heart). But for Coleridge's genuinely mysterious events and hierarchy of spirits Wordsworth substitutes natural events and an interest in psychology; Peter's conversion comes about through the awakening of faculties that he has never used before (see "Lines Left upon a Seat in a Yew-Tree," ll. 52–54), and there is nothing supernatural about any of the incidents in the poem. Wordsworth's epigraphs (from *Romeo and Juliet*, II.ii.43, and *Julius Caesar*, I.ii.146) announce the unaristocratic, commonplace matter of the tale; the Prologue, a rejection of all high-flying or hidden subjects and scenes in favor of "The common growth of mother-earth" and the marvels of the mind (133, 143), sounds a clear note of anti-romanticism in the midst of the Romantic Movement; and the tale itself, another Wordsworthian investigation of connections between the human mind and external nature, shows — for once quite plainly — that the mind creates whatever "life" it finds in the objective world.

As in "The Idiot Boy," Wordsworth's technique in the first two-thirds of *Peter Bell* involves humor that is at least partly the result of the ineptness of a fictitious narrator — a rustic storyteller who plays and dances with his narration, feeling himself "all unfit / For such high argument" (789–90). Charles E. Mounts, *PQ*, XXIII (1944), 110–13, has shown similarities between the boat-narrator relationship in the Prologue and the eagle-"Chaucer" relationship in Chaucer's *The House of Fame;* but Chaucerian influence also extends into the tale itself, e.g., where one of the auditors (like the Host after two hundred lines of *Sir Thopas*) stops the narrator and tells him how a story should be told, and where details of Peter's life and character are jumbled together in the seemingly haphazard manner of the *General Prologue* (with l. 235, "Sure never man like him did roam!" cf. the tone of "A bettre felawe sholde men noght fynde" and "Ne was ther swich another pardoner," *Gen. Prol.*, ll. 648, 693); the inn "Brim-full" of a cursing "carousing crew" (867–70) is reminiscent of the setting of the *Pardoner's Tale*. In the last 250 lines the poem grows increasingly serious, and though ll. 1111–15 recall details of the conclusion of "The Idiot Boy," the physical action here, because of the difference in circumstances, is almost unbearably pathetic. There has been a considerable change in tone from "flying horse" and "huge balloon" at the outset to Peter's "Oh! God, I can endure no more!" near the end.

In a letter of 1808, speaking of "the sickly taste of the Public in verse," Wordsworth wrote that "The *People* would love the Poem of Peter Bell, but the *Public* (a very different Being) will never love it" (*M.Y.*, I, 169–70). For obvious reasons the poem has been much parodied (by Shelley, who may have read the Prologue as an attack on *Alastor,* and by Keats's friend J. H. Reynolds, among others). Crabb Robinson thought it "one of the most delightful of Wordsworth's tales: with infinite imagination, and a great deal of profound psychology interspersed with exquisite description, psychological and natural"; Lamb considered it "one of the worst of Wordsworth's works" (*H.C.R.*, I, 96–97, 230). Modern criticism has tended to side with Lamb, though there have been some notable exceptions — e.g., Lascelles Abercrombie's essay in *The Art of Wordsworth* (1952), pp. 134–54, and Carl R. Woodring's comments in *PQ*, XXX (1951), 432–34.

128 some . . . Youth: Sometimes interpreted as a reference to Coleridge. **131–45:** See *Prel.*, V.540–41, 567, 571–77 and note. **136 magic ring:** Perhaps an allusion to Chaucer's *Squire's Tale.* **143–45:** Cf. "The Recluse," ll. 793–94. **191–200:** The Squire's rejection of the narrator's epic beginning *in medias res* marks a further descent from "ethereal height" (152). **201 Potter:** "In the dialect of the North, a hawker of earthenware is thus designated" (W., 1819, 2nd edn.). **248–50:** The point of these much ridiculed lines (and of ll. 236–72 more generally) is Peter's lack of imagination. See the I.F. note to "The Thorn"; in that poem the thorn, muddy pool, and hill of moss are "nothing more" until the narrator's imagination makes something permanently impressive of them. **268 moving time:** I.e., feeling response of the moment. **283.** Cf. "The Thorn," ll. 89, 203, 232.   **321 ff.**: With Peter characterized, the story now gets under way. Quotation marks are dropped, and beginning in l. 341 there is a shift to the present tense.   **325 river Swale**: In Yorkshire.   **501–15**: With these speculations (all having to do with the supernatural) cf. the Prologue and "The Idiot Boy," ll. 312–46. In 1819 only, following l. 515, there was an additional stanza that Wordsworth subsequently omitted so as "not to offend the pious" (*L.Y.*, I, 312): "Is it a party in a parlour? / Cramm'd just as they on earth were cramm'd — / Some sipping punch, some sipping tea, / But, as you by their faces see, / All silent and all damn'd!" Shelley used the stanza as an epigraph to "Peter Bell the Third."   **578–80**: Cf. *Prel.*, V.448–50.   **736–85**: This partly serious, partly satirical digression is a further illustration (see also ll. 916–20) of Wordsworth's statement in the dedicatory epistle that the imagination (here "Spirits of the Mind") "does not require . . . the intervention of supernatural agency."   **834–40**: Cf. *An Evening Walk*, l. 141. Miners frequently blasted in the evenings, and reverberations could be heard or felt for a distance of five miles.   **908 From Scripture**: Genesis 35:18.   **973–74**: "The notion is very general, that the Cross on the back and shoulders of this Animal has the origin here alluded to" (W., 1819).   **1134 ten months**: I.e., ten lunar months, the 280-day period of gestation — a literal rendering of rebirth (see l. 1074).

Expostulation and Reply   *Page 106*

Written (in the spring) and published 1798. This and the next piece (which were the opening poems of the 1800 *Lyrical Ballads,* and later of the section called "Poems of Sentiment and Reflection") have frequently been made the basis of a Wordsworthian nature "philosophy" that the poet himself would have been the first to reject. Rather unaccountably, few readers have been willing to accept the idea that Wordsworth is being intentionally playful in them (for an example of the controversy over this point see O. J. Campbell and Henry S. Pancoast, *MLN*, XXXVI, 1921, 408–14; XXXVII, 1922, 279–83). It ought to be clear that Wordsworth is dramatically opposing two extremes (on the one hand, men without books are "forlorn and blind," merely dreaming their time away; on the other, "*One* impulse from a vernal wood" is more instructive than the sum of all books ever written), and that, as usual, the desirable truth lies somewhere in between. See "To My Sister" and notes.

8 their kind: Perhaps purposely ambiguous, meaning both "other men" and "other *dead* men."   **15 Matthew**: It has been suggested, on not very good grounds, that the "friend who was somewhat unreasonably attached to modern books of moral philosophy" (see p. 444 in this volume) was William Hazlitt, who visited Wordsworth in the spring of 1798. It is probably equally wrong to identify this Matthew with the old man of "The Two April Mornings" and "The Fountain."   **17–20**: In *The Prelude* (e.g., XII.127–51) this "tyranny" of the senses is described as a bad condition.   **21–24**: Though it is a necessary first stage in the building up of the mind, the importance of "wise passiveness" is countered virtually throughout *The Prelude* by Wordsworth's emphasis on the mind's active faculties; cf. *Prel.*, II.384–86, and the climactic statement in XII.222–23. "Powers" (21) is a favorite word that, as Wordsworth uses it, is very nearly meaningless. **26:** Cf. *Prel.*, I.586–88, V.13, VIII.172.

The Tables Turned *Page 107*

Written and published 1798. See the notes to the preceding poem.

26–28: See "A Poet's Epitaph," ll. 17–20, and *Prel.*, II.216–19 and note. The analytic reason ("meddling intellect") is implicitly contrasted with the imagination (another kind of reason), which finds or creates unity.

Lines Composed a Few Miles above
Tintern Abbey *Page 108*

Written (in July) and published 1798. "No poem of mine was composed under circumstances more pleasant for me to remember than this. I began it upon leaving Tintern, after crossing the Wye, and concluded it just as I was entering Bristol in the evening, after a ramble of four or five days, with my Sister. Not a line of it was altered, and not any part of it written down till I reached Bristol" (I.F.). In the 1800–05 editions of *Lyrical Ballads* Wordsworth appended a note: "I have not ventured to call this Poem an Ode; but it was written with a hope that in the transitions, and the impassioned music of the versification, would be found the principal requisites of that species of composition."

The "impassioned . . . versification" tends to conceal some basic contradictions in the poem — and not just in the poet's attitude toward man, who in early and middle passages (esp. ll. 11–18, 90–102) is represented as being in union with nature but elsewhere (esp. in ll. 128–31) is described as in opposition. On the one hand, there is in ll. 88–111 (usually taken as the central passage of the poem) the strong assertion that in his maturity the poet has learned to view nature in conjunction with "The still, sad music of humanity," has felt "A presence," a "something far more deeply interfused" that rolls through all things including the mind of man, and has found in nature "the nurse, / The guide, the guardian of my heart, and soul / Of all my moral being." On the other hand, there is in much of the rest of the poem (note the tone of ll. 60, 65–66, 83–88, 111–13, 116–20, 137–39) the suggestion that this gaining of maturity is not an arrival but a falling-off, and that his sister Dorothy, who is represented as being in an earlier stage of development in relation to nature, is much better off than he is. As in the Intimations ode, with which the poem deserves careful comparison for both similarities and differences, the assertion of "Abundant recompense" (88) does not carry complete conviction; the poet looks forward to Dorothy's growing up not to the apprehension of divine presence in nature that he claims he has achieved, but to a reliance on memory, a condition in which her mind will be "a mansion for all lovely forms, / Thy memory . . . a dwelling-place / For all sweet sounds and harmonies" (137–42), and in ll. 146–49 he sounds as if he himself will be dead. Although, as Ferry points out (*The Limits of Mortality*, pp. 110–11), what we take for "a confusion of feeling . . . may be a complexity of feeling, a contemplated and contained ambivalence," it is sometimes difficult, even after many readings, to decide what the poem is primarily about. The opening emphasis on the length of time between the 1793 and 1798 visits to the Wye (1–2, and note "again" in ll. 2, 4, 14), the section describing what his recollections during the interval have meant to him (22 ff.), and the closing emphasis on remembering (141, 145, 149, 155) all suggest that the main subject is memory. See the discussions by Harold Bloom, *The Visionary Company*, pp. 127–36, and Albert S. Gérard, *Studies in Romanticism*, III (1963), 10–23. In style, structure, and some aspects of theme, the poem recalls Coleridge's much less complicated "Frost at Midnight," written five months earlier.

5–18: In the interconnection of earth and sky (7–8) and the merging of things of man with things of nature (13–18), the opening description prefigures the unity celebrated in ll. 93–102.   **22–30:** Cf. "I Wandered Lonely as a Cloud," ll. 19–24.   **28:** See *Prel.*, I.584 and note.   **30 tranquil restoration:** Cf. *Prel.*, XII.286 ("future restoration"), and the idea of "emotion recollected in tranquillity" in the 1800 Preface to *Lyrical Ballads*.   **35–49:** While it is true that in the ordinary process of recollection, when our present surroundings fade away, it may be said that "we are laid asleep / In body, and become a living soul" (i.e., alive in spirit — cf. ll. 55, 57), Wordsworth nevertheless seems to be describing something that is unexplainable in terms of association psychology; in speaking of the lightening of "the burthen of the mystery" and seeing "into the life of things" he uses the language of the mystic experience (with which the later "language of the sense," 108, does not accord). In the non-explanation that follows (49–57), however, he returns to the first idea of the paragraph (22–30), saying merely that he has mentally revisited the Wye in the interim. With ll. 38–40 cf. *Prel.*, I.21–23.   **49–57:** Cf. *Prel.*, II.419–26.   **60 sad perplexity:** Presumably owing to the discrepancy between the "recognitions dim and faint" and the scene before him (the present "picture of the mind").   **64 food:** Cf. "feed" in l. 127. Wordsworth frequently uses metaphors of feeding and drinking to describe the taking in of sense impressions; see, e.g., *Exc.*, I.152, 206, "To My Sister," l. 27, "Expostulation and Reply," l. 23, *Prel.*, I.563, II.237, IV.288, VI.481, 723, XII.325, XIII.205.   **67–102:** In these lines a number of critics (most notably Arthur Beatty, *William Wordsworth: His Doctrine and Art in Their Historical Relations*) have distinguished three stages in the poet's development in relation to nature — the first (73–74) being one of simple physical delight in running and playing out of doors (cf. the child as "best Philosopher . . . Mighty Prophet" in the Intimations ode, ll. 110–16), the second (67–72, 75–83) being a stage of purely aesthetic appreciation, and the third (88–102) involving a more philosophic view, with ethical implications at the end of the passage, in which nature and man are united by a vaguely described "something" that "rolls through all things." Wordsworth begins this passage with the second, because he was in that stage when he first visited the Wye in 1793. See *Prel.*, II.48–54, 200–203, VIII.340–56, and notes.   **71 Flying . . . dreads:** Interpreted by de Selincourt (*The Prelude*, 1959, p. 611) as a reference to Wordsworth's first moral crisis, brought about by England's declaration of war against France (see *Prel.*, X.263 ff.).   **88–102:** See the discussion of these lines by William Empson, *Seven Types of Ambiguity*, 2nd edn. (1947), pp. 151–54.   **91:** The line may refer simply to a consideration of man's mortality (see, e.g., the last eight lines of the Intimations ode, *Prel.*, VIII.1–62) or to a supposedly remediable condition like that lamented in "Lines Written in Early Spring" and "The World Is Too Much with Us"; other passages in this poem (e.g., 25–26, 51–53, 128–31) suggest not that man is inherently bad or inferior to nature but rather that he is out of tune with nature and the better way of life that it represents.   **94:** Cf. "A Night-Piece," l. 24.   **106 half create:** See the note to *Prel.*, II.255–65. The phrase (as Wordsworth acknowledged in a note) is taken from Young, *Night Thoughts*, VI.427: "[The senses] half create the wondrous world they see."   **109 nurse:** Cf. Intimations ode, l. 81.   **121 prayer:** The "prayer" begins in l. 134.   **125, 126 inform, impress:** See the note to *Prel.*, I.560.   **128–31:** See *Prel.*, VIII.303–22 and note.   **139 sober pleasure:** Cf. Intimations ode, ll. 196–98.   **140 mansion:** See the note to *Prel.*, I.407.   **152:** In December 1814, commenting on Miss Patty Smith's criticisms of *The Excursion*, Wordsworth wrote, "She talks of my being a worshiper of Nature. A passionate expression, uttered incautiously in the poem upon the Wye, has led her into this mistake; she, reading in cold-heartedness, and substituting the letter for the spirit. Unless I am greatly mistaken, there is nothing of this kind in *The Excursion*" (*M.Y.*, II, 618). He was, of course, greatly mistaken.

Nutting   *Page 111*

Written toward the end of 1798; published 1800. "Intended as part of a poem on my own life, but struck out as not being wanted there. . . . These verses arose out of the remembrance of feelings I had often had when a boy, and particularly in the extensive woods that still stretch from the side of Esthwaite Lake towards Graythwaite" (I.F.). An early MS version contains lines that were later revised and incorporated into *The Prelude* as XIII.41–47 (see *P.W.*, II, 505). The incident (in which the nook of hazels and mossy bower surrender their "quiet being" in order to foster the boy's moral sense and ultimately love of nature) is another illustration of nature's "ministry" as described in *Prel.*, I.301 ff.; a version of the poem sent to Coleridge in 1798–99 has, near the beginning, "They led me, and I followed in their steps . . . . They led me far, / Those guardian spirits" (*E.L.*, pp. 206–207). For recent critical comment see Perkins, *The Quest for Permanence*, pp. 14–16; Ferry, *The Limits of Mortality*, pp. 22–28; and Alan Grob, *JEGP*, LXI (1962), 826–32.

11 my frugal Dame: Mrs. Ann Tyson; see the note to *Prel.*, IV.28.   **48–49 unless . . . past:** See *Prel.*, IV.256–76 and note.   **54 dearest Maiden:** Dorothy Wordsworth?

Strange Fits of Passion Have I Known   *Page 113*

This poem, the next three following, and "I Travelled among Unknown Men" make up the group known as the "Lucy" poems. The first four were written in Germany in the winter of 1798–99, and published in 1800; the last seems to have been written two years later. The question of Lucy's identity, much discussed but never solved, is not very important. She is best thought of either as an imaginary character or as a now unknown early sweetheart of the poet. In any event, the focus of the poems is principally on the mental experiences of the poet-speaker — the "Strange fits of passion," the "slumber" followed by rude awakening, the "difference" to him now that she has died, the "memory of what has been." Wordsworth never printed the five poems as a group; from 1815 on, "Three Years She Grew" and "A Slumber Did My Spirit Seal" were classed with "Poems of the Imagination," the other three with "Poems Founded on the Affections."

28: Following this line, an additional stanza in a version sent to Coleridge in 1798–99 more closely links the poem with the four others, all of which mention or imply the fact of Lucy's death:

> I told her this; her laughter light
> Is ringing in my ears;
> And when I think upon that night
> My eyes are dim with tears.   (*E.L.*, p. 206)

She Dwelt among the Untrodden Ways   *Page 113*

See the notes to the preceding poem. An additional stanza preserved in MS gives the details that "slow distemper checked her bloom, / And on the Heath she died" (*E.L.*, p. 205). The curious, no doubt unintentional ambiguities in ll. 3–4, 7–8, and 9 seem not to spoil the poem. Crabb Robinson commented in 1816: "The incomparable twelve lines . . . are finely imagined. They exhibit the powerful effect of the loss of a very obscure object upon one tenderly attached to it — the opposition between the apparent strength of the passion and the insignificance of the object is delightfully conceived and the object itself well imagined" (*H.C.R.*, I, 191). Keats felt the simplicity of the last line to be "the most perfect pathos" (*The Keats Circle*, ed. H. E. Rollins, 1948, II, 276).

2 Dove: There are several English rivers and streams by this name; Wordsworth mentions the best-known of them in *Prel.*, VI.192–93.   **7–8:** Presumably a reference to Hesperus, the first star to appear in the evening.

Three Years She Grew in Sun and Shower   *Page 114*

See the notes to "Strange Fits of Passion." Readers who think that Lucy died at the age of three overlook the swelling bosom of l. 33 and the fact that "The work was done" (37). Lucy's upbringing in nature results in the perfect marriage of mind with the external world that Wordsworth celebrates in the Prospectus to "The Recluse." With ll. 9–11 cf. "Tintern Abbey," ll. 95–102.

A Slumber Did My Spirit Seal   Page 115

See the notes to "Strange Fits of Passion." A difference in verb tenses enforces the contrast between the illusory "slumber" of the first stanza and the belated awakening to an awareness of Lucy's mortality in the second. "Motion" and "force" are terms in Newtonian physics, and "diurnal" (used also in *Prel.*, I.460) has here a scientific connotation. Though in the last two lines Lucy may have become one with nature, it is better to take "rocks, and stones, and trees" as the epitome of lifelessness: more than merely touched by earthly years, she is now thoroughly *dead*. For a sampling of interpretations, see Cleanth Brooks and R. P. Warren, *Understanding Poetry*, 3rd edn. (1960), pp. 377–80.

Lucy Gray   Page 115

Written in the winter of 1798–99; published 1800. "Founded on a circumstance told me by my Sister, of a little girl who, not far from Halifax in Yorkshire, was bewildered in a snow-storm. Her footsteps were traced by her parents to the middle of the lock of a canal, and no other vestige of her, backward or forward, could be traced. The body however was found in the canal. The way in which the incident . . . [is here] treated and the spiritualising of the character might furnish hints for contrasting the imaginative influences which I have endeavoured to throw over common life with Crabbe's matter of fact style of treating subjects of the same kind" (I.F.). It is questionable whether the emphasis is on the "spiritualising" of Lucy or on the workings of the superstitious imagination (see the note to ll. 57–64). Although Lucy's solitariness is stressed in ll. 4–5 and 63 (see also the note to l. 20), it may be that the subtitle refers not so much to her manner of life and dying as to the condition of the traveler "Upon the lonesome wild" (60), whose mind plays tricks upon him.

1–4: Unless he knew her before she died (unlikely, since l. 1 implies that she is already a legendary figure), the narrator has *seen* her only in his imagination.   11–12: Cf. ll. 3–4, 59.   20: In 1816 Wordsworth told Crabb Robinson that since it was "his object to exhibit poetically entire *solitude* [see *Prel.*, IV.357–60], he represents his child as observing the day-*moon* which no town or village girl would ever notice" (*H.C.R.*, I, 190).   29–32: Cf. the stanza from "The Babes in the Wood" quoted in the 1800 Preface (p. 462 in this volume).   57–64: "Some maintain" and the whistling wind recall details of "The Thorn," another poem of contradictory statements, in which Wordsworth's purpose was "to exhibit some of the general laws by which superstition acts upon the mind."

The Danish Boy Page 117

Written 1799; published 1800. "These Stanzas were designed to introduce a Ballad upon the Story of a Danish Prince who had fled from Battle, and, for the sake of the valuables about him, was murdered by the Inhabitant of a Cottage in which he had taken refuge. The House fell under a curse, and the Spirit of the Youth, it was believed, haunted the Valley where the crime had been committed" (W., 1827).

A Poet's Epitaph Page 119

Written 1799; published 1800. Somewhat as in "The Tables Turned," but without that poem's exaggerations, Wordsworth contrasts cold analytic reasoning, enslavement to the senses, and abstract theorizing — especially in the politician (1–4), the lawyer, the natural philosopher (17–24), and the moralist — to the workings of imagination and the love of "common things" in the poet.

1 Statist: Originally (1800–32) "Statesman." **9 Man . . . cheer:** Clergyman, a "Doctor" of divinity. **17, 21 all eyes, sensual:** See "The Recluse," l. 813 and note. **19–20:** See "The Tables Turned," ll. 26–28 and note. **31–32:** See *Prel.*, VI.158–67 and note. **37–42:** Vaguely reminiscent of Gray's description of the rustic poet in "Elegy Written in a Country Church-Yard," ll. 98–106. **52 broods:** See *Exc.*, I.146–48, *Prel.*, XIV.71–74.

The Two April Mornings Page 120

Written 1799; published 1800. "This and other poems connected with Matthew [see the next selection] would not gain by a literal detail of facts. Like the Wanderer in 'The Excursion,' this School-master was made up of several both of his class and men of other occupations" (I.F. note to "Matthew," ömitted from the present volume). Four levels of time (and two sets of emotions recollected in tranquility) are brought together in the poem: the present, in which the poet speaks and Matthew is dead; the more recent of the two April mornings, when "We walked along," etc.; the earlier April morning, thirty years before, when Matthew met the "blooming Girl"; and a period still more remote, when his daughter Emma was alive.

The Fountain Page 122

Written 1799; published 1800. Wordsworth's point in ll. 15, 20, 52, 70 (also "The Two April Mornings," l. 7) is that the old man can appear mirthful even while fully aware of the "heavy laws" of mortality (45) that distinguish human beings from all other creatures and things in nature. The young speaker's lightheartedness (9–16, 59–60) is by contrast innocent and frivolous.

35–36: Age takes away youthful vigor, and leaves behind reminders (such as the fountain) of lost joy.   **49–52:** Perhaps because the "household hearts" were the ones who laughed at his jokes.   **64:** Cf. "The Two April Mornings," ll. 55–56.

To M. H. *Page 124*

Written in December 1799; published 1800. "The pool alluded to is in Rydal Upper Park" (I.F.); "M. H." is Mary Hutchinson, whom Wordsworth married in October 1802. This is the earliest of a series of "Poems on the Naming of Places," to which Wordsworth prefixed the following separate "Advertisement": "By persons resident in the country and attached to rural objects, many places will be found unnamed or of unknown names, where little Incidents must have occurred, or feelings been experienced, which will have given to such places a private and peculiar interest. From a wish to give some sort of record to such Incidents, and renew the gratification of such feelings, Names have been given to Places by the Author and some of his Friends, and the following Poems written in consequence." Other poems of this group included in the present volume are "It Was an April Morning," "To Joanna," "There Is an Eminence," "A Narrow Girdle of Rough Stones," and "When, to the Attractions of the Busy World."

Hart-Leap Well *Page 125*

Written (in January) and published 1800.

> The first eight stanzas were composed extempore one winter evening in the cottage; when, after having tired myself with labouring at an awkward passage in "The Brothers," I started with a sudden impulse to this to get rid of the other, and finished it in a day or two. My Sister and I had past the place a few weeks before in our wild winter journey from Sockburn on the banks of the Tees to Grasmere. A peasant whom we met near the spot told us the story so far as concerned the name of the Well, and the Hart, and pointed out the Stones. Both the Stones and the Well are objects that may easily be missed; the tradition by this time may be extinct in the neighbourhood: the man who related it to us was very old. (I.F.)

The poem's attitude toward man should be compared with that in "Michael." Here man is proud, unfeeling, pleasure-seeking — and the Ozymandian fate of his monuments (see ll. 73–74, 169) is entirely fitting; Michael, whose life-long efforts come to the same end, is blameless.

1: Wensley Moor lies between the rivers Swale (75) and Ure (76) in Yorkshire.   **57, 84:** "Pleasure-house" recalls Coleridge's "stately pleasure-dome" in "Kubla Khan"; "cunning artist" (61) suggests the same kind of artificiality that characterizes the products of Kubla's arrogant decree. **97 moving accident:** *Othello,* I.iii.135. See "Simon Lee," ll. 61 ff. and note.

163–68, 179–80: The moral is not unlike that of "The Ancient Mariner"; cf. "Lines Left upon a Seat in a Yew-Tree," ll. 50–54. With "meanest thing that feels" (180) cf. Intimations ode, l. 202, "meanest flower that blows."

The Brothers   *Page 130*

Begun in December 1799; completed and published 1800. "The poem arose out of the fact, mentioned to me at Ennerdale, that a shepherd had fallen asleep upon the top of the rock called The Pillar, and perished as here described, his staff being left midway on the rock" (I.F.). In a letter to Charles James Fox (14 January 1801), sent with a copy of the 1800 *Lyrical Ballads,* Wordsworth singled out "The Brothers" and "Michael" as two poems in which he

> attempted to draw a picture of the domestic affections as I know they exist amongst a class of men who are now almost confined to the North of England. . . . [They] were written with a view to shew that men who do not wear fine cloaths can feel deeply. . . . The poems are faithful copies from nature; and I hope, whatever effect they may have upon you, you will at least be able to perceive that they may excite profitable sympathies in many kind and good hearts, and may in some small degree enlarge our feelings of reverence for our species, and our knowledge of human nature . . . . I thought, at a time when these feelings are sapped in so many ways, that the two poems might co-operate, however feebly, with the illustrious efforts which you have made to stem this and other evils with which the country is labouring. (*E.L.*, pp. 261–62)

In a few details Leonard is modeled upon Wordsworth's sailor-brother John.

47–65: Cf. "When, to the Attractions of the Busy World," ll. 76–83, and *Prel.*, VI.271–74. Except that the "bodily eye" (60) is not laid asleep, this is the same process of imaginative recollection as that described in "Tintern Abbey," ll. 25 ff., and "I Wandered Lonely as a Cloud." Here, however, the imaginer is overcome by "feverish passion," and Wordsworth explained in a note, "This description of the Calenture is sketched from an imperfect recollection of an admirable one in prose, by Mr. [William] Gilbert, author of the Hurricane [1796]."   **143–44 the . . . disappeared:** Originally (1800–20) the symbolism was even more transparent — "ten years back, / Close to those brother fountains, the huge crag / Was rent with lightning — one is dead and gone." In an early note (condensed in 1815, later omitted altogether) Wordsworth explained, "The impressive circumstance here described, actually took place some years ago in this country, upon an eminence called Kidstow Pike, one of the highest of the mountains that surround Hawes-water. The summit of the pike was stricken by lightning; and every trace of one of the fountains disappeared, while the other continued to flow as before."   **182–83:** "There is not any thing more worthy of remark in the manners of the inhabitants of these mountains, than the tranquillity, I might say indifference, with which they think and talk upon the subject of death. Some of the country church-yards, as here described, do not contain a single tombstone, and most of them have a very small number" (W., 1800–05). **310–11:** "The Great Gavel, so called, I imagine, from its resemblance to the gable end of a house, is one of the highest of the Cumberland mountains. It stands at the head of the several vales of Ennerdale, Wastdale, and Borrowdale. The Leeza is a river which flows into the Lake of Ennerdale: on issuing from the Lake, it changes its name, and is called the End, Eyne, or Enna. It falls into the sea a little below Egremont" (W.).

It Was an April Morning   *Page 140*

Written and published 1800. "Suggested on the banks of the brook that runs through Easedale, which is, in some parts of its course, as wild and beautiful as brook can be. I have composed thousands of verses by the side of it" (I.F.). This and the next three poems are among the "Poems on the Naming of Places" (see the notes to "To M. H.").

39 EMMA: The poet's sister Dorothy (as in "There Is a Little Unpretending Rill"; cf. "Emmeline" in "The Sparrow's Nest" and the first poem "To a Butterfly").

To Joanna   *Page 141*

Written (by the end of August) and published 1800. "The effect of her laugh is an extravagance; though the effect of the reverberation of voices in some parts of the mountains is very striking" (I.F.). De Selincourt quotes from a MS notebook the following explanation by Wordsworth:

> The poem supposes that at the Rock something had taken place in my mind . . . which, if related, will cause the Vicar to smile. For something like this you are prepared by [ll. 32–35] . . . . I begin to relate the story, meaning in a certain degree to divert or partly play upon the Vicar. I begin — my mind partly forgets its purpose, being softened by the images of beauty in the description of the rock and the delicious morning, and when I come to [ll. 54–55] . . . I am caught in the trap of my own imagination. I entirely lose sight of my first purpose. I take fire in [ll. 56–65] . . . describing what for a moment I believed either actually took place at the time, or . . . in some fit of imagination . . . might have taken place. When the description is closed . . . I waken from the dream and see that the Vicar thinks I have been extravagating, as I intended he should. I then tell the story as it happened really . . . mingling allusions suffused with humour, partly to the trance in which I have been, and partly to the trick I have been playing on the Vicar. The poem then concludes in a strain of deep tenderness. (*P.W.*, II, 487, with punctuation slightly altered)

Joanna was Mary Hutchinson's youngest sister.

28–30: "In Cumberland and Westmoreland are several Inscriptions, upon the native rock, which, from the wasting of time, and the rudeness of the workmanship, have been mistaken for Runic. They are, without doubt, Roman" (W.).   **31:** "The Rotha . . . is the River which, flowing through the lakes of Grasmere and Rydale, falls into Wynandermere" (W.).   **56–65:** "On Helm-crag, that impressive single mountain at the head of the Vale of Grasmere, is a rock which from most points of view bears a striking resemblance to an old Woman cowering. Close by this rock is one of those fissures or caverns, which in the language of the country are called dungeons. Most of the mountains here mentioned immediately surround the Vale of Grasmere; of the others, some are at a considerable distance, but they belong to the same cluster" (W.). The passage is (as Coleridge noted, *Biog. Lit.*, ch. XX) imitated from Drayton's *Poly-Olbion*, XXX.155–64.

There Is an Eminence   *Page 143*

Written and published 1800. "The Eminence here alluded to . . . rises above the road by the side of Grasmere lake, towards Keswick, and its name is Stone-Arthur" (I.F.).
14 She: Dorothy Wordsworth.

A Narrow Girdle of Rough Stones   *Page 143*

Written (in October) and published 1800. "The friends spoken of were Coleridge and my Sister, and the facts occurred strictly as recorded" (I.F.).   **23–25 invisible . . . soul:** Perhaps intended to illustrate the fanciful mood (16, 43, 68) that produces the "rash judgment" of ll. 50–54.   **33–34 fern . . . named:** *Osmunda regalis*, the "Flowering Fern." Lines 35–38 briefly restate a main idea of the Prologue to *Peter Bell*.   **58–62:** Cf. the description of the leechgatherer in "Resolution and Independence."   **71–73:** In December 1800 Wordsworth told a correspondent that "These three lines are absolutely necessary to render the poem intelligible" (*E.L.*, p. 258).

Michael   *Page 146*

Written (in October–December) and published 1800. "The Sheepfold, on which so much of the poem turns, remains, or rather the ruins of it. The character and circumstances of Luke were taken from a family to whom had belonged, many years before, the house we lived in at Town-end, along with some fields and woodlands on the eastern shore of Grasmere. The name of the Evening Star was not in fact given to this house, but to another on the same side of the valley, more to the north" (I.F.). Writing to Thomas Poole in April 1801, Wordsworth described the poem as an attempt "to give a picture of a man, of strong mind and lively sensibility, agitated by two of the most powerful affections of the human heart; the parental affection, and the love of property, *landed* property, including the feelings of inheritance, home, and personal and family independence" (*E.L.*, p. 266). For his intention in the poem "to shew that men who do not wear fine cloaths can feel deeply," see the letter to Fox, 14 January 1801, as quoted in the notes to "The Brothers." In that letter he is thinking especially of "small independent *proprietors* of land," and he explains, "Their little tract of land serves as a kind of permanent rallying point for their domestic feelings, as a tablet upon which they are written which makes them objects of memory in a thousand instances when they would otherwise be forgotten" (*E.L.*, pp. 261–62). As in the story of Margaret (*Exc.*, I) and "The Brothers," Wordsworth's main technique in this simple, straightforward narrative is the steady accumulation of detail (with an effect that Brooks and Warren, *Understanding Poetry*, rev. edn., 1950, p. 38, call "slow-moving forcefulness"). He uses nearly four hundred lines to establish Michael's love of his land and of his son, to whom the land is to be passed on; after l. 430 the story moves swiftly to its conclusion (note the compression of detail in ll. 442–47).

2 **Green-head Ghyll:** A ravine on the eastern side of Dunmail Raise (134), a mile north of Grasmere.   **23–26:** See *Prel.*, VIII.128–317.   **33:** Cf. "The Recluse," l. 754.   **47 watchful:** See the note to *Prel.*, II.291.   **169:** "Clipping is the word used in the North of England for shearing" (W.).   **258–70:** "The story alluded to here is well known in the country. The chapel is called Ings Chapel; and is on the right-hand side of the road leading from Kendal to Ambleside" (W., 1802–05).   **324 Sheepfold:** "It may be proper to inform some readers, that a sheep-fold in these mountains is an unroofed building of stone walls, with different divisions. It is generally placed by the side of a brook, for the convenience of washing the sheep; but it is also useful as a shelter for them, and as a place to drive them into, to enable the shepherds conveniently to single out one or more for any particular purpose" (W., 1802–05).   **466:** Matthew Arnold chose this line to illustrate Wordsworth's "true and most characteristic form of expression . . . . There is nothing subtle in it, no heightening, no study of poetic style, strictly so called, at all; yet it is expression of the highest . . . kind" (*Essays in Criticism, Second Series*).   **482 boisterous:** Cf. l. 6 (also "tumultuous" in ll. 2, 322). Nature has, in a sense, the last laugh; cf. "Hart-Leap Well."

I Travelled among Unknown Men   *Page 157*

Written apparently in early 1801; published 1807. This is the fifth of the "Lucy" poems (see the notes to "Strange Fits of Passion"). If autobiographical explanation is needed, the "melancholy dream" (5) can refer either to Wordsworth's experiences in France (1791–92) or to his more recent sojourn in Germany (1798–99).

To a Young Lady   *Page 157*

Written perhaps in 1801; published in the *Morning Post*, 12 February 1802. It may or may not be relevant that in 1794 Dorothy Wordsworth was reproached by an aunt for "rambling about the country on foot" (see *E.L.*, pp. 113–14).

The Sparrow's Nest   *Page 158*

Written 1801 or 1802; published 1807. "At the end of the garden of my father's house at Cockermouth was a high terrace that commanded a fine view of the river Derwent and Cockermouth Castle. This was our favourite play-ground. The terrace-wall, a low one, was covered with closely-clipt privet and roses, which gave an almost impervious shelter to birds that built their nests there. The latter of these stanzas alludes to one of these nests" (I.F.). See Wordsworth's tribute to Dorothy in *Prel.*, XIV.232–66.

9 Emmeline: An early MS has "Dorothy."   17: De Selincourt (*P.W.*, I, 358) cites Charles Churchill, *Independence*, ll. 42–43.   18: Cf. *Prel.*, XIV.230, "Of humble cares and delicate desires."

To a Butterfly [Stay near me]   *Page 158*

Written in March 1802; published 1807. "My sister and I were parted immediately after the death of our mother, who died in 1778, both being very young" (I.F.). On this and the second butterfly poem ("I've watched you now a full half-hour") see Ferry, *The Limits of Mortality*, pp. 16–20. "Emmeline" (in an early MS "Dorothy") is used also in the preceding poem.

To the Cuckoo   *Page 159*

Written in March 1802; published 1807. Cf. the two poems "To a Butterfly."

3–4: In 1812, "In illustration of his principle of imaginative power . . . [Wordsworth] quoted his *Cuckoo,* and in particular the 'wandering voice,' as giving local habitation to an abstraction" (*H.C.R.*, I, 89). See Wordsworth's comment on the lines in the Preface of 1815 (p. 484 in this volume).   8, 19: As every birdwatcher knows, a bird's song may seem loud or soft independent of distance, and its direction is often difficult to ascertain.   12 visionary hours: Cf. *Prel.*, I.632–33.   14–18: Like Keats's invisible nightingale ("immortal Bird"), the cuckoo can be thought of as the "same" bird because it belongs to an animal species whose individuals all look and sound alike.   31 unsubstantial: Cf. the I.F. note to the Intimations ode, "I was [in childhood] often unable to think of external things as having external existence."

My Heart Leaps Up   *Page 160*

Written in March 1802; published 1807. In general the poem asserts the unity or continuity of being that is a major concern in *The Prelude.* The poet's heart-leaping response to the rainbow (an act of "natural piety"), because it is the same that he felt as a child and that he hopes he will feel as an old man, is thought of as one of "the ties / That bind the perishable hours of life / Each to the other . . . By which the world of memory and thought / Exists and is sustained" (*Prel.*, VII.461–65). Coleridge quoted the poem in *The Friend*, 10 August 1809, to illustrate the idea that men should be able "to contemplate the Past in the Present, and so to produce by a virtuous and thoughtful sensibility that continuity in their self-consciousness, which Nature has made the law of their animal Life. . . . Men are ungrateful to others only when they have ceased to look back on their former selves with joy and tenderness. They exist in fragments. Annihilated as to the Past, they are dead to the Future, or seek for the proofs of it every where, only not (where alone they can be found) in themselves." The connection of the famous paradox of l. 7 with the rest of the poem is rather tenuous. Isolated, it is often taken to mean that the adult is the product or result (hence offspring) of his childhood experiences and impressions. In context, however, Wordsworth must mean that his earlier responses to the rainbow were an essential requisite (therefore precursor, forebear) to his present strength of feeling as a man (see *Prel.*, XII.269–75, for the general idea). Lionel Trilling, *The Liberal Imagination* (1950), p. 138, explains the line in terms of "the legacy left by the child to the man." Beginning in 1815, Wordsworth printed ll. 7–9 as an epigraph to the Intimations ode.

When, to the Attractions of the Busy World   *Page 160*

Written 1800–02; published 1815. "The grove still exists, but the plantation has been walled in, and is not so accessible as when my brother John wore the path in the manner here described. The grove was a favorite haunt with us all while we lived at Town-end" (I.F.). This is the sixth of the "Poems on the Naming of Places" (see the notes to "To M. H.").

55 Visitant: After a separation of fourteen years, John had visited the Wordsworths at Grasmere in the spring and summer of 1800.   **67 Esthwaite's . . . shore:** I.e., Hawkshead, where the Wordsworth boys attended school.   **76–83:** Cf. "The Brothers," ll. 47–65.   **80 silent Poet:** John was "a Poet in every thing but words" (*E.L.*, p. 447). See the note to *Exc.*, I.77–91.   **81 watchful:** See the note to *Prel.*, II.291.   **108–10:** "This wish was not granted; the lamented Person not long after perished by shipwreck, in discharge of his duty as Commander of the Honourable East India Company's Vessel, the Earl of Abergavenny" (W.). See "Elegiac Stanzas."

To a Butterfly [I've watched you now]   *Page 162*

Written in April 1802; published 1807. With ll. 16–19, cf. the first "To a Butterfly" ("Stay near me") and "To the Cuckoo."

Stanzas Written in My Pocket-Copy of Thomson's
Castle of Indolence   *Page 163*

Written in May 1802; published 1815. "Composed in the orchard, Town-end, Grasmere, Coleridge living with us much at the time: his son Hartley has said, that his father's character and habits are here preserved in a livelier way than in anything that has been written about him" (I.F.). Though Wordsworth imitates the Spenserian style and stanza of Thomson's poem (1748), his self-portrait in the first four stanzas owes much to Beattie's *The Minstrel*.

1 One: Wordsworth.　　39 A . . . Man: Coleridge.　　42–43: In June 1805, thanking Sir George Beaumont for an engraved portrait of Coleridge, Wordsworth commented, "It is as good a resemblance as I expect to see of Coleridge, taking it altogether, for I consider C's as a face absolutely impracticable" (*E.L.*, p. 496). Part of the trouble was that Coleridge could not breathe through his nose.　　43 Phantasy: See *Prel.*, VI.297–314, VIII.435–37.

1801 [I grieved for Buonaparté]　　*Page 165*

Written in May 1802; published in the *Morning Post*, 16 September 1802. "In the cottage, Town-end, Grasmere, one afternoon in 1801 [Wordsworth's error for 1802, as also in his title], my sister read to me the Sonnets of Milton. I had long been well acquainted with them, but I was particularly struck on that occasion by the dignified simplicity and majestic harmony that runs through most of them, — in character so totally different from the Italian, and still more so from Shakspeare's fine Sonnets. I took fire, if I may be allowed to say so, and produced three Sonnets the same afternoon . . . [of which] the only one I distinctly remember is — 'I grieved for Buonaparté'" (I.F.). With Wordsworth's concept of the ideal "Governor" in this sonnet, cf. "Character of the Happy Warrior."

All told, Wordsworth wrote more than five hundred sonnets (of which thirty-three are included in the present selection). In 1833 he attempted to describe to Alexander Dyce how the majority of his, and Milton's, differ in structure from the Italian sonnet:

> It should seem that the Sonnet, like every other legitimate composition, ought to have a beginning, a middle, and an end — in other words, to consist of three parts, like the three propositions of a syllogism, if such an illustration may be used. But the frame of metre adopted by the Italians does not accord with this view, and, as adhered to by them, it seems to be, if not arbitrary, best fitted to a division of the sense into two parts, of eight and six lines each. Milton, however, has not submitted to this. In the better half of his sonnets the sense does not close with the rhyme at the eighth line, but overflows into the second portion of the metre. Now it has struck me, that this is not done merely to gratify the ear by variety and freedom of sound, but also to aid in giving that pervading sense of intense Unity in which the excellence of the Sonnet has always seemed to me mainly to consist. Instead of looking at this composition as a piece of architecture, making a whole out of three parts, I have been much in the habit of preferring the image of an orbicular body, — a sphere — or a dew-drop. All this will appear to you a little fanciful; and I am well aware that a Sonnet will often be found excellent, where the beginning, the middle, and the end are distinctly marked, and also

where it is distinctly separated into *two* parts, to which, as I before observed, the strict Italian model, as they write it, is favorable. (*L.Y.,* II, 652–53)

Resolution and Independence   *Page 165*

Written in May–July 1802; published 1807. "This old Man I met a few hundred yards from my cottage; and the account of him is taken from his own mouth. I was in the state of feeling described in the beginning of the poem, while crossing over Barton Fell from Mr. Clarkson's, at the foot of Ullswater, towards Askham. The image of the hare I then observed on the ridge of the Fell" (I.F.). Dorothy Wordsworth, who was also present, records the meeting in a journal entry of 3 October 1800:

> We met an old man almost double. . . . He was of Scotch parents, but had been born in the army. He had had a wife, and "a good woman, and it pleased God to bless us with ten children". All these were dead but one, of whom he had not heard for many years, a sailor His trade was to gather leeches, but now leeches are scarce, and he had not strength for it. He lived by begging, and was making his way to Carlisle, where he should buy a few godly books to sell. He said leeches were very scarce, partly owing to this dry season, but many years they have been scarce — he supposed it owing to their being much sought after, that they did not breed fast, and were of slow growth. . . . He had been hurt in driving a cart, his leg broke, his body driven over, his skull fractured. He felt no pain till he recovered from his first insensibility. It was then late in the evening, when the light was just going away. (D.W., *Journals,* I, 63)

On 14 June 1802, while the poem was still in progress, Wordsworth wrote to Sara Hutchinson, who had read a draft and had been displeased with "the latter part":

> I will explain to you in prose my feeling in writing that Poem, and then you will be better able to judge whether the fault be mine or yours or partly both. I describe myself as having been exalted to the highest pitch of delight by the joyousness and beauty of Nature and then as depressed, even in the midst of those beautiful objects, to the lowest dejection and despair. A young Poet in the midst of the happiness of Nature is described as overwhelmed by the thought of the miserable reverses which have befallen the happiest of all men, viz Poets — I think of this till I am so deeply impressed by it, that I consider the manner in which I was rescued from my dejection and despair almost as an interposition of Providence. 'Now whether it was by peculiar grace A leading from above' — A person reading this Poem with feelings like mine will have been awed and controuled, expecting almost something spiritual or supernatural — What is brought forward? 'A lonely place, a Pond' 'by which an old man *was*, far from all house or home' — not stood, not sat, but '*was*' — the figure presented in the most naked simplicity possible. This feeling of spirituality or supernaturalness is again referred to as being strong in my mind in this passage — '*How came he here* thought I or what can

he be doing?' I then describe him, whether ill or well is not for me to judge with perfect confidence, but this I can *confidently* affirm, that, though I believe God has given me a strong imagination, I cannot conceive a figure more impressive than that of an old Man like this, the survivor of a Wife and ten children, travelling alone among the mountains and all lonely places, carrying with him his own fortitude, and the necessities which an unjust state of society has entailed upon him. . . . You speak of his speech as tedious: everything is tedious when one does not read with the feelings of the Author — 'The Thorn' is tedious to hundreds; and so is the *Idiot Boy* to hundreds. It is in the character of the old man to tell his story in a manner which an *impatient* reader must necessarily feel as tedious. But Good God! Such a figure, in such a place, a pious self-respecting, miserably infirm . . . Old Man telling such a tale! (*E.L.*, pp. 305–306)

The main point of the poem, which (esp. in ll. 127–31) qualifies as one of those "spots of time" described in *Prel.*, XII.208 ff., is the "apt admonishment" (112) of the speaker's romanticizing on the misery and despondency traditionally suffered by poets (43–49, 113–16). The leechgatherer's troubles are much more real than those of the "mighty Poets," but instead of ending in madness he cheerfully perseveres, and the speaker, when he is finally able to take in the old man's story, "could have laughed myself to scorn" (137) at the contrast. See Anthony E. M. Conran, *PMLA*, LXXV (1960), 66–74 (good on the influences of Chaucer and Chatterton, and on the comic aspects of the poem — "the comedy of a solipsist faced with something outside himself"), and Alan Grob, *ELH*, XXVIII (1961), 89–100. Cf. "A Narrow Girdle of Rough Stones" and the meeting with the old discharged soldier in *Prel.*, IV.370–469. The stanza form, rhyme royal with a Spenserian hexameter in place of the usual final pentameter, Wordsworth would have found used earlier in Milton's "On the Morning of Christ's Nativity" and Chatterton's "An Excelente Balade of Charitie."

5: See Wordsworth's comment on this line in the Preface of 1815 (p. 484). **15:** From his situation in the present, the speaker here shifts to the past-tense recollection of an earlier day ("then"), the remainder of the poem. The pleasantness of the day, the sounds of nature, and especially the racing hare are the linking elements that arouse the recollection. **22–28:** For sadness in the midst of delight elsewhere, see, e.g., "Lines Written in Early Spring," ll. 3–4, *Prel.*, X.528–29, and the explanation in *Prel.*, I.135–39. **40–42:** Cf. *Prel.*, I.267–69. The capitalized "He" (in all editions) is misleading; Wordsworth means "anyone" (= "him . . . himself" in ll. 41–42). **43–46:** Starving in a garret, Chatterton committed suicide at the age of seventeen; like Burns (45–46) he was for the Romantics a type of neglected poetic genius. **57–65, 75–77:** Quoted in the Preface of 1815 as examples of "the conferring, the abstracting, and the modifying powers of the Imagination" (see p. 485). **69 felt:** Originally Wordsworth wrote "had," and against Mary Hutchinson's objection to the expression he argued, "The poem is throughout written in the language of men — 'I suffered much by a sickness had by me long ago' is a phrase which anybody might use" (*E.L.*, p. 304). **97–98:** Cf. *Exc.*, I.113–17.

Composed upon Westminster Bridge   *Page 170*

Written at the end of July or in September 1802; published 1807. Wordsworth said he composed the poem "on the roof of a coach, on my way to
France" (I.F.), and Dorothy's journal fixes the date of the morning that
inspired it: "we left London on Saturday morning at ½-past 5 or 6, the
31st of July. . . . We mounted the Dover Coach at Charing Cross. It was
a beautiful morning. The city, St. Paul's, with the river and a multitude of
little boats, made a most beautiful sight as we crossed Westminster Bridge.
The houses were not overhung by their cloud of smoke, and they were
spread out endlessly, yet the sun shone so brightly, with such a fierce light,
that there was even something like the purity of one of nature's own grand
spectacles" (D.W., *Journals*, I, 172–73). Wordsworth and Dorothy were
on their way to Calais, to meet Annette Vallon and his daughter Caroline.
Whether he actually wrote the sonnet then, simply erring in the date he
later gave in the title, or wrote it after returning to London in September,
has never been settled.

It Is a Beauteous Evening, Calm and Free   *Page 170*

Written in August 1802 ("on the beach near Calais" — I.F.); published
1807.
  6 mighty Being: The sea (5) or God (14), probably the first as a symbol of the second.   **9 Dear Child:** Always said to be Wordsworth's
French daughter Caroline.   **12 Abraham's bosom:** See Luke 16:22.

Composed by the Sea-Side, near Calais   *Page 170*

Written in August 1802; published 1807 (the first poem in a group of
"Sonnets Dedicated to Liberty").

Composed in the Valley near Dover   *Page 171*

Written at the end of August 1802; published 1807. Returning from France,
Wordsworth and Dorothy (the "Companion" of l. 14) landed at Dover on
August 30.

September, 1802, near Dover   *Page 171*

Written at the end of August or beginning of September 1802; published
1807.

Written in London, September, 1802   *Page 172*

Published 1807. "This was written immediately after my return from France
to London, when I could not but be struck, as here described, with the
vanity and parade of our own country, especially in great towns and cities,

as contrasted with the quiet, and I may say the desolation, that the revolution had produced in France" (I.F.). Cf. "The World Is Too Much with Us."

1 O Friend: Originally (in the early MSS) "Coleridge."

London, 1802   *Page 172*

Written in September 1802; published 1807.

Composed after a Journey across the Hambleton Hills
Page 172

Written according to Wordsworth on the day of his marriage, 4 October 1802; published 1807. Dorothy's journal entry for October 4 (which she wrote later in the month after returning to Grasmere) includes the following: "It was not dark evening when we passed the little publick house, but before we had crossed the Hambledon Hill, and reached the point overlooking Yorkshire, it was quite dark. We had not wanted, however, fair prospects before us, as we drove along the flat plain of the high hill. Far far off us, in the western sky, we saw shapes of castles, ruins among groves, a great spreading wood, rocks, and single trees, a minster with its tower unusually distinct, minarets in another quarter, and a round Grecian Temple also; the colours of the sky of a bright grey, and the forms of a sober grey, with a dome" (D.W., *Journals,* I, 178–79). See the next poem and notes.

Those Words Were Uttered   *Page 173*

Written 1802–04 (several of the sonnets are thus dated because they were composed after "I grieved for Buonaparté," May 1802, and appear in MSS known to have been finished by February or March 1804); published 1807. "Those words" are the last line and a half of the preceding poem.

12: Cf. *Prel.,* I.409–10, XIII.32. Where in the preceding poem the cloud shapes were "of the sky," superior to earthly concerns, here they exemplify "the busy dance / Of things that pass away" (*Prel.,* XIII.30–31); the "little unpretending Rill" of the next poem is, by contrast, among the "objects that endure."

There Is a Little Unpretending Rill   *Page 173*

Written 1802–04; published 1820. "This Rill trickles down the hill-side into Windermere, near Lowwood. My sister and I, on our first visit together to this part of the country, walked from Kendal, and we rested to refresh ourselves by the side of the lake where the streamlet falls into it. This sonnet was written some years after in recollection of that happy ramble, that most happy day and hour" (I.F.).

2–4 humbler . . . name: Cf. "A Narrow Girdle of Rough Stones," ll. 35–38.   **11–14:** Cf. the two preceding poems. "Immortal Spirit" here means something like unfading recollection.

To Toussaint L'Ouverture   *Page 174*

Written probably toward the end of 1802; published in the *Morning Post,* 2 February 1803. François Dominique Toussaint (1743?–1803), surnamed L'Ouverture, a self-educated slave who became general-in-chief and leader of Negro rebellion against the French in Haiti, now lay imprisoned in Paris.

On the Extinction of the Venetian Republic   *Page 174*

Written perhaps in 1802; published 1807. Napoleon proclaimed the end of the Republic of Venice in 1797. Lines 7–8 refer to the annual "wedding" of Venice to the Adriatic, a ceremony in which the doge dropped a ring into the sea.

It Is Not to Be Thought of that the Flood   *Page 174*

Written 1802–03; published in the *Morning Post,* 16 April 1803.
  4 "with . . . unwithstood"; Daniel, *The Civil Wars,* II.7.

To H. C.   *Page 175*

Written 1802–03; published 1807. Coleridge's eldest son, Hartley (1796–1849), was six years old on 19 September 1802. Cf. Wordsworth's description of the child in the Intimations ode.
  6–9: In a note of 1807 Wordsworth refers to Jonathan Carver's *Travels through the Interior Parts of North America* (1778) as the source of this image.   **10:** This is the view of the child in "We Are Seven."

To a Highland Girl   *Page 176*

Written in late September or October 1803; published 1807. This and the next poem (like the later "Stepping Westward") are products of the tour of Scotland that Wordsworth made with Dorothy and (for part of the way) Coleridge in August–September 1803. The Highland girl is described by Dorothy in her journal for August 28 (I, 279–83). Cf. "The Solitary Reaper."
  62–63: Cf. "Resolution and Independence," ll. 50–52.   **65–78:** Cf. D.W., *Journals,* I, 283, "at this day the innocent merriment of the girls [the girl of the poem and her younger companion], with their kindness to us, and the beautiful figure and face of the elder, come to my mind whenever I think of the ferry-house and waterfall of Loch Lomond, and I never think of the two girls but the whole image of that romantic spot is before me, a living image, as it will be to my dying day."   **78 Spirit:** Like "soul of

the place" in *E.L.*, p. 416, the thing that unifies all the elements of a scene. Cf. "The Soul, the Imagination of the whole" in the note to *Prel.*, XIV. 50–62.

<h3 style="text-align:center">Yarrow Unvisited   Page 178</h3>

Written probably in 1803; published 1807. "At Clovenford, being so near to the Yarrow, we could not but think of the possibility of going thither, but came to the conclusion of reserving the pleasure for some future time, in consequence of which, after our return, Wm. wrote the poem" (D.W., *Journals,* I, 391; entry for 18 September 1803). Wordsworth later said that they "declined going in search of this celebrated stream, not altogether . . . for the reasons assigned in the poem on the occasion" (I.F. note to "Yarrow Visited"). The ballad cited in the headnote is William Hamilton's "The Braes of Yarrow," which Wordsworth would have read in Percy's *Reliques.*

1 ff. Stirling castle, etc.: With the exception of "Burn-mill meadow" (42), a name borrowed from the Scottish ballad "Leader Haughs," Wordsworth had visited all the places mentioned in the poem. **35 Fair . . . rock:** Taken, as Wordsworth acknowledged in a note, from Hamilton's ballad, l. 51. **49–52:** Cf. "Yarrow Visited," ll. 1–4, *Prel.*, VI.523–28, VIII.419–20.

<h3 style="text-align:center">To the Men of Kent   Page 179</h3>

Written in October 1803; published 1807. After Napoleon's violation of the treaty of Amiens and the renewal of war in May 1803, all England (including Wordsworth, who enlisted in the Grasmere Volunteers) took to arms, daily fearing invasion by the French.

9–11: De Selincourt (*P.W.*, III, 456) explains, "There was a tradition that the inhabitants of Kent, east of the Medway, were not conquered by the Normans, but received from them a confirmation of their charters." He cites Drayton, *The Barons' Wars,* I.323–24, as Wordsworth's probable source.

<h3 style="text-align:center">Yew-Trees   Page 180</h3>

Written according to Wordsworth in 1803 (De Selincourt, however, *P.W.*, II, 504, thinks this date is several years too early); published 1815. See Wordsworth's comment cited in the notes to "A Night-Piece."

1 Lorton Vale: A few miles southeast of Wordsworth's birthplace, Cockermouth. **5 Umfraville, Percy:** Either Robert de Umfraville, Earl of Angus (1277–1325), or his nephew Sir Robert (d. 1436), both warriors against the Scots, and probably Sir Henry Percy (1364–1403), Hotspur, who fought Douglas at Otterburn. **7–8 Azincour, Crecy, Poictiers:** The three great English victories (in 1415, 1346, 1356, respectively) of the Hundred Years' War. **14 Borrowdale:** Valley stretching north from Glaramara mountain (33) to Derwent Water.

Nuns Fret Not

Written 1802–04; published 1807.

1 narrow room: In November 1802 Wordsworth told a correspondent that the music of Milton's sonnets "has an energetic and varied flow of sound crowding into narrow room more of the combined effect of rhyme and blank verse than can be done by any other kind of verse I know of" (*E.L.*, p. 312).   **6 Furness-fells:** Hills around Coniston Water, south and west of Hawkshead; the highest is Old Man of Coniston (2633').

Methought I Saw the Footsteps of a Throne   *Page 181*

Written 1802–04; published 1807.

Where Lies the Land   *Page 181*

Written 1802–04; published 1807. In 1812 Wordsworth told Crabb Robinson that the poem "expressed the delight he had felt on thinking of the first feelings of men before navigation had so completely made the world known, and while a ship exploring unknown regions was an object of high interest and sympathy" (*H.C.R.*, I, 94).

With Ships the Sea Was Sprinkled   *Page 182*

Written 1802–04; published 1807. Wordsworth explains the poem at length (in support of the declaration that "There is scarcely one of my Poems which does not aim to direct the attention to some moral sentiment, or to some general principle, or law of thought") in a letter to Lady Beaumont, 21 May 1807 (see *M.Y.*, I, 128–29).

5–8: Based, as Wordsworth acknowledged in a note of 1807, on Skelton's "The Bowge of Courte," ll. 36–38, "Methoughte I sawe a shyppe, goodly of sayle, / Come saylynge forth into that hauen brood, / Her takelynge ryche and of hye apparayle."

The World Is Too Much with Us   *Page 182*

Written 1802–04; published 1807. The sonnet is a miniature exposition of how "the regular action of the world" (*Prel.*, II.361) deadens the poetic imagination. See the note to *Prel.*, II.262.

11 pleasant lea: Spenser, "Colin Clouts Come Home Againe," l. 283. **13 Proteus . . . sea:** Cf. *P.L.*, III.603–604, "call up unbound / In various shapes old *Proteus* from the Sea."   **14 Triton . . . horn:** "Colin Clouts Come Home Againe," l. 245, "*Triton* blowing loud his wreathed horne."

Personal Talk   *Page 183*

Written 1802–06; published 1807. Each stanza is an Italian sonnet.

6 maidens . . . stalk: Cf. *A Midsummer-Night's Dream*, I.i.76–78 ("rose

... withering on the virgin thorn ... in single blessedness"), and Milton's *Comus*, ll. 743–44 ("neglected rose ... withers on the stalk"). **7–8 Forms ... floors:** I.e., markings on the floor to guide the dancers. **23 Children ... powerful:** Cf. *Prel.*, V.508–509. **25–26 melodies ... sweet:** See *An Evening Walk*, l. 237 and note. **27–28:** See *Prel.*, XII.127–51, on the tyranny of the bodily eye. **41–42:** I.e., *Othello* and *F.Q.*, I. **49 little boat:** See the Prologue to *Peter Bell*.

Ode to Duty **Page 184**

Written early in 1804; published 1807. "This Ode is on the model of Gray's Ode to Adversity, which is copied from Horace's Ode to Fortune [*Odes*, I.xxxv]" (I.F.). The epigraph, added in 1837, is adapted from Seneca, *Moral Epistles*, CXX.10, and may be translated, "Now at last [I am] not consciously good, but so trained by habit that I not only can act rightly but cannot act otherwise than rightly."

1 Daughter ... God: *P.L.*, IX.652–53, "God ... left that Command / Sole Daughter of his voice." **53 lowly wise:** *P.L.*, VIII.172–74, "Heav'n is for thee too high / To know what passes there; be lowlie wise: / Think onely what concernes thee and thy being."

Ode: Intimations of Immortality from Recollections of Early Childhood **Page 186**

Written 1802–04; published 1807. Although the evidence for dating is inconclusive, Wordsworth seems to have begun the poem toward the end of March 1802 (possibly on the next day after writing "My Heart Leaps Up"), and to have finished a version of the first four stanzas before April 4, the date given by Coleridge to his "Dejection: An Ode," in which he attempts to answer Wordsworth's questions of the present ll. 56–57. Wordsworth "added a little to the Ode" — exactly what is not known — on June 17 (D.W., *Journals*, I, 159). According to the I.F. note given just below, there was an interval of "Two years at least" between the writing of stanzas I-IV and "the remaining part" (all of V-XI?). De Selincourt argues persuasively (*P.W.*, IV, 465) that the poem was completed by the end of March 1804 (see *Prel.*, VI.48–52 and note). In 1807 the poem was headed simply "Ode"; the subtitle and the epigraph (the last three lines of "My Heart Leaps Up") were added in 1815.

The I.F. note is valuable for Wordsworth's explanation of the crucial ll. 129 ff. — *how* recollections of early childhood provide intimations of immortality — and for his declaration that he was using the notion of pre-existence of the soul as a metaphor rather than as a statement of belief:

> This was composed during my residence at Townend, Grasmere. Two years at least passed between the writing of the four first stanzas and the remaining part. To the attentive and competent reader the whole sufficiently explains itself; but there may be no harm in adverting

here to particular feelings or *experiences* of my own mind on which the structure of the poem partly rests. Nothing was more difficult for me in childhood than to admit the notion of death as a state applicable to my own being. I have said elsewhere [in "We Are Seven"] —

> "A simple child,
> That lightly draws its breath,
> And feels its life in every limb,
> What should it know of death!" —

But it was not so much from feelings of animal vivacity that *my* difficulty came as from a sense of the indomitableness of the Spirit within me. I used to brood over the stories of Enoch and Elijah, and almost to persuade myself that, whatever might become of others, I should be translated, in something of the same way, to heaven. With a feeling congenial to this, I was often unable to think of external things as having external existence, and I communed with all that I saw as something not apart from, but inherent in, my own immaterial nature. Many times while going to school have I grasped at a wall or tree to recall myself from this abyss of idealism to the reality. At that time I was afraid of such processes. In later periods of life I have deplored, as we have all reason to do, a subjugation of an opposite character, and have rejoiced over the remembrances, as is expressed in the lines —

> "Obstinate questionings
> Of sense and outward things,
> Fallings from us, vanishings;" &c.

To that dream-like vividness and splendour which invest objects of sight in childhood, everyone, I believe, if he would look back, could bear testimony, and I need not dwell upon it here: but having in the poem regarded it as presumptive evidence of a prior state of existence, I think it right to protest against a conclusion, which has given pain to some good and pious persons, that I meant to inculcate such a belief. It is far too shadowy a notion to be recommended to faith, as more than an element in our instincts of immortality. But let us bear in mind that, though the idea is not advanced in revelation, there is nothing there to contradict it, and the fall of Man presents an analogy in its favour. Accordingly, a pre-existent state has entered into the popular creeds of many nations; and, among all persons acquainted with classic literature, is known as an ingredient in Platonic philosophy. Archimedes said that he could move the world if he had a point whereon to rest his machine. Who has not felt the same aspirations as regards the world of his own mind? Having to wield some of its elements when I was impelled to write this poem on the "Immortality of the Soul," I took hold of the notion of pre-existence as having sufficient foundation in humanity for authorising me to make for my purpose the best use of it I could as a poet. (I.F.)

A letter to Catherine Clarkson, December 1814, provides a shorter statement of the meaning behind "recollections": "This poem rests entirely upon two recollections of childhood; one that of a splendour in the objects of sense which is passed away; and the other an indisposition to bend to the law of death, as applying to our own particular case. A reader who has not a vivid recollection of these feelings having existed in his mind in childhood cannot understand that poem" (*M.Y.*, II, 619).

No poem of Wordsworth has been so often discussed by the critics, mainly because of its seeming instability of tone, the obscurity of what is lost (there is no internal clue as to what the metaphorical light stands for), and the tenuousness of the connection made in stanza IX between idealism and immortality. In addition to the principal books on Wordsworth, nearly all of which treat the poem, see Herbert Hartman, *Review of English Studies*, VI (1930), 129–48; Lionel Trilling, *English Institute Annual, 1941* (1942), pp. 1–28 (the essay is reprinted in *The Liberal Imagination*, 1950); Donald A. Stauffer, *Kenyon Review*, IV (1942), 133–44; Cleanth Brooks, *The Well Wrought Urn* (1947), ch. VII; John K. Mathison, *SP*, XLVI (1949), 419–39; Thomas M. Raysor, *PMLA*, LXIX (1954), 861–75; Robert L. Schneider, *JEGP*, LIV (1955), 625–33; M. H. Abrams, *University of Toronto Quarterly*, XXVII (1958), 131–34. On the basis of the second sentence of the I.F. note, critics have frequently read the poem as a two-part structure in which stanzas I-IV ask questions about the loss of *something* (variously childhood, mystic experiences, poetic imagination), and V-XI attempt an answer and present conflicting attitudes toward a not-so-abundant recompense. If there must be two main parts, the tone will seem more consistent and the assertion of recompense more convincing if we take I-VIII as the first (with V-VIII as an expansion of I-IV, an explanation of one metaphor in terms of another) and IX-XI as the second.

1–9: Reminiscent of Coleridge's "The Mad Monk," ll. 9–16, "There was a time when earth, and sea, and skies, / The bright green vale, and forest's dark recess, / With all things, lay before mine eyes / In steady loveliness: / But now I feel, on earth's uneasy scene, / Such sorrows as will never cease; — / I only ask for peace; / If I must live to know that such a time has been!"   **23 timely utterance:** An obscure allusion. Critics usually cite "My Heart Leaps Up"; Trilling proposes the leechgatherer's words in "Resolution and Independence" (which, however, was not begun until 3 May 1802).   **28 fields of sleep:** Much written about, but never satisfactorily explained. Cf. the image of sleeping winds in "The World Is Too Much with Us," ll. 6–7.   **56–57:** Cf. "Elegiac Stanzas," ll. 14–16.   **58–128:** Cf. the reverse course of development in "Tintern Abbey," ll. 72–102, where the child is a creature of "coarser pleasures . . . glad animal movements" and it is the adult who experiences "a sense sublime . . . ." There are possible hints of the notion of pre-existence in *Prel.*, I.555–58, II.315–18, III.180–83, V.507–22, 536–38, XII.182–83 — though each of the passages can be interpreted in a less "mystical and idle sense" (see *Prel.*, II.230–32 and note).   **77–84:** Cf. *Prel.*, V.337–39. With "homely Nurse" (81) cf. "Tintern Abbey," ll. 109–11.   **85 the Child:** Always identified as Hartley Coleridge (cf. "To H. C.").   **103 "humorous stage":** Daniel, dedicatory sonnet to *Musophilus*.   **110–16, 118–20:** Cited by Coleridge (*Biog. Lit.*, ch. XXII) as an example of "thoughts and images too great for

the subject . . . an approximation to what might be called *mental* bombast."
120: Following this line, there originally appeared four additional lines —
"To whom the grave / Is but a lonely bed without the sense or sight /
Of day or the warm light, / A place of thought where we in waiting lie"
(1807–15). Wordsworth omitted them (and added the present l. 117)
after Coleridge objected to the idea of the grave as "*a place of thought!*"
and "the frightful notion of lying *awake*" in it (*Biog. Lit.*, ch. XXII).
124 inevitable yoke: Cf. *Prel.*, III.182, "yoke of earth," and V.520–21,
"yoke-fellows / To custom."   **126–28:** See *Prel.*, II.262 and note.   **131
nature:** Human nature.   **147 like . . . Thing:** *Hamlet*, I.i.48.   **152:**
Following this line, an early MS adds, "Throw off from us, or mitigate, the
spell / Of that strong frame of sense in which we dwell."   **183–84:** Cf.
Prel., XIII.246–49.   **202–203:** De Selincourt (*P.W.*, IV, 467) compares
Gray's "Ode on the Pleasure Arising from Vicissitude," ll. 49–52, "The
meanest flowret of the vale, / The simplest note that swells the gale, /
The common Sun, the air, and skies, / To him are opening Paradise."

I Wandered Lonely as a Cloud   *Page 191*

Written 1804; published 1807. Cf. Dorothy's journal for 15 April 1802:

> When we were in the woods beyond Gowbarrow Park [on the west
> side of Ullswater] we saw a few daffodils close to the water-side.
> We fancied that the lake had floated the seeds ashore, and that the
> little colony had so sprung up. But as we went along there were more
> and yet more; and at last, under the boughs of the trees, we saw that
> there was a long belt of them along the shore, about the breadth of
> a country turnpike road. I never saw daffodils so beautiful. They
> grew among the mossy stones about and about them; some rested their
> heads upon these stones as on a pillow for weariness; and the rest
> tossed and reeled and danced, and seemed as if they verily laughed
> with the wind, that blew upon them over the lake; they looked so
> gay, ever glancing, ever changing. This wind blew directly over the
> lake to them. There was here and there a little knot, and a few
> stragglers a few yards higher up; but they were so few as not to dis-
> turb the simplicity, unity, and life of that one busy highway. (D.W.,
> *Journals*, I, 131–32)

Despite Wordsworth's note of 1815, "The subject of these Stanzas is rather
an elementary feeling and simple impression (approaching to the nature
of an ocular spectrum) upon the imaginative faculty, than an *exertion* of
it," the poem is a good illustration of imagination at work (daffodils are
perceived, the ideas of dancing and jocundity are supplied from the mind,
and in the last stanza memory recreates the whole). Cf. "A Whirl-Blast
from Behind the Hill," and see the essay by Frederick A. Pottle in *Wordsworth Centenary Studies*, ed. G. T. Dunklin (1951), pp. 23–42.

    19–24: Simply vivid recollection; cf. "Tintern Abbey," ll. 22–30.   **21
flash:** See the note to *Prel.*, I.586–88.

She Was a Phantom of Delight   *Page 192*

Written 1804; published 1807. "The germ of this poem was four lines composed as a part of the verses on the Highland Girl. Though beginning in this way, it was written from my heart, as is sufficiently obvious" (I.F.). The poem is a tribute to his wife. Cf. *Prel.*, XIV.268–71.

The Prelude   *Page 193*

Although he had drafted a few isolated passages earlier, Wordsworth began serious work on his masterpiece in the winter of 1798–99, at Goslar, Germany, and by the end of 1799 had finished most of Books I and II. Much of the rest was written in 1804–05. He completed the poem in May 1805, and then for the next thirty-four years revised and retouched it, paragraph by paragraph and line by line, until he had in one way or another altered (mainly for stylistic reasons) nearly half the lines in it. Though five short excerpts appeared in print during his lifetime, the whole was first published in 1850, three months after his death. Wordsworth never gave the poem a title, referring to it simply as "the Poem on my own life"; the present title and subtitle were supplied by Mrs. Wordsworth.

That the poem was "prelude" to a larger project, never finished, does not matter. Originally thought of as part of a long work on Man, Nature, and Society (see the notes to "The Recluse"), and subsequently written as a "preparatory poem . . . [conducting] the history of the Author's mind to the point when he was emboldened to hope that his faculties were sufficiently matured for entering upon the arduous labour which he had proposed to himself" (Preface to *The Excursion*), *The Prelude* itself contains the main ideas and feelings that would have gone into the larger work. Though it was, as he told Sir George Beaumont, 1 May 1805, "a thing unprecedented in literary history that a man should talk so much about himself" (*E.L.*, p. 489), in writing of the growth of *a* poet's mind and in focusing on the development of imagination Wordsworth succeeded in generalizing autobiography into a portrayal of the essential soundness of humanity itself (see VIII.451–53).

Some of the principal ideas are touched on in the Introduction to this volume and in the notes below. Ernest de Selincourt's edition (revised by Helen Darbishire, 1959), which records variants from eighteen extant MSS and gives on facing pages the texts of the 1805 and 1850 versions, and R. D. Havens' *The Mind of a Poet* (1941) provide indispensable commentaries on the poem. See also Abbie F. Potts, *Wordsworth's "Prelude": A Study of Its Literary Form* (1953), and Herbert Lindenberger, *On Wordsworth's "Prelude"* (1963).

Book I. 1–45: Wordsworth begins by quoting himself. In these lines, the "glad preamble" to the poem (see VII.1–8), he records the spontaneous celebration of his escape from London (the "vast city" of l. 7), where he had lived from February to August 1795. Subsequently (59–

107) he describes his walk from Bristol to Racedown in September 1795, possibly merging with the account some details of his journey to Dove Cottage (which, unlike Racedown, was situated in a "Vale," 72) in December 1799. The parenthetical ll. 46–58 provide a setting in the past ("that day," 48).   **1–4:** Cf. "To My Sister," ll. 5–8.   **14 The . . . me:** An echo of *P.L.*, XII.646; but where Adam and Eve have just been expelled from their Eden, Wordsworth is about to enter his.   **21–23:** Cf. "Tintern Abbey," ll. 38–40.   **35 correspondent breeze:** A common Romantic metaphor for poetic inspiration (see l. 96, and M. H. Abrams, *Kenyon Review*, XIX, 1957, 113–30). This breeze, however, vexes its own creation (see ll. 46–47 and note).   **44–45:** The lines are a late addition to the poem. **46 Friend:** Coleridge, to whom the entire poem is addressed (and to whom Wordsworth read it aloud in January 1807).   **46–47 not . . . song:** For reasons illustrated in ll. 36–38. Cf. the statement that poetry "takes its origin from emotion recollected in tranquillity" (1800 Preface, p. 460 in this volume).   **77–78 higher . . . Fancy:** On imagination and fancy see the note to VIII.366, 373.   **96 Æolian visitations:** Further breeze-like inspirations (see l. 35); in Coleridge's "The Eolian Harp" such inspirations are erratic, sometimes producing "idle flitting phantasies."   **102–103 shed . . . influence:** *P.L.*, VII.375, "Shedding sweet influence."   **117–18 rescue . . . interference:** On Wordsworth's concern with the fading of memories see I.491–92, 614–17, VII.335, 365–66, XII.279–86, XIV.1–2. **124 That . . . discouraged:** Apparently *Lyrical Ballads* and the first version of *Exc.*, I ("present gifts / Of humbler industry," 133–34), did not constitute fulfillment of his hope.   **135–39:** Cf. "Resolution and Independence," ll. 22–28. On the likening of poet to lover, see *A Midsummer-Night's Dream*, V.i.4–17.   **139–41:** For another image of the mind brooding see XIV.70–72, and cf. *P.L.*, I.21, "Dove-like satst brooding on the vast Abyss."   **150–55:** The "vital soul" (= "living mind," 153) is the mind working imaginatively. "General Truths" may mean intellectual truths, philosophic ideas. Lines 151–53 are perhaps made clearer by Wordsworth's statement to Catherine Clarkson in December 1814, "One of the main objects of *The Recluse* is to reduce the calculating understanding to its proper level among the human faculties" (*M.Y.*, II, 619). On "Forms, images" (155) see the note to ll. 401–404.   **161 little . . . names:** I.e., a ready-made mythology, such as those available to older poets.   **168–69 some British . . . unsung:** Later (1815) Wordsworth wrote "Artegal and Elidure," according to the I.F. note to that poem, "as a token of affectionate respect for the memory of Milton. 'I have determined,' says he [Milton], in his preface to his History of England, 'to bestow the telling over even of these reputed tales, be it for nothing else but in favor of our English Poets and Rhetoricians, who by their wit will know how to use them judiciously.'" De Selincourt refers to Milton's MS list (at Trinity College, Cambridge) of subjects for a projected epic, and his plan, announced in *Epitaphium Damonis*, ll. 166–68, of writing a poem on King Arthur. **185:** The line is a late addition.   **187–90:** "After his defeat by Pompey in 66 B.C. Mithridates marched into Colchis and thence to the Cimmerian

Bosphorus, where he planned to pass round the north and west coasts of the Euxine . . . and invade Italy from the north. The connexion of Odin with Mithridates was suggested . . . by Gibbon" (de Selincourt).   190–202: "The legend is that the followers of Sertorius [Roman general assassinated in 72 B.C.], after his death, in order to escape the tyranny of Rome, fled to the Canary Islands, called by the ancients the Fortunate Isles, which were in this way peopled. It was their heroic descendants . . . who fought so valiantly and tenaciously to keep out the invading Spaniards from Teneriffe in 1493; their final subjugation was due not to the valour of the Spaniards, but to a terrible pestilence which decimated them in 1494. Their race died out completely" (de Selincourt, citing a Spanish work of 1594).   205–12: Dominique de Gourges (d. 1582) in 1567 went to Florida to avenge a massacre of the French by the Spaniards. Wordsworth read about him in Hakluyt's *Voyages*.   212–13: Gustavus I (1496–1560), who drove the Danes out of Sweden.   214–20: "There is scarce a noted glen in Scotland that has not a cave for Wallace or some other hero" (D.W., *Journals*, I, 228).   246 Locks . . . up: Pope, "The First Epistle of the First Book of Horace," l. 40, "lock up all the functions of my soul." 250–51: Cf. Milton, "Lycidas," ll. 67–69.   269, 274 this: I.e., his "lot," summed up in ll. 261–69. The questions of ll. 269–81 (whether his upbringing in nature was to end only in frustration at his inability to accomplish anything) are returned to in I.404 ff., 466–75, but are not finally answered until XIII.19 ff.   270 one . . . rivers: The Derwent (275), which flows north through Derwent Water and Bassenthwaite Lake to Cockermouth, Wordsworth's birthplace (303).   279–81, 283–84: Two early contrasts in the poem between things of man ("fretful," "shattered") and nature ("calm," "smooth").   283–86: On the "towers" (of Cockermouth Castle) and the "terrace walk" see the I.F. note to "The Sparrow's Nest."   302 fear: An important element in the poet's formative experience. See I.345, 352–56, 413, 471–74, 603, III.136, IV.252–53, V.307–309, 419, 450–51, VII.104–105, VIII.164–72, X.434–35, XII.232 ff., XIV.162–68, 244–46, 282–83, and Havens' chapter, "The Ministry of Fear," pp. 39–53. The incidents that follow — birdsnaring in autumn (306–25), nesting in spring (326–39), boatstealing in summer (357–400), skating in winter (425–63) — generally involve fear (as in *Peter Bell*, the result of nature's seeming animation), and they are described first because they impressed the child's mind directly; those of Book II, which were more pleasant (see II.48–54), operated "by means / Less often instantaneous in effect" (see VI.746–50).   304 beloved Vale: Esthwaite.   329: The "object" was stealing nests (for their eggs, to be added to a collection); by "end" Wordsworth means the effect or result of the experience (see ll. 350–51). 333–39: Nature *seems* (333, 338) to work both for and against the child. For the use of such qualifiers elsewhere see, e.g., I.3, 379, 383–84, VI.632, 636, "To My Sister," l. 6, "Lines Written in Early Spring," l. 16.   340 immortal spirit: As with "soul" (301), Wordsworth means the human mind (see the note to "The Recluse," l. 765).   342–44 reconciles . . . society: Cf. Coleridge's statement that the imagination reveals itself in the "reconciliation of opposite or discordant qualities" (*Biog. Lit.*, ch. XIV). In this and the next sentence Wordsworth celebrates the mind's ability to make a unified "calm existence" out of the various elements of past experience, many of which separately produced agitation rather than calmness. The point is more or less the same as the idea that "feeling comes in aid / Of feeling" in XII.269–71.   **357–400:** Discussed briefly in the Introduction.   **401–63:** Separately published in *The Friend*, 28 December 1809, and subsequently with Wordsworth's poems under the title "Influence of Natural Objects in Calling Forth and Strengthening the Imagination in Boyhood and Early Youth."   **401–404:** Wordsworth says in effect that God ("Wisdom and Spirit of the universe") is responsible for the mental processes so far explored — the giving to sense impressions ("forms and images") both life and permanence in the memory ("breath," "everlasting motion"; cf. "eternity of thought"). On the words "forms" and "images," which Wordsworth used variously (and frequently synonymously) to mean objects of sense perception, mental representations of such objects, and sometimes seemingly both at once, see Bennett Weaver, *SP*, XXXV (1938), 433–45; Ellen D. Leyburn, *ELH*, XVI (1949), 291–95; and C. C. Clarke, *Romantic Paradox* (1962).   **407 build up:** The metaphors of "building" and "mansion" for the mind are used in II.280, 383, IV.343, V.600, and "Tintern Abbey," l. 140.   **408–10:** See XIII.29–39 and note.   **464–66:** Inflated language for the things seen and felt in nature. Though in ll. 466–75 (as in ll. 351–56 and some other generalizing passages) nature is animated with life and purpose, in the specific incidents themselves it is the boy's own mind that "Impressed upon all forms the characters / Of danger or desire."   **484–85:** Wordsworth's "Nutting" was originally written for inclusion among these boyhood incidents.   **509–13:** Ticktacktoe. **516–35:** Modeled (with a specific borrowing in l. 522) on Pope's epic card-game in *The Rape of the Lock*, III.25–100.   **537 keen . . . tooth:** Cf. *As You Like It*, II.vii.177, where the winter wind's "tooth is not so keen." **545 extrinsic passion:** I.e., passion for "a child's pursuits" (582) — bird-snaring, skating, and the like — but not for nature herself; cf. II.7, "nourishment that came unsought."   **546 sublime:** Awful, fearful, the sense developed in Burke's *A Philosophical Enquiry into the Origin of Our Ideas of the Sublime and Beautiful* (1757).   **548–58:** As the following paragraphs make clear, Wordsworth is attempting in this difficult passage to explain how the mind responds with the pleasure of familiarity to sights apparently seen for the first time (see esp. ll. 572–80, the phenomenon we now call *déjà vu*). Most critics invoke a Platonic notion of pre-existence (like that used in the Intimations ode); but the context may suggest that Wordsworth is thinking of things in this world, and that by "first-born affinities" (555) he means very early experiences which were not retained in the "conscious memory" (e.g., Derwent's blending "his murmurs with my nurse's song," 271): see "unconscious intercourse" (562), "No conscious memory" (574), "forgotten" (585) impressions "doomed to sleep / Until maturer seasons called them forth" (594–95), "obscure feelings representative / Of things forgotten" (606–607), and the note to II.230–32.

560 stamped: Wordsworth often writes as if ideas had weight and occupied space (see, e.g., "impress" and "inform" in "Tintern Abbey," ll. 6, 125, 126); in III.362–63 he suggests that he did not learn more at Cambridge because "Those lovely forms [of nature] / Had . . . left less space within my mind."   **562–63 beauty . . . creation:** In 1805, "the eternal Beauty," by which, however, he probably meant simply what he conveys in the 1850 text, beauty so old that it seemed timeless.   **574:** Two early MSS read "No body of associated forms."   **584 along . . . blood:** Cf. II.242, IV.102, 319, and "Tintern Abbey," l. 28.   **586–88 Gleams . . . things:** Typically inflated language meaning that nature registered permanent impressions on his mind (the paragraph is a summary statement in associationistic terms; note "collisions," "accidents," "invisible links" in ll. 589, 611). For the language of fireworks elsewhere to describe the simplest ordinary mental experiences, see, e.g., the forms of "gleam" in VI.502, IX.500, "The Sparrow's Nest," l. 4, "She Was a Phantom of Delight," l. 2; the forms of "flash" in III.205, V.605, VI.502, 601, VII.437, VIII.269, XI.243, "I Wandered Lonely as a Cloud," l. 21; and "instantaneous burst" in IV.10. With "spake" (587) cf. V.13 ("speaking face of earth and heaven") and VIII.172 ("speaking monuments").   **632–36:** Cf. "To the Cuckoo," esp. l. 12.

Book II. 7 unsought: See the note to I.545.   **24 Union . . . be:** Unity of being or consciousness — one of the larger products hoped for from the unifying imagination — whereby the mental experiences of childhood and maturity are brought together in a more than merely chronological relationship (see the notes to "My Heart Leaps Up"). Continuing the melancholy tone of I.614–17, 623, 632–36 (note "almost" in l. 635), Wordsworth says here that intellect and virtue (21) are not sufficient to attain such unity, and that even with his memory functioning (30) his past and present selves seem to him "Two consciousnesses" (32).   **33 some . . . Being:** Himself as a child. The contrast of present tranquility (27) with the noisiness and "giddy motion" of childhood (9, 14–15, 47–48) emphasizes the wideness of the "vacancy" (29) between the two selves. **33–46:** Wordsworth returned to Hawkshead (where he had attended school in 1779–87) in November 1799. The Town Hall (39) had been built in 1790. An early MS identifies the "rude mass / Of native rock" as the "Stone of Rowe" (see ll. 43–44).   **48–54:** Wordsworth seems to mark a new stage of development, the boy's conscious awareness of nature — still "intervenient . . . And secondary" (201–202) — as a background to his outdoor activities. Though the experiences brought "calmer pleasures" (see the note to I.302), the difference between these and his earlier awareness of the solitary cliffs while skating (I.425–63) is not made very clear. "What distinguishes the episodes in 1 from those in the first part of this book is that the latter picture excursions some miles from Hawkshead" (Havens, p. 312).   **71 Were tempered:** The 1805 version explains more fully — "Were interfus'd with objects [the natural beauty of the island] which subdu'd / And temper'd them." The connection ("thus") with "quiet independence of the heart" is not explained.   **76–77:** For various attitudes toward solitude see III.233–36, IV.357–70, VI.419–22, VIII.222, 260–61, and Havens' chapter, "Solitude, Silence, Loneliness," pp. 54–67.   **103–107:** Furness Abbey, about twenty miles south of Hawkshead.   **134 with . . . step:** For slackening elsewhere as an important part of the process of receiving impressions from nature, see I.456–63, V.364–97 and note.   **137:** The line (referring to the estuary of the Leven) is repeated at X.603.   **140 tavern:** The White Lion, at Bowness. The boys rowed across Windermere ("Winander") to get to it.   **144 blood-red wine:** From the ballads (e.g., "Sir Patrick Spence," l. 2).   **145 the Hall:** A large circular stone house built c. 1770 on Belle Isle, in the middle of Windermere (Havens, p. 314).   **168 Minstrel . . . Troop:** Identified in Christopher Wordsworth's *Memoirs* (1851) as Robert Greenwood, afterwards Senior Fellow of Trinity College, Cambridge.   **170–74:** Wordsworth is literally submerged by the metaphors. On "lay . . . weight . . . sank down" see the note to I.560.   **183–85:** See the note to V.387–88. As with the earlier collateral attachment of nature to boyhood activities, and the later development of love for man (Book VIII), Wordsworth here comes to love something through its association with something else.   **200–203:** The beginning of a new stage (the third, if ll. 48–54 mark the second) that corresponds in some particulars to the second stage of development in "Tintern Abbey" (ll. 67–72, 75–83), though it includes the deeply-felt religious experiences (see ll. 386–418) that in "Tintern Abbey" are placed in the third stage rather than the second. See also the note to VIII.340–56.   **209–10:** Cf. Coleridge's Preface to "Christabel," on "a set of çritics . . . who have no notion that there are such things as fountains in the world . . . and who would therefore charitably derive every rill they behold flowing, from a perforation made in some other man's tank."   **216–19:** Coleridge's "secondary Imagination" (*Biog. Lit.*, ch. XIII) — what Wordsworth later in this book calls "creative sensibility" (see the note to ll. 255–65) — is primarily a unifying power (221); the "*false* secondary power" mentioned here, analytic reason, is also creative, but in a bad sense, multiplying distinctions rather than producing unity. See II.299–301 and note, 378–82, XII.155, XIII.216–20, and "The Tables Turned," ll. 26–28 and note.   **230–32:** Not in the "mystical and idle sense" of, e.g., the pre-existence metaphor used in the Intimations ode. Wordsworth must mean "Hath no beginning that reason or memory can recall," for the next paragraph (232 ff.) does show the beginnings of thought in the infant babe.   **235–38:** The 1805 version (in which the babe "Is prompt and watchful, eager to combine / In one appearance, all the elements / And parts of the same object, else detach'd / And loth to coalesce") makes clearer Wordsworth's idea that the child's first imaginative act is literally to create his mother ("one dear Presence") out of her separate parts ("arms," "breast," "eye").   **252–54:** I.e., lives imaginatively (the sense of "vital soul," "living mind" in I.150, 153). The universe is *active* (Wordsworth underlined the word in the 1805 version) because the child gives life to it.   **255–65:** Wordsworth's first theoretical statement in the poem about (as opposed to illustration of) the poetic imagination — subsequently called "infant sensibility" (270), "creative sensibility" (360), "Creative agency" (382), and the basis of "A sensitive being, a *creative* soul" in XII.207. See the Introduction; Francis Christensen, *JEGP*, XLV (1946), 361–68; and Havens, pp. 322–24. With l. 257, cf. Coleridge's statement that the primary imagination is "a repetition in the finite mind of the eternal act of creation in the infinite I AM" (*Biog. Lit.*, ch. XIII). Lines 258–60 may serve to explain "half create" in "Tintern Abbey," l. 106.   **262 uniform . . . years:** The same as "the regular action of the world" (361). See III.102–104, IV.167–68, V.516–22, VII.722–30, XII.211–14, XIV.157–62, and the Intimations ode, esp. ll. 126–28.   **276–322:** A difficult passage — for Wordsworth (see ll. 272–75, and "unknown causes" in l. 277) as well as his readers. The "trouble" of l. 276 has never been satisfactorily explained. The second sentence (277–78) may have to do with the "abyss of idealism" described in the I.F. note to the Intimations ode, but much of the rest seems to deal with the boy's first conscious awareness of memory, and of the pleasurable complexities resulting through the interaction of immediate impressions with what Wordsworth elsewhere calls "spiritual presences of absent things" (*Exc.*, IV.1234). In such a view, he marvels that his impressions ("affections . . . the building") remained when the physical objects were no longer present (279–81), and that through this "register / Of permanent relations" his perceptions were sharpened — he became more aware of changes in the seasons (288–93), and was able to see differences where others, "unwatchful," did not (299–301). His "Sublimer joy" (302), since it is "from the same source" (301), may be simply the recalling of feelings (305, 312–13) when he is in effect cut off from the surroundings that originally gave rise to them (see "form / Or image unprofaned," "night blackened," 305–307). Such ordinary mental processes were, for him, akin to the highest workings of imagination; hence the transition to "possible sublimity" (318) and the idea that there is no limit to what the imagination can create (319–22).   **280 building:** See the note to I.407.   **291 watchful:** The word had a special meaning for Wordsworth, something like "imaginatively perceptive"; see II.300, III.117, XII.12, XIII.40, "Michael," l. 47, and "When, to the Attractions of the Busy World," l. 81.   **295 "best society":** *P.L.*, IX.249.   **299–301 difference . . . is:** Not to be confused with the workings of the analytic reason (see the note to ll. 216–19); this is the same operation as that described in III.158–69, and is complementary to that mentioned in II.384–86.   **310–11 winds . . . power:** Cf. V.595–96.   **316–17 Remembering . . . not:** Cf. Coleridge to Southey, 7 August 1803, "association depends in a much greater degree on the recurrence of resembling states of Feeling, than on Trains of Idea" (*Collected Letters*, II, 961).   **319–22:** This is the first of the passages in the poem that clearly link sense experience (here the repeated "faculties") with the imaginative quest for infinity. Cf. VI.592–608 (where "the light of sense / Goes out"), VII.745–57, XIV.70–77.   **324–29:** If the antecedent of "its" (329) is "power" (324), the gist is that his perceptions were strengthened and made more pleasurable by what the poet's imagination added to "the latent qualities / And essences."   **330:** School began at 6:00 A.M. in the summer, at 7:00 in the winter (de Selincourt, citing William Knight).   **333 a Friend:** "The late Rev. John Fleming, of Rayrigg, Windermere" (note in 1850), who was at St. John's College with Wordsworth.   **348–50:** Cf. ll. 416–18 and "Tintern Abbey," ll. 35–49. **360:** "The term . . . expresses admirably both the passive and the active aspects of the poetic process: sensitivity to sense impressions and the power of transforming them" (Havens, p. 323).   **362, 363 plastic power, forming hand:** Cf. Coleridge's "shaping spirit of Imagination" in "Dejection: An Ode."   **368–70:** Cf, the metaphors of light in the Intimations ode and "Elegiac Stanzas," ll. 14–16, and the images of projection or "spreading abroad" at III.117–18, IV.170–71, V.48–49, VI.614–16, VII.752, XI.169–72, XIV.93–95 (also the idea that poetry proceeds "from the soul of Man, communicating its creative energies to the images of the external world," *M.Y.*, II, 705).   **383 building:** See the note to I.407.   **384– 86:** A specific statement that the "wise passiveness" of "Expostulation and Reply" is not enough. Cf. II.299–301, III.158–61, VII.734–36, XIV.101– 102, and Hazlitt's "This intuitive perception of the hidden analogies of things, or, as it may be called, this *instinct of imagination*" (*Complete Works*, ed. P. P. Howe, 1930–34, XVI, 8–9).   **386–418:** Especially with the reiteration of "all" in ll. 402–407, cf. "Tintern Abbey," ll. 93–102 (where the same apprehension of "one life" occurs at a later age and in a later stage of development). In the confusing "whether . . . or . . . or" of ll. 387–94 (cf. *Exc.*, I.157–62) Wordsworth offers two alternative explanations for the experience: *either* he imaginatively gave life to "unorganic natures" (from the habit of observing "affinities," 384–86, or from some "great social principle of life" that made him coerce "all things into sympathy" — cf. III.130–32), *or* he "did converse / With things that really are." The repetition of "transport" and "Communing" (410, 411 — cf. ll. 368, 376) tends to link the passage with the preceding paragraph on creative sensibility (see also l. 430).   **398–99 all . . . feeling:** Cf. the 1800 Preface, "our continued influxes of feeling are modified and directed by our thoughts, which are indeed the representatives of all our past feelings" (p. 448).   **410–14 great . . . love:** The 1805 version reads, "for in all things / I saw one life, and felt that it was joy." Wordsworth revised and expanded the passage sometime after May 1839.   **419–26:** Cf. "Tintern Abbey," ll. 49–57.   **420 pious mind:** On the heretical tendency of "one life," see Coleridge's "The Eolian Harp," esp. ll. 49 ff.   **432–40:** De Selincourt cites a letter from Coleridge to Wordsworth, September 1799, mentioning "those, who, in consequence of the complete failure of the French Revolution, have thrown up all hopes of the amelioration of mankind, and are sinking into an almost epicurean selfishness, disguising the same under the soft titles of domestic attachment and contempt for visionary *philosophes*" (*Collected Letters*, I, 527). **451–52:** Echoing Coleridge's "Frost at Midnight," ll. 51–52. Cf. VI.266–74.

Book III: Wordsworth entered St. John's College (46) at the end of October 1787. Book III covers his first year there (October–July). **30, 36 Dream, Fairy's wand:** For other uses of dream, fairy-tale, and romance imagery to suggest unreality or delusion, see V.523, VII.75–98, 455–57, 506, VIII.414–18, 435–37, 653, IX.300–302, 437–65, XI.112, 115, 125–26, 232, XII.81–83. **31 spectacle:** Cf. "show" (90, 205), "second act" (259), "pageant" (588), "spectacle" (591), and ll. 572–76. **83–87:** The parenthesis is a late addition to the poem. **89:** The 1805 version continues, "To apprehend all passions and all moods / Which time, and place, and season do impress / Upon the visible universe, and work / Like changes there by force of my own mind." **96 into herself:** Here and in ll. 116, 145–46, 174–79, 206 Wordsworth stresses the subjectivity of his experience; "genius, power, / Creation and divinity itself" lie *within* the mind, the "quickening soul" of l. 134. **117–19:** If Wordsworth intends a connection between ll. 117–18 and 119, the sense is that the more widely he spread his thoughts, the "more awful" were the "Incumbencies" that he received back. See the note to II.368–70. **130–35, 144–46:** Cf. Coleridge, "Dejection: An Ode," ll. 47–48, "we receive but what we give, / And in our life alone does Nature live." Note that Wordsworth's statements here are not qualified by the kind of alternative explanation — "did converse / With things that really are" — offered in II.392–94. After l. 135, the 1805 version adds: "Thus much for the one Presence, and the Life / Of the great whole." **139–42:** Since the paragraph generally stresses the mind's creativity, it is curious that in both of these similes Wordsworth pictures himself as passively responsive to the beauties and terrors of nature. **146 sees . . . heart:** In 1805, "look'd into my mind." **158–61:** See II.299–301, 384–86, and notes. **173–83:** Cf. V.507–509, VIII.607, XI.27–30, XII. 272–77. On the association of "genius, power, / Creation and divinity itself" with youth (173, 179, 181–83) see the Intimations ode (and the contrary notion in "Tintern Abbey"); "yoke of earth" (182) recalls "the inevitable yoke" in l. 124 of the ode. **180–84:** Cf. "The Recluse," ll. 778–94, 824. **188–89 Points . . . single:** Perhaps the "spots of time" (XII.208 ff.). **278:** Trumpington, two miles south of Cambridge, is the setting of the *Reeve's Tale*. **287:** Like Abdiel in *P.L.*, V.901–903. **288:** Cf. *P.L.*, VII.27, "In darkness, and with dangers compast round." **381–401, 430–44:** These lines "shadow forth" Wordsworth's conception of an ideal university; ll. 408–25 attack compulsory attendance at chapel. **457–60, 466–67:** In stressing the rigor and simplicity "of old," Wordsworth did not mean to suggest that the university in his own time was less democratic; see IX.222–32. **479:** The Protestant reformer Martin Bucer (1491–1551) was appointed regius professor of divinity at Cambridge in 1549; Erasmus had visited and lectured there for two and a half years during 1511–14. **512 vacation:** I.e., at-

tending Cambridge (a vacation from the real life he had experienced so
far).   564–66: De Selincourt compares *F.Q.*, III.xi.28, "goodly arras of
great maiesty, / Wouen with gold and silke so close and nere, / That the
rich metall lurked priuily . . . Yet here, and there, and every where,
vnwares / It shewd it selfe, and shone vnwillingly; / Like a discolourd
Snake . . . ."   598–611: The personified abstractions (on which see the
1800 Preface, p. 449) tend to deny the idea of ll. 592–93.   612–16:
See IV.256–76 and note.

Book IV. 1–26: "These lines describe the walk from Kendal, which
Wordsworth reached by coach, over to the Ferry on Windermere, and
after crossing the lake, up through Sawrey, past Esthwaite [19], to Hawkshead [24]" (de Selincourt). Book IV covers Wordsworth's first long vacation from Cambridge (July–October 1788).   **28 my . . . Dame:** Mrs.
Ann Tyson (d. 1796, at the age of eighty-three), with whom Wordsworth
and his brothers lodged while they attended the school at Hawkshead.
88–92: See the note to *An Evening Walk*, ll. 214–15.   **105 Like . . .
Lover:** Cf. I.135–36.   **113–17:** Adapted from Wordsworth's "The Dog —
An Idyllium" (*P.W.*, I, 264), a fragmentary poem dating from the 1780's.
119–20: Cf. "A Poet's Epitaph," ll. 39–40. Wordsworth habitually composed aloud.   **150–51 Gently . . . veil:** De Selincourt compares Exodus
34:33–35, II Corinthians 3:13–16. "Veil" may refer to the unreality in
which he participated at Cambridge; cf. the more than literal attirement as
if by "some Fairy's wand" in III.35–39. Of the various mental experiences
recorded in *The Prelude*, this (esp. in ll. 160–62) most closely resembles
that at II.302–22.   **166 God-like power:** Cf. II.257.   **167:** "Informs"
and "creates" are intransitive verbs. "Sleep" refers to "the deadening influence of custom and of the cares of life" (Havens, p. 359; see II.262 and
note).   **170 spreads abroad:** See the note to II.368–70.   **185:** Cf.
I.323.   **186–87:** The lines make a rather odd connection with the
humorous tone of the preceding paragraph.   **245 those . . . Seven:** The
Big Dipper.   **256–76:** For other passages on his merging or confusing
"naked recollection" with "after-meditation" see III.612–16, VI.237–39,
286–94, and "Nutting," ll. 48–49.   **309:** Ideas or images "rise up" also
in IV.113, V.61–62, VI.594, VII.149, 319.   **323–38:** Cf. *Exc.*, I.197–218.
Though generally read as Wordsworth's dedication of his life to poetry, ll.
333–37 are characteristically unspecific. "It is well to recall that the writing of poetry is neither mentioned nor implied in the entire passage or in
the lines that precede and follow it" (Havens, p. 365). Cf. Wordsworth's
"resolution" at an age "not . . . above fourteen," described in the I.F. note
to *An Evening Walk*.   **349–53:** The lines mean generally that he continued (at "intervals") to have elevating mental experiences. Havens paraphrases (p. 368), "I found myself as much in harmony as ever with the
end and spirit of God's works as vision reveals them, now in Nature, now
in Man, and now in the two conjoined." Line 353 is not in the 1805
version.   **354–70:** The paragraph is a late addition to the poem. With
ll. 359–60 cf. VIII.260–61. The incident that follows (370 ff.) illustrates

the potency (see "desolation" in l. 402, "ghastly" in ll. 396, 434, 458) rather than the graciousness and benignity of Solitude.   **370–469:** One of the earliest parts of the poem to be drafted (early 1798). Cf. "The Old Cumberland Beggar," "Animal Tranquillity and Decay," and (esp. with ll. 387–412, 459–60, 469) "Resolution and Independence."

Book V. 13: See I.586–88.   **17:** In place of this line, the 1805 version has "A soul divine which we participate."   **19 with herself:** I.e., with other human minds.   **26 "weep to have":** Shakespeare, Sonnet 64. **38–44:** "A strange preamble, this, to *Jack the Giant-killer!* A domed and spacious vestibule which leads only to the nursery!" — Havens (p. 376), commenting on the fact that Book V deals almost exclusively with children's books and has very little to say about serious reading of any kind. **40–41:** With this identification of "passion" with reason, cf. XIV.189–92. **48–49 gifted . . . spirit:** See the note to II.368–70.   **65–67:** On geometry and its exemption "From all internal injury" see VI.115–67. Note that in the preceding paragraph, as in the symbolic dream that follows, Wordsworth worries about perishability through *external* injury (earthquake, fire, deluge).   **70–140:** On this dream, which is based on a dream of Descartes as recorded in Baillet's *Vie de Descartes* (1691), see Jane W. Smyser, *PMLA,* LXXI (1956), 269–75. Until 1839 it was presented as the dream not of Wordsworth but of the "studious friend" (51), presumably Coleridge. **105:** Cf. VI.135–37, XI.330–33.   **108–109:** Cf. *Peter Bell,* l. 142, and Keats, "Sleep and Poetry," ll. 245–47, "the great end / Of poesy, that it should be a friend / To sooth the cares, and lift the thoughts of man." **167 living nature:** Wordsworth may mean literally alive (see XII.102–104) or something like "lively" (fresh, vivid, active — as in "Nature's living images," VI.302, and "living scene," VII.144).   **192–222:** Havens paraphrases (p. 384), "What everybody feels I will leave registered in the hearts, tongues, tears, and looks of all; what is peculiar to myself will remain working within myself; I shall merely assert the rights and honors of all books, lofty or humble, that men have loved."   **200 prose . . . verse:** *P.L.,* V.150.   **218–21 Powers . . . only less . . . Than Nature's self:** See XIII.301–12 and note.   **222 Or His:** Read "Or [less than] His." This line was added to the poem around 1820.   **227 ff.:** Wordsworth's chief protests are directed against the "modern" theorists "who, stimulated by the enthusiasm for education kindled by Rousseau, but without his genius, devoted their lives to 'child study', substituted for the old-time classics of the nursery, such as *Robin Hood* and the *Arabian Nights, etc.,* edifying tales designed to inculcate scientific information or moral truth, and invented systems which, under a show of developing the latent powers of the child, fettered that development at every turn, and produced not the child of Nature, but the self-conscious prig" (de Selincourt). "Followed," "watched," "noosed," "Stringed," "servitude," "stallèd" (238–42) emphasize Wordsworth's objection to the lack of freedom in such systems.   **260–64 Little . . . checked:** A cryptic pair of remarks. Havens (p. 387) suggests that they are "a thrust at the Cooksons, Wordsworth's mother's family . . .

[who] antagonized the homeless children by their lack of sympathy and by petty, arbitrary regulations. Lines 263–4 may mean, 'I could easily make clear the wisdom of my mother's way by contrasting it with that of the Cooksons . . . . But, as it would be an affront to her memory to criticize her mother, father, and brother, I am checked.' "   **307–309**: On the importance that Wordsworth attached to fearful experiences see the note to I.302. **329–36**: Since everything is centered in the child, he can love only himself (without vanity, he can love nothing); he has never been allowed to forget himself (cf. ll. 345–46).   **337–39**: Cf. Intimations ode, ll. 77–84. **348–49**: The image is based on the "broad Highway or Bridge over *Chaos*" built by Sin and Death "To make the Way easier from Hell to this World to and fro" (*P.L.*, Argument to Book X).   **364–97**: Written toward the end of 1798, and published in the 1800 *Lyrical Ballads*. In *Poems* of 1815 the lines were given first place among "Poems of the Imagination" (see Wordsworth's explanation in the Preface of 1815, p. 487 n. in the present volume). In the earliest surviving MS version (de Selincourt's edition, pp. 639–40) the boy is Wordsworth himself. As a comment on this passage De Quincey describes an occasion when he and Wordsworth were waiting to meet a carrier bringing London newspapers:

> At intervals, Wordsworth had stretched himself at length on the high road, applying his ear to the ground, so as to catch any sound of wheels that might be groaning along at a distance. Once, when he was slowly rising from this effort, his eye caught a bright star that was glittering between the brow of Seat Sandal, and of the mighty Helvellyn. He gazed upon it for a minute or so; and then, upon turning away to descend into Grasmere, he made the following explanation: — 'I have remarked, from my earliest days, that if, under any circumstances, the attention is energetically braced up to an act of steady observation, or of steady expectation, then, if this intense condition of vigilance should suddenly relax, at that moment any beautiful, any impressive visual object, or collection of objects, falling upon the eye, is carried to the heart with a power not known under other circumstances. Just now . . . at the very instant when the organs of attention were all at once relaxing from their tension, the bright star hanging in the air above those outlines of massy blackness, fell suddenly upon my eye, and penetrated my capacity of apprehension with a pathos and a sense of the Infinite, that would not have arrested me under other circumstances.' (De Quincey, *Literary Reminiscences*, 1861, I, 314–15)

387–88 that . . . lake: "Had I met these lines running wild in the deserts of Arabia, I should have instantly screamed out 'Wordsworth!' " (Coleridge to Wordsworth, 10 December 1798; *Collected Letters*, I, 453). Cf. the interconnection of earth and sky in II.183–85, X.516–21, XIV.61–62, "Tintern Abbey," ll. 7–8, and "Stepping Westward."   **400 erewhile**: In IV.21–23. **425**: On knowledge and power see VIII.599–601 and note.   **448–50**: Cf. *Peter Bell*, ll. 578–80.   **453–59**: A lame explanation. Wordsworth is frequently more effective (e.g., in the passages ending at IV.190, 469, VI.726) when he presents his experiences without attempting to interpret or theorize upon them.   507–22: See the notes to II.262, III.173–83.   534–38: Cf. III.170–71, 197–98. "Native continent" may refer to pre-existence (Havens, p. 401) — or simply to birth in this world, since the "humbler" ground, "not the less a tract / Of the same isthmus" that we cross in progress to maturity (the meaning of "earth and human life"), is nothing more than the "time of growing youth" (539).   540–41, 567, 571–77: Lines 540–41 and the tone of l. 567 support the main idea of the Prologue to *Peter Bell*, and ll. 571–77 seem to counter it. But by "something loftier . . ." (575–77) Wordsworth may mean that "certain colouring of imagination, whereby ordinary things should be presented to the mind in an unusual aspect" (1800 Preface, pp. 446–47). On fancy and imagination see the note to VIII.366, 373.   558–66: See II.330–35.   588 living Nature: See the note to l. 167.   591–605: The general idea is that the reader's imagination ("that transparent veil") operates creatively upon the "works / Of mighty Poets" in the same way that the mind acts creatively upon nature itself.   595–96: Cf. II.310–11.

Book VI. 6 Granta: An old name for the River Cam.   22 Two winters: 1788–89, 1789–90.   23–24 many . . . perused: Cf. Bacon, "Of Studies," "Some books are to be tasted, others to be swallowed, and some few to be chewed and digested."   48–52: "This very week" is the first week of April 1804 (Wordsworth's thirty-fourth birthday fell on a Saturday). The Intimations ode, in which life's morning radiance *has* left the hills, was completed perhaps only a week or two earlier.   55–57: Wordsworth is thinking of Milton's statement in *The Reason of Church-Government*, "I might perhaps leave something so written to aftertimes, as they should not willingly let it die."   109–14: On poetic diction see the Preface of 1800 and especially the Appendix of 1802.   115–67: On mathematics see also II.204, V.65 ff., XI.328–33, and *Exc.*, I.252–57. According to his sister, Wordsworth lost the chance of a fellowship at Cambridge because "he gave way to his natural dislike of studies so dry as many parts of the mathematics . . . . He reads Italian, Spanish, French, Greek and Latin, and English, but never opens a mathematical book" (letter of 26 June 1791; *E.L.*, p. 51).   138: Wordsworth admires in geometry what he dislikes in "classic niceties"; cf. ll. 111–13.   142–54: The source is John Newton's *An Authentic Narrative of Some Remarkable and Interesting Particulars in the Life of *********, first published in 1764 (Havens, p. 412).   158–67: Cf. ll. 297–305, 313, where he pities Coleridge for having been forced into the same kind of abstractions ("self-created sustenance of a mind / Debarred from Nature's living images") that he values here. There are a number of such conflicting passages in Book VI; Wordsworth apparently wants the best of both worlds — those of external nature and of the mind — without giving up anything of either in favor of the other.   180 the Bard: James Thomson, in *The Castle of Indolence*, I.xv.   192 That streamlet: The Dove, in Derbyshire and Staffordshire, the favorite fishing-stream of Izaak Walton.   197–98 seemed . . . noon: *P.L.*, V.310–11.

198–203: After a long separation, Wordsworth visited his sister at Penrith in the summer of 1787. The "summer" of l. 190 is ostensibly the long vacation of 1789, but in this paragraph and the next Wordsworth brings together events that took place in three summers, 1787, 1788, 1789 (de Selincourt). **205 that . . . castle:** Brougham Castle, on the Eamont (204), a mile or two southeast of Penrith. "Fame" — in this instance probably James Clarke's *Survey of the Lakes* — was wrong in reporting that Sidney visited it (207–11); the Countess of Pembroke who lived there was born several years after Sidney died (de Selincourt).   **224 Another maid:** Mary Hutchinson, whom Wordsworth married in 1802.   **233–36:** See XII.261–66 (where two of these lines are repeated nearly verbatim). Penrith Beacon is a square stone tower on a high hill a mile northeast of the town.   **237–39, 286–94:** See IV.256–76 and note.   **240:** At the beginning of April 1804 Coleridge had sailed for Malta. He was away from England (mainly at Malta, but also in Sicily, Naples, and Rome) until August 1806.   **254–56:** Cf. II.451–54. Wordsworth subsequently refers to Coleridge's schooling at Christ's Hospital, London (266–74 — see Coleridge's "Frost at Midnight" and "Sonnet to the River Otter"), his first years at Cambridge just after Wordsworth left (274–81), and the "stormy course" (281–82) that began with his runaway enlistment in the 15th Light Dragoons.   **297–305, 313:** Cf. VIII.429–37, and see the note to VI.158–67.   **322 ff.:** Wordsworth toured France and Switzerland (July–September 1790) in the company of Robert Jones, who became a lifelong friend. For their itinerary, see Havens, pp. 421–22 and accompanying maps.   **340:** Shakespeare, Sonnet 16, "stand . . . on the top of happy hours."   **346 that . . . day:** 14 July 1790 (the first anniversary of the fall of the Bastille), on which Louis XVI and others, at a great ceremony in the Champs de Mars, Paris, publicly swore fidelity to the French Assembly (see also ll. 389–90).   **420–88:** A later addition to the poem (c. 1808).   **425–26 commissioned . . . inmates:** "Wordsworth was mistaken. The armed occupation of the Chartreuse did not take place till May 1792 — the soldiers were at this time paying no more than a domiciliary visit, followed perhaps by confiscation" (de Selincourt).   **436:** St. Bruno was the founder of the Convent.   **439:** "The two streams are the *Guiers vif* and the *Guiers mort,* torrents which unite to form the river Guiers in the valley below the Grande Chartreuse" (de Selincourt).   **456–71:** "Be the house redeemed . . . [1] for the sake / Of . . . and [2] for humbler claim / Of . . . ." In this part of a 24-line sentence Wordsworth manages to extol both "conquest over sense" (458) and the consolation derived from "bodily eyes" (470–71). With ll. 466–67 cf. ll. 624–40; with ll. 469–70 ("lost . . . blank abyss") cf. ll. 594–96.   **480 Vallombre:** One of the vallies of the Grande Chartreuse.   **509–10 compassed . . . danger:** See the note to III.288.   **523–33:** Cf. VIII.419–20, "Yarrow Unvisited," ll. 49–52, and "Yarrow Visited," ll. 1–4. "Soulless image" (526) means unmodified perception. "Reconciled us to realities" (533) parallels the easy dislodgment of melancholy (617–19) following the similar disappointment of ll. 586–91; with l. 528 cf. l. 608.   **569, 571 rough stream, torrent:** In 1805, "rivulet" — which may explain the apparent ease with which they crossed this "unbridged stream" (574). **592–616:** Perhaps the most difficult passage of the entire poem. Though l. 596 may seem to refer to the travelers of the preceding paragraph, the 1805 version of the beginning of this paragraph ("Imagination! lifting up itself / Before the eye and progress of my Song . . .") makes clear that Wordsworth is describing something which happened not when he crossed the Alps in 1790 but while he was writing this part of the poem in 1804 (cf. the similar interruption in VII.316 ff.). Possibly he had begun (with the first word of the paragraph) to explain that imagination was responsible for the "melancholy slackening" (617) — just as it was earlier responsible for momentary disappointment when the "living thought" of Mont Blanc was dashed by the "soulless image" of its reality (523–28) — but then found himself "lost" (596 — cf. XII.273), in a state of confusion over seeming to blame what he everywhere else has praised. Recovery occurs between ll. 597 and 598. It is, he now recognizes, in just such questing after "infinitude" ("hopes that pointed to the clouds," 587, "hope . . . expectation . . . desire . . . something evermore about to be," 606–608) that the glory of the "conscious soul" manifests itself; the reality (the actual crossing of the Alps, the sudden fulfilling of their desires) is of secondary importance, because such "thoughts [the hopes, etc.] . . . are their own perfection and reward" (611–12). The idea is much like that of Keats in a letter to Benjamin Bailey, 13 March 1818, "every mental pursuit takes its reality and worth from the ardour of the pursuer — being in itself a nothing" (*Letters*, ed. H. E. Rollins, 1958, I, 242), and that of Imlac in Johnson's *Rasselas* (ch. VIII), "some desire is necessary to keep life in motion." The main difficulty lies in the relationship of ll. 599–602 to the rest of the paragraph (cf. II.348–50, 416–18, and "Tintern Abbey," ll. 35–49). With "usurpation" (600) cf. l. 527 (the opposite kind of seizure, sense over "living thought"). "The invisible world" (602) is presumably the same as "infinitude" (605–608; see the note to II.319–22). "Goes out" (601) is usually read as "fails" or "is extinguished," though William Empson (*The Structure of Complex Words*, pp. 294–95) suggests the meaning "proceeds from the source," and the simile at the end of the paragraph is just such an image of spreading out from a source (see the note to II.368–70). **621–40:** Separately published in the edition of 1845 under the title "The Simplon Pass." Here nature symbolizes the permanence (624–26, with which cf. ll. 466–67) and the combined "Tumult and peace" of "Eternity" — another kind, or perhaps a further example, of "infinitude" (605). With "one mind . . . same face . . . one tree" (636–37) cf. II.415, XIV.60, 74. **640:** *P.L.,* V.165, "Him first, him last, him midst, and without end." **647 innocent sleep:** *Macbeth,* II.ii.37. **651–52 river . . . Dimpling along:** Thomson, *The Seasons,* "Spring," ll. 522–23. **655 Locarno's Lake:** Maggiore. **660–62:** Como is "confined" by high mountains. Havens suggests (p. 428) that "Abyssinian privacy" is an allusion to the Happy Valley in Johnson's *Rasselas.* **662–63 I . . . thee:** In *Descriptive Sketches* (first published in 1793), ll. 77–140. **692–94, 716–18:** "The early Italian usage was to begin numbering the hours at Ave-Maria, half an hour after sunset. Today in Italy many clocks strike first the quarter and then the hour so that one forty-five (3 + 1 bells) may be mistaken for four, or two o'clock (4 + 2 bells) for six" (Havens, p. 430).   **700 Gravedona:** On the northwest shore of Lake Como.   **734:** The picturesque-seeker's reaction (see XII. 114–21).   **752–53 but . . . Heaven:** A late addition.   **757:** Cf. Milton, *Areopagitica,* "a noble and puissant Nation rousing herself like a strong man after sleep."   **764 Brabant armies:** Republican troops preparing to oppose the new Austrian emperor, Leopold II (de Selincourt).

Book VII. 1–4: Wordsworth confuses his 1795 escape from the city, when he "sang" his "glad preamble" (I.1–45), with the winter of 1798–99, when he actually started work on the poem; he is here writing in 1804.   **7 Scafell:** Scafell (3162') and Scafell Pike (3210', the highest mountain in England) are eight miles west of Grasmere.   **14:** See the note to VI.240. **18 outward hindrance:** "Mrs. Wordsworth was not well (Dora was born August 16), John (born the previous June) needed much attention, and there were many visitors. Under such conditions in a house so small as Dove Cottage work was extremely difficult" (Havens, p. 438).   **44–48:** Cf. I.35 ("correspondent breeze") and XII.329–35. The grove was "John's Grove" (see "When, to the Attractions of the Busy World").   **52 ff.:** Wordsworth returned to Cambridge in November 1790, took his degree in January 1791, and then went to live in London (February–May). Book VII records impressions not only from this sojourn but from several visits to London both before and afterward.   **69–70 concourse . . . incessantly:** Wordsworth's various epithets for London — e.g., "ant-hill" (149), "roar" (168), "throng" (189), "hubbub" (211), "concourse" (219) — prefigure the epitomizing "blank confusion" (722) of the last paragraph of the book. **77–84, 98, 111:** See the note to III.30, 36.   **99–102:** Cf. VI.589–91; here, however, his expectation is the product of "childhood's Fancy" (88), a type of "vanity" (103).   **115 Articulate music:** "Young Dick Whittington when leaving London in discouragement heard from Holloway the bells of St. Mary-le-Bow, which seemed to say to him: 'Turn again, Whittington, / Lord Mayor of London.' Whereupon, he returned to the city of which he was later thrice Lord Mayor" (Havens, pp. 440–41).   **121 Vauxhall, Ranelagh:** Fashionable pleasure-gardens. In ll. 124–26 Wordsworth is probably thinking of the Rotunda at Ranelagh.   **131 Giants:** The wooden statues of Gog and Magog.   **146 disappointment:** Because (as with Mont Blanc, VI.523–28, and the boy who had been to London, VII.93–102) the reality did not measure up to the "bold imaginations" (142).   **162 Stationed . . . door:** I.e., on signs.   **170 sequestered nook:** Milton, *Comus,* l. 500.   **193 files of ballads:** Rows of broadside ballads strung on a wire or string.   **240–59:** "Lines 248–59 describe small painted models in which no deception is attempted, but 240–7 refer to sights something like the Pantheon de la Guerre or the 'Battle of Gettysburg' in which the spectator stands in the center of a circular building and receives the impression, through the skilful merging of foreground and walls, that he sees to the horizon" (Havens, p. 442).   **267 Half-rural:** Describing both its location (in Islington, then a suburb of London) and the character of its entertainment (271 ff.). **283–84 "as . . . cave":** Milton, *Samson Agonistes*, ll. 87, 89. **288 "forms . . . time":** *Hamlet*, III.ii.27. **296–315:** "John Hatfield, a vulgar adventurer, came to Keswick in 1802, and giving himself out to be Alexander Augustus Hope, M.P. . . . imposed upon all the tradesmen of the district. He married Mary, daughter of the innkeeper of the Fish, Buttermere . . . [but] his frauds were detected, and he fled the country, leaving behind him papers which proved that he had another wife living, and several children. He was caught soon afterwards . . . tried for forgery . . . [and] hanged . . . . Wordsworth and Coleridge were much interested in the incident, and Coleridge contributed three papers upon it to the *Morning Post*" (de Selincourt). A dramatic farce based on it, *Edward and Susan; or, The Beauty of Buttermere*, by Charles Dibdin, Jr., was produced at Sadler's Wells in April 1803. **316–20:** Cf. the similar interruption while writing in VI.592–616. **336 lovely Boy:** Not Mary of Buttermere's child (325, 329, 380), but the son of a London prostitute (344–47, 365). **428:** *Macbeth*, II.i.58, "prate of my whereabout." **434 many-headed mass:** *Coriolanus*, II.iii.18, "many-headed multitude" (cf. Wordsworth's "rabblement," 273). **453–57:** This heightening of pleasure through the realization that he is seeing a play, and not real life, would seem to be the opposite of Coleridge's idea of "willing suspension of disbelief" (*Biog. Lit.*, ch. XIV). Cf. Johnson, "Preface to Shakespeare": "The delight of tragedy proceeds from our consciousness of fiction." **461–65:** "Spots of time" (XII.208 ff.) are among such ties. See also the notes to "My Heart Leaps Up." **470 tragic sufferings:** Probably in his reading (rather than in real life or on the stage). The gist of ll. 475–85 is that plays made no meaningful impression on him (his imagination "slept," the emotions did not pass "beyond the suburbs" into his mind) until he saw them acted. **496–98:** See *Henry V*, IV.iii.51–55. **512–43:** Added after 1820. (Lines 523–30 are, however, consistent with the political ideas elsewhere in the poem; de Selincourt is wrong in saying that this impression of Burke "certainly would not have been true of Wordsworth's earlier [1805] attitude to politics.") **551–72:** De Selincourt compares Cowper's "Picture of a theatrical clerical coxcomb" in *The Task*, II.414–62. **563–64 he . . . Abel:** Salomon Gessner, whose *Der Tod Abels* (1758) had gone through more than twenty editions in the English translation by Mary Collyer. **564 the Bard:** Edward Young (referring to *Night Thoughts*, 1742–45). **567 Ossian:** James Macpherson's Ossianic poems (1760–65), fraudulently put forth as translations from the works of a third-century Gaelic warrior-bard. **651 these:** E.g., seeing in the blind beggar an admonishment "from another world." The "excited spirit" is the imagination. **669–71:** I.e., are wrongly described in ll. 653–54 ("Full-formed . . . with small internal help"), because they are seen and felt only if "the mind answers to them" and the heart is prompt. For "are, are not, / As" read "are or are not according to whether." **676 the Fair:** Wordsworth had visited Bartholomew Fair with Charles Lamb in September 1802. **679 completed . . . hands:** I.e., "Full-formed" (653). But ll. 731–36 show that

imagination is at work here also.   **734–36:** Describing the unifying imagination (components of which are "Attention . . . comprehensiveness and
memory," 740–41); see II.384–86, XIV.101–102, and notes. In the lines
that follow (esp. 745–57) Wordsworth attempts to explain, as the furthest
extension of this faculty, how habitual perception of the largeness and permanence of things in nature ("everlasting . . . still stretching . . . Beyond
all compass . . . Perennial") shapes the soul's "views and aspirations . . .
To majesty" (cf. "our being's heart and home, / Is with infinitude," VI.604–
605, and see the note to II.319–22). The concluding statement of the book
(761–71), that through the imagination he found "Composure, and ennobling Harmony" in London's blank confusion, rather anticlimactically
repeats the idea of ll. 731–36.   **754 principles as fixed:** See XIII.372 and
note.

Book VIII: Turning and returning "with intricate delay" (see IX.1–8),
Wordsworth now goes back over the ground of the first seven books (which
generally treat his relationship with nature, even when he is removed from
it at Cambridge or in London) to show how love of nature led to the love
of man (key passages are ll. 256–93, 295, 340–56, 476–94, 644–50; see
Havens, p. 453, for an outline of the book). Here, however, "man" is an
abstraction (see ll. 501–502, 608–11, 673); Wordsworth does not fully
arrive at a knowledge of "individual man, / No composition of the brain,
but man / Of whom we read, the man whom we behold / With our own
eyes," until XIII.79–84.   **1–69:** The opening lines present two sides of a
contrast between man and nature — one in which men are pitifully small,
weak, and short-lived by comparison (5–7, 14–15, 55–62), and one in
which men are lordly, "For all things serve them" (62–69). The change at
l. 62 epitomizes the shift in interest and emphasis represented by the book
as a whole.   **45–52 and . . . eve":** A late addition (c. 1839). Lines 48–
52 are quoted from Joseph Cottle's *Malvern Hills* (1798), ll. 952–56.
75–97: "Strongly reminiscent in style, construction, and phrasing of *Paradise Lost,* iv.208–47, and other lines in which Milton calls to memory various scenes famed in history or fiction, only to dismiss them as unworthy of
comparison with Eden . . . . For the comparison with Gehol's matchless
Gardens Wordsworth draws on Lord Macartney's description, quoted by
John Barrow (*Travels in China,* 1804, pp. 127–33)" (de Selincourt).
84–85, 88 domes / Of pleasure, taught to melt: See the note to "Hart-Leap
Well," ll. 57, 84.   **121–28, 295, 315–17:** See "Michael," ll. 23–26, and
the note to II.183–85.   **125 of:** I.e., "in" or "as if from."   **136–43:**
Referring to *As You Like It* (136–41) and *The Winter's Tale* (142–43).
144–56: De Selincourt cites *The Shepheardes Calender,* "May," ll. 9–34,
and "Epithalamion," ll. 206–207.   **175–82 Galesus, Clitumnus, Lucretilus:**
Wordsworth read about these (rivers in Calabria and Umbria, and a mountain near Horace's Sabine farm) in Virgil's *Georgics* and Horace's *Odes.*
From drinking Clitumnus' waters, herds became "snow-white."   **185–86
I . . . seen:** In Germany, in the winter and spring of 1798–99. "Hercynian"
(215) refers to the Harz region.   **260–61:** Cf. IV.357–60.   **266:** Cf.

Thomson, *The Seasons*, "Autumn," ll. 725–30 (in which the fog similarly acts as magnifier).   **273–75:** See VI.482–88.   **303–22:** Here (as, e.g., in ll. 645–50, much of Book VII, and some of the shorter poems, most notably "Tintern Abbey") Wordsworth is well aware of evil in man; his optimism is based not on what man *is* but, rather precariously, on "what we *may* become" (650). See XIII.87–88: "Why is this glorious creature to be found / One only in ten thousand?"   **340–56:** Another summary of "stages" (see the notes to II.48–54, 200–203, 386–418, and "Tintern Abbey," ll. 67–102). The first (342–45) corresponds to Book I and part of Book II, and to "Tintern Abbey," ll. 73–74. The second (345–56) corresponds to the change marked at II.200–203, and has some things in common ("passion," "rapture") with "Tintern Abbey," ll. 67–72, 75–83 (though the reference to nature's "viewless agencies," 352, does not accord with "Tintern Abbey," ll. 82–83). The third, yet to come, is anticipated in l. 356.   **366, 373 Imagination, fancy:** In this and the next two paragraphs (399, 413, 454, and esp. 421–23), as in I.77–78 and XIV.315–20, Wordsworth seems to distinguish between the two faculties; elsewhere in the poem (e.g., in V.566–77, VII.126, 142) he merges them or uses the terms interchangeably. For his discriminations outside the poem, see the 1800–05 note to "The Thorn" and the Preface of 1815. In 1812, in a conversation at which Crabb Robinson was present, Wordsworth "was made to explain *fancy* as opposed to *imagination,* from which it results that fancy forms casual and fleeting combinations in which objects are united, *not* on a permanent relation which subsists and has its principle in the capacity of the *sensible* produced to represent and stand in the place of the abstract intellectual conception, but in a voluntary power of combination which only expresses the fact of the combination with little or no import beyond itself. This [adds Robinson] is the best explanation I can give" (*H.C.R.,* I, 93).   **389–91:** Cf. the narrator's exaggerations in "The Thorn."   **419–20:** The idea of "Yarrow Unvisited."   **429–37:** Cf. II.451–52, VI.158–67, 297–305, 313.   **459 Thurston-mere:** Another name for Coniston Water, southwest of Hawkshead.   **468–75:** Wordsworth paraphrases his "Extract from the Conclusion of a Poem, Composed in Anticipation of Leaving School" (see *P.W.,* I, 2), written in 1787.   **478 heretofore:** Especially in II.386–418 (where, however, man is in no way singled out among "all that moves and all that seemeth still"). The 1805 version of this paragraph clarifies the relationship between the bursting forth of sympathy (478–85) and the elevation of "Man" (485–94): "There came a time . . . in which / The pulse of Being everywhere was felt . . . . Then rose / Man, inwardly contemplated, and present / In my own being, to a loftier height; / As of all visible natures crown; and first / In capability of feeling what / Was to be felt . . . ."   **552–55:** Though Havens (p. 470) interprets ll. 543–59 as a mystic experience, "weight of ages" here undoubtedly refers to a powerful sense of the past that momentarily overcame Wordsworth as he entered London. The experience is preceded and followed by lines in which past and present are combined (505–507, 597–98); and the metaphor of ll. 560–89, which is intended to explain the experience (see l. 590), has to do with the way in which the mind uses the past to modify present perception. See also ll. 625–28: "a sense / Of what in the Great City had been done . . . *Weighed* with me."   562 Antiparos: A small island in the Aegean Sea. 562–64 Den . . . Yordas: Wordsworth had visited Yordas Cave (near Ingleton, Yorkshire) in the summer of 1800.   589: A one-line description of the idea of creative sensibility.   599–601 knowledge . . . power: Cf. V.425, and De Quincey's distinction between the "literature of knowledge" and the "literature of power," which he said he owed "to many years' conversation with Mr. Wordsworth" (*Collected Writings*, ed. David Masson, 1896–97, X, 48 n.).   620 their: Referring to "history" (617); in the 1805 version the antecedent is "Events" of history.   660–64 in . . . fraught: Nearly verbatim from *P.L.*, XI.203–207.   680 "busy hum": Milton, "L'Allegro," l. 118.

Book IX. 4 ravenous sea: The events in France, the subject of Books IX, X, and part of XI.   28 a year: Actually Wordsworth was in London for only four or five months, but he is bridging the gap between the end of January 1791, when he took his degree, and the end of November, when he left for France.   34: He spent the first week of December 1791 in Paris, and then went on to Orleans (December–February). He was in Blois during March–September 1792, in Orleans again during September–October, and then back in Paris until the end of the year, when he returned to England. Ostensibly he went to France "for the purpose of learning the French Language which will qualify him for the office of travelling companion to some young gentleman" (*E.L.*, p. 64).   45–53: All these places were of "recent fame" in connection with revolutionary activities. See de Selincourt's notes for specific details.   58 hubbub wild: *P.L.*, II.951.   77: Charles Le Brun's "Sainte Madeleine renonçant aux vanités de la vie" (then in the Carmelite convent in Paris, now in the Louvre).   81: His first "permanent abode" was Orleans, but the "city" of l. 126 is Blois. In Book IX he mixes experiences from both places.   132 one: Not the Royalist soldier ("One") of ll. 139–61, but Michel Beaupuy (also "one"), who is introduced in l. 288.   176 Carra, Gorsas: Jean Louis Carra and Antoine Joseph Gorsas, journalist-politicians of Girondist sympathy. They were guillotined in October 1793.   183 emigrants: Royalist fugitives who were arming to reconquer the country.   249 advocates . . . these: I.e., the Royalist officers of ll. 125 ff.   288 one: Michel Armand Beaupuy (1755–96).   363: "As individual [life is] in the wise and good [man]" (Havens, p. 503).   392–93: On the Rothay see the note to "To Joanna," l. 31. The Greta flows into the Derwent at Keswick.   398 nature: Human nature.   408–17: As a disciple of Plato, Dion attempted to exert a liberalizing influence on his relative Dionysius II, tyrant of Syracuse, but failed and was banished to Greece, where for several years he was closely attached to the Academy. Resolving on "a Deliverer's glorious task," he set forth from Zacynthus with the philosophers Eudemus and Timonides and some soldiers in two ships, entered the port of Syracuse, and in three days overthrew Dionysius (357 B.C.). Wordsworth's source is Plutarch.   451, 453

Angelica, Erminia: The heroines of Ariosto's *Orlando Furioso* and Tasso's *Gerusalemme Liberata*. By implication, ll. 437–65 show the "forbidding ways / Of custom, law, and statute" taking on "The attraction of a country in romance" (XI.110–12); see the note to III.30, 36. **456–61:** De Selincourt cites *F.Q.*, I.vi.13 and III.x.43–44, but "their unhappy thrall" better fits Serena among the cannibals in VI.viii.37 ff. **466–78:** Cf. VI.418–88. **481–91:** Romorantin, a small château twenty-five miles from Blois, was one of Francis I's boyhood homes. The "rural castle" (483, 490) is probably Beauregard, a hunting lodge built by Francis near Blois, and the lady probably Anne de Pisseleu, one of his mistresses. Chambord, nine miles southeast of Blois, was Francis' residence during 1526–30 (de Selincourt). **539–40 if . . . in:** An obscure phrase. Perhaps Wordsworth means "provided that the accused is guilty (and therefore ought not to go free)." **547–85:** Originally this tale (some 380 lines long) was included in *The Prelude,* but Wordsworth removed it and published it as a separate poem, "Vaudracour and Julia," in 1820, with an explanatory headnote that begins, "The following tale was written as an Episode, in a work from which its length may perhaps exclude it." Vaudracour's "fatal crime" (570) is the slaying of a man who has come to arrest him, at his father's instigation, in order to prevent him from marrying the low-born Julia, who is pregnant with his child. Ultimately Julia is made to enter a convent, the child dies, and Vaudracour becomes a speechless recluse. Lines 553–56 and 581–85 are nearly identical with the beginning and conclusion of the separate poem.

Book X. 10–16: Wordsworth returned to Paris (on his way to England) in October 1792. The King had been deposed and imprisoned on August 10. "Invading host" refers to the allied forces who entered France later in August, took two towns, met defeat at Valmy in September, and were evacuated early in October (see ll. 24–27). **18–19:** Based on *P.L.,* XI.391, "To *Agra* and *Lahor* of great *Mogul.*" **40–44:** The Republic was proclaimed on 21 September 1792, following the defeat of the allies at Valmy. Earlier in the month occurred the "September massacres" (73–74), in which more than a thousand Royalist suspects were dragged out of prison and butchered in cold blood. **55–56:** The Place du Carrousel, in front of the palace (53), where many among the storming mob of August 10 had been killed. **75 Saw . . . touched:** The 1805 version has "felt and touch'd them, a substantial dread." **78 The . . . manage:** *As You Like It,* I.i.13. This is the first of six images (78–84) of recurrent action or movement; cf. ll. 44–47, where the opposite idea is stated four times in as many lines. **87 "Sleep no more":** *Macbeth,* II.ii.36. **114 inglorious issue:** Although the Girondist Louvet's speech (October 29) turned public opinion against Robespierre, a week later (November 5) Robespierre answered the charges and regained his popularity. **116 one . . . man:** See III.287 and note. **130–33:** The Girondists lacked all conviction, while the Jacobins were full of passionate intensity. **186–90:** Enjoining sacrifice of either life or death (185) — dedicating one's life to the aims of truth and justice, or dying for them — regardless of (human) nature's plea against such sacrifice.   **198, 199 Harmodius, Aristogiton:** Athenian tyrannicides of the sixth century B.C.   **222:** The "necessity," as the 1805 version reveals, was "nothing less than absolute want / Of funds for my support."   **234 A . . . myself:** See the note to *Exc.*, I.77–91. **245 the . . . City:** London (until June 1793).   **247–53:** In April 1792, William Wilberforce's resolution for abolition of the slave trade had been carried in the House of Commons, but a similar motion had been "defeated" (by postponement) in the House of Lords. A bill was finally passed in 1807.   **263–76:** England declared war against France on 11 February 1793. The "shock / Given to my moral nature" is described again in XI.173–88. See Coleridge's "France: An Ode," ll. 28–42, for a similar reaction ("And hung my head and wept at Britain's name").   **321 that . . . island:** The Isle of Wight (July 1793). The British fleet was preparing to sail from Portsmouth Harbor.   **337–38 blasts . . . heaven:** *Hamlet,* I.iv.41, "airs from heaven or blasts from hell."   **356:** The Reign of Terror, September 1793–July 1794.   **381–83:** Madame Roland was a leading figure among the Girondists. As she walked to the guillotine (November 1793) she cried out, "O Liberty, what crimes are committed in thy name!" **430 second love:** His love for man (Book VIII), now sorely tried by the events of the Revolution.   **437–60:** "The thought appears to be that as the Hebrew prophets, though inspired, derived a grim human satisfaction from beholding the punishments which they had predicted would fall upon sinful cities, so I, in their spirit, lifted up at times above pity and sorrow, found something to glory in, saw in the suffering of those fierce days punishment in accord with sublime laws; and even in the chastisement which I could not understand I felt awe and a kind of sympathy with the terrible manifestations of divine power" (Havens, p. 525).   **491–502:** Arras (one of the "towns" of VI.350–53) was Robespierre's birthplace. **502 Atheist crew:** *P.L.,* VI.370.   **507 As . . . winds:** *King Lear,* III.ii.1– 24.   **511–16:** Robespierre fell on 27 July 1794, and was tried and executed on the following day. Wordsworth would have heard the news three or four weeks later. The 1805 version explains the "journey" more fully: "Having gone abroad / From a small Village where I tarried then [Rampside — see the note to "Elegiac Stanzas," ll. 1–2], / To the same . . . I was returning."   **528–29:** See "Resolution and Independence," ll. 22–28 and note.   **534 An . . . youth:** The Rev. William Taylor (1754–86), master of the Hawkshead school. He was buried in the churchyard of Cartmel Priory.   **555 rocky island:** "Known as Chapel Island [two miles southeast of Ulverton] from the remains of a small oratory, still extant in Wordsworth's time, built by the monks of Furness" (de Selincourt). **596–603:** See II.102–37 (l. 603 and II.137 are identical).

Book XI. 62–73: De Selincourt mentions the suspension of the Habeas Corpus Act early in 1793, government prosecutions of political reformers and sympathizers with France (several were tried for treason and sent to

Botany Bay), and the unsuccessful attempt in 1794 to get Thomas Hardy, founder of the reformist London Corresponding Society, condemned to death as a traitor.   **74–188:** In these lines, another "retrospect," Wordsworth turns back to describe his feelings of 1792 and 1793, the subject of Book IX and part of Book X.   **88 they:** "These . . . things" in the 1805 version, the ideas of ll. 83–86.   **105–44:** First published in *The Friend*, 26 October 1809, and subsequently with Wordsworth's poems under the title "French Revolution as It Appeared to Enthusiasts at Its Commencement." On ll. 112, 115, 125–26, see the note to III.30, 36, and cf. IX.437–65.   **169–72:** See the note to II.368–70.   **173–88:** See X.263–76.   **206–209:** Referring to French aggression in Spain, Italy, Holland, and Germany in late 1794–early 1795 (de Selincourt).   **223–305:** With the "events" of the two preceding paragraphs (esp. ll. 206–209), Wordsworth abandons practical interest in revolution and turns instead to the "wild theories" mentioned in l. 189. For these and "speculative schemes" (224) William Godwin's *An Enquiry Concerning Political Justice* (published in February 1793) is usually cited, but Havens (p. 543) quite rightly suggests that the meaning is more general — "rationalism or Jacobinism . . . [since] there is nothing in *Political Justice* that Wordsworth might not have met elsewhere." The trouble with these schemes is that they ignored man's feelings, and therefore were hopelessly unrealistic. Wordsworth "Yielded up moral questions in despair" (305) because of the terrific gap between their theoretical Man, a creature of pure reason, and his own observation of human conduct. His despair marks "the soul's last and lowest ebb" (307) in *The Prelude*. Recovery begins with l. 333.   **253–54:** De Selincourt cites Spenser, "Muiopotmos, or The Fate of the Butterflie," ll. 209–11, "What more felicitie can fall to creature, / Than to enioy delight with libertie, / And to be Lord of all the workes of Nature."   **266–67 A . . . uplifted:** Of the "Declaration of the Rights of Man" (preamble to the French Constitution of 1791) Mirabeau had said that a veil was lifted too quickly.   **283 some . . . tale:** *The Excursion* (see the next-to-last paragraph of the Preface to that work, p. 470), in which the Solitary has fallen into just such "errors" as those described in ll. 287–93.   **328 abstract science:** The 1805 version specifies "mathematics, and their clear / And solid evidence." With ll. 328–33 cf. V.105, VI.129–41, 161–67.   **359–60:** Napoleon was crowned emperor on 2 December 1804; Pope Pius VII had been summoned from Rome to take part in the ceremony.   **375–79:** Coleridge was in Sicily in August–November 1804 (see the note to VI.240). Timoleon delivered Syracuse from tyranny in 343 B.C.   **393–95 There . . . Dead:** De Selincourt compares a passage in Wordsworth's *Concerning . . . the Convention of Cintra* (1809), "There is a spiritual community binding together the living and the dead; the good, the brave, and the wise, of all ages. We would not be rejected from this community: and therefore do we hope." Cf. Coleridge, "To William Wordsworth" (1807), ll. 50–52: "The truly great / Have all one age, and from one visible space / Shed influence!"   **406 erewhile:** In VI.240–51.   **419–20 O . . . Enna:** *P.L.*, IV.268–71, "that faire field / Of *Enna*, where *Proserpin* gathring flours / Her self a fairer Floure by gloomie *Dis* / Was gatherd." **428 thy, her:** Presumably referring to modern and ancient Sicily, respectively. **443–49:** Theocritus, *Idylls*, VII.78–83.

Book XII: "Imagination, How Impaired and Restored" (1805) is, of course, the main subject of the whole poem (see XIV.188–205). "And Taste" in the title of this and the next book is a late addition (c. 1839). **11–12 breathing . . . watched:** The flowers seem to breathe *because* they are "Feelingly watched." See the note to II.291, and cf. "Lines Written in Early Spring," which is pertinent not only to "breathing flowers" but to ll. 9–32 more generally. **32–37:** Reminiscent of the Intimations ode, stanzas III and IV. **62–64:** See XI.393–95 and note. **75–76 if . . . past:** In this paragraph Wordsworth briefly reviews the "past" of XI.223–333. **103–104 overflow . . . life:** Cf. II.397. **114–21 giving . . . Insensible:** I.e., seeking out the picturesque ("a strong infection of the age," 113) in the manner of the ordinary tourist. While anatomizing "the frame of social life" (XI.280) he is concurrently anatomizing nature ("with microscopic view," "sitting thus in judgment," "barren intermeddling subtleties," XII.91, 122, 155; see II.216–19 and note). **127–51:** Cf. Wordsworth's attitude toward nature at the time of his first visit to the Wye ("Tintern Abbey," esp. ll. 81–83). Under this "tyranny" of the bodily eye (129, 131, 135, 150), the mind is entirely passive (147, 154; the "combinations" of l. 144 are found in nature, not created by the mind). Wordsworth is setting up a contrast with ll. 208 ff., in which he celebrates the mind's creativity. **151–73:** Probably Mary Hutchinson, now Wordsworth's wife. Though said to have escaped the tyranny of the eye and "rules prescribed by passive taste" (152–56), she nevertheless seems to have been only passively responsive to the beauties of nature (158–60). Wordsworth's point here, however, is that she was able to enjoy all she saw without judging (cf. Wordsworth's own earlier condition, 184–89). **193 degradation:** The superficial view of nature described in ll. 88–151. **207:** See the note on "creative sensibility," II.360. **208–335:** "Spots of time," of which Wordsworth gives two examples in ll. 225–66 and 267–335, involve the imaginative union of natural scene with human emotion and moral feeling; their "renovating virtue" as retrospective illustrations of the mind's mastery over "outward sense" (see the note to ll. 127–51) is defined in the crucial ll. 219–23. See the Introduction, and Jonathan Bishop's article in *ELH*, XXVI (1959), 45–65. **212–14:** Cf. "Tintern Abbey," ll. 39–40, 131. **225–66:** "Gordon Wordsworth has identified the scene . . . as the Cowdrake Quarry on the Edenhall side of the Penrith Beacon. Here Thomas Parker was murdered on November 18, 1766 by Thomas Nicholson who was executed near the scene of the murder on August 31, 1767" (de Selincourt). For Wordsworth's later visits to the scene (261–66), see VI.233–36 and note. **267–71:** The main point of the example. See I.340–50, VII.461–65, and notes. **272–77:** On childhood see the note to III.173–83. With "give . . . receive" cf. the lines from Coleridge quoted in the note to III.130–35. **279 hiding-places**

. . . **power:** I.e., the memory, storehouse of the "spots of time." On the fading of memory (280–82) see the note to I.117–18.   **287 Christmas-time:** December 1783.   **329–35:** Cf. VII.44–48.

Book XIII. 1–10: If the "inward agitations" of XII.329–32 exemplify emotion coming *from* nature, then this "interchange" of emotion and calmness relates to the giving and receiving of XII.276–77 and the "ennobling interchange / Of action from without and from within" in XIII.375–76 (see also ll. 290–93). Lines 7–10 restate the idea of "emotion recollected in tranquillity" (1800 Preface, p. 460).   **14:** This is Wordsworth's first declaration that his task is an easy one (cf. II.228). With the restoration of imagination in Book XII, he has now got over the hump; in ll. 19 ff. he gives a final answer to the questions of I.269–81, and later in the book (232–49) he ends the search for a theme that began in Book I.   **20–22 Power . . . reason:** See XIV.189–92.   **29–39:** Cf. I.408–10, "Those Words Were Uttered," l. 12, and the 1800 Preface, "I should be oppressed with no dishonourable melancholy, had I not a deep impression of certain inherent and indestructible qualities of the human mind, and likewise of certain powers in the great and permanent objects that act upon it, which are equally inherent and indestructible" (p. 449).   **40 watchful thoughts:** See the note to II.291.   **52 intellectual eye:** Imagination, as opposed to the "bodily eye" (XII.128).   **77–78 idol . . . Nations":** Referring not so much to Adam Smith's work (1776) as to political economists' concepts in general.   **79–84:** See the first note to Book VIII. Though Wordsworth does not say *how* he gained this "more judicious knowledge," it is clearly the result of his rediscovery of man's imaginative powers (using his own as the example) in Book XII.   **87–88:** See the note to VIII.303–22.   **94–106:** With this and subsequent passages in Book XIII on humble men and their language, cf. the fifth paragraph of the 1800 Preface (p. 447).   **142–51:** Cf. "Stepping Westward."   **167–68 appear . . . eyes:** Cf. II.299–301, 384–86.   **217–18:** Cf. II.216–19.   **220 the . . . heart:** See "The Old Cumberland Beggar," l. 153.   **224–78:** First published at the end of the "Postscript" to *Yarrow Revisited, and Other Poems* (1835).   **229:** Cf. *P.L.*, I.372, "gay Religions full of Pomp and Gold."   **232–53:** Cf. the lines included in this volume from "The Recluse," esp. ll. 788–94.   **246–49:** Cf. *Exc.*, I.922–30.   **265–75:** Silent poets; see the note to *Exc.*, I.77–91.   **290–93:** See ll. 1–10, 375–78, and notes.   **301–12, 355–60:** Both passages describe creative sensibility; see II.299–301, 384–86, and notes. With "power like one of Nature's" (312) cf. V.218–21, the second sentence of the I.F. note to "The Thorn," and Wordsworth's remark to Crabb Robinson in 1812 that he principally valued his poems "as being *a new power* in the literary world" (*H.C.R.*, I, 89).   **314 Sarum's Plain:** Salisbury Plain, in August 1793.   **352 monumental hints:** The "circles, lines, or mounds" of l. 338. The most famous of these monuments, Stonehenge, was then thought to have been the work of Druids.   **353–60:** The "unpremeditated strains" were "Guilt and Sorrow" (not published until 1842). On hearing Wordsworth recite the poem, Coleridge was immediately impressed, as he later wrote, by "the union of deep feeling with profound thought; the fine balance of truth in observing, with the imaginative faculty in modifying the objects observed; and above all the original gift of spreading the tone, the *atmosphere,* and with it the depth and height of the ideal world around forms, incidents, and situations, of which, for the common view, custom had bedimmed all the lustre" (*Biog. Lit.,* ch. IV).   **370 a new world:** Cf. III.144–46.   **372 fixed laws:** Cf. l. 23 ("steadfast laws"), and Wordsworth's description of imagination as "denoting operations of the mind upon . . . [external] objects, and processes of creation or of composition, governed by certain fixed laws" (Preface of 1815, p. 483).   **375–78:** Cf. ll. 1–10, 290–93. Here, as perhaps also in the more ambiguous earlier passages, Wordsworth describes "an ennobling interchange" between the external world and the human mind in which nature's role is principally that of existing in order to be seen ("action from without" refers to nature's "action" on the perceiver's senses). This "interchange" strikes an ideal medium between "The self-created sustenance of a mind / Debarred from Nature's living images, / Compelled to be a life unto herself" (VI.301–303) and the opposite danger represented by the "tyranny" of the bodily eye (XII.127–51). It is the same as the exquisite "fitting" of mind and external world that Wordsworth proclaims in "The Recluse," ll. 816–24, and it is the main point that the final episode of *The Prelude,* the ascent of Mt. Snowdon, is intended to illustrate (see "mutual domination," "interchangeable supremacy," "Willing to work and to be wrought upon," "By sensible impressions not enthralled," XIV.81, 84, 103, 106).

Book XIV. 1–6: Wordsworth climbed Snowdon, the highest mountain in Wales ("Cambria"), in the summer of 1791. The "youthful friend" was Robert Jones (see VI.322 ff. and note). The village of Beddgelert, six miles south of the mountain, is one of the common starting-points for tourists.   **17–18, 35–41, 50–56, 64:** See "A Night-Piece" and notes.   **50–62:** In the 1805 version, ll. 50–56 are represented by a line and a half, "Meanwhile, the Moon look'd down upon this shew / In single glory," and ll. 61–62 by a passage of six lines — "The universal spectacle throughout / Was shaped for admiration and delight, / Grand in itself alone, but in that breach [the "rift" of l. 56] / Through which the homeless voice of waters rose, / That dark deep thoroughfare had Nature lodg'd / The Soul, the Imagination of the whole" (see the note to "To a Highland Girl," l. 78). In the final text, by giving greater emphasis to the moon, and introducing the ideas of "encroachment none" and the moon's sovereignty, Wordsworth considerably clarified the way in which the scene emblemizes both the "ennobling interchange" mentioned at the end of Book XIII and the "type / Of a majestic intellect" described in the following paragraph. For discussion of these revisions see Havens, pp. 611–13, and Michael Goldman, *Explicator,* XVIII (1960), item 41.   **66–77:** Though the antecedent of "it" (66) is "vision" (64 — "scene" in 1805), the "type / Of a majestic intellect" (= "mind" and "higher minds" in ll. 70, 90 — the human mind, not God's) is specifically the moon, looking down upon the rift in the ocean of mist ("infinity . . . the dark abyss" in ll. 71–74). For "that broods . . . privilege" (71–77), the 1805 version has "That is exalted by an under-presence, / The sense of God, or whatsoe'er is dim / Or vast in its own being." Wordsworth may have been thinking of this paragraph (63–129) when he wrote to W. S. Landor, 21 January 1824, that "in poetry it is the imaginative only, viz., that which is conversant [with], or turns upon infinity, that powerfully affects me . . . those passages where things are lost in each other, and limits vanish, and aspirations are raised" (*L.Y.*, I, 134–35). **71–72 broods . . . abyss:** See the note to I.139–41. **81, 84, 103, 106:** See the note to XIII.375–78. **87–88 Nature . . . exhibits:** I.e., in the "vision" or scene of the preceding paragraph. **93–95:** See the note to II.368–70. **101–102 they . . . suggestions:** Cf. VII.734–36. De Selincourt cites Wordsworth's 1800–05 note to "The Thorn": "imagination . . . the faculty which produces impressive effects out of simple elements." **103 work . . . upon:** A parallel with "create . . . and . . . catch" (94–96). **115 Of Whom:** Ostensibly "from the Deity" (112). But the capital may not be Wordsworth's (1805 reads "whom"), and the word may refer to self rather than God. Cf. the Preface of 1815, where Wordsworth says that creative workings of the imagination proceed from and are governed by "a sublime consciousness of the soul in her own mighty and almost divine powers" (p. 486). **119–20 Soul . . . intuitive:** *P.L.*, V.486, 488. **126–27 peace . . . understanding:** Philippians 4:7. **130–32:** I.e., freedom from the thraldom of "sensible impressions" (106), from the "growing weight of vulgar sense" (159). On "his whole life long" see II.262–65. **160 universe of death:** The phrase (from *P.L.*, II.622) refers to a universe of outward forms only — in Coleridge's terms "essentially fixed and dead" (*Biog. Lit.*, ch. XIII) until the imagination informs it with light and life. Cf. Coleridge to Wordsworth, 30 May 1815: "the philosophy of mechanism . . . in every thing that is most worthy of the human Intellect strikes *Death*" (*Collected Letters*, IV, 575). **162–88, 207–209:** This "love," requisite to the imagination and at the same time dependent on it, is closely akin to Coleridge's "Joy" in "Dejection: An Ode," ll. 64–77, 134–39. For ll. 181–87, the 1805 version reads: "but there is higher love / Than this, a love that comes into the heart / With awe and a diffusive sentiment; / Thy love is human merely; this proceeds / More from the brooding Soul, and is divine." **189–92:** Cf. V.40–41, XIII.20–22. **204–205:** The 1805 version reads, "The feeling of life endless, the great thought / By which we live, Infinity and God." Havens comments (pp. 624–25): "It is not immediately clear in what part of *The Prelude* ('lastly,' 203, implies in the later books) Wordsworth has drawn from the progress of the imagination 'the feeling of life endless' . . . . He may have thought that the growth of the individual in spiritual power by the aid of the imagination implies the existence of God and 'endless occupation for the Soul' (119), or immortality; and he may have felt that he had 'drawn' this feeling or faith throughout lines 63–129." **233 elsewhere:** See "The Sparrow's Nest" (l. 18 of which

Wordsworth echoes in XIV.230).   **244–46:** See *P.L.*, IX.489–91.   **260 a nobler:** I.e., man.   **267 One:** Mary Hutchinson. With ll. 268–70 cf. "She Was a Phantom of Delight."   **293–95:** Cf. II.394–418.   **295–98 chastened . . . duty:** Cf. Intimations ode, stanza X, and "Ode to Duty." **311 a Work:** See the first paragraph of notes to the selection from "The Recluse."   **315 secondary grace:** Fancy; see the note to VIII.366, 373. **355 Calvert:** Raisley Calvert, who died in January 1795, leaving Wordsworth £900.   **395–96:** "Wordsworth was at Alfoxden from July 1797 to June 1798; Coleridge was living three miles off at Nether Stowey; the Quantock hills rise behind both places. . . . the 'summer' . . . was the warm spring and early summer of 1798" (de Selincourt).   **399–400 that . . . Mariner:** "The Ancient Mariner," ll. 19–20, 39–40.   **404 him:** Johnny, in "The Idiot Boy."   **419 private grief:** The death of his brother John on 5 February 1805.   **448 the mind of man:** As always, the "haunt, and the main region of my song" ("The Recluse," ll. 793–94). On "becomes" see VIII.650, and the note to VIII.303–22.

Stepping Westward   *Page 36?*

Written in June 1805; published 1807. The poem is based on an incident of the 1803 Scottish tour that Dorothy reports as follows: "The sun had been set for some time, when, being within a quarter of a mile of the ferryman's hut, our path having led us close to the shore of the calm lake we met two neatly dressed women, without hats, who had probably been taking their Sunday evening's walk. One of them said to us in a friendly soft tone of voice, 'What! you are stepping westward?' I cannot describe how affecting this simple expression was in that remote place, with the western sky in front, *yet* glowing with the departed sun" (D.W., *Journals*, I, 367; entry for 11 September 1803). Cf. *Prel.*, XIII.142–51.

The Solitary Reaper   *Page 367*

Written in November 1805; published 1807. "This Poem was suggested by a beautiful sentence in a MS Tour in Scotland written by a Friend the last line being taken from it *verbatim*" (W., 1807). The sentence (from Thomas Wilkinson's MS published in 1824 as *Tours to the British Mountains*) is the following: "Passed a female who was reaping alone she sung in Erse as she bended over her sickle; the sweetest human voice I ever heard: her strains were tenderly melancholy, and felt delicious, long after they were heard no more." Cf. "To a Highland Girl."

Character of the Happy Warrior   *Page 368*

Written in the winter of 1805–06; published 1807. "[These] Verses were written soon after tidings had been received of the Death of Lord Nelson, which event directed the Author's thoughts to the subject" (W., 1807). Nelson died on 21 October 1805, and was buried in London on the fol-

lowing January 9). "The course of the great war with the French naturally
fixed one's attention upon the military character, and, to the honour of our
country, there were many illustrious instances of the qualities that constitute its highest excellence. Lord Nelson carried most of the virtues that the
trials he was exposed to in his department of the service necessarily call
forth and sustain . . . . I will add, that many elements of the character
here pourtrayed were found in my brother John, who perished by shipwreck, as mentioned elsewhere" (I.F.). Wordsworth intends "Warrior" in
the broadest sense — political leader, statesman, ideal governor. On the
relationship of the ideas of the poem to classical and Renaissance ethical
thought, see J. B. Hamilton, *Modern Language Quarterly*, XVI (1955),
311–24.

4–5 hath . . . thought: Another instance of the idea that the child is
father of the man.   **6–7, 15–18, 45–47:** Cf. *Prel.*, IV.168–71.   **75–76
persevering . . . better:** Taken, as Wordsworth acknowledged in a note of
1807, from "The Flower and the Leaf" (then thought to have been written by Chaucer), ll. 548–50.

Power of Music   Page 370

Written 1806; published 1807. "Taken from life" (I.F.). This and the
next poem resulted from Wordsworth's visit to London in April–May 1806.

Star-Gazers   Page 371

Written 1806; published 1807. "Observed by me in Leicester-square
[London], as here described" (I.F.). The "little boat" of ll. 3–4 may
recall the Prologue to *Peter Bell;* the largely unanswered questions of ll.
9–28 all concern the subject of that earlier work, the imagination.

Yes, It Was the Mountain Echo   Page 372

Written in June 1806; published 1807. "The echo came from Nab-scar,
when I was walking on the opposite side of Rydal Mere" (I.F.).

Elegiac Stanzas Suggested by a Picture
of Peele Castle   Page 373

Written in the summer of 1806 (Wordsworth saw his friend Beaumont's
painting in London in April–May, and wrote the poem after returning to
Grasmere); published 1807. His brother John's death by drowning in a
shipwreck on 5 February 1805 was for Wordsworth, as his letters show, a
major blow from which he never fully recovered. The present poem, written more than a year after the event, and "with mind serene" (40), announces a rejection of two ideas that are of first importance in his poetry

up to this time — the beneficence of nature and the supremacy of the poetic imagination. There is an awakening concern with humanity (36, 53–54) similar to that seen earlier in, e.g., "Tintern Abbey," the Intimations ode, and *The Prelude*, but it is no longer the love of nature that leads him to it. Here the "glassy sea," "tranquil land," and "sky of bliss" give way to a "sea in anger," "lightning, the fierce wind, and trampling waves"; the imagination — though Wordsworth's attitude is ambiguous (see the note to l. 35) — is exposed as a "fond illusion," the empty dream of men who are "to be pitied"; and the castle, which displaces the sea as the dominant symbol of the poem, is valued for its "unfeeling armour." Although it was a temporary revulsion (as, e.g., his concern with imagination in *The White Doe of Rylstone*, begun toward the end of the following year, may show), the fact is that Wordsworth did not write more than a relative handful of first-rate poems in the forty-odd years of life remaining to him.

1–2: Peele (Piel) Castle is on an island just off the southern extremity of the Furness Peninsula, in N. Lancashire. Wordsworth lived within sight of it while visiting a cousin at Rampside in August 1794.   14–16 gleam . . . dream: See the Intimations ode, esp. ll. 56–57, and *Prel.*, II.368–70. 34 new control: Cf. "Ode to Duty," written more than two years earlier. 35: Reminiscent of the Intimations ode (e.g., ll. 177–78). Along with the idea of "consecration" (16), the line tends to counter the assertions elsewhere in the poem that the imagination is a "fond illusion." Cf. Wordsworth's statement in a letter to James Losh, 16 March 1805: "I feel that there is something cut out of my life which cannot be restored" (*E.L.*, pp. 465–66).   57 fortitude: Wordsworth several times mentions fortitude, resignation, and duty in his letters following John's death, and on 12 March 1805 he transcribed for Beaumont a passage from Aristotle on "the property of fortitude" (*E.L.*, p. 462).

Thought of a Briton on the Subjugation
of Switzerland   *Page 375*

Written in 1806–07; published 1807. Switzerland had been under French domination since 1802. Although Wordsworth in 1808 thought it his best sonnet (*M.Y.*, I, 241), and Coleridge called it "one of the noblest Sonnets in our Language, and the happiest comment on the line of Milton — 'The *mountain* Nymph, sweet Liberty' ["L'Allegro," l. 36]" (*The Friend*, 21 December 1809), the poem does not stand up well under close reading. The "Two Voices," associated with England (1) and Switzerland (2), are not voices of Liberty but merely sounds heard by her — metaphorical equivalents of the two geographic locations; and because they are natural sounds (the torrent's murmur, ocean's bellow) they will continue whether or not Liberty can hear them. As a consequence, while the individual phrases are grandly Miltonic, the poem as a whole represents a rather unnecessarily roundabout way of enjoining Englishmen to preserve their freedom. It concludes almost as a warning to Liberty that *she* is in danger of losing the other half of her "chosen music."

The White Doe of Rylstone   *Page 376*

Written in October 1807–January 1808; corrected and enlarged in 1809–10; published 1815.

> The Poem of the White Doe of Rylstone is founded on a local tradition, and on the Ballad in Percy's Collection, entitled, "The Rising of the North." The tradition is as follows: — 'About this time,' not long after the Dissolution, 'a White Doe,' say the aged people of the neighbourhood, 'long continued to make a weekly pilgrimage from Rylstone over the fells of Bolton, and was constantly found in the Abbey Churchyard during divine service; after the close of which she returned home as regularly as the rest of the congregation.' — DR. [Thomas Dunham] WHITAKER's *History [and Antiquities] of the Deanery of Craven* [1805]. — Rylstone was the property and residence of the Nortons, distinguished in that ill-advised and unfortunate Insurrection; which led me to connect with this tradition the principal circumstances of their fate, as recorded in the Ballad. (W. — for the rest of this and the other fairly lengthy notes that Wordsworth printed with the poem, a few of which are quoted below, see *P.W.*, III, 535–56)

Wordsworth's comments on the poem in his letters and conversation all stress the importance of imagination and the idea that the main action of the poem is spiritual rather than physical (cf. the 1800 Preface to *Lyrical Ballads*, p. 448: "feeling . . . gives importance to the action and situation, and not the action and situation to the feeling"). On 19 April 1808, for example, he described to Coleridge his side of an argument with Charles Lamb:

> I . . . told Lamb that I did not think the Poem could ever be popular first because there was nothing in it to excite curiosity, and next, because the main catastrophe was not a material but an intellectual one; I said to him further that it could not be popular because some of the principal objects and agents, such as the Banner and the Doe, produced their influences and effects not by powers naturally inherent in them, but such as they were endued with by the Imagination of the human minds on whom they operated: further, that the principle of action in all the characters, as in the Old Man, and his Sons, and Francis, when he has the prophetic vision of the overthrow of his family, and the fate of his sister, and takes leave of her as he does, was throughout imaginative; and that all action (save the main traditionary tragedy), i.e. all the action proceeding from the will of the chief agents, was fine-spun and inobtrusive, consonant in this to the principle from which it flowed, and in harmony with the shadowy influence of the Doe, by whom the poem is introduced, and in whom it ends. It suffices that everything tends to account for the weekly pilgrimage of the Doe, which is made interesting by its connection with a human being, a Woman, who is intended to be honoured and loved for what she *endures*, and the manner in which she endures it; accomplishing a conquest over her own sorrows (which is the true subject of the Poem) by means, partly, of the native strength of her character, and partly by the persons and things with whom and which

she is connected; and finally, after having exhibited the 'fortitude of patience and heroic martyrdom' [*P.L.*, IX.31–32], ascending to pure etherial spirituality, and forwarded in that ascent of love by communion with a creature not of her own species, but spotless, beautiful, innocent and loving . . . . (*M.Y.*, I, 197–98)

A letter of nearly eight years later, to Francis Wrangham, 18 January 1816, repeats the same basic points:

I hope it [*The White Doe*] will be acceptable to the intelligent, for whom alone it is written. It starts from a high point of imagination, and comes round through various wanderings of that faculty to a still higher; nothing less than the Apotheosis of the Animal, who gives the first of the two titles to the Poem. And as the Poem thus begins and ends with pure and lofty Imagination, every motive and impulse that actuates the persons introduced is from the same source, a kindred spirit pervades, and is intended to harmonize, the whole. Throughout, objects (the Banner, for instance) derive their influence not from properties inherent in them, not from what they are actually in themselves, but from such as are bestowed upon them by the minds of those who are conversant with or affected by those objects. Thus the Poetry, if there be any in the work, proceeds whence it ought to do, from the soul of Man, communicating its creative energies to the images of the external world. (*M.Y.*, II, 704–705; see also the I.F. note, in *P.W.*, III, 542–43)

For discussion of the poem, see the critical edition by Alice P. Comparetti (1940); the articles by Ellen D. Leyburn, *SP*, XLVII (1950), 629–33, and Martin Price, *PQ*, XXXIII (1954), 189–99; and Danby, *The Simple Wordsworth*, pp. 130–45.

The first epigraph (added in 1837) is of Wordsworth's own composition, ll. 1–6 being taken from his early play, *The Borderers*, ll. 1539–44. The second (printed with the poem from the beginning) is from Bacon's "Of Atheism." In 1815 and 1820 the sonnet "Weak Is the Will of Man" was also used as an epigraph. In a 64-line dedicatory poem to his wife (here omitted) Wordsworth records his debt to Spenser's story of Una and her milk-white lamb.

1: Bolton Priory (or Abbey), which Wordsworth visited in the summer of 1807, is on the river Wharfe (6) in the West Riding of Yorkshire. Rylstone is seven miles to the northwest.   **226–34:** This tradition of the founding of Bolton Priory (which he got, along with the suggestion for ll. 236–37, from Whitaker's *History*) Wordsworth made the subject of a separate poem, "The Force of Prayer," published with *The White Doe* in 1815.   **252–53:** Defeated in an encounter near Banbury in July 1469, Sir William Herbert, Earl of Pembroke, was taken prisoner and beheaded (at Northampton, however, rather than on the porch of Banbury church). **267–307:** The "Shepherd-lord," Henry de Clifford, fourteenth Baron Clifford (1455?–1523), who fought at Flodden (1513), where the Scots king James IV was slain, is the subject of Wordsworth's "Song at the Feast of

Brougham Castle," written and published in 1807. Barden Tower (294) is two miles northwest of Bolton Priory. **314–15:** Reminiscent of the *Squire's Tale*, ll. 189 ff., and *F.Q.*, I.xii.9. **357:** "The Rising in the North," l. 108. **360 ff.:** In November 1569 Sir Thomas Percy, seventh Earl of Northumberland (1528–72), joined forces with Charles Neville, sixth Earl of Westmorland (1543–1601), in an effort to release Mary Queen of Scots from prison and restore the Catholic religion to England.

> Their common banner (on which was displayed the cross, together with the five wounds of Christ), was borne by an ancient gentleman, Richard Norton . . . . Having entered Durham, they tore the Bible, &c., and caused mass to be said there: they then marched on to Clifford Moor near Wetherbye, where they mustered their men. Their intention was to have proceeded on to York; but, altering their minds, they fell upon Barnard's castle, which Sir George Bowes held out against them for eleven days. The two earls . . . were masters of little ready money . . . [and] were not able to march to London, as they had at first intended. In these circumstances, Westmoreland began so visibly to despond, that many of his men slunk away, though Northumberland still kept up his resolution, and was master of the field till December 13, when the Earl of Sussex, accompanied with Lord Hunsden and others, having marched out of York at the head of a large body of forces, and being followed by a still larger army under the command of Ambrose Dudley, Earl of Warwick, the insurgents retreated northward towards the borders, and there dismissing their followers, made their escape into Scotland. (from Percy's headnote to "The Rising in the North")

400 dying fall: *Twelfth Night,* I.i.4. **511:** "The Rising in the North," l. 90. **527 O . . . prophesy:** *1 Henry IV,* V.iv.83. **588:** *P.L.,* VIII.452, "He ended, or I heard no more." **595:** "Brancepeth Castle stands near the river Were [602, usually "Wear"], a few miles from the city of Durham. It formerly belonged to the Nevilles, Earls of Westmoreland" (W.). **667–68 Dove . . . brood:** Cf. *P.L.,* I.21, "Dove-like satst brooding." **687 towers . . . Cuthbert:** Durham Cathedral. **696:** Raby Castle, near Staindrop in Durham, was Neville's peacetime seat. **716–17:** "From the old Ballad [ll. 99–100]" (W.). Wetherby is on the Wharfe a dozen miles southwest of York. **787 Dudley:** Ambrose Dudley, Earl of Warwick (1528?–90). **796:** "From the Old Ballad [l. 144]" (W.). **798:** Barnard Castle (also ll. 940–42, 1116). **800, 801:** Leonard Dacre (d. 1573) was a chief promoter of the northern rebellion; Thomas Howard, fourth Duke of Norfolk (1536–72), who had projected a marriage with Mary Queen of Scots, was at this time imprisoned in London. **814–24:** Thurstan or Turstin (d. 1140), archbishop of York, aided in defeating the Scots at the Battle of the Standard (1138). Roger de Mowbray, second Baron Mowbray (d. 1188?), who was then in his early teens, is said to have been present at the battle. **828–34:** Referring to the Battle of Neville's Cross in 1346. **883–84 her . . . laid:** I.e., Francis' and Emily's mother, who taught "The faith reformed and purified" (1041). **1069 stand and wait:** Milton, "When I Consider How My

Light Is Spent," l. 14.   **1175:** *The Battle of Flodden Field,* V.9, "From Penigent to Pendle Hill."   **1328:** Sir Thomas Radcliffe, third Earl of Sussex (1526?–83), president of the Council of the North.   **1387 blank awe:** Milton, *Comus,* l. 452.   **1446:** Sir George Bowes (1527–80), provost marshal of Sussex's army.   **1550/51:** The epigraph (added in 1837) is from Wordsworth's "Address to Kilchurn Castle, upon Loch Awe," ll. 6–9.   **1707, 1711:** "At the extremity of the parish of Burnsal, the valley of Wharf forks off into two great branches, one of which retains the name of Wharfdale, to the source of the river; the other is usually called Littondale, but more anciently and properly, Amerdale. Dernbrook . . . runs along an obscure valley from the N. W." (W., quoting Whitaker). **1721:** Cf. *F.Q.,* I.iii.9, "by her lookes conceiued her intent."   **1762 𝕲𝖔𝖉 𝖚𝖘 𝖆𝖞𝖉𝖊:** "On one of the bells of Rylstone Church, which seems coeval with the building of the tower, is this cypher, '𝕵. 𝕹.' for John Norton, and the motto, '𝕲𝖔𝖉 𝖚𝖘 𝖆𝖞𝖉𝖊' " (W.).

Characteristics of a Child Three Years Old   *Page 420*

Written 1811; published 1815. "Picture of my Daughter, Catharine, who died the year after" (I.F.). With the last two lines cf. *Prel.,* V.386–88.

Surprised by Joy   *Page 420*

Written 1812–15; published 1815. "Thee" of the third line and following is Wordsworth's daughter Catharine, who died in June 1812 at the age of three. See the preceding poem.

The Shepherd, Looking Eastward   *Page 421*

Written 1807–15; published 1815.

Yarrow Visited   *Page 421*

Written in the autumn of 1814; published 1815. On the relationship of this to his earlier Yarrow poem Wordsworth commented, in a letter of 23 November 1814 to R. P. Gillies, "Second parts, if much inferior to the first, are always disgusting, and as I had succeeded in *Yarrow Unvisited,* I was anxious that there should be no falling off; but that was unavoidable, perhaps, from the subject, as imagination almost always transcends reality" (*M.Y.,* II, 611). See also "Yarrow Revisited."

1–4: See "Yarrow Unvisited," ll. 49–52 and note.   **25–32:** Wordsworth here merges stories associated with (1) the flower Love-lies-bleeding (*Amaranthus caudatus*), (2) Mary Scott of Dryhope, the "Flower of Yarrow" (see J. C. Shairp, *Aspects of Poetry,* 1881, p. 335), (3) slain lovers lamented in the ballads (e.g., in William Hamilton's "The Braes of Yarrow").   **55 Newark's Towers:** The setting of Scott's *The Lay of the Last Minstrel.*

Laodamia   Page 423

Written 1814; published 1815. "The incident of the trees growing and
withering [167–74] put the subject into my thoughts, and I wrote with
the hope of giving it a loftier tone than, so far as I know, has been given
to it by any of the Ancients who have treated of it. It cost me more trouble
than almost anything of equal length I have ever written" (I.F.). At the
end of the poem Wordsworth supplied a note concerning sources: "For the
account of these long-lived trees, see Pliny's Natural History, lib. xvi. cap.
44.; and for the features in the character of Protesilaus see the Iphigenia
in Aulis of Euripides. Virgil places the Shade of Laodamia in a mournful
region, among unhappy Lovers [*Aeneid,* VI.440–49]."

27–29 unsubstantial . . . re-unite: Cf. *P.L.*, VI.330–31, "th'Ethereal
substance clos'd / Not long divisible" (parodied by Pope, *The Rape of the
Lock*, III.152).   158–63: Wordsworth's changes here show a succession
of attitudes. Originally (1815–20) the stanza began, "Ah, judge her gently
who so deeply loved! / Her, who, in reason's spite, yet without crime . . ."
and she was consigned to the "unfading bowers" with the rest of the happy
ghosts. In 1827, however, she was "not without . . . crime," and "doomed
to wander in a grosser clime." The mitigating *"as* for a wilful crime" first
appeared in 1845.   167–74: It is curious that this ending, the original
stimulus of the poem (see the I.F. note), symbolizes not the general "moral"
(73–76, 139–50) or Protesilaus' mission to inculcate it — the main business
of the poem — but rather Protesilaus' heroic action against the Trojans.

"Weak Is the Will of Man"   Page 428

Written 1807–15; published 1815 (as one of the epigraphs to *The White
Doe of Rylstone*). For imagination as a source of faith, see *Prel.*, XIV,
esp. ll. 188–205.

November 1   Page 428

Written in December 1815; published in both the *Examiner* and the *Champion* on the same day, 28 January 1816. "Suggested on the banks of the
Brathay by the sight of Langdale Pikes" (I.F.).

September, 1815   Page 428

Written in December 1815; published in the *Examiner*, 11 February 1816.

Composed upon an Evening of Extraordinary
Splendour and Beauty   Page 429

Written in the summer of 1817; published 1820. Wordsworth appended
the following note to the poem: "The multiplication of mountain-ridges,

described at the commencement of the third Stanza of this Ode, as a kind of Jacob's Ladder, leading to Heaven, is produced either by watery vapours, or sunny haze; — in the present instance by the latter cause. Allusions to the Ode, entitled 'Intimations of Immortality,' pervade the last Stanza."

49–52: "In these lines I am under obligation to the exquisite picture of 'Jacob's Dream,' by Mr. Alstone [Washington Allston], now in America" (W.). Cf. Keats, "Sleep and Poetry" (published in March 1817), ll. 81–84: "I'd . . . my spirit teaze / Till at its shoulders it should proudly see / Wings to find out an immortality."

Sole Listener, Duddon! *Page 431*

Written perhaps in 1818; published 1820 (in *The River Duddon, A Series of Sonnets*).

After-Thought *Page 431*

Written 1818–20; published 1820 (the concluding sonnet of *The River Duddon*). For sources and interpretation see Stewart C. Wilcox, *PQ*, XXXII (1953), 210–12, and *PMLA*, LXIX (1954), 139–41.

7–9: "The allusion to the Greek Poet will be obvious to the classical reader" (W., referring to Moschus, "Lament for Bion," ll. 102–104). **14:** *P.L.*, VIII.282, "And feel that I am happier then I know" (cited by Wordsworth).

Inside of King's College Chapel, Cambridge *Page 432*

Written at the end of 1820 or in 1821; published 1822. This and the next poem are among the "Ecclesiastical Sonnets" (first published separately under the title *Ecclesiastical Sketches*), a series treating the history and offices of the Church of England.

1 royal Saint: Henry VI, who founded King's College in 1441. The Chapel was begun in 1446.

Mutability *Page 432*

Written 1821; published 1822.

10–14: Cf. ll. 66–70 of a fragmentary Gothic tale written by Wordsworth in the early 1790's, "The unimaginable touch of time / Or shouldering rend had split with ruin deep / Those towers that stately stood, as in their prime, / Though shattered stood of undiminished height, / And plumed their heads with trees that shook before the night" (*P.W.*, I, 288). The first of these lines (identical with the last five words of the sonnet) echoes a phrase in *Of Education* where Milton speaks of "unimaginable touches" of music (S. H. Monk, *MLN*, LII, 1937, 503–504).

To —— [Look at the fate of summer flowers] *Page 432*

Written 1824; published 1827. "Prompted by the undue importance attached to personal beauty by some dear friends of mine" (I.F.). It has been suggested that the poem is addressed to Wordsworth's daughter Dora, who was twenty years old in August 1824.

20, 22: The quotations are adapted from Spenser, "An Hymne in Honour of Beautie," ll. 213–14.

To a Sky-Lark [Ethereal minstrel!] *Page 433*

Written 1825; published 1827.

Scorn Not the Sonnet *Page 433*

Written 1820–27; published 1827.
2–3 with . . . heart: Browning commented in "House," l. 40, "Did Shakespeare? If so, the less Shakespeare he!"

If Thou Indeed Derive Thy Light *Page 434*

Written 1820–27; published 1827. Lines 2, 14–16 were added in 1837. From 1845 on, the poem was printed at the beginning of the collected poems, where Wordsworth intended it "to serve as a sort of preface" (*L.Y.*, III, 1263).

Yarrow Revisited *Page 434*

Written in September or October 1831; published 1835. "Yarrow Unvisited" and "Yarrow Visited" are alluded to in ll. 1–4, 75–80, 109–10. Scott died a year later, in September 1832.

93–95: More or less the point of *Prel.*, XII.208 ff. **99–104:** Alluding to the "Introduction" to Scott's *The Lay of the Last Minstrel*. **109–12:** Cf. ll. 29–30, 93–95. "Yarrow Unvisited" looked toward the future (sights unseen); "Yarrow Visited" concerned the present ("common sunshine"); "Yarrow Revisited" is a "Memorial tribute" (84) to the past.

Calm Is the Fragrant Air *Page 437*

Written 1832; published 1835.

Steamboats, Viaducts, and Railways *Page 438*

Written 1833; published 1835.

Most Sweet It Is with Unuplifted Eyes *Page 438*

Written 1833; published 1835.

Extempore Effusion upon the Death of James Hogg
Page 439

Written in November 1835; published in the Newcastle *Journal* early in
December, and in the *Athenaeum*, 12 December 1835. "These verses
were written extempore, immediately after reading a notice of the Ettrick
Shepherd's death [on November 21], in the Newcastle paper . . . . The
persons lamented . . . were all either of my friends or acquaintance"
(I.F.). Scott (8–10) had died in September 1832, Coleridge (15–18) in
July 1834, Lamb (19–20) in December 1834, Crabbe (31–34) in February
1832, and Felicia Hemans (37–40) in May 1835. The first two stanzas
refer to the occasions of "Yarrow Visited" and "Yarrow Revisited."

INDEX OF TITLES

[Page numbers in italic type refer to notes to the poems.]

579